BIOLOGICAL ANTHROPOLOGY
OF THE HUMAN SKELETON

BIOLOGICAL ANTHROPOLOGY OF THE HUMAN SKELETON

Edited by

M. ANNE KATZENBERG
Department of Archaeology
University of Calgary

SHELLEY R. SAUNDERS
Department of Anthropology
McMaster University

A JOHN WILEY & SONS, INC., PUBLICATION

New York • Chichester • Weinheim • Brisbane • Singapore • Toronto

This book is printed on acid-free paper. ∞

Copyright © 2000 by Wiley-Liss, Inc. All rights reserved.

Published simultaneously in Canada.

No part of this publication may be reproduced, stored in a retrieval system or transmitted in any form or by any means, electronic, mechanical, photocopying, recording, scanning or otherwise, except as permitted under Section 107 or 108 of the 1976 United States Copyright Act, without either the prior written permission of the Publisher, or authorization through payment of the appropriate per copy fee to the Copyright Clearance Center, 222 Rosewood Drive, Danvers, MA 01923, (978) 750-8400, fax (978) 750-4744. Requests to the Publisher for permission should be addressed to the Permissions Department, John Wiley & Sons, Inc., 605 Third Avenue, New York, NY 10158-0012, (212) 850-6011, fax (212) 850-6008, E-Mail: PERMREQ@WILEY.COM.

For ordering and customer service call, 1-800-CALL-WILEY.

Library of Congress Cataloging-in-Publication Data:
    Biological anthropology of the human skeleton / edited by Mary Anne Katzenberg,
Shelley R. Saunders.
      p. cm.
    Includes index.
    ISBN 0-471-31616-4 (cloth : alk. paper)
    1. Human skeleton.   2. Human remains (Archaeology).   3. Bones—Analysis.
I. Katzenberg, Mary Anne.   II. Saunders, Shelley Rae.

GN70.B55 2000
599.9′47—dc21   99-054718

Printed in the United States of America.

10 9 8 7 6 5 4 3

To our families (including pets), with love and affection.

CONTENTS

PREFACE

What's Bred in the Bone, a novel by Robertson Davies, begins with the proverb, "What's bred in the bone will not out in the flesh." The story is about a man who supposedly reflects his "breeding" since his behavior and characteristics are direct reflections of what he has inherited from his family. While biological determinism may work in fiction, it is anathema to the biological anthropologist. The cornerstone of biological anthropology is the interaction of culture and human biology. What is manifested in the physical and behavioral characteristics of any living being is a result of the intertwining of an inherited genome with environmental factors. Human osteologists have struggled with this concept from the earliest beginnings of skeletal studies and continue to struggle with it today. Ancient DNA studies suggest that we ultimately want to know the "inherent" properties coming out of the bones. If we cold read the genome, we would "know" the person. But of course, we understand that, as living tissues, bones and teeth are influenced by environmental forces. Bones respond to mechanical forces and thus they alter in response to activities and stresses. Craniometric studies attempt to study population relationships, assuming that cranial shape and size reflect inherited features, but we know that cranial shape and size can be altered purposefully (e.g., head binding) or unintentionally (chewing stresses). It is the job of the human osteologist to study the interactions between inherited characteristics and their modification by the environment in order to understand, not just what is "bred" in the bone but what bones can tell us about the flesh, that is, the lives of earlier peoples.

Each of the following chapters deals with a specific type of advanced analysis of bones and teeth. The original plan for the book was to be a second edition of our earlier edited book, *Skeletal Biology of Past People: Research Methods.* However as work progressed it seemed that with five additional chapters and many new contributors, it is really something different. The differences are directly related to changes that have occurred in the analysis of human skeletal and dental remains over the past few years. Most notably these changes include heightened ethical concerns about studying the skeletal remains of aboriginal peoples in many countries where those people are no longer the dominant culture. These concerns and the resulting legislation in some jurisdictions have radically changed the way physical anthropologists and archaeologists carry out their work. A second change is the rise of forensic anthropology and the fact that research in forensic anthropology, while still overlapping with more traditional approaches, now includes topics not central to studies of archaeological skeletons. We begin this book with chapters on the ethics of studying human remains and forensic anthropology.

An important theme that is found throughout the book is the progress of new methods. We were training to become anthropologists in the 1970s when many new research areas were emerging in physical anthropology. The earlier practice of providing descriptive osteological reports either as stand-alone works or, more commonly, as appendices to archaeological site reports was fading out and more problem-oriented research was emerging. Biological distance studies using both metric and nonmetric traits of human bones and teeth were carried out in order to investigate prehistoric migration and relatedness through time and space. Paleopathology was emerging as a means of addressing questions about prehistoric adaptations in contrast to the earlier emphasis on unusual cases of specific diseases. Paleodemography, similarly, addressed questions of adaptation of earlier populations. Since the initial enthusiastic studies, all of these topics have undergone criticism and have emerged as, perhaps, humbled, but also strengthened by the critiques. The same is true of the more recently introduced methods involving biochemical analyses of bones and teeth. These include analyses of trace elements, stable isotopes, and ancient DNA.

Each of these methods has undergone a series of stages that may be characterized as follows:

1. Discovery—either entirely new or new to physical anthropology, a new method is discovered and the potential application are explored.
2. Applications to questions of interest regarding reconstructing past peoples.
3. Critique, introspection, experimentation.
4. Emergence in a stronger, more reasoned form.

NAGPRA (Native American Graves Protection and Repatriation Act) and similar legislation in other countries have led to a reconfiguring of how skeletal studies of past peoples are carried out. Some of these changes can be viewed in a positive light. For example, standards have been developed in the expectation that collections will not be curated indefinitely. These standards were needed even before the prospect of reburial emerged. In addition, an interesting configuration of events happened in the 1990s. As some Native Americans voiced their disapproval of skeletal studies, expanding urban development led to archaeological excavations of several large, historic cemeteries dating from the eighteenth and nineteenth centuries. These cemeteries contained the remains of Euro-Americans and African Americas as well as other groups. At the same time, the growing number of students trained in human osteology provided a pool of individuals to excavate and study these remains. Debates about excavation and study continued, but in many cases some period of time was allowed for proper scientific study. One special example of the cooperation between scientists and concerned descendants is the work being conducted at Howard University on a large African-American slave cemetery discovered in New York City. In Europe, there is a long history of excavating historic cemeteries and the increasing number of trained human osteologists has led to larger scale studies (the St. Brides' skeletal collection in London, England, is a good example). The increased scientific study of skeletons from historic cemeteries has also provided opportunities for testing methods. In many cases, the identities of at least some of the individuals are known from legible coffin inscriptions or detailed cemetery maps. It has been possible to investigate the accuracy of methods of determining sex and age at death and to detect biases in mortality samples that are directly related to causes of death.

This book is organized into five parts. Part I, theory and application, features two chapters that describe recent shifts in skeletal studies. Walker's chapters provides information on how humans have regarded the dead over time and across cultures. He grapples with the issues surrounding the ethics of skeletal research, the clash with cultural beliefs about treatment of the dead, and the politics of communities. Taking a clearly anthropological approach to these questions, he shows us that there is a tremendous diversity of attitudes about the physical remains of the dead. He makes a strong case for the value of and the justification of scientific research. Ubelaker focuses on the development of forensic anthropology with its roots in descriptive osteology and its present form as an applied specialization of human osteology. He discusses the major comparative collections used for establishing standards including the recently developed forensic data bank. He then takes the reader through the various steps in forensic anthropology, including recovery, identification, sex and age determination, stature estimation, and positive identification. He concludes with information on training opportunities and professional organizations dedicated to forensic anthropology.

Part II includes chapters on morphological analyses of bones and teeth and age changes. Four of these contributors prepared chapters for our earlier book and, while the topics are similar, each chapter includes contributions and advances that have occurred throughout the 1990s. Ruff describes biomechanical analyses of bones and the applications of such studies to understanding past human behavior ranging from fossil hominids through to early historic human groups. He draws from his own extensive research to provide examples of how biomechanical studies have improved our understanding of past activity patterns. Examples include changes in robusticity throughout human evolution, the relationships between subsistence and bone strength, and the relationship between gender roles and their biological manifestation in bone structure. Mayhall covers dental morphology, highlighting newer methods of characterizing tooth size and shape, and the applications of such studies to biological and behavioral characteristics of past peoples. He emphasizes the importance of achieving precision of observations of both dental measures and dental morphological traits. He also argues for maintaining simplicity in our methodological approaches. Both of these aspects of the research process are absolutely necessary for us to make meaningful comparisons of the results obtained by different observers. Mayhall shows that knowledge in the field of dental morphology remains limited because the precision necessary for properly evaluating population variability has still not been achieved. Saunders covers the various types of studies that are specific to subadults, focusing on age determination but also considering sex determination and variations in growth and development. One problem with proceeding to studies of growth and development is that of sampling. Differential burial practices, differential preservation, and biases related to cause of death can all cause problems in assessing past growth patterns from subadult burials. Some of these problems have been addressed in studies of a large historic cemetery where parish records are available for comparison. This cemetery has also provided opportunities for assessing historic variation in growth and development as well as testing methods of age determination. Saunders and her students have demonstrated how careful study of historic samples can tell us not only more about those particular people, but can help us to evaluate methods used on prehistoric samples. Fitz-Gerald and Rose present information on age determination for subadult remains through dental microstructure analysis. The use of newer image analysis techniques (which are now easy to install in most anthropology laboratories) improves precision and relieves the tedium of collecting these data. This research shows great promise. If we can get a clearer picture of the amount of inter- and intrapopulation variation in dental development we will know more about how tissue growth is buffered from stress and whether meaningful population differences really do exist. As these authors explain, it is only very recently that the investigation of microstructural growth markers in dental tissues has become accepted as appropriate for estimating tooth crown formation times. Robling and Stout provide details as well as examples of adult age determination based on bone histomorphometry. They review the principles of bone modeling and remodeling as a prelude to explaining how cortical bone microstructure is used in age determination. Variations due to activity, sex, disease, and population affinity are discussed. Appendices to their chapter allow one to practice the methods of histological age determination on photomicrographs from a femur and a rib.

Part III is titled Prehistoric Health and Disease and includes three chapters. As in Part II, the sequence of chapters is: studies based on gross observations of bones, gross observations of teeth, and microscopic studies. Lovell focuses on paleopathology and diagnosis of bony lesions. She provides detailed information on various diagnostic methods including radiology and microscopy. Steps toward diagnosis are discussed with emphasis on accurate description and consideration of the distribution of lesions within an individual skeleton as well as the distribution within skeletal samples. Hillson presents methods for analyzing and describing dental pathology, with detailed information on the underlying causes of various conditions. He stresses the importance of careful observation, demonstrating how different ways of scoring pathological changes can dramatically alter determinations of disease prevalence. If care is taken with observations, so that the surviving jaws and teeth in skeletal collections really do represent what was buried, then the distribution of dental disease can tell us a lot about the diets and activities of past populations. Then we can seek correspondence between dental data and data from stable isotopes, faunal and botanical assemblages, and artifacts used in daily life. Pfeiffer covers the subject of bone histology with respect to healthy bone turnover and various disease states. This chapter ties in nicely with those of Ruff, and Robling and Stout in that it covers information on bone structure at the histological level and the factors that account for variation. Her work includes variation in bone histology over recent human evolution with examples drawn from Neanderthals to recent European immigrants to Canada. Procedures for preparing bones in thin sections are reviewed with cautions regarding diagenetic alteration.

Part IV, Chemical and Genetic Analyses of Hard Tissues, includes chapters on stable isotope analysis, trace element analysis, and ancient DNA. Katzenberg provides background information on stable isotope studies and examples of applications to questions regarding paleodiet, migration, and life history. She demonstrates how isotopic analysis of archaeological tissues has advanced dramatically over a relatively short time span. Rather than simply confirming information that was already available from other sources, she shows how this field has called into question various archaeological hypotheses about subsistence adaptations as well as adding to our understanding of human ecology. She discusses three areas of research that are particularly promising because of their implications for a more detailed reading of the past. These include reconstructing infant feeding practices, detecting pathological changes in bones, and the management of animal and plant species by earlier human populations. Sandford and Weaver provide information on the current status of trace element studies. These include attempts to control for postmortem changes. They focus their discussion on the dietary indicators strontium and barium, and the toxic element lead. This chapter nicely illustrates the states of new methods, discussed early in the preface. Sandford and Weaver have labeled these "inaugural" (discovery and early applications), "intermediate" (reevaluation and testing), and "modern" (emphasis on experimental and simulation studies). The chapters on stable isotope analysis and trace element analysis both emphasize the importance of training in the physical sciences. Stone discusses advances in the isolation and analysis of ancient DNA. A great wave of excitement was ushered in with the first developments in the extraction and amplication of ancient DNA. If we can retrieve fragments of genes from long-deceased humans, surely we can reconstruct the evolutionary and population history of past human groups. But the early claims for the retrieval of ancient DNA from dinosaurs and other fossils were cast aside when it was shown that the amplified DNA came from modern contaminants. The promise of ancient DNA research lost some of its luster. Yet, more recently, Stone herself has been part of the research team able to offer clear evidence for the sequencing of Neanderthal DNA. Nevertheless, she cautions us about the difficulties of proving positive results and warns us that the promise is there, but the road ahead is still difficult.

Part V, Quantitative Methods and Population Studies, includes three chapters. Pietrusewsky discusses cranial measurement techniques and their applications to biological distance studies. He takes the reader through the various statistical procedures used to visualize biological relationships. These include a range of multivariate statistics such as clustering techniques, multidimensional scaling, and Mahalanobis' generalized distance. Craniometric analysis has been one of the transitional realms of osteological research. Pietrusewsky shows how this approach is still appropriate for the investigation of widespread museum collections, where destructive analyses are prohibited. Further, he demonstrates by using examples from his own extensive research in the Pacific, that multiple lines of evidence, including craniometric, dental, linguistic, and molecular data are all necessary to contribute to our understanding of human population history. Jackes tackles the problem of adult age determination and evaluates recent attempts to circumvent some of the problems. She surveys and evaluates all of the different approaches to age-at-death estimation including single methods, such as metamorphosis of the public symphysis and cranial suture closure, as well as complex methods. She emphasizes the difficulties of dealing with the biases of reference samples and the effects of skeletal preservation on efforts to produce age distributions for archaeological samples. She takes the position that statistical investigation and manipulation cannot substitute for the ne-

cessity of having accurate biological age estimates. Finally, Milner, and Wood and Boldsen evaluate the current status of paleodemography by focusing on some of the questions that have fueled past debates within the field. They address problems of sampling, age and sex estimation, non-stationarity, heterogeneous risk, and selective mortality. Paleodemography draws from many of the types of studies covered in previous chapters and attempts to tie together the success of populations based on factors such as diet, disease experience, activity patterns, growth and development, and population interactions. Milner and colleagues provide a frank view of the potential and the limitations of achieving the goal of being able to determine the level of adaptation of past populations.

All of these chapters have the common theme of determining information about past peoples from their skeletal and dental remains. Adult age determination is an important theme that appears in many of the chapters. Similarly, postmortem change, sampling, and the relationship between cemetery samples and living populations recurs throughout the book. Ethical considerations have had a major impact on all of the topics discussed. It is our hope that this information will provide both breadth and depth for advanced studies in human osteology and will serve as a guide to more intensive study.

M. Anne Katzenberg
Shelley R. Saunders

ACKNOWLEDGMENTS

M.A.K. wishes to acknowledge the Killam Foundation for awarding her a Killam Resident Fellowship at the University of Calgary for the fall term, 1998. The release time provided by this program made it possible to complete her chapter and to work on the various editor's tasks. Brenda Shaw, University of Calgary, provided editorial assistance in reviewing and formatting references for the various chapters.

S.R.S. would like to thank Anne Keenleyside and Marlene Ellerker for their help during various phases of the writing and editing process. The staff of the Deer Lodge in Lake Louise, Alberta provided a splendid working environment for our final editing sessions.

We also thank the staff at Wiley for their efficiency and encouragement.

CONTRIBUTORS

JESPER L. BOLDSEN, received his Ph.D. in biology from the Department of Theoretical Statistics, Aarhus University (Denmark) in 1983. He is professor of paleodemography at the Danish Centre for Demographic Research and the Institute for Community Health, Odense University. He is head of the Anthropological Data Base, Odense University, adjunct professor of anthropology at the University of Utah, and associate editor of the *Journal of Biosocial Science.* Research interests revolve around human population biology, epidemiology, demography, and evolution. A long-standing interest in growth and sexual maturation combined with work on population structure led him to study the effect of the structure of the sexual network among young Danes on the spread of HIV. In recent years he has concentrated much of his research effort on analyzing the structure of the medieval population of Denmark. This work has been based on studies of extensively excavated medieval cemeteries. He has published widely in biological an anthropological journals. Several recent publications include "Two methods for reconstruction of the empirical mortality profile," *Human Evolution*, 1988; "Patterns of advanced age mortality in the medieval village Tirup," in *Exceptional Longevity: From Prehistory to the Present,* edited by B. Jeune and J. Vaupel (Odense University Press, 1995); "Body proportions in a medieval village population: effects of early childhood episodes of ill health," *Annals of Human Biology*, 1998.

CHARLES FITZGERALD, received his Ph.D. in biological anthropology from Cambridge University in 1996. He is currently completing a postdoctoral fellowship sponsored by the Social Sciences and Humanities Research Council of Canada at McMaster University. The focus of his doctoral and postdoctoral research has been on the validation, standardization, and application of dental histological age and development assessment techniques. In addition to growth and development, his research interests include skeletal biology and paleoanthropology. Recent publications include "Do enamel microstructures have regular time dependency? Conclusions from the literature and a large-scale study," *Journal of Human Evolution*, 1998; "Is reproductive synchrony an evolutionarily stable strategy for hunter-gatherers?" (with R.A. Foley), *Current Anthropology,* 1996; and a co-edited volume with R.D. Hoppa, *Human Growth in the Past: Studies from Bones and Teeth,* Cambridge University Press, 1999.

SIMON HILLSON, Ph.D. (University of London, 1979), is currently reader in bioarchaeology at the Institute of Archaeology, University College London. Dr. Hillson's main research interests are in the biology of past human populations, ranging from the most recent post-medieval populations of London to Predynastic Egyptians, and remains from Upper Paleolithic contexts. In particular, he works with dental remains, studying their morphology, microstructure, and pathology. As well as a number of journal articles, he has published three books: *Dental Anthropology* (Cambridge University Press, 1996), *Mammal Bones and Teeth* (Institute of Archaeology, UCL, 1992), and *Teeth* (Cambridge University press, 1986). Currently he is writing a fully revised second edition of *Teeth*.

MARY JACKES, received her Ph.D. from the University of Toronto in 1977 and is currently adjunct professor in the Department of Anthropology at the University of Alberta. She has participated in archaeological and paleontological fieldwork and osteological analysis in Australia, Algeria, Canada, China, Italy, Kenya, and Portugal and, Tanzania. Her major interest is in testing methods by analyzing collections representative of major transitions in human history, using data from contact period Ontario and the Mesolithic-Neolithic transition in the western Mediterranean. Recent publications include "Pubic symphysis age distributions," *American Journal of Physical Anthropology*, 1985, "Human skeletal biology and the Mesolithic-Neolithic transition in Portugal," in *Epipaléolithiques et Mésolithique en Europe,* edited by P. Bintz, 1999 (with D. Lubell); and "Birth rates and bones," in *Strength in Diversity*, edited by A. Herring and L. Chan, (Canadian Scholars Press, 1994).

M. ANNE KATZENBERG, received her Ph.D. in anthropology from the University of Toronto in 1983. She is currently professor in the Department of Archaeology, University of Calgary. Her research interests include diet and health in past peoples. In particular she explores the various applications of stable isotope analysis to reconstructing paleodiet, paleodemography, and ecology. She is an associate editor of the *American Journal of Physical Anthropology* and is past president of the Canadian Association for Physical Anthropology. Recent publications include "Stable isotope variation in pathological bone," *International Journal of*

Osteoarchaeology, 1999 (with N. Lovell); "Stable isotope ecology and paleodiet in the Lake Baikal region of Siberia," *Journal of Archaeological Science,* 1999 (with A. Weber); and "Weaning and infant mortality: evaluating the skeletal evidence," *Yearbook of Physical Anthropology*, 1996 (with D.A. Herring and S.R. Saunders). She is co-editor, with Stanley Ambrose, of *Close to the Bone: Biogeochemical Approaches to Paleodietary Analyses in Archaeology* Plenum Press (in press).

NANCY C. LOVELL, received her Ph.D. from Cornell University in 1987 and is currently professor and head of anthropology at the University of Alberta. She specializes in skeletal biology and paleopathology and has carried out field research in India and Egypt. Recent publications include "Trauma analysis in paleopathology," *Yearbook of Physical Anthropology,* 1997; "A biocultural analysis of anemia in the ancient Indus Valley," *International Journal of Osteoarchaeology,* 1997; "Physical Anthropology" in *Encyclopedia of the Archaeology of Ancient Egypt*, edited by K.A. Bard (Routledge, 1999); and "Patterns of dental enamel defects at ancient Mendes, Egypt" (with Whyte I), *American Journal of Physical Anthropology*, 1999. Dr. Lovell is the recipient of grants from the Social Sciences and Humanities Research Council of Canada to support research on the skeletal biology of ancient Egyptians and has conducted cemetery excavations in Egypt for several years. She is a past president of the Canadian Association for Physical Anthropology and a member of the American Association of Physical Anthropologists, the Paleopathology Association, and the Dental Anthropology Association.

JOHN T. MAYHALL, (D.D.S., Indiana University, 1963; Ph.D., University of Chicago, 1976) is professor and head of oral anatomy at the Faculty of Dentistry, University of Toronto. He specializes in dental morphology, the genetics of tooth shape and size, and three-dimensional methods for the study of morphology. He has worked with various groups throughout the world including Canadian Inuit and Indians; Alaskan Eskimos, Indians, and Aleuts; southwestern United States Indians; Australian Aboriginals; Ecuadorian Indians; and individuals in Finland with sex-chromosome disorders. Some of his recent publications include "A new, three-dimensional method of measuring tooth wear," *American Journal of Physical Anthropology,* 1997 (with Ikuo Kageyama); "Dental morphology of 47, XYY males: molar cusp area, volume, shape and linear measurements, *University of Oregon Anthropological Papers,* 1998 (with Lassi Alvesalo and Grant Townsend); and "The dental complex: a morphological smokescreen or compass?", *Perspectives in Human Biology,* 1999. He is co-editor with Tuomo Heikkinen of the proceedings of the 11th International Symposium of Dental Morphology, *Dental Morphology '98* (University of Oulu Press). Professor Mayhall is a member of the American Association of Physical Anthropologists, Canadian Association for Physical Anthropology, Japanese Dental Anthropology Association, International Association for Dental Research, and Canadian Association for Dental Research as well as being a member and current president of the Dental Anthropology Association.

GEORGE R. MILNER, received his Ph.D. in anthropology from Northwestern University in 1982. He is currently professor of anthropology at The Pennsylvania State University. Before coming to Penn State, he was a postdoctoral fellow in physical anthropology at the Smithsonian Institution and director of the Museum of Anthropology at the University of Kentucky. His research has focused on both archaeology and human osteology, with an emphasis on the prehistory of eastern North America. He has conducted fieldwork on mortuary and habitation sites in several midwestern states and in the Pacific. Currently he is serving as an associate editor for the *Journal of Anthropological Archaeology* and the *American Journal of Physical Anthropology.* His most recent book is *The Cahokia Chiefdom: The Archaeology of a Mississippian Society* (Smithsonian Institution Press, 1998). Among his osteological publications is the co-authored article "The osteological paradox: problems of inferring prehistoric health from skeletal samples," *Current Anthropology,* 1992 (with J.W. Wood, H.C. Harpending, and K.M. Weiss). He is co-editor with C.S. Larsen of *In the Wake of Contact: Biological Responses to Conquest* (John Wiley & Sons, 1993).

SUSAN PFEIFFER, completed her Ph.D. in anthropology at the University of Toronto in 1976. Her chapter was prepared while she was an associate professor in the Department of Human Biology and Nutritional Science at the University of Guelph, Ontario, Canada. She is currently an associate professor in the Department of Anthropology, University of Toronto. Her interests in human skeletal biology focus on reconstructing life characteristics from the skeleton, with a special interest in hunting-gathering people of the past. She has published analyses of bone mass, adult age at death methods, and interpreting ossuary remains. Recent publications include "Variability in osteon size in recent human populations," *American Journal of Physical Anthropology,* 1998; "A morphological and histological study of the human humerus from Border Cave," *Journal of Human Evolution,* 1996 (with J. Zehr); and "Violent human death in the past: a case from the Western Cape," *South African Journal of Science,* 1999 (with N.J. van der Merwe, J.E. Parkington, and R. Yates).

MICHAEL PIETRUSEWSKY, received his Ph.D. in anthropology from the University of Toronto in 1969 and is currently professor of anthropology at the University of Hawaii, Honolulu, Hawaii. His research, which focuses on studies of human skeletal remains from Australia, the Pacific, East Asia, and Southeast Asia, includes physical anthropology, skeletal biology, studies of biological distance involving the use of multivariate statistical procedures, and forensic anthropology. Recent publications include "Ban Chiang, a prehistoric village site in northeast Thailand II: the human skeletal remains," *The University Museum, University of Pennsylvania, Memoir Series,* in press (with M.T. Douglas); "Multivariate craniometric investigations of Japanese, Asians, and Pacific Islanders," *Interdisciplinary Perspectives on the Origins of the Japanese. International Symposium 1996,* edited by K. Omoto, International Research Center for Japanese Studies, Kyoto, Japan, 1996; and "An osteological assessment of health and disease in precontact and historic (1778) Hawai`i" (with M.T. Douglas), in *In the Wake of Contact: Biological Responses to Conquest,* edited by C.S. Larsen and G. R. Milner (Wiley-Liss, Inc., 1994). Dr. Pietrusewsky is a member of the American Association of Physical Anthropologists, fellow of the American Academy of Forensic Sciences, diplomat of the American Board of Forensic Anthropologists, and member of the editorial board of the Anthropological Society of Japan. He has been a visiting professor/ scholar to numerous countries including Japan, Peoples Republic of China, Taiwan (Republic of China), Australia, Canada, France, and Germany.

ALEXANDER G. ROBLING, received his Ph.D. from the University of Missouri in 1998 and is currently a postdoctoral fellow in the departments of Anatomy and Orthopedic Surgery at Indiana University—Purdue University, Indianapolis. He specializes in the effects of mechanical loading on bone modeling and remodeling dynamics. His publications include "Morphology of the drifting osteon," *Cells, Tissues, Organs,* 1999 (with S. Stout), and "Sex estimation from the metatarsals," *Journal of Forensic Sciences,* 1997 (with D. Ubelaker). Dr. Robling is a member of the American Anthropological Association, the International Bone and Mineral Society, and the American Society for Bone and Mineral Research.

JEROME C. ROSE, received his Ph.D. in anthropology/biological anthropology from the University of Massachusetts, Amherst, in 1973. He is currently professor of anthropology at the University of Arkansas, Fayetteville, and a member of the department of anthropology, Institute of Archaeology and Anthropology, Yarmouk University, Irbid, Jordan. Dr. Rose's early research interest was dental anthropology with a particular focus upon dental histology including the study of enamel microdefects and enamel hypoplasias. Methodological specialties include light and electron microscopy and thin sectioning technology. He has conducted bioarcheological excavations in Illinois, Arkansas, Texas, Egypt, and Jordan. Research on the origins of agriculture and the economic determinants of health provided the motivation to begin a speciality in the bioarchaeology of the Middle East. He is currently working in Jordan on the excavation and analysis of Byzantine tombs. Recent publications include "NAGPRA is forever: osteology and the repatriation of skeletons," *Annual Review of Anthropology,* 1996 (with T.J. Green and V.D. Green); "Skeletal biology of the prehistoric Caddo" (with M.P. Hoffman, B.A. Burnett, A.M. Harmon, and J.E. Barns), in *The Native History of the Caddo: Their Place in Southwestern Archaeology and Ethnohistory,* edited by T.K. Perttula and J.E. Bruseth (Texas Archeological Research Laboratory, University of Texas, Austin, 1998); and "Gross dental wear and dental microwear in historical perspective" (with P.S. Ungar), in *Dental Anthropology: Fundamentals, Limits and Prospects,* edited by K.W. Alt, F.W. Rösing, and M. Teschler-Nicola, Springer-Verlag, (1998). He also edited "Bioarcheology of the South Central United States," *Arkansas Archeological Survey Research Series* No. 55, Fayetteville, AR, 1999.

CHRIS RUFF, received his Ph.D. in biological anthropology from the University of Pennsylvania in 1981 and is currently a professor in the Department of Cell Biology and Anatomy, Johns Hopkins University School of Medicine. His research interests are in skeletal biology and biomechanics, primate functional morphology and evolution, osteoporosis, and climatic adaptation. Recent publications include "Biomechanics of the hip and birth in early *Homo,*" *American Journal of Physical Anthropology,* 1995; "Body mass and encephalization in Pleistocene *Homo*" *Nature,* 1997 (with E. Trinkaus and T.W. Holliday); and "Evolution of the hominid hip," in *Primate Locomotion: Recent Advances,* edited by E. Strasser, J. Fleagle, H. McHenry, and A. Rosenberger (Plenum Press, 1998). He is a member of the AAAS Section Committee on Anthropology, the Executive Committee of the American Association of Physical Anthropologists, the Orthopaedic Research Society, and the American Society for Bone and Mineral Research, and is the editor of the *Yearbook of Physical Anthropology.*

MARY K. SANDFORD, (Ph.D., University of Colorado, 1984) is associate dean of the College of Arts and Sciences and associate professor of Anthropology at the University of North Carolina at Greensboro. Her research interests include bone chemistry, bone physiology, paleopathology, epidemiology, science education, and scientific visualization. She is currently directing a project sponsored by the National Science Foundation under the Research Experiences for Undergraduates Directorate involving the analysis of an Archaic period skeletal collection. She has conducted bioarchaeological field research in Crete, Western Mexico, and the Caribbean and recently completed the analysis of human skeletal remains from the pre-Columbian Tutu site on the island of St. Thomas. She recently coauthored *A View to the Past: Bioarchaeological Analysis of Human Remains from the Tutu site, St. Thomas, US Virgin Islands,* 1997 (with G. Bogdan and G. E. Kissling), a technical report on the Tutu material. She is the editor of the book series *Interpreting the Remains of the Past,* published by Gordon and Breach, and the editor of *Investigations of Ancient Human Tissue: Chemical Analyses in Anthropology,* 1993. She is currently section chair (program editor) for the Biological Anthropology Section of the American Anthropological Association.

SHELLEY R. SAUNDERS, received her Ph.D. in anthropology from the University of Toronto in 1977. She is currently professor in the Department of Anthropology, McMaster University and a research fellow of the Royal Ontario Museum, Toronto. Her research covers macroscopic and microscopic human skeletal growth, dental growth and development, dental pathology, sexual dimorphism in human skeletons, and ancient DNA studies. She is an associate editor of the *American Journal of Physical Anthropology* and currently director of the Institute for the Study of Ancient and Forensic DNA, McMaster University. Recent publications include "What can be done about the infant category in skeletal samples?" (with L. Barrans) in *Human Growth in the Past,* edited by R.D. Hoppa and C.M. FitzGerald (Cambridge University Press, 1999) "Sex determination: XX or XY from the human skeleton," (with D. Yang), in *Forensic Osteological Analysis: A Book of Case Studies,* edited by S. Fairgrieve (Charles C. Thomas, 1999); and "Enamel hypoplasia in a Canadian historic sample," *American Journal of Human Biology,* 1999 (with Anne Keenleyside). She is co-editor (with D.A. Herring) of *Grave Reflections: Portraying the Past Through Cemetery Studies* (Canadian Scholars' Press, 1995).

ANNE C. STONE, received her Ph.D. from Pennsylvania State University in 1996 and is currently an assistant professor in the Department of Anthropology at the University of New Mexico. She specializes in human and chimpanzee population genetics and evolution. Her publications include "Analysis of ancient DNA from a prehistoric Amerindian cemetery" (with M. Stoneking), *Philosophical Transactions of the Royal Society, London, B,* 1999; "MtDNA analysis of a prehistoric Oneota population: implications for the peopling of the New World," *American Journal of Human Genetics,* 1998 (with M. Stoneking); "Neandertal DNA sequences and the origin of modern humans," *Cell,* 1997 (with M Krings, R.W. Schmitz, H. Krainitzki and S. Pääbo); and "Sex determination of ancient human skeletons using DNA," *American Journal of Physical Anthropology,* 1996 (with G. Milner, S. Pääbo and M. Stoneking). Dr. Stone is a member of the American Association of Physical Anthropologists, the American Anthropological Association, the Society of Molecular Biology and Evolution, and the American Association of Anthropological Genetics.

SAM D. STOUT, received his Ph.D. from Washington University, St. Louis, in 1976 and is currently professor of anthropology at the University of Missouri, Columbia. He specializes in histomorphometric analysis of bone, and its applications in skeletal biology, bioarchaeology, paleopathology, and forensic anthropology. Recent publications include "Computer assisted 3D reconstruction of serial sections of cortical bone to determine the 3D structure of osteons," *Calcified Tissue International* (1999) (with B. Brunsden, C. Hildebolt, P. Commean, K. Smith, and N.C. Tappen); "Morphology of the drifting osteon," *Cells, Tissues, Organs,* 1999) (with A. Robling); "Methods for improving the efficiency of estimating total osteon density in the human anterior mid-diaphyseal femur," *American Journal of Physical Anthropology,* 1998 (with U.T. Iwaniec, T.D. Crenshaw, M.J. Schoeninger, and M.F. Ericksen); and "Bone remodeling rates and maturation in three archaeological skeletal populations," *American Journal of Physical Anthropology,* 1995 (with R. Lueck). Dr. Stout is a member of the American Association of Physical Anthropologists, the American Academy of Forensic Sciences, the Paleopathology Association, and the American Association for the Advancement of Science.

DOUGLAS H. UBELAKER, received his Ph.D. from the University of Kansas in 1973. Currently, he is curator of physical anthropology at the Smithsonian Institution's National Museum of Natural History. His research interests are focused within human skeletal biology and forensic applications. He has also worked extensively with prehistoric skeletal samples from highland Ecuador and from eastern North America. Recent publications include "The evolving role of the microscope in forensic anthropology," in *Forensic Osteology: Advances in the Identification of Human Remains,* second edition, edited by K.J. Reichs (Charles C. Thomas, 1998); "Comparison of macroscopic cranial methods of age estimation applied to skeletons from the Terry collection," *Journal of Forensic Sciences,* 1998 (with V. Galera and L. Hayek); and "Taphonomic applications in forensic anthropology," in *Forensic Taphonomy,* edited by W.D. Haglund and M.H. Sorg (CRC Press, 1997). Dr. Ubelaker is also co-editor, with J.W. Verano, of *Disease and Demography in the Americas,* Smithsonian Institution Press, 1992.

PHILLIP L. WALKER, received his Ph.D. from the University of Chicago in 1973. He is currently professor of anthropology at the University of California, Santa Barbara. His interests include bioarchaeology, paleopathology, forensic anthropology, and human evolution. Some of his recent publications include "Marriage patterns of California's early Spanish-Mexican colonists (1742–1876)," *Journal of Biosocial Science,* 1997 (with C. Garcia-Moro and D.I. Toja); "Wife beating, boxing, and broken noses: skeletal evidence for the cultural patterning of interpersonal violence" in *Troubled Times: Violence and Warfare in the Past,* edited by D. Martin and D. Frayer (Gordon and Breach, 1997); and "Diet, dental health, and cultural change among recently contacted South American Indian hunter-horticulturists," in *Human Dental Development, Morphology, and Pathology: A Tribute to Albert A. Dahlberg,* edited by John R. Lukacs, University of Oregon Anthropological Papers, No. 54, 1998, (with L. Sugiyama and R. Chacon). Professor Walker is currently a member of the American Anthropological Association ethics Committee. He also serves as a member of the American Association of Physical Anthropology Executive Committee, an associate editor of the International Journal of Osteoarchaeology, and an advisor to the Society for American Archaeology Task Force on Repatriation. He is past president of the Dental Anthropology Association and served as a member of the Department of Interior Native American Graves Protection and Repatriation Act Review Committee between 1992 and 1997.

DAVID S. WEAVER, received his Ph.D. from the University of New Mexico in 1977 and is currently professor of anthropology and associate professor of comparative medicine at Wake Forest University in Winston-Salem, North Carolina. His research interests include bone biology, bone physiology, paleopathology and osteology, osteoporosis, and treponematosis in modern prehistoric contexts. Among his recent publications are "Osteoporosis in the bioarchaeology of women," in *Sex and Gender in Paleopathological Perspective,* edited by A.L. Grauer and P. Stuart MacAdam (Cambridge University Press, 1998); "Forensic aspects of fetal and neonatal skeletons" in *Forensic Osteology: Advances in the Identification of Human Remains,* edited by K.J. Reichs, (Charles C. Thomas, 1998); and "Two cases of facial involvement in probable treponemal infection from late prehistoric coastal North Carolina," *International Journal of Osteoarchaeology,* 1998 (with D.L. Hutchinson).

JAMES W. WOOD, received his Ph.D. from the University of Michigan in 1980 and is currently professor of anthropology and senior research scientist in the Population Research Institute at Pennsylvania State University. He has carried out fieldwork on demography, reproductive biology, and population genetics. Recent publications include "A theory of preindustrial population dynamics: demography, economy, and well-being in Malthusian systems," *Current Anthropology,* 1998; "The osteological paradox: problems of inferring prehistoric health from skeletal samples," *Current Anthropology,* 1992 (with G.R. Milner, H.C. Harpending, and K.M. Weiss); and *Dynamics of Human Reproduction: Biology, Biometry, Demography* (Aldine de Gruyter, 1994).

PART I

THEORY AND APPLICATION IN STUDIES OF PAST PEOPLES

CHAPTER 1

BIOARCHAEOLOGICAL ETHICS: A HISTORICAL PERSPECTIVE ON THE VALUE OF HUMAN REMAINS

PHILLIP L. WALKER

INTRODUCTION

The rapidity of technological and cultural change in current times is forcing us to confront a myriad of moral dilemmas over issues as wide ranging as the ethics of cloning humans, the ownership of our genetic material, and the rights of animals relative to those of humans. These ethical issues concern the very nature of what it means to be human and our relationships, not only to other people, but also to the plants and animals that sustain us.

The enormous strides we have taken toward human equality during this century mean that formerly disenfranchised and enslaved members of minority groups are beginning to gain power and control over their lives. In many countries there has been a decline in the political dominance and moral authority of organized religions. Notions of multiculturalism and a growing acceptance of the moral principle of not discriminating against people based on gender, ethnicity, or religious beliefs mean that there is no longer a shared set of cultural values we can use for guidance in dealing with moral issues (Cottingham, 1994).

This increased tolerance of cultural diversity poses ethical dilemmas because, as the range of value systems and religious beliefs that are considered socially acceptable increases, so does the probability of social conflict. To deal with these issues, many scientific associations are beginning to reconsider ethical principles that underlie their research activities. The field of bioarchaeology is especially problematic in this respect, positioned as it is between medicine, with its ethical focus on generating scientific knowledge for use in helping individual patients, and anthropology, with its ethical principles that stem from deep belief in the power of cultural relativism to overcome ethnocentrism and encourage tolerance.

It is in this context that skeletal biologists are increasingly being forced to adapt their activities to the value systems of the descendants of the people they study. Human skeletal remains are more than utilitarian objects of value for scientific research. For many people, they also are objects of religious veneration of great symbolic and cultural significance. Over the past thirty years, formerly disenfranchised groups such as Native Americans and Australian Aborigines have increasingly been able to assert their claims of moral authority to control the disposition of both the remains of their ancestors and the land their ancestors occupied (Howitt, 1998; Scott, 1996). This trend toward repatriating museum collections and granting land rights to indigenous people can only be

Biological Anthropology of the Human Skeleton, Edited by M. Anne Katzenberg and Shelley R. Saunders.
ISBN 0-471-31616-4 Copyright © 2000 by Wiley-Liss, Inc.

understood within a broader social and historical context.

To provide this historical perspective, I will describe the evolution of religious beliefs about the proper treatment of the dead and conflicts that have arisen over the centuries between these beliefs and the value scientists place on the empirical information that can be gained through research on human remains. This is followed by a discussion of the generally accepted ethical principles that are beginning to emerge in the field of bioarchaeology. Finally, some practical suggestions are offered for dealing with conflicts that arise when these ethical principles conflict with those of descendant groups.

THE HISTORY OF BELIEFS ABOUT THE DEAD

Early in our evolutionary history people began to develop a keen interest in the remains of their dead comrades. At first this was undoubtedly simply a response to the practical considerations of removing the decaying remains of a dead relative from one's domicile or preventing scavengers from consuming the body. More elaborate patterns of mortuary behavior soon began to develop. Cut marks on the crania of some of the earliest members of our species show that as early as 600,000 years ago people living at the Bodo site in Ethiopia were defleshing the heads of the dead (White, 1986). It has been suggested that such practices reflect a widespread belief among our ancestors concerning the role of the brain in reproduction (La Barre, 1984).

By 50,000 to 100,000 years ago mortuary practices had evolved into elaborate rituals that involved painting bodies with red ochre and including food or animal remains with the body as offerings. Through time these cultural practices became associated with increasingly complex religious beliefs that helped people cope with the uncertainties of death. Depositing utilitarian items and valuables such as ornaments in graves became commonplace in the Upper Paleolithic period. Such practices suggest continued use of these items was anticipated in the afterlife. Expressions of such beliefs can be found in some of the earliest surviving religious texts. The Egyptian Book of the Dead, for instance, provides spells and elaborate directions for use by the souls of the deceased during their journeys in the land of the dead (Allen, 1960; Ellis N, 1996).

The belief that the soul persists in an afterworld has deep roots in Western religious traditions. The ancient Greeks held elaborate funeral rituals to help a dead person's soul find its way across the River Styx to a community of souls in the underworld. Once in the underworld, there was continued communion between the living and the dead. For example, the soul of a dead person could be reborn in a new body if their living family members continued to attend to their needs by bringing them honey cakes and other special foods on ceremonial occasions (Barber, 1988). By medieval times most people continued to view death as a semipermanent state in which the living and the spirit of the dead person could maintain contact with each other. Folktales about ghosts and corpses coming to life were widespread and contributed to the idea of the dead functioning in society with the living (Barber, 1988; Caciola, 1996). The issue of integrity of the corpse and the relationship of this to the afterlife dominated medieval discussions of the body: salvation became equated with wholeness, and hell with decay and partition of the body (Bynum, 1995:114).

After the Reformation, conservative Protestant groups continued to emphasize the profound significance of a person's physical remains after death. In fact, one of the more troublesome issues facing Protestant reformers after the abolition of purgatory in the early sixteenth century was the need to provide a rational explanation for the status of body and soul in the period intervening between death and resurrection (Spellman, 1994). One strategy for dealing with this vexing problem is provided by the constitution for the Old School Presbyterian Church, published in 1822, which asserts that the bodies of deceased members of the church "even in death continue united in Christ, and rest in the graves as in their beds, till at the last day they be again united with their souls . . . the self same bodies of the dead which were laid in the grave, being then again raised up by the power of Christ" (Laderman, 1996:54).

Such beliefs in the continuance of life after death remain prevalent in modern Western societies (Cohen, 1992). Recent surveys show that 25% of European adults report having contact with the dead (Haraldsson and Houtkooper, 1991), and a significant number of Americans believe in reincarnation (Donahue, 1993; Walter, 1993). About half of the people in the United States believe that hell is a real place in which people suffer eternal damnation (Marty, 1997). In another survey, 80% of the North American population believes in some kind of an afterlife (Goldhaber, 1996; Tonne, 1996). Among Canadians, 40% believe in the Devil and 43% in hell (Belief in the Devil, 1995).

Surveys also show that, in spite of speculation about the secularizing effects of education and academia, most highly educated people, including professors and scientists, are about as religious as other Americans. Anthropologists are one of the few groups that deviate significantly from the majority view that individual human beings continue to exist in some kind of an afterlife. Compared to faculty in the physical sciences, anthropologists are almost twice as likely to be irreligious, to never attend church, and one in five actually declare themselves "opposed" to religion (Iannaccone et al., 1998). This is significant in the context of the ethical issues considered in this paper because it means that the values of the anthropologists who do skeletal research will often differ dramatically from those of descendants of the people they study.

Although the prevalence of conviction in an afterlife appears to have changed relatively little during the twentieth century, the cultural context in which it occurs has been dramatically transformed. The familiarity with death

that characterized earlier societies in which people were forced to confront the dead directly on a daily basis has been replaced by avoidance of the dead. With the commercialization of the burial process by the "death-care" industry in wealthy countries, traditions such as wakes and ritual preparation of the dead for burial by family members have been replaced by the processing of the dead in remote settings (Badone, 1987; Horn, 1998; Rundblad, 1995). This cultural trend toward lack of contact with the dead has greatly increased the cultural gulf between a public that has little familiarity with death and skeletal researchers, such as bioarchaeologists, who confront the dead on a daily basis.

THE HISTORY OF RESEARCH ON HUMAN REMAINS

Ambivalence toward scientific research on human remains has deep roots in Western societies. From its onset, scientific research on the dead has been the domain of physicians who were often forced to work under clandestine conditions on the bodies of social outcasts. The earliest recorded systematic dissections of a human body were conducted in the first half of the third century B.C., by two Greeks, Herophilus of Chalcedon and Erasistratus of Chios. These studies were performed in Alexandria, a city where traditional Greek values were weakened by Ptolemic influences, and probably involved vivisection and the use of condemned criminals (Von Staden, 1989: 52–53, 1992). In the ancient world, scientific research of this kind was extremely problematic because it violated Greco-Roman, Arabic, and early Judeo-Christian beliefs about the afterlife, impurity, and pollution (Bynum, 1994; Eknoyan, 1994; Von Staden, 1992). In the Christian world, anatomical studies of the dead were especially troublesome because many people feared resurrection would be impossible if their body had been dissected. This belief derived from the conviction that at resurrection the actual body is reconnected with the soul. People thus feared that dissection would somehow interfere with this process and leave the soul eternally wandering around in search of lost parts (Bynum, 1994).

During the Renaissance the strength of religious sanctions against dissection began to weaken and, by the sixteenth century, surgeons in Protestant countries such as England were officially given the authority to take the bodies of hanged criminals for use in their anatomical studies. This practice had the dual purpose of furthering the healing arts and serving as a deterrent to criminals who feared the desecration of their bodies (Humphrey, 1973; Wilf, 1989). The repugnance of being dissected was so great that riots sometimes erupted after executions over the disposition of the bodies. Samuel Richardson observed one of these spectacles: "As soon as the poor creatures were half-dead, I was much surprised, before such a number of peace-officers, to see the populace fall to hauling and pulling the carcasses with so much earnestness, as to occasion several warm encounters, and broken heads. These, I was told, were the friends of the person executed, or such as, for the sake of tumult, chose to appear so, and some persons sent by private surgeons to obtain bodies for dissection. The contests between these were fierce and bloody, and frightful to look at" (Richardson, 1987).

As appreciation for the medical value of the information that could be gained through dissection increased, so did the need for anatomical specimens. Soon the demand for bodies for use in teaching and research outstripped the legal supply of executed criminals, and physicians increasingly began to obtain cadavers through robbing graves and hiring body-snatchers who were referred to as "resurrectionists" (Hutchens, 1997; Millican, 1992; Schultz, 1992). This practice was widespread and persisted well into the twentieth century in some parts of the United States. The desire for bodies even led to the series of infamous murders committed by William Burke and William Hare in Edinburgh in the 1820s, with the aim of supplying dissection subjects to Dr. Robert Knox, the anatomist. Hare turned king's evidence, Burke was hanged for his crimes, and

the incident led to controlling legislation in Britain.

Grave-robbing activities sometimes met with violent public resistance. In 1788, for example, New Yorkers rioted for three days after some children peered through windows of the Society of the Hospital of the City of New York and discovered medical students dissecting human cadavers, one of whom turned out to be their recently deceased mother. A mob of five thousand eventually stormed the hospital and the jail where several doctors had taken refuge. The militia had to be called in and finally dispersed the crowd by firing muskets into it.

To avoid problems such as this, the professional body snatchers hired by medical schools concentrated on robbing the graves of the poor and powerless. The cemeteries of almshouses were favorite targets and, in the United States, African-American graveyards were favored as places to plunder. Upon visiting Baltimore in 1835, Harriet Martineau commented that the bodies used for dissection were exclusively those of African Americans "because the whites do not like it, and the coloured people cannot resist" (Martineau, 1838:140).

Although much of the early anatomical research focused on resolving issues concerning physiology and surgical anatomy, from the beginning skeletal studies with a decidedly anthropological flavor were done to answer questions related to human variation and adaptation. As early as 440 B.C., Herodotus (484– 425 B.C.) reported on an investigation into the effect of the environment on the strength of the skull:

> On the field where this battle was fought I saw a very wonderful thing which the natives pointed out to me. The bones of the slain lie scattered upon the field in two lots, those of the Persians in one place by themselves, as the bodies lay at the first—those of the Egyptians in another place apart from them. If, then, you strike the Persian skulls, even with a pebble, they are so weak, that you break a hole in them; but the Egyptian skulls are so strong, that you may smite them with a stone and you will scarcely break them in. They gave me the following reason for this

difference, which seemed to me likely enough: The Egyptians (they said) from early childhood have the head shaved, and so by the action of the sun the skull becomes thick and hard. (Herodotus, 1990)

Much of the early anatomical work on human variation had its roots in the belief of Aristotle and his contemporaries that Nature was organized hierarchically as a continuous chain. He was certain that all other animals existed for the sake of Man. This view of the world provided a useful framework for comprehending the enormous complexity of the natural world and also had the appeal of rationalizing the stratified nature of Greek society with powerful rulers and a social elite at the top and the slaves at the bottom (Clutton-Brock, 1995).

By the Middle Ages this hierarchical view of the world had been transformed into the Christian doctrine in which the world was seen as a perfect expression of God's will that descended in continuous succession through a "Great Chain of Being" from the perfection of the creator to the dregs of things at the very bottom of creation. This perspective permeated much of the work of early natural historians such as John Ray, who developed the doctrine of "natural theology," in which he argued that the power of God could be understood through the study of his creation, the natural world (Ray, 1692). In this context, the description of biological variation, including that found among humans, was a frankly religious activity in which the exploration of the fabric of the natural world at both its macroscopic and microscopic levels was seen as a way of revealing the "divine architect's" plan for the universe.

The expanded view of biological diversity provided by the specimens brought back by Columbus and other early European explorers stimulated a frenzy of species description and the first detailed anatomical studies of the differences between apes and humans. Through his careful dissections of a chimpanzee, Edward Tyson (1650–1708) was able to debunk myths based on the reports of classical authors such as Homer, Herodotus, and Aris-

totle that humankind contained several species including "satyrs," "sphinges," and "pygmies," and in 1779 Charles Bonnet (1720–1793) wrote a detailed account of the orangutan in which he noted a close relationship to us, albeit with the "lowest races" of our species (Bonnet, 1779; Clutton-Brock, 1995; Tyson, 1966).

After resolving the issue of whether humans and apes are members of the same species, Enlightenment scholars were still faced with the problem of interpreting the previously unsuspected extent of human biological and cultural diversity revealed by European colonial expansion into remote areas of the world. Linnaeus, for example, recognized five divisions of our genus, which included "Homo monstrosus," a catchall category for a variety of mythical creatures reported by early explorers. The debate soon took on a strong religious flavor and began to focus upon how the empirical facts of human variation could be made congruent with biblical accounts of Adam and Eve and the Tower of Babel. Interpretations of human diversity became sharply divided between the adherents of the theory of monogenesis, which traced all humans to a single origin in the Garden of Eden, and the adherents of polygenesis, who rejected the criteria of interfertility as the basis for the identification of biological species and took the unorthodox position that Europeans, Africans, Asians, and Native Americans were derived from different ancestral forms.

By the end of the eighteenth century, evidence obtained from human skeletal remains began to assume an increasingly important role in these debates over the origins and significance of human biological and cultural differences. Cranial evidence (a total of 82 skulls), for instance, figured prominently in the famous doctoral thesis of Johann Friedrich Blumenbach (1752–1840) in which he argued that modern human diversity had arisen as a consequence of the degeneration of a primordial type (varietas primigenia) whose closest living approximation could be found in the people of the Caucasus Mountains (Blumenbach et al., 1865). Such studies generated considerable interest in human cranial variation, and soon systematic efforts were begun to assemble research collections of human skeletal material from throughout the world.

In the United States, research on population differences in cranial morphology was dominated by Samuel George Morton (1799–1851), a physician from Philadelphia. Morton studied medicine at the University of Edinburgh where he was influenced by theories of polygenism and the hereditarian views of phrenologists that were in vogue at the time (Spencer, 1983). Underlying Morton's careful craniometric research was the basic theoretical assumption of phrenology: differences in skull shape corresponded to differences in the shape of the brain and consequent differences in brain function. To test these theories, Morton amassed a large collection of human crania from all over the world that he compared using cranial measurements. From this he derived a hierarchy of racial types with blacks at the bottom, American Indians intermediate, and whites at the top (Morton, 1839).

Morton's craniometric approach to understanding human variation set the stage for much of the osteological research done by physical anthropologists during the rest of the nineteenth century. Most of this work was typological in orientation and focused upon the classification of people into broad categories such as brachycephalic (round-headed) or dolichocephalic (long-headed) based on ratios of measurements. Although acceptance of the monogeneticists' theory that all humans trace their ancestry to a single origin gradually increased, especially after the publication of Darwin's theory of natural selection, a typological, craniometrically oriented approach emphasizing taxonomic description and definition over functional interpretation persisted well into the middle of the twentieth century in the work of influential skeletal biologists such as Aleš Hrdlička (1869–1943) and Ernest Hooton (1887–1954).

There are several reasons for the remarkable tenacity of the typological emphasis in research on human skeletal remains. First, there is the idea that human variation can be adequately accommodated by a few fundamentally different racial types, which conveniently coincides with beliefs in racial inferiority and superiority that continue to persist in modern societies. The idea of a straightforward relationship between the shape of a person's skull and their genetic makeup also was seductive to physical anthropologists because it meant that cranial differences could be used as a powerful tool to further one of anthropology's principle goals: producing detailed reconstructions of population movements and historical relationships. Finally, there is a practical consideration behind the persistence of the typological orientation of skeletal research. Until recently, the computational problems of someone attempting to statistically compare quantitative observations made on skeletal collections of any meaningful size were practically insurmountable. The typological approach, with all of its simplifying assumptions and loss of information on within-group heterogeneity, offered a cost-effective alternative to this practical dilemma.

The last point is nicely illustrated by the anthropometric work of Franz Boas (1858–1942), the founder of American anthropology and a strong opponent of simplistic hereditarian interpretations of human variation. Through his anthropometric studies of Europeans who immigrated to the United States, Boas showed that the shape of the cranial vault, a trait nineteenth-century racial typologists had fixated upon, is highly responsive to environmental influences and thus of limited value in taxonomic analysis (Boas, 1912). Boas realized the potential of anthropometric research for elucidating the cultural and biological history of our species and from 1888 to 1903 worked to assemble anthropometric data on 15,000 Native Americans and 2,000 Siberians (Jantz et al., 1992). In contrast to Hrdlizčka and many of his other contemporaries, Boas realized the necessity of statistical analysis for understanding the variability within these samples. Unfortunately, the computational capabilities of the data processing tools that were available at the beginning of the nineteenth century (i.e., pencil and paper) made meaningful analysis of the information on human variation contained within this monumental collection of anthropometric observations impossible (Jantz, 1995). Consequently, almost nothing was done with these data until a few years ago when availability of computers with adequate data storage and processing capability made their analysis possible (see Pietrusewsky, Chapter 14).

During the past thirty years, physical anthropology has finally escaped from the methodological and conceptual shackles of nineteenth-century racial typology. Research on the skeletal remains of earlier human populations has entered a vibrant new phase in which the great potential Boas saw in studies of human variation as a source of insights into the biological and cultural evolution of humankind is beginning to be realized. This paradigm shift has involved replacing the futile nineteenth-century preoccupation with drawing stable boundaries around populations, whose biological and cultural makeup is constantly in flux, with new evolutionary ecological approaches that recognize the complexity and adaptive significance of interactions between genetic variability and developmental plasticity. This theoretical reorientation has resulted in a new bioarchaeological approach to the analysis of skeletal remains from earlier human populations that uses cultural, biological, and paleoenvironmental evidence to illuminate the processes of human adaptation (Larsen, 1997). With this new approach has come an increasing appreciation for the many ways the remains of our ancestors can help us to both better understand and devise solutions to the many seemingly intractable problems of violence, disease, and social inequity that we currently face.

THE SOURCES OF SKELETAL COLLECTIONS

To fully appreciate the concerns that modern indigenous people have about collections of human skeletons, it is necessary to understand the historical and social context in which skeletal collections have been made throughout history. The practice of collecting human skeletal remains as war trophies and for religious purposes has deep historical roots. It has been argued that taking the heads of the dead to obtain their power is among the earliest of ritual practices (La Barre, 1984). In the past, the taking of heads, scalps, and other body parts during warfare was a widespread practice, especially among Native Americans and Melanesians, and can nearly be considered a cultural universal (Driver, 1969; Harner, 1972; Olsen and Shipman, 1994; Owsley et al., 1994; White and Toth, 1991; Willey and Emerson, 1993). Although suppressed in modern societies, such practices continue in the form of the collection of "trophy skulls" from battlefields by modern soldiers (McCarthy, 1994; Sledzik and Ousley, 1991).

Among Christians, the belief that proximity to the bones and other body parts of saints could bring miracles was common as early as the fourth century A.D. This use of human remains as objects of religious veneration gradually resulted in the accumulation of substantial skeletal collections. By the ninth century the remains of martyrs had become so valuable that competition between religious centers created a regular commerce that sometimes degenerated to the point of melees between monks attempting seize the bodies of martyrs by force of arms (Gauthier, 1986; Geary, 1978; Thurston, 1913). The belief that the miraculous powers of important religious figures could be accessed through their bones stimulated a lively market in human remains. At one point 19 churches claimed to possess the mandible of John the Baptist (Collin de Plancy, 1821). Philip II (1556–1598) of Spain, a zealous Catholic, commissioned an envoy to collect the remains of as many saints and martyrs as he could, and assembled a collection of 11 complete skeletons along with thousands of skulls, long bones, and other miscellaneous skeletal elements at his residence, the Escorial near Madrid (Wittlin, 1949). Belief in the magical powers of human remains was not limited to those of Catholic saints. When an Egyptian mummy was obtained by Leipzig,

Germany, in 1693 it soon became a tourist attraction owing to the common belief "that it pierceth all parts, restores wasted limbs, consumption, heckticks, and cures all ulcers and corruption" (Wittlin, 1949).

Until the middle of the eighteenth century, Europe had no museum collections in the modern sense. Instead, there were vast collections held by monarchs and the Catholic Church that functioned as reliquaries, storehouses, and treasuries. During the Enlightenment, a strong belief in the power of empirical investigations of the natural world as a method for the discovery of God's laws brought with it a need for museums whose purpose was the preservation of historical artifacts and natural objects for scientific scrutiny. At first these collections took the form of "curio cabinets" maintained by wealthy aristocrats for their personal research and the edification of their friends. Many of these early collectors were physicians and, owing to their professional interest in human anatomy, they naturally included human skeletons and preserved anatomical specimens in their cabinets. For example, the large collection amassed by Sir Hans Sloane (1660–1753), the personal physician to Queen Anne and King George II, included a number of human skeletons. Upon Sloane's death, these skeletons and the rest of his collection were bequeathed to the British Parliament at a nominal sum and served as the nucleus of the British Museum's natural history collection. In America, scholarly associations such as The Library Company of Philadelphia, which was formed in 1731 by Benjamin Franklin and his colleagues, began to maintain collections that included anatomical specimens and, around the same time, the Pennsylvania Hospital in Philadelphia established its teaching cabinet with the acquisition of a human skeleton and a series of anatomical models (Orosz, 1990:16–17).

These collections of skeletons and anatomical specimens were of great value because they made it possible to provide instruction in surgical anatomy without offending Christians who had religious objections to the dissection of cadavers. During the last half of the eighteenth century, the inadequacies of the old system of learning anatomy by studying models and occasionally observing a demonstrator dissect a criminal's body became increasingly apparent. With the growth of medical knowledge, aspiring surgeons began clamoring for more hands-on experience so they could avoid the horrifying prospect of learning their trade through the butchery of their first living patients. This desire was reinforced by a growing public recognition of the value of being operated upon by someone with practical experience in dissection.

These social pressures resulted in an exponential increase in the demand for cadavers. To meet this need, "anatomical acts" were eventually passed that expanded the legal sources of cadavers to include the victims of duels, suicides, and, most importantly, unclaimed bodies. The demand was so great that this new legal supply of bodies was often inadequate and, throughout the nineteenth century, medical schools were still enlisting the services of body snatchers to obtain their instructional materials (Blake, 1955; Blakely et al., 1997; Newman, 1957).

Although the increase in dissections opened the possibility of increasing the scope of skeletal collections, this potential was not fully realized. Collections were made of specimens with interesting anomalies and pathological conditions but, as a rule, the rest of the dissected person's skeleton was disposed of in what often seems to have been a cavalier fashion (Blakely, 1997:167). From what can be discerned from the remnants of nineteenth-century medical school collections that survive today, little effort was made to create carefully documented skeletal collections of known age and sex for use in assessing the normal range of human variation. The failure to create such systematic collections probably stems in part from the prevalence of racist views that minimized the importance of variation within groups and exaggerated the significance of population differences.

The immensity of the carnage brought by the Civil War profoundly affected attitudes toward the dead in the United States (Laderman,

1996). The war desensitized people to death and this made it possible to view corpses with increasing detachment. At the same time, the logistic problems the military faced in preserving the bodies of so many dead soldiers for transportation back to their families turned corpses into commodities that needed to be processed by professionals such as doctors and undertakers. In this context of mass slaughter, rising professionalism, and growing rejection of religious beliefs in the resurrection of the body, surgeons struggling to devise standardized treatments for the sometimes horrifying injuries they faced began to view autopsies and other medical research on dead soldiers as an ethical imperative. To accommodate this research the Army Medical Museum was founded in 1862 as a repository for thousands of skeletal specimens, preserved organs, photographs, and other medical records obtained during the treatment and autopsy of military casualties (Barnes et al., 1870; Otis and Woodward, 1865).

At the close of the Civil War, army doctors shifted the focus of their collecting activities toward medical concerns arising from the Indian wars in the western United States, such as the treatment of arrow wounds (Bill, 1862; Parker, 1883; Wilson, 1901). One aspect of this work involved the collection of Native American crania and artifacts from battlefields and cemeteries. This was implemented through a letter from the Surgeon General's Office, dated January 13, 1868, that stated: "Will you allow me to ask your kind interposition in urging upon the medical officers in your departments the importance of collecting for the Army Medical Museum specimens of Indian Crania and of Indian Weapons and Utensils, so far as they may be able to procure them." Other documents make it clear that these collections were made under the protest of the Indians whose graves were being raided and that such activities could even result in further hostilities with the Indians (Bieder, 1992). Although government sanctioned grave robbing of this kind eventually stopped, it understandably continues to provoke outrage among the descendants of

the people whose bodies were stolen (Riding In, 1992).

Beginning in the middle of the nineteenth century, large public natural history museums began to be established whose goals were both popular education and scholarly research (Orosz, 1990). These museums provided an institutional framework within which the large skeletal collections could be consolidated from the smaller private collections of physicians and wealthy amateur archaeologists. These new museums had the resources necessary to maintain staffs of professional research scientists and to augment their osteological collections through purchases from private collectors and the sponsorship of archaeological expeditions throughout the world.

In the United States, the most important natural history museums from the perspective of collections of human skeletal remains are the Smithsonian Institution, founded in 1846, the Peabody Museum of Archaeology and Ethnology, founded 1866, the American Museum of Natural History, founded in 1869, the Harvard Peabody Museum of Archaeology and Ethnology, founded in 1866, the Columbian Museum of Chicago (now the Chicago Field Museum), founded in 1893, the Lowie Museum of Anthropology (now the Phoebe Hearst Museum), founded in 1901, and the San Diego Museum of Man, founded in 1915. During the twentieth century the number of museums with significant holdings of human skeletal remains rapidly increased and by 1998 about 700 federal and private institutions possessed skeletal remains from an estimated 110,000 individuals.

The research value of these collections varies enormously depending upon the conditions under which they were collected. Owing to the cranial typology orientation of nineteenth-century physicians, most of the material collected before the beginning of the twentieth century consists of isolated crania, lacking associated mandibles or infracranial remains. Because of the predisposition of these researchers to interpret human variation within a framework of stable types that were comparatively immune to environmental influences, most of them lack adequate provenience information and are simply labeled in terms of preconceived racial categories or broad geographical regions. All of these factors greatly reduce the value of such collections for research purposes. Fortunately, most of the skeletal material in museums derives from the work of professional archaeologists and is associated with at least some contextual information that allows the individual to be placed in a meaningful historical, environmental, and cultural context. This type of information is essential for modern bioarchaeological research, which relies heavily on contextual information to reconstruct the cultural ecology of earlier human populations.

During the first half of the twentieth century, several visionary anatomists realized the value of having skeletons from individuals of known age, sex, and ethnic background for use in anthropological and forensic research on the effects that environmental and genetic factors have on health, disease, and morphological variation. Working in conjunction with the teaching programs of medical schools, these researchers carefully recorded anthropometric data, vital statistics, health histories, and other relevant information on the people scheduled for dissection. Afterwards they prepared their skeletons for curation in research collections. Three of the largest of these dissection room collections were established in the United States, at the Washington University School of Medicine in St. Louis, the Western Reserve University in Cleveland, and Howard University in Washington, D.C.

A central figure in the creation of these collections is William Montague Cobb (1904–1990). Cobb, an African-American, who was an acknowledged activist leader in the African American community, realized the value that empirical data on human variation has as an antidote to racism (see also Ubelaker, Chapter 2). After receiving his medical degree at Howard University, he did postgraduate studies at the Western Reserve University where he helped T. Wingate Todd (1885–1938) assemble that university's skeletal collection.

After writing a doctoral dissertation on anthropological materials, which included information on the geographic and ethnic origins of the people who contributed their skeletons to the Western Reserve collection, Cobb returned to Washington where he created a similar collection at Howard University (Cobb, 1936). A prolific author and dedicated teacher of anatomy, Cobb used his understanding of human biology, which in part was derived from dissections and skeletal research, to improve the health and reinforce the civil rights of African Americans (Cobb, 1939; Cobb, 1948; Rankin-Hill and Blakey, 1994).

In Great Britain and Europe, a different approach has been taken to the creation of known age and sex skeletal collections for use in anthropological research. The crypts outside Saint Bride's Church, London, were disturbed through bombing during World War II. Restoration of the church has resulted in a documented collection of skeletal remains dating from the mid-eighteenth century (Huda and Bowman, 1995; Scheuer and Bowman, 1995). Similar collections of people of known age and sex from historic cemeteries have been established in Coimbra, Portugal (Cunha, 1995), Lisbon, Portugal, Geneva, Switzerland (Gemmerich, 1997) and Hallstatt, Austria (Sjøvold, 1990, 1993). However, a great many anatomical collections of skeletons of nineteenth- and twentieth-century individuals exist in anatomy departments and medical schools throughout Europe, Britain, and other countries.

THE VALUE OF HUMAN SKELETAL REMAINS

In the ongoing debate over the disposition and scientific analysis of ancient human remains in museum collections, there is a tendency for the ethical issues surrounding skeletal research and the maintenance of skeletal collections to be reduced to simplistic oppositions: science versus religion, right versus wrong, and so on. Although framing the complex social issues underlying the debate in this way may be politically expedient, it is counterproductive for anyone seeking a solution that balances the concerns of descendants against those of the scientific community.

From my brief discussion of the evolution of beliefs about human remains, it is obvious that the details of the rituals people have devised for the treatment of the dead have varied enormously among the cultures of the world through time. The practice of funeral rites by friends and relatives and the use of a method of disposing of the body appear to be human universals but, beyond that, there is little uniformity (Brown, 1991; Murdock, 1945). This diversity of beliefs about how the dead should be treated poses ethical dilemmas for bioarchaeologists when their scientific work conflicts with the beliefs of the descendants of the people whose remains they study.

One approach to resolving disputes over research on ancient skeletal remains is to view such disagreements as cultural issues arising from competing value systems (Goldstein and Kintigh, 1990). Conceiving of disputes over the treatment of the dead as products of conflicting value systems avoids polemics and self-righteous posturing in which each side battles for moral superiority and instead promotes communication and mutual understanding. This can eventually result in the discovery of solutions that are consistent with the value systems of both parties in the dispute.

The only justification for the study of skeletal remains from earlier human populations is that such research yields information that is useful to modern people. Although the value of skeletal research seems self-evident to the people who conduct it, there are many indigenous people who feel that such work is not only useless, but also extremely harmful owing to the damage it does to them and the spirits of their ancestors. This conflict between the values scientists and descendant groups attach to human remains is central to the most important ethical dilemmas bioarchaeologists face. Since mutual understanding is a prerequisite for finding a common ground between these apparently incommensurable world views, it is useful to briefly describe the values scientists and descendant groups attach to ancient human remains.

Bioarchaeologists focus their research on ancient human skeletal remains, not out of idle scientific curiosity, but instead because they believe that the information contained within the remains of our ancestors is of great value to modern people. Human skeletal remains are a unique source of information on the genetic and physiological responses our ancestors made to the challenges posed by past natural and sociocultural environments. Consequently, they provide an extremely valuable adaptive perspective on the history of our species.

Most of what we know about our recent history is based on inferences derived through analysis of artifacts, documents, oral histories, and other products of human cultural activity. Owing to their symbolic content, such cultural artifacts are difficult to interpret and often consistent with multiple, sometimes contradictory views of the past. The subjective aspects of attempting to interpret cultural artifacts from the perspective of our current cultural milieu are well recognized: Historical works often reveal more about the cultural values and political biases of the historian than they do about the reality of the historical event being described. All historians are products of the culture in which they live, and they are always selective in what they report.

Because of its biological basis in the physiological processes of growth, development, and acclimatization to environmental change, the information about interactions with past environments encoded in human remains provides an extremely valuable comparative basis for evaluating interpretations of the past based on artifacts, documents, and other culture-based sources. The historical data provided by skeletal studies are of such great value because the methodological problems inherent in extracting evidence from a skeleton are completely different from those historians face when they attempt to interpret the historical significance of the cultural products with which they work. The only way we can reduce the cultural biases that distort our understanding of past events is through collecting a diversity of evidence from sources that are susceptible to different types of interpretative error. The greater the diversity of the evidence we have about the past, the easier it is to rule out alternative interpretations that are unlikely to reflect actual events. By using a series of data sources that, standing alone, would be open to many different interpretations, it is in this way possible to triangulate on what really happened in the past.

The unique perspective that skeletal evidence provides on the history of our species makes it a potent weapon against cultural relativists and historical revisionists who view the past as a source of raw materials they can exploit to refashion history into whatever narrative is currently considered *au courant* or politically expedient. In some schools of postmodernist thought, history is viewed as a symbolic construct devoid of any objective truth: all we are left with is an endless process of constructing conflicting narratives about the past that are all of equal merit or are only of merit because they are different. In some rarified corners of the humanities, the possibility of knowing with certainty that voluminously documented historical events such as the Holocaust actually occurred is actively debated (Braun, 1994; Friedman, 1998; Jordan, 1995; Kellner, 1994). In the world of these theorists, people interested in discovering what happened in the Holocaust are doomed to an academic life of continuously revisualizing and recontextualizing subjective impressions of subjective descriptions of the slaughter of millions of people into new, contradictory, and, from their perspectives, more meaningful imaginations of the past.

In contrast to the symbolic problems inherent in historical reconstructions based upon written records and oral histories, human skeletal remains provide a direct source of evidence about the lives and deaths of ancient and modern people that is, at a fundamental level, free from cultural bias (Walker, 1997). The skeletons of the people buried row upon row at concentration camps such as Terezin, the racks of skulls from the Cambodian killing fields at Tuol Sleng Prison, and the cut marks on the skeletons of the hundreds of massacred prehistoric Native Americans unceremoniously buried at the Crow Creek site in South Dakota speak volumes about real historical events that ended the lives of real people.

In certain respects, bones do not lie. To give a specific example from my own research, the presence of lesions indicative of severe, repeated physical abuse in the skeletons of children murdered by their parents says something very specific about a history of traumatic experiences that a child suffered during its short life (Walker, 2000; Walker et al., 1997). Although multiple "narratives" can be constructed based on the presence of such lesions (the child was extraordinarily clumsy or accident prone, the child's parents repeatedly beat him over a prolonged period until he died, and so on), at a fundamental level such skeletal evidence says something indisputable about a physical interaction that took place between the dead child and his or her physical environment. Unlike written records or oral histories, human remains are not culture-dependent symbolic constructs. Instead they provide an extraordinarily detailed material record of actual physical interactions that occurred between our ancestors and their natural and sociocultural environments. As such, human remains are extremely valuable sources of evidence for reconstructing what actually happened in the past.

This esoteric view that bioarchaeologists hold concerning the central role that collections of human skeletal remains play in helping us to obtain an objective view of history is not widespread. The vast majority of the world's population views human remains with a mixture of morbid fascination and dread because they serve as such vivid reminders of one's own mortality and impending death. The symbolic saliency of directly confronting a dead person has been deftly exploited for a diversity of religious, political, and economic purposes. Throughout the world, in many different settings, human remains are placed on public display and used in ways designed to foster group cohesion and legitimize religious or political authority. During times of social instability, it is common for these same remains to be destroyed or humiliated to weaken and disrupt the group solidarity they once fostered (Cantwell, 1990). The controversy over the continued display of Lenin's remains in Red Square and the disposition of the recently discovered remains of Czar Nicholas II and his family provide good examples of how human remains can be used as tools to advance or suppress political ideas and facilitate or disrupt social cohesion (Caryl, 1998; Fenyvesi, 1997).

The strong symbolic power of human remains has encouraged people to devise an amazing number of uses for them. Throughout the world, displays of human remains are among the most effective tools for luring people into museums. At the British Museum, for example, postcards of mummies rival the Rosetta Stone in public popularity (Beard, 1992). In many places displays of human remains are such popular tourist attractions that they have become the mainstays of local economies. The Museo de los Momias in Mexico, where the naturally mummified bodies of poor people who could not afford to purchase permanent graves are on display, is touted as Mexico's second most popular museum, bested only by the anthropological museum in Mexico City (Osmond, 1998). Two similar examples are the awe-inspiring creativity of displays of thousands of disinterred human bones in the All Saints Cemetery Chapel near Kutna Hora in the Czech Republic and in the Church of the Capuchins in Rome (Fig. 1.1).

In some cases the symbolic value of retaining human remains for display is sufficient to override religious sanctions against it. Medieval Chinese Ch'an Buddhists practiced mummification of eminent priests as demonstrations of the relationship between spiritual attainment and the incorruptibility of the body even though they espoused a religious doctrine that accorded little value to the corpse. A similar example is the recent decision that the value of the display of bones from Khmer Rough victims at the Tuol

Sleng Prison Museum as evidence of the Cambodian genocide outweighed Buddhist religious beliefs that mandate cremation (Erlanger, 1988; Peters, 1995). The denial of burial in Christian countries as a form of posthumous punishment and object lesson for the living has already been mentioned. In England, the heads of people such as Oliver Cromwell were displayed on poles erected on the roof of the Great Stone Gate of London Bridge, and gibbets containing the rotting bodies of famous pirates such as Captain Kidd were strategically placed along the banks of the Thames to greet sailors as they returned from the sea. During the nineteenth century, the heads of Miguel Hidalgo and three other leaders of the Mexican war of independence met a similar fate when they hung on public display in cages for ten years as grim reminders of the folly of revolution. Ironically, these same skulls of Mexico's founding fathers have recently been resurrected and again put on public display for the opposite purpose: they rest next to each other under glass on red velvet in a dimly lit crypt where they remind school children of the heroism of the country's founders (Osmond, 1998).

As is illustrated by the case of Hidalgo's skull, the strong symbolic value of human remains endow those who control them with a powerful tool that can be used to vividly express multiple, sometimes contradictory, meanings. Owing to this great symbolic power, it is not surprising that issues surrounding the control, treatment, and disposition of human remains pose some of the most vexing ethical dilemmas skeletal biologists face. Bioarchaeologists do not view human remains primarily as symbols. Instead they value them as sources of historical evidence that are key to understanding what really happened during the biological and cultural evolution of our species. This lack of concern with symbolic issues is in stark contrast to the richness of the symbolic connotations human skeletons have for most people. This conflict in worldviews is especially acute in areas of the world that were subjected to European colonization. In North America, Hawaii, and Australia, where the

Figure 1.1   The interior of the All Saints Cemetery Chapel in Sedlec, a suburb of Kutna Hora in the Czech Republic. The chapel is decorated with the bones of some 40,000 people whose remains were excavated by from a nearby graveyard by Monks of the Cistercian order.

indigenous people suffered the greatest devastation at the hands of European colonists, ancient human remains have assumed great significance as symbols of cultural integrity and colonial oppression. In this postcolonial world, gaining control over ancestral remains is increasingly considered essential to the survival and revitalization of indigenous cultures.

That the views of indigenous people concerning this issue have changed dramatically during the past forty years is amply illustrated by archaeological reports that describe the enthusiastic participation of Native Americans in the excavation of burials, some of whose study by bioarchaeologists are currently under dispute (Benson and Bowers, 1997; Brew, 1941;

Fewkes, 1898; Hewett, 1953; Hrdlička, 1930a, 1930b, 1931; Hurt et al., 1962; Judd, 1968; Neuman, 1975; Roberts, 1931; Smith, 1971; Smith et al., 1966). As late as the 1960s, Inuit people in the Northwest Territory of Canada who I worked with seemed little concerned about the excavation of ancient skeletal remains. In fact, they were extremely cordial to the members of the expedition I was on and assisted us in any way they could. Although they expressed mild concerns about carrying human skeletons in their boats, they otherwise were supportive of and expressed considerable interest in our bioarchaeological work.

To comprehend the urgency of the current concerns Native Americans have about the treatment of their ancestral remains it is necessary to understand the magnitude of the recent disruptions of their cultures. Beginning at the end of the nineteenth century, systematic attempts began to be made to separate Native American children from their families, suppress their Native identities, and inculcate them with Christian values (Ellis C, 1996; Lomawaima, 1993). Simultaneously, the isolation that formerly characterized life on the remote reservations in marginal areas that the government relegated them to began to break down owing to the development of interstate highways, radio, television, and the intrusions of tourists. These developments have had such a devastating effect on the transmission of traditional beliefs and practices that the remnants of earlier times preserved in museums have increasingly become a cultural focus. Control over these collections is an important political issue for Native Americans because, by gaining control over the biological and cultural remains of their ancestors, they can begin to reassert their cultural identity within the dominant Euro-American culture.

When viewed within this context of cultural marginalization and repression, it is easy to see why many indigenous people see little value in what to them are the very nebulous goals of bioarchaeologists. Zimmerman (Ubelaker and Grant, 1989) presents evidence supporting the depth of Indian concern about the retention of museum collections. He cites an unpublished survey that John S. Sigstad conducted in 1972 of Indian tribes in the BIA Aberdeen region. All respondents agreed that human remains in museums should be reburied, 95% indicated bones should not be displayed in museums, and only 35% of the respondents believed that human remains should be excavated for scientific research (Ubelaker and Grant, 1989).

Some indigenous people have the erroneous belief that only the remains of their ancestors are studied and cite this as a reflection of the racist attitudes of the European colonists who robbed them of their land (Tobias, 1991; Vizenor, 1986). They feel that such research degrades them by singling them out to be "made fun of and looked at as novelties" (Mihesuah, 1996; Walters, 1989). Bioarchaeologists respond to this charge by pointing out the vast collections of non–Native American skeletal remains in European museums and arguing that it would be racist not to have collections of Native American remains in New World museums, since this would imply that knowledge of the history of the indigenous people of the New World had nothing to contribute to the understanding of our common past (Ubelaker and Grant, 1989).

Some indigenous people reject the epistemology of science, at least as it applies to their history and cultural affairs, and instead prefer to view the past as it is revealed through traditional ways of knowing, such as oral history, legend, myth, and appeal to the authority of revered leaders. For people with this perspective, scientific research directed toward documenting the past is not only superfluous, but also potentially culturally subversive owing to the capacity of scientific evidence to conflict with traditional beliefs about the past and, in this way, undermine the authority of traditional religious leaders. From this perspective, scientific investigations into the history of indigenous cultures are simply another manifestation of the attempts of an oppressive imperialist colonial power to control and weaken the belief systems of indigenous people so that they will be easier to exploit (Bray, 1995; Dirlik, 1996; Riding In, 1996).

In academia, this position clearly resonates with radical postmodernist theorists of the humanities who believe that reconstructing history as an objective reality is a hopeless endeavor and instead argue that history is a symbolic weapon that ethical people should use to help the marginal political and cultural constituencies of the world in their struggles against the holders of power (Hodder et al., 1995).

This tension between traditional and scientific views of the past has recently been brought into sharp focus through the controversy over the disposition of the 9,300-year-old human remains found at the Kennewick site on the banks of the Columbia River in Washington State (Hastings and Sampson, 1997; Lemonick, 1996; Morell, 1998; Petit, 1998; Preston, 1997; Slayman, 1997). Scientists who have examined these remains say they possess characteristics unlike those of modern Native Americans. They believe that research into reasons for this difference has the potential to make an important contribution to our understanding of the history of humankind. Members of the five Native American tribes that have claimed the skeleton, on the other hand, believe that the question of the cultural affiliation of this individual has already been resolved by their elders who tell them that they have lived in the area where the skeleton was found since the beginning of creation. The complexity of this dispute increased further when members of the Asutru Folk Assembly, a traditional European pagan religion, sued for the right to use scientific research to decide if this individual is one of their ancestors. They claim that "It's not an accident that he came to us at this time and place . . . Our job is to listen to (the bones) and hear what they have to say" (Lee, 1997).

Modern indigenous people often frame such disputes over the power to control the interpretation of tribal history in spiritual terms. It is a common pan-Indian religious belief that all modern Native Americans are spiritually linked to all other Indian people living and dead (Walters, 1989). Another widely held belief is that space is spherical and time is cyclical (Clark, 1997). All living Indians thus have a responsibility for the spiritual well-being of their ancestors that requires them to assure that their ancestors are buried in the ground where they can be reintegrated into the earth and complete the circle of life and death (Bray, 1995; Halfe, 1989). Contemporary Native Americans who hold these beliefs argue that, so long as ancestral spirits are suffering because their bones are not buried in the earth, living people will continue to suffer a myriad of adverse consequences. Thus, any activity inconsistent with reburial, such as excavation, study, museum curation, and storage, is considered an act of desecration and disrespect. For indigenous people with such views, there is no middle ground upon which scientific research can be conducted on human skeletal remains and associated artifacts. These remains are of great spiritual and psychological importance and their reburial is required to heal the wounds of colonial oppression (Emspak, 1995; Murray and Allen, 1995)

ETHICAL RESPONSIBILITIES OF SKELETAL BIOLOGISTS

Given these sharply polarized views concerning the value of scientific research on human remains, what are the ethical responsibilities of skeletal biologists? On one hand, we have bioarchaeologists who believe that the historical evidence obtained from human remains is critical for defending humankind against the historical revisionist tendencies of repressive, genocidal political systems, and, on the other, we have indigenous people who believe that the spirits of their ancestors are being tortured on the shelves of museums by racist, genocidal, colonial oppressors. If we can accept the relativist perspective that both of these views have some validity, then it is possible to envisage a compromise that gives due recognition to both value systems.

Although there is still a broad spectrum of perceptions of what is right and what is wrong among modern people, with the precipitous decline in cultural diversity that has occurred owing to the expansion of modern communication systems, we are seeing a worldwide convergence of values, at least concerning certain areas of human affairs (Donaldson, 1992). These shared values are developing as part of the evolution of the transnational political and economic systems that are beginning to unite the world's disparate cultures. The Declaration of Human Rights of the United Nations, for example, provides a generally accepted set of rules for ethical human behavior that most people can accept in principle, if not in practice. They include recognition of the right to equality, freedom from discrimination, freedom from torture and degrading treatment, freedom from interference with privacy, and freedom of belief and religion (UN, 1948). Other attempts to devise a set of ethical rules that encompass what some people believe is emerging as a culturally universal system of moral principles include widespread humanistic values such as the recognition that it is wrong to be indifferent to suffering, that tolerance of the beliefs of others is good, and that people ought to be free to live as they choose without having their affairs deliberately interfered with by others (Hatch, 1983).

The cultural values expressed by the assertion of basic human rights and universal moral principles such as these can be criticized as hegemonic attempts to use Western cultural ideas as tools for gaining power and political control for transnational business interests. For example, the Chinese government has recently criticized allegations concerning its suppression of the rights of political dissidents as insensitive to unique Chinese cultural values such as obedience to authority, collectivism, family, and other dispositions (Li, 1998).

This issue of developing universal, government-sponsored standards of ethical behavior is of more than theoretical interest to bioarchaeologists since it is commonly asserted that the maintenance of skeletal collections for use in scientific research is a violation of a fundamental human right. For example, Article X of the draft of the "Inter-American Declaration on

the Rights of Indigenous Peoples" approved by the Inter-American Commission on Human Rights of the Organization of American States in a section entitled "Spiritual and Religious Freedom" specifically states that when "sacred graves and relics have been appropriated by state institutions, they shall be returned" to indigenous people (IACHR, 1995).

At the opposite end of the spectrum of political inclusiveness and governmental authority from the UN and OAS statements on human rights are the ethics statements that professional associations develop for their members to use as guides for the decisions they make during their everyday activities. The decline in the capacity of organized religions and other traditional social institutions to impose a unifying set of ethical principles acceptable to modern multicultural societies, and the constant stream of ethical challenges posed by new technological developments has stimulated enormous interest in the formulation of standards for ethical conduct in many areas of professional activity (Behi and Nolan, 1995; Bulger, 1994; Fluehr-Lobban, 1991; Kruckeberg, 1996; Kuhse et al., 1997; Kunstadter, 1980; Lynott, 1997; Muller and Desmond, 1992; Navran, 1997; Parker, 1994; Pellegrino, 1995; Pyne, 1994; Salmon, 1997; Scanlon and Glover, 1995; Schick, 1998).

Many professional associations and governmental agencies have developed ethical guidelines for use by researchers in the biomedical and social sciences that contain information directly relevant to resolving the ethical dilemmas bioarchaeologists face when they work with ancient human remains (AAA, 1986, 1997; AIA, 1991, 1994; CAPA, 1979; MRCC, 1998; NAPA, 1988; NAS, 1995; SAA, 1996; SAP, 1983; SPA, 1976; UNESCO, 1995).

Although only a few of these statements deal specifically with issues surrounding the study of human remains, a comparison of the principles for ethical behavior they espouse suggests considerable agreement on a few fundamental rules that can be used to guide researchers who work with ancient human remains: (1) human remains should be treated with dignity and respect, (2) descendants should have the authority to control the disposition of the remains of their relatives, and (3) owing to their importance for understanding the history of our species, the preservation of collections of archaeological collections of human remains is an ethical imperative.

Each of these principles is based upon a complicated set of value judgments whose implications for the real-world practices of skeletal biologists depend in many ways upon the cultural lens through which they are viewed. For example, what is considered the dignified treatment of human remains varies widely depending on a person's cultural background. These ethical principles also contain an inherent contradiction since recognizing the rights of descendants may at times conflict with the preservation ethic.

Respect for Human Dignity

The ethical principle that human remains should be treated with respect and dignity is consistent with, and can be seen as an extension of, respect for human dignity, which is the cardinal ethical principle for modern research on human subjects in the biomedical and social sciences (Margareta, 1996; MRCC, 1998; UNESCO, 1995). This ethical principle is based upon the belief that it is unacceptable to treat human remains solely as a means (mere objects or things), because doing so fails to respect the intrinsic human dignity of the person they represent and thus impoverishes all of humanity. An argument can be made that since the remains of dead people are just "decaying organic matter" that "feels nothing, conceptualizes nothing, has no interests, and cannot suffer," in other words, that there is no person here to respect or disrespect, the respect is not for the body, but the antemortem person from whom the remains are derived (Lynch, 1990). Although it is true that, for most skeletal biologists, human remains are viewed as depersonalized and desanctified, there is still general agreement that they are nevertheless highly meaningful and should be treated with dignity

and respect (Buikstra, 1981; Ubelaker and Grant, 1989).

A skeptic might question the wisdom of extending the concept of human dignity to the dead: What does the treatment of human remains have to do with human rights or human dignity? In view of the atrocities currently being perpetrated on helpless people by repressive governments throughout the world, would it not be more productive to focus the fight for human rights on living people who could actually benefit from the results? In my view, a convincing argument can be made that, although the human being that skeletal remains are derived from no longer exists, their former intimate association with a living person is more than sufficient to earn them respectful treatment. The logic of this argument is similar to that used by animal rights activists who admit that, although animals by definition do not have human rights, their ill-treatment does demean humans and thus has implications for human behavior (McShea, 1994; Man's Mirror, 1991). In the same way it can be argued that disrespectful treatment of human remains is morally repugnant because of its potential to desensitize people in a way that is likely to encourage a lack of respect for and consequent ill-treatment of the living (Grey, 1983:105–153).

If we accept the premise that it is unethical to treat human remains with disrespect, we are still faced with the problem that respectful treatment is a highly subjective concept. The cultures of the world have devised an enormous variety ways of respecting the dead that include hanging the skulls of close relatives from the rafters of huts, using skulls of parents as pillows, and letting vultures feed upon dead relatives. Some modern people believe that pumping dead relatives full of chemicals, dressing them up, and burying them in the ground is respectful. Others believe that incinerating them, grinding up what's left in a mill, and putting the resulting bone meal in a cardboard box is respectful. In the cultural context of scientific research, respect for human remains derives not only from their association with a person who was once alive, but also from an appreciation of the information about the past they can yield. To a scientist, respectful treatment of human remains includes taking measures to insure the physical integrity of the remains and the documentation associated with them, avoiding treatments that will contaminate or degrade their organic and inorganic constituents, and so on.

These convoluted academic arguments about the definition of and justification for treating human remains with respect, of course, seem bizarre to indigenous people who view ancestral remains not as inanimate objects devoid of life but instead as living entities that are imbued with ancestral spirits. From the perspective of some Native Americans, for example, ancient human skeletons are "not just remains, they're not bone to be studied, you're dealing with spirits as you touch those remains" (Augustine, 1994). As Rachel Craig, a Native Alaskan put it, "I feel an obligation to give back to them, to speak for them. Our grandmothers have told us the importance of the spirit world. The spirits of those people cannot rest and make their progress in the spirit world unless they know that those bones are put back in the earth where they belong. That is our teaching" (Craig, 1994). This same view of the retention of skeletons in museums as interfering with the afterlife and separating the spirits of the dead from the community of the living is forcefully expressed by William Tallbull, a member of the Northern Cheyenne tribe: "We talk about people coming home. When the people came home from the museum and are buried at home, they all go and visit every house. This is where the joy comes in. They are home. They are here. They walk around through the village and become part of us again. That's all we are asking" (Tallbull, 1994).

Descendant Rights

Since disputes over who should have the right to control the disposition of ancient human remains are central to many of the ethical dilemmas bioarchaeologists face, it is useful to consider this issue in as broad a perspective as possible. Giving close relatives authority to make decisions about the disposition of the remains of the recent dead appears to be a cultural universal. Only in exceptional circumstances, such as the special dispositions mandated for the bodies of executed criminals as part of their punishment, and the control that coroners are given over bodies that might yield evidence relevant to legal proceedings, is the right of close relatives to decide the disposition of a body denied. Many cultures have special rules governing the disposition of the bodies of people who die under unusual circumstances, and some of these make exceptions to the rule of kin control over the dead. Herodotus, for example, observed that the Egyptians gave special treatment to the bodies of people who drown in the Nile or were eaten by crocodiles: "No one may touch the corpse, not even any of the friends or relatives, but only the priests of the Nile, who prepare it for burial with their own hands—regarding it as something more than the mere body of a man—and themselves lay it in the tomb" (Herodotus, 1990).

Considering the universal recognition of the rights of relatives, it not surprising that this is one issue upon which, as far as I know, all bioarchaeologists agree: if skeletal remains can be identified as those of a known individual for whom specific biological descendants can be traced, the disposition of those remains, including possible reburial, should be decided by the closest living relatives.

Many of the ethical dilemmas that skeletal biologists face arise not out of a disagreement over this fundamental principle of ethical behavior but, instead, over how the rights of descendants should be recognized in real-world situations. The first problematic area concerns how the rights of relatives with different relationships to the dead person should be balanced against each other. In modern legal systems authority over the dead is judged using a rigid hierarchy of rights. For example, the Uniform Anatomical Gifts Act establishes the following order of priority for people authorized to make decisions about the authorization of removal of body parts: (1) the spouse, (2) an adult son or daughter, (2) either parent, (4) adult brother or sister, (5) the person's legal guardian at the time of death, (6) any other person authorized to dispose of the body. Even here, there is considerable room for cultural variation in rules governing control over the dead. In China, for example, because of its the pervasive patriarchal family structure, authority of the wife regarding funeral arrangements is likely to be less than that of the male members of his patriline (Cooper, 1998).

In contrast to the agreement about giving lineal descendants control over the disposition of the remains of close relatives, there is a no consensus concerning the question of the appropriate way to decide the disposition of human remains that are distantly related to living people. What is the ethical way to decide the disposition of the remains of people who are many generations removed from any living person? How shall we weigh the many attenuated genetic and cultural ties that link large numbers of living people to ancestors who lived thousands, hundreds of thousands, or even millions of years ago? Which living individuals should be granted the moral authority to decide the disposition of our ancient ancestors?

The basic elements of the dilemma can be better understood from a scientific perspective by considering how the genetic and cultural connections that link modern people and earlier generations vary as a function of time. The first problem is that the more distant an ancestor is from a descendant, the more descendants there are sharing the same genetic relationship to that ancestor. The variables that influence the number of shared ancestors that living people have are complex. However, one fact is indisputable: as we probe more deeply into our family tree, the probability of discovering an ancestor we share with a large number of other living people increases dramatically. In a lineage of people who each had two children and did not marry relatives, it would take seven generations, or about 250 years, to produce over five billion modern descendants. People, of course, tend to marry relatives and not

everyone has the same number of children. Even if we account for these complicating variables, the fact remains that many living people are likely to be related to an individual who lived many generations ago.

If we really believe that relatives should decide the disposition of ancestral remains, how can we identify those descendants and allow them to make a collective decision about the proper treatment of their relative's bones? The problem of linking modern people to our hunter-gatherer ancestors is complicated by the highly mobile lifestyle of such populations. This decreases the likelihood that the ancestral remains of a modern group will be found in the territory in which that modern group currently resides. In situations of population replacement, it is in fact more likely that the modern people who now live in an area were directly responsible for the extermination of the ancient people who formerly occupied that same territory.

Even in cases where it is clear that descendants continue to occupy the land of their ancestors, there is still the problem posed by the expansion of living descendants with increasing genealogical remoteness. In an area such as Europe, with a relatively stable gene pool, someone who died more than a few hundred years ago is likely to be related to hundreds of thousands, if not millions of living people. For instance, DNA studies conducted on the 5000-year-old mummified body recently found in the Tyrolean Alps suggest a genetic relationship between this person and the 300 million or so contemporary people living in central and northern Europe (Handt et al., 1994). This of course does not include many millions of additional people living in North America and elsewhere with ancestral ties to northern Europe.

In the Western Hemisphere the problem of assigning rights for the control of ancestral remains to living descendants is complicated by gene flow between indigenous Americans and the people of Europe, Africa, and Asia. For example, geneticists estimate that 31% of the contemporary gene pool of people identified as

Hispanic or Mexican Americans is derived from their Native American ancestors (Gardner et al., 1984; Hanis et al., 1991). These Native American descendants are thus numerically a very significant component of the New World population and, if demographic trends continue, are likely to replace non-Hispanic Euro-Americans as the ethnic majority in the United States in less than one life span (Edmondson, 1996; Nicklin, 1997). If we believe that descendants should have a right to decide the disposition of the remains of their ancestors, then we need to find a way to incorporate the views of Hispanic Americans into the process through which the disposition of ancient American remains is decided.

Some people see focusing on genetic relationships in this way as a myopic and misguided biological reductionism. After all, is not a person's cultural background more important than the genetic links that tie them to earlier generations? From this perspective, there are two types of ancestors, genetic and cultural, and it is the cultural link that a person feels they have with the people who lived in the past that counts. Although the idea of limiting authority to make decisions about the disposition of ancient human remains to people who share the deceased person's cultural identity makes some sense, applying this ethical principle is extremely problematic in real-world situations. If the strength of a modern person's belief in their cultural link to an earlier person's remains is to be the measure of moral authority, how are we to evaluate the relative validity of such beliefs?

To give a specific example, many Native Americans see the intrusions of the "New Age" movement into their cultural identity as the appropriation of Native American spiritual traditions by outsiders who are destroying Indian spirituality and contributing to white racism and genocide (Geertz, 1996; Hernandez-Avila, 1996; Jocks, 1996; Johnson W, 1996b; Kehoe, 1996; Smith, 1991; Specktor, 1989). Is it ethically acceptable to give the same authority to the beliefs of people who received their cultural identity during a psychotherapy session in

which it was revealed to them that they are the reincarnation of an Inca princess, that we give to descendants with demonstrable genetic links to earlier populations? This is where the rejection of scientific evidence and the unconditional acceptance of cultural relativism can become problematic (Goldstein and Kintigh, 1990:587–588).

It is also fair to ask at what point does a living person's cultural connection to a dead person become so attenuated that it merges into the common cultural heritage of all people, and thus no longer provides a moral basis for special rights and control. Several cultural variables could be considered relevant here: a shared language, common religious practices, and so on. The difficulty is weighing the significance of such disparate cultural traits, especially in the context of ancient remains and cultural evolution.

This issue of cultural continuity is a contentious one, in part, because when indigenous cultures are marginalized, disrupted, and driven to the brink of extinction, remnants of the past, including ancestral human remains, become increasingly important as symbols of cultural oppression and survival. This inverse relationship between concern over ancestral remains and cultural continuity is illustrated by the differences between Latin America and North America in concern over ancestral remains and repatriation issues. In Latin American countries where a strong sense of "Indianness" has been integrated into the national identity, human remains are excavated and displayed without opposition in museums. In this context, they serve as symbols of a national past that is shared by and important to all citizens (Ubelaker and Grant, 1989). The government of the United States, in contrast, has historically considered Native Americans as outsiders to be dealt with by isolating them on reservations and suppressing their indigenous languages and beliefs to facilitate converting them into functional members of the dominant Euro-American culture. These government policies have devastated Native American cultures and contributed enormously to the hostility Indian people feel over issues related to the control of ancestral remains.

In the United States, a legislative attempt has been made to use a combination of biological and cultural continuity as the basis for giving modern indigenous groups the rights over ancient skeletal remains. The Native American Graves Protection and Repatriation Act (NAGPRA) gives federally recognized tribes that can demonstrate a "cultural affiliation" to ancestral remains the authority to control their disposition. In this legal context, cultural affiliation means "a relationship of shared group identity which can be reasonably traced historically or prehistorically between a present day group and an identifiable earlier group." In this statute, cultural affiliation is established when "the preponderance of the evidence—based on geographical, kinship, biological, archeological, linguistic, folklore, oral tradition, historical evidence, or other information or expert opinion—reasonably leads" to the conclusion that a federally recognized tribe is culturally affiliated with an "earlier group."

Although NAGPRA has benefited many federally recognized tribes and has had the positive effect of increasing communication between Native Americans and bioarchaeologists, its exclusion of Native Americans who lack federal recognition raises serious ethical issues. It is derided by some Native Americans who see it as another step in the long history of attempts to define "Native American groups" in ways that facilitate their control and manipulation by oppressive governmental agencies. In California, for instance, many groups that by any even-handed definition are authentic "tribes" have failed to receive official recognition by the federal government, or have had their federal recognition removed, and thus are denied full access to the provision of NAGPRA (Goldberg, 1997; Walker, 1995).

Again, these legalistic considerations and academic concerns over how to establish a connection between the living and the dead seem strange to indigenous people whose religious beliefs resolve such issues for them. Many indigenous people are creationists who reject the idea that all modern people share a common ancestor. Instead, some believe that their tribe is the result of a special creation and that they have lived in the area currently occupied by their tribe since the beginning of time. Such beliefs remove any uncertainties regarding ancestral relationships and result in acrimonious disputes between scientists and tribal members such as those that have occurred over the Kennewick skeleton (Hastings and Sampson, 1997; Lemonick, 1996; Morell, 1998; Petit, 1998; Preston, 1997; Slayman, 1997).

The Preservation Ethic

The final universally accepted principle of bioarchaeologists is the preservation ethic. Human remains are a source of unique insights into the history of our species. They constitute the "material memory" of the people who preceded us and thus provide a direct means through which we may come to know our ancestors. Because we believe that the lessons that the remains of our ancestors can teach us about our common heritage have great value to modern people, it is an ethical imperative to work to preserve as much as possible of this information for future generations. This position is championed by governments throughout the world who support archaeological research, encourage the conservation and preservation of archaeological resources, and discourage unnecessary destruction of archaeological sites (Knudson, 1986:397).

As caretakers of this fundamental source of information on the biological history of our species, we need to promote the long-term preservation of skeletal collections and in this way ensure that future generations will have the opportunity to learn from them and in this way know about and understand that history (Turner, 1986). Prehistoric research, including osteological study, is one way that our common heritage can be fully revealed (White and Folkens, 1991:418–423). This position is forcefully expressed in the Society for American Archaeology Statement Concerning the Treatment of Human Remains:

WHEREAS human remains constitute part of the archaeological record and provide unique information about demography, genetic relationship, diet, and disease which is of special significance in interpreting descent, health and nutritional status in living and ancient human groups; and

WHEREAS education and research in the anthropological, biological, social and forensic sciences require that collections of human skeletal remains be available to responsible scholars; and

WHEREAS the study of humankind's past should not discriminate against any biological or cultural group:

THEREFORE BE IT RESOLVED that the Society for American Archaeology deplores the indiscriminant reburial of human skeletal remains and opposes reburial of any human skeletal remains except in situations where specific lineal descendants can be traced and it is the explicit wish of these living descendants that remains be reburied rather than being retained for research purposes; and that no remains should be reburied without appropriate study by physical anthropologists with special training in skeletal biology unless lineal descendants explicitly oppose such study.

AND BE IT FURTHER RESOLVED that the Society for American Archaeology encourage close and effective communication with appropriate groups and with individual scholars who study human remains that may have biological or cultural affinity to those groups (SAA, 1984).

The preservation ethic is based on the scientific premise that there are aspects of our shared reality that have the potential to be brought into sharper focus through the examination of ancient human skeletal remains. The fact that each person sees the world through a slightly different cultural lens does not mean that it is impossible to translate between these different experiences to find a common basis of understanding. The physical facts that we have for deciding what happened in the past are not infinitely plastic and this places material constraints on our culturally biased interpretations.

The progressive aspect of creating the more accurate view of reality that we strive for is an important justification for the preservation of skeletal collections. Most scientists recognize the cultural influences that focus their observations on certain aspects of reality and color the inferences they make based on those observations (Glock, 1995; Tomaskova, 1995; Wylie, 1989). Although we know that our conclusions are to some extent distorted by our cultural biases, we take comfort in the fact that these distortions will be detected and corrected through future research by others with different cultural perspectives.

For this self-correcting aspect of the scientific method to be operative, the evidence upon which our conclusions are based must be available for scrutiny by future researchers. In experimental fields such as physics, this is accomplished through repeating experiments. In historical sciences such as bioarchaeology, our reconstructions of what happened in the past are refined and corrected through the reexamination of collections using new analytical techniques and theoretical perspectives.

During the past twenty years, the rate at which this self-correcting process operates has increased markedly as a result of the restudy of skeletal collections in museums using newly developed analytical techniques that have greatly expanded the types of information we can retrieve from ancient human remains. Especially exciting are new chemical techniques that provide precise information on the types of food people ate (Hult and Fessler, 1998; Stott and Evershed, 1996; Tuross and Stathoplos, 1993; and see Katzenberg, Chapter 11, and Sandford and Weaver, Chapter 12), procedures for reconstructing ancestral relationships through DNA analysis (Hagelberg et al., 1994; Stone and Stoneking, 1993; Von Haeseler et al., 1996, and see Stone, Chapter 13). New techniques are also being developed for reconstructing the disease histories of human populations through the analysis of pathogen-specific bone proteins (Drancourt et al., 1998; Hoffman, 1998; Ortner et al., 1992).

The development of these new, enormously informative, analytical techniques underscores how valuable human remains are as a source of insights into the history of our species. The information content of a cultural product such as stone tool is very meager in comparison to the wealth of biological and cultural information that can be extracted from a human skeleton. The historical information an artifact yields is limited to data on the activity patterns and mental processes that can be inferred from its physical properties, form, and archaeological context. As Carver (1996) has pointed out, there is a subjective aspect to the identification of the artifacts of human cultural activity that are measurable, historically meaningful entities within the corpus of mud and stones that humans have left as the traces of their past activities. Through archaeological research, what was once muck is transformed into monuments and the thunderstones of one generation become the flint axes of the next.

The information contained within the structure of the human skeleton, in contrast, is of a different sort. It is not a culture-dependent symbolic construct. Skeletal remains instead have their basis in adaptive physiological and demographic processes operating at the individual and species levels. Encoded within the molecular and histological structure of skeletal tissues is a detailed record of the person's childhood development and adult history of metabolic responses to the challenges encountered in his or her natural and sociocultural environment. This information can be supplemented by an equally rich record of ancestral relationships and the evolutionary history of our species recorded in the structure of the DNA molecules preserved within a skeleton. The information about historical events encoded in the skeletons of our ancestors can be thought of as a complex message from the past that we can decode through bioarchaeological research. Each skeleton has a unique story to tell about that individual's life as well as the evolutionary events that constitute the history of our species. By working to preserve ancient skeletal remains, we

ensure that future generations will be able to gain access to the important historical information they contain.

SOURCES OF CONFLICT

The ethical principles described above have an inherent potential for conflict. The preservation ethic, with its basis in the belief that the information that skeletal studies can yield is of great value to all people, can easily conflict with the ethical principle that the descendants should have the right to decide the disposition of their ancestor's remains. If we recognize the validity of the interests of both descendants and scientists in human skeletal remains, how do we deal with the ethical problems that arise when the preservation ethic conflicts with the desires of descendants?

When the remains of close relatives are involved, there is unanimity among bioarchaeologists that the concerns of descendants should override any scientific interests in those remains. Ethical dilemmas, however, frequently do arise when the ancestor-descendant relationship is less clear-cut. How do we balance the scientific value of very ancient skeletal remains against the concerns of modern people who are remotely related to those same individuals?

In balancing the scientific value of archaeological collections against descendant rights, most scientists see the strength of the ancestor-descendant relationship as a continuum that becomes attenuated with succeeding generations. At one end of this continuum we have remains of people with living children and grandchildren who have an undisputed right to determine the disposition of their close relative's remains. At the other we have the remains of very distant relatives, such as the earliest members of our species, to which all modern people are equally related. From this evolutionary perspective, descendant rights are seen as decreasing as the number of generations separating the living and the dead increases. At some point, claims by one modern group of descendants to decide the disposition of ancient human remains are counterbalanced by the right of all people to have access to the unique source of evidence on the history of our species that human skeletal remains provide. How do we decide when the scientific value of skeletal evidence is sufficient to override the concerns of remotely related descendants?

There is no easy answer to the question of how to balance descendant rights against the right of all people to know about the past, because the values skeletal biologists and descendants attach to human remains are essentially incommensurable. Part of the problem arises from the fact that many modern indigenous people do not accept the idea that the ancestor-descendant relationship becomes attenuated with time. Instead they see the spirits of their ancestors, no matter how distant, as an integral part of the modern community of the living. Nor do they see themselves as closely related to the rest of humanity. Instead they believe that they are the products of a special creation that occurred in the area their tribe currently occupies and this is an issue of faith about which scientific evidence is irrelevant (Johnson G, 1996). For instance, Armand Minthorn, a member of the Umatilla tribe, which claims the 9500-year-old Kennewick skeleton, made this point when he stated: "We know how time began and how Indian people were created. They can say whatever they want, the scientists" (The Invisible Man, 1996). The implication of such beliefs is that all human remains, no matter how ancient, if they are from the area in which a group believes they were created, are those of their direct ancestors.

Although such creationist interpretations of the history of our species seem strange to many scientists, they are shared by a substantial number of nonindigenous people. For example, a recent survey found that about 20% of the people in the United States shared the Christian belief derived from a literal interpretation of the bible that God created the cosmos about 5000 to 10,000 years ago (Goldhaber, 1996).

Some archaeologists argue that the utilitarian approach of attempting to balance scientific value against descendant rights is an ethnocentric attempt to frame the problem within the "Eurowestern" system of cultural values that emphasizes finding solutions to problems that maximize benefits and minimize costs (Klesert and Powell, 1993). We can all agree that we will never find a culture-free metric for weighing the value of knowing what actually happened in the past against the concerns descendants have about ancestral remains. However, even if we agree that the benefit of giving control over ancestral remains to people who identify themselves as descendants always outweighs their value as a source of scientific information, we still face the problem of determining who should be able to claim standing as a descendant and what is the ethical thing to do when there are competing claims.

When dealing with close relatives, where the genealogical link between ancestor and descendant is known, allocating descendant rights over the remains of their relatives is fairly straightforward. For example, we might establish a hierarchy that gives a person's spouse, children, parents, and siblings the authority to control the disposition of their remains. Even such a simple scheme as this is open to charges of ethnocentrism because it reifies western kinship systems that emphasize the importance of genetic relatedness as a criteria for moral authority and invests the rights to make such decisions in a person's nuclear family. Other societies might give greater authority to elder members of a person's patriline or matriline, or disregard the modern Western preoccupation with genetic relatedness altogether in favor of another culture-dependent conception of relatedness.

Such cultural differences in ways of conceiving the ancestor-descendant relationship can even transcend the species boundary. For example, I know people who claim the moral authority to remove the bones of dinosaurs from museum collections because they believe, based on their creation myths, that these remains are those of their ancestors before they were transformed into human form. What are we to do with people with sincerely held beliefs about an ancestor-descendant relation-ships such as this when those beliefs conflict with our own?

Even if we are willing to recognize the va-lidity of such claims and agree that the moral authority of belief in a close ancestor-descen-dant relationship always outweighs any scien-tific value skeletal collections might have, we are still faced with the dilemma of deciding what to do when there are conflicting claims for the same skeletal collections. This problem is vividly illustrated by several recent cases in the United States in which people with differ-ent beliefs about the past have disputed each other's assertions of moral authority to control archaeological collections. In Hawaii, 15 feder-ally recognized native groups became involved in a dispute over the disposition of ancestral re-mains from Mokapu on the island of Oahu (NAGPRA, 1994). One of these groups in-sisted that scientific research be conducted on the remains of these ancient individuals to de-termine their ancestral relationships while oth-ers viewed such work as a deep insult to the spirits of the their ancestors. In a similar case, Stanford University acceded to the reburial de-mands of one group of Ohlone Indians without scientific analysis over the objections of other Ohlone people who, from the Western ge-nealogical perspective, were equally related to those remains (Gross, 1989; Workman, 1990). Another acrimonious fight over descendant rights has arisen in the American Southwest between the Navajo and Zuni Indians as part of a government-instigated land deal that pro-hibits the Navajo from burying their dead in certain traditional burial areas and requires them to renounce claims on sacred sites (Benedek, 1992; Cockburn, 1997). Both tribes have publicly asserted their ancestral rights to the remains of what archaeologists call the Anasazi culture. In other disputes, people who have documentary evidence that they are de-scendant of the indigenous people from an area have objected to the descendant rights claimed by people who lack such documentation (Erlandson et al., 1998; Haley et al., 1997; Kelley, 1997).

One option for dealing with the conflicts that arise when several groups of people assert the moral authority that comes with belief in descendancy from distant ancestors is to take refuge in the legal system where lawyers, politicians, government functionaries, and po-litically astute special interest groups can wres-tle with each other to find a solution to the vexing question of who should have legal standing as a descendant. Although they appear to envisage possible exceptions in cases of "ex-traordinary scientific value," this is in essence what Klesert and Powell (1993) suggest when they argue that "we must abide by the prefer-ences of the legally recognized descendants" in disputes concerning the excavation and analy-sis of ancient burials. For those who view our legal systems as distillations of the moral prin-ciples of the people that laws govern, turning the ethical problem of defining "real" descen-dants over to the courts is very appealing. This political strategy, of course, has the added prac-tical advantage of not eliciting legal sanctions. The moral problem of relying on laws to decide which groups have the right to determine the disposition of human remains has its basis in the faulty assumption that we all live in just so-cieties. Laws have, after all, in the recent past been used as the mechanisms through which groups have been defined by democratically elected governments for purposes of apartheid, slavery, and genocide.

The difficulties associated with legislative solutions to the ethical problem of determining the disposition of skeletal collections are illus-trated by the problems that have arisen in Israel and the United States through legislative at-tempts to resolve disputes over the control of skeletal collections. Ultraorthodox Jewish or-ganizations in Israel, such as the Atra Kadisha, who regard all academic study involving hu-man remains a violation of Jewish law, have long been at loggerheads with physical anthro-pologists over the excavation and the handling of human remains, including skeletons of ex-treme antiquity such as those of Neanderthals (Watzman, 1996a, 1996b, 1996c). Owing to the compromises necessary for coalitions of political parties to maintain control of the Israeli government, court rulings have been issued that make the study of unearthed human remains impossible.

In the United States, the Native American Graves Protection and Repatriation Act institutionalizes long-standing inequities in the treatment of federally recognized and non-federally recognized descendants (Walker, 1998). Particularly troubling from an ethical standpoint is its failure to acknowledge the existence of authentic descendant groups that, for one reason or another, have either failed to receive or rejected federal tribal recognition. This omission is especially unfortunate for the many federally unrecognized descendants in California and the eastern United States where the vagaries of the colonial process allowed the government to avoid giving Indian tribes the rights of self-determination that go along with federal recognition. Even if such federally unrecognized groups were given legal standing as descendants, the law would still present ethical problems because, with the minor exception of granting rights to people who can show a direct genealogical connection to the remains of known individual, it fails to recognize the rights of the many people of Native American descent who lack any tribal affiliation.

RESOLVING CONFLICTS

If we cannot rely on our legal systems to make difficult ethical decisions concerning who descendants are and under what conditions their rights should take precedence over the preservation ethic, what basis is there for finding equitable solutions that balance these potentially conflicting ethical principles? First, it is important to recognize that there is no inherent conflict between the maintenance of skeletal collections for scientific research and respect for the dead. As I previously mentioned, in many countries research upon and the public display of ancestral remains are matters of national pride. In other situations, arrangements can often be made that satisfy the religious and

symbolic concerns of modern descendants while allowing scientific research on ancestral remains to continue. At St. Bride's Church, London, the skeletons of people with known descendants whose burials were disturbed during the German bombings of World War II are respectfully maintained in a special room where they are available for scientific research (Huda and Bowman, 1995; Scheuer and Bowman, 1995). In this way, the religious and symbolic concerns of descendants are respected, while at the same time making it possible for these remains to continue to yield important insights into the lives of eighteenth- and nineteenth-century Londoners that are not adequately documented in written records (Walker, 1997, 2000).

In all societies, cultural understandings of sacredness and ethical behavior are constantly being reshaped in response to changing social realities. This is especially true for the issues surrounding the treatment of ancient human remains because the social context of bioarchaeological research is a modern one not confronted by earlier generations. For many indigenous societies the curation of ancestral remains and their study is a new phenomenon that presents practical problems requiring the development of new rituals, new conceptions of sacredness, and new beliefs concerning what is respectful and disrespectful behavior. In other societies, especially sedentary ones accustomed to maintaining large, intensively used cemeteries, a long history of facing the practical and symbolic problems posed by the disturbance and handling of ancestral remains has resulted in traditional solutions. For example, the Chumash Indians of southern California, with whom I have worked for the past twenty-five years, had specialists called *li-wimpshit*, which means "custodian of the algebra," who were familiar with the human skeleton and the art of arranging bones. These medical practitioners not only could set bones, but they could also arrange all the bones of the human skeleton properly, and determine whether those ancestral bones had once belonged to a man or a woman (Walker and

Hudson, 1993:46, 48). The need for someone qualified to deal with human bone derived from Chumash burial practices, which emphasize the importance of having the remains of the dead near to the living. Cemeteries were, therefore, located adjacent to or within villages. As the size of Chumash settlements grew, so did the size of their cemeteries, and this frequently necessitated the excavation and disturbance of ancestral remains (King, 1969).

Although the social context of the issues surrounding the treatment of the dead that the modern Chumash face are very different from those they confronted in the past, traditional beliefs about the treatment of the dead have served as a basis for creating a situation in which bioarchaeological research can continue while ensuring that due respect is shown for their dead. Through working with tribal members over the years, my colleagues and I have developed a cooperative arrangement through which Chumash ancestral remains and associated burial objects are being repatriated from other universities and museums to a safe keeping place at my campus. This is highly desirable from the perspective of descendants because of our location near the center of the area historically occupied by the tribe. We have constructed a specially designed subterranean ossuary to receive these remains as part of the construction of our new social sciences and humanities building. This ossuary was designed through consultation with both federally and non-federally recognized tribal members to ensure that it meets their spiritual needs, and also solves the practical problem of providing security against future disturbance that would be unavailable in an unguarded reburial area. The ossuary also makes it possible for scientific research on these collections to continue under the supervision of descendants so that future generations can gain a deeper understanding of the history and accomplishments of the tribe.

Mutually acceptable solutions such as this, which balance spiritual and practical concerns of descendants against the important historical information skeletal research can provide, are the outcome of personal relationships, mutual

trust and respect, and the recognition of common interests. Such relationships require time to nurture. My academic colleagues and I have spent our entire professional careers working with Chumash descendants to protect and learn from the archaeological record left by their ancestors. This has involved assisting descendants and local law enforcement authorities in the apprehension and prosecution of grave robbers and looters and actively working to minimize the threats urban development poses for their sacred sites and archaeological resources. At the request of descendants we have given seminars and workshops on archaeology, osteology, and the intricacies of the laws that govern the management and protection of archaeological resources. Whenever possible, we have actively involved descendants in our research projects. Such collaborations are enormously rewarding, not only on a personal level, but also professionally, because of the important insights descendants can provide into the history of their culture.

Not all groups have religious traditions that can be easily built upon to allow scientific research conducted on the remains of the dead. The strong objections ultraorthodox Jewish have to any skeletal studies already have been mentioned (Watzman, 1996c). As the claims of Hopi and the Navajo to archaeological remains from the ancient Anasazi culture show, it is easy for the control of bones and burial sites to become enmeshed in larger battles over unrelated economic and social issues concerning the control of land and natural resources, environmental preservation, and so on. This of course greatly complicates the problem of finding a basis for compromise. Sometimes collaboration with descendants may be difficult or impossible owing to antagonism toward Western science, and strong traditional beliefs about the retention of a person's spirit within their bones. Some native Hawaiians, for example, believe that people possess *mana*, which after death resides in the bones, and have argued in court that the publication of information about skeletal collections is offensive and will steal the *mana* of their ancestors (Kanahele, 1993). Many Plains Indian tribes also have strong beliefs about the residence of souls in their ancestral remains. This, along with animosity stemming from racism, genocidal attacks by the U.S. military, cultural suppression in boarding schools, and economic marginalization on reservations makes the prospects for the preservation of skeletal collections from most of the Plains area bleak (Ubelaker, 1994:395).

In situations such as these it may be impossible to obtain a compromise that allows skeletal research to continue. However, from the personal experiences I have had in working with many different groups of indigenous people, once the shroud of mystery associated with what osteologists actually do is removed through direct contacts between people, it is often possible to find a foundation upon which mutual understanding and cooperation can be built. The most obvious basis for developing such collaborations is in the identification and analysis of ancient human remains that are inadvertently disturbed through erosion, for example, or during construction projects. In such situations, the value of close collaboration between osteologists and descendants is obvious. After it has been decided that remains are indeed human, the issue of whether or not they are modern (and thus possibly relevant to a forensic investigation) needs to be resolved. If they are indeed ancient, the question of which modern group of people they are affiliated with needs to be considered. This issue is especially important to some indigenous people who have strong religious sanctions against the burial of non-group members in their cemeteries. The value of osteological research is also self-evident in forensic investigations relating to the prosecution of grave robbers. I have collaborated with Native Americans in several of such cases. In one, we matched a fragment of a mandible confiscated from a suspect's home, with another piece of the same mandible that tribal members had recovered from the area of an ancient grave disturbed by looters. This incontrovertible evidence connecting the defendant with the crime scene resulted in a guilty plea. In another case, we used skeletal evidence to successfully refute a grave robber's attempt to exonerate himself by claiming that the Native American remains he excavated were from a person of European ancestry, and thus not protected by the state's Native American graves protection law. Through the process of working on such cases, I have seen the views of people who once saw little value in skeletal research change dramatically as they increasingly became aware of many important insights skeletal studies can give us into the lives of those who have gone before us.

When skeletal collections are lost owing to our inability to find equitable solutions that balance the concerns of modern descendants against the need to preserve collections so that future generations will have substantive information about the past, it is perhaps of some solace to remember that we live in an entropic world in which the natural processes of decay and disintegration and the economic and social realities of modern life continuously conspire to destroy the faint traces our ancestors have left for us in the archaeological record. We cannot turn this tide. All we can do is work to preserve as much of the physical evidence of our common heritage as possible. Those ancestral remains and the facts about the history of our species that they reveal will be our legacy to future generations.

REFERENCES

[AAA] American Anthropological Association. 1986. Principles of Professional Responsibility Adopted by the Council of the American Anthropological Association, May 1971 (as amended through November 1986). Arlington, Va.: AAA.

[AAA] American Anthropological Assocation. 1997. Code of Ethics of the American Anthropological Association. Arlington, Va.: AAA.

[AIA] Archaeological Institute of America. 1991. Code of Ethics. American Journal of Archaeology 95:285.

[AIA] Archaeological Institute of America. 1994. Code of Professional Standards. Boston: AIA.

Allen TG. 1960. The Egyptian Book of the Dead. Chicago: University of Chicago Press.

Augustine D. 1994. Minutes: Native American Graves Protection and Repatriation Review Committee Seventh Meeting, May 12–14, 1994, Rapid City, South Dakota.

Badone E. 1987. Changing Breton responses to death. Omega: Journal of Death and Dying 18:77–83.

Barber P. 1988. Vampires, Burial, and Death: Folklore and Reality. New Haven: Yale University Press.

Barnes JK, Woodward JJ, Smart C, Otis GA, Huntington DL. 1870. The Medical and Surgical History of the War of the Rebellion (1861–65). Washington: U.S. Government Printing Office.

Beard M. 1992. Souvenirs of culture: deciphering (in) the museum. Art History 15:505–532.

Behi R, Nolan M. 1995. Ethical issues in research. British Journal of Nursing 4:712–716.

Belief in the Devil. 1995. Gallup Poll 55:1–4.

Benedek E. 1992. The Wind Won't Know Me: A History of the Navajo-Hopi Land Dispute. New York: Alfred A. Knopf.

Benson A, Bowers S. 1997. The Noontide Sun: The Field Journals of the Reverend Stephen Bowers, Pioneer California Archaeologist. Menlo Park, Calif.: Ballena Press.

Bieder RE. 1992. The collecting of bones for anthropological narratives. American Indian Culture and Research Journal:21–35.

Bill JH. 1862. Notes on arrow wounds. Medical Record Oct 1862; 365–367.

Blake JB. 1955. The development of American anatomy acts. Journal of Medical Education 8: 431–439.

Blakely RL, Harrington JM, Barnes MR. 1997. Bones in the Basement: Postmortem Racism in Nineteenth-Century Medical Training. Washington: Smithsonian Institution Press.

Blakely RLH, Judith M. 1997. Grave consequences: the opportunistic procurement of cadavers at the Medical College of Georgia. In: Blakely RL, Harrington JM, Barnes MR, editors. Bones in the Basement: Postmortem Racism in Nineteenth-Century Medical Training. Washington: Smithsonian Institution Press. pp. 162–183.

Blumenbach JF, Wagner R, Marx KFH, Flourens P, Hunter J, Bendyshe T. 1865. The anthropological treatises of Johann Friedrich Blumenbach. London: Published for the Anthropological Society by Longman, Green, Longman, Roberts & Green.

Boas F. 1912. Changes in bodily form of descendants of immigrants. Am Anthropol 14:530–562.

Bonnet C. 1779. Ouvres d'histoire naturelle et de philosophie. Neuchatel: S. Fauche.

Braun R. 1994. The Holocaust and problems of historical representation. History and Theory 33: 172–195.

Bray T. 1995. Repatriation: A Clash of World Views. AnthroNotes—National Museum of Natural History Bulletin for Teachers 17. vol. 17, no. 1/2 winter/spring.

Brew J. 1941. Preliminary report of the Peabody Museum Awatovi Expedition of 1939. Plateau 13:37–48.

Brown D. 1991. Human Universals. New York: McGraw-Hill.

Buikstra J. 1981. A specialist in ancient cemetery studies looks at the reburial issue. Early Man 3:26–27.

Bulger RE. 1994. Toward a statement of the principles underlying responsible conduct in biomedical research. Acad Med 69:102–107.

Bynum CW. 1994. Images of the resurrection body in the theology of late antiquity. Catholic Historical Review 80:7–30.

Bynum CW. 1995. The Resurrection of the Body. New York: Columbia University Press.

Caciola N. 1996. Wraiths, revenants and ritual in medieval culture. Past and Present 152:3–45.

Canadian Association for Physical Anthropology 1979. Statement on the excavation, treatment, analysis and disposition of human skeletal remains from archaeological sites in Canada. 1:32–36.

Cantwell A-M. 1990. The choir invisible: reflections on the living and the dead. Death Studies 14:613–628.

Carver M. 1996. On archaeological value. Antiquity 70:45–56.

Caryl C. 1998. Russia buries the czar but not its squabbles. U.S. News & World Report. vol. 125 p. 36.

Clark PA. 1997. Notes on suffering, death and Native American spirituality. America 177:21–24.

Clutton-Brock J. 1995. Aristotle, the Scale of Nature, and modern attitudes to animals. Social Research 62:420–441.

Cobb WM. 1936. The Laboratory of Anatomy and Physical Anthropology of Howard University. Washington: Howard University.

Cobb WM. 1939. The First Negro Medical Society; A History of the Medico-Chirurgical Society of the District of Columbia, 1884–1939. Washington: The Associated Publishers.

Cobb WM. 1948. Progress and Portents for the Negro in Medicine. New York: National Association for the Advancement of Colored People.

Cockburn A. 1997. Alexander Cockburn's America: the Navajo Indians are resisting pressure to capture their lands. New Statesman 126:32.

Cohen S. 1992. Life and death: a cross-cultural perspective. Childhood Education 69:107–108.

Collin de Plancy JAS. 1821. Dictionnaire critique des reliques et des images miraculeuses. Paris: Guien.

Cooper G. 1998. Life-cycle rituals in Dongyang County: time, affinity, and exchange in rural China. Ethnology 37:373–394.

Cottingham J. 1994. Religion, virtue and ethical culture. Philosophy 69:163–180.

Craig R. 1994. Minutes: Native American Graves Protection and Repatriation Review Committee Eighth Meeting, Nov 17–19, 1994, Albany, New York.

Cunha E. 1995. Testing identification records: evidence from Coimbra identified skeletal collection (nineteenth and twentieths centuries). In: Herring A, Saunders S, editors. Grave Reflections: Portraying the Past Through Skeletal Studies. Toronto: Canadian Scholars' Press. pp. 179–198.

Dirlik A. 1996. The past as legacy and project: postcolonial criticism in the perspective of indigenous historicism. American Indian Culture and Research Journal 20:1–30.

Donahue MJ. 1993. Prevalence and correlates of New Age beliefs in six Protestant denominations. Journal for the Scientific Study of Religion 32:177–184.

Donaldson T. 1992. Can multinationals stage a universal morality play? Business and Society Review 81:51–55.

Drancourt M, Aboudharam G, Signoli M, Dutour O, Raoult D. 1998. Detection of 400-year-old Yersinia pestis DNA in human dental pulp: an approach to the diagnosis of ancient septicemia. Proceedings of the National Academy of Sciences of the United States 95:12637–12640.

Driver HE. 1969. Indians of North America. Chicago: University of Chicago Press.

Edmondson B. 1996. The minority majority in 2001. American Demographics 18:16–17.

Eknoyan G. 1994. Arabic medicine and nephrology. Am J Nephrol 14:270–278.

Ellis C. 1996. Boarding school life at the Kiowa-Comanche agency, 1893–1920. Historian 58:777–793.

Ellis N. 1996. Ba and khu. Parabola 21:23–27.

Emspak J. 1995. Repatriation battles. Progressive 59:14–15.

Erlandson JM, King CRL, Ruyle EE, Wilson DD, Winthrop R, Wood C, Haley BD, Wilcoxon LR. 1998. The making of Chumash tradition. (Includes related articles.) Curr Anthropol 39:477–510.

Erlanger S. 1988. A museum for the things too painful to forget. New York Times. December 30 pp. A4(N), A4(L).

Fenyvesi C. 1997. The communist cult of the dead. U.S. News & World Report 123(3):12.

Fewkes J. 1898. Archeological Expedition to Arizona in 1895: Seventeenth Annual Report of the Bureau of American Ethnology to the Secretary of the Smithsonian Institution, 1895–96. Washington: Smithsonian Institution. pp. 519–744.

Fluehr-Lobban C. 1991. Professional ethics and anthropology: tensions between its academic and applied branches. Business and Professional Ethics Journal 10:57–68.

Friedman M. 1998. Why Joseph Campbell's psychologizing of myth precludes the Holocaust as touchstone of reality. Journal of the American Academy of Religion 66:385–401.

Gardner LI, Jr., Stern MP, Haffner SM, Gaskill SP, Hazuda HP, Relethford JH, and Eifler CW 1984. Prevalence of diabetes in Mexican Americans. Relationship to percent of gene pool derived from native American sources: Diabetes 33(1): 86–92.

Gauthier M-M. 1986. Highways of the faith: relics and reliquaries from Jerusalem to Compostela. Secaucus, N.J.: Wellfleet.

Geary PJ. 1978. Furta sacra: thefts of relics in the central Middle Ages. Princeton: Princeton University Press.

Geertz AW. 1996. Contemporary problems in the study of Native North American religions with special reference to the Hopis. American Indian Quarterly 20:393–414.

Gemmerich I. 1997. Collection I. Gemmerich: squelettes récent vaudois 1992–1993 (CH) Dossier documentaire. Bull Soc Suisse d'Anthrop 3:1–12.

Glock A. 1995. Cultural bias in the archaeology of Palestine. Journal of Palestine Studies 24:48–49.

Goldberg C. 1997. Acknowledging the repatriation claims of unacknowledged California tribes. American Indian Culture and Research Journal 21:183–190.

Goldhaber G. 1996. Religious belief in America: a new poll. Free Inquiry 16:34–40.

Goldstein L, Kintigh K. 1990. Ethics and the reburial controversy. Am Antiq 55:585–591.

Grey TC. 1983. The legal Enforcement of Morality. New York: Borzoi Books.

Gross J. 1989. Stanford agrees to return ancient bones to Indians. New York Times. June 24 p. 1(L).

Hagelberg E, Quevedo S, Turbon D, Clegg JB. 1994. DNA from ancient Easter Islanders (DNA from human bones from Easter Island near Chile). Nature 369:25–26.

Haley BD, Wilcoxon LR, Brown MF, Friedman J, Handler R, Jackson JE, Kealiinohomoku J, Kelley KB, Linde-Laursen A, O'Meara JT, Spiegel AD, Trigger DS. 1997. Anthropology and the making of Chumash tradition. Curr Anthropol 38:761–794.

Halfe LB. 1989. The circle: death and dying from a native perspective. J Palliat Care 5:36–41.

Handt O, Richards M, Trommsdorff M, Kilger C, Simanainen J, Georgiev O, Bauer K, Stone A, Hedges R, Schaffner W, et al. 1994. Molecular genetic analyses of the Tyrolean Ice Man. Science 264:1775–1778.

Hanis CL, Hewett-Emmett D, Bertin TK, and Schull WJ 1991. Origins of U.S. Hispanics. Implications for diabetes: Diabetes Care 14(7):618–27.

Haraldsson E, Houtkooper JM. 1991. Psychic experiences in the multinational human values study: Who reports them? Journal of the American Society for Psychical Research 85:145–165.

Harner MJ. 1972. The Jivaro: People of the Sacred Waterfalls. Los Angeles: University of California.

Hastings D, Sampson D. 1997. Q: Should scientists be allowed to "study" the skeletons of ancient American Indians? Insight on the News 13:24–27.

Hatch E. 1983. Cultures and Morality: The Relativity of Values in Anthropology. New York: Columbia University Press.

Hernandez-Avila I. 1996. Mediations of the spirit: Native American religious traditions and the ethics of representation. American Indian Quarterly 20:329–352.

Herodotus. 1990. The History of Herodotus. Chicago: Encyclopedia Britannica, Inc.

Hewett E. 1953. Pajarito Plateau and Its Ancient People. Albuquerque: The University of New Mexico Press.

Hodder I, Shanks M, Alexandri A, Buchli V, Carman J, Last J, Lucas G. 1995. Interpreting Archaeolgy: Finding Meaning in the Past. New York: Routledge.

Hoffman M. 1998. New medicine for old mummies (molecular diagnoses of mummies reveal infectious diseases). Am Sci 86:233–234.

Horn M. 1998. The deathcare business: the Goliaths of the funeral industry are making lots of money off your grief. U.S. News & World Report 124:50–58.

Howitt R. 1998. Recognition, respect and reconciliation: steps towards decolonisation? Australian Aboriginal Studies 1998:28–34.

Hrdlička A. 1930a. The Ancient and Modern Inhabitants of the Yukon: Explorations and Field-Work of the Smithsonian Institution in 1929. Washington: Smithsonian Institution. pp. 137–146.

Hrdlička A. 1930b. Anthropological Survey in Alaska. Forty-Sixth Annual Report of the Bureau of American Ethnology to the Secretary of the Smithsonian Institution 1928–1929. Washington: Government Printing Office.

Hrdlička A. 1931. Anthropological Work on the Kuskokwim River, Alaska: Explorations and Field-Work of the Smithsonian Institution in 1930. Washington: Smithsonian Institution. pp. 123–134.

Huda TF, Bowman JE. 1995. Age determination from dental microstructure in juveniles. Am J Phys Anthropol 97:135–150.

Hult M, Fessler A. 1998. Sr/Ca mass ratio determination in bones using fast neutron activation analysis. Applied Radiat Isot 49:1319–1323.

Humphrey DC. 1973. Dissection and discrimination: the social origins of cadavers in America, 1760–1915. Bull N Y Acad Med 49:819–827.

Hurt WJ, Buckles WG, Fugle E, Agogino GA. 1962. Report of the Investigations of the Four Bear Site, 39DW2, Dewey County, South Dakota, 1958–1959. Vermillion, S.D.: W.H. Over Museum, State University of South Dakota.

Hutchens MP. 1997. Grave robbing and ethics in the 19th Century. JAMA 278:1115.

[IACHR] Inter-American Commission on Human Rights. 1995. Draft of the Inter-American Declaration on the Rights of Indigenous Peoples. Inter-American Commission on Human Rights of the Organization of American States. (Draft approved by the IACHR at the 1278 session held on September 18, 1995).

Iannaccone L, Stark R, Finke R. 1998. Rationality and the "religious mind." Economic Inquiry 36:373–389.

Jantz RL. 1995. Franz Boas and Native American biological variability. Hum Biol 67:345–353.

Jantz RL, Hunt DR, Falsetti AB, Key PJ. 1992. Variation among North Amerindians: analysis of Boas's anthropometric data. Hum Biol 64: 435–461.

Jocks CR. 1996. Spirituality for sale: sacred knowledge in the consumer age. American Indian Quarterly 20:415–431.

Johnson G. 1996. Indian tribes' creationists thwart archeologists: New York Times. Oct. 22 pp. A1(N), A1(L).

Johnson W. 1996. Contemporary Native American prophecy in historical perspective. Journal of the American Academy of Religion 64:575–612.

Jordan T. 1995. The philosophical politics of Jean-Francois Lyotard. Philosophy of the Social Sciences 25:267–285.

Judd N. 1968. Men Met Along the Trail, Adventures in Archaeology. Norman: University of Oklahoma Press.

Kanahele E. 1993. Minutes: Native American Graves Protection and Repatriation Review Committee Fourth Meeting, Feb 26–28, 1993, Honolulu, Hawaii.

Kehoe AB. 1996. Eliade and Hultkrantz: the European primitivism tradition. American Indian Quarterly 20:377–394.

Kelley KB. 1997. Comment on: anthropology and the making of Chumash tradition. Curr Anthropol 38:782–783.

Kellner H. 1994. "Never Again" is now. History and Theory 33:127–144.

King L. 1969. The Medea Creek Cemetery (LAn-243): an investigation of social organization from mortuary practices. University of California Archaeological Survey Annual Report 11:23–68.

Klesert AL, Powell S. 1993. A perspective on ethics and the reburial controversy. Am Antiq 58: 348–354.

Knudson R. 1986. Contemporary cultural resource management. In: Meltzer DJ, Fowler DD, Sabloff JA, editors. American Archaeology Past and Future: A Celebration of the Society for American Archaeology 1935–1985. Washington: Smithsonian Institution Press. pp. 395–414.

Kruckeberg D. 1996. A global perspective on public relations ethics: the Middle East. Public Relations Review 22:181–189.

Kuhse H, Singer P, Rickard M, Cannold L, Van Dyk J. 1997. Partial and impartial ethical reasoning in health care professionals. J Med Ethics 23: 226–232.

Kunstadter P. 1980. Medical ethics in cross-cultural and multi-cultural perspectives. Soc Sci Med: Med Anthropol 14B:289–96.

La Barre W. 1984. Muelos: a Stone Age superstition about sexuality. New York: Columbia University Press.

Laderman G. 1996. The Sacred Remains: American Attitudes Toward Death, 1799–1883. New Haven: Yale University Press.

Larsen CS. 1997. Bioarchaeology: Interpreting Behavior from the Human Skeleton. New York: Cambridge University Press.

Lee M. 1997. Ancient ritual pays tribute to Kennewick Man. Tri-City Herald. Kennewick, Pasco and Richland, Washington. August 28: A1–A2.

Lemonick MD. 1996. Bones of contention. Time 14818:81. October 14.

Li X. 1998. Postmodernism and universal human rights: why theory and reality don't mix. Free Inquiry 18:28–31.

Lomawaima KT. 1993. Domesticity in the federal Indian schools: the power of authority over mind and body. American Ethnologist 20:227–240.

Lynch A. 1990. Respect for the dead human body: a question of body, mind, spirit, psyche. Transplantation Proceedings 22:1016–1018.

Lynott MJ. 1997. Ethical principles and archaeological practice: development of an ethics policy. Am Antiq 62:589–599.

Margareta A. 1996. Respect for the patient's integrity and self-determination—an ethical imperative called upon in the Swedish Health and Medical Care Act. Med Law 15:189–193.

Martineau H. 1838. Retrospect of western travel. London: Saunders and Otley.

Marty ME. 1997. Certain punishment. Christian Century 114:1143.

McCarthy P. 1994. American headhunters: ghoulish war souvenirs turn up in living rooms and landfills. Omni 16:14.

McShea DW. 1994. On the rights of an ape. Discover 15:34–37.

Mihesuah DA. 1996. American Indians, anthropologists, pothunters, and repatriation: ethical, religious, and political differences. American Indian Quarterly 20:229–237.

Millican F. 1992. Body snatching: the robbing of graves for the education of physicians. Lancet 340:899.

Man's Mirror. 1991. Economist 321(3):21.

Morell V. 1998. Kennewick Man's trials continue. Science 280:190–192.

Morton SG. 1839. Crania Americana: Or, a Comparative View of the Skulls of Various Aboriginal Nations of North and South America: To Which Is Prefixed an Essay on the Varieties of the Human Species. Philadelphia: J. Dobson.

[MRCC] Medical Research Council of Canada. 1998. Tri-Council Policy Statement: Ethical Conduct for Research Involving Humans of the Medical Research Council of Canada. Ottawa: Public Works and Government Services of Canada.

Muller JH, Desmond B. 1992. Ethical dilemmas in a cross-cultural context. A Chinese example. West J Med 157:323–327.

Murdock GP. 1945. The common denominator of cultures. In: Linton R, editor. The Science of Many in the World Crisis. New York: Columbia University Press. pp. 123–142.

Murray T, Allen J. 1995. The forced repatriation of cultural properties to Tasmania. Antiquity 69:871–877.

[NAGPRA] Native American Graves Protection and Repatriation Act. 1994. Minutes: Native American Graves Protection and Repatriation Review Committee Eighth Meeting, Nov. 17–19, 1994, Albany, New York.

[NAPA] National Association for the Practice of Anthropology. 1988. Ethical Guidelines for Practitioners. Arlington, Va.: NAPA.

[NAS] National Academy of Science. 1995. On Being a Scientist: Responsible Conduct in Research. Washington: National Academy Press.

Navran F. 1997. Twelve steps to building a best-practices ethics program. Workforce 76:117–120.

Neuman R. 1975. The Sonata Complex and Associated Sites on the Northern Great Plains: Nebraska State Historical Society Publications in Anthropology. Lincoln: Nebraska State Historical Society.

Newman C. 1957. The evolution of medical education in the nineteenth century. London: Oxford University Press.

Nicklin JL. 1997. A larger and wealthier Hispanic community draws the attention of college fund raisers. Chronicle of Higher Education 44(3):A43.

Olsen SL, Shipman P. 1994. Cutmarks and perimortem treatment of skeletal remains on the Northern Plains. In: Owsley DW, Jantz RL, editors. Skeletal Biology in the Great Plains: Migration, Warfare, Health, and Subsistence. Washington: Smithsonian Institution Press. pp. 363–376.

Orosz JJ. 1990. Curators and Culture: The Museum Movement in America, 1740–1870. Tuscaloosa: University of Alabama Press.

Ortner DJ, Tuross N, Stix AI. 1992. New approaches to the study of disease in archeological New World populations. Hum Biol 64:337–360.

Osmond SJ. 1998. Mummies and martyrs. World and I 13:212–221.

Otis GA, Woodward JJ. 1865. Reports on the Extent and Nature of the Materials Available for the Preparation of a Medical and Surgical History of the Rebellion. Philadelphia: Printed for the Surgeon General's Office by J.B. Lippincott & Co.

Owsley DW, Mann RW, Baugh TG. 1994. Culturally modified human bones from the Edwards Site. In: Owsley DW, Jantz RL, editors. Skeletal Biology in the Great Plains: Migration, Warfare, Health, and Subsistence. Washington: Smithsonian Institution Press. pp. 363–376.

Parker LS. 1994. Bioethics for human geneticists: models for reasoning and methods for teaching. Am J Hum Genet 54:137–147.

Parker WT. 1883. Concerning arrow wounds. Philadelphia Medical Times 14:127–129.

Pellegrino ED. 1995. Toward a virtue-based normative ethics for the health professions. Kennedy Institute of Ethics Journal 5:253–277.

Peters HA. 1995. Cambodian history through Cambodian museums. Expedition 37:52–62.

Petit CW. 1998. A fight over the origins of ancient bones. U.S. News & World Report 125:64.

Preston D. 1997. The Lost Man. New Yorker 73: 70–80.

Pyne R. 1994. Empowerment through use of the Code of Professional Conduct. British Journal of Nursing 3:631–634.

Rankin-Hill LM, Blakey ML. 1994. W. Montague Cobb. Am Anthropol 96:74–96.

Ray J. 1692. The Wisdom of God Manifested in the Works of the Creation. London: S. Smith.

Richardson R. 1987. Death, Dissection, and the Destitute. London: Routledge & Kegan Paul.

Riding In J. 1992. Six Pawnee crania: historical and contemporary issues associated with the massacre and decapitation of Pawnee Indians in 1869. American Indian Culture and Research Journal 16:101–119.

Riding In J. 1996. Repatriation: a Pawnee's perspective. American Indian Quarterly 20:238–251.

Roberts FJ. 1931. The Ruins at Kiatuthlanna, Eastern Arizona: Smithsonian Institution, Bureau of American Ethnology, Bulletin. Washington: Government Printing Office.

Rundblad G. 1995. Exhuming women's premarket duties in the care of the dead. Gender & Society 9:173–192.

[SAA] Society for American Archaeology. 1984. Resolution. Am Antiq 49:215–216.

[SAA] 1996. Principles of Archaeological Ethics. Washington: SAA.

Salmon MH. 1997. Ethical considerations in anthropology and archaeology, or relativism and ustice for all. Journal of Anthropological Research 53:47–60.

[SOPA] Society of Professional Archaeologists. 1983. Professional and Ethical Responsibilities. Baltimore, MD: SOPA.

Scanlon C, Glover J. 1995. A professional code of ethics: providing a moral compass for turbulent times. Oncol Nurs Forum 22:1515–1521.

Scheuer JL, Bowman JE. 1995. Correlation of documentary and skeletal evidence in the St. Bride's crypt population. In: Herring A, Saunders S, editors. Grave Reflections: Portraying the Past Through Skeletal Studies. Toronto: Canadian Scholars' Press. pp. 49–70.

Schick T Jr. 1998. Is morality a matter of taste? Why professional ethicists think that morality is not purely "subjective." Free Inquiry 18:32–34.

Schultz SM. 1992. Body Snatching: The Robbing of Graves for the Education of Physicians in Early 19th Century America. Jefferson, N.C.: McFarland.

Scott C. 1996. Indigenous self-determination and decolonization of the international imagination: a plea. Human Rights Quarterly 18:814–820.

Sjøvold T. 1990. Brachycephalization in microevolutionary terms: the evidence from the Hallstatt cranial collection. Sbornik Narodniho Muzea v Praze Rada B Prirodni Vedy 46: 196–201.

Sjøvold T. 1993. Testing assumptions for skeletal studies by means of identified skulls from Hallstatt Austria. Am J Phys Anthropol (suppl) 16:181.

Slayman AL. 1997. A battle over bones: lawyers contest the fate of an 8,400-year-old skeleton from Washington State. Archaeology 50:16–22.

Sledzik PS, Ousley S. 1991. Analysis of six Vietnamese trophy skulls. J Forensic Sci 36:5 20–530.

Smith A. 1991. For all those who were Indian in a former life. Ms. Magazine 2:44–45.

Smith W. 1971. Painted Ceramics of the Western Mound at Awatovi. Reports of the Awatovi Expedition: Papers of the Peabody Museum of Archaeology and Ethnology. Cambridge: Harvard University Peabody Museum.

Smith W, Woodbury R, Woodbury N. 1966. Report of the Hendricks-Hodge Expedition, 1917–1923: Contributions from the Museum of the American Indian Heye Foundation. New York: Museum of the American Indian Heye Foundation.

[SPA] Society of Professional Archaeologists. 1976. Code of Ethics, Standards of Research Performance and Institutional Standards. Oklahoma City: SPA.

Specktor M. 1989. Shamans or charlatans? Do some teachers of Native American spirituality distort Indians' culture? Utne Reader : 15–17.

Spellman WM. 1994. Between death and judgment: conflicting images of the afterlife in late seventeenth-century English eulogies. Harvard Theological Review 87:49–65.

Spencer F. 1983. Samuel George Morton's doctoral thesis on bodily pain: the probable source of Morton's polygenism. Trans Stud Coll Physicians Phila 5:321–328.

Stone AC, Stoneking M. 1993. Ancient DNA from a pre-Columbian Amerindian population. Am J Phys Anthropol 92(9):463.

Stott AW, Evershed RP. 1996. delta 13C analysis of cholesterol preserved in archaeological bones and teeth. Anal Chem 68:4402–4408.

Tallbull W. 1994. Minutes: Native American Graves Protection and Repatriation Review Committee Seventh Meeting, May 12–14, 1994, Rapid City, South Dakota.

The Invisible Man. 1996. Economist 341(7988): 84–85.

Thurston H. 1913. Relics. In: Herbermann CG, Pace EA, Pallen CB, Shahan TJ, Wynne JJ, MacErlean AA, editors. The Catholic Encyclopedia; An International Work of Reference on the Constitution, Doctrine, Discipline, and History of the Catholic Church. New York: Encyclopedia Press.

Tobias PV. 1991. On the scientific, medical, dental and educational value of collections of human skeletons. International Journal of Anthropology 6:277–280.

Tomaskova S. 1995. A site in history: archaeology at Dolni Vestonice/Unterwisternitz. Antiquity 69(16):301.

Tonne H. 1996. It is hard to believe. Free Inquiry 16:40.

Turner CG. 1986. What is lost with skeletal reburial? I. Adaptation. Quarterly Review of Archaeology 7:1–3.

Tuross N, Stathoplos L. 1993. Ancient proteins in fossil bones. Methods Enzymol 224:121–129.

Tyson E. 1966. Orang-outang; sive, Homo Sylvestris; or, The anatomy of a pygmie: a facsimile. London: Dawsons.

Ubelaker DH. 1994. An overview of Great Plains human skeletal biology. In: Owsley DW, Jant RL, editors. Skeletal Biology in the Great Plains: Migration, Warfare, Health, and Subsistence. Washington: Smithsonian Institution Press. pp. 391–395.

Ubelaker DH, Grant LG. 1989. Human skeletal remains: preservation or reburial? Yrbk Phys Anthropol 32:249–287.

[UN] United Nations. 1948. Universal Declaration of Human Rights. G.A. res. 217A (III), U.N. Doc A/810 at 71.

[UNESCO] United Nations Educational, Scientific, and Cultural Organization. 1995. UNESCO Revised Outline of a Declaration on the Human Genome and Its Protection in Relation to Human Dignity and Human Rights. Eubios Journal of Asian and International Bioethics 5:150–151.

Vizenor G. 1986. Bone courts: the rights and narrative representation of tribal bones. American Indian Quarterly 10:319–331.

Von Haeseler A, Sajantila A, Paabo S. 1996. The genetical archaeology of the human genome. Nat Genet 14:135–140.

Von Staden H. 1989. Herophilus: the art of medicine in early Alexandria. Cambridge: Cambridge University Press.

Von Staden H. 1992. The discovery of the body: human dissection and its cultural contexts in ancient Greece. Yale J Biol Med 65:223–241.

Walker PL. 1995. Minutes: Native American Graves Protection and Repatriation Review Committee Ninth Meeting, Feb 16–18, 1995, Los Angeles, California.

Walker PL. 1997. Wife beating, boxing, and broken noses: skeletal evidence for the cultural patterning of interpersonal violence. In: Martin D, Frayer D, editors. Troubled Times: Violence and Warfare in the Past. Toronto: Gordon and Breach. pp. 145–175.

Walker PL. 1998. Clarifying the Terms of NAGPRA. Anthropology Newsletter: American Anthropological Association 39:17.

Walker PL. 2000. Is the battered-child syndrome a modern phenomenon? Proceedings of the Tenth European Meeting of the Paleopathology Association. In press.

Walker PL, Cook DC, Lambert PM. 1997. Skeletal evidence for child abuse: a physical anthropological perspective. J Forensic Sci 42:196–207.

Walker PL, Hudson T. 1993. Chumash Healing: Changing Health and Medical Practices in an American Indian Society. Banning, Calif.: Malki Museum Press.

Walter T. 1993. Death in the New Age. Religion 23:127–145.

Walters AL. 1989. Esther under glass. Christianity and Crisis 49:133–134.

Watzman H. 1996a. Digging away at the foundations. New Sci 150:49.

Watzman H. 1996b. Outcome of Israeli election could have major impact on colleges. Chronicle of Higher Education 42:A48.

Watzman H. 1996c. Religion, politics, and archaeology: scholars fear that new Israeli government will block excavations of ancient graves. Chronicle of Higher Education 42:A31–A32.

White TD. 1986. Cut marks on the Bodo cranium: a case of prehistoric defleshing. Am J Phys Anthropol 69:503–509.

White TD, Folkens PA. 1991. Human Osteology. San Diego: Academic Press.

White TD, Toth N. 1991. The question of ritual cannibalism at Grotta Guattari. Curr Anthropol 32(21):118.

Wilf SR. 1989. Anatomy and punishment in late 18th-century New York. Journal of Social History 22:507–530.

Willey P, Emerson TE. 1993. The osteology and archaeology of the Crow Creek massacre. Plains Anthropologist 38:227–269.

Wilson T. 1901. Arrow wounds. American Anthropologist New Series. 3:513–531.

Wittlin AS. 1949. The Museum, Its History and Its Tasks in Education. London: Routledge & Kegan Paul.

Workman B. 1990. Ohlones split over reburial of ancestors: letter to Stanford asks that bones be studied. San Francisco Chronicle Thursday, April 12 p.A6.

Wylie AM. 1989. The interpretive dilemma. In: Pinsky V, Wylie A, editors. Critical Traditions in Contemporary Archaeology. Cambridge: Cambridge University Press. pp. 18–27.

CHAPTER 2

METHODOLOGICAL CONSIDERATIONS IN THE FORENSIC APPLICATIONS OF HUMAN SKELETAL BIOLOGY

DOUGLAS H. UBELAKER

At times, the study of the skeletal biology of past peoples includes those of the relatively recent past whose remains have been recovered in a medicolegal context. Examination of such remains traditionally has been referred to as *forensic anthropology*. This subfield of physical anthropology can include the examination of soft tissues, but most practitioners use their skills as physical anthropologists to examine skeletal remains. The aim of this work is basically twofold: to assist in the identification of human remains and to help figure out what happened to them. To stay within the parameters of this volume, this chapter focuses primarily on the examination of skeletal remains in this forensic context.

HISTORICAL DEVELOPMENT

The academic ancestry of forensic anthropology extends back into the nineteenth century when anatomists and early physical anthropologists occasionally were asked to bring their academic skills to focus on problems of human identification. Stewart (1979a) credits Thomas Dwight (1843–1911) for writing the essay "The Identification of the Human Skeleton: A Medico-Legal Study" in 1878 and launching professional anthropological interest in this area of physical anthropology. Although an anatomist, working before physical anthropology emerged as an organized discipline, Dwight demonstrated a significant research interest in forensic applications and problems of skeletal anatomy. He recognized the research need to develop procedures to estimate age at death, sex, and living stature from skeletonized human remains (Dwight, 1878, 1881, 1890a, 1890b, 1894a, 1894b, 1905).

Other notable early pioneers included George A. Dorsey (1869–1931) (Stewart, 1978; Ubelaker, 1999a) and Harris Hawthorne Wilder (1864–1928) (Stewart, 1977, 1979a, 1979b, 1982). Dorsey received his Ph.D. from Harvard University in 1894 (the first Ph.D. awarded by Harvard in anthropology) where he likely was exposed to medicolegal applications of human osteology through contact with Thomas Dwight, who had been appointed Parkman Professor of Anatomy in 1883. Following Dwight's lead, Dorsey published on the medicolegal applications of knowledge of skeletal anatomy (1897, 1899). In 1897 and 1898, Dorsey testified in a high-profile murder trial in Chicago. A local sausage manufacturer, Adolph Luetgert, was accused of the murder of his wife and the disposal of her remains in a vat at the sausage factory. Dorsey's testimony regarding small fragments found

Biological Anthropology of the Human Skeleton, Edited by M. Anne Katzenberg and Shelley R. Saunders.
ISBN 0-471-31616-4   Copyright © 2000 by Wiley-Liss, Inc.

within the vat was debated. Following this experience, his research interests shifted to ethnology and journalism.

After receiving his doctorate in anatomy in Germany, H.H. Wilder began a career appointment (1892–1928) at Smith College in Massachusetts teaching zoology and anthropology. At Smith, Wilder contributed to two major areas of forensic science. He enlarged on F. Galton's dermatoglyphic studies to include observations of prints on the palm and sole and advocated the use of dermatoglyphics over the Bertillon system of anthropometric traits for positive identification. Wilder also conducted research on the restoration of soft tissue and facial reproduction (Stewart, 1982).

Recent research has also demonstrated that the early leader in physical anthropology, Aleš Hrdlička (1869–1943) had broad forensic interests, reported on skeletal cases, and initiated a relationship of forensic service provided by the Smithsonian Institution to the Federal Bureau of Investigation that continues today (Ubelaker, 1999b). Hrdlička is well known for his seminal role in the development of American physical anthropology. In a career largely spent at the Smithsonian Institution (1903–1943), he founded the *American Journal of Physical Anthropology* in 1918 and the American Association of Physical Anthropologists (first meeting in 1930). His works on the evidence for an early human presence in the New World, anthropometry, and many other areas of physical anthropology are well known. Less recognized are Hrdlička's training and work in legal medicine. Over his long career, Hrdlička researched broad medicolegal issues including insanity, and the possible contributions of biological attributes to criminal and other abnormal behavior. He also presented opinions on cases involving insanity, skeletal identification, and ancestry of living peoples. His skeletal casework included trauma interpretation and an early example of photographic superimposition. Hrdlička's expertise in the identification of skeletonized human remains was recognized as early as 1918 by the Federal Bureau of Investigation. By the time of his death, Hrdlička

consulted regularly with the FBI on skeletal issues and was highly regarded by them as a resource in investigation (Ubelaker, 1999b).

In more recent times, as physical anthropology grew as a discipline, increasingly professional research attention focused on the medicolegal applications. Through pioneering efforts by Wilton Marion Krogman (1903–1987), Thomas Dale Stewart (1901–1997), and others, forensic anthropology became recognized by anthropologists and law enforcement personnel not only as an intriguing secondary interest of skeletal biologists, but a legitimate and deserving area of scientific inquiry. Three texts were written, synthesizing much of the available information (Krogman, 1962; Stewart, 1970, 1979a) along with numerous journal articles.

In 1972, growth of activity in forensic anthropology led to the formation of a physical anthropology section of the American Academy of Forensic Sciences with 14 founding members. Membership in the section increased steadily to 236 in 1998. Professionalism within forensic anthropology received another boost in 1977 when a certification process was developed. Board membership of 22 in 1978 grew to about 48 in 1998. Currently, to become a board-certified diplomate of the American Board of Forensic Anthropology, a forensic anthropologist must hold a Ph.D. in physical anthropology with a specialty in skeletal biology, have experience doing casework, and must pass a written and practical examination usually given in association with the annual meeting of the American Academy of Forensic Sciences. Certification (diplomate status) provides the recipient with a useful credential for work within forensic anthropology.

Increasingly, forensic anthropologists have published results of their work in forensic journals, especially the *Journal of Forensic Sciences* (Ubelaker, 1996). Such research has focused on specific forensic applications and has greatly increased the capability of forensic anthropologists to do their work.

Through the involvement of the diplomates and other forensic anthropologists in the medicolegal system, each year more than 1000 cases are reported on in North America (Reichs, 1995). These cases represent mostly skeletonized remains, but also include fresh, mummified, decomposed, and burned remains.

Information regarding the professional activity of the diplomates is available, courtesy of the American Board of Forensic Anthropology. Preservation of diplomate status requires of each diplomate an annual summary of professional activity. The reports for 1996 from all diplomates but one suggest that 1439 cases were studied by diplomates in that year. The data reveal that in 1996 about 19% of the cases originated from civil disputes (Fig. 2.1) and the remaining 81% were forwarded from agencies (i.e., local law enforcement, state police, military, coroners, medical examiners, or sheriffs' departments). Of the agency submissions (Fig. 2.2), the majority (73%) originated from medical examiners' or coroners' offices. The military was the next largest contributor. Of the civil cases (Fig. 2.3), the majority were requested by the plaintiff.

Diplomates are also requested to report on the types of cases on which they work. For 1996 (Fig. 2.4), skeletons represented the most common type of case, followed by decomposed and fresh cases. Cases involving burned remains, nonhuman material, and remains of archeolog-

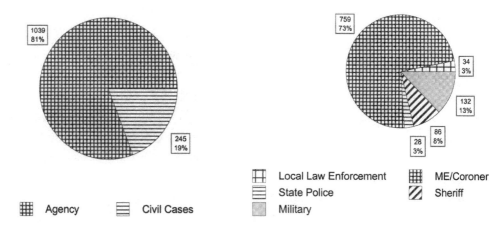

Figure 2.1 Sources of casework reported by diplomates, 1996.

Figure 2.2 Agencies submitting cases to diplomates, 1996.

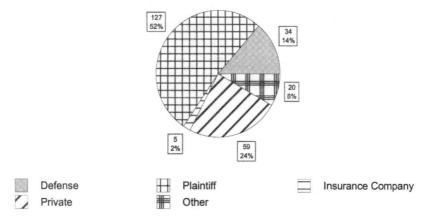

Figure 2.3 Sources of civil cases reported by diplomates, 1996.

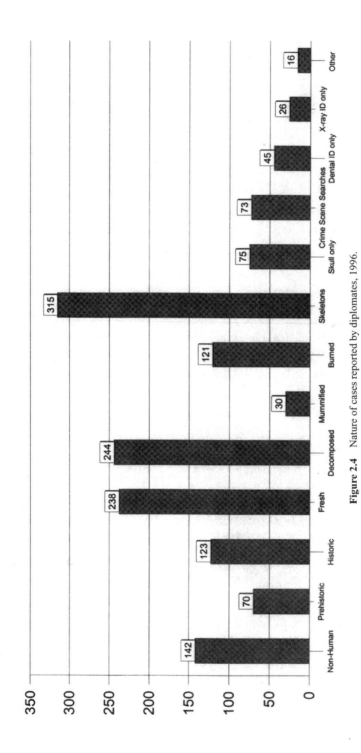

Figure 2.4   Nature of cases reported by diplomates, 1996.

ical origin were also common. Comparison of these data with those for 1992 (Reichs, 1995) reveals an increase in the study of fresh and decomposed remains (Fig. 2.5). This pattern likely represents the increased awareness of medical examiners and others of the potential contributions of forensic anthropologists to the study of remains that are not skeletonized.

Figure 2.6 compares the relative percentage of cases of historic, prehistoric, and nonhuman to others of greater legal interest between 1992 (from Reichs, 1995) and 1996. This figure suggests these proportions have remained relatively stable.

Data are also available on requests for special techniques of analysis from the diplomates. Examples of such techniques are dental aging from microscopic structure, age determination from microscopic examination of cortical bone, facial reproduction, photographic superimposition, and photographic comparison. In Fig. 2.7, these data for 1996 are compared with those from 1984, 1988, and 1992 (from Reichs, 1995). These data suggest a recent increase in age estimation from bone histology and photographic superimposition, but decreases in requests for the other specialized techniques.

Direct testimony in court remains relatively uncommon for forensic anthropologists. In 1996, the use of written reports in court was much more common, followed by depositions. In 1996, the diplomates delivered 158 lectures to professional groups and 169 public lectures. They taught 19 general classes of skeletal biology, and 28 classes of forensic anthropology. The diplomates reported 123 students working with them, of which 31 were affiliated with the American Academy of Forensic Sciences. Thirty-five presentations on forensic topics were given at professional meetings and the diplomates reported 45 forensic-related manuscripts completed. Interest in forensic anthropology has grown in Europe as well, although much of this work continues to done by non-anthropologists, mostly physicians. The Smithsonian's annual week-long workshop in forensic anthropology was presented in France in 1992, 1994, 1996,

and 1998. The first three European courses were jointly sponsored by the Smithsonian Institution and the Université de Bretagne Occidentale, Brest. The fourth was sponsored by the Smithsonian and the Université Montpellier. The courses have been well attended by interested parties mostly from France, but also from Italy, Norway, England, Ireland, Portugal, Hungary, Romania, Iceland, Netherlands, Spain, and the United States.

Training courses also have been offered in England and Mexico with considerable student interest in this emerging field. For three years (1996–1998), the National Museum of Health and Medicine in Washington, D.C., has jointly sponsored a course in forensic anthropology with the University of Bradford in England. The course has largely been attended by law enforcement personnel from England.

RELATIONSHIP OF FORENSIC ANTHROPOLOGY TO SKELETAL BIOLOGY

As indicated above, the roots of forensic anthropology reach back to early anatomists and pioneer physical anthropologists who responded positively to requests from the law enforcement community to apply their skills. Prominent past forensic anthropologists such as Hrdlička, Stewart, Krogman, and J. Lawrence Angel (1915–1986) represented physical anthropologists who shared their forensic interests with broader issues in anthropology. Hrdlička did some forensic work, including issues of insanity and ancestry of then-living individuals but also pursued interests in all other areas of physical anthropology and some areas outside of physical anthropology (Ubelaker, 1999b). Stewart considered forensic anthropology only one of three broad interests, the other two being anthropometry and paleoanthropology. Angel was highly regarded for his forensic contributions, but initiated them late in his career, focusing first on skeletal biology of the Near East and anatomy issues (Buikstra and Hoshower, 1990), research that he continued

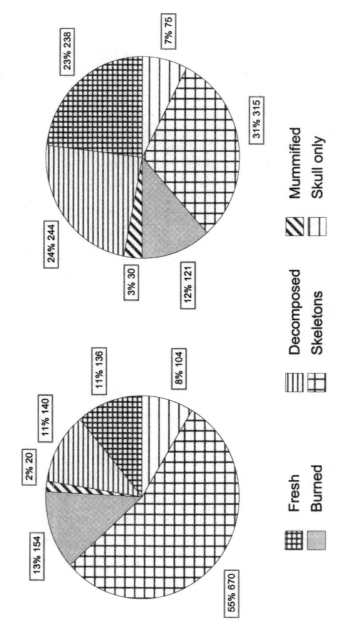

1992   **1995**

Figure 2.5 Types of cases reported by diplomates, 1992 versus 1996.

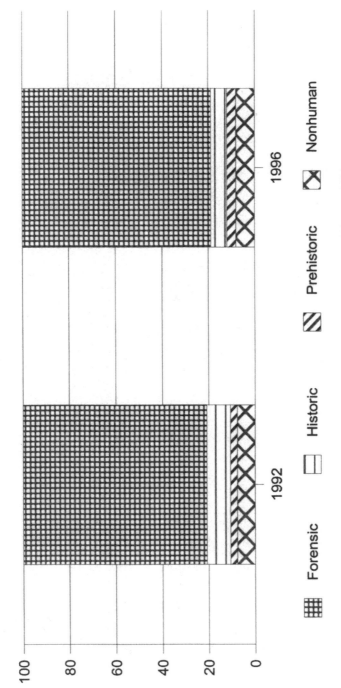

Figure 2.6 Percentage of cases by type reported by diplomates, 1992 versus 1996

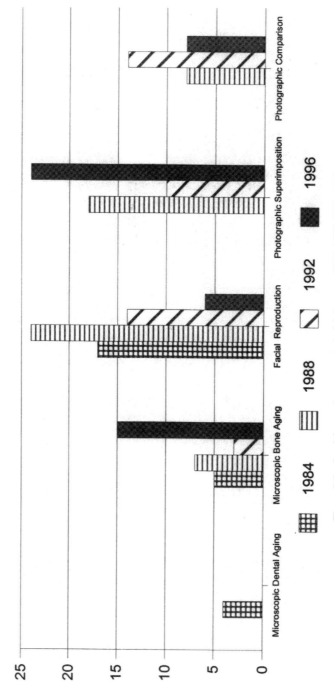

Figure 2.7 Special procedures requested of diplomates, 1984, 1988, 1992, 1996.

along with his forensic work. Krogman pioneered the modern era of forensic anthropology in North America and also was an expert in growth and development (Johnston, 1997). These early workers likely were drawn into forensic applications by their reputations and expertise in the relevant areas of physical anthropology. It is also likely that they welcomed these applications because of the new information the forensic experience provided them. The forensic work represents not only an opportunity for public service and to demonstrate the relevance of our science, but also a unique chance to acquire information about contemporary populations and problems. This information and the experience gained through case analysis and court testimony frequently sharpens the skills of the skeletal biologist and improves analysis of remains recovered from archeological contexts.

THEORETICAL ISSUES

At first glance, it might appear that forensic anthropology differs from the more general field of skeletal biology in that the former concentrates on the individual while the latter addresses larger population issues. Upon closer examination, this simplistic dichotomy breaks down. Many studies within skeletal biology, especially paleopathology, concentrate on the individual, if not the individual specimen. As with forensic anthropology, the skeletal biologist/paleopathologist uses scientific knowledge from the literature and experience to diagnose a disease or interpret a cultural modification.

As in skeletal biology, the forensic anthropologist considers the individual specimen in the context of total human variation and uses information about the individual to improve techniques and gain insight into broader issues. The immediate goals of forensic anthropology are specific: primarily to help identify the person and figure out what happened to them. The secondary goals are to gather biological/skeletal information about contemporary populations and to further our understanding of human variation for a number of skeletal variables.

Broad anthropological knowledge is almost always needed to properly interpret a forensic case. The seemingly simple determination of human versus nonhuman requires experience not only in human variation, the human disease process, and the taphonomic effects on human bone, but also awareness of the diverse materials that can resemble human bones and teeth. The more fragmentary and altered the materials, the more difficult this process becomes. A submitted bone fragment may not resemble normal human bone, but it could represent a pathological condition, a fragment from a very young or very old individual, or human bone altered by heat or exposure to postmortem influences. A small fragment may appear to fall within the range of variation of human bone, especially in consideration of the diverse factors outlined above, but can nonhuman sources be completely eliminated? These interpretations call for broad knowledge of skeletal biology and even other related fields that ultimately shape the language utilized within the final report or testimony on the witness stand. Similarly, a broad perspective is needed to address issues of age at death, sex, ancestry, living stature, time since death, facial reproduction, evidence of foul play, and other identifying features frequently involved in forensic anthropology.

The theoretical approach employed in forensic anthropology basically involves a broad anthropological, population perspective applied to the individual. Forensic issues and goals are addressed using anthropological data, techniques, and perspectives. Some of the foci of forensic anthropological analysis such as interpretation of gunshot wounds and identification of foul play would seem to be unique to the forensic anthropology experience. However, even these areas call for broader anthropological knowledge of bone biomechanics and structural variation for proper interpretation.

As anthropologists, forensic anthropologists also recognize the unique opportunities presented by the casework to improve procedures and to gain knowledge about key issues within contemporary society. The cases examined nearly always present a special problem or reflect materials from unusual contexts that broaden our knowledge. Many of the cases represent known individuals at the time or those who are later identified, offering an opportunity to expand our knowledge about various aspects of human variation. The practice of forensic anthropology clearly expands the experience and expertise of the individual skeletal biologist conducting the work. Through publications and presentations at professional meetings, this special knowledge improves the science.

THE FORENSIC DATA BANK

Angel's work (1974, 1976) offers examples of how forensic anthropologists have used the opportunity offered by casework to gather information about the skeletal biology of contemporary people (Ubelaker, 1990). In 1962, J. Lawrence Angel joined the staff of the Smithsonian Institution and succeeded T. Dale Stewart in consultation with the nearby F.B.I. headquarters in forensic anthropology. In about 1978, the author assumed responsibility for the F.B.I. work, but Angel continued to report on cases for others. By 1986, his caseload had risen to about 565. He not only learned a lot from doing all of the cases, but he also attempted to apply the data from them to larger anthropological questions. These data became the "modern" sample that added perspective to his studies of long term temporal change in patterns of fractures (Angel, 1974) and other variables (Angel, 1976). In an internal 1977 Smithsonian document, Angel described his forensic work as both public service and research. Angel noted: "Much time at present goes to careful study of human skeletons brought for identification . . . since almost all of these are research data. It has taken years to collect adequate samples of modern, and Colonial American adults. The time invested is just beginning to pay off

. . . Applied science is not a dirty word" (Ubelaker, 1990:197).

As increasing numbers of skeletal biologists became involved in forensic applications, the need for improved techniques and knowledge of the contemporary population was recognized. Many of the procedures available for estimating sex, age, ancestry, stature, etc. were based upon existing museum collections of human remains, especially the Terry Collection at the Smithsonian Institution in Washington, D.C., and the Hamann-Todd Collection in Cleveland, Ohio.

The Hamann-Todd Collection consists of approximately 3157 skeletons and associated records housed at the Cleveland Museum of Natural History (Lovejoy et al., 1985). The Department of Anatomy of Western Reserve University assembled this collection between 1912 and 1938. According to Lovejoy and colleagues, cause of death information is available for about 9% of the adults and only about 512 are of relatively known age at death. Others show discrepancies between the stated age of the individual and observations on age made by anatomists at the time.

The Terry Collection consists of the remains of over 1600 individuals who mostly were dissected at the Washington University School of Medicine in St. Louis, Missouri, during the twentieth century. This collection of mostly older individuals contains primarily those classified as either "white" or "black." The collection was assembled mostly by Robert J. Terry (1871–1966) and Mildred Trotter (1899–1991) following dissection. The collection, with associated records, hair samples, and some death masks, is located in the Department of Anthropology of the Smithsonian's National Museum of Natural History in Washington, D.C.

Both the Terry and Hamann-Todd collections have been extensively utilized in skeletal biology research and both represent individuals whose deaths date from the early part of the twentieth century. As valuable as these collections are, concerns grew about the extent to which they represent human populations from other gene pools, geographic areas, and time periods. Such concern from the forensic anthropologists led to the formation of a forensic data bank in 1984, sponsored by the physical anthropology section of the American Academy of Forensic Sciences. The concept was that as forensic anthropologists throughout North America worked on contemporary forensic cases, they would gather noninvasive data from them which would facilitate the research process. A prominent group of forensic anthropologists met to agree on the data to be collected and standardized forms were made available to all involved with casework (Jantz and Moore-Jansen, 1988).

By June 1998, the number of individuals in the data bank had increased to about 1550, a size comparable to the older Terry and Hamann-Todd collections. Emerging from this effort is a large pool of measurements and observations on the skeletal remains of known individuals who were examined as forensic cases. These data not only have obvious utility in supplying anthropological information about the contemporary population but also offer an opportunity to develop improved techniques directly applicable to forensic work.

In 1993, a major product of the database effort emerged, FORDISC 1.0 (Jantz and Ousley, 1993), a DOS computer program that enables the classification of an adult cranium by sex and ancestry. The advantages of this system over previously published discriminant function equations were: (1) FORDISC was based on the large, diverse, contemporary forensic data bank, of obvious direct applicability to modern forensic cases, and (2) the interactive program allowed the formation of custom functions when not all measurements were available. With FORDISC 1.0, a powerful new tool was added that resulted directly from data generated from the forensic casework.

Three years later, the FORDISC product was upgraded (2.0) (Ousley and Jantz, 1996), utilizing the enlarged data bank and adding additional online assistance, including a pictorial guide to measurements and improved graphics. Other additions include postcranial measurements to improve classification of sex and ancestry and allow estimation of living stature, mandibular measurements, and world-wide data collected by W.W. Howells (1973, 1989). The new system represents a substantial improvement and demonstrates the interplay between skeletal biology and forensic anthropology.

Comparison of data in the forensic data bank with those generated from the Terry and Hamann-Todd collections documents the temporal variation involved and the need to maintain the data bank. Such a comparison was made by Ousley and Jantz (1998) using measurements derived from both types of collections and by applying discriminant functions in the literature developed from older collections to cases in the data bank. This exercise demonstrated differences between these samples and documented the importance of the modern data in forensic applications.

EVIDENCE RECOVERY

Proper recovery of human remains constitutes an increasingly important aspect of forensic analysis. Most discoveries of human remains that lead to forensic investigation are not made by professionals. Construction workers, hikers, hunters, berry pickers, and family dogs usually are the first to notice human remains in these contexts. Most cases studied by forensic anthropologists are skeletonized and unidentified. Usually this means that they originate in areas not frequently traveled by humans, sites where they can remain undetected while soft tissue decomposition progresses. Frequently such sites are isolated, rural, wooded areas where ground cover discourages immediate discovery. In many areas of North America, discovery must wait until seasonal activities (hiking, hunting, etc.) bring a potential human discoverer into visual contact with the remains. In areas with cold winter seasons, low temperatures bring reduced foliage and increased ground visibility. This, coupled with winter treks to the woods by hunters and hikers, leads to discovery.

Once discovery of human remains is made, it is important to recover the remaining evidence as thoroughly and carefully as possible. Although much progress in this area has been made in recent years, much more can be done. If human remains are known or thought to be involved, recovery by a forensic anthropologist can be a great help. Shovels, trowels, and other sharp tools may be necessary to properly excavate the materials, but in the hands of nonprofessionals, these tools may produce alterations on the remains that would complicate analysis. Increasingly, forensic anthropologists are involved in recovery or those involved have had some exposure to principles of excavation through courses or seminars. Publications are available to advise those involved on the principles of recovery of human remains (e.g., Haglund and Sorg, 1997; Pickering and Bachman, 1997; Ubelaker, 1989).

Most recovery missions remain an exercise in common sense using careful archeological techniques. Advanced technology increasingly is available to supplement the traditional approaches. Ground-penetrating radar, soil resistivity equipment, metal detectors, and other sophisticated equipment can assist, particularly in cases with other evidence suggesting buried remains in a general area. In some circumstances, cadaver dogs can help as well. Use of these approaches, along with surface topography, aerial photography, vegetation patterns, and other indicators can facilitate difficult decisions on where labor-intensive excavation should be employed. Such a complex search clearly calls for a team approach, since no single expert likely will be knowledgeable in all the specialized procedures and equipment involved.

The major issues involved in evidence recovery are similar to those of traditional archeology or the recovery of ancient human remains. Decisions must be made regarding the amount of time and effort directed toward recovery. Ideally, all resources available should be utilized and directed toward the maximum

recovery of information. Just as with an archaeological excavation, the recovery operation is destructive and offers a mostly one-time opportunity to learn as much as possible. Practical decisions must be made regarding the use of available resources and time. Frequently these decisions must be made in consideration of other priorities. At the time of recovery, it is difficult to predict what information might prove important later in the investigation. Thus it is important to have the decisions guided by the most experienced and trained personnel available.

NONHUMAN VERSUS HUMAN REMAINS

Although most forensic anthropologists can easily distinguish intact, well-preserved human remains from those of nonhumans, fragmentary or otherwise altered material can be challenging. Detailed knowledge of human skeletal anatomy is usually sufficient to recognize that evidence is consistent with a human origin. The more precise opinion that remains are of human origin requires some recognition of the many other materials that can mimic the human condition. With the reality that molecular approaches potentially offer positive identification from minute bits of evidence, forensic anthropologists can expect to see increasing frequencies of submission of such evidence. Since the molecular procedures are costly and time consuming, an initial determination by the anthropologist of human versus nonhuman can be important.

Such determinations usually rely upon the experience of the anthropologist, supplemented by comparative collections. Other experts, especially zooarchaeologists or other naturalists, may need to be consulted. In my experience, microscopic examination can provide important diagnostic information. Examination of small evidence with a high-quality dissecting-type microscope (I currently use a Carl Zeiss SV 11 Stereomicroscope with photographic capability) allows clear viewing of morphological surface details that facilitate diagnosis. With fragmentary evidence, the examination of the visible internal surface may reveal helpful aspects of structure.

For especially difficult fragments, it may be desirable to prepare thin sections for even more detailed microscopic study (see Pfeiffer, Chapter 10). In particular, the osteon organization may present a nonhuman pattern (Ubelaker 1989). Although human/nonhuman differences in bone histology are recognized in the literature, more research is needed to clarify the distribution of these differences throughout the skeleton and among different species (Enlow, 1962, 1963; Enlow and Brown, 1956, 1957, 1958; Foote, 1916; Ubelaker, 1989).

If soft tissues are sufficiently preserved, they may provide additional clues on human/nonhuman status. Hair analysis or serological techniques may be able to clarify if remains are of human origin and perhaps identify species, genus, etc. Both of these approaches have proven to be useful in determining that some forensic cases of submitted cranial remains represented calves with hydrocephaly rather than human infants (Ubelaker et al., 1991). In this forensic application, extracts were prepared from desiccated soft tissue associated with the specimens. Double diffusion test methods were employed using the extract and antibodies of bovine, deer, horse, sheep, swine, and human. A precipitin line formed in the presence of anti-bovine serum which with additional testing contributed to the final diagnosis that the remains represented calves with hydrocephaly. Hair examination and cranial morphology also contributed diagnostic information.

AGE AT DEATH

Scientific progress in the estimation of age at death involves greater awareness of the variability involved, new techniques available for different structures, and greater appreciation of the importance of regional and temporal variation in the aging process.

Forensic anthropology strives for an accurate estimation of age at death. Such "accuracy" involves coming as close as possible to actual chronological age at death and realistically conveying the probabilities associated with the estimate. The process is complicated by the fact that many individual techniques are available that have been developed by different researchers working with diverse samples. On the positive side, many techniques are now available reflecting age changes in different populations around the world at varying periods in history. The downside is that comparison of the accuracy of techniques can be difficult if they were developed from different samples. The situation also creates some uncertainty when a method is applied to an individual originating from a population that differs from the one that contributed to the development of the method. Increasingly, the scientific literature respects these problems through utilization of diverse samples and testing of methods on different samples.

Decisions regarding which methods to utilize in estimation of age at death result not just from the relative accuracy of the methods but also the experience of the investigator, available equipment, and the preservation of the remains. For example, adult age estimation through microscopic examination of long bone cortical microstructure offers one of the most accurate single approaches according to the literature, but requires time-consuming specimen preparation and equipment that is not universally available. This technique also requires assessment of complex histological structures, a process not familiar to all forensic anthropologists (see Robling and Stout, Chapter 7). A technique that may have been quite accurate when developed by a specialist in a particular process may not be as accurate in the hands of a less-experienced researcher.

Although some techniques for age estimation appear more accurate than others, usually it is advisable to consult as many age indicators as possible in assessing age at death, especially for adults (see Jackes, Chapter 15). For immature skeletons, the extent of dental development provides the most accurate age indicator. If teeth are fragmented, absent, or otherwise difficult to recognize, then the size and overall morphology of bones (including epiphyses) or bone fragments can be useful (see Saunders, Chapter 5).

For adults, age assessment is more difficult because the increased number of years have allowed potentially greater internal differences to develop in the various age indicators. A skeleton may present a relatively youthful-appearing pubic symphysis and sternal end of the fourth rib, yet show premature arthritic development and extensive tooth loss. All of these aging systems are variable and not entirely linked. For these reasons an assessment of all available data is important.

The application of different techniques to the same sample of individuals of known age at death offers some insight into the relative accuracy and reliability of the methods. With such an approach, Virginia Galera, Lee-Ann Hayek, and I (Galera et al., 1995) applied various techniques of estimation of age at death that are popular in both Europe and North America to 963 skeletons of known age at death in the Terry Collection of the Smithsonian Institution. The evaluation included four approaches to cranial suture closure (Acsádi and Nemeskéri, 1970; Baker, 1984; Masset, 1982; Meindl and Lovejoy, 1985), antemortem tooth loss, vertebral osteophytosis (Stewart, 1958), sternal rib morphology (İşcan et al., 1984a, 1984b, 1985; İşcan and Loth, 1986a, 1986b), the pubic symphysis (Acsádi and Nemeskéri, 1970; Gilbert and McKern, 1973; McKern and Stewart, 1957; Suchey and Katz, 1986; Suchey et al., 1986, 1988; Todd, 1920, 1921) and auricular surface changes (Bedford et al., 1989; Lovejoy et al., 1985).

Statistical testing revealed no significant differences in the scoring of these techniques by the three investigators. This suggests that the techniques are not difficult to interpret and apply even with investigators with minimal anthropological preparation (Galera et al., 1995). Application of the cranial methods suggested that those relying upon endocranial closure

were more accurate than the ectocranial ones (Galera et al., 1998). The different methods demonstrated different strengths when applied to different subsets of the sample, but overall the European methods were more accurate, at least when applied to the crania of the Terry Collection.

In another test, various methods of estimating age at death of adults were applied to a sample of 19 French autopsy individuals of known age at death (Ubelaker et al., 1998). Individual techniques tested consisted of the Lamendin et al. (1992) procedure of assessing single-rooted teeth, the morphology of the sternal end of the fourth rib (İşcan et al., 1984a, 1984b, 1985; İşcan and Loth, 1986a, 1986b), the Suchey-Brooks system for the pubic symphysis (Brooks and Suchey, 1990) and the Kerley method (Kerley, 1965, 1970; Kerley and Ubelaker, 1978) of assessing femoral cortical remodeling. In addition, three comprehensive approaches were employed: (1) a mathematical average of the ages derived from the individual approaches, (2) a two-step procedure (Baccino and Zerilli, 1997) that combines aspects of the pubic symphysis assessment with the dental technique, and (3) an overall assessment by each investigator of all available information.

Statistical analysis of the results indicated that the comprehensive approaches were more accurate than any of the individual approaches. Of the single approaches, the dental technique offered the best results. The relative success of the seven methods employed reflected not only the nature of the methods but also the experience of the investigators and the complexity of the structures requiring interpretation. This was most apparent with the complex Kerley method, which yielded much more accurate results when applied by an experienced investigator in comparison to those produced by a professional with less familiarity with the technique. The value of experience in assessing age at death has been emphasized by others as well (Saunders et al., 1992).

Estimation of age at death in a forensic context concentrates on the individual, utilizing experience and data from the literature on age changes within populations throughout the world. Such estimates offered in reports or court testimony should utilize appropriate language to convey the proper associated probabilities. For example, in the analysis of a forensic case, a particular technique might suggest an age at death of about 34 years. It is appropriate to call attention to this result in a forensic report but equally important to convey the possible range around this estimate. Without this perspective, the authorities may limit their search of missing persons to those of age 34 and not discover the actual missing person whose age varied somewhat from that estimate. When age at death is known, the cases offer an opportunity to augment our knowledge of skeletal age changes and the influencing factors involved.

SEX

In forensic anthropology, as in the more general field of skeletal biology, the estimation of sex (not gender [Walker and Cook, 1998]) of the adult is generated most accurately from observations of the pelvis. (For a discussion of sex determination of the subadult skeleton, see Saunders, Chapter 5). In the absence of the pelvis, in incomplete remains, or those with excessive deterioration of the pelvis, the morphology, especially the size, of bones can provide important information. Most recent research in this area has been directed toward making data available on sex differences in parts of the skeletons that may be recovered in unusual circumstances.

Such research is reflected by recent work on bones of the feet. These data are relevant in the forensic context because bones of the foot can be protected within shoes and stockings from taphonomic forces that otherwise destroy or separate the rest of the skeleton. Boots recovered from water contexts may contain the bones of the foot as the only skeletal representation of the individual, otherwise lost or distributed by decomposition and fluvial factors. Footwear

containing bones of the foot also may be separated from the other remains by animals, forcing a specialized analysis of just those remains if only the foot bones are recovered.

To help meet this forensic problem, Introna et al. (1997) examined 80 right calcanei from 40 males and 40 females from a contemporary southern Italian collection. Eight measurements were taken leading to both univariate and multivariate analyses that complement earlier work in estimating sex from this bone. The Italian study is especially useful in a comparative sense to help document not only sex differences but how the expression of these differences may vary in populations around the world.

Smith, and Robling and Ubelaker turned to the Smithsonian's Terry Collection for data on sex differences in the metatarsals (Robling and Ubelaker, 1997; Smith, 1997) and foot phalanges (Smith, 1997). Discriminant function equations were generated to facilitate sex identification of these bones.

ANCESTRY

In studying remains of unknown identity, forensic anthropologists usually attempt to estimate the ancestry of the individual or the group with which this person would likely have been identified in their community (the so-called "race" of the individual). This information can be useful to law enforcement in attempting to narrow the search for the identity. Knowledge of the ancestry is also useful in other aspects of analysis, especially stature estimation in which different regression equations are available for blacks, whites, etc., since there is group variability in stature and body proportions. It is important however, to recognize the social dimensions of these categories and not confuse this effort with past typological classifications that suggested greater biological grouping than actually exists.

In forensic anthropology, the estimation of ancestry is accomplished through observation of characteristics such as dental morphology and features of the facial skeleton and through measurements, usually with discriminant function analysis. The former approach has been augmented by increased attention on the variety of anatomical features that display variation (see Gill and Rhine, 1990). The latter approach has grown primarily through the acquisition of measurements from larger, more diverse samples, with special effort aimed at the needs of the forensic community.

In recent years, the estimation of ancestry has been strengthened considerably in forensic anthropology through the forensic data bank discussed earlier in this chapter. The data bank and the computer program FORDISC 2.0 have improved the ability of forensic anthropologists to predict ancestry (Ousley and Jantz, 1996). Like any other discriminant function program, FORDISC forces a classification into the groups defined within the database. Intelligent use of this program, and any other such functions, must interpret these classifications using all available information.

As an example of the application of this system, measurements from a recent forensic case of known identity were entered into the program. The individual was an adult female of known living stature of about 63 in (160 cm) and was known in the community as being white. Once the data were entered on a standard IBM compatible computer, only a few seconds were required to classify the measurements as originating from a white female with a posterior probability of 0.969 and a typicality of 0.842 (Ubelaker, 1997). Posterior probability relates the likelihood that the unknown originates within the group it is classified into, assuming it originates from one of the groups used in the analysis. Typicality probability presents the likelihood that the unknown originates within any of the groups used in the analysis. For additional detail on these statistics, see Ousley and Jantz (1996).

A second classification using the database of W.W. Howells (1973, 1989) required 9 min to classify the "unknown" as a Zalavar female from western Hungary, ninth to tenth century. The other close groupings using the Howells database were Egyptian and Taiwanese (fe-males). Like the forensic database, the Howells system had correctly classified the measurements as originating from a female, but the closest population classifications were quite disparate geographically. Intelligent use of this system must regard the classifications within the context of other information. It obviously would be incorrect to conclude from the Howells classification that the individual originated from the Zalavar group of western Hungary, ninth to tenth century, as suggested by the face value of the analysis. Rather, an individual classified in that manner by the Howells database likely would have been socially classified as white in contemporary North American society. The Howells database is mostly comprised of archeologically recovered remains. While such ancient samples may not be represented directly by a modern forensic case, they can provide useful perspective to assist in the overall evaluation.

The estimation of ancestry calls upon our skills as physical anthropologists to assess the biological information displayed by the forensic remains in the context of world-wide human variation. This aspect of forensic analysis also requires broader anthropological interpretation of how an individual with certain skeletal characteristics would likely be regarded (social classification or "race") by the community in which they lived. Once again, language on this issue must be carefully selected to convey the proper levels of probability involved.

LIVING STATURE

Recent progress in the estimation of living stature has been registered on three fronts: (1) the detection of errors and clarification of past formulae for estimating stature, (2) improvements in methods with the new forensic data bank, and (3) recognition of the potential error involved in "known" living stature.

In recent years, most skeletal biologists in North America have relied heavily upon the published stature regression equations of Trotter (1970). These formulae were generated from multiple databases of measurements of long bones from individuals of known stature, many of military origin whose statures were likely measured and thus accurately documented. Of all the long bones, the tibia is especially problematic to measure because it presents extensions from the articular surfaces on both the proximal (intercondylar eminence) and distal (medial malleolus) ends. Research with Trotter's original measurements raised questions about the manner in which she measured the tibia. Her published definition of the measurement used in the stature calculation from the tibia excluded the intercondylar eminence but included the medial malleolus. Since Trotter had measured individuals in the Terry Collection, those tibiae were available and could be remeasured for comparison with her original measurements (Jantz et al., 1995). This procedure suggested that, at least in the Terry sample, the medial malleolus was excluded, but questions remain on how the measurement was taken on other skeletons utilized in Trotter's research. The example is illustrative of the importance of careful definition of measurements and the need to critically evaluate such information in the existing literature.

Improvements in stature estimation also result from the incorporation of new information from additional skeletal samples. Most relevant to forensic anthropology are revisions resulting from the forensic data bank. Using the new contemporary information in the data bank, Jantz (1992) offered new regression equations for both sexes and the various population groups. Comparison of these formulae with those previously published revealed differences, but it was difficult to determine if they represented secular trends in the groups represented, or relative error in the reporting of living stature.

The error involved in so-called known living stature remains a persistent problem, not only in developing new equations from the forensic data bank but also applying estimates to cases. Research has shown a human tendency to erroneously report living stature, especially in males (Himes and Roche, 1982; Willey and Falsetti, 1991). Thus, even if stature can be ac-

curately estimated from skeletal remains, the "known" statures of missing persons available for comparison may be sufficiently different from actual stature to complicate the identification process. Estimates of stature from remains can be useful not only to help identify unknown remains, but also for exclusion and to assist in the sorting of commingled remains.

FACIAL REPRODUCTION

A central goal of forensic anthropology is the accumulation of information about an individual from their remains to facilitate identification. At times, even with individuals thought to be deceased only short periods of time, information on sex, age at death, ancestry, living stature, and other information still does not lead to an identification. There are many reasons for this, but among them is the possibility that the lifestyle of the individual is such that the community has not considered the possibility of death, or for other reasons the individual is not officially registered as a missing person. In such cases, authorities may request a facial reproduction. The goal here is to estimate the living facial appearance of the individual so that the image can be presented to the public through the media. Hopefully, such visual public exposure will trigger the memory of an acquaintance and lead to identification. The facial reproduction is not used directly for the positive identification; however, it may help generate the recognition and documents needed for such identification.

Techniques of facial reproduction can consist of three-dimensional reproduction using clay or a similar material deposited on the skull or a cast of the skull, an artist's sketch prepared from visual examination of the skull, or various computer approaches (Ubelaker, 1993; Ubelaker and O'Donnell, 1992). While these approaches have varying procedures and advantages, they all require considerable experience and rely upon estimates of the depth of the soft tissue at various points on the skull. Current research seeks to improve data on soft tissue depth through studies of ultrasound

(Manhein et al., 1998) and magnetic resonance imaging (MRI) (Marks et al., 1998).

PHOTOGRAPHIC SUPERIMPOSITION

The closely related procedure of comparing a recovered skull with a photograph taken during life has been augmented by computer technology (Ubelaker et al., 1992). This technique is termed *photographic superimposition* and is employed in cases when identification of remains is suspected but not confirmed by other evidence. The technique is largely used for exclusion, to demonstrate that the recovered skull could not have originated from the individual depicted in the photograph. Although it is possible that the technique also could be used for positive identification, usually when a "match" is made, it only can establish that the remains could have originated from the person shown in the photograph.

An early example of a variant of this technique is provided by the 1935 analysis of John Glaister and colleagues who compared photographs of two missing persons with recovered remains (Glaister, 1953; Glaister and Brash, 1937). They compared the photographs of the living with photographs taken of the remains, arranged to approximate the positions of the heads in the living photographs. The comparisons contributed to the identification of the skeletons.

The method of comparison was enhanced by the introduction of the use of video (Brown, 1982, 1983; Helmer and Grüner 1976a, 1976b). Use of two video cameras, an electronic mixing device, and a viewing screen offered a more dynamic method of comparing the two images.

The computer-assisted approach involves the use of a video camera and a computer. Images of both the remains and the photograph of the living individual are captured with the video camera, digitized, and stored within the computer. Software then allows both images to be brought up on the screen simultaneously and manipulated for detailed comparison (Ubelaker et al. 1992). Variations of the above techniques can be used to compare any two objects to evaluate their similarity of shape. They have proven most useful in forensic anthropology to compare recovered skulls with antemortem photographs, but applications are not limited to these materials. Since the technique is usually not used for positive identification, it can be used for exclusion or in support of other evidence for identification. The technique merely facilitates comparison. The success of the evaluation of the comparison depends upon the experience of the investigator. For example, the technique can be used to establish that the two images are consistent. The investigator must then use knowledge of variation to determine if the features examined are sufficiently unique to warrant identification.

TIME SINCE DEATH

Determination of the postmortem interval can prove important in forensic investigation. Research using controlled specimens (especially such as that conducted at the facility at the University of Tennessee) has contributed a great deal to improving our understanding of the complex factors operating on postmortem alteration. Controlled studies have revealed the role of arthropods and other animal activity, as well as such factors as burial depth, temperature, state of the body when deposited, etc. In addition to entomological evidence, volatile fatty acids in the soil (Vass et al., 1992), plant growth (Willey and Heilman, 1987), mechanical trampling (Ubelaker and Adams, 1995), and many other factors can influence the process. Haglund and Sorg have edited a book (1997) that summarizes much of this recent research. Much of this information limits specific anthropological interpretation since patterns can vary greatly and frequently not all of the influencing factors are known in a case.

POSITIVE IDENTIFICATION

Positive identification is achieved when unique characteristics known to exist within an individual are found in recovered remains. Traditionally, such evidence usually originates from dental records. These are most commonly radiographs, which can be compared to radiographs of unidentified jaws and teeth. Other useful dental characteristics include restorations, fillings, and crowns. Unique aspects of dental or skeletal morphology may also be useful. Increasingly, positive identifications are made using molecular techniques, frequently from minute evidence.

Usually, positive identifications from dental work or molecular evidence are made by specialists in those areas (forensic odontologists and geneticists, respectively). Forensic anthropologists are involved in the analysis that leads to identification by narrowing the range of possibilities and directly in the interpretation of skeletal and dental morphology from photographs, radiographs, and other evidence. This is an interpretative endeavor that calls for experience and judgment. In my experience, positive identifications from forensic anthropology result primarily from comparison of skeletal anatomical details with antemortem radiographs. If identical features are found, attention focuses on the uniqueness of those features. Are the points observed unusual enough that positive identification can be established? On the other hand, if differences are found are they of the nature and magnitude to preclude identification? Differences may reflect only techniques of preparing the radiographs, the length of time between death and the date the antemortem radiographs were taken, taphonomic factors, or others. Experience and knowledge of human skeletal anatomy are needed to sort all this out and draw a reasonable conclusion.

MOLECULAR APPROACHES

Recent years have witnessed a surge of activity in molecular approaches to forensic science. Aspects of this research have an impact and complement efforts in forensic anthropology.

The areas of greatest impact are positive identification, sex determination, and, potentially, ancestry evaluation.

Techniques of DNA extraction and amplification have increased dramatically (Cattaneo et al., 1997; Evison et al., 1997). Sources of valuable molecular evidence have grown from recent soft tissue to skeletal remains (Boles et al., 1995; Hochmeister et al., 1995; Holland et al., 1993; Primorac et al., 1996; Rankin et al., 1996; Yamamoto et al., 1998). Such techniques have proven useful in establishing positive identification, even in such cases as a dead infant kept by the alleged mother for 16 years (Yamamoto et al. 1998), war victims from mass graves in Croatia, Bosnia, and Herzegovina (Primorac et al., 1996), mass graves from Guatemala (Boles et al., 1995), and remains originating from the U.S. Civil War (Fisher et al., 1993). In cases in which forensic anthropological analysis does not clearly indicate sex, molecular techniques may be able to provide the necessary information (Nesser and Liechti-Gallati, 1995)

Considerable information is also being compiled on molecular patterns in world-wide populations (Allen et al., 1993; Ambach et al., 1997; Bell et al., 1997; Budowle et al., 1994, 1996, 1997a, 1997b; Busque et al., 1997; Chow et al., 1993; Gené et al., 1998; Glock et al., 1996; Hartmann et al., 1997; Hayes et al., 1995; Jin et al., 1997; Khatib et al., 1997; Lorente et al., 1994; Medintz et al., 1997; Melton and Stoneking, 1996; Melton et al., 1997a, 1997b; Moura-Neto and Budowle, 1997; Park et al., 1997; Pfitzinger et al., 1995; Pinheiro et al., 1997; Rodriguez-Calvo et al., 1996; Romero Palancho et al., 1996; Scholl et al., 1996; Spinella et al., 1997; Walkinshaw et al., 1996; Watanabe et al., 1997). In the future, this information may allow estimates of ancestry with increased precision. Even with these developments, the role of the forensic anthropologist is still important in providing rapid initial descriptions and narrowing the field of identification in cases where investigators have no preliminary suspicions of who the person might be.

EVIDENCE OF FOUL PLAY

Forensic anthropologists are in a unique position to offer opinions about some types of evidence relating to foul play. A careful eye (sometimes aided by a microscope) is needed to spot some evidence for trauma. Knowledge of the reaction of bone to a variety of stimuli is then required to determine the nature of the alterations and if they represent antemortem, perimortem or postmortem conditions. A single forensic case may present evidence of all types. Evidence of bone response, remodeling (or lack of it), coloration patterns, and related observations all contribute to the solution of the puzzle. Since anthropologists routinely work with human remains from many different contexts (archaeologically recovered skeletons, museum collections, autopsy specimens, etc.), they, more than any other professionals, have the necessary knowledge.

The exposure to evidence of foul play in modern cases also facilitates interpretation of trauma in the archaeologically recovered remains encountered in skeletal biology. This area of forensic anthropology represents a clear example of the desirable "two-way street" interplay between forensic work and the more general field of skeletal biology. Knowledge of diverse taphonomic processes operating on human bone gained through work with archaeological samples is needed to interpret examples of trauma in forensic cases. Conversely, the knowledge gained about perimortem trauma through forensic work is critical to proper interpretation of such evidence in skeletal biology.

Such involvement has lead to significant research by anthropologists in trauma interpretation. Examples are especially noteworthy in interpretation of gunshot wounds and sharp-force trauma. Ross (1996) used her research approach as a forensic anthropologist to address the long-standing recognized difficulty in estimating bullet caliber from characteristics of cranial alterations. She examined the cranial alterations in 73 individuals with cranial gunshot trauma of known bullet caliber. Measurements were recorded on the alterations and the data were analyzed using sophisticated statistics. The study revealed that the size of the alterations produced in gunshot trauma results not only from the caliber of the bullet but also from the thickness of the bone at the site of impact. Information was generated by the study that assists in the interpretation of gunshot skeletal trauma.

In another innovative research approach to better understanding skeletal trauma, Houck (1998) devised a "cutting machine" to examine aspects of sharp-force trauma in bone. Bovine tibial diaphyses were cut with three different knives using the machine. All resulting cutmarks were examined for class and individual characteristics. As with Ross' study cited above, the data were analyzed statistically by Houck producing information of great importance in the forensic interpretation of sharp-force trauma. Additional discussion of anthropological interpretation of skeletal trauma is provided by Berryman and Symes (1998), Reichs (1998), Sauer (1998), and Symes et al. (1998).

FUTURE PROSPECTS

Interest and participation in forensic anthropology has grown steadily since the casual, occasional encounters of a few pioneers early in the history of American physical anthropology. The sustained growth of this area of physical anthropology can be measured in student interest, the numbers of anthropologists involved in casework, increases in the memberships of the physical anthropology section of the American Academy of Forensic Sciences and the diplomates of the American Board of Forensic Anthropology, and the increase in the number of research publications focusing on topics in forensic anthropology. This growth shows no sign of diminishing and has led to the recognition of forensic anthropology as a vigorous subfield of physical anthropology. Slowly, job opportunities have expanded from the traditional anthropological employment sites of universities and museums to specific research and teaching in forensic anthropology, as well as employment in crime laboratories, medical examiners' offices, and the military. Increasingly, forensic anthropologists are integrated into evidence recovery teams and the medicolegal investigation of death. Forensic anthropologists have provided important perspective in the international investigation of possible war crimes and human rights issues.

The field of forensic anthropology has progressed so far that one might think that few research problems remain. Such is not the case. In fact, progress has highlighted the tremendous need for new data and anthropological perspective on most areas of forensic anthropology. Major questions remain regarding population variation in many of the problems routinely assessed by forensic anthropologists. Much more work needs to be done in the areas of assessment of time since death, animal versus human recognition, taphonomic change, environmental factors, foul play, and positive identification. Even more traditional areas of scholarship such as the estimate of sex, age at death, stature, and ancestral origins would benefit greatly from new research and perspective.

Most training in forensic anthropology is centered in university departments of anthropology with an emphasis in human skeletal biology and its forensic applications. For students seeking education in this area, I recommend consulting the guide to departments of anthropology published by the American Anthropological Association (American Anthropological Association, 1997) along with the list of current diplomates of the American Board of Forensic Anthropology, Inc. (website: http://www.csuchico.edu/anth/ABFA). University degree programs can be supplemented with various courses and seminars in forensic anthropology that are offered periodically. Such a week-long course is offered annually by the Smithsonian Institution (alternating course location each year between Washington, D.C., and Europe). The National Museum of Health and Medicine of Washington, D.C., offers a similar annual course and others are available regionally. Students seeking experience should also consider internships with professional forensic anthropologists who are active with casework.

Training remains firmly entrenched within skeletal biology, but increasingly students are acquiring skills in additional areas including law and various technical specialties. While this additional perspective is undoubtedly valuable, I feel it should supplement and not displace the traditional anthropological education. Anthropologists working in the forensic arena need to be aware of the increasingly specialized contributions made in medicolegal cases. However, it is primarily the anthropological training with archaeological techniques and samples and other experiences within anthropology that separate the contributions of forensic anthropologists from those of others and make us unique. The future is indeed bright for those skeletal biologists willing to accept the challenge of applying their skills to the resolution of forensic problems.

REFERENCES

Acsádi GY, Nemeskéri J. 1970. History of Human Life Span and Mortality. Budapest: Akadémiai Kiadó.

Allen M, Saldeen T, Pettersson U, Gyllensten U. 1993. Genetic typing of HLA class II genes in Swedish populations: application to forensic analysis. J Forensic Sci 38:554–570.

Ambach E, Parson W, Niederstätter H, Budowle B. 1997. Austrian Caucasian population data for the quadruplex plus amelogenin: refined mutation rate for HumvWFA31/A. J Forensic Sci 42: 1136–1139.

American Anthropological Association. 1997. AAA Guide, 1997–1998. Arlington, Va.: American Anthropological Association.

Angel JL. 1974. Patterns of fractures from Neolithic to modern times. Anthropologiai Kozlemenyek 18:9–18.

Angel JL. 1976. Colonial to modern skeletal change in the U.S.A. Am J Phys Anthropol 45:723–736.

Baccino E, Zerilli A. 1997. The two step strategy (TSS) or the right way to combine a dental

(Lamendin) and an anthropological (Suchey-Brooks System) method for age determination [abstract]. In: Proceedings of the 49th Annual Meeting of the American Academy of Forensic Sciences, February 17–22, 1997 New York, NY p. 150. Am Acad For Sci 3:150.

Baker RK. 1984. The relationship of cranial suture closure and age analyzed in a modern multi-racial sample of males and females. M.A. Thesis. California State University, Fullerton.

Bedford ME, Russell KF, Lovejoy CO. 1989. The utility of the auricular surface aging technique. Am J Phys Anthropol 78:190–191. Abstract.

Bell B, Budowle B, Martinez-Jarreta B, Casalod Y, Abecia E, Castellano M. 1997. Distribution of types for six PCR-based loci; LDLR, GYPA, HBGG, D7S8, GC and HLA-DQA1 in central Pyrenees and Teruel (Spain). J Forensic Sci 42:510–513.

Berryman HE, Symes SA. 1998. Recognizing gunshot and blunt cranial trauma through fracture interpretation. In: Reichs KJ, editor. Forensic Osteology, 2nd edition. Springfield, Ill.: Charles C. Thomas. pp. 333–352.

Boles TC, Snow CC, Stover E. 1995. Forensic DNA testing on skeletal remains from mass graves: a pilot project in Guatemala. J Forensic Sci 40:3 49–355.

Brooks S, Suchey JM. 1990. Skeletal age determination based on the os pubis: a comparison of the Acsádi-Nemeskéri and Suchey-Brooks methods. Hum Evol 5:227–238.

Brown KA. 1982. The identification of Linda Agostini. Am J Forensic Med Pathol 3(2):131–141.

Brown KA. 1983. Developments in cranio-facial superimposition for identification. J Forensic Odonto-Stomatol 1:57–64.

Budowle B, Jankowski LB, Corey HW, Swec NT, Freck-Tootell S, Pino JA, Schwartz R, Kelley CA, Tarver ML. 1997a. Evaluation of independence assumptions for PCR-based and protein-based genetic markers in New Jersey Caucasians. J Forensic Sci 42:223–225.

Budowle B, Monson KL, Giusti AM, Brown BL. 1994. Evaluation of Hinf I-generated VNTR profile frequencies determined using various ethnic databases. J Forensic Sci 39:988–1008.

Budowle B, Smerick JB, Keys KM, Moretti TR. 1997b. United States population data on the multiplex short tandem repeat loci—HUMTH01, TPOX, and CSF1P0—and the variable number tandem repeat locus D1S80. J Forensic Sci 42:846–849.

Budowle B, Woller J, Koons BW, Furedi S, Errera JD, Padar Z. 1996. Hungarian population data on seven PCR-based loci. J Forensic Sci 41:667–670.

Buikstra JE, Hoshower LM. 1990. Introduction. In: Buikstra J, editor. A Life in Science: Papers in Honor of J. Lawrence Angel. U.S.A. Center for American Archeology. Scientific Papers Number 6 pp. 1–16.

Busque L, Desmarais D, Provost S, Schumm JW, Zhong Y, Chakraborty R. 1997. Analysis of allele distribution for six short tandem repeat loci in the French Canadian population of Québec. J Forensic Sci 42:1147–1153.

Cattaneo C, Craig OE, James NT, Sokol RJ. 1997. Comparison of three DNA extraction methods on bone and blood stains up to 43 years old and amplification of three different gene sequences. J Forensic Sci 42:1126–1135.

Chow ST, Tan WF, Yap KH, Ng TL. 1993. The development of DNA profiling database in an HAE III based RFLP system for Chinese, Malays, and Indians in Singapore. J Forensic Sci 38:874–884.

Dorsey GA. 1897. A sexual study of the size of the articular surfaces of the long bones in aboriginal American skeletons. Boston Med Surg J 137(4):80–82.

Dorsey GA. 1899. The skeleton in medicolegal anatomy. Chicago Med Recorder 16:172–179.

Dwight T. 1878. The Identification of the Human Skeleton. A Medico-Legal Study. Boston: Massachusetts Medical Society.

Dwight T. 1881. The sternum as an index of sex and age. J Anat Physiol London 15:327–330.

Dwight T. 1890a. The sternum as an index of sex, height and age. J Anat Physiol London 24:527–535.

Dwight T. 1890b. The closure of the cranial sutures as a sign of age. Boston Med Surg J 122(17):389–392.

Dwight T. 1894a. Methods of estimating the height from parts of the skeleton. Med Rec NY 46:293–296.

Dwight T. 1894b. The range and significance of variations in the human skeleton. Boston Med Surg J 13:73–76, 97–101.

Dwight T. 1905. The size of the articular surfaces of the long bones as characteristics of sex; an anthropological study. Am J Anat 4:19–32.

Enlow DH. 1962. A study of the post-natal growth and remodeling of bone. Am J Anat 110(2): 79–101.

Enlow DH. 1963. Principles of Bone Remodelling. Springfield, Ill.: Charles C. Thomas.

Enlow DH, Brown SO. 1956. A comparative histological study of fossil and recent bone tissues. Part I. Tex J Sci VII(4):405–443.

Enlow DH, Brown SO. 1957. A comparative histological study of fossil and recent bone tissues. Part II. Tex J Sci IX(2):186–214.

Enlow DH, Brown SO. 1958. A comparative histological study of fossil and recent bone tissues. Part II. Tex J Sci X(2):187–230.

Evison MP, Smillie DM, Chamberlain AT. 1997. Extraction of single-copy nuclear DNA from forensic specimens with a variety of postmortem histories. J Forensic Sci 42:1032–1038.

Fisher DL, Holland MM, Mitchell L, Sledzik PS, Willcox AW, Wadhams M, Weedn VW. 1993. Extraction, evaluation, and amplification of DNA from decalcified and undecalcified United States Civil War bone. J Forensic Sci 38:60–68.

Foote JS. 1916. A contribution to the comparative histology of the femur. Smithsonian Contributions XXXV:3.

Galera V, Ubelaker DH, Hayek LA. 1995. Interobserver error in macroscopic methods of estimating age at death from the human skeleton. Int J Anthropol 10(4):229–239.

Galera V, Ubelaker DH, Hayek LAC. 1998. Comparison of macroscopic cranial methods of age estimation applied to skeletons from the Terry Collection. J Forensic Sci 43:933–939.

Gené M, Fuentes M, Huguet E, Piqué E, Bert F, Corella A, Pérez-Pérez A, Corbella J, Moreno P. 1998. Quechua Amerindian population characterized by HLA-DQα, YNZ22, 3´APO B, HUMTH01, and HUMVWA31A polymorphisms. J Forensic Sci 43:403–405.

Gilbert BM, McKern TW. 1973. A method for aging the female os pubis. Am J Phys Anthropol 38(1): 31–38.

Gill GW, Rhine S, editors. 1990. Skeletal Attribution of Race: Methods for Forensic Anthropology. Albuquerque: Maxwell Museum of Anthropology. Anthropological Papers No. 4.

Glaister J. 1953. The Ruxton Case. In: Glaister J, editor. Medical Jurisprudence and Toxicology. Edinburgh: E. & S. Livingstone. pp. 99–108.

Glaister J, Brash JC. 1937. The skulls and the portraits. In: Medico-Legal Aspects of the Ruxton Case. Edinburgh: E. & S. Livingstone. Chapter IX.

Glock B, Schwartz DWM, Schwartz-Jungl EM, Mayr WR. 1996. Allelic ladder characterization of the short tandem repeat polymorphism in Intron 6 of the lipoprotein lipase gene and its application in an Austrian Caucasian population study. J Forensic Sci 41:579–581.

Haglund WD, Sorg MH, editors. 1997. Forensic Taphonomy: The Postmortem Fate of Human Remains. Boca Raton, Fla.: CRC Press.

Hartmann JM, Houlihan BT, Keister RS, Buse EL. 1997. The effect of ethnic and racial population substructuring on the estimation of multi-locus fixed-bin VNTR RFLP genotype probabilities. J Forensic Sci 42:232–240.

Hayes JM, Budowle B, Freund M. 1995. Arab population data on the PCR-based loci: HLA-DQA1, LDLR, GYPA, HBGG, D7S8, Gc, and D1S80. J Forensic Sci 40:888–892.

Helmer R, Grüner O. 1976a. Vereinfachte Schädelidentifizierung nach dem Superprojektionsverfahren mit Hilfe einer Video-Anlage. Vortr. auf dem X. Kongreβ der internat. München: Akademie für Gerichtliche und Soziale Medizin 14.

Helmer R, Grüner O. 1976b. Vereinfachte Schädelidentifizierung nach dem Superprojektionsverfahren mit Hilfe einer Video-Anlage. Forensic Science 7(3):202.

Himes JH, Roche AF. 1982. Reported versus measured adult statures. Am J Phys Anthropol 58(3):335–341.

Hochmeister MN, Budowle B, Borer UV, Rudin O, Bohnert M, Dirnhofer R. 1995. Confirmation of the identity of human skeletal remains using multiplex PCR amplification and typing kits. J Forensic Sci 40:701–705.

Holland MM, Fisher DL, Mitchell LG, Rodriguez WC, Canik JJ, Merril CR, Weedn VW. 1993. Mitochondrial DNA sequence analysis of human skeletal remains: identification of remains from the Vietnam War. J Forensic Sci 38:542–553.

Howells WW. 1973. Cranial Variation in Man. Cambridge, Mass: Papers of the Peabody Museum 67.

Howells WW. 1989. Skull Shapes and the Map. Cambridge, Mass.: Papers of the Peabody Museum 78.

Houck MH. 1998. Skeletal trauma and the individualization of knife marks in bones. In: Reichs KJ, editor. Forensic Osteology, 2nd edition. Springfield, Ill.: Charles C. Thomas. pp. 410–424.

Introna F, Di Vella G, Campobasso CP, Dragone M. 1997. Sex determination by discriminant analysis of calcanei measurements. J Forensic Sci 42:725–728.

İşcan MY, Loth SR 1986a. Determination of age from the sternal rib in white females: a test of the phase method. J Forensic Sci 31:990–999.

İşcan MY, Loth SR. 1986b. Determination of age from the sternal rib in white males: a test of the phase method. J Forensic Sci 31:122–132.

İşcan MY, Loth SR, Wright RK. 1984a. Age estimation from the rib by phase analysis: white males. J Forensic Sci 29:1094–1104.

İşcan MY, Loth SR, Wright RK. 1984b. Metamorphosis at the sternal rib: a new method to estimate age at death in males. Am J Phys Anthropol 65:147–156.

İşcan MY, Loth SR, Wright RK. 1985. Age estimation from the rib by phase analysis: white females. J Forensic Sci 30:853–863.

Jantz RL. 1992. Modification of the Trotter and Gleser female stature estimation formulae. J Forensic Sci 37:1230–1235.

Jantz RL, Hunt DR, Meadows L. 1995. The measure and mismeasure of the tibia: implications for stature estimation. J Forensic Sci 40(5):758–761.

Jantz RL, Moore-Jansen PH. 1988. A Data Base for Forensic Anthropology: Structure, Content and Analysis. Knoxville: The University of Tennessee Department of Anthropology. Report of Investigations No. 47.

Jantz RL, Ousley SD. 1993. FORDISC 1.0: Personal Computer Forensic Discriminant Functions. Knoxville: The University of Tennessee.

Jin L, Underhill PA, Buoncristiani M, Robertson JM. 1997. Defining microsatellite alleles by genotyping global indigenous human populations and non-human primates. J Forensic Sci 42:496–499.

Johnston FE. 1997. Krogman, Wilton Marion (1903–1987). In: Spencer F, editor. History of Physical Anthropology: An Encyclopedia, vol. 1. New York: Garland Publishing, Inc. pp. 586–587.

Kerley ER. 1965. The microscopic determination of age in human bone. Am J Phys Anthropol 23:149–163.

Kerley ER. 1970. Estimation of skeletal age: after about age 30. In: Stewart TD, editor. Personal Identification in Mass Disasters. Washington, D.C.: Smithsonian Institution. pp. 57–70.

Kerley ER, Ubelaker DH. 1978. Revisions in the microscopic method of estimating age at death in human cortical bone. Am J Phys Anthropol 49:545–546.

Khatib H, Ezzughayyar M, Ayesh S. 1997. The distribution of the vWF alleles and genotypes in the Palestinian population. J Forensic Sci 42:504–505.

Krogman WM. 1962. The Human Skeleton in Forensic Medicine. Springfield, Ill.: Charles C. Thomas.

Lamendin H, Baccino E, Humbert JF, Tavernier JC, Nossintchouk RM, Zerilli A. 1992. A simple technique for age estimation in adult corpses: the two criteria dental method. J Forensic Sci 37:1373–1379.

Lorente JA, Lorente M, Budowle B, Wilson MR, Villanueva E. 1994. Analysis of the HUMTH01 allele frequencies in the Spanish population. J Forensic Sci 39:1270–1274.

Lovejoy CO, Meindl RS, Pryzbeck TR, Mensforth RP. 1985. Chronological metamorphosis of the auricular surface of the ilium: a new method for the determination of adult skeletal age at death. Am J Phys Anthropol 68:15–28.

Manhein MH, Listi G, Barrow NE, Barsley RE, Musselman R, Ubelaker DH. 1998. New tissue depth measurements for American adults and children [abstract]. Proceedings of the 50th Annual meeting of the American Academy of Forensic Sciences IV February 9–14, 1998, San Francisco, CA:187–188.

Marks MK, Tufano DR, Uberbacher EC, Flanery RE, Olman VN, Xu Y. 1998. Computational approach to facial reconstruction [abstract]. Proceedings of the American Academy of Forensic Sciences IV, February 9–14, 1998, San Francisco, CA:188.

Masset C. 1982. Estimation de l'âge au décès par les sutures crâniennes. Université Paris VII. Thèse de Sciences Naturelles, multigraphiée.

McKern TW, Stewart TD. 1957. Skeletal Age Changes in Young American Males. Natick, Mass.: Headquarters, Quartermaster Research and Development Command. Technical Report EP–45.

Medintz I, Levine L, McCurdy L, Chiriboga L, Kingston C, Desnick RJ, Eng CM, Kobilinsky L. 1997. HLA-DQA1 and polymarker allele frequencies in two New York City Jewish populations. J Forensic Sci 42:919–922.

Meindl RS, Lovejoy CO. 1985. Ectocranial suture closure: a revised method for the determination of skeletal age at death based on the lateral-anterior sutures. Am J Phys Anthropol 68:57–66.

Melton T, Ginther C, Sensabaugh G, Soodyall H, Stoneking M. 1997a. Extent of heterogeneity in mitochondrial DNA of sub-Saharan African populations. J Forensic Sci 42:582–592.

Melton T, Stoneking M. 1996. Extent of heterogeneity in mitochondrial DNA of ethnic Asian populations. J Forensic Sci 41:591–602.

Melton T, Wilson M, Batzer M, Stoneking M. 1997b. Extent of heterogeneity in mitochondrial DNA of European populations. J Forensic Sci 42:437–446.

Moura-Neto RS, Budowle B. 1997. Fixed bin population data for the VNTR loci D1S7, D2S44, D4S139, D5S110, D10S28, and D14S13 in a population sample from Rio de Janeiro, Brazil. J Forensic Sci 42:926–928.

Neeser D, Liechti-Gallati S. 1995. Sex determination of forensic samples by simultaneous PCR amplification of α-satellite DNA from both the X and Y chromosomes. J Forensic Sci 40: 239–241.

Ousley SD, Jantz RL. 1996. FORDISC 2.0: Personal Computer Forensic Discriminant Functions. Knoxville: The University of Tennessee.

Ousley SD, Jantz RL. 1998. The forensic data bank: documenting skeletal trends in the United States. In: Reichs KJ, editor. Forensic Osteology, 2nd edition. Springfield, Ill.: Charles C. Thomas. pp. 441–458.

Park SJ, Lee WG, Lee SW, Kim SH, Koo BS, Budowle B, Rho HM. 1997. Genetic variations at four tetrameric tandem repeat loci in Korean population. J Forensic Sci 42:125–129.

Pfitzinger H, Ludes B, Kintz P, Tracqui A, Mangin P. 1995. French Caucasian population data for HUMTH01 and HUMFES/FPS short tandem repeat (STR) systems. J Forensic Sci 40:270–274.

Pickering RB, Bachman DC. 1997. The Use of Forensic Anthropology. New York: CRC Press.

Pinheiro F, Pontes L, Gené M, Huguet E, Costa JPD, Moreno P. 1997. Population study of the HUMTH01, HUMVWA31A, HUMF13A1, and HUMFES/FPS STR polymorphisms in the North of Portugal. J Forensic Sci 42:121–124.

Primorac D, Andelinovic S, Definis-Gojanovic M, Drmic I, Rezic B, Baden MM, Kennedy MA, Schanfield MS, Skakel SB, Lee HC. 1996. Identification of war victims from mass graves in Croatia, Bosnia, and Herzegovina by the use of standard forensic methods and DNA typing. J Forensic Sci 41:891–894.

Rankin DR, Narveson SD, Birkby WH, Lai J. 1996. Restriction fragment length polymorphism (RFLP) analysis on DNA from human compact bone. J Forensic Sci 41:40–46.

Reichs KJ. 1995. A professional profile of diplomates of the American Board of Forensic Anthropology: 1984–1992. J Forensic Sci 40: 176–182.

Reichs KJ. 1998. Postmortem dismemberment: recovery, analysis and interpretation. In: Reichs KJ, editor. Forensic Osteology, 2nd edition. Springfield, Ill.: Charles C. Thomas. pp. 353–388.

Robling AG, Ubelaker DH. 1997. Sex estimation from the metatarsals. J Forensic Sci 42:1062–1069.

Rodríguez-Calvo MS, Bellas S, Souto L, Vide C, Valverde E, Carracedo A. 1996. Population data on the loci LDLR, GYPA, HBGG, D7S8, and GC in three southwest European populations. J Forensic Sci 41:291–296.

Romero Palanco JL, Rodriguez Morales R, Vizcaya Rojas MA, Gamero Lucas JJ, Arufe Martinez MI. 1996. Genetic polymorphism of the inter-alpha-trypsin inhibitor (ITI) in Càdiz Province, Southern Spain. J Forensic Sci 41:664–666.

Ross AH. 1996. Caliber estimation from cranial entrance defect measurements. J Forensic Sci 41:629–633.

Sauer NJ. 1998. The timing of injuries and manner of death: distinguishing among antemortem, perimortem and postmortem trauma. In: Reichs KJ, editor. Forensic Osteology, 2nd edition. Springfield, Ill.: Charles C. Thomas. pp. 321–332.

Saunders SR, Fitzgerald C, Rogers T, Dudar C, McKillop H. 1992. A test of several methods of skeletal age estimation using a documented archaeological sample. Can Soc Forensic Sci J 25:97–118.

Scholl S, Budowle B, Radecki K, Salvo M. 1996. Navajo, Pueblo, and Sioux population data on the loci HLA-DQA1, LDLR, GYPA, HBGG, D7S8, Gc, and D1S80. J Forensic Sci 41:47–51.

Smith SL. 1997. Attribution of foot bones to sex and population groups. J Forensic Sci 42:186–195.

Spinella A, Marsala P, Biondo R, Montagna P. 1997. Italian population allele and genotype frequencies for the AmpliType7 PM and the HLA-DQ-alpha loci. J Forensic Sci 42:514–518.

Stewart TD. 1958. The rate of development of vertebral osteoarthritis in American whites and its significance in skeletal age identification. The Leech 28:144–151.

Stewart TD, editor. 1970. Personal Identification in Mass Disasters. Washington: Smithsonian Institution.

Stewart TD. 1977. History of physical anthropology. In: Wallace AFC, Angel JL, Fox R, McLendon S, Sady R, Sharer R, editors. Perspectives on Anthropology 1976. Washington: American Anthropological Association. pp. 70–79. Special Publication No. 10.

Stewart TD. 1978. George A. Dorsey's role in the Luetgert case: a significant episode in the history of forensic anthropology. J Forensic Sci 23:786–791.

Stewart TD. 1979a. Essentials of Forensic Anthropology, Especially as Developed in the United States. Springfield, Ill.: Charles C. Thomas.

Stewart TD. 1979b. Forensic anthropology. In: Goldschmidt W, editor. Washington: American Anthropological Association. pp. 169–183. Special Publication No. 11.

Stewart TD. 1982. Pioneer contributions of Harris Hawthorne Wilder, Ph.D., to forensic sciences. J Forensic Sci 27:754–762.

Suchey JM, Brooks ST, Katz D. 1988. Instructions for use of the Suchey-Brooks system for age determination of the female os pubis. Instructional materials accompanying female pubic symphyseal models of the Suchey-Brooks system. Distributed by France Casting (Diane France, 2190 West Drake Road, Suite 259, Fort Collins, CO 80526).

Suchey JM, Katz D. 1986. Skeletal age standards derived from an extensive multiracial sample of modern Americans. Am J Phys Anthropol 69:269. Abstract.

Suchey JM, Wiseley DV, Katz D. 1986. Evaluation of the Todd and McKern-Stewart methods for aging the male os pubis. In: Reichs KJ, editor. Forensic Osteology. Springfield, Ill.: Charles C. Thomas. pp. 33–67.

Symes SA, Berryman HE, Smith OC. 1998. Saw marks in bone: introduction and examination of residual kerf contour. In: Reichs KJ, editor. Forensic Osteology, 2nd edition. Springfield, Ill.: Charles C. Thomas. pp. 389–409.

Todd TW. 1920. Age changes in the pubic bone: I. The male white pubis. Am J Phys Anthropol 3:285–334.

Todd TW. 1921. Age changes in the pubic bone. Am J Phys Anthropol 4:1–70.

Trotter M. 1970. Estimation of stature from intact limb bones. In: Stewart TD, editor. Personal Identification in Mass Disasters. Washington: Smithsonian Institution. pp 71–83.

Ubelaker DH. 1989. Human Skeletal Remains: Excavation, Analysis, Interpretation, 2nd edition. Washington: Taraxacum.

Ubelaker DH. 1990. J. Lawrence Angel and the development of forensic anthropology in the United States. In: Buikstra JE, editor. A Life in Science: Papers in Honor of J. Lawrence Angel. Center for American Archeology. pp. 191–200. Scientific Papers 6.

Ubelaker DH. 1993. Facial reproduction. In: Wecht CY, editor. Forensic Sciences. New York: Matthew Bender and Co.

Ubelaker DH. 1996. Skeletons testify: anthropology in forensic science, AAPA Luncheon Address: April 12, 1996. Yrbk Phys Anthropol 39: 229–244.

Ubelaker DH. 1997. Review of FORDISC 2.0: Personal Computer Forensic Discriminant Functions, by Ousley SD and RL Jantz. Int J Osteoarch 8:128–133.

Ubelaker DH. 1999a. George Amos Dorsey. In; Garraty JA, Carnes MC, editors. American National Biography, vol. 6. New York: Oxford University Press. pp. 764–765

Ubelaker DH. 1999b

. Aleš Hrdlička's role in the history of forensic anthropology. J Forensic Sci. 44:724–730.

Ubelaker DH, Adams BJ. 1995. Differentiation of perimortem and postmortem trauma using taphonomic indicators. J Forensic Sci 40:509–512.

Ubelaker DH, Baccino E, Zerilli A, Oger E. 1998. Comparison of methods for assessing adult age at death on French autopsy samples [abstract]. Proceedings of the American Academy of Forensic Sciences IV:174–175.

Ubelaker DH, Berryman HE, Sutton TP, Clayton ER. 1991. Differentiation of hydrocephalic calf and human calvariae. J Forensic Sci 36:801–812.

Ubelaker DH, Bubniak E, O'Donnell G. 1992. Computer-assisted photographic superimposition. J Forensic Sci 37:750–762.

Ubelaker DH, O'Donnell G. 1992. Computer-assisted facial reproduction. J Forensic Sci 37: 155–162.

Vass AA, Bass WM, Wolt JD, Foss JE, Ammons JT. 1992. Time since death determinations of human cadavers using soil solution. J Forensic Sci 37:1236–1253.

Walker PL, Cook DC. 1998. Gender and sex: vive la difference. Am J Phys Anthropol 106:255–259.

Walkinshaw M, Strickland L, Hamilton H, Denning K, Gayley T. 1996. DNA profiling in two Alaskan native populations using HLA-DQA1, PM, and D1S80 loci. J Forensic Sci 41:478–484.

Watanabe Y, Yamada S, Nagai A, Takayama T, Hirata K, Bunai Y, Ohya I. 1997. Japanese population DNA typing data for the loci LDLR, GYPA, HBGG, D7S8, and GC. J Forensic Sci 42: 911–913.

Willey P, Falsetti T. 1991. Inaccuracy of height information on driver's licenses. J Forensic Sci 36:813–819.

Willey P, Heilman A. 1987. Estimating time since death using plant roots and stems. J Forensic Sci 32:1264–1270.

Yamamoto T, Uchihi R, Kojima T, Nozawa H, Huang X, Tamaki K, Katsumata Y. 1998. Maternal identification from skeletal remains of an infant kept by the alleged mother for 16 years with DNA typing. J Forensic Sci 43:701–705.

PART II

MORPHOLOGICAL ANALYSES AND AGE CHANGES

CHAPTER 3

BIOMECHANICAL ANALYSES OF ARCHAEOLOGICAL HUMAN SKELETONS

CHRISTOPHER B. RUFF

Biomechanics is the application of mechanical principles to biological systems (Wainwright et al., 1982). It has been used extensively in many fields of study, including orthopedics (Frankel and Nordin, 1980; Mow and Hayes, 1991), human industrial design (Easterby et al., 1982), and evolutionary biology (Rayner and Wooton, 1991). The widespread use of biomechanics theory in anthropology dates back to the mid-1970s, where its utility was demonstrated in such diverse areas as primate locomotion (Wells and Wood, 1975), mastication (Hylander, 1975), and long bone structural analysis (Lovejoy et al., 1976). This last study is particularly relevant to the present chapter, since it showed how engineering concepts could be applied to human archaeological samples. Since then there have been many investigations of archaeological and palaeontological skeletal material that have used a biomechanical approach to reconstruct past behavioral patterns (for recent reviews see Bridges, 1996; Ruff, 1999; also this chapter). Such studies have ranged from those of long-term evolutionary trends in skeletal robusticity (e.g., Grine et al., 1995; Ruff et al., 1993) to recent environmental adaptations to subsistence changes (e.g., Brock and Ruff, 1988; Bridges, 1989; Ruff et al., 1984).

This chapter provides an overview of these studies, as well as some currently ongoing investigations, and demonstrates the rich potential of this kind of approach in addressing many bioarchaeological questions. First, though, to place these studies into context and provide necessary background, I begin with some more general comments on bone biology, followed by a brief introduction to biomechanics theory and measurement techniques.

Many factors contribute to the development of bone form (Figure 3.1). Genetic (or intrinsic) factors are particularly important in early development (Murray, 1936). Nongenetic factors include both systemic influences—those that affect the entire skeleton—and more localized influences. Examples of systemic influences include hormonal effects, nutritional deficits, and various disease states (Jowsey, 1977). Mechanical influences may also have a general systemic effect on growth of the skeleton, possibly acting through hormonal mediators (Lieberman, 1996). More localized factors include traumatic injuries (e.g., fractures), diseases affecting limited areas (e.g., periostitis), and mechanical loading of (application of force to) particular skeletal elements. All of these factors are important potential sources of information when examining archaeological samples (see Larsen, 1997, and other chapters in this volume). However, because mechanical influences on bone are often both localized and

Biological Anthropology of the Human Skeleton, Edited by M. Anne Katzenberg and Shelley R. Saunders.
ISBN 0-471-31616-4   Copyright © 2000 by Wiley-Liss, Inc.

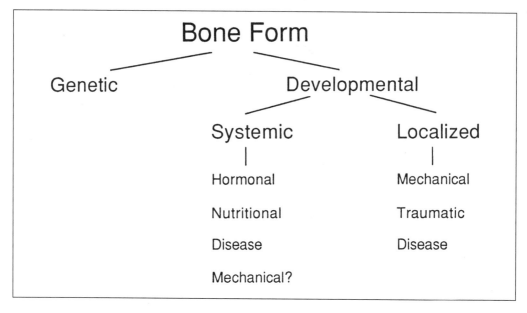

Figure 3.1   Determinants of bone form.

directly functionally interpretable, mechanically based analyses can be especially valuable in reconstructing past behavioral patterns from skeletal material.

There are a number of different structural levels on which biomechanical analyses of the skeleton may be carried out (Fig. 3.2). On the microstructural level, bone histological features such as osteon size and density can provide information on bone remodeling rates in past populations (Abbott et al., 1996; Burr et al., 1990). On a slightly larger measurement scale, the density and orientation of trabeculae can be related to differences in mechanical loading of joints (Heller, 1989; Rafferty, 1998; Rafferty and Ruff, 1994). The primary focus of this chapter will be on macroscopic features of bones, in particular long bone diaphyses, which can be modeled fairly simply as engineering structures, as described below. With newer imaging methods, such as computed tomography, these features can be studied noninvasively, that is, without destroying any part of a specimen, and are also relatively simple to interpret. Furthermore, it has been shown (e.g., Woo et al., 1981) that the primary response of long bone diaphyses to

changes in mechanical loading during life is through alterations in diaphyseal geometry or structure, rather than material properties (e.g., bone density, intrinsic material strength). The structural plasticity of bone can be quite dramatic, as illustrated in many experimental and observational studies (Trinkaus et al., 1994). Thus, long bone cross-sectional geometry can provide in effect a window into the past mechanical environment of that bone, which in turn can be related to individual behavior.

BIOMECHANICAL MODELS

It has been shown experimentally that long bone diaphyses can be modeled as engineering beams (Huiskes, 1982). In a beam analysis, cross-sectional properties of a bone are used to estimate its rigidity and strength under particular kinds of loadings or applied forces (Lovejoy et al., 1976; Ruff and Hayes, 1983a) (see Fig. 3.3). For example, the area of cortical bone (CA) in a section is a measure of its resistance to compressive or tensile loadings. Second moments of area (also called "moments of inertia") are measures of resistance to bending and torsional loadings. Second moments of area can be calculated about an axis through a section, in which case they are referred to using a capital I, together with a subscript indicating the axis about which they were calculated (e.g., I_x). These are measures of bending rigidity in the plane *perpendicular* to that axis. *Maximum* and *minimum* bending rigidities of a section are referred to as I_{max} and I_{min}, respectively, and are always perpendicular to each other. Second moments of area are calculated as products of unit areas and their squared distances from an axis or point, and are thus in linear dimensions to the fourth power (e.g., mm^4). Bending *strength* is represented by the section modulus Z (with subscript as appropriate), calculated as I/y, with y equal to the perpendicular distance from the

axis to the outermost edge of the section, and are expressed in linear dimensions to the third power (e.g., mm^3). Second moments of area can also be calculated about the center, or centroid of a section, in which case they are referred to as J, the polar second moment of area, proportional to torsional rigidity. J is equal to the sum of any two second moments of area calculated about perpendicular axes (e.g., I_{max} + I_{min}). Torsional strength is again calculated as J/y (with y the distance from the centroid to the outermost fiber). The general principles underlying the calculation and interpretation of these section properties have been discussed in the anthropological literature (Lovejoy et al., 1976; Ruff and Hayes, 1983a; Sumner et al., 1989) as well as in many engineering textbooks (e.g., Timoshenko and Gere, 1972). An example of such an analysis is shown in Figure 3.3.

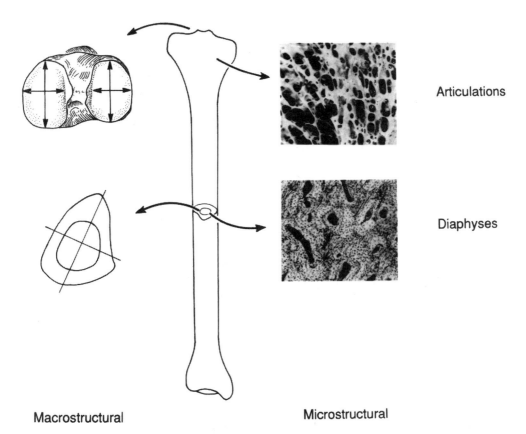

Articulations

Diaphyses

Macrostructural

Microstructural

Figure 3.2 Levels of structural analysis of long bones. (Reproduced from Ruff and Runestad, 1992, with permission, from the Annual Review of Anthropology, Volume 21, © 1992, by Annual Reviews.)

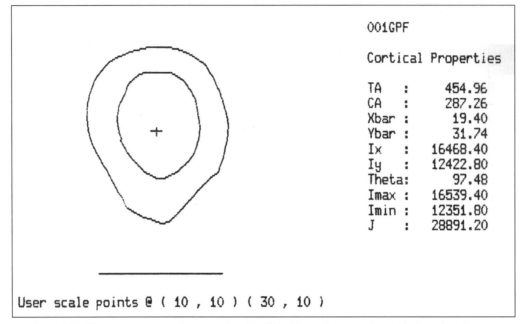

Figure 3.3 Computer reconstructed cross section of a midshaft femur from an archaeological sample, using program SLICE (also see Figure 3.4). Cross indicates position of section centroid; scale bar is oriented along x (mediolateral) axis. Geometric section properties: TA: total periosteal area; CA: cortical area; Xbar, Ybar: centroid coordinates; I_x, I_y: second moments of area about x and y axes; Theta: orientation of greatest bending rigidity (major axis of section), measured counterclockwise from the x axis; I_{max}, I_{min}: maximum and minimum second moments of area; J: polar second moment of area. Centroid coordinates in mm, areas in mm², second moments of area in mm⁴, theta in degrees.

While early studies employed relatively laborious manual methods for calculating these properties (e.g., Lovejoy et al., 1976; Martin and Atkinson, 1977), advances in technology have made possible more automated methods, and thus inclusion of much larger sample sizes. Digitizing of section images, by tracing periosteal and endosteal boundaries with an electronic stylus, with perimeter point coordinates automatically input to an analysis program, results in very rapid (several minutes per section) data collection (Fig. 3.4). Using this technique, large numbers of sections can be analyzed, allowing truly demographic and comparative studies (Bridges, 1989; Brock and Ruff, 1988; Churchill, 1994; Robling, 1998; Ruff 1987b, 1994a, 1999; Ruff and Hayes, 1983a, 1983b, 1988; Ruff et al., 1993; Weiss, 1998). It is also possible to analyze cross-sectional image data directly from digital data files generated by, for example, computed tomography (Sumner et al., 1989) or other photographic scanning techniques.

Various methods can be used to obtain cross-sectional images of long bones. Natural breaks can be photographed (being careful to use only perpendicular breaks or to correct for obliquity in images), or bones can be physically sectioned and photographed. Computed tomographic (CT) scanning is an excellent noninvasive technique for acquiring image data, provided care is taken in setting appropriate bone boundary thresholds, which will vary depending on the physical characteristics (including preservation) of the specimen and whether it is scanned in air or water (Ruff and Leo, 1986; Sumner et al., 1989). When CT is not available, multiple plane radiography can be an adequate substitute, particularly when combined with physical molding of external contours (Churchill, 1994; Sakaue, 1998;

Trinkaus and Ruff, 1989). In this technique the periosteal contour is obtained by tracing the inside of a ring of molding material placed around the bone, and an approximate endosteal contour is reconstructed by taking cortical breadths from radiographs at several points and measuring in from the perimeter. In a slight variation, casts of the bones can be sectioned to obtain the periosteal contour, and then combined with radiographic measurements for the endosteal boundary (Ruff, 1995; Ruff et al., 1993). These techniques have been used to study Pleistocene fossils, as well as more recent archaeological samples (see references above). Even biplanar radiographs alone can yield reasonably accurate results when applied to fairly cylindrical diaphyseal regions (Runestad et al., 1993), although not when applied to very irregular sections (Biknevicius and Ruff, 1992). Formulas are available to con-

vert such bone breadth data to area and second moment of area variables (Biknevicius and Ruff, 1992; Runestad et al., 1993). Finally, information from bone mineral absorptiometric scans can be converted to cross-sectional geometric data (Martin and Burr, 1984); this technique has been used successfully in a variety of contexts (Beck et al., 1990, 1993, 1996; Jungers and Burr, 1994).

In order to compare the biomechanical properties of individuals or samples of different body size, it is necessary to incorporate some kind of size standardization. One relatively simple method is to divide cross-sectional properties by powers of bone length (e.g., Ruff et al., 1984). Cross-sectional areas are in linear dimensions squared (e.g., mm^2), so they could be divided by bone length^2. Similarly, second moments of area could be divided by bone length^4. While an early allometric study supported this

Figure 3.4 Digitizer with backprojected photographic slide of bone cross section for manual tracing; section reconstruction by SLICE shown on screen at left. (*Note*: not the same section as shown in Figure 3.3).

approach (Ruff, 1984), later studies have shown that this is oversimplified (Ruff, 2000; Ruff et al., 1993). First, both theoretical considerations and empirical testing using better line-fitting techniques indicate that cross-sectional areas and second moments of area vary in proportion to bone length^3 and bone length$^{5.33}$, respectively, in individuals of similar body shape (Ruff et al., 1993). Second, if there is significant variation in body proportions (i.e., the length of limb segments relative to stature, and body breadth relative to stature) then this variation should be incorporated if possible into the procedure (Ruff, 2000; Ruff et al., 1993; Trinkaus et al., 1999). This can be done in a variety of ways: by including body shape correction factors along with bone length powers (Ruff et al., 1993; Trinkaus, 1997), or by actually estimating body mass, allowing for differences in body proportions (Trinkaus et al., 1998, 1999).[1] Body mass itself can be estimated from skeletal remains using different techniques that rely on different underlying assumptions (Ruff et al., 1997).

One relatively simple procedure for at least partially controlling for differences in body size in such analyses is to compare cross-sectional diaphyseal properties to articular size. This is based on the observation that cross-sectional diaphyseal dimensions are much more plastic, or environmentally sensitive, than articular dimensions during growth and development (Ruff and Runestad, 1992; Ruff et al., 1994; Trinkaus et al., 1994). Thus, for example, Pleistocene *Homo*, who were very likely more physically active and muscular than modern humans, have more robust femoral shafts relative to femoral head size than modern humans (Ruff et al., 1993; also see below).

The importance of factoring in body size and body shape when evaluating differences in skeletal robusticity can be illustrated by considering some long bone external metric data collected by Collier (1989) on a number of different modern human skeletal samples. Collier's main purpose in carrying out his study was to place Australian Aborigines into a wider geographic/cultural context and to evaluate competing claims of either gracility or increased robusticity of their infracranial skeletons relative to those of other modern humans. Figure 3.5 shows his results for a traditional femoral midshaft "robusticity index"— the square root of the product of midshaft A-P and M-L breadths divided by femoral length—in his six male samples. This clearly illustrates that relative to bone length, Australian Aborigines have narrower diaphyses than the other groups, which include two samples of Eskimos, recent Euro-American whites from the Terry Collection, Arikara Amerindians, and a Romano-British sample. On the face of it, this supports assertions of greater long bone "gracility" among the Australians, which in turn could imply lower activity levels. However, comparing femoral midshaft breadth to femoral head size in these groups produces a very different picture. As shown in Figure 3.6, relative to femoral head size, the Australian sample has the *greatest* diaphyseal breadth of the six samples. Thus, relative to a body size (not limb length) index, Australian Aborigines have very robust shafts, consistent with their active lifestyles. Their lower traditional "robusticity index" is due to their very long limbs relative to trunk length and body mass (Abbie, 1967), which itself is most likely a climatic adaptation to their hot environment (Roberts, 1978; Ruff, 1994b). Among the other samples in Figure 3.6, whites from the Terry Collection have among the lowest diaphyseal breadths relative to body size, consistent with a more sedentary lifestyle (see Ubelaker, Chapter 2, for information on the Terry Collection). The even lower value for "riverine" Eskimos may be due in part to a relatively sedentary subsistence strategy (which relied principally on salmon runs, according to Collier), and to sampling error (the samples for femoral midshaft breadth and femoral head data were not perfectly matched in the available tabulation of raw data, with riverine Eskimos hav-

---

[1]It should be noted that the best "size" measure against which to compare *non*-weight-bearing skeletal elements, for example, those of the human upper limb, is uncertain at present (Churchill et al., n.d.; Ruff, 1999, 2000; Ruff et al., 1993; Trinkaus et al., 1999).

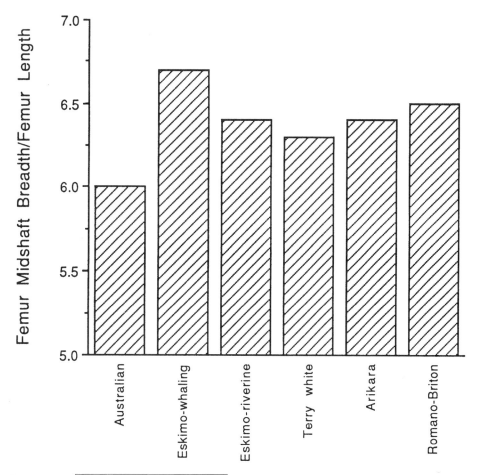

Figure 3.5 ($\sqrt{\text{Femoral Midshaft AP} \cdot \text{ML Breadth}}$/Femoral Length) · 100 in six skeletal samples compiled by Collier (1989).

ing the greatest mismatch in sample sizes). Also, the external diaphyseal breadths measured in this study encapsulate only a part of cross-sectional geometric variation, not reflecting differences in endosteal dimensions, which vary significantly among human populations and are important in bone mechanical adaptation (Kimura and Takahashi, 1982; Ruff et al., 1991, 1993; also see below).

This example also illustrates the potential danger of using external diaphyseal dimensions themselves as "size" measures for standardizing cortical bone area or mass in comparisons between individuals or populations. This is the implicit assumption underlying use of indices such as %CA (percent

cortical area: cortical area/periosteal area), or BMD (bone mineral density: bone mineral content/ external breadth), both still commonly employed in the anthropological and clinical literature (see discussion in Ruff and Hayes, 1984a; Beck et al., 1992). Such an approach ignores the mechanical significance of variation in bone periosteal dimensions and the contribution of the entire cortex to structural integrity (Beck, 1996), a theme that is further developed below.

The remainder of this chapter is devoted to illustrations of how biomechanical approaches can be applied to different kinds of problems in human evolutionary and adaptational studies. The general order of topics is arranged

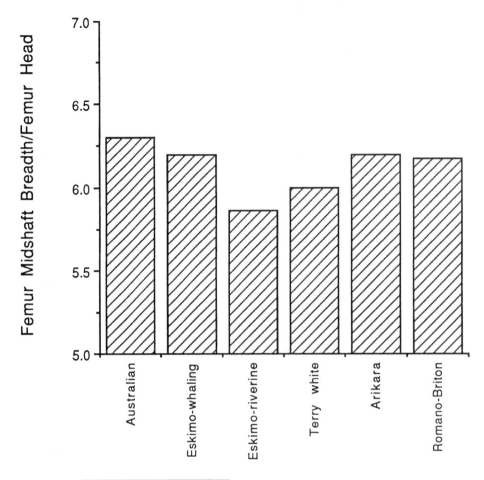

Figure 3.6 $\sqrt{\text{Femoral Midshaft AP} \cdot \text{ML Breadth}}$ /Femoral Head Breadth) · in six skeletal samples compiled by Collier (1989). (Ratios calculated for this figure from available raw data.)

from larger to smaller scale, beginning with long-term evolutionary trends within hominids, followed by variation between and within populations of modern (Holocene) humans, and finally variation within individual lifetimes.

LONG-TERM EVOLUTIONARY TRENDS

The study of long-range temporal trends in hominid skeletal structure, besides being of intrinsic palaeontological interest, provides an important context within which to consider variation among more recent population sam-

ples. In fact, some findings later applied to the analysis of archaeological remains were first developed in response to issues raised in studying earlier hominids. For example, it has long been recognized that the long bones of pre-Holocene hominids appear "robust," with larger external dimensions and thicker cortices than those of modern humans (e.g., Boule, 1911; Endo and Kimura, 1970; Kennedy, 1983; Lovejoy and Trinkaus, 1980; Weidenreich, 1941). This issue was addressed through an allometric study of biomechanical properties in a large sample of both modern and earlier humans (Ruff et al., 1993). Results from the study have been used in "size" standardizing of such properties in archaeological samples (Ruff, 1999).

Figure 3.7 summarizes trends in average cortical area and polar second moment of area (i.e., axial and bending/torsional rigidities, respectively) of the femoral midshaft over the past two million years within the genus *Homo*. The data are based on 30 Pleistocene and 229 Holocene specimens, standardized for differences in body size (see Ruff et al., 1993). The temporal scale in the figure is logarithmic, thus, the approximately linear decline in cross-sectional properties indicates an exponentially increasing decline in bone rigidity relative to body size. The simplest explanation for this general trend is that as cultural mechanisms for interacting with the physical environment elaborated during the last two million years (i.e., technological sophistication increased), biological mechanisms—in this case, bone strength—

decreased in importance. In fact, there is an inverse relationship between cranial capacity and long bone robusticity within this evolutionary lineage, although declines in bone robusticity lag behind increases in cranial capacity (Ruff et al., 1993). This explanation is also supported by the finding of no concurrent change in relative femoral head size among the same samples (Ruff et al., 1993)—articular size is much less plastic than diaphyseal cross-sectional size (Ruff et al., 1991; Trinkaus et al., 1994), and thus would be less likely to reflect the increased mechanical loadings characteristic of Pleistocene *Homo*. This also argues that developmental rather than genetic mechanisms were responsible for increased bone robusticity in these earlier humans. The degree of difference between the most robust early *Homo* sample in Figure 3.7 and the average for modern humans is equivalent to that which can be produced

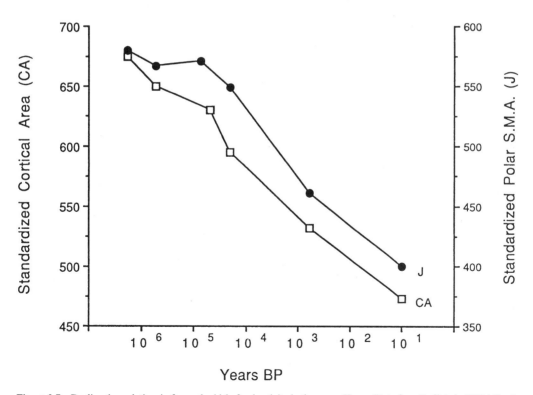

Figure 3.7 Decline through time in femoral midshaft robusticity in the genus *Homo*. (Data from Ruff et al., 1993.) X axis scale is exponential. Both cortical area and polar second moment of area divided by appropriate powers of bone length (see original reference for details). (Modified from Ruff et al., 1993 [one point in J curve corrected from original].)

simply by increasing exercise in experimental animals (Woo et al., 1981). Several other authors have also demonstrated a consistent pattern of relatively increased cortical bone thickness and/or robusticity in Pleistocene samples, including upper limb bones (Churchill et al., 1996; Grine et al., 1995; Pearson and Grine, 1997; Pfeiffer and Zehr, 1996).

It can be shown through analyses of even earlier hominids, including australopithecines such as AL 288-1 ("Lucy") (Ruff, 1998; Ruff et al., 1999) that the temporal trend in Figure 3.7 in relative long bone strength continues, that is, earlier hominid specimens are progressively stronger. Australopithecine long bones are equivalent in strength to those of living great apes (Ruff et al., 1999), while modern humans are much weaker relative to body size (Ruff, 2000). Thus, during their evolution humans have become progressively further distanced from the rest of the animal kingdom in terms of relative skeletal strength, again most likely explained by the increasing substitution of technology for pure physical strength. While the variation in skeletal robusticity found among more recent human populations is small compared to these species-scale differences (since all modern humans employ technology), it is governed by the same general principles of bone mechanical adaptation.

VARIATION AMONG AND WITHIN HOLOCENE POPULATIONS

Subsistence Strategy and Terrain

Subsistence strategy has long been considered among the most important factors influencing the skeletal biology of recent human populations (Cohen and Armelagos, 1984; Larsen, 1997; Powell et al., 1991). The focus of many such studies has been primarily nutritional, that is, the direct dietary effects of a subsistence transition on the skeleton. However, changes in subsistence economy also affect behavioral patterns (Murdock and Provost, 1973; Watanabe, 1977), which in turn should leave their marks on the skeleton.

An early example of the application of long bone biomechanical analysis to this kind of problem is a study of tibial diaphyseal cross-sectional geometry reported by Lovejoy and colleagues in 1976. Although this study was primarily methodological and examined only a small sample, the results were used to support a general biomechanical explanation for differences in bone cross-sectional shape, whereby tibiae from preindustrial populations are adapted for more active locomotion (greater bending and torsional loads) than those from industrial populations.

In 1984 we reported the results of a study of changes in femoral diaphyseal cross-sectional properties with the transition from a hunting-gathering to an agricultural subsistence strategy in populations living along the prehistoric Georgia coastline (Ruff et al., 1984). The agricultural sample showed declines in bone strength, even when properties were standardized by dividing by powers of bone length (Figure 3.8). They were also rounder, indicating a decline in bending in specific planes (M-L in the proximal femur, A-P in the midshaft femur), a trend that was particularly marked among males. As shown later in this chapter, this pattern seems to be associated with declines in mobility. Thus, these results supported the hypothesis of a general decrease in mechanical loading of the lower limb in agriculturalists compared to preagriculturalists, associated with reduced mobility and perhaps workload. Interestingly, in comparisons with similar data collected for Southwest Amerindians from Pecos Pueblo, New Mexico (Ruff and Hayes, 1983a), who were agriculturalists but living in a very different environment, bone *shape* was similar to Georgia coast agriculturalists, while bone robusticity (strength relative to body size) was more similar between Pecos and Georgia preagriculturalists. This suggested that both subsistence strategy and physical environment could be important in contributing to mechanical loadings of the lower limb, a theme that is further developed below.

Bridges (1989) carried out a similar study of changes in femoral and humeral cross-sectional geometry in prehistoric hunter-gatherer and agricultural Amerindian samples

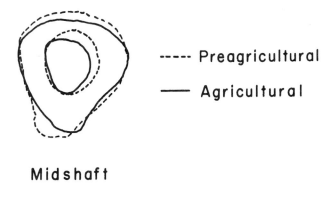

Midshaft

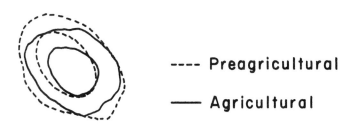

Subtrochanteric

Figure 3.8 Changes in cross-sectional geometry of femora with the transition to agriculture on the Georgia coast (outlines scaled for equal bone lengths). Agricultural femora are both relatively weaker and rounder than preagricultural femora. (Reproduced from Ruff et al., 1984.)

from the Tennessee River Valley. Her results were somewhat different from those of the Georgia coast samples. Specifically, she found that some measures of relative strength of the limbs increased rather than decreased with the transition to agriculture in this region, particularly in the lower limb in males and the upper limb in females. The change in the upper limb in females was attributed to increased mechanical loading due to corn grinding. The reason for the changes in the lower limb was not entirely clear, but these were provisionally interpreted as reflecting a general increase in activity level in the agricultural period. Thus,

these results may indicate that the transition to agriculture in inland regions of the southeastern United States was associated with a different behavioral change than that found in coastal regions. Possible explanations for this include regional differences in intensity of agricultural reliance as well as difficulty in hoe agriculture itself, relative to prior hunting and gathering subsistence techniques. Bridges (1985) did find some similarities in the pattern of temporal change in cross-sectional bone shape to those documented for the Georgia coast, however (decrease in A-P/M-L bending strength of the femoral midshaft in the agricultural sample). The type of change observed appears to indicate a similar increase in sedentism per se with the adoption of agriculture across the southeastern United States (Ruff and Larsen, 1990). Bridges (1989) also emphasized the need to examine changes in bone structure in multiple skeletal regions in order to distinguish local mechanical effects from general systemic effects such as diet.

Several other studies have used limb bone structure to explore variation in subsistence-related behavior in different regions of the United States, including the Southwest (Brock and Ruff, 1988; Ruff and Hayes, 1983a, 1983b), the Great Plains (Ruff, 1994a), and the Great Basin (Larsen et al., 1995; Ruff, 1999). Thus, pooling results, it is possible to simultaneously evaluate the effects of both subsistence strategy and physical terrain on limb bone structure (Ruff, 1999). Table 3.1 shows the samples used in the analysis. Because far more data are available for the femoral midshaft than for any other skeletal location (268 individuals), only data for this section are included here. All cross-sectional data are standardized over appropriate powers of bone length, as described in detail in the original report (Ruff, 1999). (Previous studies (Ruff et al., 1993) had indicated relatively similar body shapes in these samples, so that use of bone length as a "size" measure should not introduce any significant bias.)

Three-way analyses of variance of these sections, with "subsistence," "terrain," and "sex" as factors, yield some surprising results. As shown in Figure 3.9, neither cortical area (axial compressive rigidity) nor the polar second moment of area (bending/torsional rigidity) vary significantly between preagricultural and agricultural samples ($p > .30$), once the other two factors are accounted for. However, as shown in Figure 3.10, terrain has a marked effect on femoral midshaft rigidity, with samples from mountainous regions being significantly greater in bending/torsional rigidity (J) than those from the plains or coastal regions, again adjusting for the other two factors. The plains and coastal samples are not significantly different from each other (Tukey post-hoc tests). Males are significantly stronger than females ($p < .05$), but when broken down by subsistence strategy only preagricultural samples show this difference. The effects of sex as a factor are further considered in the next section.

Thus, it appears that subsistence strategy does not have a consistent effect on at least the overall level of mechanical loading of the lower limb for populations as a whole. This is concordant with the earlier cited studies of the Pecos, Georgia, and Tennessee samples. On the contrary, physical terrain has a strong effect on lower limb bone loading, with the largest difference occurring between mountainous and other regions, exactly as one might predict from general biomechanical considerations. A preliminary comparison of much more limited data for the humerus indicates that terrain has a much less marked effect on the upper limb (Ruff, 1999), again as would be predicted biomechanically. It would be very interesting to

TABLE 3.1   Amerindian Samples for Comparison of the Effects of Subsistence and Terrain on Femoral Midshaft Structure

Region	Subsistence	Terrain	Males	Females	Total
Georgia	Preagricultural	Coastal	8	12	20
Georgia	Agricultural	Coastal	11	9	20
South Dakota	Preagricultural	Plains	27	21	48
South Dakota	Agricultural	Plains	33	25	58
Great Basin	Preagricultural	Mountains	28	34	62
New Mexico	Agricultural	Mountains	30	30	60
Total			137	131	268

(Data from Ruff, 1999.)

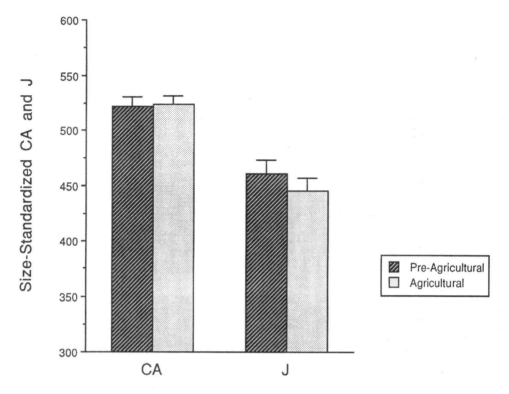

Figure 3.9 Effects of subsistence strategy on femoral midshaft robusticity in prehistoric Amerindians (see Table 3.1 for samples). Means + 1 SE of cortical area (CA) and polar second moment of area (*J*), adjusted for effects of terrain and sex. All data divided by appropriate powers of bone length (see original reference for details). Differences between preagricultural and agricultural samples nonsignificant ($p > .30$). (Data from Ruff, 1999.)

see whether these patterns hold up in other areas of the world.

Sexual Dimorphism

Sexual division of labor is a fundamentally important aspect of human culture, and is tremendously variable between modern human societies (Murdock and Provost, 1973). Because different physical tasks should place different physical loads on the body, sexual division of labor should be reflected, to some degree at least, in skeletal structure. Differences between the sexes in overall body size have indeed been linked to long-term trends in subsistence strategy (Frayer, 1980, 1984), although the relationship between sexual dimorphism in body size and subsistence on a smaller localized scale may be more complex

and variable (Hamilton, 1982). Sex differences in bone *structure* have been less commonly studied, yet specific behavioral inferences may be more easily made from structure than from size alone, in part because localized structure is more mechanically driven, while body size is more influenced by nutrition and other systemic factors (Figure 3.1).

Sex differences in long bone cross-sectional shape have long been recognized (e.g., Hrdlicka, 1898; Kimura, 1971b), although no systematic attempt was made to relate such variation to behavioral differences until relatively recently. The Pecos Pueblo sample demonstrated marked sexual dimorphism in femoral and tibial diaphyseal shape, in particular an increase in A-P bending rigidity among males in sections centered around the knee (Ruff and Hayes, 1983b). This sex-related difference was not found among

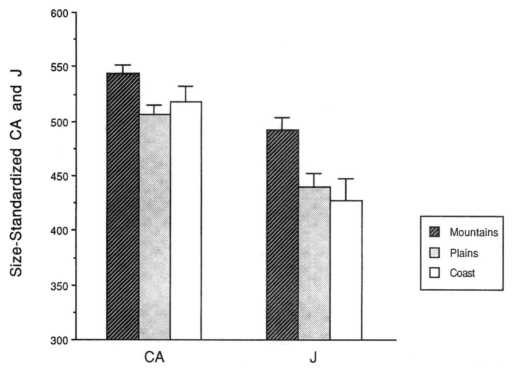

Figure 3.10   Effects of terrain on femoral midshaft robusticity in prehistoric Amerindians (see Table 3.1 for samples). Means + 1 SE of cortical area (CA) and polar second moment of area (*J*), adusted for effects of terrain and sex. All data divided by appropriate powers of bone length (see original reference for details). Significant (*p* < .05) differences in J between "mountains" and two other samples, and in CA between "mountains" and "plains"; all differences between "plains" and "coast" samples nonsignificant (*p* > .70). (Reproduced from Ruff, 1999, courtesy of University of Utah Press.)

modern U.S. whites (Ruff, 1987a). A survey of available data from a number of studies showed that this difference between samples was part of a broader trend, in which hunter-gatherers show the greatest sexual dimorphism in cross-sectional shape, agriculturalists less dimorphism, and industrial samples almost no dimorphism (Ruff, 1987a). The trend parallels a reduction in the sexual division of labor across these subsistence groups, in particular a reduction in the general mobility of males (Murdock and Provost, 1973), which should be reflected in decreased A-P bending loads of the lower limb. Interestingly, sexual dimorphism in the shape of the *proximal* femoral shaft did not vary between subsistence groups. This is probably because proximal femoral shape primarily reflects bending loads related to pelvic morphology (Ruff, 1995), which shows relatively constant sexual

dimorphism across different populations (because of the relatively constant physical demands of childbirth in females).

A number of new cross-sectional geometric studies of archaeological samples have been carried out since these earlier analyses. Sexual dimorphism in the ratio of A-P to M-L bending rigidity of the femoral midshaft in 14 Amerindian samples is shown in Figure 3.11, arranged from greatest to least dimorphism. Hunter-gatherers clearly have greater dimorphism than agriculturalists, although there is also variability within each subsistence category.[2] Although not plotted here, industrial samples have even less dimorphism than agri-

[2]Interestingly, the lowest hunter-gatherer data point in Figure 3.11, "New Mexico (HG)," was derived from samples that may have included some mixed subsistence strategy, that is, maize agriculture (Brock and Ruff, 1988)

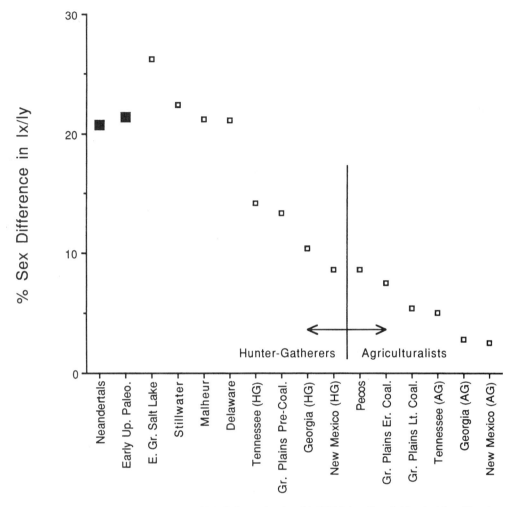

Figure 3.11 Sexual dimorphism in midshaft femoral ratio of A-P/M-L bending rigidity in 14 prehistoric Amerindian and two paleolithic samples: [(male–female)/female] · 100. HG (hunter-gatherer) and AG (agricultural) refer to temporal sequences within the same region. (Modified from Ruff, 1999. For Georgia samples, see Ruff and Larsen, in press. See Ruff, 1999, and text for data sources.)

culturalists (Ruff, 1987a). Using the samples shown in Table 3.1, when subsistence strategy, terrain, and sex are analyzed together using three-way analysis of variance (ANOVA), sex is a highly significant factor ($p < .0001$) in determination of femoral midshaft A-P/M-L bending rigidity. There is also a significant ($p < .05$) interaction between sex and subsistence strategy, with only preagricultural samples showing significant ($p < .0001$) differences between males and females. This was also found

to be true for levels of overall femoral shaft robusticity, as noted above.

Thus, among Holocene populations, there is clear evidence for an effect of subsistence strategy on sex differences in femoral midshaft shape. Subsistence-related variation in the sexual division of labor, and consequent mobility patterns, seems to be the most likely explanation for this finding. Also shown in Figure 3.11 are cross-sectional data for two Late Pleistocene samples—an archaic *Homo sapiens* (i.e., Neanderthal) sample (*n* = 13), and an early anatomically modern *Homo sapiens* sample (Skhul-Qafzeh and Early Upper Paleolithic-associated material from Europe) (*n* = 27) (Ruff et al., 1993; Trinkaus and Ruff, 1999; Trinkaus, pers. comm.). The Pleistocene samples demonstrate levels of sexual dimorphism in femoral midshaft AP/M-L bending rigidity in the high range of modern hunter-gatherers, indicating a similar sexual division of labor. These new data complement and extend a previous analysis of external breadth ratios of pre-Holocene samples (Ruff, 1987a). Interestingly, a similar degree of sexual dimorphism in bone shape in both earlier samples is present despite the fact that overall shape of Neanderthals is quite different from that of later humans, probably reflecting differences in basic body shape (Trinkaus and Ruff, 1989, 1999). Thus, using a biomechanical approach, it is possible to distinguish the effects of behavioral differences from those of overall body form (Trinkaus et al., 1998).

These observations should be confirmed on other samples, in particular samples from other geographic regions with different cultural histories and environments. Archaeological and modern samples from Japan and Australia do fit the predicted patterns well (Ruff, 1987a). A sample of twentieth-century East Africans (Ruff, 1995), probably representing a mix of "agricultural" and "industrial" subsistence strategies, also fits predictions: sexual dimorphism in femoral midshaft AP/M-L bending rigidity in this sample is less than 4%. Populations undergoing direct transitions from one subsistence strategy to another provide the best controlled tests of the hypothesis (e.g., Ruff et al., 1984). It should also be noted that these patterns have forensic implications, that is, the sexing of skeletal remains, as discussed in more detail elsewhere (Ruff, 1987a).

Effects of European Contact

A special case of environmental impact on human biology and behavior is represented by contact between radically different cultures, with subsequent rapid change in one of them

(Larsen and Milner, 1994). Such an event took place during the period of European contact with Native Americans in North America (Baker and Kealhofer, 1996; Thomas, 1991). In a series of studies we have examined the impact of European contact and colonization on native populations from La Florida—the present day Georgia coast and Florida (Larsen et al., 1996; Larsen and Ruff, 1994; Ruff, 1997; Ruff and Larsen, 1990). The most recent of these studies (Ruff and Larsen, in press) incorporated cross-sectional properties of the femoral and humeral shafts of more than 200 individuals from this region, including a dozen precontact sites and five postcontact sites.

We found that Spanish contact and missionization in La Florida had mixed effects on body size and mechanical loadings of the skeleton of native populations. Stature did not change on average from immediate precontact to postcontact periods. Relative strength of the femur and humerus increased after contact, although the femoral shaft also became rounder. This was interpreted to indicate an increase in overall workload (and possibly body mass relative to stature) following missionization, combined with a general reduction in mobility, both of which are consistent with the historical record of forced labor and increased sedentism in this region after contact (Ruff and Larsen, 1990). Finer-grained analyses of the data yield some other interesting insights. Among the postcontact samples, only those two from the Guale people, who were more extensively incorporated into the mission system, show increases in relative long bone strength, while another sample from the Yamassee, who lived nearby but were more independent of the Spanish, do not. Furthermore, there is evidence for variation in use of native labor even within culturally/temporally defined samples. Sexual dimorphism in femoral midshaft shape increases greatly in the two Guale samples over precontact values, as shown in Figure 3.12. At the same time, variability among males in this index also increases dramatically (see

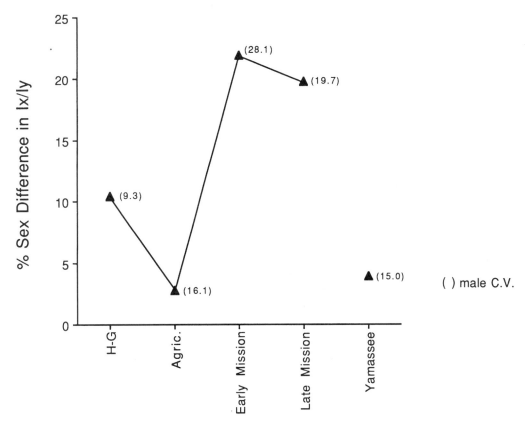

Figure 3.12   Sexual dimorphism in midshaft femoral ratio of A-P/M-L bending rigidity in five prehistoric and early historic Amerindian samples from the Georgia coast: [(male–female)/female] · 100. H-G: hunter-gatherers; Agric.: agriculturalists. "Early" and "Late Mission" refer to Guale living in Spanish missions; "Yamassee" were contemporaneous with these samples but lived outside the missions. Numbers in parentheses refer to the coefficients of variation for males within each sample (see text). (Data from Ruff and Larsen, in press.)

male coefficients of variation in Fig. 3.12). Thus, some contact period males show A-P/M-L values more similar to those of females, while others exhibit very high values. This is again concordant with historical records, which indicate that only certain males were recruited into forced labor that involved long-distance traveling (Ruff and Larsen, 1990). Again, the less acculturated Yamassee do not show this increase in sexual dimorphism or male variability in A-P/M-L bending loading of the femur (Fig. 3.12).

This kind of analysis demonstrates the potential for structural approaches to distinguish even relatively subtle variations in behavior between populations and individuals. The following section shows how these same approaches can be applied to intraindividual variation.

VARIATION WITHIN INDIVIDUALS

Ontogenetic Studies

Study of changes in skeletal morphology during growth and development can shed light on many interesting questions, including the general health of a population (i.e., growth disruptions and their causes), age-related behavioral changes, and the relative effects of genetics and environment in determining skeletal form (see Larsen, 1997, also Saunders, Chapter 5). The last factor is particularly significant in terms of better understanding fundamental principles of bone adaptation, principles that can then be applied to the interpretation of any human sample, recent or earlier (e.g., Ruff et al., 1994). Ontogenetic studies of skeletal samples are strictly not "intraindividual," since by necessity they rely on cross-sectional sampling of different age groups rather than longitudinal sampling of single individuals (for some potential problems in using such an approach, see Saunders, Chapter 5). However, the aim of these analyses is to define age changes that should be characteristic of individuals within a population, so they are appropriately considered in this section.

A biomechanical study of femoral growth in the Pecos Pueblo archaeological sample was used to examine changing long bone proportions during childhood and adolescence (Ruff et al., 1994). The study was stimulated in part by the discovery of the early adolescent *Homo erectus* specimen KNM-WT 15000 (Walker and Leakey, 1993), which was shown to have unusual articular to diaphyseal proportions when compared to adult early *Homo* specimens (Ruff et al., 1994). Femora from 31 juveniles, ages 5 to 19 years old, were obtained from the Pecos collection, with cross-sectional diaphyseal properties determined using CT; femoral head breadth and femoral length were also measured. "Adult" values for these properties were obtained from a previous study (Ruff, 1988; Ruff and Hayes, 1983a) of the Pecos sample, using the mean values for 20- to 24-year-olds. Sex was determined for individuals 15 years of age and older using pelvic criteria.

Figure 3.13 shows the age changes in femoral length, head breadth, and midshaft cortical area between age 5 and early adult-

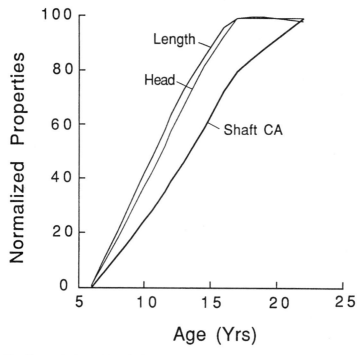

Figure 3.13 Changes in femoral length, femoral head breadth, and midshaft cortical area (CA) from 6 to 22 years of age in the Pecos Pueblo archaeological sample. Properties are expressed as percent distance traveled between these two endpoints; mean tendencies are plotted using the LOWESS technique. (Reproduced from Ruff et al., 1993; see original reference for details.)

hood, expressed as the percent distance traveled between these two endpoints. It is clear that articular size (head breadth) follows a growth trajectory similar to that of bone length, while shaft cross-sectional area follows a different pattern, first falling behind, then "catching up" with articular and length parameters by early adulthood. The growth pattern in shaft CA during childhood-adolescence is very similar to that of body weight (as measured in living samples) (Ruff et al., 1994), while articular size follows a trend more like that of linear body growth, that is, long bone length and stature. In fact, evidence from other studies indicates that the direct mechanical effect of body weight may be the most important stimulus for growth in cross-sectional diaphyseal dimensions in adolescents, at least in weight-bearing elements (Moro et al., 1996; van der Meulen et al., 1996).

Sumner and Andriacchi (1996) reported very similar findings based on an analysis of archaeological remains from Grasshopper Pueblo, extending the age range down to one year and including the humerus as well as femur. The humerus showed patterns of growth in cross-sectional properties and length similar to those of the femur, but cross-sectional properties of the humerus progressively fell behind those of the femur from age 1 to age 10, corresponding to a period of adjustment of the limbs to their different functions, that is, weight-bearing versus non-weight-bearing. Interestingly, humeral and femoral bone lengths did not show the same age changes in proportions, consistent with the mechanical stimulus hypothesis (articulations were not measured). The authors also noted the possible effects of continuing muscular growth after cessation of growth in length as an explanation for the humeral cross-sectional pattern.

These results help explain why the early *Homo* juvenile skeleton, KNM-WT 15000, aged about 11 to 12 years, shows what appears to be small cross-sectional diaphyseal dimensions relative to femoral head size (Ruff et al., 1994), since in early adolescence the former lags behind the latter, mirroring differences in

growth in body weight versus linear growth. In fact, relative to modern human children of his age range, KNM-WT 15000 has a stronger diaphysis compared to femoral head size, similar to Pleistocene *Homo* adults (Ruff et al., 1993). This is also consistent with other evidence cited earlier that articulations are more genetically canalized than diaphyseal cross-sectional dimensions, following patterns of change in general growth of the skeleton (which may be affected by systemic factors—see Fig. 3.1) rather than localized mechanical influences. This was one rationale for using femoral head size rather than cross-sectional diaphyseal size for estimating body mass, and encephalization, in a large sample of Pleistocene *Homo* (Ruff et al., 1997).

As shown earlier, there are systematic differences in cross-sectional shape of the mid-femur through mid-tibia that reflect behavioral differences between adult males and females in preindustrial societies (Ruff, 1987a). Analyses of individuals at different ages can reveal the developmental timing of these behavioral changes. Figure 3.14 is a plot of mid-distal femoral shaft AP/M-L bending rigidity in the same 31 juveniles from Pecos Pueblo, together with the means and standard deviations for 20- to 24-year-old adults from the same population sample. Assuming this cross-sectional sample represents an accurate picture of growth, there is a clear increase in the A-P/M-L ratio from early childhood through late adolescence. (This same general trend can be seen in the series of bone cross sections shown in figure 3.1 of Sumner and Andriacchi, 1996.) Sex cannot be determined reliably for juveniles less than 15 years old. Among the mid- to late adolescents for whom sex could be determined, on average the two sexes have begun to diverge along the same lines (males have greater values) as adults, although there is almost complete overlap between the male and female ranges. In fact, the sex difference in the ratio among 15 to 19 year olds is statistically significant ($p = .05$, t = test), and the mean percentage difference between them (12.7%) is similar to that between Pecos adults as a whole (13.3%; Ruff,

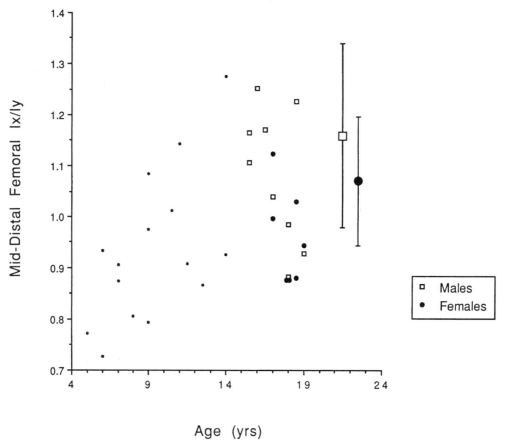

Figure 3.14 Individual age changes in the ratio of A-P/M-L bending rigidity of the mid-distal femoral shaft (35% of bone length from the distal end) in the Pecos Pueblo archaeological sample. Individuals under 15 years of age not sexed; means (± 1 SD for 20 to 24 year olds ($n = \pm 10$ for each sex) shown. (See Ruff et al., 1994, for methodological details.)

1987a). Thus, the greater mobility of males inferred from the adult data was apparently characteristic of adolescents as well, implying that adult behavioral patterns were established relatively early. It is interesting, too, that adolescent males show a greater range of values for the shape index than females; this pattern is also present among adults (Figure 3.14; also see Ruff, 1987a). This may indicate a greater range of behavioral patterns among males, an explanation that is consistent with ethnographic data for agricultural societies (Murdock and Provost, 1973). It would be quite interesting to see whether the same ontogenetic patterns are characteristic of societies with other subsistence strategies, that is, hunter-

gatherers, and/or those with different social structures.

Another study that examined ontogenetic changes in cross-sectional diaphyseal geometry was an investigation of tibial modeling in a Medieval Nubian juvenile sample by Van-Gerven and colleagues (Van Gerven et al., 1985). This study clearly demonstrated the danger in using periosteal area or breadth to "size standardize" either cortical area or bone mineral content (BMC). While %CA declined during adolescence in this sample, due to concurrent subperiosteal expansion, second moments of area showed large *increases* over the same age range. Also, while BMC standardized over bone width showed a continuous increase with age, BMC over true bone area remained almost constant after age 6 years (also see Ruff and Hayes, 1984b). These observations helped resolve some apparent anomalies noted earlier in the pattern of adolescent skeletal growth and development in this sample, that is, normal growth in long bone length and bone areas but apparently "abnormal" change in %CA (Hummert, 1983). In another analysis of the Pecos ontogenetic sample (Ruff et al., 1994), we similarly showed that periosteal, medullary, and cortical areas followed different growth trajectories throughout development, resulting in smaller %CA among adolescents. This helped explain why KNM-WT 15000 has relatively small %CA compared to modern (and early *Homo*) adults, yet relatively large %CA compared to modern juveniles of his age range. Interestingly, two juvenile Neanderthals did not show this apparent age pattern, indicating possibly different growth trajectories, although larger samples will be needed to verify this observation.[3]

Osteoporosis

Loss of bone with aging is another kind of change in bone structure that is really part of the same life-long developmental sequence but is usually considered separately. Strictly speaking, loss of bone mass can occur through either loss in volume (osteoporosis) or loss in material density (osteomalacia), and "osteopenia" is the general term that applies to both. However, since bone loss with aging normally is mainly geometric (i.e., volumetric) (Ruff and Hayes, 1988), and osteoporosis is the more widely used term to describe bone loss under a variety of conditions (e.g., see Marcus et al., 1996), I will refer to age-related bone loss here simply as osteoporosis.

Osteoporosis and its clinical manifestation—increase in fracture incidence—is a major medical and societal problem in the modern

world (Marcus et al., 1996). Many studies have also demonstrated bone loss with aging in archaeological populations (for reviews see Pfeiffer and Lazenby, 1994; Ruff and Hayes, 1983b). Archaeological samples have the advantages of being (usually) more genetically and behaviorally homogeneous than most modern clinical or autopsy samples; conversely however, they present problems associated with inaccurate age assignments and uncertain dietary and other environmental factors. Despite these limitations, analysis of archaeological remains is important, first, for broadening temporal and geographic ranges within which to identify and study this problem, and second, for establishing a kind of preindustrial baseline with which to compare modern populations. Both factors may help to identify causes of the current "epidemic" of osteoporosis-related fractures, particularly among women of northern European descent (Cooper and Melton, 1996; Villa and Nelson, 1996).

Figure 3.15 is a schematic representation of adult age changes in cortical bone geometry of the femoral and tibial diaphyses in the Pecos Pueblo sample (Ruff and Hayes, 1983b) and a sample of modern U.S. whites (Ruff and Hayes, 1988). Both samples undergo endosteal resorption with aging, greater among females than among males. Both male samples also undergo periosteal expansion with aging. However, among females only the Pecos sample exhibits periosteal expansion, while U.S. white females do not. Periosteal expansion with aging, due to slow periosteal appositional growth, has been termed "compensatory," since it tends to mechanically compensate for endosteal loss of bone and some decline in bone material strength with aging (Martin and Atkinson, 1977). Thus, in these samples, the geometric component of bending/torsional rigidity remains constant or actually increases with aging, except in U.S. white females, where it declines. The same pattern of difference between U.S. white men and women has more recently been confirmed for the femoral neck, using structural data extracted from hip bone mineral scans (Beck et al., 1992, 1993).

---

[3]Dodo and coworkers (1998) have very recently presented evidence for relatively thick long bone cortices in another juvenile Neanderthal, the two-year-old child from Dederiyeh Cave, Syria.

This difference in geometric remodeling with aging may, in part, explain why older U.S. white females are subject to higher risk of fractures. The stimulus for continued periosteal expansion of long bones with aging is unclear, but several lines of evidence indicate that it may very well be mechanical in nature, that is, higher levels of activity lead to relatively greater periosteal apposition of bone throughout life (Ruff and Hayes, 1983b, 1988). This argues strongly in favor of physical activity as a preventive measure against age-related fractures (Snow et al., 1996). The analysis of a physically active, preindustrial sample (Pecos) helped to highlight this factor, and demonstrated the value of archaeological "baselines" in this kind of study (also see Pfeiffer and Lazenby, 1994).

Bilateral Asymmetry

The human upper limb is virtually unique among mammals in that it is freed from locomotor functions, and thus is not constrained to be bilaterally symmetric. Upper limb bilateral asymmetry in bone length, weight, and various other dimensions has been demonstrated in many modern, archaeological, and palaeontological samples (Bridges, 1989; Churchill and Formicola, 1997; Fresia et al., 1990; Roy et al., 1994; Ruff and Jones, 1981; Sakaue, 1998; Stirland, 1993; Trinkaus et al., 1994; and references therein). (Lower limb bone asymmetry also exists, but is usually much smaller and/or more variable; Ruff and Jones, 1981; Trinkaus et al., 1994). Measurements of bilateral asymmetry have been used to infer behavioral characteristics of past populations (see references above). Assessment of bilateral asymmetry is also a useful way to address more fundamental bone structure/function questions (e.g., Trinkaus et al., 1994), since this approach inherently controls for such factors as variation in body size and many systemic physiological and life history variables (Fig. 3.1).

Two studies of archaeological material demonstrated changes in upper limb bone dia-physeal asymmetry associated with subsistence changes (Bridges, 1989; Fresia et al., 1990). In both cases a transition from a hunting-gathering economy to one that included food production led to a decline in asymmetry, with the decline much more marked among females. Bridges (1989) attributed the decline in her Tennessee River Valley samples to the introduction of corn processing involving mortar and pestle pounding by both arms (and ostensibly performed by women), an explanation that may also apply to the Georgia coast samples studied by Fresia and coworkers (1990). The latter study also documented a continued decline in asymmetry after Spanish contact, in this case more marked among males than females. This is consistent with other evidence that males of this society were increasingly recruited to perform traditionally "female" (i.e., agricultural) tasks by the Spanish colonialists (Ruff and Larsen, 1990).

Even more specific behavioral inferences have been drawn from studies of upper limb bilateral asymmetry. Stirland (1993) compared two medieval British samples and found that one that included longbow archers had less humeral asymmetry, purportedly due to the more equal use of the two upper limbs during this activity. Asymmetry also declined with age, confirming a trend noted earlier for another, archaeological sample (Ruff and Jones, 1981; also see Trinkaus et al., 1994).

All of these studies compared right versus left-side dimensions and expressed results as degree of right "dominance." This is reasonable, since at least 90% of humans are right-handed (Coren and Porac, 1977). However, this will systematically underestimate the true magnitude of asymmetry, since some left-handers will normally be present, and left-handers show equal and opposite asymmetry to right-handers in bone structural parameters (Roy et al., 1994). This problem can be circumvented by calculating asymmetry as (max–min)/min (Churchill and Formicola, 1997; Trinkaus et al., 1994; some authors have calculated asymmetry both this way and as right versus left, e.g., Sakaue, 1998). Figure 3.16 summarizes

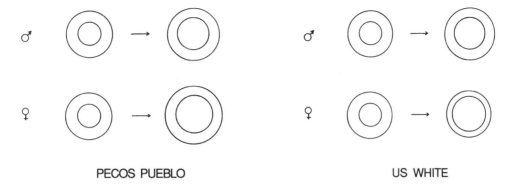

Figure 3.15 Schematic representation of adult changes with aging in lower limb bone cross-sectional geometry in samples from Pecos Pueblo (Ruff and Hayes, 1983b) and U.S. whites (Ruff and Hayes, 1988).

humeral bilateral asymmetry data of this kind for a number of different modern, archaeological, and palaeontological samples (Churchill, 1996; Trinkaus et al., 1994). Two structural parameters are shown: average mid-distal humeral shaft strength (the polar section modulus, derived from J using a procedure described in Ruff, 1995) and a measure of distal humeral articular surface area (the square of distal humeral articular breadth).[4] A few samples did not have articular breadth data available. Because of potential skewing of data distributions, median rather than mean values are used (Trinkaus et al., 1994).

As shown in Figure 3.16, all three Late Pleistocene samples, which include both Neanderthals and "early anatomically modern" (Early and Late Upper Paleolithic-associated) humans, show much greater asymmetry in humeral shaft strength than any of the Holocene samples. They are slightly exceeded in shaft asymmetry only by a sample of modern professional tennis players (Jones et al., 1977;

Ruff et al., 1994; Trinkaus et al., 1994). The next highest shaft asymmetry is found among Aleuts (early post-European contact), then two archaeological Amerindian samples, and finally samples of recent Euro-Americans, Jomon (prehistoric Japanese), and Spanish missionized Amerindians from the Georgia coast. Asymmetry in humeral articular surface area is much smaller, and much less variable, with comparable levels of asymmetry in Pleistocene and post-Pleistocene samples.

These results are consistent with other evidence presented earlier that long bone articulations are much less sensitive to alterations in mechanical loadings throughout life than are diaphyses (cross-sectional dimensions). Late Pleistocene *Homo* appears to have engaged in activities involving strong unilateral loading of the upper limb, which produced relative hypertrophy of the "dominant" side (the right side in all cases; Churchill, pers. comm.; Trinkaus et al., 1994). Articular asymmetry remained relatively low, however, similar to that of Holocene humans. (Distal humeral articular breadth per se was not measured in the professional tennis player sample, but other epiphyseal dimensions of the elbow region showed much less asymmetry than shaft dimensions; Ruff et al., 1994; Trinkaus et al., 1994). Interestingly, the smallest difference between articular and cross-sectional diaphyseal asymmetry is found among the recent Euro-American sample. Because articulations are in general less

[4]Distal articular breadth (combined breadth of the trochlea and capitulum) squared is a good approximation of distal humeral articular surface area. In a study that included a much more complex method of estimating articular surface areas, including approximation of the trochlea and capitulum as a partial cylinder and partial sphere (Ruff, in prep., also see Churchill, 1996), the correlation between (distal articular breadth)^2 and surface area calculated in the more complex way in 100 modern human humeri was $r = .85$, with a percent standard error of estimate of 8.8% and a slope nonsignificantly different from 1.0

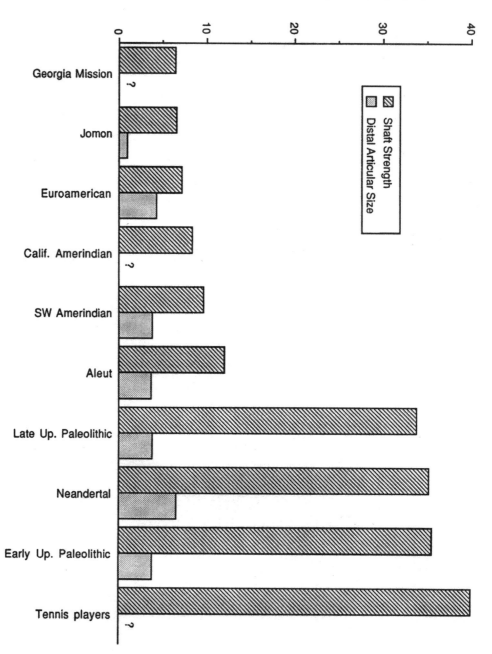

Figure 3.16 Median bilateral asymmetry in mid-distal humeral shaft strength (polar section modulus) and distal articular size (the square of trochlear plus capitular breadth) in modern, archaeological, and paleontological samples. Question mark indicates no data available for that sample. (Data from Trinkaus et al., 1994, and Churchill and Formicola, 1997.)

mechanically sensitive, and in particular cannot respond after mid- to late adolescence when long bone epiphyses fuse, this may reflect the generally smaller mechanical loads on the upper limb that would be expected in this industrial population, especially among adults. Of course, relatively large but *symmetric* loads on the upper limbs may also produce low asymmetry in structural parameters (Bridges, 1989); this may explain the reduction in shaft asymmetry in the Georgia coast missionized sample. One possible method of disentangling these alternatives is to also estimate strength of each limb relative to an appropriate body size measure, then compare each to other samples of "dominant" and "nondominant" limbs (Churchill and Formicola, 1997). Difficulties in choosing the best method for "size" standardizing of upper limb bone dimensions complicates this approach, however (Churchill et al., n.d.; Ruff, 1999, 2000; Ruff et al., 1993; Trinkaus et al., 1999).

The high shaft strength asymmetry in the Aleut sample is interesting, since in some ways this sample may represent the closest behavioral analogy to the Late Pleistocene samples. In this context, the lower asymmetry in the California Amerindian and Jomon samples, both of which were also preagricultural (albeit probably more sedentary and less dependent on hunting than Aleuts) is more difficult to explain, although it should be noted that the difference between articular and shaft asymmetry is moderately large in the Jomon sample (Fig. 3.16) (no articular data are available for the California sample). Following the reasoning presented above, it may be that articular asymmetry can be used as a kind of "control" against which to evaluate shaft asymmetry, and that this difference may better reflect continued asymmetry in use of the limbs throughout life. This certainly seems to be the case among individuals with known extreme asymmetry in upper limb use, for example, professional tennis players and individuals with physical disabilities and consequent functional disuse of one limb (Churchill and Formicola, 1997; Ruff et al., 1994; Trinkaus et

al., 1994). This hypothesis should be further tested in additional samples with known functional differences in limb use.

CONCLUSIONS AND FUTURE DIRECTIONS

Many different scales of analysis are amenable to biomechanical studies, from long-term evolutionary trends to microevolutionary changes and variation within an individual's lifetime. However, all levels of analysis employ the same basic principles of bone mechanics, physiology, and adaptation. For example, when carrying out a mechanically based interpretation, it is important to consider that mechanical loadings on bone are influenced by both the size of the person (i.e., body mass) and the particular behavioral use of a skeletal element. Thus, body size must be controlled for in some way to carry out meaningful comparisons of behavioral differences. One such approach is to compare cross-sectional diaphyseal properties, which have been shown to be very responsive to mechanical loadings throughout life, to articular size, which is less plastic and apparently more regulated by general systemic influences on body size. Comparisons of bilateral asymmetry (e.g., right humerus with left humerus) also inherently control for body size differences between individuals.

Long-term biomechanical studies within hominids have documented a gradual, but accelerating trend toward skeletal gracilization over the past 2 to 3 million years, concomitant with the replacement of physical strength with technology as our primary means of adaptation to the environment. Within populations of the last few thousand years, physical terrain may be the most important single variable in determining robusticity (bone strength relative to body size) of the lower limb bones. Subsistence strategy does not have a consistent effect on overall skeletal robusticity, but it does have a marked effect on sexual dimorphism in both robusticity and bone cross-sectional shape. Variation in lower limb bone cross-sectional properties is consistent with differences in sexual division of labor, with the greatest differences in hunting-gathering societies, an intermediate level in agriculturalists, and minimal dimorphism in industrialists. This trend can be distinguished in male-female comparisons of skeletal material as far back as the Late Pleistocene. European contact with Native American populations is another environmental change that has been explored using biomechanical analysis. These studies have documented a number of changes resulting from Spanish missionization of native populations in La Florida: generally increased workload and decreased mobility, increased variation in mobility among males (with some males recruited for long-distance burden carrying), and increased variation in behavior between missionized and less acculturated contemporaneous populations in the region.

Ontogenetic studies can shed light on the timing of events and basic physiological mechanisms underlying the development of adult skeletal form. Different skeletal features grow at different rates and are most responsive to mechanical influences at different ages. This must be appreciated when interpreting variation in skeletal morphology both between different age groups within the same population, and between juveniles of different populations and/or time periods, for example, comparisons between the early juvenile *Homo erectus* KNM-WT 15000 and modern children. Ontogenetic analyses can also provide insights into the age of onset of adult patterns of behavior such as sexual division of labor. Studies of age-related bone loss, or osteoporosis, are a special extension of growth and development studies to the complete adult lifespan. Analysis of archaeological samples has demonstrated the probable importance of activity level in maintaining bone strength with aging, and the value of such samples as preindustrial "baselines" against which to compare modern populations. Studies of bilateral asymmetry in bone structural properties have revealed interesting patterns of differences between earlier (Pleistocene) and later (Holocene) samples, and between different Holocene

samples that may reflect systematic differences in behavioral use of the upper limb. Comparisons between cross-sectional diaphyseal and articular properties may help in interpreting bilateral asymmetry results.

As attested by the foregoing summary, the application of biomechanical approaches in bioarchaeological settings has expanded greatly over the past 20 years. However, there are several areas in particular that deserve more emphasis in the future. First, the great majority of functionally oriented studies of archaeological skeletal material have been macroscopic in nature, that is, concerned with the cross-sectional diaphyseal and external articular properties that have been discussed herein. However, bone adaptation occurs on other structural levels as well, as summarized earlier in Figure 3.2. Properties such as trabecular bone orientation and cortical bone microstructure are more difficult to measure, especially noninvasively, but new techniques such as three-dimensional microcomputed tomography (Thompson and Illerhaus, 1998) may make at least some of these parameters more accessible in the future. Combined micro- and macrostructural approaches can shed new light on the basic cellular mechanisms underlying bone adaptation (Abbott et al., 1996; Burr et al., 1990). Similarly, analysis of trabecular architecture can provide clues to the various constraints and potential responses of articulations to mechanical factors. For example, in interspecies comparisons among primates, it appears that relative articular size primarily reflects relative joint mobility, whereas the magnitude of mechanical loading across the joint has more of an effect on trabecular mass and density (Rafferty and Ruff, 1994). Similar comparative studies within humans have not, to my knowledge, yet been carried out.

Another area that is ripe for further study is the mechanical significance of variation in muscle insertion scar morphology (Hawkey and Merbs, 1995). While many authors have assumed a direct relationship between muscle scar size on bones and mechanical usage, this relationship has not been systematically investigated and is probably more complex (Wilczak, 1998). Again, combining analysis of muscle scars with other types of structural characteristics such as cross-sectional diaphyseal strength and articular size may help to shed further light on their behavioral significance, as well as the optimal means of quantifying observed scar morphology.

Finally, the geographic representation of archaeological samples used in biomechanical analyses should be expanded. By far the majority of such studies have concentrated on North American samples (although a number of investigations of Japanese samples have also been carried out, e.g., Kimura, 1971a; Kimura and Takahashi, 1984; Sakaue, 1998). Truly worldwide comparisons are important, first, because these greatly increase the range of morphological and behavioral variation encompassed, and thus the robustness of structure-function conclusions reached (e.g., see Ruff, 1995), and second, because most of human evolution has taken place outside of any one limited geographic range, creating opportunities to study skeletal adaptation to many unique cultural and other environmental challenges. The general principles of biomechanics should be universally applicable, but their potential expression among different human populations has only begun to be explored.

ACKNOWLEDGMENTS

Among the many colleagues who have contributed to the work described in this chapter, I would like to acknowledge in particular the past and continuing collaborations with Dr. Clark Larsen and Dr. Erik Trinkaus. This research has been supported by grants from the National Science Foundation, the Wenner-Gren Foundation, and the National Institutes of Health.

REFERENCES

Abbie AA. 1967. Skinfold thickness in Australian Aborigines. Phys Anthrop Oceania 2:207–219.

Abbott S, Trinkaus E, Burr DB. 1996. Dynamic bone remodeling in later Pleistocene fossil hominids. Am J Phys Anthropol 99:585–601.

Baker BJ, Kealhofer L, editors. 1996. Bioarchaeology of Native American Adaptation in the Spanish Borderlands. Gainesville: Univ. Press of Florida, 232 p.

Beck TJ. 1996. On measuring bone to predict osteoporotic fracture: moving beyond statistical inference. J Radiol 199:612–614.

Beck TJ, Ruff CB, Bissesur K. 1993. Age-related changes in female femoral neck geometry: implications for bone strength. Calcif Tiss Intl Suppl 1:541–546.

Beck TJ, Ruff CB, Mourtada FA, Shaffer RA, Maxwell-Williams K, Kao GL, Sartoris D, Brodine S. 1996. Dual-energy X-ray absorptiometry derived structural geometry for stress fracture prediction in male U.S. Marine Corps recruits. J Bone Min Res 11:645–653.

Beck TJ, Ruff CB, Scott WW, Plato CC, Tobin JD, Quan CA. 1992. Sex differences in geometry of the femoral neck with aging: a structural analysis of bone mineral data. Calcif Tiss Intl 50:24–29.

Beck TJ, Ruff CB, Warden KE, Scott WW, Rao GU. 1990. Predicting femoral neck strength from bone mineral data: a structural approach. Invest Radiol 25:6–18.

Biknevicius AR, Ruff CB. 1992. Use of biplanar radiographs for estimating cross-sectional geometric properties of mandibles. Anat Rec 232: 157–163.

Boule M. 1911. L'homme fossile de La Chapelleaux-Saints. Annales de Paléontologie 6:111–172.

Bridges PS. 1985. Changes in Long Bone Structure with the Transition to Agriculture: Implications for Prehistoric Activities. Ann Arbor: Univ. Michigan (Ph.D.Thesis), 247 p.

Bridges PS. 1989. Changes in activities with the shift to agriculture in the southeastern United States. Curr Anthropol 30:385–394.

Bridges PS. 1996. Skeletal biology and behavior in ancient humans. Evol Anthropol 4:112–120.

Brock SL, Ruff CB. 1988. Diachronic patterns of change in structural properties of the femur in the prehistoric American Southwest. Am J Phys Anthropol 75:113–127.

Burr DB, Ruff CB, Thompson DD. 1990. Patterns of skeletal histologic change through time: comparison of an archaic Native American population with modern populations. Anat Rec 226: 307–313.

Churchill SE. 1994. Human Upper Body Evolution in the Eurasian Later Pleistocene. Albuquerque: University of New Mexico (Ph.D. Thesis), 395 p.

Churchill SE. 1996. Particulate versus integrated evolution of the upper body in Late Pleistocene humans: a test of two models. Am J Phys Anthropol 100:559–583.

Churchill SE, Formicola V. 1997. A case of marked bilateral asymmetry in the upper limbs of an Upper Palaeolithic male from Barma Grande (Liguria), Italy. Intl J Osteoarch 7:18–38.

Churchill SE, Pearson OM, Grine FE, Trinkaus E, Holliday TW. 1996. Morphological affinities of the proximal ulna from Klasies River main site: archaic or modern? J Hum Evol 31:213–237.

Churchill SE, Wall CE, Schmitt D. n.d. Bone strength to body size scaling in non-weight bearing structures: the human upper limb.

Cohen MN, Armelagos GJ. 1984. Paleopathology at the Origins of Agriculture. New York: Academic Press, 615 p.

Collier S. 1989. The influence of economic behaviour and environment upon robusticity of the post-cranial skeleton: a comparion of Australian Aborigines and other populations. Archaeol Oceania 24:17–30.

Cooper C, Melton LJ. 1996. Magnitude and impact of osteoporosis and fractures. In: R Marcus, Feldman D, Kelsey J, editors. Osteoporosis. New York: Academic Press, pp. 419–434.

Coren S, Porac C. 1977. Fifty centuries of right-handedness: the historical record. Science 198: 632–633.

Dodo Y, Kondo O, Muhesen S, Akazawa T. 1998. Anatomy of the Neandertal infant skeleton from the Dederiyeh Cave, Syria. In: T Akazawa, Aoki K, Bar-Yosef O, editors. Neandertals and Modern Humans in Western Asia. New York: Plenum Press, pp. 323–338.

Easterby R, Kroemer KHE, Chaffin DB, editors. 1982. Anthropometry and Biomechanics. Theory and Application. New York: Plenum Press, 327 p.

Endo B, Kimura T. 1970. Postcranial skeleton of the Amud Man. In: Suzuki H, Takai F, editors. The Amud Man and His Cave Site. Tokyo: Academic Press, pp. 231–406.

Frankel VH, and Nordin M, editors. 1980. Basic Biomechanics of the Skeletal System. Philadelphia: Lea and Febiger, 303 p.

Frayer DW. 1980. Sexual dimorphism and cultural evolution in the late Pleistocene and Holocene of Europe. J Hum Evol 9:399–415.

Frayer DW. 1984. Biological and cultural change in the European Late Pleistocene and Early Holocene. In: Smith FH, Spencer F, editors. The Origins of Modern Humans: A World Survey of the Fossil Evidence. New York: Wiley-Liss, pp. 211–250.

Fresia A, Ruff CB, Larsen CS. 1990. Temporal decline in bilateral asymmetry of the upper limb on the Georgia coast. Anthropol Papers Am Mus Nat Hist 68:121–132.

Grine FE, Jungers WL, Tobias PV, Pearson OM. 1995. Fossil *Homo* femur from Berg Aukas, northern Namibia. Am J Phys Anthropol 97:151–185.

Hamilton ME. 1982. Sexual dimorphism in skeletal samples. In: Hall RL, editor. Sexual Dimorphism in *Homo Sapiens*. New York: Praeger, pp. 107–163.

Hawkey DE, Merbs CF. 1995. Activity-induced musculoskeletal stress markers (SMA) and subsistence strategy changes among ancient Hudson Bay Eskimos. Int J Osteoarch 5:324–338.

Heller JA. 1989. Stress trajectories in the proximal femur of archaic *Homo sapiens* and modern humans. Am J Phys Anthropol 78:239.

Hrdlicka A. 1898. Study of the normal tibia. Am Anthropol 11:307–312.

Huiskes R. 1982. On the modelling of long bones in structural analyses. J Biomech 15:65–69.

Hummert JR. 1983. Cortical bone growth and dietary stress among subadults from Nubia's Batn El Hajar. Am J Phys Anthropol 62:167–176.

Hylander WL. 1975. The human mandible: lever or link? Am J Phys Anthropol 43:227–242.

Jones HH, Priest JD, Hayes WC, Tichenor CC, Nagel DA. 1977. Humeral hypertrophy in response to exercise. J Bone Joint Surg 59A:204–208.

Jowsey J. 1977. Metabolic Diseases of Bone. Philadelphia: Saunders, 312 p.

Jungers WL, Burr DB. 1994. Body size, long bone geometry and locomotion in quadrupedal monkeys. Z Morphol Anthropol 80:89–97.

Kennedy GE. 1983. Some aspects of femoral morphology in *Homo erectus*. J Hum Evol 12: 587–616.

Kimura T. 1971a. Cross-section of human lower limb bones viewed from strength of materials. J Anthropol Soc Nippon 79:323–336.

Kimura T. 1971b. Sex determination on the cross-section of human lower leg bones. Jap J Legal Med 25:431–438.

Kimura T, Takahashi H. 1982. Mechanical properties of cross section of lower limb long bones in Jomon man. J Anthropol Soc Nippon 90: 105–117.

Kimura T, Takahashi H. 1984. Mechanical properties of cross section of lower limb long bones in Jomon man. J Anthropol Soc Nippon 90 (Suppl):105–118.

Larsen CS. 1997. Bioarchaeology: Interpreting Behavior from the Human Skeleton. Cambridge: Cambridge Univ. Press, 461 p.

Larsen CS, Milner GR, editors. 1994. In the Wake of Contact. New York: Wiley-Liss, 206 p.

Larsen CS, Ruff CB. 1994. The stresses of conquest in Spanish Florida: structural adaptation and change before and after conquest. In: Larsen CS, Milner GR, editors. Biological Landscapes of Change. New York: Wiley-Liss, pp. 21–34.

Larsen CS, Ruff CB. in press. A biohistory of health and behavior in the Georgia Bight: 2. Behavioral changes and skeletal adaptation. In: Steckel RH, Rose JC, editors. The Backbone of History: Health and Nutrition in the Western Hemisphere, Vol. II. Cambridge: Cambridge Univ. Press.

Larsen CS, Ruff CB, Griffin MC. 1996. Implications of changing biomechanical and nutritional environments for activity and lifeway in the Eastern Spanish Borderlands. In: Baker BJ, Kealhofer L, editors. Bioarchaeology of Native American Adaptation in the Spanish Borderlands. Gainesville: Univ. Press of Florida, pp. 95–125.

Larsen CS, Ruff CB, Kelly RL. 1995. Structural analysis of the Stillwater postcranial human remains: behavioral implications of articular joint pathology and long bone diaphyseal morphology. In: Larsen CS, Kelly RL, editors. Bioarchaeology of the Stillwater marsh: Prehistoric Adaptation in the Western Great Basin. New York: American Museum of Natural History pp. 107–133. Anth. Pap. Am. Mus. Nat. Hist. Vol. 77.

Lieberman DE. 1996. How and why humans grow thin skulls: experimental evidence for systemic cortical robusticity. Am J Phys Anthropol 101: 217–236.

Lovejoy CO, Burstein AH, Heiple KG. 1976. The biomechanical analysis of bone strength: a method and its application to platycnemia. Am J Phys Anthropol 44:489–506.

Lovejoy CO, Trinkaus E. 1980. Strength and robusticity of the Neandertal tibia. Am J Phys Anthropol 53:465–470.

Marcus R, Feldman D, Kelsey J, editors. 1996. Osteoporosis. San Diego: Academic Press, 1373 p.

Martin RB, Atkinson PJ. 1977. Age and sex-related changes in the structure and strength of the human femoral shaft. J Biomech 10:223–231.

Martin RB, Burr DB. 1984. Non-invasive measurement of long bone cross-sectional moment of inertia by photon absorptiometry. J Biomech 17:195–201.

Moro M, Van der Meulin MCH, Kiratli BJ, Marcus R, Bachrach LK, Carter DR. 1996. Body mass is the primary determinant of midfemoral bone acquisition during adolescent growth. Bone 19: 519–526.

Mow VC, Hayes WC, editors. 1991. Basic Orthopaedic Biomechanics. New York: Raven Press, 453 p.

Murdock GP, Provost C. 1973. Factors in the division of labor by sex: a cross-cultural analysis. Ethnology 12:203–225.

Murray PDF. 1936. Bones. Cambridge: Cambridge Univ. Press, 203 p.

Pearson OM, Grine FE. 1997. Re-analysis of the hominid radii from Cave of Hearths and Klasies River Mouth, South Africa. J Hum Evol 32:5 77–592.

Pfeiffer S, Zehr MK. 1996. A morphological and histological study of the human humerus from Border Cave. J Hum Evol 31:49–59.

Pfeiffer SK, Lazenby RA. 1994. Low bone mass in past and present aboriginal populations. In: Draper HH, editor. Advances in Nutritional Research, Vol. 9. New York: Plenum, pp. 35–51.

Powell ML, Bridges PS, Mires AMW, editors. 1991. What Mean These Bones? Studies in Southeastern Bioarchaeology. Tuscaloosa: Univ. Alabama Press, 229 p.

Rafferty KL. 1998. Structural design of the femoral neck in primates. J Hum Evol 34:361–383.

Rafferty KL, Ruff CB. 1994. Articular structure and function in *Hylobates*, *Colobus*, and *Papio*. Am J Phys Anthropol 94:395–408.

Rayner JMV, Wooton RJ, editors. 1991. Biomechanics in Evolution. Cambridge University Press, 273 p.

Roberts DF. 1978. Climate and Human Variability, 2nd ed. Menlo Park, Calif.: Cummings, 123 p.

Robling AG. 1998. Histomorphometric Assessment of Mechanical Loading History from Human Skeletal Remains: The Relation Between Micromorphology and Macromorphology at the Femoral Midshaft. Columbia: Univ. Missouri (Ph.D. Thesis), 174 p.

Roy TA, Ruff CB, Plato CC. 1994. Hand dominance and bilateral asymmetry in structure of the second metacarpal. Am J Phys Anthropol 94: 203–211.

Ruff CB. 1984. Allometry between length and cross-sectional dimensions of the femur and tibia in *Homo sapiens sapiens*. Am J Phys Anthropol 65:347–358.

Ruff CB. 1987a. Sexual dimorphism in human lower limb bone structure: relationship to subsistence strategy and sexual division of labor. J Hum Evol 16:391–416.

Ruff CB. 1987b. Structural allometry of the femur and tibia in Hominoidea and *Macaca*. Folia Primatol 48:9–49.

Ruff CB. 1988. Hindlimb articular surface allometry in Hominoidea and *Macaca*, with comparisons to diaphyseal scaling. J Hum Evol 17:687–714.

Ruff CB. 1994a. Biomechanical analysis of Northern and Southern Plains femora: behavioral implications. In: Owsley DW, Jantz RL, editors. Skeletal Biology in the Great Plains: A Multidisciplinary View. Washington: Smithsonian Institute Press, pp. 235–245.

Ruff CB. 1994b. Morphological adaptation to climate in modern and fossil hominids. Yrbk Phys Anthropol 37:65–107.

Ruff CB. 1995. Biomechanics of the hip and birth in early *Homo*. Am J Phys Anthropol 98:527–574.

Ruff CB. 1997. Structural analysis of long bones from La Florida: interpreting behavior. Am J Phys Anthropol Suppl 24:201.

Ruff CB. 1998. Evolution of the hominid hip. In: Strasser E, Rosenberger A, McHenry H, Fleagle J, editors: Primate Locomotion: Recent Advances. Davis, Calif.: Plenum Press, pp. 449–469.

Ruff CB. 1999. Skeletal structure and behavioral patterns of prehistoric Great Basin populations. In: Hemphill BE, Larsen CS, editors. Understanding Prehistoric Lifeways in the Great Basin Wetlands: Bioarchaeological Reconstruction and Interpretation. pp. 290–320.

Ruff CB. 2000. Body size, body shape, and long bone strength in modern humans. J Hum Evol 38:269–290.

Ruff CB, Hayes WC. 1983a. Cross-sectional geometry of Pecos Pueblo femora and tibiae—a biomechanical investigation. I. Method and general patterns of variation. Am J Phys Anthropol 60:359–381.

Ruff CB, Hayes WC. 1983b. Cross-sectional geometry of Pecos Pueblo femora and tibiae - a biomechanical investigation. II. Sex, age, and size differences. Am J Phys Anthropol 60:383–400.

Ruff CB, Hayes WC. 1984a. Age changes in geometry and mineral content of the lower limb bones. Ann Biomed Eng 12:573–584.

Ruff CB, Hayes WC. 1984b. Bone mineral content in the lower limb: relationship to cross-sectional geometry. J Bone Joint Surg 66A: 1024–1031.

Ruff CB, Hayes WC. 1988. Sex differences in age-related remodeling of the femur and tibia. J Orthop Res 6:886–896.

Ruff CB, Jones HH. 1981. Bilateral asymmetry in cortical bone of the humerus and tibia—sex and age factors. Hum Biol 53:69–86.

Ruff CB, Larsen CS. 1990. Postcranial biomechanical adaptations to subsistence changes on the Georgia Coast. Anth Pap Am Mus Nat Hist 68: 94–120.

Ruff CB, Larsen CS. in press. Reconstructing behavior in Spanish Florida: the biomechanical evidence. In: Larsen CS, editor. Bioarchaeology of La Florida: Human Biology in Northern Frontier New Spain. Gainesville: Univ. Press of Florida.

Ruff CB, Larsen CS, Hayes WC. 1984. Structural changes in the femur with the transition to agriculture on the Georgia coast. Am J Phys Anthropol 64:125–136.

Ruff CB, Leo FP. 1986. Use of computed tomography in skeletal structure research. Yrbk Phys Anthropol 29:181–195.

Ruff CB, McHenry HM, Thackeray JF. 1999. The "robust" australopithecine hip: cross-sectional morphology of the SK 82 and 97 proximal femora. Am J Phys Anthropol 109:509–521.

Ruff CB, Runestad JA. 1992. Primate limb bone structural adaptations. Ann Rev Anthropol 21: 407–433.

Ruff CB, Scott WW, Liu AY-C. 1991. Articular and diaphyseal remodeling of the proximal femur with changes in body mass in adults. Am J Phys Anthropol 86:397–413.

Ruff CB, Trinkaus E, Holliday, TW. 1997. Body mass and encephalization in Pleistocene *Homo*. Nature 387:173–176.

Ruff CB, Trinkaus E, Walker A, Larsen CS. 1993. Postcranial robusticity in *Homo*, I: Temporal trends and mechanical interpretation. Am J Phys Anthropol 91:21–53.

Ruff CB, Walker A, Trinkaus E. 1994. Postcranial robusticity in *Homo*, III: Ontogeny. Am J Phys Anthropol 93:35–54.

Runestad JA, Ruff CB, Nieh JC, Thorington RW, Teaford MF. 1993. Radiographic estimation of long bone cross-sectional geometric properties. Am J Phys Anthropol 90:207–213.

Sakaue K. 1998. Bilateral asymmetry of the humerus in Jomon people and modern Japanese. Anthropol Sci 105:231–246.

Snow CM, Shaw JM, Matkin CC. 1996. Physical activity and risk for osteoporosis. In: Marcus R, Feldman D, and Kelsey J, editors. Osteoporosis. New York: Academic Press, pp. 511–528.

Stirland AJ. 1993. Asymmetry and activity-related change in the male humerus. Intl J Osteoarch 3:105–113.

Sumner DR, Andriacchi TP. 1996. Adaptation to differential loading: comparison of growth-related changes in cross-sectional properties of the human femur and humerus. Bone 19:121–126.

Sumner DR, Olson CL, Freeman PM, Lobick JJ, Andriacchi TP. 1989. Computed tomographic measurement of cortical bone geometry. J Biomech 22:649–653.

Thomas DH, editor. 1991. Columbian Consequences, Vol. 2: Archaeological and Historical Perspectives on the Spanish Borderland East. Washington: Smithsonian Institution Press, 586 p.

Thompson JL, Illerhaus B. 1998. A new reconstruction of the Le Moustier 1 skull and investigation of internal structures using 3-D-μCT data. J Hum Evol 35:647–665.

Timoshenko SP, Gere JM. 1972. Mechanics of Materials. New York: Van Nostrand Reinhold, 541 p.

Trinkaus E. 1997. Appendicular robusticity and the paleobiology of modern human emergence. Proc Nat Acad Sci 94:13367–13373.

Trinkaus E, Churchill SE, Ruff CB. 1994. Postcranial robusticity in *Homo*, II: Humeral bilateral asymmetry and bone plasticity. Am J Phys Anthropol 93:1–34.

Trinkaus E, Churchill SE, Ruff CB, Vandermeersch B. 1999. Long bone shaft robusticity and body proportions of the Saint-Césaire 1 Châtelperronian Neandertal. J Arch Sci. 26:753–773.

Trinkaus E, Ruff CB. 1989. Diaphyseal cross-sectional morphology and biomechanics of the Fond-de-Forêt 1 femur and the Spy 2 femur and tibia. Bull Soc Roy Bel Anthrop Prehist 100:33–42.

Trinkaus E, Ruff CB. 1999. Diaphyseal cross-sectional geometry of Near Eastern Middle Paleolithic humans: the femur. J Arch Sci 26: 409–424.

Trinkaus E, Ruff CB, Churchill SE, Vandermeersch B. 1998. Locomotion and body proportions of the Saint-Césaire 1 Châtelperronian Neandertal. Proc Nat Acad Sci 95:5836-5840.

Trinkaus E, Stringer CB, Ruff CB, Hennessy RJ, Roberts MB, Parfitt SA. 1999. Diaphyseal cross-sectional geometry of the Boxgrove 1 Middle Pleistocene human tibia. J Hum Evol 37:1–25.

van der Meulen MCH, Ashford MW, Kiratli BJ, Bachrach LK, Carter DR. 1996. Determinants of femoral geometry and structure during adolescent growth. J Orthop Res 14:22–29.

Van Gerven DP, Hummert JR, Burr DB. 1985. Cortical bone maintenance and geometry of the tibia in prehistoric children from Nubia's Batn el Hajar. Am J Phys Anthropol 66:275–280.

Villa LV, Nelson L. 1996. Race, ethnicity, and osteoporosis. In: Marcus R, Feldman D, Kelsey J, editors. Osteoporosis. New York: Academic Press, pp. 435–447.

Wainwright SA, Biggs WD, Currey JD, Gosline JM. 1982. Mechanical Design in Organisms. Princeton University Press, 423 p.

Walker A, Leakey R, editors. 1993. The Narioko- tome *Homo Erectus* Skeleton. Cambridge: Harvard Univ. Press, 457 p.

Watanabe H. 1977. The human activity system and its spatiotemporal structure. In: Watanabe H, ed- itor. Human Activity System: Its Spatiotemporal Structure. Tokyo: Univ. Tokyo Press, pp. 3–39.

Weidenreich F. 1941. The extremity bones of *Sinanthropus pekinensis*. Paleont Sinica (NS D) 5D:1–150.

Weiss E. 1998. Sexual Differences in Activity Patterns of a Central Californian Hunter-

Gatherer Population. Sacramento: California State University (MA Thesis), 110 p.

Wells JP, Wood GA. 1975. The application of bio- mechanical motion analysis to aspects of green monkey (*Cercopithecus a. sabaeus*) locomotion. Am J Phys Anthropol 43:217–226.

Wilczak CA. 1998. A New Method of Quantifying Musculoskeletal Stress Markers (MSM): A Test of the Relationship Between Enthesis Size and Habitual Activity in Archaeological Populations. Ithaca: Cornell University (Ph.D. Thesis).

Woo SLY, Kuei SC, Amiel D, Gomez MA, Hayes WC, White FC, Akeson WH. 1981. The effect of prolonged physical training on the properties of long bone: a study of Wolff's law. J Bone Joint Surg 63A:780–787.

CHAPTER 4

DENTAL MORPHOLOGY: TECHNIQUES AND STRATEGIES

JOHN T. MAYHALL

Dental morphology may be defined as the study of the form and structure of teeth. This chapter takes a broad view of the macroscopic form of the teeth and includes topics such as mensuration and pathology as it affects the shape and size along with tooth shape as it might be more narrowly defined. (See Ten Cate, 1998, for an extensive description of the microscopic structure of teeth and their development.) All of these topics are related to the "look" of the teeth and are valuable in describing the dentition of skeletal samples and individual skeletons as well as living individuals (dental morphology can be compared directly between skeletal and living samples). Much of what follows is from the dental literature or the specialized volumes dealing with tooth development, pathology, growth, and physiology of the oral structures and data on dental morphology and mensuration that may be read infrequently by biological anthropologists (Alt et al., 1998; Brothwell, 1963; Butler and Joysey, 1978; Dahlberg, 1971; Dahlberg and Graber, 1977; Hillson, 1986, 1996; Kurtén, 1982; Lukacs, 1998; Mayhall and Heikkinen, 1999; Moggi-Cecchi, 1995; Pedersen et al., 1967; Radlanski and Renz, 1995; Russell et al., 1988; Smith and Tchernov, 1992; Woelfel and Scheid, 1997). The references provided are rather ex-tensive but certainly not exhaustive. In addition, one may wish to consult the *Journal of Dental Research*, *Archives of Oral Biology*, *American Journal of Physical Anthropology*, *Human Biology, Dental Anthropology*, or any number of dental and anthropological journals that have published numerous papers on dental morphology. The references here are intended to allow the reader to go to several sources for further study on a particular topic and to direct the reader toward rewarding papers that may be the basis for your investigation.

The use of dental morphology along with other important areas such as tooth wear, oral pathology, enamel hypoplasia, and other microscopic changes in the tooth structure allows the skeletal biologist to reconstruct much of the lifestyle of the individual being studied. It is clear that the teeth are a very important component in any in-depth study of skeletal material, not only because of their endurance but because of their ability to record the biology of the body during an important time in the life of an individual. The dentition begins its formation very early in gestation and has not completed its development until the third decade of life. The insults that the body and the dentition have received may be recorded permanently in the teeth while bone has the opportunity to remodel during the life of an individual thus obliterating the earlier changes.

For many studies the insults of living may not be as important as being able to reconstruct

Biological Anthropology of the Human Skeleton, Edited by M. Anne Katzenberg and Shelley R. Saunders.
ISBN 0-471-31616-4   Copyright © 2000 by Wiley-Liss, Inc.

the population affinities of the groups under examination. Here, the use of tooth size and shape are very important since there is evidence of a genetic basis to much of the variation that is observed. There is a strong possibility that we will better understand the genetics of tooth size and shape soon and we will be able to use this knowledge to accurately determine the affinities of individuals and groups. When one surveys the literature it becomes clear that the major problems confronting dental anthropologists are ones of consistency in observation. These problems can be overcome and the skeletal biologist can use the techniques described below to further identify the biological and cultural background of much of the skeletal material still relatively unstudied.

This chapter takes a conservative approach to the techniques that are described. The reader can be assured that the methods are ones that are easily achievable and are generally accepted, not esoteric ones that can only be achieved with highly specialized, very expensive equipment. However, there are references to new, somewhat more complicated methods that appear to be very useful to the skeletal biologist. This is not to suggest that there are not other methods that can be applied to the study of dental morphology, but one must be careful to use methods that are, as much as possible, comparable throughout the field of dental morphology. The reader will notice that some of the methods proposed here are criticized as well. This does not mean that the techniques are inappropriate but rather suggests that they must be carefully considered to determine if they are the correct ones for the particular goal of the researcher. As with any technique, there are deficiencies that must be considered before embarking on a particular study; the perfect technique has yet to appear. The appropriate technique for one study may not be so for another. The criticisms are based on my use or attempted use of them in realistic situations.

The chapter is divided into three principal areas: tooth size, tooth morphology, and a very brief synopsis of dental pathology and wear as

they affect the morphology of the dentition. (Hillson, Chapter 9, presents a more thorough coverage of dental pathology.) These are not mutually exclusive. The morphology of a tooth is closely related to the size of the tooth (four-cusped mandibular molars are generally smaller than five-cusped ones). A tooth with a complex groove pattern is more likely to be carious than one with a simple pattern because the complex tooth has more furrows to trap food. It has long been thought that a molar with three roots will be more prone to severe periodontal disease than one with two roots simply because it has more furcations (the areas of the tooth where the roots divide) and will trap more food and be more difficult to keep clean. However, the complex-patterned molar is probably more efficient for mastication than the simple molar primarily because it will have more cutting and grinding surfaces and a three-rooted molar will be more difficult to dislodge from the maxillae than one with a simpler root configuration. A classic example of the relationship of morphology and pathology is the shovel-shaped incisor. This tooth, because of its I-beam cross section, is a very strong tooth that resists chipping and breaking; few individuals with this feature have broken or chipped teeth. However, the morphology of the lingual surface is such that there is a food trap created by the joining in the cingulum area of the extra tooth material of the marginal ridges that creates this strength. This food trap is not a problem in populations that subsist on a non-cariogenic diet, but with the advent of processed foods and increased levels of caries these teeth become the nidus of early, difficult-to-detect decay. Further, because the extra enamel and dentin forming the marginal ridges increases the faciolingual diameter of the tooth at the mesial and distal proximal surfaces, it is difficult for an examiner to transmit light through those areas of the tooth and detect the dark shadow of small carious lesions. In a small study of Canadian Indians, who have very well-developed shovel-shaped incisors, we found that as many as 60% of the lesions detected using radiographs were missed using direct transmitted light examination techniques, a much higher figure than would be expected in a population where shovel-shaped incisors are not found (Titley and Mayhall, unpublished). Here we can see the practical results of a change in morphology resulting in increased tooth size and the resultant liability of undetected dental caries.

The reader may have noticed the use of some specialized dental terms above. It may be of assistance to briefly outline some of the more common terms that one encounters in perusing the dental literature. First, that portion of the tooth and the dentition in general that is nearer the midline is referred to as the *mesial* surface while the more distant surface is the *distal*. The surface nearer the tongue is the *lingual*. There are several terms used to describe the surface that is close to the lips or cheek. An all-encompassing term would be the *facial surface*, but the surface on the anterior teeth (incisors and canines) is generally the *labial surface* while that on the posteriors (premolars and molars) that is near the cheek is referred to as the *buccal surface*. The biting surface is called the *incisal* on the anterior teeth while on the posteriors it is the *occlusal*. Areas that contact the adjacent tooth are referred to as the *contact areas*. These contact areas are on the proximal surfaces (mesial and distal ones).

There are several tooth numbering systems that are in general use (Figs. 4.1 and 4.2). The universal system numbers the permanent teeth from the maxillary right third molar (1) to the maxillary left third molar (16) and then continues from the mandibular left third molar (17) around to the mandibular right third molar (32), while in the deciduous dentition letters from A to T are used. The Palmer and Haderup systems are very similar to each other with a symbol being used to indicate the position of the occlusal surface and the midline and the number indicating the position of the tooth counting from the midline. The other notation system in general use is the F.D.I. system where each quadrant of the dentition is assigned a prefix that precedes the tooth position number. The initial number is 1 for the permanent maxillary right quadrant, 2 for the maxillary left, 3 for the mandibular left, and 4 for the

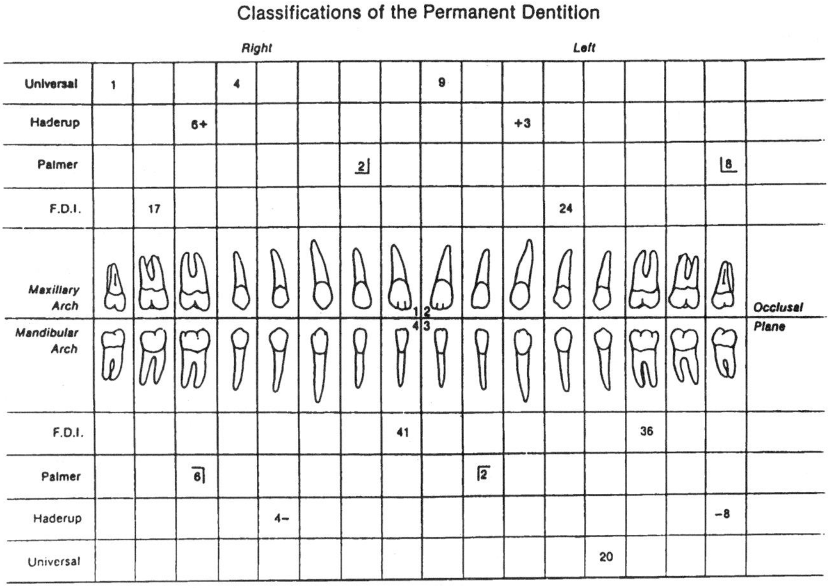

Figure 4.1 The most common notation systems for the permanent dentition. The maxillary right third molar would be 1 in the Universal system, 8+ in the Haderup system, 8| in the Palmer system, and 18 in the F.D.I. system.

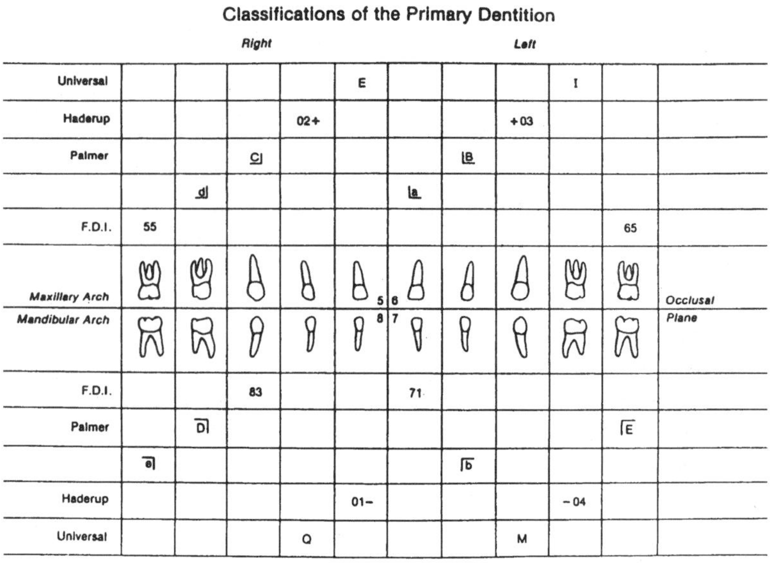

Classifications of the Primary Dentition

	Right									Left	
Universal					E				I		
Haderup				02+				+03			
Palmer			c|				|B				
		d|			|a						
F.D.I.	55									65	
Maxillary Arch					5|6						Occlusal
Mandibular Arch					8|7						Plane
F.D.I.		83			71						
Palmer	D|							|E			
	a|				|b						
Haderup			01–				–04				
Universal			Q			M					

Figure 4.2 The deciduous dentition notation systems. Note that both uppercase and lowercase letters may be used.

mandibular right. In the deciduous dentition the numbers are 5, 6, 7, and 8, respectively. In the anthropological literature you may also find reference to the tooth being described with a letter and a superscript or a subscript. In this case, a permanent maxillary incisor is I^2, a deciduous mandibular lateral incisor is i_2, and a permanent mandibular first molar is M_1. There is not a comprehensive dental dictionary available; this is because those that are available are primarily of interest to dentists. These volumes generally lack any mention of palaeontological terminology or terms that are in common usage in dental anthropology.

TOOTH SIZE

The traditional measurement of teeth was confined to two crown measurements and from these came several indices that have been useful in describing tooth crown proportions and basic shapes. This is not to suggest that there are only two measurements; there are several that can be used to describe the entire tooth. However, the vast majority of the literature will describe the tooth crown with the mesiodistal

diameter and the faciolingual (buccolingual) diameter. The former is the one that has to be considered very carefully before embarking on the measurement of any large sample. Two sets of landmarks can be used, both with their justifications. First, some investigators describe the mesiodistal diameter of the crown as the distance between the contact points of the tooth (Fig. 4.3), the area where the tooth contacts its neighbour (Moorrees, 1957; Thomsen, 1951). (Even though we refer to "contact points," these are, in reality, *areas* of contact which become larger with interproximal attrition, the wear of the enamel that occurs when the adjacent teeth move against each other during mastication.) In this case, the calipers are held parallel to the occlusal plane of the tooth and the (sharpened) beaks of the calipers are placed on the mesial and distal contact points of the crown. One advantage of this measurement is the ability to sum all the mesiodistal measurements and derive the length of the dental arcade. This method has the disadvantage that if there is any interproximal attrition (see Hillson, Chapter 9, for a detailed description), a very common situation in skeletal materials, the mesiodistal measurement will be reduced. If one uses this method the sample sizes will be reduced, sometimes drastically, by the number of rejected measurements due to mesial or distal attrition.

The other method (Fig. 4.3) measures the maximum width of the crown in the mesiodistal plane (Mayhall, 1979; Pedersen, 1949). This will usually be wider than the former method and may be the easier method to employ. Theoretically, this method provides somewhat more information about the development of the tooth since it is measuring the largest amount of growth in the mesiodistal plane. There are instances, especially in the anterior teeth, when the two methods will be using the same landmarks and derive the same values (Fig. 4.4). It is important to decide before the study which will be used. This will require a comprehensive literature search to determine what studies one wishes to use for comparative purposes. Both methods require the investigator to have a reasonable sense of dental morphology, especially when the teeth are not in the alveolus or are rotated in the tooth row. Any good dental anatomy text (Jordan and Abrams, 1992; Osborn, 1981;

Woelfel and Scheid, 1997) or, more to this area of interest, works by Goose (1963) and Hillson (1986, 1996) can be of assistance if one is not sure of the morphological landmarks of the particular teeth included in the study. The landmarks may vary considerably depending on the tooth type being measured.

Once the mesiodistal measurement is determined, the faciolingual meaurement can be ascertained (Fig. 4.3) by holding the calipers perpendicular to the plane that was used for the mesiodistal and determining the widest diameter of the tooth (Goose, 1963). This measurement is subject to error because for many of the molars the most protruding portion of the facial aspect of the tooth will be toward the mesial and the corresponding point for the lingual will be toward the distal side of the crown. This requires that the calipers be carefully positioned so as not to be anything other than perpendicular to the mesiodistal axis. Also, the two points probably will not be in the same plane occlusocervically. The calipers must also be held parallel to the occlusal plane. For the anterior teeth, the faciolingual measurement is difficult because the heights of contour of the

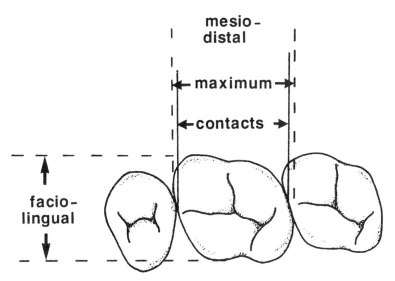

Figure 4.3 Illustration of the dimensions included in the two principal methods for determining the mesiodistal diameters (contact points or maximum diameter). The faciolingual measurement is obtained by holding the caliper beaks perpendicular to the mesiodistal measurement and parallel to the occlusal plane.

facial and lingual surfaces are so disparate (Fig. 4.4). It is important here, and with the premolars and canines, to ensure that the caliper beaks are parallel to the long axis of the tooth and not the crown (the long axis of the crown is often not in the same plane as the axis for the entire tooth). Care should be taken to ascertain that the heights of contour on the cingulum area of the incisors and canines are accessible to the caliper points. Often, the cingulum area, the portion of the lingual surface that forms a protuberance in the cervical third of the crown, is obscured by the lingual plate of bone if the tooth is partially erupted. More commonly, this becomes a problem when measuring dental stone models where the cingulum is not fully revealed because of the overlying soft tissue gingiva.

With these two measurements one can construct indices that crudely describe the proportions of the tooth, the approximate area of the occlusal surface, etc. (Goose, 1963; Jacobson, 1982; Middleton Shaw, 1931; Pedersen, 1949; Selmer-Olsen, 1949). The *crown index* is the faciolingual diameter of the crown divided by the mesiodistal diameter multiplied by 100. This index is designed to display the ratio between the two measurements and illustrate the shape of the crown. Rosenzweig (1970) used it to study sexual dimorphism and population differences of Middle Eastern groups and cautiously promoted it as a distinguishing factor. The *crown module* is derived by the addition of the mesiodistal and faciolingual measurements and division by 2. This is claimed to be an expression of the mass of the crown although Pedersen (1949) correctly notes that it is "a rather imperfect one." The third index is *crown robustness*, which is the mesiodistal dimension multiplied by the faciolingual one (Kajava, 1912; Weidenreich, 1937). This last index has also been termed the *crown area* by Wolpoff (1971) and has been used by Lukacs (1988) in a study of early agriculturists. Most of these in-

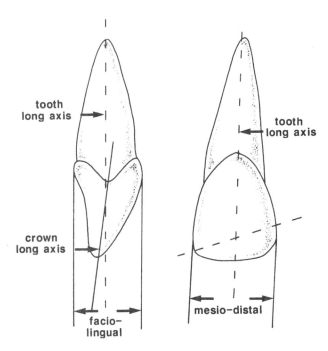

Figure 4.4 The landmarks for measuring the anterior teeth. Note that the long axis of the crown may not be the same as the long axis of the tooth. The determination of the mesiodistal distance is through the contact points and perpendicular to the long axis of the tooth.

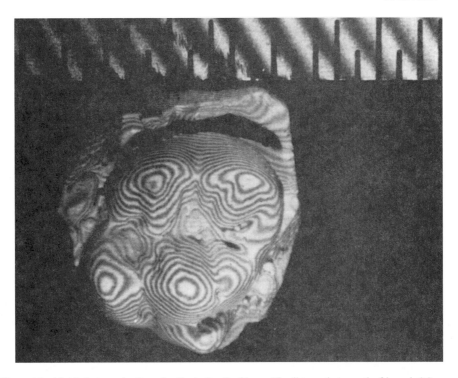

Figure 4.5 Moiré photograph of a molar illustrating the fringes. The distance between the fringes is 0.2 mm.

dices have been overtaken by more sophisticated techniques that are available to accurately describe not only the occlusal area but the heights of the cusps, the distance between them, and their position on the crown.

One technique that has gained popularity recently is the use of moiré fringe photography. The general technique is not new (Takasaki, 1970; 1973) but with the advent of grids that indicate differences in contour of as little as 50 μm it is possible to quickly and accurately describe the tooth crowns of the molars and, to some extent, the other teeth. Until now, the work has concentrated on the molars because they are the easiest to orient reliably (Kageyama et al., 1999; Kanazawa et al., 1984; Mayhall and Kanazawa, 1989; Sekikawa et al., 1988).

The tooth to be analysed is oriented with the occlusal plane parallel to a grid with inscribed parallel lines through which collimated light and a macro lens of a 35-mm camera are aimed (see Ozaki and Kanazawa, 1984, for a detailed description). The result of the light passing through the grid and striking the uneven surface of the tooth is the production of contour lines (fringes) that are an easily determined distance apart (Fig. 4.5). These contour lines are captured with high-speed, high-contrast film and enlarged. The resulting photographs are then measured and the heights of cusps can be determined by counting the number of contour lines. Distance determinations that have been reported recently include intercuspal distances, position of the cusps on the occlusal surface, heights of the cusps, and the depths of the fossae and their positions. Moiré contourography techniques are not limited to teeth. Kanazawa (1980) has successfully used the technique for craniometry and found that many of the problems that have made craniometrics difficult can be overcome. Kamura and colleagues (1984) have investigated the differences in facial contours using moiré techniques while Rass and colleagues (1995) have used stereophotogrammetry to accomplish the same thing.

One further advance that has the potential to describe the basal areas of tooth crowns utilizes the moiré methodology. Researchers attempted to determine the basal area of the tooth crown, an area with differing definitions depending on the study, by photographing the tooth from directly above (Biggerstaff, 1970; Hanihara et al., 1970) and tracing the resultant outline of the crown with a planimeter (Williams, 1979). In this way an approximation of the area of each cusp and the entire crown could be reported. Hanihara and his co-workers used a novel method to determine the relative size of the cusps. They photographed the teeth as above and then printed the images on photographic paper that was very consistent in size and weight. Next, they divided the tooth images into the cusps by simply cutting them along the separating grooves and the cusp outlines. When this was accomplished they weighed each cusp image and could then determine the proportions of the cusps. The method of using two-dimensional photos has one important drawback: the heights of contour of the crown are not at the same level occlusocervically on all surfaces of the crown. Thus, the plane that was measured might be tilted or different for each cusp. Using moiré contourography and digital image analysis it is possible to achieve the basal areas of the crown and cusps at the same level throughout the crown (Mayhall and Alvesalo, 1991; Mayhall et al., 1998). In other words, one can make an imaginary cross section of the crown at any distance from the occlusal plane to the heights of contour and determine the area at that level.

Townsend and Alvesalo (1999) have photographed casts of premolars with a small pencil mark delineating each cusp tip. With a scale introduced into the photo it is possible to accurately determine the intercuspal distance. This technique is one that holds promise because of its low technical requirements. One only needs a camera, high-contrast film, some method of ensuring that the occlusal plane is parallel to the focal plane of the camera, a scale introduced into each photograph, and a pencil to produce accurate photos that are easily measured. The distance between cusp tips is important because it is seemingly less affected by sexual differences than the "outer" measurements such as the mesiodistal and faciolingual dimensions (Mayhall and Kanazawa, 1989). The importance of this becomes obvious in measuring loose teeth when there is the possibility of a significant amount of sexual dimorphism in the mesiodistal and faciolingual dimensions but the sex of the teeth is unknown.

A rather interesting technique using a variant of photography is the use of photocopying equipment to reproduce in two dimensions the intercuspal distances and the intra-arch distances. In these cases one simply puts the cast of the arch or a tooth on the photocopying plate and reproduces it in a flat plane (Singh and Savara, 1964). McKeown (1981) suggested a photographic method for recording the three-dimensional form of individual teeth. The tooth to be analysed is placed in a metal frame cube that allows the tooth to be photographed from all sides. Five photographs are taken from a standard distance (150 cm) and from these the dimensions can be determined. One other technique that utilizes standardized photographs has been reported by Yamada and Brown (1988). Occlusal photographs were used to determine the contours of maxillary molars by measuring the distances from the central pit to the perimeter of the crown at 10° intervals. These last two determinations may suffer from the same constraints that limited earlier studies; the maximum contours of the crown are not in the same plane. There are other techniques that attempt to characterize the tooth in three dimensions that may prove to be valuable (Brook et al., 1999; Lambrechts et al., 1984; Pirttiniemi et al., 1999).

The use of standardized measurement techniques allows the skeletal biologist to accurately compare individual teeth and those of populations and various subgroups. However, it must be remembered that there is a wide range of variability in tooth size, both interpopulationally (Brabant, 1973; Garn et al., 1968; Lavelle, 1970, 1971) and intrapopulationally (Dahlberg, 1990). Care must be taken that the results of mensuration are accurate and comparable with other studies and that samples are of sufficient size to allow for meaningful comparisons. This last caveat is one that plagues skeletal biologists as well as other dental researchers. When beginning a study of the dentition, be prepared to lose a large proportion of the teeth to wear, pathology, and antemortem and postmortem loss. In some studies populations of several hundred living people revealed the number of suitable teeth in a particular class that were usable to be less than a dozen (Mayhall, 1979). These small numbers may be further reduced by ante- and postmortem loss. They may be so reduced that studies of fluctuating asymmetry, for instance, are impossible due to the lack of suitable antimeres (Mayhall et al., 1991).

Upon determining the techniques that are apropos to the material to be examined the researcher is still confronted with the problem of the usefulness of the various techniques. How are these mensurational determinations to be used? Are they valuable for genetic studies, population comparisons, sexual dimorphism comparisons, evolutionary studies, or asymmetry studies? Is there so much variation within the populations under investigation that any meaningful comparisons would be compromised? While there is, obviously, no single answer to these questions, it may be of value to show how dental measurements have been used in studies that include the above areas.

Genetic studies can be of a populational nature or they can be used to determine the role of genes in tooth size. Some of the results of studies by Alvesalo and his colleagues provide clues to anomalous teeth or dentitions that may be found in skeletal samples (Alvesalo, 1971, 1985, 1997; Alvesalo and Portin, 1980; Alvesalo and Varrela, 1979; Garn et al., 1965; Kari et al., 1980; Kirveskari and Alvesalo, 1981, 1982; Mayhall et al., 1991; Townsend et al., 1984). Alvesalo and co-workers have used various measurements of the tooth to describe groups of individuals with abnormalities in their sex chromosomes and to compare these with their normal first degree relatives

(Townsend et al., 1988). For instance, the greater thickness of enamel and dentin and a larger overall tooth size in 47,XYY males when compared to their normal relatives supports the view that the extra Y chromosome exerts a promoting effect on both the function of the ameloblasts and, possibly, on the growth of dentin (Alvesalo, 1985, 1997). By examining males with portions of the Y chromosome missing it is possible to suggest a growth-promoting gene in the nonfluorescent part of the long arm (Alvesalo, 1985). Similarly, it is now becoming clear that the X chromosome's short arm contains gene(s) for tooth crown growth (Alvesalo, 1997). This evidence comes partly from studying the tooth size of 46,X,i(Xq)[1] females and comparing it with the size of 45,X females (Turner syndrome) and normal female relatives. The isochromosome females have smaller teeth than the 45,X females who in turn have smaller teeth than the normal 46,XX females (Mayhall et al., 1991). It may be worth identifying individuals in a skeletal population with extremely small tooth sizes and speculating about the possibility of a syndrome such as Turner syndrome being a causative factor.

Teeth have the unique asset of being comparable between skeletal samples and living populations. In living individuals one can utilize dental stone models of the dentition for accurate measurements while for teeth from archaeological sites the measurements can be done directly. Several studies have used this "crossover" ability to their advantage (Campbell, 1925; Mayhall, 1976; Pedersen, 1949) while others have compared the tooth size among skeletal groups (Brabant, 1973; Perzigian, 1976; Selmer-Olsen, 1949; Turner, 1967) or among living groups (Garn et al., 1968; Hanihara, 1977; Harris, 1977; Jacobson, 1982; Lavelle, 1970, 1971). These comparisons must be carefully examined due to the possibility that two samples of any one population may show large variation (Lavelle, 1970). By using univariate and multivariate statistics, popula-

[1]46,X,I (Xq) females are those with one normal X chromosome (a single long arm [q] and one short arm [p] and an isochromosome, an X chromosome having two long arms.

tions may be defined using tooth size alone although the investigator must be aware of the effect of tooth size variability on any results.

The sexual dimorphism of tooth size has been the subject of various studies of populations as diverse as Swedish children (Lysell and Myrberg, 1982), Australian Aborigines (Brown et al., 1980; Hanihara, 1976), Ecuadorian Indians (Mayhall and Karp, 1983), and French-Canadians (Buschang et al., 1988). The Swedish study noted that "although the sex differences are small, especially in the deciduous dentition, they are statistically significant for both dentitions" (p. 113). The permanent canines displayed a 5–6% difference while the sexual dimorphism for the rest of the teeth was about 2–4%. These figures are claimed to agree with other studies of peoples of European ancestry. This rather small amount of dimorphism leads to a cautionary note; in most skeletal samples the samples are small and this 2–6% dimorphism will not be apparent. In short, it is probably not possible to use univariate analysis of the size of the teeth for any sexual discrimination. De Vito and Saunders (1990) recognized the problem of using single teeth and deciduous teeth to determine the sex of individuals. In a discriminant function analysis of deciduous teeth from the Burlington, Ontario, growth study (Canadians of British origin) they were able to reach an acceptable level of discrimination. They caution that the application of the discriminant functions they utilized may not be applicable to other populations due to their variations in dimorphism.

Moiré contourography has also been used to determine the amount of sexual dimorphism in the molar crowns. This is especially valuable because for the first time the heights of the cusps have been accurately measured and compared. Studies of Japanese (Sekikawa et al., 1988) have noted that the cusps of the deciduous second molars (maxillary and mandibular) and permanent first molars are consistently higher in males than in females. Kanazawa et al. (1983) determined that the sex differences were found primarily around the distal cusps of

the maxillary teeth while Mayhall and Kanazawa (1989) noted that the differences in Canadian Inuit were consistently higher in males for all cusps in the maxillary first molar. Mayhall and Alvesalo (1992) extended the use of moiré contourography by including digital image analysis in studying the sexual dimorphism of a Finnish population. In this study, cusp height, basal area, cusp volume, and position of the cusps were compared between the sexes. The broadest comparisons between populations and between males and females were in the paper by Kanazawa and co-workers (1988) where the authors claimed that the three-dimensional shape of the occlusal surface was distinguishable for four general racial populations. In evolutionary studies, particularly microevolutionary ones, tooth size has been a valuable adjunct. Japanese studies have used tooth dimensions for analyzing geographically isolated populations (Hanihara, 1989), investigating temporal and biological relationships (Mizoguchi, 1988), and demonstrating the effects of hybridization on Japanese children's dentition (Hanihara and Ueda, 1979). Two other studies that demonstrate the use of tooth size for evolutionary studies are the work of Rosenzweig and Smith (1971), who noted that highly inbred isolates were found to display the same amount of variability as more heterogeneous groups, and Henderson and Greene's (1975) application of dental field theory to primate evolution. Some workers have attempted to use tooth size and changes in it to analyze evolutionary trends (Brace et al., 1991; Calcagno and Gibson, 1991; Hinton et al., 1980; Lukacs, 1984; Perzigian, 1975; 1984). Many of the studies suggest that there has been a reduction in tooth size over time. However, the cause of these reductions is speculation at present for, as Lukacs (1984) states, there are at least two barriers to this line of research: the absence of a mechanism consistent with known evolutionary principles for producing the reduction and the absence of accurate data on many of the living and prehistoric populations. There are those who would contend that mechanisms are identifiable that give an indication of the reasons, if not for tooth size reduction through time, then for changes in the occlusion (Brace et al., 1991; Seguchi, 1998). Presumably, changes in occlusion are closely related to changes in tooth size. Mayhall (1977) in a study of the Eskimos of northern Alaska noted that these people were renowned for their use of their teeth as a "third hand" and for heavy mastication, but this role may have been exaggerated by observers. In fact, many Eskimos have functioned well both physically and reproductively without teeth while consuming frozen whale, seal, and fish, thus casting doubt on the dogma that teeth were necessary for survival in prehistoric human populations. It appears premature to suggest that the mechanisms of tooth reduction are known. Lukacs (1984:253) correctly notes, "Final determination of the precise evolutionary mechanism(s) of dental reduction will come from experimental studies of laboratory animals rather than from analysis of the fossil or skeletal record."

One final area that has been popular with those interested in tooth size is the amount of fluctuating asymmetry seen in the dentition. These seemingly random differences between antimeres[2] may indicate an inability of an individual to buffer disturbances in development and could be valuable to the skeletal biologist in that they may indicate local developmental disturbances. Perzigian (1977:81), using skeletal samples, has suggested that, "environmentally mediated growth disturbance may be sensitively reflected by fluctuating asymmetry." It would be of benefit in reconstructing the lifestyles of skeletal populations if we could use dental asymmetry to determine the levels of insults to the growth of the individuals in that population. However, before embarking on the study of asymmetry one is cautioned that there are several factors that may influence the validity of the results. Townsend (1981) and Townsend and Brown (1980) caution that the methodology of the data collection is very im-

portant in comparisons. Measurement methods must be comparable between studies, the methods of quantifying the asymmetry should be the same, and the methods of obtaining the dental casts measured should be alike. Garn and co-workers (1979) and Smith and her colleagues (1982) demonstrate that large sample sizes are required to be able to make statistically valid comparisons. Garn and colleagues state, "Since most published studies on left-right dental asymmetry are based on small samples (generally below 100 and in some cases as small as 15), it is increasingly likely that apparent intergroup differences in crown asymmetry may reflect sampling limitations" (1979:2012). Smith and co-workers summarize their research by concluding that, ". . . fluctuating asymmetry is not yet established as a useful and reliable measure of general stress in human populations" (1982:288)., Finally, Mayhall and Saunders (1985) felt that it was practically impossible to overcome the "noise" level and test recent hypotheses regarding fluctuating dental asymmetry. The case for caution should be apparent; so that if one is to explore the hypothesized benefits of this area a rigorous protocol and large samples are a must.

TOOTH MORPHOLOGY

Tooth morphology is an area of dental research that suffers from a lack of standardization. In many instances tooth crown morphology is the only visible way of comparing large populations. Novice (and experienced) researchers in this area have been frustrated by this lack of standardization and an inability to accurately observe the range of variation of dental morphological traits. They have also had the uneasy feeling that their observations were not comparable to those of others. It is not possible to solve these problems here, but it is possible to steer the observer toward techniques that have been used successfully by experienced researchers.

The use of dental morphology and the observation of dental morphological traits have a long

[2]An antimere is one of the opposite corresponding teeth in the dental arch. Examples are the right and left mandibular canines, the right and left maxillary first molars, etc.

history in dental anthropology. Some of the earliest pioneers such as Campbell (1925), Dahlberg (1945, 1950, 1951, 1958, 1963, 1965), and Pederson (1949) cautioned the researcher that there were problems in comparing results from one investigator with those from another. A.A. Dahlberg attempted to alleviate the problem by constructing a set of dental stone models that displayed the range of variability of about a dozen morphological traits of the permanent dentition (Fig. 4.6 illustrates an example of his plaque demonstrating the variation in the maxillary incisors). These are still the most widely used materials. Soon after Dahlberg issued the permanent series, Kazuro Hanihara issued a set for the deciduous dentition (Fig. 4.7 illustrates the variation in shovel-shaped deciduous maxillary central incisors). These plaques are not as widely available and none is produced at present. Turner has issued a series of plaques (Fig. 4.8) that deal with the permanent dentition, and

these are available from the Department of Anthropology, Arizona State University. (Turner and co-workers [1991] published a description of many of the traits that they considered important and their presumed variations. While helpful, two-dimensional photographs are not a suitable substitute for the three-dimensional plaques.) If one is to do any comparative studies of dental morphological traits the three-dimensional plaques are invaluable and should be available for consultation. These are the only three-dimensional materials generally available to reduce interobserver error in trait determinations. However, the majority of papers using the standards do not describe which variations of a particular trait were used or they collapse observations into a few categories, which obliterates the fine differences between traits making it difficult to compare one's studies with published materials. This deficiency in comparing population traits is usually overcome by a single inves-

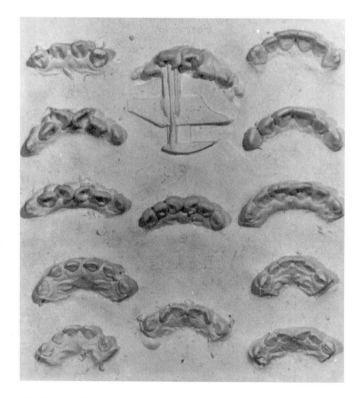

Figure 4.6   The shovel-shaped maxillary permanent incisor plaque devised by A.A. Dahlberg.

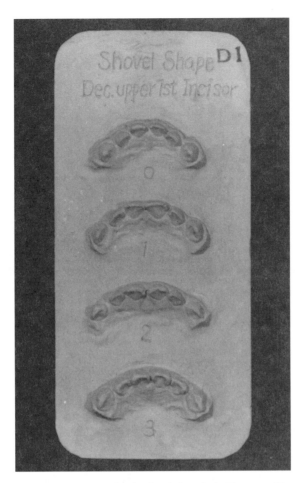

Figure 4.7   Kazuro Hanihara's plaque illustrating the shovel-shape in deciduous maxillary central incisors.

tigator doing all of the observations on all the populations to be studied; a cumbersome, time-consuming, and expensive process. Another way of attempting to overcome problems has been to use the presence or absence of a trait as the description for comparative purposes, but this method suffers from the lack of an accurate description of the threshold for the presence of the trait (Mayhall, 1999a).

An example of the problems with shifting thresholds of what constitutes presence of a trait can be see in Table 4.1. It provides data on the expression of the Carabelli's trait and is from various sources but categorizes the trait into three cells: smooth (no indication of any expression), intermediate structures (grooves,

Y, etc.), or cusps. These examples are used for the sake of simplicity; it would have been preferable to report about seven categories. These data demonstrate the pitfalls of combining data to gain better sample sizes. If we were to regard as "absent" the smooth category, we would note that there is a major difference between the Eskimos, Indians, and British whites on one hand and the American whites and Easter Islanders on the other. If, however, we decide that only the cusp expressions constitute "presence," we note that the Easter Islanders are unique. The other populations have about 20–25% of their expressions in the present or cusp category while the Easter Islanders have less than half the prevalence of the cusps. It is

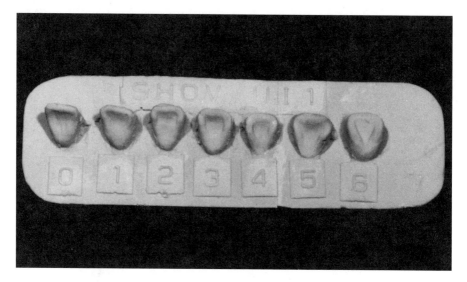

Figure 4.8   Arizona State University shovel-shaped maxillary central incisor plaque.

doubtful that the observer of these data would intuitively place Eskimos, Indians, and whites in the same general population. (The differences noted in the table may be due to differing methods of observation of the expressions.) This example illustrates the point that the use of present/absent categories without careful consideration of the subcategories included in each can produce results that are easily misinterpreted.

The use of dental morphological traits such as Carabelli's trait, shovel-shaped incisors, molar cusp and groove patterns, and protostylid continues to be valuable in general population identification and comparison. It is difficult to "learn" the variation in the dozen or so traits generally used without consulting the standards above and/or working with an experienced investigator to observe the variation of the traits and their scoring. The comparison of the results of such studies is also difficult because the traits are quasi-continuous variables but the descriptions of the traits are not. Thus, many of the usual statistical tests are not applicable to these trait comparisons.

Carabelli's trait is frequently referred to as Carabelli's cusp, although the range of expression encompasses variations from a pit to

grooves to cusps on the lingual surface of the mesiolingual cusps of maxillary molars (Dahlberg, 1951; Townsend and Brown, 1981). The plaques of Dahlberg and Turner for the permanent molars and Hanihara for the deciduous molars (Fig. 4.9) are invaluable for accurately describing the range of variation seen for this cusp. Probably more has been written about this trait than any other. While this may be admirable, it has resulted in a varied and contradictory literature about such topics as the description of the expressions of the trait, the frequency of occurrence of the trait in various populations, and the role of heredity in its expression. For instance, there has been discussion about whether the pit that is found in the same location as the cusp is a negative expression of the trait or completely unrelated to the other expressions. (This discussion is even more intense when pondering the protostylid, to be discussed later.) The mode of inheritance has continued to be enigmatic with some claiming a simple dominant-recessive mode (Tsuji, 1958), others opting for two allelic genes with no dominance (Kraus, 1951; Turner, 1967), and still others pointing out that the simple models are just that and suggesting that the inheritance may be multifactorial

(Goose and Lee, 1971; Townsend and Brown, 1981).

The interpopulation expression of the trait is confused by the lack of consistent reporting. Many of the papers report the cusp expressions only while others report the prevalence of the varying expressions of the trait. In general, one can state that the larger expressions such as a cusp or a bulge can be found in a high percentage of people of European ancestry (Dahlberg, 1963; Mayhall et al., 1982), a high frequency of the moderate to absent expressions in Asiatic groups (Mayhall, 1976; Pedersen, 1949; Tratman, 1950), and in Australian Aborigines the frequency varies in trait occurrence and expression. However, Townsend and Brown (1981) note that the frequency in Australian Aborigines is comparable to that reported for Bushman and Bantu whereas the cusp frequency is similar to South African whites and Hawaiians. (These data further confirm the difficulty of comparisons between reports by different authors and, in some cases, the same author.)

The protostylid (Fig. 4.10), or Tubercle of Bolk (DeSmet and Brabant, 1969), is found on the facial surface of the mesiofacial cusps of mandibular molars. It displays about the same range of variation in expression as does Carabelli's trait (Dahlberg, 1951, 1986). The pit expression has been difficult to characterize because it falls along the facial groove of the crown and in some populations there is another pit (foramen caecum) that may occur at the same location. Because of this confusion some studies have reported only the bulge and cusp expressions (Hanihara et al., 1975). The figures for the frequency of occurrence of this trait are variable and subject to the same problems noted for expressions of Carabelli's trait. Until 1950, the protostylid appears to have escaped scrutiny with only 10 instances being reported (Dahlberg, 1950). Dahlberg reported that 31% of Pima Indians displayed the trait, which suggested that this might be associated with populations of Asiatic origins. However, subsequent studies have been only mildly supportive of this. In 1963 Dahlberg found that 42% of Old Harbor Eskimos displayed a complete absence of the trait on the first molar while Sioux Indians and American whites showed complete absence in 20% and 26%, respectively. Hanihara and colleagues (1975) noted that people of European origin displayed none of the positive expressions while 29% of the Eskimos he studied had "swelling or tubercle type" expressions on the first molar. (Hanihara et al. [1975] indicate that the expressions on the second deciduous molar are much more prevalent.) This trait is unusual in that the cusplike expressions are more common on the third molars than on the first, a feature quite different than the pattern for most traits where the most mesial tooth in a group is the most stable and demonstrates the greatest expressions of a trait.

The most famous variation in crown morphology is the shovel-shaped incisor. This trait can be found on any of the incisors but is generally more highly expressed in the maxillary ones rather than the mandibular incisors. The range of variation (Figs. 4.6, 4.7, 4.8) is truly amazing (Aas and Risness, 1979a, 1979b; Mizoguchi, 1985). The shovel is generally seen on the lingual surface of the incisors where the lingual marginal ridges are enlarged, thus

TABLE 4.1 Carabelli's Trait Expressions

Population	Source	Smooth (%)	Intermediate (%)	Cusp (%)
Wainwright Eskimos	Hershey, 1979	8	66	26
Pima Indians	Dahlberg, 1963	17	59	24
American whites	Keene, 1968	40	38	22
British whites	Goose and Lee, 1971	21	58	19
Easter Islanders	Turner and Scott, 1977	67	23	10

After Hershey, 1979.

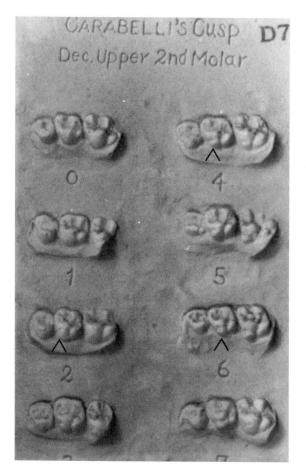

Figure 4.9   Kazuro Hanihara's plaque illustrating the range of variation of Carabelli's trait in the deciduous maxillary second molar. Arrows indicate three expressions.

forming the sides of the shovel. Additionally, there are double-shovel incisors where the facial marginal ridges are also enlarged creating two areas of depression, one on the lingual and one on the facial surface. The greatest expression is the barrel-shaped incisor, where the lingual marginal ridges are so enlarged that they contact on the lingual surface creating a depression surrounded by the incisal edge and the marginal ridges, forming a barrel as viewed from the incisal surface. These generally occur on the maxillary lateral incisors.

The determination of the amount of "shovelling" can be done visually, or several researchers (Aas, 1979, 1983; Aas and Risness, 1979a, 1979b; Hanihara et al., 1970; Kirveskari, 1974)

have successfully measured the lingual fossa using a depth gauge (see Fig. 4.6.) When the depth is measured it becomes clear that the visual determinations can be biased by the distance between the lingual marginal ridges. It may be that the depth of the fossa is approximately the same in the central and lateral incisors, but because the laterals are narrower mesiodistally the fossa appears to be deeper resulting in a higher rating than the central. The investigator must be extremely careful to use standards for visual comparisons and to continually refer to them during any data collection.

The frequency of the occurrence of shovel-shaped incisors is generally held to be greatest in populations of Asian origin and lower in other groups. Mizoguchi (1985) in a thorough analysis of the trait has presented the data from 148 studies that used visual determination of the expression and 44 that utilized depth measurements. In general, populations native to Asia and North America have the deepest lingual fossae (larger than 0.9 mm) with South American natives intermediate (0.5–1.0 mm) and Europeans the shallowest (0.3–0.7 mm). If only the larger expressions (shovel and semi-shovel) are included, then one can generalize that North and South American natives demonstrate an occurrence of 70–95%, Asians about the same as the Amerindians, Melanesians approximately 6–20%, Australian Aborigines about 60-90%, Europeans 5–50% and Teso and Bantu from Africa between 10 and 20% (Mizoguchi, 1985). In North America, Indians and Inuit (Eskimos) have about the same frequency of occurrence of the trait but the Indians have the larger expressions (Mayhall, 1972).

There has been much written about the cusp and groove patterns of the mandibular teeth. Most skeletal biologists know of the Dryo-pithecus or Y-5 pattern. What may be overlooked is that the number of cusps varies independently of the groove pattern. So when we describe the molar as having a +4 pattern we are really describing two phenomena, the number of cusps, in this case four, and the groove pattern, a plus. Without going into the detail that is available in works by Dahlberg (1945, 1951), Jorgensen (1956), or Kirveskari (1974), there are three generally recognized patterns of the primary grooves on the mandibular molars, a Y, an X, and a +. These describe the manner in which the grooves contact each other and separate the cusps from each other. The cusp number, at first glance, appears to be simple, just count the cusps. It is not quite this easy as the number refers only to the principal cusps. This means that a five-cusped tooth may have as

Figure 4.10 Plaque from A.A. Dahlberg's series illustrating protostylid variation (double arrows) on permanent and deciduous mandibular molars (left) and Carabelli's trait expression (single arrows) on permanent and deciduous maxillary molars (right).

many as seven cusps since two of them are accessory cusps. Also, a four-cusped tooth may have five or six cusps for the same reason. The accurate description of the cusp and groove patterns requires a basic knowledge of crown morphology, which can be obtained from any of the dental anatomy texts mentioned earlier or several papers that deal with the trait variability (Axelsson and Kirveskari, 1981; Dahlberg, 1951). Hillson (1986, 1996) provides an excellent discussion of the traits.

As noted above, mandibular molars can have accessory cusps, two of which—the sixth cusp and the seventh cusp—are commonly described. The seventh cusp is also known as the tuberculum intermedium, metaconulid, tuberculum accessorium mediale internum, or c7, and the sixth as the tuberculum sextum, entoconulid, tuberculum accessorium posteriore internum, or c6 (Kirveskari, 1974). The expression of these traits can be observed from the standard plaques of Turner or Hanihara. The sixth cusp and seventh cusp have been de-

scribed for such diverse groups as Canadian Eskimos (Hartweg, 1966), Skolt Lapps (Kirvekari, 1974), American whites (Dahlberg, 1945; Mayhall et al., 1982), Australian Aborigines (Hanihara, 1976), Japanese (Suzuki and Sakai, 1955), and Ainu (Hanihara et al., 1975). Generally, it has been suggested that nonwhite and large-toothed peoples show higher frequencies of cusp 6 while the frequencies for cusp 7 are mixed depending on the molar examined. It is probably fair to assume that part of the difficulty with the reported frequencies for these accessory cusps is the different definitions of what constitutes a cusp. In some studies expressions that would usually be assigned a "large" category are only reported while in others making use of the standardized plaques report a much wider range of variation.

A trait that is rarely discussed and that has no "standard" for it is the premolar occlusal tubercle found on all premolars (Fig. 4.11). This is included here because this trait is seen occasionally in native North American populations and can

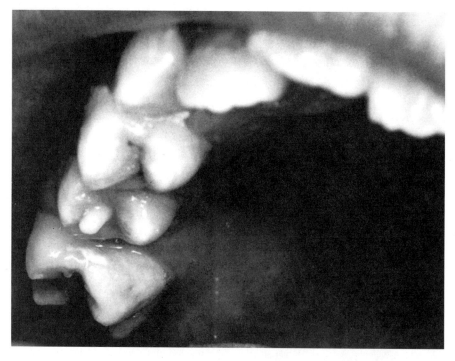

Figure 4.11 The premolar occlusal tubercle on a maxillary second premolar.

result in tooth loss and malocclusion. Kirveskari (1974) noted that this trait has been described in the literature as a dilated composite odontome (Tratman, 1949), occlusal enamel pearl (Pedersen, 1949), odontome of the axial core type (Lau, 1955), tuberculated premolar (Oehlers, 1956), premolar cone (Coon, 1962), and occlusal anomalous tubercle (Merrill, 1964). The trait has been described as having two, possibly three, types of expression. Merrill (1964) described a buccal triangular ridge type, which is confined to the lingual aspect of the buccal cusp, and a central groove type, found in the center of the occlusal surface obliterating the central groove. Kirveskari (1974) and co-workers (1972) tentatively describes another manifestation that may be related to the first two, a bulging of the lingual aspect of the buccal cusps. This is not as well defined as the buccal triangular ridge type. The range of occurrence in North American populations is between 0% in Sadlermiut Inuit (Alexandersen, 1970) and 38% in Koyukon, Alaska Indians (Mayhall, 1979).

One should be aware that all of the cusps have names based on the theories of molar evolution. Generally, these follow the names assigned by Osborn, Gregory, and Cope (see Hillson, 1986:14–16, 1996:85). For a detailed examination of molar evolution and the names assigned to the cusps, Peyer's (1968) description is one of the most complete. In the mandibular molars the mesiofacial cusp is termed the *protoconid*, the distofacial is the *hypoconid*, the distal is the *hypoconulid*, the mesiolingual is the *metaconid*, and the distolingual is the *entoconid*. In the maxillary molars the mesiofacial cusp is termed the *paracone*, the distofacial is the *metacone*, the mesiolingual is the *protocone*, and the distolingual cusp is the *hypocone*. Names ending in -cone refer to the maxillary cusps and those ending in -id refer to the mandibular cusps. It should be kept in mind that there is general agreement on the nomenclature for the mandibular molars but there are varying opinions about the correctness of the nomenclature for the maxillary ones.

The maxillary cusp number is much simpler than the mandibular. The greatest amount of the variation is found in the size of the distolingual cusp. Again the standardized plaques are useful in identifying the range of variation. The hypocone may be well developed (4), somewhat smaller (4–), vestigial (3+) or absent (3) (Dahlberg, 1945). The first molars almost always display a well-developed cusp while the second and third molars are more variable. As a broad generalization, populations of Asian origin are more conservative with larger expressions found on all molars while those of European origin tend toward a reduction in the hypocone size in the second and third molars. The hypocone tends to reduce in size as one goes distally in the molar series.

The volume of cusps has been described recently by Mayhall and Alvesalo (1991). We used the moiré technique and then determined the area within each contour line on each cusp of the maxillary molars of a Finnish population and combined these areas multiplying by the "thickness" of the contour lines to achieve an approximate volumetric determination. This has the advantage of not only demonstrating the three dimensions of a cusp but also identifying the actual growth of the cusp using its volume since growth is not two-dimensional. We found that there is little sexual dimorphism in the basal area and volume of the hypocone but the other major cusps (trigon) do show significant differences in these two determinations. We have suggested that growth of the later developing hypocone slows down in relation to the growth of the rest of the crown.

Another area of interest to dental anthropologists is the artificial deformation of teeth, either intentional (Aquirre, 1963; Fastlicht, 1976; Migraine, 1987; Romero, 1958; Singer, 1953) or unintentional, (Brown and Molnar, 1990; Patterson, 1984; Schulz, 1977), which can provide clues to cultural practices and relationships. Romero's classic monograph includes illustrations helpful for the identification of the various alterations of tooth form he found in North America.

Finally, there is odontoglyphics, a neglected area of study. Zubov (1977) studied the groove patterns on molars and noted that they were as individualistic as dermatoglyphics. These groove patterns are important because, as Zubov notes, they are a result of the calcification waves meeting during ontogenesis of the teeth, a phenomenon that is genetically determined. He also points out that most of the furrows on the occlusal surface of the teeth are set prior to the formation of the enamel cap. Another advantage of this system is the usefulness of the groove patterns when the cusps have been worn away, although many of the superficial furrows may also be lost to investigation. Zubov proposed several "Laws and Principles of Odontoglyphics," which divided the furrows into "intertubercular furrows" (those that completely isolate cusps and are deep) and "tubercular furrows" (those passing over cusps and providing incomplete differentiation of the elements). The description of the patterns can be converted into symbols based on the intersections of the furrows (Fig. 4.12). There are varying patterns in different populations and ethnic groups but little has been published in English. This technique has rarely been used outside the Soviet Union, but it appears to hold promise for individual identification (Zubov and Nikityuk, 1974, 1978) since all skeletal biologists know the teeth are the part of the body that is usually best preserved.

To this point we have concentrated exclusively on the crown of the tooth. The roots may be the only portion of the tooth remaining in a jaw postmortem. Even when the roots are not present it is possible to determine the number of roots present and their position by examining the alveolus that may remain after recent ante- or postmortem loss. It may be possible to determine how long before death a tooth was lost by the amount of "new" bone replacing the now empty alveolus. Many of the oral anatomy textbooks give the impression that the number of roots and their morphology is immutable. This is not the case (Alexandersen and Carlsen, 1998). While most of the anterior teeth have a single root, the mandibular canines occasionally have two roots, a buccal one and a lingual one. The maxillary first premolars are usually described as having two roots, but observers have noted that about 40% of these teeth have a single root. There are some upper first premolars that have three roots, two buccal roots and a single lingual one. On the other hand, the maxillary second premolar is usually described as having a single root, but there are many with two roots. This is mentioned here because in attempting to identify teeth it is important to remember that crowns are the better part of the tooth to use for drawing a conclusion. The crowns of teeth appear to be less affected by their surroundings as they develop than the roots. Roots are commonly seen with dilacerations (sharp bends in the root), blunted apices, and fractures probably caused by trauma.

The mandibular premolars also show variation in their root number. Varrela (1995) studied the root structure of 45,X females and

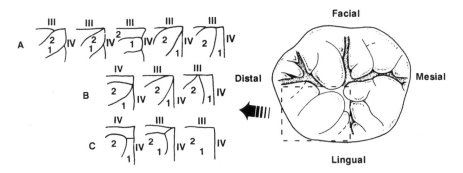

Figure 4.12 Possible positions of furrows 1 and 2 on the entoconid as illustrated by Zubov. See Zubov (1977) for a detailed explanation.

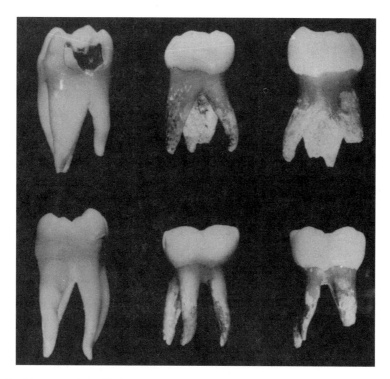

Figure 4.13 Three-rooted mandibular permanent first and deciduous second molars. In each case the "extra" root appears to be the distolingual one.

found that a significant number of these teeth had two roots. Thirty-two percent of the 45,X females had mandibular second premolars with two roots while 28% of them had first premolars showing the same condition. Overall, 46% of the females studied had at least one two-rooted mandibular premolar. These figures contrast with only 2–3% of the female control sample's two-rooted first premolar and an absence of the two roots in the second premolar.

The molars demonstrate a wide range of variation in roots and structure. Even the most stable of the molars, the mandibular permanent first molar and the deciduous second molar, sometimes have three roots instead of the usual two (Mayhall, 1972, 1981; Swindler et al., 1997; Tratman, 1938). In this case there is a mesial root and two distal roots (Fig. 4.13). One should be guarded in determining the occurrence of this trait in skeletal material. The three roots of the molar may provide the tooth with a better chance of remaining in the oral

cavity than would a two-rooted one. Thus, it is possible that there might be an unusually high number of these teeth because the two-rooted ones have been exfoliated antemortem, and the alveolus may have healed so that it is impossible to tell the number of roots that were present. Swindler and his co-workers (1998) have compiled data from other studies and present a range of frequencies from 3.1% (Melanesians) to 28.8% in their study of precontact Easter Islanders. The figure for North American natives is given as 8.2%. European populations have the lowest frequency—less than 1% (Turner and Benjamin, 1989). See Tasa (1998) for a comprehensive survey of the studies of three-rooted mandibular premolars.

Multiple roots occur frequently in the third molars. It is impossible to make a definitive statement about the "correct" number of roots for these teeth. The range is from one root, usually a fusion of the "normal" number of roots, to as many as five or six. Both maxillary and mandibular third molars will demonstrate wild variations in root number.

This section on morphology has been brief and has discussed only some of the major traits. It is not unusual when conducting a study to find that a sample contains other traits or expressions of the above traits that are not identified by any of the usual works or standards. (This is the chance to have a cusp or a pit named after you!) As in the section on size of the teeth, the same general questions can be asked about the usefulness of these traits. In the case of the few traits discussed above, there has been a broad description of the range of expressions of the traits and their frequency of occurrence in different populations. These data suggest that there is a genetic determination for the traits, but we do not understand the complex interaction between the environment and heredity in producing the expressions that can be observed. Berry (1976) has cautioned that, before morphological traits are used for biological distance studies, it is necessary to ascertain how environmental factors, such as diet, affect their expression. If there are effects from the interaction of pathological conditions and the traits, these might render large numbers of teeth unable to be scored. This last point is important because it has been shown that the expression of a trait can have an effect on the amount of pathology seen in an individual or a population (Mayhall, 1972). Three examples of this relationship can be observed: in shovel-shaped incisors, where the junction of the increased ridges on the lingual surface of the incisor may meet near the cingulum and form a deep pit allowing for food entrapment and, subsequently, dental caries (Mayhall, 1972); the buccal pits on molars of some Asiatic groups have no enamel lining in them and are regularly seen with early caries (Mayhall, 1972; Pedersen, 1949); and in enamel projections into the bifurcations of roots, periodontal pockets often occur (Masters and Hoskins, 1964). Pathological conditions such as dental caries or periodontal disease may obliterate the trait or cause a tooth to be lost. Consequently, morphological traits can affect the probability of tooth loss thus skewing the results of morphological studies.

The sexual dimorphism of dental traits has been reported for most of the foregoing traits but these have been inconclusive. Canadian Inuit groups show no sexual dimorphism (Mayhall, 1976); there is no sexual difference in Japanese shovel-shaping but there are differences in some of the other traits above (Mizoguchi, 1985); and Lapps (Kirveskari, 1974) demonstrate an inconsistent pattern with no dimorphism for shoveling or protostylid but moderate dimorphism for Carabelli's and cusps 6 and 7. North American whites (Mayhall et al., 1982) revealed no dimorphic expressions. Harris (1980) in a study of 38 samples of living populations found that many groups of females possess significantly higher frequencies of shoveling on maxillary central incisors than do males. American blacks did not display a sex difference in the frequency of shoveling. This varying amount of sexual dimorphism poses a problem for those who are examining unattributed teeth. However, the literature is full of studies that have not taken sex into consideration. The differences in expression and prevalence are small, even in those populations that are dimorphic, and it is generally permissible to combine the sexes if it is not possible to report them separately.

The mode of inheritance of dental morphological traits is not well understood (Mayhall, 1999b). Kirveskari and Alvesalo (1982) have examined the dental morphology of 45,X females and compared it with their normal relatives and the general population. The reduced expressions of nonmetric dental traits in this study suggests that there is a size-independent reduction in tooth crowns that is associated with the loss of an X chromosome. There is some indication that the reductions seen in Turner syndrome patients are not as uniform as first suspected (Mayhall and Alvesalo, 1992). Sofaer (1970) noted that the Hardy-Weinberg law has been applied to population data and the claims by these analyses that various morphologic characters were controlled by single autosomal genes were flawed. He concluded by emphasizing that "the nature of the genetic control can only be derived from a study of related individuals" (Sofaer, 1970:1508).

Alvesalo (1997) has summarized our present knowledge of the expression of sexual dimorphism when he notes that the differences result from the differential effects of the X and Y chromosomes on dental growth. Mayhall and Alvesalo (1992) demonstrated that there were differences in cusp shape between the sexes. Many of the differences seen in tooth shape and size are the result of sexual dimorphism in the thicknesses of enamel and dentin. Alvesalo and his colleagues have published many studies demonstrating the effects of the sex chromosomes on crown size and shape. (See Alvesalo, 1997, for a summary.) Molecular studies have shown that the loci for human amelogenin, the main protein component of the organic matrix in enamel, are on both the X and Y chromosomes although the amino acid sequences of the genes on the X and Y chromosomes appear to differ (Lau et al., 1989; Nakahori et al., 1991; Salido et al., 1992).

Asymmetry of morphological traits on the antimeres has historically been assumed to be negligible. Most studies that have examined only one side of the jaw have used the other side if a particular trait could not be scored on the side under study. The reasoning was that there were few examples contradicting the assumption of antimere symmetry and, thus, sample size could be increased. But as early as 1954, Meredith and Hixon stressed that there was a noticeable difference in the expression of Carabelli's trait between sides of the maxilla. Biggerstaff (1973) and Harris (1977) reported relatively high levels of asymmetry for traits as well. Townsend and Brown (1980, 1981) in their study of Australian Aboriginals found almost 10% asymmetry in the deciduous second molar and about 9% asymmetry in the first molar for Carabelli's trait. The comparisons in different groups of the amount of dental asymmetry in nonmetric traits are more recent phenomena (Baume and Crawford, 1980; Perzigian, 1977). If these are to be reported, one must be careful to: (1) specify how the asymmetry was scored, (2) insure that the sample

sizes are adequate (Garn et al., 1979; Smith et al., 1982), (3) take into account population differences in overall trait presence, and (4) take into account the duration of the development of the trait (Saunders and Mayhall, 1982).

Investigation of the dental morphology literature brings the realization that some groups have sets of traits that appear to be combined into aggregations—the dental complexes. These aggregations of traits and their varying expressions and occurrences were first proposed by Hanihara (1966, 1967, 1968), who identified the Mongoloid dental complex. Sofaer and his co-workers (1972) noted that the value of phylogenetic comparisons based on tooth morphology depends on a knowledge of the extent to which the observed morphological variation is genetic in origin, and this can be derived only from the analysis of family data. Lasker and Lee already had anticipated the use of the dental complexes and the forensic value of teeth when they commented, "'Races' are abstractions whereas racial traits actually occur in varying frequencies among members of smaller breeding populations. . . . local evolution, the widening circles of intermarriage, and the large measure of inter-individual variability in any group will probably continue to restrict the usefulness for forensic purposes of racial criteria of the teeth." (1957:417). There has been extensive use of the trait complexes recently (Irish, 1997; Turner, 1987, 1990) but Mayhall (1999a) has questioned the value of the use of the traits when the traits' expressions and frequencies are only reported as present or absent.

ORAL PATHOLOGY RELATED TO SIZE AND SHAPE

The pathological condition of the teeth and maxillae has been of value to the skeletal biologist and this is directly related to the gathering of data about the morphology and size of the teeth and the diet and culture of the individuals being studied. The reader should refer to any of the comprehensive oral pathology texts or the more specialized texts on particular oral conditions to discover the wide variety of conditions and techniques that are of value to the study of the teeth from archaeological sites. One work that has a detailed description of pathological conditions in skeletal materials and the problems of their accurate description is Patterson's study of the pre-Iroquois and Iroquois populations of Ontario (1984). Another volume covering some of these topics is Kelley and Larsen (1991). Hillson, Chapter 9, deals with dental pathology and should be the starting point for any study of the relationships of dental morphology and dental pathology.

Dental Caries

The most common and obvious pathological condition that has been studied in skeletal series is dental caries (a singular and plural form). Dental caries can be characterized as the number of teeth decayed, missing, or filled per individual, although this is a simplistic descriptor in studies of skeletal materials. This is an important descriptive method if the study is to compare skeletal samples with living populations. However, this is rarely possible because seldom are all of the teeth recovered in archaeological contexts. Any study should indicate the location on the tooth surface of the lesion. The location of the lesion may vary by population and age (Keene and Keene, 1985; Parfitt, 1955; Zadik, 1976). Root caries is more prevalent in older individuals (Keene, 1986; Nikiforuk, 1985), and the modern North American Indian populations apparently have fewer interproximal lesions. They may, however, demonstrate more occlusal lesions because of their complex crown morphology (Mayhall, 1972; Pedersen, 1949). The skeletal biologist who wants in depth knowledge of all aspects of dental caries is referred to the volumes by Nikiforuk (1985).

Periodontal Disease

Periodontal disease(s) is an area of controversy when we examine skeletal material (Alexandersen, 1967). The most benign form of periodontal disease is gingivitis, which is an inflammation of the gingiva with no obvious effects on the underlying bone. On the other hand, there are generalized periodontal diseases that may be observed on the alveolar bone of the maxillae. One of the possible signs of periodontal disease is a blunting of the alveolar crest bone. The crest appears porous and notched on the facial and lingual portions. This is probably due to inflammatory processes. It is problematic whether horizontal bone loss is pathological or physiological. There is evidence that this bone loss is associated with attrition, which may be considered physiological, and age related. It is difficult to attribute generalized bone loss to a pathological condition or directly to attrition (Barker, 1975).

This very brief summary of two major pathological conditions and the chapter by Hillson (this volume) should suggest to the skeletal biologist that oral pathological conditions may significantly influence the results of any dental morphological study. As was mentioned earlier, there is a close relationship between tooth size, discrete traits, and pathology, and this relationship must be taken into consideration in any study.

Tooth Wear (Attrition and Abrasion)

One further condition that greatly affects tooth size and morphology is tooth wear. It seems that in populations that exhibit wear, that wear is the primary reason for the elimination of teeth from analyses. Sixth and seventh cusps, shovel-shaping, and groove patterns may be impossible to record accurately because of wear. The wear may be pathological or, more commonly, physiological. In the first category might be included bruxism, the grinding of the teeth sometimes due to stress or abrasion, or the nonmasticatory wearing of the teeth. The latter can be produced by activities such as habitually gripping a smoking pipe with the teeth, use of devices such as toothbrushes and floss for cleaning the teeth, and holding any external materials in the teeth (dog traces, grasses used in basketry, etc.). The characterization of tooth wear has been extensively documented (Miles, 1963; Molnar, 1971; Molnar et al., 1983; Murphy, 1959; Richards and Brown, 1981; Tomenchuk and Mayhall, 1979; Walker et al., 1991) and there are many techniques proposed for the characterization of it. A major problem that you may encounter is that none of the techniques is appropriate for your study group because the types and patterns of wear do not fit any of the models already published. In these cases you may have to devise another method that will adequately describe your observations. This may further confuse your readers and disallow any comparisons with other studies. If possible, the use of quantitative descriptions is preferable to purely qualitative ones. Walker and co-workers (1991) have proposed methods that are accurate and comprehensive and Mayhall and Kageyama (1997) have used a three-dimensional measurement system to detail the loss of tooth substance over time.

CONSISTENT AND APPROPRIATE MORPHOLOGICAL OBSERVATIONS

As noted at the beginning of this chapter, some of the major problems confronting dental anthropologists are ones of consistency in observation. The foregoing will, hopefully, allow the skeletal biologist to use the techniques described to further identify the biological and cultural background of skeletal material. While this chapter has taken a conservative approach to the techniques, the reader can be assured that the methods here and in the other chapters of this volume are easily achievable and are generally accepted. The biologist must be careful to use methods that are, as much as possible, comparable throughout the field of dental morphology. As with any study the researcher must carefully plot the methods to be utilized for a particular study. It is incumbent on all of us to understand the deficiencies of a particular technique as well as its strengths before embarking on a particular study; the perfect technique has yet to appear. The appropriate technique for one study may not work for an-

other. Carefully assess your goals for your research and then find the techniques that will best help you to achieve them. The techniques described in this chapter may allow you to provide comparable, accurate results that others can utilize in their studies.

REFERENCES

Aas IH. 1979. The depth of the lingual fossa in permanent maxillary incisors of Norwegian Lapps. Amer J Phys Anthropol 51:417–420.

Aas IH. 1983. Variability of a dental morphological trait. Acta Odontol Scand 41:257–263.

Aas IH, Risness S. 1979a. The depth of the lingual fossa in permanent incisors of Norwegians: I. Method of measurement, statistical distribution and sex dimorphism. Amer J Phys Anthropol 50:335–340.

Aas IH, Risness S. 1979b. The depth of the lingual fossa in permanent incisors of Norwegians: II. Differences between central and lateral incisors, correlations, side asymmetry and variability. Amer J Phys Anthropol 50:341–347.

Aquirre OC. 1963. Odontologia y Mutilaciones Dentarias Mayas. Guatemala: Editorial Universitaria San Carlos. 255 pp. (in Spanish).

Alexandersen V. 1967. The pathology of the jaws and the temporomandibular joint. In: Brothwell D, Sandison AT, editors. Diseases in Antiquity. Springfield, Ill.: Charles C. Thomas. pp. 551–595.

Alexandersen V. 1970. Tandmorfologisk variation hos Eskimoer og andre Mongoloide populationer. Tandlaegebladet 74:587–602. (in Danish).

Alexandersen V, Carlsen O. 1998. Supernumerary roots of mandibular molar teeth. In: Lukacs JR, editor. Human Dental Development, Morphology, and Pathology. Eugene: Univ. Oregon pp. 201–214. Anthropol Pap. 54.

Alt KW, Rösing FW, Teschler-Nicola M, editors. 1998. Dental Anthropology: Fundamentals, Limits, and Prospects. New York: Springer-Wein. 564 pp.

Alvesalo L. 1971. The influence of the sex-chromosome genes on tooth size. Proc Finn Dent Soc 67:3–54.

Alvesalo L. 1985. Dental growth in 47,XXY males and in conditions with other sex-chromosome anomalies. In: Sandberg AA, editor. The Y

Chromosome. Part B: Clinical Aspects of Y Chromosome Abnormalities. New York: Liss. pp. 227–300.

Alvesalo L. 1997. Sex chromosomes and human growth: a dental approach. Hum Genet 101:1–5.

Alvesalo L, Portin P. 1980. 47,XXY males: sex chromosomes and tooth size. Am J Hum Genet 32:955–959.

Alvesalo L, Varrela J. 1979. Permanent tooth sizes in 46,XY females. Am J Hum Genet 32:736–742.

Axelsson G, Kirveskari P. 1981. Cusp number and groove pattern of lower molars in Icelanders. Acta Odontol Scand 39:361–366.

Barker BCW. 1975. Periodontal disease and tooth dislocation in aboriginal remains from Lake Nitchie N.S.W., West Point Tasmania and Limestone Creek Victoria. Arch Phys Anthropol Oceania 10:185–217.

Baume RM, Crawford MH.1980. Discrete dental trait asymmetry in Mexican and Belizean groups. Amer J Phys Anthropol 52:315–321.

Berry AC. 1976. The anthropological value of minor variants of the dental crown. Amer J Phys Anthropol 45:257–268.

Biggerstaff RH. 1970. A Quantitative and Qualitative Study of the Post-Canine Dentition of Twins. Ann Arbor: University Microfilms. 292 pp.

Biggerstaff RH. 1973. Heritability of the Carabelli cusp in twins. J Dent Res 52:40–44.

Brabant H. 1973. Etude odontologique des restes humains decouverts dans la necropole Gallo-Romaine et Merovingienne de Dieue Meuse en France. Bull Group Int Rech Sci Stomatol Odontol 16:239–261. (in French).

Brace CL, Smith SL, Hunt KD. 1991. What big teeth you had grandma! Human tooth size, past and present. In: Kelley MA, Larsen CS, editors. Advances in Dental Anthropology. New York: Wiley-Liss. pp. 33–57.

Brook A, Smith R, Elcock C, Al-Sharood M, Shah A, Karmo M. 1999. The measurement of tooth morphology: development and validation of a new image analysis system. In: Mayhall JT, Heikkinen T, editors. Dental Morphology 1998. Oulu, Finland: 11th International Symposium on Dental Morphology. pp. 380-387.

Brothwell DR, editor. 1963. Dental Anthropology. New York: Pergamon, 288 pp.

Brown T, Margetts B, Townsend GC. 1980. Comparison of mesiodistal crown diameters of the deciduous and permanent teeth in Australian Aboriginals. Aust Dent J 25:28–33.

Brown T, Molnar S. 1990. Interproximal grooving and task activity in Australia. Amer J Phys Anthropol 81:545–554.

Buschang PH, Demirjian A, Cadotte L. 1988. Permanent mesiodistal tooth size of French-Canadians. J Can Dent Assoc 54:441–444.

Butler PM, Joysey KA, editors. 1978. Development, Function and Evolution of Teeth. London: Academic Press. 523 pp.

Calcagno JM, Gibson KR. 1991. Selective compromise: evolutionary trends and mechanisms in hominid tooth size. In: Kelley MA, Larsen CS, editors. Advances in Dental Anthropology. New York: Wiley-Liss.pp. 59–76.

Campbell TD. 1925. Dentition and Palate of the Australian Aboriginal. Adelaide: Hassell Press. 123 pp.

Coon CS. 1962. The Origin of the Races. New York: Knopf. 724 pp.

Dahlberg AA. 1945. The changing dentition of man. J Amer Dent Assoc 32:676–690.

Dahlberg AA. 1950. The evolutionary significance of the protostylid. Amer J Phys Anthropol 8:15–25.

Dahlberg AA. 1951. The dentition of the American Indian. In: Laughlin WS, editor. Papers on the Physical Anthropology of the American Indian. New York: Viking Fund. pp. 138–176.

Dahlberg AA. 1958. Rotated maxillary central incisors among various tribes of American Indians. J Jap Orthod Soc 17:157–169. (in Japanese).

Dahlberg AA. 1963. Analysis of the American Indian dentition. In: Brothwell DR, editor. Dental Anthropology. New York: Pergamon. pp. 149–177.

Dahlberg AA. 1965. Geographic distribution and origin of dentitions. Intl Dent J 15:42–49.

Dahlberg AA, editor. 1971. Dental Morphology and Evolution. Chicago: Univ. of Chicago, 350 pp.

Dahlberg AA. 1986. Ontogeny and dental genetics in forensic problems. Forensic Sci Int 30: 163–176.

Dahlberg AA. 1990. The face and dentition of Australasian population: preface and overview. Am J Phys Anthropol 82:245–246.

Dahlberg AA, Graber TM, editors. 1977. Orofacial Growth and Development. The Hague: Mouton. 354 pp.

DeSmet R, Brabant H. 1969. Observations anthropologiques sur la denture des Indiens Javagos. Bull Soc Roy Belge Anthropol Prehist 80:97–123. (in French).

De Vito CLH, Saunders SR. 1990. A discriminant function analysis of deciduous teeth to determine sex. J Forensic Sci 35:845–858.

Fastlicht S. 1976. Tooth Mutilations and Dentistry in Pre-Columbian Mexico. Berlin: Quintessence. 164 pp.

Garn SM, Cole PE, Smith BH. 1979. The effect of sample size on crown size asymmetry. J Dent Res 58:2012.

Garn SM, Lewis AB, Kerewsky R. 1965. X-linked inheritance of tooth size. J Dent Res 44:439–441.

Garn SM, Lewis AB, Walenga AJ. 1968. Crown-size profile pattern comparisons of 14 human populations. Arch Oral Biol 13:1235–1242.

Goose DH. 1963. Dental measurement: an assessment of its value in anthropological studies. In: Brothwell DR, editor. Dental Anthropology. New York: Pergamon. pp. 125–148.

Goose DH, Lee GTR. 1971. The mode of inheritance of Carabelli's trait. Hum Biol 43:64–69.

Hanihara K. 1966. Mongoloid dental complex in the deciduous dentition. J Anthropol Soc Japan 74:61–72.

Hanihara K. 1967. Racial characteristics in the dentition. J Dent Res 46:923–926.

Hanihara K. 1968. Mongoloid dental complex in the permanent dentition. Tokyo and Kyoto: Proceedings of the VIIIth International Congress of Anthropological and Ethnological Sciences. pp. 298–300.

Hanihara K. 1976. Statistical and comparative studies of the Australian Aboriginal dentition. Univ Mus, Univ Tokyo Bull 11:1–57.

Hanihara K. 1977. Distances between Australian Aborigines and certain other populations based on dental measurements. J Hum Evol 6:403–418.

Hanihara K, Matsuda T, Tanaka T, Tamada M. 1975. Comparative studies of the dentition. In: Watanabe S, Kondo S, Matsunaga E, editors. Anthropological and Genetic Studies on the Japanese Part III. Anthropological and Genetic Studies of the Ainu. Tokyo: Univ. of Tokyo. pp. 256–264.

Hanihara K, Tamada M, Tanaka T. 1970. Quantitative analysis of the hypocone in the human upper molars. J Anthropol Soc Nippon 78: 200–207.

Hanihara K, Tanaka T, Tamada M. 1970. Quantitative analysis of the shovel-shaped character in the incisors. J Anthropol Soc Nippon 78:90–98.

Hanihara K, Ueda H. 1979. Crown diameters in Japanese-American F1 hybrids. Ossa 6:105–114.

Hanihara T. 1989. Comparative studies of geographically isolated populations in Japan based on dental measurements. J Anthropol Soc Nippon 97:95–107.

Harris EF. 1977. Anthropologic and Genetic Aspects of the Dental Morphology of Solomon Islanders, Melanesia. Ann Arbor: University Microfilms. 465 pp.

Harris EF. 1980. Sex differences in lingual marginal ridging on the human maxillary central incisor. Amer J Phys Anthropol 52:541–548.

Hartweg R. 1966. La dentition des Esqimaux de Ungava et des Indiens Wabemakustewatsh de la cote Orientale de la Baie Hudson. Univ. of Laval Centre d'Etudes Nordiques Travaux Divers. 13:1–156. (in French).

Henderson AM, Greene DL. 1975. Dental field theory: an application to primate evolution. J Dent Res 54:344–350.

Hershey SE. 1979. Morphology of the Wainwright Eskimo dentition: Carabelli's structures. Ossa 6:115–124.

Hillson S. 1986. Teeth. Cambridge: Cambridge Univ. Press. 376 pp.

Hillson S. 1996. Dental Anthropology. Cambridge: Cambridge Univ Press. 373 pp.

Hinton RJ, Smith MO, Smith FH. 1980. Tooth size changes in prehistoric Tennessee Indians. Hum Biol 52:229–242.

Irish JD. 1997. Characteristic high- and low-frequency dental traits in sub-Saharan African populations. Amer J Phys Anthropol 102:455–467.

Jacobson A. 1982. The Dentition of the South African Negro. Birmingham: Alexander Jacobson. 365 pp.

Jordan RE, Abrams L. 1992. Kraus' Dental Anatomy and Occlusion. St. Louis: Mosby Yearbook. 371 p.

Jorgensen KD. 1956. The deciduous dentition: a descriptive and comparative anatomical study. Acta Odontol Scand 14(suppl. 20):1–202.

Kageyama I, Mayhall JT, Townsend G. 1999. Three-dimensional analysis of deciduous and permanent molars in Australian Aborigines. Perspec Hum Biol 4(3):103–108.

Kajava Y. 1912. Die zahne der Lappen. Suomen Toimistuksia 10:1–64, as cited by Pedersen, 1949.

Kamura H, Soejima W, Fukuchi Y, Goto M, Katsuki T. 1984. The racial differences between the faces of Japanese and Taiwanese females using moire-topography. Proc 10th Ann Meeting Jap Soc Moiré Contourography, Tokyo pp. 11–12. (in Japanese).

Kanazawa E. 1980. Principal component analysis of three-dimensional coordinates of landmarks on the Japanese skull. J Anthropol Soc Nippon 88:209–228. (in Japanese).

Kanazawa E, Sekikawa M, Ozaki T. 1983. Three-dimensional measurements of the occlusal surface of upper first molars in a modern Japanese population. Acta Anat 116:90–96.

Kanazawa E, Sekikawa M, Ozaki T. 1984. Three-dimensional measurements of the occlusal surfaces of upper molars in a Dutch population. J Dent Res 63:1298–1301.

Kanazawa E, Morris DH, Sekikawa M , Ozaki T. 1988. Comparative study of the upper molar occlusal table morphology among seven human populations. Amer J Phys Anthropol 77: 271–278.

Kari M, Alvesalo L, Manninen K. 1980. Sizes of deciduous teeth in 45,X females. J Dent Res 59:1382–1385.

Keene HJ. 1968. The relationship of the Carabelli's trait and the size, number, and morphology of the maxillary molars. Arch Oral Biol 13:1023–1025.

Keene HJ. 1986. Dental caries prevalence in early Polynesians from the Hawaiian islands. J Dent Res 65:935–938.

Keene HJ, Keene AJ. 1985. Dental caries prevalence in early Hawaiian children. Pediatr Dent 7: 271–277.

Kelley MA, Larsen CS, editors. 1991. Advances in Dental Anthropology. New York: Wiley-Liss. 389 pp.

Kirveskari P. 1974. Morphological traits in the permanent dentition of living Skolt Lapps. Proc Finn Dent Soc 70 (suppl.) II:1–90.

Kirveskari P, Alvesalo L. 1981. Shovel shape of maxillary incisors in 47,XYY males. Proc Finn Dent Soc 77:79–81.

Kirveskari P, Alvesalo L. 1982. Dental morphology in Turner's syndrome 45,X females. In: Kurtén B, editor. Teeth: Form, Function and Evolution. New York: Columbia Univ. pp. 298–303.

Kirveskari P, Hedegard B, Dahlberg AA. 1972. Bulging of the lingual aspects of buccal cusps in posterior teeth of Skolt Lapps from Northern Finland. J Dent Res 51:1513.

Kraus BS. 1951. Carabelli's anomaly of the maxillary molar teeth. J Hum Biol 3:348–355.

Kraus BS, Jordan RE, Abrams L. 1969. Dental Anatomy and Occlusion. Baltimore: Williams and Wilkins. 317 pp.

Kurtén B. 1982. Teeth: Form, Function and Evolution. New York: Columbia Univ. 393 pp.

Lambrechts P, Vanherle G, Vuysteke M, Davidson CL. 1984. Quantitative evaluation of the wear resistance of posterior dental restorations: a new three-dimensional measuring technique. J Dent 12:252–267.

Lasker GW, Lee MMC. 1957. Racial traits in the human teeth. J Forensic Sci 2:401–419.

Lau EC, Mohandas TK, Shapiro U, Slavkin HC, Snead ML. 1989 Human and mouse amelogenin gene loci are on the sex chromosomes. Genomics 4:162–168.

Lau TC. 1955. Odontomes of the axial core type. Br Dent J 99:219–225.

Lavelle CLB. 1970. Comparison of the deciduous teeth between caucasoid, negroid, and mongoloid population samples. Dent Pract 21:121–124.

Lavelle CLB. 1971. Mandibular molar tooth dimensions in different human racial groups. Bull Group Int Rech Sci Stomatol Odontal 14: 273–289.

Lukacs JR. 1984. Cultural variation and the evolution of dental reduction: an interpretation of the evidence from south Asia. In: Basu A, Malhotra KC, editors. Human Genetics and Adaptation, Vol. 2. Delhi: Indian Statistical Institute. pp. 252–269.

Lukacs JR. 1988. Dental morphology and odontometrics of early agriculturalists from neolithic Mehrgarth, Pakistan. In: Russell DE, Santoro J-P, Sigogneau-Russell D, editors. Teeth Revisited: Proceedings of the VIIth International Symposium on Dental Morphology. Mem Mus Nat Hist Nat, Paris, ser C 53:285–303.

Lukacs JR, editor. 1998. Human Dental Development, Morphology and Pathology. Eugene: Univ. Oregon Anthropol Pap. No. 54. 447 pp.

Lysell L, Myrberg N. 1982. Mesiodistal tooth size in the deciduous and permanent dentitions. Eur J Orthod 4:113–122.

Masters DH, Hoskins SW. 1964. Projection of cervical enamel into molar furcations. J Periodontal 35:49–53.

Mayhall JT. 1972. Dental morphology of Indians and Eskimos: its relationship to the prevention and treatment of caries. J Can Dent Assoc 38:152–154.

Mayhall JT. 1976. The Morphology of the Permanent Dentition of Prehistoric and Modern Central Arctic Eskimoid Peoples: A Study of Their Biological Relationships. Unpub Ph.D. thesis, Univ of Chicago. 175 pp.

Mayhall JT. 1977. Cultural and environmental influences on the Eskimo dentition. In: Dahlberg AA, Graber TM, editors. Orofacial Growth and Development. The Hague: Mouton. pp. 216–227.

Mayhall JT. 1979. The biological relationship of Thule culture and Inuit populations: an odontological investigation. In: McCartney AP, editor. Thule Eskimo Culture: An Anthropological Retrospective. Archaeol Surv Can 88:448–473.

Mayhall JT. 1981. Three-rooted deciduous mandibular second molars. J Can Dent Assoc 47: 319–321.

Mayhall JT. 1999a. Dichotomy in human dental morphology: a plea for complexity. In: Mayhall JT, Heikkinen T, editors. Dental Morphology 1998. Oulu: Oulu University Press. pp. 43–47.

Mayhall JT. 1999b. The dental complex: A morphological smokescreen or a compass? Perspec Hum Biol 4(3):1–7.

Mayhall JT, Alvesalo L. 1991. Sexual dimorphism in the three-dimensional determinations of the maxillary first molar: cusp height, area, volume and position. In: Smith P, Tchernov E, editors. Structure Function and Evolution of Teeth. London: Freund Publishing House. pp. 425–436.

Mayhall JT, Alvesalo L. 1992. Dental morphology of 45,XO human females: molar cusp area, volume, shape and linear measurements. Arch Oral Biol 37:1039–1043.

Mayhall JT, Alvesalo J, Townsend G. 1991. Tooth crown size in 46,X,iXq human females. Arch Oral Biol 36:411–414.

Mayhall JT, Alvesalo L, Townsend G. 1998. Dental dimensions of 47,XYY males: molar cusp area, volume, shape, and linear dimensions. In: Lukacs JR, editor. Human Dental Development, Morphology, and Pathology. Eugene: Univ. Oregon Anthropol Pap. 54:29–39.

Mayhall JT, Heikkinen editors. 1999. Dental Morphology 1998. Oulu: Oulu University Press. 492 pp.

Mayhall JT, Kageyama I. 1997. A new three-dimensional method for determining tooth wear. Am J Phys Anthropol 103:463–469.

Mayhall JT, Kanazawa E. 1989. Three-dimensional analysis of the maxillary first molar crowns of Canadian Inuit. Amer J Phys Anthropol 78: 73–78.

Mayhall JT, Karp SA. 1983. Size and morphology of the permanent dentition of the Waorani Indians of Ecuador. Can Rev Phys Anthropol 3:55–67.

Mayhall JT, Saunders SR. 1985. Dimensional and discrete dental trait asymmetry relationships. Amer J Phys Anthropol 69:403–411.

Mayhall JT, Saunders SR, Belier PL. 1982. The dental morphology of North American whites: a reappraisal. In: Kurtén B, editor. Teeth: Form, Function and Evolution. New York: Columbia Univ. pp. 245–258.

McKeown M. 1981. A method of analyzing the form of individual human teeth. J Can Dent Assn 47:534–537.

Meredith HV, Hixon EH. 1954. Frequency, size, and bilateralism of Carabelli's tubercle. J Dent Res 33:435–440.

Merrill RG. 1964. Occlusal anomalous tubercles on premolars of Alaskan Eskimos and Indians. Oral Surg 17:484–496.

Middleton Shaw JC. 1931. The Teeth, the Bony Palate and the Mandible in Bantu Races of South Africa. London: John Bale & Sons. 134 pp.

Migraine D. 1987. Les mutilations dentaires dans les civilisations exotiques et leur signification. J Can Dent Assoc 53:831–834. (in French).

Miles AEW. 1963. Dentition in the assessment of individual age in skeletal material. In: Brothwell DR, editor. Dental Anthropology. London: Pergamon. pp. 191–209.

Mizoguchi Y. 1985. Shovelling: a statistical analysis of its morphology. Univ. Mus, Univ. Tokyo Bull 26:1–176.

Mizoguchi Y. 1988. Tooth crown diameters of the permanent teeth of the Epi-Jomon people from the Usu-10 and other sites in the Seaside region of Funkawan Bay, Hokkaido, Japan. Mem Nat Sci Mus 21:211–220. (in Japanese).

Moggi-Cecchi J, editor. 1995. Aspects of Dental Biology: Palaeontology, Anthropology and Evolution. Florence: International Institute for the Study of Man. 460 pp.

Molnar S. 1971. Human tooth wear, tooth function and cultural variability. Am J Phys Anthropol 34:175–190.

Molnar S, McKee JB, Molnar IM, Prezybeck TR. 1983. Tooth wear rates among contemporary Australian Aborigines. J Dent Res 62:562–565.

Moorrees CFA. 1957. The Aleut Dentition. Cambridge: Harvard University Press. 196 pp.

Murphy T. 1959. The changing pattern of dentine exposure in human tooth attrition. Am J Phys Anthropol 17:167–178.

Nakahori Y, Takenaka O, Nakagome T. 1991. A human X-Y homologous region encodes "amelogenin." Genomics 9:262–269.

Nikiforuk G. 1985. Understanding Dental Caries. 2 vols. Basel: Karger.

Oehlers FAC. 1956. The tuberculated premolar. Dent Practit Dent Rec 6:144–148.

Osborn JW. 1981. Dental Anatomy and Embryology. Oxford: Blackwell. 447 pp.

Ozaki T, Kanazawa E. 1984. An application of the moiré method to three-dimensional measurements of the occlusal aspects of molars. Acta Morphol Neerl-Scand 22:85–91.

Parfitt GJ. 1955. The distribution of caries on different sites of the teeth in English children from the age of 2–15 years. Br Dent J 99:423–427.

Patterson DK. 1984. A Diachronic Study of Dental Palaeopathology and Attritional Status of Prehistoric Ontario Pre-Iroquois and Iroquois Populations. Ottawa: Archaeol Sur Can 122: 1–428.

Pedersen PO. 1949. The East Greenland Eskimo dentition. Medd øm Grönland 1423:1–244.

Pedersen PO, Dahlberg AA, Alexandersen V, editors. 1967. Proceedings of the International Symposium on Dental Morphology. J Dent Res 46 (pt.1):769–992.

Perzigian AJ. 1975. Natural selection on the dentition of an Arikara population. Am J Phys Anthropol 42:63–69.

Perzigian AJ. 1976. The dentition of the Indian Knoll skeletal population: odontometrics and cusp number. Am J Phys Anthropol 44: 113–122.

Perzigian AJ. 1977. Fluctuating dental asymmetry: variation among skeletal populations. Am J Phys Anthropol 47:81–88.

Perzigian AJ. 1984. Human odontometric variation: an evolutionary and taxonomic assessment. Anthropologie 22:193–198.

Peyer B. 1968. Comparative Odontology. Chicago: Univ. Chicago Press. 347 pp.

Pirttiniemi P, Alvesalo L, Pirilä-Parkkinen, Silven O, Heikkilä J, Julku J, Karjalahti P. 1999. A new method for measuring three-dimensional dental morphology. In: Mayhall JT, Heikkinen T, editors. Dental Morphology 1998. Oulu, Finland, 11th International Symposium on Dental Morphology. pp. 407–413.

Radlanski RJ, Renz H, editors. 1995. Proceedings of the 10th International Symposium on Dental Morphology. Berlin: M Marketing Services. 471 pp.

Rass F, Habets LLMH, van Ginkel FC, Prahl-Andersen B. 1995. Method for quantifying facial asymmetry in three dimensions using stereophotogrammetry. Angle Ortho 65:233–239.

Richards LV, Brown T. 1981. Dental attrition and age relationships in Australian Aborigines. Archaeol Oceania 16:94–98.

Romero J. 1958. Mutilaciones Dentarias Prehispanicas de Mexico Y America en General. Instituto Nacional de Anthropologica e Historia Investigaciones Serie 3:1–326. (in Spanish).

Rosenzweig KA. 1970. Tooth form as a distinguishing trait between sexes and human populations. J Dent Res 49:1423–1426.

Rosenzweig KA, Smith P. 1971. Dental variability in isolates. J Dent Res 50:155–160.

Russell DE, Santoro J-P, Sigogneau-Russell D, editors. 1988. Teeth Revisited: Proceedings of the VIIth International Symposium on Dental Morphology. Mem Mus Nat Hist ser C Sci Terre 53, Paris: Editions du Paris. 462 pp.

Salido EC, Yen PH, Koprivnikar K, Yu LC, Shapiro U. 1992. The human enamel protein gene amelogenin is expressed from both the X and the Y chromosomes. Am J Hum Genet 50:303–316.

Saunders SR, Mayhall JT. 1982. Developmental patterns of human dental morphology traits. Arch Oral Biol 27:45–49.

Schulz PD. 1977. Task activity and anterior tooth grooving in prehistoric California Indians. Amer J Phys Anthropol 46:87–92.

Seguchi N. 1998. Secular change in occlusion: the frequency of the overbite and its association with food preparation techniques and eating habits. [abstract]. Am J Phys Anthropol 26(suppl):199.

Sekikawa M, Kanazawa E, Ozaki T. 1988. Cusp height relationships between the upper and lower molars in Japanese subjects. J Dent Res 67:1515–1517.

Selmer-Olsen R. 1949. An Odontometrical Study on the Norwegian Lapps. Oslo: I Kommisjon Hos Jacob Dybwad. 167 pp.

Singer R. 1953. Artificial deformation of teeth: a preliminary report. S Afr J Sci 50:116–122.

Singh IJ, Savara BS. 1964. A method for making tooth and dental arch measurements. J Amer Dent Assoc 69:719–721.

Smith BH, Garn SM, Cole PE. 1982. Problems of sampling and inference in the study of fluctuating dental asymmetry. Am J Phys Anthropol 58:281–289.

Smith P, Tchernov E, editors. 1992. Structure, Function and Evolution of Teeth. London: Freund. 570 p.

Sofaer JA. 1970. Dental morphologic variation and the Hardy-Weinberg law. J Dent Res 49:1505–1508.

Sofaer JA, Niswander JD, MacLean CJ, Workman PL. 1972. Population studies on Southwestern Indian tribes V. Tooth morphology as an indicator of biological distance. Am J Phys Anthropol 37:357–366.

Suzuki M. Sakai T. 1955. On the "tuberculum accessorium sic mediale internum" in recent Japanese. Anthropol Soc Nippon J 64:135–139. (in Japanese).

Swindler DR, Drusini AG, Christino C. 1997. Variation and frequency of three-rooted first permanent molars in pre-contact Easter Islanders: anthropological significance. J Polynesian Soc 106:175–183.

Swindler DR, Drusini AG, Christino C, Ranzato C. 1998. Molar crown morphology of precontact Easter Islanders compared with molars from other islands. In: Stevenson CM, Lee G, Morin FJ, editors. Easter Island in Pacific Context South Seas Symposium. Santa Barbara: Easter Island Foundation. pp.163–168.

Takasaki H. 1970. Moiré topography. Appl Optics 9:1457–1472.

Takasaki H. 1973. Moiré topography. Appl Optics 12:845–850.

Tasa GL. 1998. Three-rooted mandibular molars in Northwest Coast populations: Implications for Oregon prehistory and peopling of the new world. In: Lukacs JR, editor. Human Dental Development, Morphology, and Pathology. Univ Oregon, pp. 215–244. Anthropol Pap. 54.

Ten Cate AR. 1998. Oral Histology: Development, Structure, and Function. 5th ed. St. Louis: Mosby. 497 p.

Thomsen S. 1951. Dental morphology and occlusion in the people of Tristan da Cunha. Results of the Norwegian Scientific Expedition to Tristan Da Cunha 1937–1938. 25:1–61.

Tomenchuk J, Mayhall JT. 1979. A correlation of tooth wear and age among modern Igloolik Eskimos. Am J Phys Anthropol 51:67–77.

Townsend GC. 1981. Fluctuating asymmetry in the deciduous dentition of Australian Aboriginals. J Dent Res 60:1849–1857.

Townsend GC, Alvesalo L. 1999. Premolar crown dimensions in 47,XXY Klinefelter syndrome males. Perspec Hum Biol. 4(3):71–76.

Townsend GC, Brown T. 1980. Dental asymmetry in Australian Aboriginals. Hum Biol 52:661–673.

Townsend G, Brown T. 1981. The Carabelli trait in Australian Aboriginal dentition. Archs Oral Biol 26:809–814

Townsend G, Alvesalo A, Jensen B, Kari M. 1988. Patterns of tooth size in human chromosomal aneuploidies. In: Russell DE, Santoro J-P, Sigogneau-Russell D, editors. Teeth Revisited: Proceedings of the VIIth International Symposium on Dental Morphology. Mem Mus Nat Hist Nat, Paris. ser C 53:25–45.

Townsend GC, Jensen BL, Alvesalo L. 1984. Reduced tooth size in 45,X Turner syndrome females. Am J Phys Anthropol 65:367–372.

Tratman EK. 1938. Three-rooted lower molars in man and their racial distribution. Br Dent J 64:264–267.

Tratman EK. 1949. An unrecorded form of the simplest type of the dilated composite odontome. Br Dent J 86:271–275.

Tratman EK. 1950. A comparison of the teeth of people: Indo-European racial stock with the Mongoloid racial stock. Yrbk Phys Anthropol. pp. 272–314.

Tsuji T. 1958. Incidence and inheritance of the Carabelli's cusp in a Japanese population. Jap J Hum Genet 3:21–31.

Turner CG. 1967. The Dentition of Arctic Peoples. Ann Arbor: University Microfilms. 284 pp.

Turner CG. 1987. Pleistocene and Holocene population history of East Asia based on dental variation. Am J Phys Anthropol 73:305–321.

Turner CG. 1990. Major features of sundadonty and sinodonty, including suggestions about East Asian microevolution, population history, and late Pleistocene relationships with Australian Aboriginals. Amer J Phys Anthropol 82:295–317.

Turner CG, Benjamin O. 1989. World variation in three-rooted lower first permanent molars. Unpublished, presented at VIII International Symposium on Dental Morphology, Jerusalem.

Turner CG, Nichol CR, Scott GR. 1991. Scoring procedures for key morphological traits of the permanent dentition: the Arizona State University dental anthropology system. In: Kelley MA, Larsen CS, editors. Advances in Dental Anthropology. New York: Wiley-Liss. pp. 13–31.

Turner CG, Scott GR. 1977. Dentition of the Easter Islanders. In: Dahlberg AA, Graber TM, editors. Orofacial Growth and Development. The Hague: Mouton. pp. 229–249.

Varrela J. 1995. Multirooted mandibular premolars in 45,X females: frequency and morphological types. In: Smith P, Tchernov E, editors. Structure, Function and Evolution of Teeth. London: Freund. pp. 519–526.

Walker PL, Dean G, Shapiro P. 1991. Estimating age from tooth wear in archaeological populations. In: Kelley MA, Larsen CS, editors. Advances in Dental Anthropology. New York: Wiley-Liss. pp. 169–178.

Weidenreich F. 1937. The Dentition of Sinanthropus Pekinensis. A Comparative Odontography of the Hominids. Palaeon Sin New Ser D, no.1. 180 pp.

Williams LR. 1979. A Photogrammetrical Analysis of Pongid Molar Morphology. unpub. Ph.D. dissertation, Univ. of Toronto. 211 pp.

Woelfel JB, Scheid RC. 1997. Dental Anatomy: Its Relevance to Dentistry. Baltimore: Williams & Wilkins. 449 pp.

Wolpoff MH. 1971. Metric trends in hominid dental evolution. Case Western Reserve University Studies in Anthropology 2:1–244.

Yamada H, Brown T. 1988. Contours of maxillary molars studied in Australian Aboriginals. Amer J Phys Anthropol 76:399–407

Zadik D. 1976. Caries experience in deciduous and permanent dentition of the same individuals. J Dent Res 55:1125–1126.

Zubov AA. 1977. Odontoglyphics: the laws of variation of the human molar crown microrelief. In: Dahlberg AA, Graber TM, editors. Orofacial Growth and Development. The Hague: Mouton. pp. 269–282.

Zubov AA, Nikityuk BA. 1974. New odontological methods of twin types diagnostics. Voprosy anthropologii 46:108–128. (in Russian).

Zubov AA, Nikityuk BA. 1978 Prospects for the application of dental morphology in twin type analysis. J Hum Evol 7:519–524.

CHAPTER 5

SUBADULT SKELETONS
AND GROWTH-RELATED STUDIES

SHELLEY R. SAUNDERS

INTRODUCTION

In 1968, Johnston was justified in claiming that physical anthropologists studying the skeletal biology of earlier human populations concentrated upon adults and excluded infants and children from their research (Johnston, 1968). This neglect is all the more surprising since typical mortality curves for nonindustrial and pre-twentieth-century groups graphically portray the precariousness of the growth period with its great nutritional requirements and susceptibility to disease. Since the 1960s, and in large part influenced by Johnston's early efforts (Johnston, 1961, 1962, 1969) on the Indian Knoll skeletal sample from Kentucky, there have been a number of attempts to redress the oversight and look for prehistoric population differences in subadult mortality, child growth, and development.

The assessment of general population health has also become a fundamental part of the interpretation of the life ways of extinct or past populations, with a shifting focus on multiple rather than single indicators of physiological stress (Buikstra and Cook, 1980; Goodman et al., 1988; Mensforth et al., 1978; Ubelaker, 1995; Verano and Ubelaker, 1992). There is a general confidence that it is now possible to test hypotheses and assess the relationship be-

tween a population and its environment from the study of cemetery skeletal remains (Johnston and Zimmer, 1989). But the question remains, is this confidence justified, especially when trying to study juvenile mortality?

This chapter examines in some detail the practical problems of analyzing the skeletons of immature individuals from archeological samples and whether these problems are surmountable. Questions of sampling, the determination of sex, and the estimation of age are addressed. The balance of the chapter focuses on the assessment of growth and development using population comparisons, studies of growth rates, and the influence of environmental factors on growth. The possible detection of health stress or cause of death of juveniles are broad fields that are not included here because of space limitations. Readers wishing to find more information should consult relevant chapters in this book and the following sources: Larsen, 1997; Ortner, 1998; Ortner and Mays, 1998; Saunders and Barrans, 1999; Schultz, 1989, 1992, 1995. It is clear that certain theoretical and methodological difficulties cannot be overcome. Since this is so, what is possible? The chapter concludes with recommendations for future research.

SAMPLING

First and foremost in any study of skeletal samples is the evaluation of bone preservation.

Biological Anthropology of the Human Skeleton, Edited by M. Anne Katzenberg and Shelley R. Saunders.
ISBN 0-471-31616-4 Copyright © 2000 by Wiley-Liss, Inc.

Counts of juvenile skeletons from prehistoric and historic cemeteries are commonly very low, introducing a bias into skeletal samples (Guy et al., 1997; Jackes, 1992; Saunders, 1992). Several authors have identified three factors as responsible for the underrepresentation of immature individuals: cultural beliefs about infants and children influencing mortuary behavior, the effects of biological and environmental processes causing differential preservation of immature bones, and incomplete archeological recovery due to biased excavation techniques.

There is considerable evidence for differential burial practices that will frequently bias against infants and children or alter the proportions of subadult and adult skeletons from a cemetery. The practice of infanticide has been and still is widespread and relatively common among many human cultures (Scrimshaw, 1984). Both the deliberate killing of babies and "passive infanticide" in the form of neglect, decrease the likelihood that some deceased infants will receive formal cemetery burial. In addition, the definition of life after birth is usually dependent upon a cultural definition of when life begins. Some groups acknowledge infant life several days after birth, while others do not consider children fully human for several years (Saunders and Barrans, 1999).

Infants are frequently buried far away from cemeteries, under house floors or entry ways, or in other contexts. *Taran* is a well-known Gaelic term referring to the ghosts of unbaptized babies who were usually buried outside of normal cemeteries. The burial practices of prehistoric Iroquoians of southern Ontario are another illustration. Ethnohistoric sources refer to the burial of infants along pathways so that their souls might re-enter the womb of a passing woman (Thwaites, 1896–1901). Modern excavations of Iroquoian village sites have uncovered high proportions of newborn infants buried in long house floors (Saunders and Spence, 1986), and it appears that the choice of the central corridor of the long house often represented the "path" along which an appropriate woman might walk (Saunders and Fitzgerald, 1988).

It is also widely believed that the bones of infants and children, because they are small and fragile, do not preserve and therefore are often lost to the excavator (Johnston and Zimmer, 1989). Certainly, the bones of young individuals have high organic and low mineral content and are less dense than the bones of adults, making them more susceptible to decay (Currey and Butler, 1975; Specker et al., 1987). Gordon and Buikstra (1981) found soil acidity levels to be significantly correlated with bone preservation in the skeletons of both adults and children, with juvenile bone durability declining rapidly with decreasing soil pH.

Walker and colleagues (1988) were able to compare mortality profiles derived from an analysis of burial records and skeletal collections from a nineteenth-century Franciscan mission cemetery in California. The baptismal and death records of the mission indicated that most of the people buried in the cemetery were either infants or elderly adults, fitting the typical U-shaped distribution of mortality seen in this period. But the skeletal sample contains mainly young adults. Even though the skeletal sample size is small (only 2% of all people buried in the cemetery), a random sample of burials should not deviate so much from the known age distribution of people buried in the cemetery. The authors concluded that age-specific differences in preservation account for the missing children and elderly adults. More recently, Guy and colleagues (1997) state that the proportion of infants (under one year) in archeological cemeteries generally fluctuates around 5 or 6% while the proportion of infants dying in prevaccination populations recorded by historical demographers should never fall below 25% of live births. They identify taphonomic variability (susceptible bones in poor burial environments) as the main cause of low percentages of juvenile bones in skeletal samples, arguing as a consequence that paleodemographic reconstruction is uniformly restricted.

On the other hand, Sundick (1978) argues that even the smallest growth centers and the most fragile of the flat bones of the vault of the skull or the scapula of subadult skeletons can be as well preserved as the bones of the robust adult skeleton. He attributes incompleteness to the degree of skill of the excavators and the need to be able to recognize juvenile bones. Few researchers would care to admit that excavation methods at a site had been less than perfect but obviously deficient training may contribute to inadequate recovery of skeletal remains.

We should expect that explanations for juvenile sample bias in skeletal collections are diverse, multifactorial, and often unique to the cultural and archeological context of the site (see for example, Hoppa and Gruspier, 1996; Hoppa and Saunders, 1998; Nawrocki, 1996; Paine and Harpending, 1998; Saunders, 1992). On the other hand, Guy and colleagues (1997) reject cultural explanations for the lack of infant skeletons, citing an example from a historic French cemetery where the proportion of infants represents a fifth of the recorded proportion in the parish registers. They note that this population punished infanticide and practiced the baptism of neonates, presuming then that most infant skeletons should have been found. Yet a number of examples exist from historic cemeteries where it is clear that spacial locations of burials are age-specific (Lilley et al., 1994; McWhirr, et al., 1982; Molleson et al., 1993), or where substantial proportions of immature individuals, even infants, are present (Cook and Buikstra, 1979; Farwell and Molleson, 1993; Hutchins, 1998; Owsley and Jantz, 1985; Saunders et al., 1993; Sperduti et al., 1997).

Almost ten years of research has been conducted on a large nineteenth-century church cemetery sample from Canada, where skeletal observations could be compared to a complete set of burial records as well as other documents (Saunders et al., 1995b). This work has shown that a complex of factors explains the relative proportions of juveniles and infants in the skeletal sample when compared to documentary information. In 1989, archaeologists excavated 597 burials at St. Thomas' Anglican Church cemetery in Belleville, Ontario (Herring et al., 1991; McKillop et al., 1989). The cemetery was used from 1821–1874 and the 1989 excavation recovered 40% of all interments as recorded in parish registers covering the entire cemetery period. The estimated proportion of all subadults to adults in the skeletal sample matches closely with adult and subadult burials recorded in the registers (Herring et al., 1991). But the proportion of infants in the skeletal sample significantly exceeds that recorded in the registers over the full period of cemetery use, contrary to widely held expectations. Initially, we interpreted this difference as a temporal bias in the archaeological excavation of the site. During the 1820s and 1830s, many of the region's pioneer inhabitants avoided the distance required to travel to town and buried dead infants in family plots. The proportions of infant burials increased over the decades as the population grew and infant mortality rates increased, and these may have been recovered disproportionately during excavation.

Further work on the St. Thomas' sample has shown that infant deaths were probably also underreported, a common phenomenon in many past documents (Lynch et al., 1985), since estimates of infant mortality rates are low given what is typically reported for the time period (Sawchuk and Burke, in press). But there may be other cultural reasons for the presence of surreptitious infant burials whose interment was simply not known by the minister. The local newspaper provides accounts of probable infanticide cases (Saunders et al., 1995b), and other historical documents of the time refer to concealed infant burials in church cemeteries by those avoiding the payment for a plot (Daechsel, pers. comm.).

Another factor particularly relevant to skeletal analyses is the degree of preservation of important age and sex determining criteria on subadult and adult skeletons. In intracemetery comparisons, identification criteria and other markers are the variables that are compared. Are these criteria less likely to be preserved on subadult than adult skeletons?

Table 5.1 shows that, in fact, a similar or even better proportion of the subadults (individuals aged under 16 years although most are

TABLE 5.1   Frequency of Preserved Age Estimation Indicators for Subadult Skeletons and Adult Skeletons from the St. Thomas' Anglican Church Sample

Age	Frequency	Percentage
Subadults		
Dental and/or diaphyseal data	275/281	97.9
Dental formation data	240/281	85.4
Diaphyseal data	242/281	86.1
No information for age	6/281	2.1
Adults		
Auricular surface data	238/278	85.6
Pubic symphysis data	171/278	61.5
Intact cranium (analysable)	232/278	83.5
Infracranial measurements	255/278	91.7

under 6 years) in the St. Thomas' sample preserved usable age indicators. In 98% of the subadult skeletons, dental, diaphyseal, or both indicators were preserved sufficiently for age estimation. Special care had been taken to search for and recover developing tooth germs and bone growth centers. In another example, Spence (1986) anticipated the discovery of fetal skeletons from within an early Iroquoian village site and arranged to have all maxillae and mandibles prewrapped in the field to preserve fetal tooth germs and thus, estimate fetal ages more accurately. These examples suggest that factors such as differential burial practices and excavation techniques can sometimes prove more important to subadult skeletal preservation than differential tissue survival.

SEX DETERMINATION

One universal problem presents itself with the study of subadult skeletons, the apparent difficulty of determining sex (Workshop of European Anthropologists, 1980). Knowing the sex of the individual has a bearing on determination of age because of sex variability in growth. Generally, females grow faster than males, meaning that non sexspecific age estimates of subadult skeletons will be much broader than if sex is known. Yet knowledge of the sex of the

individual is important to anthropological inquiry since it provides the opportunity to study gender-biased care and status differences among children.

The differentiation between the sexes is in large part determined by the testes, because if cells are not masculinized by the presence of androgen they will develop along ovarian lines (Stini, 1985). This is illustrated by the fact that fetal testosterone is present by the tenth week, peaks around the time of major sexual differentiation at 15 weeks, and decreases again until just before puberty (Weaver, 1980). Multiple loci have been implicated in the ultimate genetic control of sex differentiation. Endocrine function then contributes to producing human sexual dimorphism. Before the onset of puberty, male infants and children are, on average, larger than females for such features as head for weight index (Ounsted et al., 1981), bone thickness, and bone density (Mazess and Cameron, 1972; Specker et al., 1987). But, in addition, from the twentieth week of life in utero the female foetus is approximately 10% more mature than the male and this growth difference will persist until the attainment of full maturity (Stini, 1985). It is likely that the difference in maturation rate between the sexes is influenced by a complex of factors.

Because of the sex difference in maturation, the sex of subadolescent human skeletons might be inferred by comparing dental development with bone development in the same individual, since males mature more slowly skeletally than females, while the rate of dental formation is more similar in males and females (Hunt and Gleiser, 1955). The procedure is to estimate age independently from dental and skeletal remains using both male and female standards. If the dental and skeletal age estimates from male standards are closer to one another than those found for female standards, then the unknown individual would be male. A test of this method using dental and skeletal radiographs from living children obtained accuracy levels of 73–81% (Hunt and Gleiser, 1955). In this study, skeletal ages were based on hand bone maturation, an impractical method for excavated skeletons, but the authors suggest using bone formation at the knee joint. Sundick (1977) reported success with this approach in skeletons of individuals over 12 years where sex was confirmed by pelvic morphology and skeletal age was estimated from diaphyseal lengths, but accuracy rates were not reported. More recently, Goode-Null (1996) achieved high accuracy by comparing skeletal development at the knee to a generalized (not sex-specific) estimate of dental age in a documented sample of fetal and infant remains. While questions arise about the influences of population variation and pathological stress on the effectiveness of this method, the reports of success suggest it warrants further testing.

Choi and Trotter (1970) used long bone weight and length ratios to produce a sex classification accuracy of 72% for fetal skeletons, but the use of bone weights makes this method presently inapplicable for exhumed bones. Further, the classification accuracy is low; a minimum criterion for classification accuracy should be 50% better than chance or at least 75% (De Vito and Saunders, 1990).

Since the pelvis is the most sexually dimorphic part of the adult skeleton it would make sense to look for dimorphism in the subadult pelvis, and there is a long literature on this subject (Boucher, 1955, 1957; Morton, 1942; Morton and Hayden, 1941; Reynolds, 1945, 1947; Thomson, 1899). Infant males are said to have longer ilia, ischia, and femoral necks, and females to have longer pubic bones and wider greater sciatic notches. Weaver (1980) reevaluated some of the earlier metric methods using a large fetal dry bone sample of known sex but found almost no significant sex differences for measurement indices. Schutowski (1987) used the raw data from hip and femur dimensions of fetuses and neonates gathered by Fasekas and Kósa (1978) to examine sex differences. Discriminant functions were derived from these measurements, but the maximum classification accuracy was only 70%. A further application of his calculated functions to two samples of known age and sex was unsuccessful (Majó et al., 1993).

Weaver (1980, 1986) proposed that subjectively recorded variation in the height of the iliac auricular surface is sex dependent in fetal and infant skeletons. He tested this nonmetric trait on a known sample and obtained a classification accuracy of 43 to 75% for females and 73 to 92% for males. In an attempt to test the reliability of the trait, Hunt (1990) compared the ratio of raised to nonraised auricular surfaces with a 1:1 expected sex distribution in a large sample of subadult ilia from several archeological sites (where sex was unknown). Although burial practices and other factors could alter an expected 1:1 infant sex ratio in archeological samples, Hunt found severely unrealistic sex ratios, including an age-related shift from newborns to young adolescents. A later study of a small known sex sample (Mittler and Sheridan, 1992) also identified an age influence on this trait. More recently, Holcomb and Konigsberg (1995) explored sciatic notch shape in a large fetal sample using an objective morphometric approach. While they did find significant sexual dimorphism in the shape of the notch, overlap between males and females was too great for the notch to be used as a sex indicator at early ages.

The fact that significant sexual dimorphism occurs in the permanent dentition has prompted the claim that, for children, the teeth might represent the only factor useful for sex diagnosis (Workshop of European Anthropologists, 1980). But the magnitudes of dimorphism are small and most data come from permanent teeth that cannot be studied in the large samples of young infants. Several studies have determined that a small but significant dimorphism does exist in the deciduous dentition but only two studies have employed classificatory procedures for separating the sexes. One of these, (Black, 1978) concluded that deciduous teeth show much less dimorphism than permanent teeth and that discriminant functions calculated from the diameters of deciduous teeth are much less accurate

TABLE 5.2   Discriminant Function Equations for Distinguishing Males from Females by Various Combinations of Deciduous and Permanent Tooth Dimensions [a,b,c]

Group/Equation

4 Maxillary and 1 Mandibular Variables

A 1.500 (FL R max li) + 1.091(FL R) + 0.654 (FL L max dm2) − 1.489 (FL L max c) + 1.640 (MD R mand c) − 20.342

B 1.380 (FL R max li) + 0.896 (FL R max ci) + 0.357 (FL L max dm2) − 1.474 (FL L max c) + 2.266 (MD R mand c) − 19.36

3 Maxillary and 1 Mandibular Variables

D 1.899 (FL R max li) + 1.174 (FL L max dm2) − 1.750 (FL L max c) + 1.653 (MD R mand c) − 20.138

4 Maxillary Variables

A 1.625 (FL R max li) + 1.239(FL R max ci) + 1. 135 (FL L max dm2) − 1.141 (F L L max c) − 18.564

B 1.690 (FL R max li) + 0.967 (FL R max ci) + 1. 184 (FL L max dm2) − 1.097 (FL L max c) − 18.192

3 Maxillary Variables

D 2.084 (FL R max li) + 1.688 (FL L max dm2) − 1.353 (FL L max c) − 18.425

1 Mandibular Variable

A 3.079 (MD R mand c) − 18.861

B 3.051 (MD R mand c) − 18.699

D 3.000 (MD R mand c) − 18.407

4 Deciduous and 3 Permanent Maxillary and Mandibular Variables

C 0.542 (FL R max li) + 0.279 (FL L max dm2) − 0.723 (FL L max c) + 1.058 (MD R mand c) + 1.837 (F L L max Ml) + 0.628 (MD L mand Ml) − 1.692 (FL L mand M1) − 17.423

3 Deciduous and 1 Permanent Maxillary Variables

C 0.574 (FL R max li) + 0.393 (FL L max dm2) − 0.371 (FL L max c) + 1.521 (F L L max MI) − 21.314

1 Deciduous and 2 Permanent Mandibular Variables

C 2.049 (MD R mand c) + 0.887 (MD L mand Ml) − 0.516 (F L L mand Ml) − 16.872

[a]Reproduced from DeVito and Saunders (1990), with permission of the publisher.

[b]Abbreviations: F faciolingual; MD, mesiodistal; L, left; R, right; max, maxillary; mand, mandibular.

[c]Results above 0 are male and those below 0 are female.

for sex classification. De Vito and Saunders (1990), using three to five measurements of deciduous teeth as well as combinations of deciduous and permanent measurements, produced discriminant functions in which 76 to 90% of holdout samples were correctly classified by sex, which means that the level of classification accuracy of the deciduous teeth at least approaches the levels achieved using the permanent teeth (Table 5.2). But the pattern and degree of sexual dimorphism reported for various groups shows considerable population variation.

A test of these discriminant function equations was conducted using a small sample of personally identified skeletons of children from two historic nineteenth-century pioneer cemeteries (Saunders, 1992). Of the seven females represented, six were correctly classified, but of the eight males only three were correctly classified. The teeth of the individuals from the archeological samples are smaller than the living Canadian reference sample so that males were more often assessed as females. This suggests bias against size and/or maturity in the skeletal sample, which is influenced by mortality bias.

Hopes have sometimes been expressed for methods of chemical or elemental identification of sex from the skeleton (Beattie, 1982; Dennison, 1979; Gibbs, 1991; Lengyel, 1968). But sex differences in bone chemical composition are usually dependent upon postpubertal physiological differences and can be dramatically altered by the burial environment. The end of the long arm of the Y chromosome is visible with special staining in living cells undergoing division. This method of sex determination has been attempted with forensic cases (Mudd, 1984; Sundick, 1985) but human cells do not remain patent for long and investigators may identify artifacts as stained chromosomes.

With the advent of molecular techniques for sequencing human cellular DNA, sex can be defined at the molecular level because the X and Y chromosomes have their own distinctive DNA sequences. Unlike direct microscopic observations of the chromosomes, molecular analysis does not require that the DNA be in a viable condition as long as DNA molecules are chemically available. Now that several researchers have successfully determined sex in archaeological skeletons by extracting DNA (Faerman et al., 1995; Hummel and Herrmann, 1994; Stone et al., 1996; Yang et al., 1998; see also Stone, Chapter 13) the problem of subadult sex classification seems solved. But aDNA (ancient DNA) analysis is far from foolproof and the methodology is not readily available to bioarchaeologists. The cost of testing large samples is still prohibitive and problems with extraction and contamination of archaeological specimens have not been overcome (Saunders and Yang, 1999). Significant proportions of archaeological samples do not yield any DNA that can be amplified, and for those samples that do, several independent tests are needed to avoid the high likelihood of error (there is a 50% chance of being right). Nevertheless, we should be optimistic. Sex determination by DNA analysis offers some of the greatest potential for future research because laboratory techniques in molecular biology continue to make great strides.

AGE ESTIMATION

Most critical, of course, to the identification of immature individuals from skeletal samples is the problem of age estimation. Subadult age-at-death estimations can be considered more accurate than adult age estimations because of the telescoped time span of human growth relative to the total life span over which age variability is assessed. But present difficulties with determining sex in subadults increase the range of error.

Age estimation of the skeleton involves establishing physiological age (developmental changes in the tissues) and then attempting to correlate this with chronological age at death. Additional sources of error besides the sex difference contribute to the discrepancy between physiological and chronological age. These include random individual variation in maturation and the systematic effects of environmental and genetic factors on growth. Tooth emergence, a piercing of the gum or alveolar bone by the developing tooth, has been studied extensively and used widely in archeological and forensic efforts to estimate age at death of unknown skeletons. But many local factors can affect tooth emergence such as infection or premature extraction of the deciduous predecessor (c.f. Demirjian, 1978; El-Nofely and İşcan, 1989) and published data from living populations refers to emergence through the gums, not the bony alveolus that skeletal biologists observe.

Dental formation is a better measure of physiological maturity (see Ubelaker, 1989). The formation of tooth crowns and roots is much less affected by hormonal influences, local and general environmental factors, and nutrition and social factors than tooth emergence, skeletal development, weight, or height (Demirjian, 1978; El-Nofely and İşcan, 1989; Smith, 1991). Developing teeth show morphologically distinct stages of formation and mineralization, which can be identified radiographically and microscopically. Human biologists studying growth in living children started in the middle of this century to use dental formation (or sometimes calcification, which microscopically evaluates the mineralization process) rather than emergence as a maturity indicator. There are two major advantages to this approach. First of all, dental formation is independent of skeletal maturity and most closely approximates chronological age (Demirjian et al., 1973; Garn et al, 1958; Lewis and Garn, 1960; Moorrees et al, 1963a; Nolla, 1960). In addition, the dental formation system is the only system that is uniformly applicable for estimating age from prenatal stages to late adolescence since formation is a continuous process (Demirjian, 1978).

What methods should be followed to record dental maturation and what standards exist for estimating chronological age from dental age? Since skeletal biologists studying archeological samples now seem to recognize that dental formation is the preferred method, it is important that careful and consistent methodologies be employed. Research over the past decade has shown that chronological age can be determined most accurately from microscopic assessments of incremental structures in tooth tissues (see Chapter 6 by FitzGerald and Rose). But this area of research is still under development so that currently, the simplest and cheapest method of assessing large archeological samples comes from X rays. Obtaining good radiographs of all subadult dentitions from cemetery samples should be common practice. Many researchers now have their own X-ray facilities and most have ready access to medical or dental X-ray services. Even small, portable X-ray units with independent power sources are becoming more widely available for those having to work in difficult field situations. Besides their value for comparing tooth formation to existing standards, which are all based on X rays, the films also serve as primary data sources when skeletons must be reburied.

During tooth maturation a series of morphological stages are recognizable, beginning with actual formation of the tooth crypt and ending with closure of the apex of the fully formed root. Every tooth follows the same sequence, but in order to study the process some system of mensuration is required. Most researchers have chosen ordinal or ranked systems of observation, but the numbers of tooth formation stages in the different systems have ranged from 3 to 20 (Table 5.3—see Demirjian, 1978, for a detailed discussion of these systems). The difficulties with this type of observation include problems of defining stages and subjectivity in identifying stages such as the difference between one-quarter and one-half formation of root length (Macho and Wood, 1995). Collapsing of categories reduces inter- and intraobserver error. Demirjian and Goldstein (1976) described eight carefully defined stages of formation using X-ray pictures, diagrams and, written criteria, which are probably easier to follow, although this method has not yet been widely used in archeological studies, mainly because of the attendant difficulties with choosing and applying their age standards. The standards are presented as maturity scores on percentile

TABLE 5.3 Comparatibe Table of "Stages of Dental Formation" According to Different Authors[a]

	Fanning (1961)	Moorrees et al. (1963a)	Hunt and Gleiser (1955)	Nanda and Chawla (1966)	Nolla (1960)	Demirjian et al. (1973)	Garn et al. (1958)
Presence of crypt	1	—	—	—	1	—	—
Initial cusp formation	2	1	—	—	2	1(A)	1
Coalescence of cusps	3	2	1	—	—	—	—
Occlusal surface completed	4	3	2	1	—	2(B)	—
Crown $1/3$	—	—	—	—	3	—	—
Crown $1/2$	5	4	3	2	—	3(C)	—
Crown $2/3$	6	—	4	—	4	—	—
Crown $3/4$	—	5	—	3	5	—	—
Crown formation completed	7	6	5	4	6	4(D)	—
Initial radicular formation	8	7	6	$5(1/8)$	—	—	2
Initial radicular bifurcation	8 A,B	8	—	—	—	—	—
Root $1/4$	9	9	7	6	—	5(E)	—
Root $1/3$	10	—	8	$7(3/8)$	7	—	—
Root $1/2$	11	10	9	8	—	—	—
Root $2/3$	12	—	10	$9(5/8)$	8	6(F)	—
Root $3/4$	13	11	11	10	—	—	—
Root completed	14	12	12	$11(7/8)$	9	7(G)	—
Apex $1/2$ closed	—	13	—	—	—	—	—
Apex closed[b]	15	14	13	12	10	8(H)	3

[a] Reproduced from Demirjian (1978), with permission of the publisher.

[b] Apex closure: $1/4$; $1/2$; $3/4$.

charts and require a minimum of four different tooth types to assign a score.

Precision of observations might be improved by measuring the absolute lengths of developing teeth. A study of a sample of infants and young children of known age from an eighteenth- and nineteenth-century church crypt in England (Liversidge et al., 1993) showed a clear relationship between developing root length and the age of the individuals, which could then be used to estimate age in unknown cases. In this study, deciduous tooth length appears to grow faster than permanent tooth length. Further information is needed on other and larger population samples to evaluate the reliability of this method across populations.

No matter what methodological approach is used, the skeletal researcher must decide what aging standards are to be used and how to report them. Published standards for tooth formation are mainly derived from samples of white North American and northern European children, although even these standards are relatively few (Anderson et al., 1976; Demirjian et al., 1973; Haavikko, 1970; Moorrees, et al., 1963a, 1963b; Nielsen and Ravn, 1976). There is very little information on other populations, although there have been efforts in this direction (Harris and McKee, 1990; Loevy, 1983; Nichols et al., 1983; Trodden, 1982). Clear evidence for the existence of population differences in dental development is sparse. It is difficult to evaluate population differences because it is very hard to determine both the start points (specific age at which a tooth crown begins to form) and the rates of dental formation among different groups. Smith (1991) examined the methodological problems involved in assessing variability in the timing of dental development in detail and concluded that statistical treatment of the data is responsible for much of the reported variability. But, in one of the few studies that has directly compared the development of teeth among living groups, Harris and McKee (1990) found that African-Americans from the U.S. mid-south were advanced for all teeth in the age of attainment of tooth formation stages compared to European-Americans in the same area of the United States. There is also some preliminary evidence to show that black South Africans are advanced in dental development over white South Africans (Chertkow, 1980), and that the French-Canadian sample studied by Demirjian and colleagues (1973) is slower in dental maturation than Latino, African-American, and European-American children. Owsley and Jantz (1983) compared the relative stages of formation achieved between tooth pairs within two samples, Native American Arikara from several archeological sites and American whites derived from the standards of Moorrees and co-workers (1963a, 1963b). They found a significant difference in the ages assigned to tooth pairs between the two groups with the Native Americans showing advancement in tooth maturation. More recently, Tompkins (1996) assessed the differences in patterns of dental development by directly comparing formation stages of various teeth relative to the attained maturation status of a reference tooth in three samples—French-Canadians, black South Africans, and a mixed group of Native Americans. He found evidence of delayed molar development in the French-Canadian sample when compared to both the African and Native American samples. Other researchers have begun to follow Tompkins' approach, with mixed results (Liversidge, 1998, Saunders et al., 1998; Watt and Lunt, 1998). Careful evaluations of population variability re-

quire large samples and careful sampling. Until there is widespread population data on microscopic crown and root formation rates (Antoine et al., 1998; FitzGerald et al., 1998) this question will not be resolved for skeletal biologists studying past populations.

Some years ago, Lovejoy and colleagues (1990) took a novel approach to the issue and attempted to numerically correct for population differences in chronological age estimation of a prehistoric Indian sample by comparing data on gingival emergence in Euro-Americans compared to Amerindians. The average absolute time of emergence is earlier in Amerindians and appears to increase with increasing age. Since the average discrepancy was calculated as .69 years at age 12, these authors applied a sliding scale of correction of .69/12 or .0575 years of delay per year to both deciduous and permanent tooth evaluations of developmental age using formation. Though ingenious, some of their assumptions are in error. For one, dental emergence is not closely correlated with dental development and can be strongly affected by premature tooth loss, itself exacerbated by high rates of dental pathology (Brauer and Bahador, 1942; Garn et al., 1960).

Accuracy of Age Estimation Methods

Tests of age prediction using children of known age have been reported from studies of living children (see Smith, 1991, for a review). The accuracy of age prediction is dependent upon the age range that is studied and the number of teeth observed. Variation in accuracy increases at older ages as sources of variability in dental development increase, but the more teeth that are examined, the more accurate the estimates. Smith's (1991) own comparison of the chronological age of several children to the stages of permanent mandibular tooth formation derived from the data of Moorrees et al. (1963a) suggests that dental age can be estimated to within 2 months for young children (the children ranged in age from 4 to 10 years).

A few researchers have examined the accuracy of dental age estimates in archeological

Estimated Ages of Burials
Three Age Methods, Same Sample

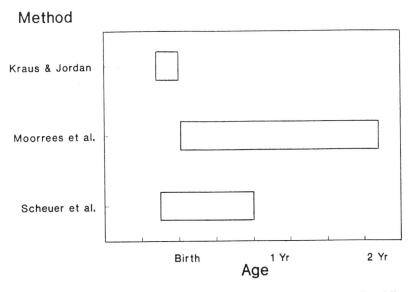

Figure 5.1 Ranges in estimated ages for the same sample of young infants are shown using three different methods: fetal dental development (Kraus and Jordan, 1965); postnatal dental development (Moorrees et al., 1963a), and diaphyseal length (Scheuer et al., 1980).

or forensic samples. Several of these have been tests of small samples of personally identified individuals (Bowman et al., 1992; Saunders et al., 1993; Liversidge, 1994) but they have used different methods and achieved variable results. Saunders and colleagues (1993a) also compared the overall distribution of age estimations from tooth formation in a large nineteenth-century Canadian sample to documented ages from burial records for the cemetery to determine the representativeness of the skeletal sample. Trying out several combinations of published dental formation standards, they observed that the combination of permanent and deciduous mandibular tooth standards based on the sample of children studied by Moorrees et al. (1963a, 1963b) produced the best comparisons of the skeletal sample to the age distributions recorded in the parish registers. They argue, mainly for methodological reasons, that the mandibular standards of Moorrees and colleagues work best, at least for North American or European

samples.[1] While other workers might prefer other standards, these authors point out that care must be taken not to apply truncated reference standards to cases of young children. For example, the standards of Anderson and colleagues (1976) begin at three years of age making them inappropriate for estimating the ages of infants and toddlers. As has been shown with age estimation reference standards for adults, the distributions of subadult age estimates for archaeological samples may be biased by and thus reflect the samples that were used to assign age. This is illustrated in Figure 5.1 in which several different standards were used to calculate age for a group of fetuses and newborns. Depending upon which standard is used, there are tendencies to under- or overage the individuals (Saunders and Spence, 1986).

[1]The standard of Moorrees and co-workers still suffers from problems. The high number of formation stages create problems with precision of observation and, most seriously, the charts of results of age variability for each stage are poorly reproduced and hard to interpolate,

Age evaluation for the prenatal and perinatal periods is generally based on fewer standards produced from much smaller samples. But Kraus and Jordan (1965) published data on very early crown coalescence from a sample of 737 human fetuses examined between 1954 and 1963. These standards have been applied to archaeological specimens in several cases known to this author (see Spence, 1986, and Saunders and Spence, 1986, for examples). Deutsch and colleagues (1985) have also provided data on deciduous anterior tooth crown length measurements and weights from a sample of 50 anatomically normal fetuses and infants aged 0–46 weeks, based on their total body size (actual gestational age is almost never known for fetal samples). Obviously, only the developing crown length standards can be used on archaeological samples. Skinner and Goodman (1992) have noted that there is still a distinct shortage of detailed standards for the early formation of deciduous tooth crowns that can be applied to late fetal and neonatal skeletons.

Physiological age of the immature skeleton, minus the teeth, must be assessed from either the appearance and union of bony epiphyses or from bone size. Diaphyseal length measurements are the common sources of skeletal age estimates from before birth to mid-teens because long bone epiphyses are assumed to be frequently lost at excavation. Even if they are recovered, trying to attach them to separate diaphyses would simply introduce more error. This limits the bone size technique of skeletal age estimation to a shorter portion of the total growth period, approximately late fetal to 12 years.

Since epiphyseal appearance is not readily applicable to excavated skeletons because of recovery problems, epiphyseal union becomes the favored method in the mid-teens when the process of gradual union of the epiphyses begins. Ubelaker (1989) provides a thorough discussion of the various standards available for age estimation from epiphyseal union. Important points to bear in mind are that sex differences also exist in the timing and sequence of epiphyseal union, there is a failure of many published studies to report full ranges of variation for the timing of union of epiphyses, and there are methodological problems with observation of the process and duration of union. Several years can elapse between the beginning and final closure of an epiphysis (McKern and Stewart, 1957) so that various "stages" of union can be defined. However, others have shown that interobserver error increases with the number of ranked stages of union defined for any one epiphysis (Webb and Suchey, 1985). There are some studies that have proposed using specific examples of growth center appearance, size increase, and early union for estimating skeletal age of infants and young children. These include the mandibular symphysis (Becker, 1986), the tympanic plate of the temporal bone (Curran and Weaver, 1982; Weaver, 1979), and development of the occipital bone (Redfield, 1970), but the age ranges appropriate to these criteria are often limited. More recently, careful examinations of the development of individual bones in the fetal, infant, and child skeleton have begun to produce more useful standards (Scheuer and MacLaughlin-Black, 1994).

Diaphyseal length is often used as an estimate of skeletal age when calcifying teeth are missing. But it must be remembered that bone development studies using skeletal samples require both dental and skeletal data so that dental age may be treated as the closest approximation to chronological age while skeletal age serves as a marker for alterations and defects of growth. Sources of diaphyseal length data include the radiographic samples mentioned above and dry bone measurements taken from archaeological samples (Armelagos et al., 1972; Hoffman, 1979; Hummert and Van Gerven, 1983; Johnston, 1962; Mensforth, 1985; Merchant and Ubelaker, 1977; Sundick, 1972; y'Edynak, 1976). The purpose of recording diaphyseal measurements from archaeological samples using dental development as an approximation of chronological age (true chronological age is unknown) is to try to account for population variation in bone size as well as to attempt assessments of population variation in growth. Ubelaker (1989) has shown that the calculated age at death from femur diaphyses using a number of different population standards varies widely. The total number of years within the range of estimates he calculated varies from 3.5 to 8.5 years and increases as bone size increases. Consequently, it is important to choose skeletal age standards appropriate for the known or suspected population affiliation of the individual or sample because this will greatly increase accuracy.

There also exist specific bone size standards for estimating fetal and perinatal age (Fasekas and Kósa, 1978; Kósa, 1989; Malinowski and Mllodziejowski, 1978; Olivier and Pineau, 1960; Palkama et al., 1962; Scheuer et al., 1980).[2] Here again, population variation is a factor (Scheuer et al., 1980). Ubelaker (1989) showed that there is a considerable range of variation in fetal age estimations, exceeding one-half lunar month, when using the Fazekas and Kósa regression equations. One other potential source of data for fetal and perinatal age estimation is fetal femur length measured using ultrasound (O'Brien and Queenan, 1981). An examination of mean ultrasound femur length at term is very close to mean length based on cadaver samples (Fasekas and Kósa, 1978; Olivier and Pineau, 1960).

The sample reported by Fasekas and Kósa (1978) is one of the most important because of its large size, although skeletal size is compared to body size in this sample and not to true gestational age. Fortunately for skeletal researchers, meticulous analysis of the Fasekas and Kósa data as well other samples by Sellier and colleagues (Bruzek et al., 1997; Sellier et al., 1997) has produced new equations for estimating body length—and therefore, age—from diaphyseal length in the skeletons of stillborns and neonates. This provides opportunities for researchers to con-

---

[2]Malinowski and Młodziejowski provide a useful review of early studies of the size of limb bones of fetuses and infants.

centrate on fetal and infant mortality as indicators of population health in past populations when these bones are well preserved in skeletal samples (Saunders and Barrans, 1999).

Other Age Estimation Methods

While the dental and skeletal methods described above are the main means of estimating age, there is also the possibility of using histological methods with subadult bones. Several important studies of cortical bone histology have included assessments of infants and children (Amprino and Bairati, 1936; Jowsey, 1960; Kerley, 1965). Bone turnover in the growing skeleton is usually seen as too complex to be used in age estimation because of the superimposition of bone modeling over remodeling of cellular based structures (Stout, 1992). Nevertheless, there may be some useful applications in the future (Saunders and DeVito, 1990).

One other possibility is to use a modification of the method of functional dental wear developed by A.E.W. Miles (1962, 1963, 1978). The advantage of this method is that it is specifically tailored to each population to which it is applied. One begins with dental age estimates from formation and emergence of pre-adult dentitions seriated from youngest to oldest. The degree of occlusal molar wear observed on *permanent* molars of age-estimated children and adolescents is then used to assign ages to the adults in a sample. The method is based on the premise that the first permanent molar will average six more years of wear than the second permanent molar, and so on. "Functional molar age" is then defined as the number of years for which the molar had been in use. Functional dental age estimates based on wear might be applied to older children and adolescents while deciduous tooth wear could also be examined as a check on dental age variability among individuals. Jackes (1992) indicates that wear assessments for estimating age should be supplemented with dental measurements.

GROWTH STUDIES OF ARCHAEOLOGICAL SKELETAL SAMPLES

While he was one of the first to attempt to study growth using archaeological skeletal samples, Johnston (1962) was also the first to caution that these samples do not represent the normal, healthy children in the population who lived but those who died to become part of a biased mortality sample. On the other hand, Lovejoy and colleagues (1990) have argued that most infant deaths among earlier groups were the result of not chronic but acute diseases and should not drastically alter dental or osteological maturation. They claim, as did Sundick (1978), that skeletal samples compare favorably to their counterparts who survived to adulthood. Other researchers are more conservative, arguing that deceased juveniles represent the minima rather than the modes of those who lived (Buikstra and Cook, 1980). To some, differential selection at death and the heterogeneity of mortality samples is a given (Whittington, 1991). Saunders and Hoppa (1993) addressed this issue by examining the literature on survivors and nonsurvivors in living populations. They observed that nonsurvivors have higher morbidity per age and higher levels of stress resulting in shorter height-for-age than survivors. After modeling the potential magnitude of biological mortality bias on linear growth by generating survivor and nonsurvivor distributions of height-for-age, they found that the difference in stature between survivors and nonsurvivors is significant, but the actual measurable difference in total femoral length is probably never more than several millimeters. These findings suggest that the effect of mortality bias on long bone lengths of juvenile skeletons from archaeological samples is minimal. Other factors such as sample sizes, aging methodologies, and preservation status probably have a greater impact on efforts to investigate growth retardation resulting from elevated stress in earlier populations.[3]

[3]But note my earlier comments about the possibility of mortality bias being reflected in tooth size.

One of the difficulties with the earliest growth-related studies is that chronological age was often estimated from combinations of dental and osseous criteria or from dental emergence alone (Armelagos et al., 1972; Johnston, 1962; Lallo, 1973; y'Edynak, 1976) (see Table 5.4). Some early researchers also attempted to separate male and female juveniles without any methodological justification. A turning point came with the use of dental development to estimate chronological age at death (Merchant and Ubelaker, 1977; Sundick, 1972). Nevertheless, because of constant efforts to "tinker" with age estimation methodologies, few existing publications are comparable even if we ignore the problem of mortality bias.

Measures of diaphyseal length when compared to estimated dental age in archaeological samples are necessarily cross-sectional, but with the superimposed problems of sex and age estimation. Longitudinal growth studies of living children, which follow a series of individuals continuously over substantial periods of time can examine individual growth patterns, the timing of significant growth events, and the relative velocities of growth. Only longitudinal growth studies can adequately examine individual variability in growth rates and patterns. Many who have studied juvenile long bone size in archaeological samples persist in referring to their results as growth curves. It must be remembered that these are not true growth curves in the sense that they are used in living growth studies, either cross-sectional or longitudinal since, of course, the dimensions represent deceased individuals who never reached maturity. There have even been attempts to examine the relative increase in percent diaphyseal size by dental age group to plot "growth in velocity." Again, these are analyses of velocity changes in long bone size, not true velocity curves as growth researchers use them.

Bearing in mind the above limitations, until recently studies of growth-related change in archaeological samples have been restricted to examining the adequacy of growth of children as an index of overall community health, or the adaptation of the population to its environment

(Johnston and Zimmer, 1989). No one has discovered any major differences in the direction or apparent pattern of skeletal size in the past. It could be argued that this means there have not been any major changes in human growth patterns over time, but such changes would have to be drastic to be detected in archaeological skeletal samples. Most or all skeletal samples of past groups appear shorter for age than modern groups. Might this represent genetic differences (see y'Edynak, 1976) or the effects of a harsh environment on the growth of disadvantaged children (Johnston and Zimmer, 1989)? Given what is known about the effects of the environment on the growth of the skeleton, we would expect that most cases represent environmental effects, that is, populations suffering from nutritional and disease-related stress. But a study of the historic-era skeletal sample from St. Thomas' Anglican Church, Belleville, Ontario, by Saunders and co-workers (1993b) suggests that these children followed a pattern of growth not unlike that of modern American children, up to at least 12 years of age, with perhaps the exception of those under 2 years who are slightly smaller than modern standards. This is contrasted with a sample of skeletons from the Raunds Site, a tenth century A.D. Anglo-Saxon cemetery (Hoppa, 1992) and a sample of skeletons from the Roman period cemeteries at Poundbury in England (Farwell and Molleson, 1993) as well as several other medieval and later period cemeteries from Britain (Molleson et al., 1993; Ribot and Roberts, 1996; Wiggins and Rogers, 1995), where individuals of comparable dental age had much shorter diaphyses.

There are several ways of assessing alterations to the growth process in skeletal samples: through examination for temporal changes that reflect changes in environmental quality within groups, or through comparison to modern samples with adequate control of population factors (age estimation, etc.). As long as we know that population migration was minimal, rapid changes over relatively short time periods are easily attributable to environmental changes since genetic change takes place much more slowly. Several studies have identified temporal changes in growth-related bone size. Lallo (1973; see also Goodman et al., 1984) found a decrease in the attained size of diaphyseal lengths in the Mississippian period (A.D. 1200–1300) in the central Illinois River valley and associated this with a dietary change from mixed foraging and farming to intensive maize agriculture.

Jantz and Owsley in their series of papers on the Arikara (Jantz and Owsley, 1984a, 1984b; Owsley and Jantz, 1985) showed that the latest group (in the late eighteenth and early nineteenth century) experienced the lowest rates of diaphyseal increase in size, particularly in late childhood and in the perinatal group (late fetal/early neonatal) of the archaeological samples. This is attributed to undernutrition, introduction of epidemic diseases, depopulation and intertribal conflict, and especially stress effects on the mother, later reflected in the perinatals. One might ask here how epidemic diseases would influence altered growth characteristics in the later samples since most contact period epidemics were acute and not chronic. They suggest that the native groups were undergoing declines in health status as European influence and encroachment from other tribes increased over time.

It is also possible to look for an association between smaller individuals in specific growth periods and other skeletal indicators of bone pathology. Hummert and associates (Hummert, 1983a, 1983b; Hummert and Van Gerven, 1983) have examined the relationship between diaphyseal lengths and cortical bone volume, Harris lines, and histomorphology in two medieval period samples from Sudanese Nubia. They identified differences between the early and late samples. However, while increases in bone lengths appear to have been fairly well maintained, percent cortical area revealed excessive endosteal resorption. This was attributed to nutritionally related stress. However, a later study of the geometric properties of these bones (Van Gerven et al., 1985; see also Ruff, Chapter 3) suggested that the reduction in percent cortical area could just as easily be interpreted as a response to increased bending

TABLE 5.4 Some Previous Growth Studies of Archaeological Samples

Source	Sample and Temporal Context	Sample Size	Age Range	Method
Johnston, 1962	Indian Knoll, Kentucky, Archaic Period. 3000 B.C.	165	fetal–5.5 yrs	Dental erupt. & osseous.
Mahler, 1968 (see Armelagos et al., 1972)	Nubians, Wadi Halfa 350 B.C.–A.D. 1350	115	6 mos.–31 yrs.	Dental erupt. & osseous
Walker, 1969	Lake Woodland, Illinois	43	nb[a]–12 yrs.	?
Sundick, 1972	Indian Knoll, Kentucky, Archaic Period. 3000 B.C.	128	nb–18 yrs.	Dental development
Lallo, 1973 (see Goodman et al., 1984)	Dickson Mounds, Woodland–Mississippian	557	nb–35 yrs.	Multiple
y'Edynak, 1976	Eskimo and Aleut	109	nb–20 yrs.	Dental erupt. & osseous.
Merchant & Ubelaker, 1977	Mobridge Site, Arikara, A.D. 1700–1750	193	nb–18.5 yrs.	Dental development
Sundick, 1978	Altenerding, W. Germany, 6–7th centuries A.D.	82	nb–18 yrs.	Dental development
Jantz and Owsley, 1984a, 1984b, 1985	Arikara, seven samples	~500	nb–12 yrs.	Adjusted dental development
Hummert, 1983a, 1983b	Kulubnarti, Nubia, early and late Christian A.D. 550–1450	180	nb–16 yrs.	Dental development
Cook, 1974	Illinois Valley, Woodland and Mississippian	ca. 244	nb–6 yrs.	Dental development
Mensforth, 1985	Libben Late Woodland & Bt-5 Archaic	85 45	nb–10 yrs.	Dental development
Saunders & Melbye, 1990	Late Ontario Iroquois, A.D. 1615	147 146	nb–15 yrs.	Dental development

Reference	Site	N	Age range	Study
Lovejoy et al., 1990	Libben Site, Ohio, Late Woodland, A.D. 800–1100	152	nb–12 yrs.	Dental development
Hoppa, 1992	Raunds, Berinsfield and Exeter, Anglo-Saxon medieval	90	nb–16 yrs.	Dental development
Saunders et al., 1993b	St. Thomas' Anglican Church cemetery, 19th cent. 1821–1874	281	Fetal–15 yrs.	Dental development
Farwell and Molleson, 1993	Poundbury Camp, Dorchester, U.K. Late Roman	>400	<20 yrs.	Dental development
Molleson et al., 1993	Spitalfields Crypt, East London, U.K. late 18th–early 19th centuries	187	<20 yrs.	Dental development
Wiggins and Rogers, 1995	Barton-on-Humber, U.K. Medieval England	650 of 850	?	Dental development
Miles and Bulman, 1994	Ensay, Scotland A.D. 1500–1850	120	Fetal–20 yrs.	Dental development
Dillingham, 1996	Toqua Site, Tennessee Late Mississippian Dalla Phase A.D. 1200–1650	145 subadults 33 femora	Prenatal–2.5yrs.	Dental development
Ribot and Roberts, 1996	Raunds, Chicester 8th–12th centuries A.D.	180	<18–20 yrs.	Dental & osseous development
Hutchins, 1998	Milwaukee County Almshouse late 19th–early 20th centuries	138	Fetal–6 mos.	Dental development

[a]nb = newborn

strength (developed as the children grew normally) and that there might not be any evidence of environmental stress on growth at all. On the other hand, there is definite evidence that bone growth in length will be maintained at the expense of growth in cortical thickness in the face of nutritional and disease stress (Himes, 1978; Huss-Ashmore, 1981). These kinds of comparisons require further study.

Several examinations of temporal and within-site variations in growth-related features have also been conducted by Mensforth (1985) and Lovejoy and colleagues (1990) on prehistoric sites in Kentucky and Ohio. Mensforth (1985) identified early long bone growth retardation in the Late Woodland Libben, Ohio, sample (A.D. 800–1100) when compared to Late Archaic period foragers from the Carlston Annis Bt-5 site in Kentucky (2655–3992 B.C.), specifically in the 6- month to 4-year age range, and suggested high levels of infectious disease in the first years of life as the implicating factor. This was based on the identification of a high prevalence of periosteal reactive bone in the subadults, indicating infection. Lovejoy and co-workers (1990) have provided documentation of this situation in their study of the normalized values for the Libben sample compared to healthy Euro-American children. Both studies note that there is evidence that the Libben people ate a nutritionally adequate diet. They attribute elevated disease loads to higher population density and a greater degree of sedentism compared to seasonally mobile hunter-gatherers. While this is difficult to demonstrate for past populations, it is a compelling argument that has been used in other investigations (Katzenberg, 1992; Larsen, 1997; Ribot and Roberts, 1996; Saunders et al., 1992).

SUGGESTIONS FOR FUTURE RESEARCH

Sex Determination

Logic says that there should be sufficient dimorphism for sex separation in fetal and early infant skeletons because of the presence of high levels of testosterone. Dimorphism should increase again at adolescence as pubertal changes begin to occur. But the percentages of observed subadult skeletal dimorphism are believed to be low compared to levels observed in the adult pelvis. In Weaver's (1980) study of hip bones, two indices, although not significantly different between the sexes but which fit expected patterns, showed dimorphism ranging from 0.2–9.9%. Specker and colleagues (1987), in their analysis of bone mineral index in 5- to 7-year-old children, observed 17.7%— surprisingly high dimorphism. The ranges of dimorphism for a variety of adult pelvic indices (Kelley, 1979; MacLaughlin and Bruce, 1986; Schulter-Ellis, 1983) are between 10 and 26% with the highest levels deriving from Kelley's sciatic notch/acetabular index.

The teeth, because of their constancy of size after development, should be good indicators of subadult sexual dimorphism. However, the magnitude of tooth dimorphism is also fairly low, as indicated above. Here, dimorphism is attributed to protracted amelogenesis in the developing male tooth crowns, which results in thicker enamel, a process that will also be affected by individual variability (Moss and Moss-Salentjin, 1977). There has been some success with sex discrimination using measurements of the permanent teeth (De Vito and Saunders, 1990; and see Mayhall, Chapter 4) and more recently, with combinations of permanent and deciduous teeth and even deciduous teeth alone (DeVito and Saunders, 1990). But population variation in both tooth size and dimorphism remain the stumbling blocks to the application of discriminant functions derived from specific groups. It should also be pointed out that population differences in tooth size are independent of population differences in tooth size dimorphism, further complicating the issue (DeVito, 1989). Problems of tooth preservation and postmortem damage are less of an issue here. Interest in permanent tooth dimorphism as an indicator of sex was generated from a desire to characterize fragmentary samples where teeth are the best preserved or least destroyed elements. However, if deciduous tooth dimorphism could be used with some reliability, it would be applicable to teeth that are generally in better condition than permanent teeth, less affected by caries, wear, and other trauma. Here, careful excavation is crucial since it is certainly possible to recover incompletely calcified tooth crowns still in their crypts.

It would be helpful if, in the future, skeletal researchers could have access to large samples of subadult skeletons of known sex and age, be they accumulations of data from forensic cases (which are, fortunately, still rare) or more likely, from identified individuals excavated from historically documented cemeteries. Recently, Humphrey (1998) has examined subadult sexual dimorphism in a documented church crypt sample from a growth perspective. She found clear differences within the infracranial skeleton in terms of the relative contributions of sexual differences in growth rate and duration to adult sexual dimorphism. The development of sexual dimorphism is clearly a result of a complex pattern of interacting factors.

Sex determination of archeological samples using DNA extraction and analysis of sex specific gene fragments is of great promise but not yet ready to solve all our problems. There are still issues of consistency, control, false negatives, and false positives to deal with in DNA analysis as well as the current cost and expense of testing large samples from which substantial proportions may never yield amplifiable DNA. But this is an exciting area of research that holds the most potential for the future.

Age Estimation

There is still a need for further examination of dental development in a variety of population groups. In particular, we need information on deciduous tooth development (quantified at macroscopic and microscopic levels) gathered from living individuals. While there will not be much in the way of longitudinal tooth development data in the future, since the widespread use of research X rays has been curtailed, there is still the possibility of amassing large samples of cross-sectional data from clinical, radiographic databases (Trodden, 1982). Yet, archaeological samples themselves may be the best sources of data for devising and improving on methods of skeletal and even dental age estimation. Identified cases from historic archaeological sites can, again, act as a database for exploring deciduous crown and root development, dental wear as a subadult age estimation technique, and histological age changes in cortical and possibly even trabecular bone.

If population differences in the rates and timing of dental development exist, then the problem of how to compare two samples using consistent estimates of dental age and thereby search for meaningful differences in skeletal growth must still be solved. This work is only beginning and perhaps will be solved by analyses of microscopic enamel and dentine formation to determine the range of variability in dental development.

Growth-Related Research

To continue to pursue growth-related research on archaeological skeletal samples we need some solutions to the problems identified above. Pragmatically, the most useful research at present would be to utilize ranges established for population variation in growth and development in the kinds of living groups that are comparable to the archaeological samples we are studying. We will never be able to conduct longitudinal studies of growth in the past but we can refine our cross-sectional comparisons between archaeological samples and modern group data.

Since there is little likelihood of examining the skeletons of willed bodies of subadults, occasional forensic cases of immature individuals serve as very important sources of data for improving our methods of identification. One other source that has considerable potential is the recovery of identified individuals from historic cemeteries with associated documentation. Stored databases of clinical radiographs might also prove useful in this regard.

This survey has been cautionary but it is not pessimistic. There is considerable potential for the analysis of growth-related phenomena in archaeological skeletal samples. Studies of historical samples, especially those with associated documentation, may allow us to test some of our assumptions about the nature of human mortality samples so that we can reach confident conclusions about prehistoric peoples.

ACKNOWLEDGMENTS

Work conducted on the St. Thomas', Belleville, sample was made possible by collaboration with Dr. Heather McKillop and thanks to the permission for study provided by St. Thomas' Anglican Church and its congregation. The skeletal research on the St. Thomas' sample has been supported by grants from the Ontario Heritage Foundation, the Bridge St. Foundation, the Arts Research Board of McMaster University, and the Social Sciences and Humanities Research Council of Canada. This chapter could not have been written without the collaboration and support of the SSHRC grant team, Gerry Boyce, Ann Herring, and Larry Sawchuk. I would also like to thank Rob Hoppa for stimulating research discussions and for his association as a scientific colleague.

REFERENCES

Amprino J, Bairati EA. 1936. Processi di reconstruzione e di riassorbimento nella sostansa compaata delle osa dell nomo. Richerche see cento soggetto della nascita sino a tarda eta. Z Zellforsch Mikrosk Anat 24:439–511.

Anderson DL, Thompson GW, Popovich F. 1976. Age of attainment of mineralization stages of the permanent dentition. J Forensic Sci 21:191–200.

Antoine D, Dean MC, Hillson S. 1998. Periodicity of incremental structures in dental enamel based on the developing dentition from post medieval known-age children. 11th International Symposium on Dental Morphology. August 26–30, 1998, Oulu, Finland. Abstract #10.

Armelagos GJ, Mielke JH, Owen KH, Van Gerven DP. 1972. Bone growth and development in prehistoric populations from Sudanese Nubia. J Hum Evol 1:89–119.

Beattie O. 1982. An assessment of X-ray energy spectroscopy and bone trace element analysis for the determination of sex from fragmentary human skeletons. Can J Anthropol 2:205–215.

Becker MJ. 1986. Mandibular symphysis (medial suture) closure in modern Homo sapiens: preliminary evidence from archaeological populations. Am J Phys Anthropol 69:499–501.

Black TK. 1978. Sexual dimorphism in the tooth-crown diameters of the deciduous teeth. Am J Phys Anthropol 48:77–82.

Boucher BJ. 1955. Sex differences in the foetal sciatic notch. J Forensic Med 2:51–54.

Boucher BJ. 1957. Sex differences in the foetal pelvis. Am J Phys Anthropol n.s. 15:581–600.

Bowman JE, MacLaughlin SM, Scheuer JL. 1992. The relationship between biological and chronological age in the juvenile remains from St. Bride's Church, Fleet Street. Ann Hum Biol 19:216.

Brauer JC, Bahador MA. 1942. Variation in calcification and eruption of the deciduous and permanent teeth. J Am Dent Assoc 29:1373.

Bruzek J, Sellier P, Tillier AM. 1997. Variabilité et incertitude de l'estimation de l'âge des non-adultes: le cas des individus morts en période périnatale. Actes des 7e Journées anthropologiques." L'Enfant, Son Corps, Son Histoire." Editions APDCA.

Buikstra JE, Cook DC. 1980. Paleopathology: an American account. Ann Rev Anthropol 9: 433–470.

Chertkow S. 1980. Tooth mineralization as an indicator of the pubertal growth spurt. Am J Orthod 77:79–91.

Choi SC, Trotter M. 1970. A statistical study of the multivariate structure and race-sex differences of American white and Negro fetal skeletons. Am J Phys Anthropol 33:307–312.

Cook DC. 1984 Subsistence and health in the Lower Illinois Valley: osteological evidence. In: Cohen MN, Armelagos GJ, editors. Paleopathology at the Origins of Agriculture. Orlando, Fla.: Academic Press. pp. 237–271.

Cook DC, Buikstra JE. 1979. Health and differential survival in prehistoric populations: pre-natal dental defects. Am J Phys Anthropol 51: 649–664.

Curran BK, Weaver DS. 1982. The use of the coefficient of agreement and likelihood ratio test to examine the development of the tympanic plate using a known-age sample of fetal and infant skeletons. Am J Phys Anthropol 58:343–346.

Currey JD, Butler G. 1975. The mechanical properties of bone tissue in children. J Bone Joint Surg 57A:810–814.

Demirjian A. 1978. Dentition. In: Falkner F, Tanner JM, editors. Human Growth. Vol 2, Postnatal Growth. New York: Plenum Press. pp. 413–444.

Demirjian A, Goldstein H. 1976. New systems for dental maturity based on seven and four teeth. Ann Hum Biol 3:411–421.

Demirjian A, Goldstein H, Tanner JM. 1973. A new system of dental age assessment. Hum Biol 45:211–228.

Dennison J. 1979. Citrate estimation as a means of determining the sex of human skeletal remains. Arch Phys Anthropol Oceania XIV:136–143.

Deutsch D, Tam O, Stack MV. 1985. Postnatal changes in size, morphology and weight of developing postnatal deciduous anterior teeth. Growth 49:202–217.

De Vito C. 1989. Discriminant Function Analysis of Deciduous Teeth to Determine Sex. M.A. Thesis. McMaster University.

De Vito C, Saunders SR. 1990. A discriminant function analysis of deciduous teeth to determine sex. J Forensic Sci 35:845–858.

Dillingham PC. 1996 Long bone growth variation in children from the Toqua site (40MR6). Am J Phys Anthropol Suppl 22:98 (abstract).

El-Nofely A, İşcan MY. 1989. Assessment of age from the dentition in children. In: İşcan MY, editor. Age Markers in the Human Skeleton. Springfield, Ill.: Charles C Thomas. pp. 237–254.

Fanning, EA. 1961. A longitudinal study of tooth formation and tooth resorption. N.Z. Dent. J. 57:202.

Faerman M, Filon D, Kahila G, Greenblatt CL, Smith P, Oppenheim A. 1995. Sex identification of archaeological human remains based on amplification of the X and Y amelogenin alleles. Gene 167:327–332

Farwell DE, Molleson TI. 1993. Poundbury. Vol. 2, The Cemeteries. Dorset Natural History and Archaeological Society, Monograph Series Number 11.

Fasekas IG, Kósa F. 1978. Forensic Fetal Osteology. Budapest: Akadémiai Kiadó.

FitzGerald C, Saunders SR, Macchiarelli R, Bondioli L. 1998. Deciduous crown formation times of a large archaeological sample determined by histological microstructural analysis. 11th International Symposium on Dental Morphology. August 26–30, 1998, Oulu, Finland. Abstract #9, pp. 92–101.

Forfar JO, Arneil GC. 1978. Textbook of Pediatrics. Edinburgh: Churchill Livingstone.

Garn SM, Lewis AB, Koski PK, Polachek DL. 1958. Variability of tooth formation. J Dent Res 38:135.

Garn SM, Lewis AB, Polachek DL. 1960. Interrelations in dental development. 1. Interrelationships within the dentition. J Dent Res 39:1049.

Gibbs LM. 1985. Preliminary report on the use of citrate levels from human skeletal remains as a possible determinant of sex. Paper presented at the 13th Canadian Association for Physical Anthropology Meetings, Thunder Bay, Ontario.

Gibbs LM. 1991. Citrate, Sex and Skeletal Remains. M.A. Thesis. McMaster University. Hamilton, Ontario.

Goode-Null SK. 1996. A comparative evaluation of two juvenile sexing techniques. Am J Phys Anthropol Suppl 22:114–115.

Goodman AH, Brooke TR, Swedlund AC, Armelagos GJ. 1988. Biocultural perspectives on stress in prehistoric, historical and contemporary population research. Yrbk Phys Anthropol 31:169–202.

Goodman AH, Lallo J, Armelagos GJ, Rose JC. 1984. Health changes at Dickson Mounds, Illinois (A.D. 950–1300). In: Cohen MN, Armelagos GJ, editors. Paleopathology at the Origins of Agriculture. Orlando, Fla.: Academic Press. pp. 271–306.

Gordon CC, Buikstra JE. 1981. Soil pH, bone preservation, and sampling bias at mortuary sites. Am Antiq 48:566–571.

Guy H, Masset C, Baud C. 1997. Infant taphonomy. Int J Osteoarch 7:221–229.

Haavikko K. 1970. The formation and the alveolar and clinical eruption of the permanent teeth. Suomen Hammaslaak Toim 66:103–170.

Harris EF, McKee JH. 1990. Tooth mineralization standards for blacks and whites from the middle southern United States. J Forensic Sci 35: 859–872.

Herring A, Saunders S, Boyce G. 1991. Bones and burial registers: infant mortality in a 19th-century cemetery from Upper Canada. Northeast Hist Arch 20:54–70.

Himes JH. 1978. Bone growth and development in protein-calorie malnutrition. World Rev Nutr Diet 28:143–187.

Hoffman JM. 1979. Age estimations from diaphyseal lengths: two months to twelve years. J Forensic Sci 24:461–469.

Holcomb SMC, Konigsberg LW. 1995. Statistical study of sexual dimorphism in the human fetal sciatic notch. Am J Phys Anthropol 97:113–126.

Hoppa RD. 1992. Evaluating human skeletal growth: an Anglo-Saxon example. Int J Osteoarch 2:275–288.

Hoppa RD, Gruspier KL. 1996. Estimating diaphseal length from fragmentary subadult skeletal remains: implications for palaeodemographic reconstructions of a southern Ontario ossuary. Am J Phys Anthropol 100:341–354.

Hoppa RD, Saunders SR. 1998. The MAD legacy: How meaningful is mean age-at-death in skeletal samples. Intl J Anthropol 13(3):1–14.

Hummel S, Herrmann B. 1994. Y-chromosome DNA from ancient bones. In: Herrmann B, Hummel S, editors. Ancient DNA. New York: Springer-Verlag. pp. 205–210.

Hummert JR. 1983a. Childhood Growth and Morbidity in a Medieval Population from Kulubnarti in the "Batn El Hajar" of Sudanese Nubia. Ph.D. Dissertation. University of Colorado at Boulder.

Hummert JR. 1983b. Cortical bone growth and dietary stress among subadults from Nubia's Batn el Hajar. Am J Phys Anthropol 62:167–176.

Hummert JR, Van Gerven DP. 1983. Skeletal growth in a medieval population from Sudanese Nubia. Am J Phys Anthropol 60:471–478.

Humphrey LT. 1998. Growth patterns in the modern human skeleton. Am J Phys Anthropol 105: 57–72.

Hunt DR. 1990. Sex determination in the subadult ilia: an indirect test of Weaver's nonmetric sexing method. J Forensic Sci 35:881–885.

Hunt EE, Gleiser I. 1955. The estimation of age and sex of preadolescent children from bones and teeth. Am J Phys Anthropol 13:479–487.

Huss-Ashmore R. 1981. Bone growth and remodeling as a measure of nutritional stress. In: Martin DL, Bumsted MP, editors. Biocultural Adaptation: Comprehensive Approaches to Skeletal Analysis. Amherst, Mass.: Department of Anthropology, University of Massachusetts at Amherst. pp. 84–95. Research Reports No. 20.

Hutchins LA 1998. Standards of infant long bone diaphyseal growth from a late nineteenth century and early twentieth century almshouse cemetery. M.Sc. Thesis. The University of Wisconsin–Milwaukee.

Jackes M. 1992. Paleodemography: problems and techniques. In: Saunders SR, Katzenberg MA, editors. The Skeletal Biology of Past Peoples: Advances in Research Methods. New York: Wiley-Liss. pp. 189–224.

Jantz RL, Owsley DW. 1984a. Temporal changes in limb proportionality among skeletal samples of Arikara Indians. Ann Hum Biol 11:157–164.

Jantz RL. Owsley DW. 1984b. Long bone growth variation among Arikara skeletal populations. Am J Phys Anthropol 63:13–20.

Jantz, RL, Owsley DW. 1985. Patterns of infant and early childhood mortality in Arikara skeletal populations. In: Status, Structure and Stratification. M. Thompson, MT Garcia, and FJ Kense, eds. Proceeding of the Sixteenth Annual Conference, Chacmool, University of Calgary, Calgary, Alberta.

Johnston FE. 1961. Sequence of epiphyseal union in a prehistoric Kentucky population from Indian Knoll. Hum Biol 33:66–81.

Johnston FE. 1962. Growth of the long bones of infants and young children at Indian Knoll. Am J Phys Anthropol 20:249–254.

Johnston FE. 1968. Growth of the skeleton in earlier peoples. In: Brothwell DR, editor. The Skeletal Biology of Earlier Human Populations. Oxford: Pergamon Press. pp. 57–66.

Johnston FE. 1969. Approaches to the study of developmental variability in human skeletal populations. Am J Phys Anthropol 31:335–341.

Johnston FE, Zimmer LO. 1989. Assessment of growth and age in the immature skeleton. In: İşcan MY, Kennedy KAR, editors. Reconstruction of Life from the Skeleton. New York: Alan R. Liss. pp. 11–22.

Jowsey J. 1960. Age changes in human bone. Clin Orthop 17:210–218.

Katzenberg, MA. 1992. Changing diet and health in pre- and proto-historic Ontario. In: Huss-Ashmore R, Schall J, Hediger M, editors. Health and Lifestyle Change. The University Museum of Archaeology and Anthropology, University of Pennsylvania, Philadelphia pp. 23–31. MASCA Research Papers in Science and Archaeology.

Kelley MA. 1979. Sex determination with fragmented skeletal remains. J Forensic Sci 24: 154–158.

Kerley ER. 1965. The microscopic determination of age in human bone. Am J Phys Anthropol 23: 149–163.

Kósa F. 1989. Age estimation from the fetal skeleton. In: İşcan MY, editor. Age Markers in the Human Skeleton. Springfield, Ill.: Charles C. Thomas. pp. 21–54.

Kraus BS, Jordan RE. 1965. The Human Dentition Before Birth. Philadelphia: Lea & Febiger.

Lallo J. 1973. The Skeletal Biology of Three Prehistoric American Indian Societies from Dickson Mounds. Ph.D. Dissertation. Department of Anthropology, University of Massachusetts, Amherst.

Larsen CS. 1997. Bioarchaeology: Interpreting Behavior from the Human Skeleton. Cambridge; Cambridge University Press.

Lengyel I. 1968. Biochemical aspects of early skeletons. In: Brothwell DR, editor. Skeletal Biology of Earlier Human Populations. Oxford: Pergamon Press. pp. 271–278.

Lewis AB, Garn SM. 1960. The relationship between tooth formation and other maturational factors. Angle Orthod 30:70.

Lilley JM, Stroud G, Brothwell DR, Williamson MH. 1994. The Jewish Burial Ground at Jewbury. York: York Archaeological Trust, Council for British Archaeology.

Liversidge HM. 1994. Accuracy of age estimation from developing teeth of a population of known age (0–5.4 years). Int J Osteoarch 4:37–46.

Liversidge H. 1998. Relative dental formation in humans before the emergence of M_1. 11th International Symposium on Dental Morphology. August 26–30, 1998, Oulu, Finland. Abstract #44.

Liversidge HM, Dean MC, Molleson TI. 1993. Increasing human tooth length between birth and 5.4 years. Am J Phys Anthropol 90:307–314.

Loevy HT. 1983. Maturation of permanent teeth in black and Latino children. J Dent Res 62A:296.

Lovejoy CO, Russell KF, Harrison ML. 1990. Long bone growth velocity in the Libben Population. Am J Hum Biol 2:533–542.

Lynch KA, Mineau GP, Anderton DL. 1985. Estimates of infant mortality on the western frontier: the use of genealogical data. Historical Methods 18:155–164.

MacLaughlin SM, Bruce MF. 1986. The sciatic notch/acetabular index as a discriminator of sex in European skeletal remains. J Forensic Sci 31:1380–1390.

Macho GA, Wood BA. 1995. The role of time and timing in hominid dental evolution. Evol Anthropol 4:17–31.

Mahler, PE. 1968. Growth of the long bones in a prehistoric population from Sudanese Nubia. MA dissertation. University of Utah.

Majó T, Tillier A-M, Bruzek J. 1993. Test des fonctions discriminantes de Schutkowski impliquant l'ilium pou la determination du sexe dans des series d'enfants de sex et d'age connus. Bull Mem Soc D'Anthropol Paris. 5:61–68.

Malinowski A, Młodziejowski B. 1978. Development of long bones of lower limbs in human fetuses. Colleg Anthropolog 2:196–205.

Mazess RB, Cameron JR. 1972. Growth of bone in school children: comparison of radiographic morphometry and photon absorptiometry. Growth 36:77–92.

McKern TW, Stewart TD. 1957. Skeletal age changes in young American males analysed from the standpoint of age identification. Environmental Protection Research Division Quartermaster Research and Development Center. U.S. Army Tech, Report EP-45, 1957. Natick, Massachusetts.

McKillop H, Marshall S, Boyce G, Saunders S. 1989. Excavations at St. Thomas' Church, Belleville, Ontario: A Nineteenth Century Cemetery. Paper presented at the Ontario Archaeological Symposium, London, Ontario.

McWhirr AL, Viner L, Wells C. 1982. Romano-British Cemeteries at Cirencester. Cirencester Excavation Committee, Corinium Museum, Cirencester, England.

Mensforth RP. 1985. Relative tibia long bone growth in the Libben and Bt-5 prehistoric skeletal populations. Am J Phys Anthropol 68:247–262.

Mensforth RP, Lovejoy CO, Lallo JW, Armelagos GJ. 1978. The role of constitutional factors, diet, and infectious disease in the etiology of porotic hyperostosis and periosteal reactions in prehistoric infants and children. Med Anthropol 2:1–59.

Merchant VL, Ubelaker DH. 1977. Skeletal growth of the protohistoric Arikara. Am J Phys Anthropol 46:61–72.

Miles AEW. 1962. Assessment of the ages of a population of Anglo-Saxons from their dentitions. Proc R Soc Med 55:881–886.

Miles AEW. 1963. The dentition in the assessment of individual age in skeletal material. In: Brothwell DR, editor. Dental Anthropology. New York: Pergamon Press. pp. 191–209.

Miles AEW. 1978. Teeth as an indicator of age in man. In: Butler PA, Joysey KA, editors. Development, Function and Evolution of Teeth. London: Academic Press. pp. 455–464.

Miles AEW, Bulman JS. 1994. Growth curves of immature bones from a Scottish island population c.1600 A.D. Int J Osteoarch 4(2):121–136.

Mittler DM, Sheridan SG. 1992. Sex determination in subadults using auricular surface morphology. J Forensic Sci 37:1068–1075.

Molleson T, Cox M, Waldron AH, Whittaker DK. 1993. The Spitalfields Project. Vol. 2, The Anthropology, The Middling Sort. Council for British Archaeology. CBA Research Report 86. York, England.

Moorrees CFA, Fanning EA, Hunt EE. 1963a. Age variation of formation stages for ten permanent teeth. J Dent Res 42:1490–1501.

Moorrees CFA, Fanning EA, Hunt EE. 1963b. Formation and resorption of three deciduous teeth in children. Am J Phys Anthropol 21:205–213.

Morton DG. 1942. Observations of the development of pelvic conformation. Am J Obstet Gynecol 44:789–819.

Morton DG, Hayden CT. 1941. A comparative study of male and female pelves in children with a consideration of the etiology of pelvic conformation. Am J Obstet Gynecol 41:485–495.

Moss ML, Moss-Salentijn L. 1977. Analysis of developmental processes possibly related to human sexual dimophsim in permanent and deciduous canines. Am J Phys Anthropol 46:407–414.

Mudd JL. 1984. Determination of sex from forcibly removed hairs. J Forensic Sci 29:1072.

Nanda RS, Chawla TN. 1966. Growth and development of dentitions in Indian school children. I. Development of permanent teeth. Am J. Orthod 52:837.

Nawrocki SP. 1995. Taphonomic processes in historic cemeteries. In: Grauer, AL, editor. Bodies of Evidence: Reconstructing History Through Skeletal Analysis. New York: Wiley-Liss. pp. 49–68.

Nichols R, Townsend E, Malina R. 1983. Development of permanent dentition in Mexican American children. Am J Phys Anthropol 60:232.

Nielsen HG, Ravn JJ. 1976. A radiographic study of mineralization of permanent teeth in a group of children aged 3–7 years. Scand J Dent Res 84:109–118.

Nolla CM. 1960. The development of the permanent teeth. J Dent Child 27:254.

O'Brien GD, Queenan JT. 1981. Growth of the ultrasound fetal femur length during normal pregnancy. Am J Obstet Gynecol 141:833–837.

Olivier G, Pineau H. 1960. Nouvelle determination de la taille foetale d'apres les longueurs diaphysaires des os longs. Ann Med Leg 40:141–144.

Ortner DJ. 1998. Workshop X: Human skeletal disease with an emphasis on diseases caused by malnutrition. Paleopathology Association Meetings, Salt Lake City, Utah.

Ortner DJ, Mays S. 1998. Dry-bone manifestations of rickets in infancy and early childhood. Int J Osteoarch 8:45–55.

Ounsted M, Scott A, Moar V. 1981. Proportionality and gender in small-for-dates and large-for dates babies. Early Hum Devel 5:289–298.

Owsley DW, Jantz RL. 1983. Formation of the permanent dentition in Arikara Indians: timing differences that affect dental age assessments. Am J Phys Anthropol 61:467–471.

Owsley DW, Jantz RL. 1985. Long bone lengths and gestational age distributions of post-contact period Arikara Indian perinatal infant skeletons. Am J Phys Anthropol 68:321–329.

Paine RR, Harpending HC. 1998. Effect of sample bias on paleodemographic fertility estimates. Am J Phys Anthropol 105:231–240.

Palkama A, Virtama P, Telkka A. 1962. Estimation of stature from radiographs of long bones in children. II. Children under one year of age. Annales Medicinae Experimentalis et Biologiae Fenniae (Helsinki) 40:219–222.

Redfield A. 1970. A new aid to aging immature skeletons: development of the occipital bone. Am J Phys Anthropol 33:207–220.

Reynolds EL. 1945. The bony pelvic girdle in early infancy. Am J Phys Anthropol n.s. 3:321.

Reynolds EL. 1947. The bony pelvis in prepubertal childhood. Am J Phys Anthropol n.s. 5:165–200.

Ribot I, Roberts C. 1996. A study of non-specific stress indicators and skeletal growth in two mediaeval subadult populations. J Arch Sci 23:67–79.

Saunders SR. 1992. Subadult skeletons and growth related studies. In: Saunders SR, Katzenberg MA, editors. Skeletal Biology of Past Peoples: Research Methods. New York: Wiley-Liss. pp. 1–20.

Saunders SR, Barrans L. 1999. What can be done about the infant category in skeletal samples? In: Hoppa RD, FitzGerald CM, editors. Human Growth in the Past: Studies from Bones and Teeth. Cambridge Studies in Biological and Evolutionary Anthropology 25. Cambridge University Press, pp. 153–209.

Saunders SR, DeVito C. 1990. Variability in cortical bone microstructure in the subadult human femur. Am J Phys Anthropol 81:290–291.

Saunders SR, DeVito C, Herring A, Southern R, Hoppa R. 1993a. Accuracy tests of tooth formation age estimations for human skeletal remains. Am J Phys Anthropol 92:173–188.

Saunders SR, Fitzgerald W. 1988. Life and death in sixteenth century Ontario. Paper presented to the McMaster Symposium, Hamilton, Ontario.

Saunders SR, Herring DA, Boyce G. 1995b. Can skeletal samples accurately represent the living populations they come from? The St. Thomas' cemetery site, Belleville, Ontario. In: Grauer AJ, editor. Bodies of Evidence: Reconstructing History Through Skeletal Analysis. New York, John Wiley & Sons. pp. 69–89.

Saunders SR, Herring DA, Ramsden PG. 1992. Transformation and disease: precontact Ontario Iroquoians. In: Verano JW, Ubelaker DH, editors. Disease and Demography in the Americas.

Washington: Smithsonian Institution Press. pp. 117–126.

Saunders SR, Herring DA, Sawchuk LA, Boyce G. 1995a. The nineteenth-century cemetery at St. Thomas' Anglican Church, Belleville: skeletal remains, parish records, and censuses. In: Saunders SR, Herring DA., editors. Grave Reflections: Portraying the Past Through Cemetery Studies. Toronto: Canadian Scholar's Press. pp. 93–118.

Saunders SR, Hoppa RD. 1993. Growth deficit in survivors and non-survivors: biological mortality bias in subadult skeletal samples. Yrbk Phys Anthropol 36:127–152.

Saunders SR, Hoppa R, Southern R. 1993b. Diaphyseal growth in a nineteenth century skeletal sample of subadults from St. Thomas' Church, Belleville, Ontario. Int J Osteoarch 3:265–281.

Saunders SR, Hoppa RD, Sperduti A, Bondioli L, Macchiarelli R. 1998. The juvenile skeletal sample of the imperial Roman site of Portus Romae, Italy. Canadian Association for Physical Anthropology, 26th Annual Meeting. Calgary; Alta. p. 25.

Saunders SR, Melbye FJ. 1990. Subadult mortality and skeletal indicators of health in Late Woodland Ontario Iroquois. Can J Arch 14: 61–74.

Saunders SR, Spence MW. 1986. Dental and skeletal age determinations of Ontario Iroquois infant burials. Ont Arch 46:21–26.

Saunders SR, Yang D. 1999. Sex determination: XX or XY from the human skeleton. In: Fairgrieve SI, editor. Forensic Osteological Analysis: A Book of Case Studies. Springfield, Ill.: Charles C. Thomas. pp. 36–59.

Sawchuk LA, Burke SDA. 1998. Out of the darkness and into first light: assessing mortality in the early Canadian community of Belleville, Ontario, 1876–1885. Urban History, (in press).

Scheuer L, MacLaughlin-Black S. 1994. Age estimation from the pars basilaris of the fetal and juvenile occipital bone. Int J Osteoarch 4: 377–382.

Scheuer JL, Musgrave JH, Evans SP. 1980. The estimation of late fetal and perinatal age from limb bone length by linear and logarithmic regression. Ann Hum Biol 7:257–265.

Schulter-Ellis FP, Schmidt DJ, Hayek LA, Craig J, 1983. Determination of sex with a discriminant analysis of new pelvic bone measurements: Part 1. J Forensic Sci 28:169–179.

Schultz M. 1989. Causes and frequency of diseases during early childhood in Bronze Age populations. Adv Paleopathol 1:175–179.

Schultz M. 1992. Paleopathologie erkenntnisse aus kinderskeletten. Archaologie in Deutschland 8:18–23.

Schultz M. 1995. The role of meningeal diseases in the mortality of infants and children in prehistoric and historic populations. Am J Phys Anthropol Suppl 20:192 (abstract).

Schutowski H. 1987. Sex determination of fetal and neonate skeletons by means of discriminant analysis. Int J Anthropol 2:347–352.

Scrimshaw SCM. 1984. Infanticide in human populations: societal and individual concerns. In: Hausfater G, Blaffer Hrdy S, editors. Infanticide; Comparative and Evolutionary Perspectives. New York: Aldine. pp 439–462.

Sellier P, Tillier A-M, Bruzek J. 1997. The estimation of the age at death of perinatal and postnatal skeletons: methodological reassessment and reliability. Am J Phys Anthropol Suppl 24:208.

Skinner M, Goodman AH. 1992. Anthropological uses of developmental defects of enamel. In: Saunders SR, Katzenberg MA, editors. Skeletal Biology of Past Peoples: Research Methods. New York: Wiley-Liss. pp. 153–174.

Smith BH. 1991. Standards of human tooth formation and dental age assessment. In: Kelley MA, Larsen CS, editors. Advances in Dental Anthropology. New York: Wiley-Liss. pp. 143–168.

Specker BL, Brazerol W, Tsang RC, Levin R, Searcy J, Steichen J. 1987. Bone mineral content in children 1 to 6 years of age. Am J Dis Child 141: 343–344.

Spence MR. 1986. The excavation of the Keffer Site burials. Report on file at the Museum of Indian Archaeology, London, Ontario.

Sperduti A, Bondioli L, Prowse TL, Salomone F, Yang D, Hoppa RD, Saunders SR, Macchiarelli R. 1997. Reconstructing life conditions of the juvenile population of Portus Romae in 2nd–3rd cent. A.D. Canadian Association for Physical Anthropology Meetings, London, Ontario.

Stini WA. 1985. Growth rates and sexual dimorphism in evolutionary perspective. In: Gilbert RI, Mielke JH, editors. The Analysis of Prehistoric Diets. Orlando, Fla.: Academic Press. pp. 191–226.

Stone AC, Milner GR, Paabo S, Stoneking M. 1996. Sex determination of ancient human skeletons using DNA. Am J Phys Anthropol 99:231–238.

Stout SD. 1992. Methods of determining age at death using bone microstructure. In: Saunders SR, Katzenberg MA, editors. Skeletal Biology of Past Peoples: Research Methods. New York: Wiley-Liss pp. 21–36.

Sundick RI. 1972. Human skeletal growth and dental development as observed in the Indian Knoll population. Ph.D. Dissertation. University of Toronto.

Sundick RI. 1977. Age and sex determination of subadult skeletons. J Forensic Sci 22:141–144.

Sundick RI. 1978. Human skeletal growth and age determination. Homo 29:228–249.

Sundick RI. 1985. Sex determination of unidentified remains by Y-chromosome fluorescence techniques. Paper presented at the American Academy of Forensic Sciences, Las Vegas, Nevada.

Thomson A. 1899. The sexual differences of the foetal pelvis. J Anat Phys 33:359.

Thwaites RG, editor. 1896–1901. The Jesuit Relations and Allied Documents. 73 volumes. Cleveland: Burrows Brothers.

Tompkins RL. 1996. Human population variability in relative dental development. Am J Phys Anthropol 99:79–102.

Trodden BJ. 1982. A Radiographic Study of the Calcification and Eruption of the Permanent Teeth in Inuit and Indian Children. National Museum of Man Mercury Series, Archaeological Survey of Canada, Paper No. 112.

Ubelaker DH. 1989. The estimation of age at death from immature human bone. In: İşcan MY, editor. Age Markers in the Human Skeleton. Springfield, Ill.: Charles C. Thomas. pp. 55–70.

Ubelaker DH. 1995. Osteological and archival evidence for disease in historic Quito, Ecuador. In: Saunders, SR, Herring A, editors. Grave Reflections: Portraying the Past Through Cemetery Studies. Toronto: Canadian Scholars' Press. pp. 223–240.

Van Gerven DP, Hummert JR, Burr DB. 1985. Cortical bone maintenance and geometry of the tibia in prehistoric children from Nubia's Batn el Hajar. Am J Phys Anthropol 66:275–280.

Verano JW, Ubelaker DH. 1992. Disease and Demography in the Americas. Washington: Smithsonian Institution Press.

Walker PL. 1969. The linear growth of long bones in Late Woodland Indian children. Proc Ind Acad Sci 78:83–87.

Walker PL, Johnson J, Lambert P. 1988. Age and sex biases in the preservation of human skeletal remains. Am J Phys Anthropol 76:183–188.

Watt M, Lunt DA. 1999. Stages of tooth development relative to the first permanent molar in a medieval population from the southwest of Scotland. Proceedings of the 11th International Symposium on Dental Morphology. August 26–30, 1998, Oulu, Finland. pp. 120–127.

Weaver DS. 1979. Application of the likelihood ratio test to age estimation using the infant and child temporal bone. Am J Phys Anthropol 50: 263–270.

Weaver DS. 1980. Sex differences in the ilia of a known sex and age sample of fetal and infant skeletons. Am J Phys Anthropol 52:191–195.

Weaver DS. 1986. Forensic aspects of fetal and neonatal skeletons. In: Reichs KJ, editor. Forensic Osteology. Springfield, Ill.: Charles C. Thomas. pp. 90–100.

Webb PAO, Suchey JM. 1985. Epiphyseal union of the anterior iliac crest and medial clavicle in a modern multiracial sample of American males and females. Am J Phys Anthropol 68:457–466.

Whittington SL. 1991. Detection of significant demographic differences between subpopulations of prehispanic Maya from Copan, Honduras, by survival analysis. Am J Phys Anthropol 85: 167–184.

Wiggins R, Rogers J. 1995. Skeletal growth deficits and dental development in the Barton on Humber skeletal population. Am J Phys Anthropol Suppl 20:221.

Workshop of European Anthropologists 1980. Recommendations for age and sex diagnoses of skeletons. J Hum Evol 9:517–549.

Yang DY, Eng B, Waye JS, Dudar JC, Saunders SR. 1998. A new strategy for DNA sex determination from ancient human skeletons. Am J Phys Anthropol Suppl 26:236.

y'Edynak G. 1976. Long bone growth in western Eskimo and Aleut skeletons. Am J Phys Anthropol 45:569–574.

CHAPTER 6

READING BETWEEN THE LINES: DENTAL DEVELOPMENT AND SUBADULT AGE ASSESSMENT USING THE MICROSTRUCTURAL GROWTH MARKERS OF TEETH

CHARLES M. FITZGERALD AND JEROME C. ROSE

INTRODUCTION

Accurate estimation of the age-at-death of a person is a common problem, and certainly one of the most difficult, faced by anthropologists confronted with unknown skeletal and dental material. This difficulty is significantly increased when the bones or teeth belonged to someone who lived in the distant past—and who may not even have been an anatomically modern *Homo sapiens*. There are particular methodological difficulties associated with each of the many age estimation approaches available, but there is also one essential problem that almost all approaches share. Most conventional methods must use growth and aging standards developed from living peoples for determining the ages of specimens from the past. A very troubling question arises from this approach: How applicable or appropriate can such modern standards be to an archaeological or early hominid population? Indeed, even the use of standards derived from one modern population of a particular geographic affinity for use on another with a different affinity may be considered questionable,

particularly since many standards are based on well-nourished populations of European descent.

This chapter presents an approach to age estimation that overcomes this essential difficulty. It is based on the interpretation of certain microstructures in the enamel and dentine of teeth that act as markers of growth, providing an endogenous record of development. This obviates the need to apply standards of any sort, allowing accurate assessments based on calibrations internal to the tooth itself. There are a number of other histological methods of age determination from teeth, such as counting layers in cementum (Stott et al., 1982, but see Miller et al., 1988), Gustafson's method of multiple determination (Burns and Maples, 1976; Gustafson, 1950; Lucy and Pollard, 1995; Lucy et al., 1994), and dentine sclerosis (Bang and Ramm, 1970; Johanson, 1971; Lucy et al., 1994), but this chapter is only concerned with the approach, actually more correctly a series of different techniques, that interprets development from dental microstructural growth markers. A limitation of this method is that it can only be used to determine age in subadults, that is in individuals who have not reached dental maturity and who still have at least one tooth that has not completed its growth. Given this limitation, a frequently asked question is "Why would we

Biological Anthropology of the Human Skeleton, Edited by M. Anne Katzenberg and Shelley R. Saunders.
ISBN 0-471-31616-4   Copyright © 2000 by Wiley-Liss, Inc.

chose to use such a laborious technique for age determination in circumstances other than the study of rare fossil specimens?"

Even a cursory review of the literature provides abundant answers to this question. There are many fundamental problems involved in using modern dental growth data to determine age at death of subadults recovered from archaeological excavations (Smith, 1991), but accurate ages with limited ranges of error are crucial to bioarchaeology and the interpretation of demographic and palaeopathological data. Forensic anthropologists require accurate ages at death and methods for determining the timing of past traumatic events seen in the teeth to match them with medical records or to establish the presence of past child abuse (e.g., Skinner and Anderson, 1991; Walker et al., 1997). Enamel hypoplasia and histological indicators of physiological perturbations known as Wilson bands have recently played a major role in bioarchaeological analyzes and, yet, their full potential as analytical tools cannot be reached without improved methods for accurately determining the ages at which they developed (Goodman and Rose, 1990). Furthermore, there are debates concerning the interpretation of hypoplasias of various widths and depths and how these may relate to the length and severity of the physiological stress that produced them that can only be resolved with methods that can precisely determine the timing of dental growth (Goodman and Rose, 1990).

Before embarking on a description of these analytical techniques and the methods of histological preparation of teeth required for their application, some background to their use in anthropology will be discussed. The literature providing the theoretical underpinning to dental histological age assessment is also briefly surveyed.

BACKGROUND

Dental histological aging first appeared on the anthropological stage amidst a flurry of controversy. Bromage and Dean's 1985 paper, which reevaluated the age estimates for a number of Plio-Pleistocene hominids using one of the enamel microstructures, introduced the histological aging approach to the field, and immediately created contention. The particular technique that these authors utilized in their study, and the notion that dental microstructures were produced with regular periodicity throughout tooth growth, was challenged (e.g., Mann et al., 1987). The reasons for the controversy may have had less to do with technical issues than with the results of the study, which contradicted the then prevailing view that the extended period of childhood development characteristic of modern humans came early in hominid evolution (see Mann, 1975, for the evidence supporting this point of view). Bromage and Dean's results suggested that the pattern of early hominid dental growth was more like that of modern apes, who lack the particularly lengthy and delayed maturation and prolonged infant dependency of modern humans.

Since the beginning of the debate there has been an expanding corpus of published material in support, and few challenges in the literature presenting hard evidence against the use of histological aging techniques. Although there are still a few who disagree, the time dependency of dental microstructures is no longer seriously questioned (cf. Dean, 1987, and a special issue of the *Journal of Human Evolution*—in particular FitzGerald,, 1998; Risnes, 1998; and Shellis 1998). Most dental experts concur that microstructures record normal growth in a way that permits the developmental and chronological history of a tooth to be accurately reconstructed.

DENTAL ANATOMY AND THE HISTOLOGY OF TOOTH GROWTH

Although they did not come widely to the attention of anthropology until the publication of Bromage and Dean's provocative paper, dental microstructures and their regular periodicity through tooth growth have an extensive history in the dental literature that extends back to the nineteenth century. Their pedigree as estimators of subadult aging is not as long, dating to the early 1960s. For those interested in pursuing this literature in more detail, the following are recommended: for the histology of tooth growth and dental microstructures, see Aiello and Dean, 1990; Avery, 1987, 1992; Boyde, 1976, 1989; Hillson, 1986; Ten Cate, 1989; Warshawsky, 1988; for a review of the literature surrounding issues of time dependency, see Dean, 1987, 1989, 1995, 1998a, 1999; Fitz-Gerald 1996, 1998.

Hominid teeth comprise a crown and a root (see Fig. 6.1). The crown denotes that part of the tooth covered by the hard, whitish tissue called enamel. It contains no living cells and is the hardest biological substance known, consisting of about 97% (by weight) of inorganic material made up mainly of hydroxyapatite crystallites, a calcium phosphate. Enamel is secreted as an organic matrix by specialized columnar secretory cells called ameloblasts. Within 24 hours after secretion this matrix undergoes initial mineralization, after which the proportion of hydroxyapatite in the tissue increases steadily through a process of maturation until the enamel reaches its final state of hardness.

The root and the bulk of the crown of the tooth are composed mainly of dentine. Dentine is a hard, elastic, avascular, vital, yellowish-white tissue that is less brittle than enamel. It is only about 70% (w/w) mineralized with hydroxyapatite crystals and contains a dense mat of elastic collagen, providing a resilient support. Dentine, like enamel, is a secretory product, manufactured by columnar cells called odontoblasts, which produce an organic matrix that later mineralizes. Dentine encloses a central chamber, which is filled with a connective tissue called pulp that becomes more fibrous in nature throughout life. This is lost in dried teeth.

Very early in tooth development, histodifferentiation results in the formation of the hard tissue-producing cells. Odontoblasts first begin to form dentine along the future junction between the enamel and dentine of the tooth

crown (called the enamel-dentine junction or EDJ) at the site of future cusp tips. Inductive influences from the odontoblasts result in differentiation and formation of ameloblasts, which then begin to secrete enamel matrix. Both types of cells produce hard tissue in their wake as they move away from the EDJ in opposite directions toward their ultimate destinations—the surface in the case of ameloblasts, and the pulp chamber in the case of odontoblasts. Crowns and roots thus increase appositionally (i.e., they grow thicker) at the same time that they increase in length by differentiation of new ameloblasts and odontoblasts. The rate at which length increases, that is, the pace of recruitment of new ameloblasts and odontoblasts, is called the extension rate.

Enamel is composed of many hundreds of thousands of unbroken, interlaced prisms or rods that extend from the EDJ to the tooth surface (see Fig. 6.1). Prisms are formed by ameloblasts that secrete enamel matrix from their distal ends as they slowly make their way to the surface of the tooth. Very shortly after its secretion, this matrix begins to mineralize and mature into enamel. After the ameloblasts reach the tooth surface, they transform into a maturative phase and are eventually shed during tooth eruption. Because of this, enamel cannot subsequently undergo repair during the lifetime of the tooth.

Dentine formation differs in several respects and is a far more complex process than enamel formation. The odontoblasts that form dentine first lay down a predentine matrix, which then goes through a process that may take a number of days and which involves the degradation and removal of some of the matrices' components, the modification of others, and finally mineralization. Unlike ameloblasts, odontoblasts do not die after the primary formation of dentine is complete, but remain alive and are able to add small amounts of tissue to the mature tooth throughout the lifetime of the individual. Except in pathological conditions, they do not replace lost dentine but only add to it appositionally along the edge of the pulp chamber. The living odontoblasts remain lining the pulp

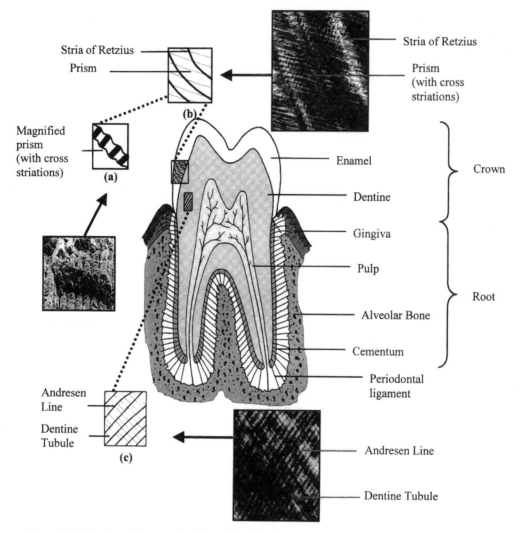

Figure 6.1   A tooth and its supporting tissues, illustrating some of the internal microstructures of enamel and dentine. A small section of enamel has been magnified to show the relationship between enamel prisms that follow a course from the EDJ to the enamel surface, and striae of Retzius that crosscut prisms at an angle. The inset micrograph relating to the schematic (b) shows an actual longitudinal enamel section examined under polarized light with prisms running from right to left and three brown striae of Retzius crosscutting them diagonally from bottom right to top left. Cross striations, marking daily appositional increments, can be clearly seen as bands on the prisms in this photograph. The same number of cross striations can be counted between all adjacent regular striae in one tooth, and this circaseptan interval is also identical in all of the teeth in one dentition. The schematic (a) shows one prism highly magnified, with cross striations illustrated as dark bands on prism varicosities (one cross striation is defined as running from the end of one dark band to the beginning of another). The inset photomicrograph relating to box (a) is a taken with an SEM (scanning electron microscope) and it shows a small portion of enamel fractured in an oblique transverse plane. Prisms and their three-dimensional relationship to each other can be seen as well as the varicosities on each prism, which are cross striations as they appear in the SEM. The schematic (c) at the bottom of the figure depicts a section of dentine, with long period Andresen lines running diagonally from lower left to upper right and dentine tubules crosscutting them obliquely. The photomicrograph relating to (c) is a longitudinal section taken in polarized light.

chamber and they have long cell processes that extend behind the cell along the route it has taken as it passed from the EDJ (or CDJ, the cement dentine junction, in the case of the root). Each odontoblast process lies in a dentine tubule that therefore reveals the former direction of travel of the odontoblast during tooth formation.

Teeth by their very nature are extremely durable, and because they are protected from any functional influences during their morphological development while contained within the jaws, and following emergence into occlusion there is only minimal influence on their development, great significance can be attached to studies of tooth morphology and microstructure (Aiello and Dean, 1990). Since enamel's mineralization occurs so rapidly after secretion by ameloblasts, it is particularly useful since it retains an accurate histological record of its development unmodified by remodeling or turnover throughout life.

DENTAL MICROSTRUCTURAL GROWTH MARKERS

The premise that underlies the use of histological aging techniques is that matrix secretion is governed by various metabolic rhythms, which change the rate and/or mineral density of secretion over a cycle with a regularly recurring periodicity. This leaves microstructural time markers that are preserved in the secretion products—enamel and dentine. Since remodeling of dental tissues does not take place, or is minimal in the case of dentine, these growth markers are permanently preserved and can be histologically examined and interpreted.

In the discussion so far no distinction has been made between enamel and dentine, since both retain microstructural growth markers in their tissues that are presumed to have formed from the same underlying metabolic rhythms. However, dentine is a more complex and difficult tissue to analyze and studies in anthropology utilizing it have only begun within the last few years, mainly by M.C. Dean (Dean, 1995,

1998a, 1999; Dean and Scandrett, 1995, 1996). A problem that has hindered the study of dentine by anthropologists is that the dentine of archaeologically recovered teeth is sometimes rendered opaque by taphonomic processes taking place during burial in the ground. On the other hand, diagenetic changes, particularly if of very long duration (as in the case of early hominoid fossils), sometimes have the opposite effect, making dentine microstructures more discernible. In any event, since there is a much larger body of work on enamel, and it is intrinsically an easier tissue to study, it is the prime focus of discussion through the rest of this chapter.

Short Period Markers

The microstructural growth markers of teeth can be grouped into two basic categories: short period markers and long period markers. Short period markers result from the metabolic changes arising through one of the body's central regulators, the circadian rhythm. Daily clocks are ubiquitous in all multicelled organisms and such a rhythmic regulatory variation appears to be fundamental in the physiological activity of all cells (Scheving and Pauly, 1974). Since dentine and enamel are formed through secretory activity, it would therefore be surprising not to find evidence of such an elemental cycle in their structure.

The short period growth markers produced by this 24-hour rhythm in enamel are called cross striations, and in dentine von Ebner's lines. Under polarized light microscopy (PLM) cross striations appear as bands consisting of fine, transverse, dark striations along the length of enamel prisms, and under the SEM (scanning electron microscope), and sometimes also in PLM, these bands are seen to be associated with enlargements or varicosities of the prism (see Fig. 6.1 for examples). Cross striations are found in the enamel of all primates and many other mammalian groups, and their form varies only slightly in the relative width of bright and dark bands and the regularity of their spacing (Hillson, 1986).

The evidence for circadian rhythmicity of cross striations and von Ebner's lines is considerable. Perhaps most telling is direct experimental evidence, and this will be briefly reviewed. Schour and colleagues (Massler and Schour, 1946; Schour and Hoffman, 1939; Schour and Poncher, 1937) presented results that correlated daily rates of enamel production with cross striations. These data had been derived from studies that administered injections of substances that leave permanent tracer labels in growing enamel and dentine to infants with inoperable hydrocephalus. Another group of investigators working at the about the same, but in Japan, headed by Okada and Mimura (see Okada, 1943, as well as Rosenberg and Simmons, 1980a, 1980b; Shinoda, 1984, for a review of the work of the Japanese group), provided quantified, experimentally established evidence of the daily nature of cross striations. Okada and colleagues used injections of sodium fluoride and lead acetate administered at irregular but known intervals to demonstrate that cross striations were daily increments in growing dogs, rabbits, pigs, and monkeys. These substances produced visible lines in the enamel of these animals and the number of cross striations between labels were counted and found to correspond to the number of days between injections. They also labeled dentine and, using a similar technique, this group was able to establish that von Ebner's lines were also daily markers in dentine. Finally, Bromage (1989, 1991) administered three different fluorescent labeling compounds at known intervals to two postnatal pig-tailed macaques. The compounds chosen labeled both enamel and dentine. First permanent molars were sectioned and examined under ultraviolet light to reveal the fluorescent labels, but in only one specimen was there sufficient optical contrast in the lines to allow study of the enamel. Bromage was able to count the number of cross striations between the labels in this animal and also the number from the last line to the occlusal edge. The tallies agreed precisely with the known intervals between dosages and the interval between the last dosage and the sacrifice of the animal.

A number of hypotheses have been put forward to account for the appearance and particular mineral properties of cross striations, but perhaps the most plausible is from Boyde (1964, 1979, 1989; also elaborated by Risnes, 1998). He suggested that the carbon dioxide (carbonate/bicarbonate) available for incorporation in the enamel mineral component would be greater during those phases of the 24-hour cycle when metabolic activity was the greatest. This variation in the rate of metabolic activity will result in variation in the secretion rate of enamel matrix, enamel being secreted faster at times of most intense metabolic activity. During the time when enamel is forming most quickly (and ameloblast movement is fastest), because of its effect on the distribution and orientation of growing crystallites that make up the prism, the prism body will in fact become wider. This mechanical explanation adds to the fundamental biochemical one, which also explains the variation in mineral density that is found to be associated with cross striation areas along the prism.

Long Period Markers

The long period markers of enamel are called brown striae of Retzius, and those of dentine, Andresen lines. Some striae of Retzius project onto and crop out at the surface of the crown, and these can be thought of as constituting a separate long period marker of enamel, called perikymata.

In longitudinal sections (i.e., in two dimensions), brown striae of Retzius appear to form successive layers (or "caps") around the dentine horn (see Fig. 6.2c), which, after the first cap reaches the occlusal surface, become discontinuous cuspally on either side of it (see Fig. 6.2c). Striae layers continue down on either side of the crown all the way to the cervix of the tooth, most striae appearing to run obliquely from the EDJ to the occlusal surface so that they form an acute angle with the prisms they cross (see Fig. 6.1b). In transverse sections, striae of Retzius appear as concentric rings that encircle the tooth. However, it is necessary to mentally reconstruct the views in Figure 6.2 in three dimensions to understand the real architecture of the striae. In three dimensions, the continuous striae around the dentine horn are more aptly imagined as "domes" (a term used by Hillson, 1986) rather than caps, and the striae down the crown that are discontinuous cuspally, as circumferential "sleeves" (Hillson, 1986).

Striae differ in their visibility and they are variably expressed, even within one tooth. They are most clearly discernable in the outer enamel, and particularly also in the cervical third of crowns. In modern humans, striae are more widely spaced in the occlusal part of the crown and they become closer together toward the cervical portion. This difference in spac-ing—30–45 μm at the widest and 15–20 μm at the narrowest—reflects differences in the rate of enamel formation, which are fastest cuspally and which slow toward the cervix where striae become more closely packed together. The angle that striae form with the surface (and with the EDJ) also changes, being most acute cuspally and becoming more obtuse through the crown cervically. Again, this reflects changes in the rate of enamel production and the enamel extension rate.

Striae of Retzius are only visible in sectioned or broken teeth, however those striae that terminate at the enamel surface are projected onto it as fine, transversely oriented, circular "wrinkles" consisting of a series of ridges separated by corresponding grooves. The totality of

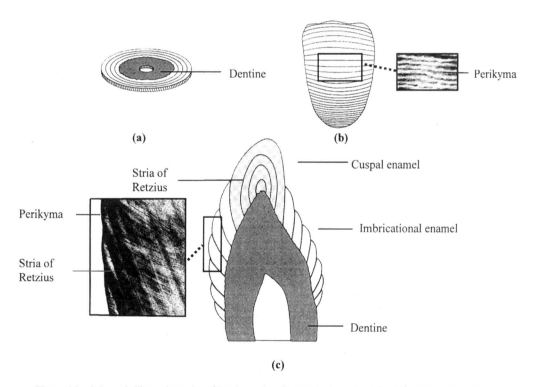

Figure 6.2 Schematic illustrating striae of Retzius and perikymata in three views. Top left (a) is a transverse section through a tooth in which striae appear as concentric rings. Top right (b) is a view looking at the outside surface of the crown in which perikymata appear as ridges encircling it. The inset is an actual photograph of perikymata. On the bottom (c) is a longitudinal section showing striae as continuous domes around the dentine horn. The first discontinuous layer to emerge at the surface terminates as a perikymata, and striae and perikymata continue down either side of the crown to the cervix. The inset photomicrograph is a longitudinal section of enamel.

the excrescence, that is, both the ridge and groove (see Fig. 6.2), is known as a perikyma (from Greek, *peri* meaning around and *kyma* meaning wave), perikymata in the plural. From Figure 6.2 it is clear that only the sleeved striae crop out at the surface as perikymata; all but one of the domed striae remain buried within the cusp. These hidden striae are often referred to as cuspal (or appositional) striae and those terminating at the surface as imbricational (or lateral) striae.

It is now well established that the number of daily increments between adjacent long period lines in enamel is uniform within one tooth and is consistent among all of the teeth in one dentition (FitzGerald, 1998). This is likely also to be the case with von Ebner's and Andresen lines in dentine (Dean, 1999). However, the number of cross striations between adjacent striae, although uniform in all teeth in one individual, commonly varies from 7 to 10 days among different individuals. The range of this period, called a circaseptan interval (because it is "around seven [days]"), is even greater than this, and intervals have been recorded as low as 5 days and as high as 14 days in modern humans (FitzGerald, 1996; Hillson, 1996). Fukuhara (1959) in a very careful study using

ground sections of teeth, calculated circaseptan intervals that ranged between mean values of 2 and 8 for 10 other primate species (with a modal value of 7 or 8).

Such a range of rhythms does not seem to be related to any known astronomical or natural cadences and although a number of possible explanations have been proposed, none has yet been unreservedly accepted as correct. Among the likeliest are several put forward by Newman and Poole (1974, 1993), who suggest that a near-weekly rhythm might arise from interference beats between several interacting rhythms. For instance, an eight-day periodicity will result from interference between two rhythms, one of 24 hours and the other of 27—two rhythms running independently of each other interacting to produce a third. It has also been suggested that the circaseptan interval may be chaotic in origin (FitzGerald, 1996).

Although the precise nature of the rhythm is unclear at this time, the etiology of striae of Retzius formation is better understood. Boyde (1964, 1979, 1989) has extended his hypothesis for the formation of cross striations (already discussed) to embrace the formation of striae of Retzius and perikymata. Risnes (1990, 1998) has made meticulous SEM observations of

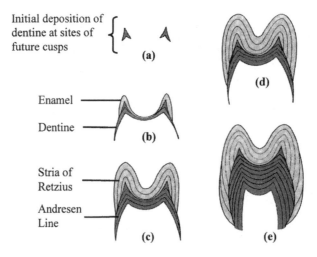

Figure 6.3 The pattern of incremental growth illustrating formation of long period lines in enamel and dentine. Growth begins with initial dentine deposition at (a) and proceeds through to the early stages of crown formation at (e).

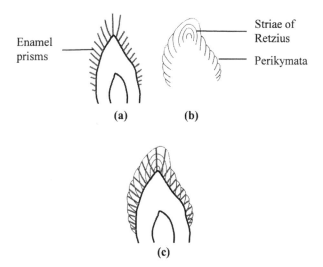

Enamel prisms

Striae of Retzius

Perikymata

(a)   **(b)**

(c)

Figure 6.4 Schematic drawing representing a way of conceptualizing long period incremental growth lines. The upper two diagrams show two aspects of the lower diagram, which represents the cuspal area of a tooth sectioned longitudinally. Diagram (a) illustrates a few of the many enamel prisms that run from the EDJ to the surface, drawn schematically as straight lines. Diagram (b) decouples striae of Retzius from prisms, envisioning them as an epiphenomenon superimposed on prism growth. Diagram (c) is (b) overlaid on (a).

striae and incorporated some of Boyde's ideas to come up with a convincing explanation for their production. In the same way that prism varicosities (see Fig. 6.1a) are regarded as a rhythmic, reciprocal expansion and reduction of prism growth, regular striae of Retzius may be regarded as an accentuation of the same phenomenon (Risnes, 1998:345). Striae result from growth discontinuities (i.e., disturbances in mineralization) affecting all ameloblasts secreting at the time of the disturbance or perturbation (and it is likely that the same underlying rhythm that produces striae in enamel also produces Andresen lines in dentine). These long period lines therefore mark successive layers or sheets of enamel (or dentine) formed at regular circaseptan intervals throughout tooth development (see Fig. 6.3). Each layer (or more correctly, shell in three dimensions) represents the external profile of the tooth as it existed at the end of each circaseptan interval.

Because of the layering that is observed, tooth growth is usually described as being appositional or incremental, but in its strictest sense this is incorrect, and in fact may con-

tribute to the confusion that exists in the minds of some people on this topic. Layers of enamel are not "added," rather individual prisms continuously increase in length, growing away from the EDJ, and from time to time their growth is perturbed slightly, producing a discontinuity. The collective result of this discontinuity, which occurred coevally in all developing ameloblasts, assumes the appearance of a layer. Thinking of striae of Retzius as epiphenomena (as represented in Fig. 6.4) makes it easier to understand the rhythmic superposition on growth that in fact is occurring. It is the circaseptan rhythm that is the phenomenon, not the stria. Cross striations may be seen in precisely the same way, as epiphenomena of a circadian regulatory rhythm.

Perikymata are formed by the same slowing down or discontinuity of enamel production that occurs at the end of a circaseptan interval. The systemic trigger that produces striae causes ameloblasts at the surface to cease their matrix secretion phase slightly prematurely. Those cells that were about to cease production do so immediately and slightly earlier than their cervical neighbors. These are the cells associated with the troughs of the perikymata, and in fact, the plane of projection of the floor of a trough corresponds with the plane of the associated stria. The ridges represent ameloblasts undergoing a normal terminal phase process in the interval before the next perturbation in growth (Boyde, 1976, 1989).

IRREGULAR STRIAE OF RETZIUS

Not all striae of Retzius are formed through the action of the regular circaseptan rhythm. One very prominent stria, called the neonatal line, can be seen in the enamel of deciduous teeth and permanent first molars (and sometimes permanent incisor crowns, which can occasionally begin mineralizing before birth) (Eli et al., 1989; Schour, 1936; Weber and Eisenmann, 1971; Whittaker and Richards, 1978). This line develops at parturition and is thought to relate to the physiological stresses of birth, and, in fact, a relationship has been shown to exist with wider lines in babies who suffered severe birth trauma (Eli et al., 1989). This neonatal line is essentially the first accentuated striae of Retzius, since prenatal enamel does not normally contain striae, except in cases where there was extensive prenatal stress often associated with birth defects (Hillson, 1996). Because they record the birth event and thus "zero" developmental chronology, neonatal lines are important in age estimation techniques, as will be discussed later.

A second group of irregular striae have been associated with various types of physiological stresses, such as infection, disease, and malnutrition, and these are called Wilson bands, or sometimes pathological striae (Rose, 1977, 1979; Goodman and Rose, 1990; Wilson and Schroff, 1970). Wilson bands are thought to relate to the same growth disrupting factors that cause enamel hypoplastic defects on crowns. Because it is believed that these disruptions in enamel growth arise from metabolic disturbances, enamel hypoplasias and Wilson bands have been intensively studied in many living

and past populations by anthropologists who use them as indicators of environmental stress (see Hillson, Chapter 9). This means that accurate timing of the duration and frequency of the stress episode are important in helping to isolate the cause of the stressor.

Wilson bands can be distinguished from regular striae of Retzius because they are broader, more accented, and exhibit irregular prism structure, and generally also because they tend to be visible along more of their length than regular striae. Wilson bands may in fact be visible along their full length from the EDJ to the surface, not often the case for striae of Retzius. Goodman and Rose (1990) considered, in their minimum definition of a Wilson band, that it need be continuous for only three-quarters of its length.

The same uncertainty surrounding causation that pertains with regular striae exists with Wilson bands. However, it is likely that irregular striae are formed like regular striae as a response, albeit a heightened or exaggerated one, of the active ameloblast sheet to some disruption to growth. In the case of Wilson bands, the trigger clearly does not arise from a regular circaseptan rhythm, but instead likely can be attributed to an external stressor. The extent of the growth disruption is also probably either of greater duration or intensity than provided by the disruption from regular metabolic cycling (for further discussion of etiology see Goodman and Rose, 1990; Simpson, 1999).

Together with regular striae, irregular striae serve an important function in histological aging. Because irregular striae are distinctive, and because they are triggered by a stimulus that affects all growing teeth at a point in time, they can be used as "registration lines," which trace positions of contemporaneity from tooth to tooth in the dentition (Condon and Rose, 1992). There is usually a well-defined sequence in variation in width and appearance of striae (of both regular and irregular types) within one crown, and a number of authors have noted that that this sequence is the same in any crown that was forming in an individual at the same time (Fujita, 1939; Gustafson, 1955; Hillson, 1992; Takiguchi, 1966). The sequence of striae in different teeth from one individual can be matched and an extended sequence of striae built up covering the whole length of crown formation for all of the dentition.

Irregular striae appear to have counterparts in dentine. Neonatal lines can be observed in dentine, and accentuated Andresen lines have been matched with counterpart Wilson bands (Dean, 1995). This effect on both hard tissues implies that the upset causing irregular striae and Andresen lines has a systemic origin, adding weight to the belief that it is a stressor that influences the dental development environment.

PREPARING TEETH FOR HISTOLOGICAL EXAMINATION

In order to interpret internal microstructural growth markers, teeth must be microscopically examined and this means cutting thin longitudinal sections from them and mounting these on glass slides. This is a technical challenge and there are a number of ways to accomplish it, which are well described in the literature (e.g., Beasley et al., 1992; Marks et al., 1996; Schenk et al., 1984; Schmidt and Keil, 1971; also particularly recommended is Hillson, 1996, which discusses sectioning and allied techniques that are particularly useful for archaeological specimens, and which in the same volume also gives a primer in microscopy for novices).

Here we will discuss one method for section preparation that is intended to give some idea of what is involved for those who have never sectioned teeth. This methodology was developed because it is comparatively easy to carry out, and because it cuts down the time involved not only in preparation, but also in sectioning, grinding, and polishing, since teeth are not embedded. However, it must be stressed that it is intended to be used in large-scale investigations and, although the quality of the finished slide will likely be acceptable, it will be more difficult to achieve outstanding results using this "quick and dirty" approach. Despite these limitations, these are the ideal circumstances for most bioarchaeological investigations. It is

not appropriate for use with very precious specimens, like fossil teeth, nor for teeth that are very brittle and prone to damage, nor for teeth that will be subjected to additional investigative approaches (such as, for instance, transmission electron microscopy). A more conventional procedure (see references in the previous paragraph) that embeds the tooth in a block before sectioning is recommended for specimens of this sort, or for any tooth whose state of preservation is uncertain.

Prior to sectioning, a line marking the cutting plane should be dotted-in around the whole tooth with a permanent fine-tipped marker since cutting accuracy is important: sections must pass through the maximum thickness of enamel and run nonobliquely through the long axis of the longest growing cusp (normally the mesio-buccal cusp of molars). It is usual to embed specimens in a hard supporting material prior to sectioning, but tooth preparation in this approach consists only of soaking teeth in cyanoacrylate cement (Super Glue® or Krazy Glue®), which fills in surface micro-cracks and provides support to fragile enamel. In other words, the cement keeps the enamel from falling off during the sectioning process. After immersing and rotating teeth in Super Glue, it is easiest to allow the film to harden on a layer of "dental sticky wax" (Dental Model Cement Sticky Wax, readily available from most dental supply companies) that has been melted and poured into a petri dish. They can then easily be removed simply by softening the wax slightly on a hot plate.

Teeth must be sectioned using a special low-speed saw, which is available from several manufacturers and in a variety of models. One of the simplest, and probably the type in widest use (but not the most technically superior), are peripheral-bladed saw models made by Buehler Ltd. (41 Waukegan Rd., Lake Bluff, IL 60044). These have rotating diamond-edged blades against which the specimen is held by a counterweighted arm. The tooth should be precisely oriented and attached to the cutting chuck by coating with dental sticky wax that has been applied with a small-bladed hot knife (the wax also provides additional support for brittle enamel). Distilled water serves as an adequate cutting coolant, and after sectioning, the chuck is dismounted and the cut face of the tooth is dried and coated with a film of Super Glue, which is allowed to set. A microscope slide is then attached to this coated face (parallel to the tooth surface) with a layer of dental sticky wax. The chuck is then remounted on the saw and a slice about 250–300 μm thick is cut.

The tooth section, still attached to its slide, is then lapped (or polished) with a medium grade (e.g., 3 micron) aluminium oxide slurry (an abrasive compound mixed with water) to remove any saw marks. Lapping may be done by hand on a glass plate or with a rotary machine, which is much faster. If a grinding/polishing wheel is employed then a diamond paste of the same size spread on a nylon cloth covered wheel may also be used. After lapping, the slide is cleaned in an ultrasonic bath and then dried in a vacuum chamber over silica gel. A small amount of adhesive is spread over the surface of the section, and another glass slide placed onto it (a number of adhesives are available for cementing specimens to glass, including Super Glue and different types of epoxy resins, but highly recommended is a UV-cured resin, acrylic acid and hydroxypropyl methacrylate, obtainable from Logitech Ltd. [Erskine Ferry Rd., Glasgow, G60 5EU, UK]). The two should be clamped together until the new slide is firmly cemented to the specimen. The slide "sandwich" is then placed on a hot plate and the sticky wax attaching the specimen to the first glass slide is melted off. The first slide can then be removed and discarded, leaving the polished face of the tooth now permanently attached to a glass slide.

The other face of the section is then lapped with a course aluminium oxide slurry (e.g., 9 micron) to remove any remaining wax, the superglue layer, and any saw marks, to within about 40 μm of the desired 100-μm thickness. Lapping is then continued with a fine grade of aluminium oxide (e.g., 0.5 micron) until the remaining excess material has been removed. The slide and section are then cleaned thoroughly in an ultrasonic bath. We do not routinely etch our specimens, but if it is desired to do so, then it should be done at this stage. Etching is done to enhance cross striations or striae of Retzius and is also particularly valuable for identifying Wilson bands. After polishing and cleaning, the slide and section are suspended in any one of a variety of acid solutions, for instance hydrochloric, phosphoric, or EDTA (ethylenediaminetetraacetic), depending on the purpose of the treatment. (For details on alternative treatments to accentuate various structures, see Boyde et al., 1978; Grine, 1986; Hillson, 1986; Schmidt and Keil, 1971; Wilson and Schroff, 1970.)

The specimen on its slide is dehydrated in absolute ethyl alcohol and thoroughly dried under vacuum over silica gel. It should then be immersed in xylene and kept under vacuum until air bubbles stop coming from the specimen. After removal from the xylene, the coverslip is mounted by floating it over the section on a drop of mounting medium (see Fitz-Gerald, 1996). Finished slides should be left for several weeks to set.

AGE ESTIMATION AND TIMING OF DEVELOPMENTAL EVENTS

There are a number of approaches available, depending on which incremental growth markers are utilized, for estimating crown development time or chronological age, or for establishing the timing of certain developmental events, like the formation of Wilson bands. Fundamentally, they may be grouped into two categories: those that interpret internal markers, the most accurate; and those that employ (surface) perikymata, less accurate. The former, which have the advantage of yielding often very exact chronologies, suffer the downside of requiring that teeth be sectioned. This is neither always practical nor appropriate, as in the case of rare early hominid teeth, and for these there is no other recourse available but to use the less accurate perikymata approach.

Determinations of crown formation time and developmental event timing are made on single teeth, which can be either fully mature or still immature. Subadult age estimation requires a more specific set of criteria, the primary one being that at least one tooth in the dentition not be fully grown. Also, the most accurate age estimates can be made when at least one of the teeth being analyzed has a neonatal line (these are all deciduous teeth, first permanent molars, and sometimes permanent lower central and lateral incisors and upper central incisors). Lastly, if the dentition is nearly complete, for instance, if the only crown not fully developed is the M3, then examples of all teeth that provide a full chronological history of the dentition must be histologically analyzed, and nonoverlapping results summed (e.g., in the example cited this might involve analyzes of an M1, a C, an M2, and an M3; the method for determining the nonoverlapping portions of their development time will be described later). The focus of the following will be a discussion of techniques involving single teeth; age estimation will simply require extrapolation of the method being discussed to the relevant number of teeth in the dentition.

A special case of age estimation arises where crowns in the dentition are fully mature, but apical closure of all teeth has not yet occurred (i.e., root development of at least one tooth is incomplete). This means that a summation of enamel development will fall short of total age by the amount of root development that extends beyond it. Since we have confined ourselves here to techniques that analyze enamel microstructures, interested readers are referred to Beynon et al. (1991), Dean (1993), and Dirks (1998) for information on how to estimate incomplete root development.

Noninvasive Estimates Utilizing Perikymata

In their 1985 paper, Bromage and Dean counted all of the perikymata on the surface of the Plio-Pleistocene hominid teeth that they were studying. They assumed that the circaseptan interval in all of these teeth was seven days, and by multiplying the number of perikymata they counted by this number, they calculated the time in days taken to form the imbricational

enamel portion of the crown (the "sleeves" in Fig. 6.2c). In order to arrive at total crown formation time they had to add an estimate of cuspal enamel time to this figure (the "domes" of enamel in Fig. 6.2c). Since the crowns of all of their specimens were not yet fully mature, this permitted the age of the specimens rather than simply crown formation times to be determined. However, it meant that for incisors they had to estimate a third factor—the time elapsed from birth to initial calcification (since these teeth do not usually begin to mineralize prenatally). These authors estimated the total time for these two factors for the incisors in their study to be six months. This was based on some of their own investigations of modern human teeth and the limited data that were then available in the literature.

The obvious weaknesses to this method are the errors arising from the estimates that are required. The database for circaseptan intervals is certainly much larger than that available for initial calcification and cuspal enamel formation times. Table 6.1 shows most of the extant published data on circaseptan intervals, and from the table it is clear from the larger studies where statistical data has been provided that modal values and means suggest that circaseptan intervals occur commonly in a range from 7 to 9 or 10 days. However, these data are almost wholly derived from modern humans and since nondestructive estimates are most appropriate for early hominid teeth, the most apposite data is simply not known with certainty. Since 1985, the database for cuspal enamel formation time has increased, but because cuspal enamel varies by tooth type, the data must be also be subdivided in this way, making the already small sample too poor to allow any potentially helpful statistical conclusions to be drawn, even for modern humans.

The confidence that can be attached to estimates for these three factors is therefore not great and this problem is irremediable without more research data, particularly on early hominids. This is not likely to be substantial without an enhancement in technology that will permit these variables to be established from

TABLE 6.1

Study	Date	Sample Size	Circaseptan Interval[1]			
			Range	Mean	SD[2]	Mode[2]
Asper[3]	1916	10	5–10			
Gysi[3]	1931			7		
Komai	1942	10	8–11			
Okada	1943		7–10			
Fukuhara	1959			8		
Kajiyama	1965	140		8–9		
Newman and Poole	1974		7–8			
Bromage and Dean	1985	20	6–9	7–8	0.69	8
Beynon and Reid	1987	100	6–10	7.7	0.83	8
Bullion—modern sample	1987	40	7–10	8.2	0.83	8
Bullion—archaeoligical	1987	10	6–10	8.2	1.03	8
Dean and Beynon	1991	1	7	7		
Beynon	1992	17	7–10	8.1	0.86	8
Dean, B, R, W	1993	1	8	8		
Dean, B, T, M—*P. robustus*	1993	1	9	9		
Ramirez-Rozzi-Neanderthal	1993	1	8	8		
Huda and Bowman	1994	9	4–11			
Dean	1995	2	8	8		
Beynon & Reid	1995	20				7
FitzGerald	1996	96[4]	7.8–12.3	9.7	1.02	9.2
Reid et al.	1998	4	8–9	8.3	0.52	8
Risnes	1998					10–11

[1] Unless otherwise indicated, data is from anatomically modern humans

[2] Data inserted where available

[3] Reliability of study is open to question

[4] It is difficult to know whether sample sizes in some of the other studies are on a strictly comparable basis to this study. For instance, the Bullion (1987) study certainly included multiple teeth from the same individual in her sample. This is not a statistically legitimate approach. Using it for this study would increase the sample size to 158.

fossil teeth nondestructively. Nonetheless, in the absence of any other noninvasive endogenous approach for estimating the development of extinct species, this method still has an important role to play.

However, it is strongly recommended that when perikymata-based approaches are used, a range of estimated ages should be provided. This range will reflect the recognition that there is variation within the three parameters of circaseptan interval, cuspal enamel, and initial calcification that have been input into the calculation. It is also imperative that perikymata counts be taken from photomontages of the whole buccal/labial surface of the tooth being

analyzed, and these should preferably be taken in an SEM. Attempting to count perikymata "by eye" under a low-power stereomicroscope is a very difficult task since the tooth surface must be illuminated by direct light, the angle of which is critical and changes down the curved surface of the tooth. Perikymata should be marked on the photomontage and counts should be repeated until a clear consensus figure is reached.

Histologically Established Estimates

In order to view dental microstructures, a good light microscope with polarizing attachments is required. These attachments consist of two polarizing filters, one fitted to the condenser below the ground section being viewed, called the polarizer, and other above the section in the objective, called the analyzer. These filters polarize the transmitted light, that is, they "comb out" incoming light and only permit light rays vibrating in one plane to emerge. The polarizer and analyzer are adjusted so that the vibration planes of light transmitted through them are perpendicular to each other. In this "crossed" position, with no tooth section on the microscope stage, no light is transmitted through the analyzer and the field appears dark when viewed through the objective. However, crystalline substances, like the hard tissues of teeth, exhibit a property called birefringence, or the ability to be "doubly refracting." Light waves traversing them are reorganized into two sets of waves vibrating in perpendicular planes, with the refractive indices of the two planes usually being different. In other words, the light vibrations in one plane travel faster through the tooth section than those in the plane perpendicular to them. The effect of this is to "twist" the emerging rays, which will now no longer be polarized in the same plane. When resolved by the analyzer and viewed through the objective, these twisted rays from the ground tooth section will appear in a range of interference colors that is related to the amount of birefringence and the thickness of the section.

Enamel microstructures are therefore more easily observed under polarized light, with polarizer and analyzer "crossed" to give maximum contrast. (see Hillson, 1986, 1996; Schmidt and Keil, 1971). Ideally, the microscope used should be able to magnify in powers as low as 100×, with at least one or two more increments through to 600x. A camera attachment, or a device capable of capturing digital images, is also a necessity.

Counting All Cross Striations

Boyde (1963) was the first to use dental histological analyses to estimate subadult age. He matched distinctive striae in different growing teeth in an archaeological specimen and counted cross striations from one tooth to the next. The objective was to count the total number of all cross striations formed from birth (registered by the neonatal line) until death (the end of enamel production). In his paper, Boyde sectioned the first permanent molar and the maxillary central incisor of a child from an Anglo-Saxon grave. He identified the neonatal line in M1 and counted the cross striations along a prism from it to the surface (see Fig. 6.5, which also elaborates on the rationale). He then traced the stria of Retzius that intersected with this prism back to the EDJ. Picking up the prism from the point of intersection, he again counted cross striations along it to the surface and repeated the process until he reached a stria that was distinctive enough to be matched with a homologous stria in the incisor. Carrying the total count of days forward, he continued the same procedure on the incisor until the last prism in the cervix was counted. He was then able to arrive at the total number of days from birth to death of this child.

Although highly accurate, this methodology, which involves counting all cross striations, is tedious and it also requires excellent visibility of both cross striations and striae of Retzius throughout the whole enamel, which is not often the case. There are a number of other approaches that are easier, some of which exploit the uniformity of the circaseptan interval, and these will be examined next.

Using Short Period and Long Period Markers

Techniques for calculating crown formation times that rely on uniformity of circaseptan intervals must derive the two components of enamel growth, imbricational enamel formation and cuspal enamel formation, and these are usually obtained separately. Imbricational growth can be calculated by multiplying the total number of striae of Retzius to emerge at the surface, by the circaseptan interval, the number of cross striations between adjacent striae of Retzius (see Fig. 6.6). Since, as has been said, the circaseptan interval may differ from individual to individual, but is identical within all

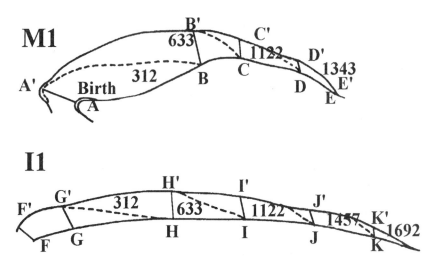

Figure 6.5 Schematic illustrating Boyde's histological age estimation technique. The two outline drawings are longitudinal sections of teeth, the upper a mandibular first molar and the lower a mandibular central incisor. The numbers are cross striation counts. The dotted lines represent significant striae of Retzius that could be identified in both teeth. The labeled vertical lines, (e.g., AA′) represent prisms. Boyde, in fact, used more prisms than shown, but those illustrated demonstrate the technique using the significant Retzius lines. Cross striations are first counted from the neonatal line in M1 out to the surface along prism AA′. Note that when the ameloblast forming prism AA′ reached the surface at A′, the incremental layer was situated along the Retzius line approximated by AB′, and the next ameloblast to start secreting enamel was at point B. Therefore the next cross striation count is made along prism BB′, the next along CC′, and so on. Looking at the lower drawing the pattern of significant striae shows the same cross striation counts up to the incremental line at 1122. Counting is then continued until the final total of 1692 days is reached. This is the point where enamel formation ceased at death. (After Boyde, 1963.)

the teeth of one individual, it is therefore only necessary to determine the number of days between striae once within one tooth from any dentition being studied. This is done in whichever tooth cross striations and striae are most clearly discernible in one field of view. Cross striations should be counted along a prism between two adjacent regular striae.

Once the circaseptan interval has been established, the first stria of Retzius to terminate at the surface is identified (at P_1 on Fig. 6.6). In a permanent tooth this stria will emerge as a distinct perikymata, but this is not the case with deciduous teeth, in which perikymata are not well defined. In either instance, this point, which marks the junction between cuspal and imbricational enamel, is often difficult to determine, and the section should be carefully scrutinized to ensure that the correct location is accurately identified. Once established, all of the striae terminating at the surface are counted

away from it cervically down the face of the crown (labelled P_2 to P_n on Fig. 6.6). Particular care should be exercised to ensure that the enamel at the CEJ, which is fragile and may have broken away postmortem, is present.

Imbricational growth is then determined according to the following formula:

$$CI \cdot P_n$$

where CI is circaseptan interval in days, and P_n is the total number of striae to terminate at the crown surface).

There are a number of ways to estimate the time taken to form cuspal enamel, but in all cases, the highest accuracy is obtained by working from montages of the cuspal area, rather than by eye directly through the microscope. Montages have traditionally been assembled by pasting together individual photomicrographs, taken across the area of interest. However, if digital images are available, either captured directly through the microscope using a digital video camera, or by photographing with an analogue video camera and converting the signal with a digitizing frame grabber, or by digitally scanning photomicrographs, then photomontages can be assembled on the computer. This offers the very real advantage of being able to use image analysis software to take measurements and counts from the digital montage. Montages may be put together using the computer program Adobe Photoshop. There are a variety of sophisticated image analysis packages available, but at the point of going to press there are also two freeware programs that can be downloaded from the Internet that do an adequate job. One, called NIH Image, is a public domain image processing and analysis program for the Macintosh, now also available for PCs. It was developed at the Research Services

Branch of the National Institute of Mental Health (NIMH). The other is UTHSCSA Image Tool, also a public domain image processing and analysis program, but developed at the University of Texas Health Science Center at San Antonio, Texas, and available only for a PC platform.

Dean (1998b) has recently evaluated four ways of determining cuspal enamel formation times, but he found little differences among them. Each may be "expected to provide equally valid results, with each having different practical advantages in different situations" (Dean, 1998b:460). A variant of one of these approaches will be described here.

A prism running from the tip of the dentine horn (or near to it) to the point at the junction of cuspal and imbricational enamel (prism A at P_1 in Fig. 6.6) represents the time elapsed since the initiation of crown growth. A montage should be pieced together that visualizes the

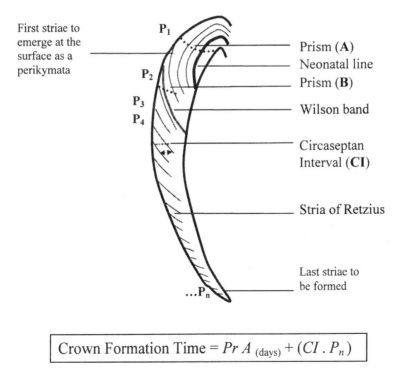

$$\text{Crown Formation Time} = Pr\,A_{\text{(days)}} + (CI \cdot P_n)$$

Figure 6.6 Schematic diagram of a longitudinally sectioned tooth showing derivation of formula for calculating total crown formation time and the timing of developmental events, like Wilson bands.

full run of this prism from the EDJ to the occlusal surface (digital images or photomicrographs taken at 200× to 400× magnification will probably be most appropriate). If cross striations are easily discernible along the full length of this prism then counting all of them will yield cuspal enamel formation in days. If cross striation clarity is good but not complete on Prism A, then cross striations need not be counted along its full length, but counts can be occasionally transferred from one adjacent prism to another at different levels along prominent striae of Retzius (see Fig. 6.7 and see Dean and Beynon, 1991; Risnes, 1986).

However, counting all cross striations can be a time-consuming process and sometimes they cannot be visualized through the full length of the enamel mantel, particularly in deciduous teeth. In these circumstances, the time taken to form prism A (in Fig. 6.6) can be estimated, and this is most easily done using image analysis software and a computer spreadsheet. First, the apparent path taken by the prism on the digital montage is traced out and this path is then measured using image analysis software. The prism is closely scrutinized and

wherever cross striations are discernible, either on the prism itself, or more commonly, on adjacent prisms, their positions are recorded on the montage. Next, a cross striation repeat interval, representing the average daily appositional growth rate of as large a group of cross striations as can be clearly discerned, is calculated at each of these points on the prism path. For example, a group of prisms, say six, is measured and then divided by 6 to arrive at an average cross striation repeat interval (representing one day's mean growth of enamel at this point on the prism). The distance between each of these recording points is measured. Using a computer spreadsheet, the average rates can then be interpolated in 5% lengths along the prism. Finally, knowing the total distance of the prism and the average rates of production at 19 points along it, the total time taken for its formation can then be calculated. If image analysis software is not available, then estimates of length of both the prism and groups of cross striations can be made by using needlepoint callipers on the photomontage, and the number of percentiles reduced if necessary (e.g., to 10 or 20% increments). The resulting

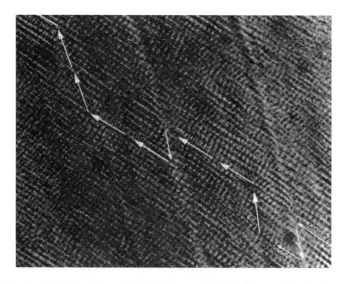

Figure 6.7   A longitudinal photomicrograph (at 200× magnification) of enamel showing how cross striations (which have been marked by thin white lines) can be tracked across a series of striae and transferred from one striae to another so that clearer fields of view are utilized (Dean and Beynon, 1991).

estimate will not be as accurate, but it will still be very good. After cuspal enamel time is calculated, it is added to imbricational enamel to arrive at total crown formation time.

As illustrated in the schematic in Figure 6.6, it is possible using this technique to time particular developmental events like the neonatal line (in absolute terms from prenatal initiation of calcification) and Wilson bands. The timing of the neonatal line, which will usually cross the cuspal/imbricational prism, will simply involve subdividing the estimate of prism A made above into prenatal and postnatal portions. This split will also permit chronological age of the specimen (rather than total crown formation time) to be established.

Depending on where they are found in the crown, Wilson bands can be timed by modifying the techniques for arriving at imbricational and cuspal enamel timing just discussed. In the example shown in Figure 6.6, for instance, where the Wilson band is found in the imbricational enamel, the number of striae from P_1 to the striae just cuspal to the Wilson band are counted and multiplied by the circaseptan interval (in Figure 6.6 there are none). The prism that intersects the junction of the next regular striae after the Wilson band is identified (prism B at P_2 in Figure 6.6) and the number of cross striations along this prism from the cuspal striae is counted. The age of occurrence of the Wilson band in this case would therefore be calculated as:

$$(\text{prism A}_{(\text{days})} - \text{prenatal enamel formation time}) + (\text{CI} \cdot P_x) + (\text{NCS})$$

where P_x equals the number of striae from P_1 cervically up to the Wilson band, and NCS equals the number of cross striations from the striae at P_x to the Wilson band.

It is known that prisms do not pursue straight courses through the enamel mantel; they weave or decussate from the EDJ to the surface (Boyde, 1989; FitzGerald, 1996; Osborn, 1990; Risnes, 1986). Under the cusp, directly over the tip of the dentine horn and on the true axis of the cusp, prisms spiral toward the surface in an area known as "gnarled

enamel." More laterally away from the center of the cusp, decussation is reduced, but prisms still weave from side to side in both the longitudinal and semitransverse dimensions. This means that the prism path that appears to be continuous in a two-dimensional longitudinal section is actually a composite of several prisms that weave into and out of the plane of section. Decussation is greatest in the inner third of the cuspal enamel lateral to the cusp center, and prisms pursue a much straighter course in the outer two-thirds. Prisms also become straighter moving laterally and cervically in a tooth. This movement has represented a point of potential concern in that it was thought that the effect might be significant enough to underestimate cross striation counts in areas at the junction of cuspal and imbricational enamel. Suggestions on how to correct this count upward have been made (FitzGerald, 1996). However, the recent paper by Dean (1998b) that compared cuspal enamel formation times determined from cross striation counts with times independently determined in three other ways found no significant differences. Dean established cuspal enamel formation times four ways in *Pan* and *Pongo* as well as in *Homo* and discovered that the cross striation count was understated against the other methods only in *Homo*, implying that decussation was greatest in our species. However, the difference in *Homo* was not significant (less than 3%) and may well have reflected measurement error. On this basis therefore, no adjustments to cross striation counts need be made to account for possible decussation.

Cuspal enamel formation time may be calculated in other ways, for instance by counting all striae under the cusp tip (Bullion, 1987; Dean, 1985) and then multiplying this number by the circaseptan interval. A number of other approaches rely on a formula derived by Shellis (1984) that determines the enamel extension rate (also see Dean, 1998b). This is the daily rate at which, during crown development, new enamel formation extends in the cervical direction. The extension rate can be estimated at each point where a stria of Retzius intersects the EDJ and it can therefore be used to calculate not only cuspal enamel formation time, but also total crown formation time, if the calculations are continued cervically along the EDJ all the way to the CEJ.

CONCLUSIONS AND FUTURE RESEARCH DIRECTIONS

More research needs to be done by dental biologists, anatomists, and histologists into the nature of dental microstructures and the fundamental causes of their observed regular periodicity. Large-scale testing against known-aged specimens will ultimately provide the most convincing proof for anthropologists, although considerable difficulties stand in the way of collecting large, statistically valid samples. Nevertheless, a recent careful study by Antoine et al. (1999) of a small sample of known-aged subadults has added more compelling proof of the efficacy of the techniques. There is certainly already enough convincing evidence to validate their use in dental development studies by anthropologists.

There are still problems to be resolved in the routine anthropological application of dental histological techniques. Observation of the microstructures remains a technical challenge, but this will become easier with the development and widespread use of more sophisticated techniques that use laser confocal microscopy, computed tomography, micro-ultrasound scanning, digital image analysis equipment, and other powerful computer-based technologies. One of these, or some other as yet unimagined technology, will one day allow accurate nondestructive determination of circaseptan intervals, striae counts, and information on cuspal enamel from whole teeth. Until this becomes a reality, more large-scale studies need to be done to increase knowledge about the variability of dental microstructures within and between modern human and ape populations, and to increase the database of information that will lead to better estimates of some of the microstructural vari-

ables. This will increase the accuracy of perikymata-based approaches and also increase the simplicity of other methods by allowing population-specific standards to be substituted for components that must now be calculated for each tooth being analyzed.

This chapter has focused on histological analyzes of enamel, although the information provided on the microstructures of dentine and their incremental growth will have suggested that this tissue also has trapped in it growth and development data, if only we can improve techniques for its interpretation. So far dentine has only had limited exploitation, but clearly, because it comprises the bulk of a tooth, it offers perhaps a greater potential than enamel. A better understanding of the complexities of dentine growth and advances in techniques for its histological analysis are areas of research that hold out enormous future promise.

However, perhaps the most exciting areas of research are not associated with validating histological techniques or making them easier to apply. They lie instead in the potential that these techniques have for resolving some fundamental anthropological problems. Quite simply, dental histological assessment using microstructures can provide information that is not obtainable in any other way. No better illustration of this potential can be found than the predicament facing biological anthropologists trying to assess growth and development from skeletal material. A fundamental problem centers on the use of appropriate exogenous reference standards, a question raised at the beginning of this chapter. However, the problem extends beyond the correctness of the use of one population standard on a different population—there are also concerns about the accuracy of the standards themselves. Tooth formation as traditionally measured by the appearance of growing teeth on radiographs is fraught with methodological problems (e.g., Aiello and Dean, 1990; Beynon et al., 1991, 1998; Risnes, 1986) and, in addition, studies have used idiosyncratic approaches in the way that they collect data and assess tooth maturity; some have been cross-sectional, others semi-longitudinal, and some have used as little as three fractional stages to gauge tooth development, others as many as twenty. Histological techniques that provide an accurate endogenous record of tooth development can overcome these difficulties. Not only do they obviate the need to use radiographs, but they also furnish a continuous history of both rate and total time taken for dental development. More, importantly, they also avert the necessity of having to select an appropriate reference population, or the best modern analogue in the case of an extinct species.

While finding their greatest application so far in evolutionary ontogeny and studies of premodern hominid growth, dental microstructural analyses are beginning to be exploited in bioarchaeological studies (e.g., FitzGerald et al., 1999; Hoppa and FitzGerald, 1999; Huda and Bowman, 1995). The time and labor required to make assessments on large samples of subadult individuals have so far precluded widespread use of these techniques for bioarchaeological studies. But the potential benefits are clear, and improvement and standardization of methods and incorporation of computer-based digital imaging procedures will make dental microstructural analysis more accessible to nonspecialists, and make assessment of large samples feasible. Ultimately, of course, the ability to accurately assess dental formation patterns and timing is crucially necessary to reconstructing with confidence the age-at-death and other palaeodemographic variables of recently dead, long dead, or fossil specimens.

ACKNOWLEDGMENTS

We would like to gratefully acknowledge funding support from a postdoctoral fellowship from The Social Sciences and Humanities Research Council of Canada (CF).

Particular acknowledgment is extended to Professor David Beynon and to Mr. Don Reid, both of the University of Newcastle upon Tyne Dental School, U.K., for generously sharing their expert technical knowledge of tooth sectioning during development and modification of the approach briefly outlined here.

REFERENCES

Aiello L, Dean C. 1990. An Introduction to Human Evolutionary Anatomy. New York: Academic Press.

Antoine D, Dean MC, Hillson S. (1999). The periodicity of incremental structures in dental enamel based on the developing dentition from post-medieval known-age children. In: Mayhall JT, Heikkinen T, editors. Proceedings of the 11th International Symposium of Dental Morphology, Aug 26–30, 1998, Oulu, Finland. Oulu: Oulu University Press, pp. 48–55.

Avery JK. 1987. Oral Development and Histology. Baltimore: Williams and Wilkins.

Avery JK. 1992. Essentials of Oral Histology and Embryology. St. Louis: Mosby Year Book Inc.

Bang G, Ramm E. 1970. Determination of age in humans from root dentine transparency. Acta Odontol Scand 28:3–35.

Beasley MJ, Brown WA, Legge AJ. 1992. Incremental banding in dental cementum: methods of preparation for teeth from archaeological sites and for modern comparative specimens. Int J Osteoarch 4:37–50.

Beynon AD, Clayton CB, Ramirez Rozzi F, Reid DJ. 1998. Radiographic and histological methodologies in estimating the chronology of crown development in modern humans and great apes: a review with some applications for studies on juvenile hominids. J Hum Evol 35:351–370.

Beynon AD, Dean MC, Reid DJ. 1991. Histological study on the chronology of the developing dentition in gorilla and orang-utan. Am J Phys Anthropol 86:189–203.

Boyde A. 1963. Estimation of age at death of young human skeletal material from incremental lines in the dental enamel. In: Third International Meeting in Forensic Immunology, Medicine, Pathology, and Toxicology (16–24 April 1963), London. pp. 36–46.

Boyde A. 1964. The structure and development of mammalian enamel. Ph.D. Thesis. University of London.

Boyde A. 1976. Amelogenesis and the structure of enamel. In: Cohen B, Kramer IRH, editors.

Scientific Foundations of Dentistry. London: Heinemann. pp. 335–352.

Boyde A. 1979. Carbonate concentration, crystal centres, core dissolution, caries, cross striations, circadian rhythms, and compositional contrast in the SEM. J Dent Res 58b:981–983.

Boyde A. 1989. Enamel. In: Oksche A, Vollrath L, editors. Handbook of Microscopic Anatomy, Vol. V/6, Teeth. Berlin: Springer-Verlag. pp. 309–473.

Boyde A, Jones SJ, Reynolds PS. 1978. Quantitative and qualitative studies of enamel etching with acid and EDTA. In: Johari O, O'Hare AMF, editors. Scanning Electron Microscopy, Vol. 2. Chicago, Ill.: SEM Inc. pp. 991–1002.

Bromage TG, Dean MC. 1985. Re-evaluation of the age at death of immature fossil hominids. Nature 317:525–527.

Bromage TG. 1989. Experimental confirmation of enamel incremental periodicity in the pigtail macaque. Am J Phys Anthropol 78:197.

Bromage TG. 1991. Enamel incremental periodicity in the pig-tailed macaque: a polychrome fluorescent labelling study of dental hard tissues. Am J Phys Anthropol 86:205–214.

Bullion SK. 1987. The biological application of teeth in archaeology. Ph.D. Thesis. University of Lancaster.

Burns KR, Maples WR. 1976. Estimation of age from individual adult teeth. J Forensic Sci 21:343–356.

Condon K, Rose JC. 1992. Intertooth and intratooth variability in the occurrence of developmental enamel defects. In: Bapasso LL, AH Goodman, editors. Recent Contributions to the Study of Enamel Developmental Defects. Chieti (Italy): J Paleopathology, Monogr Publ 2. pp. 61–78.

Dean MC. 1985. The eruption pattern of the permanent incisors and first permanent molars in *Australopithecus* (*Paranthropus*) *robustus*. Am J Phys Anthropol 67:251–257.

Dean MC. 1987. Growth layers and incremental markings in hard tissues; a review of the literature and some preliminary observations about enamel structure in *Paranthropus boisei*. J Hum Evol 16:157–172.

Dean MC. 1989. The developing dentition and tooth structure in hominoids. Folia Primatol 53: 160–176.

Dean MC. 1993. Daily rates of dentine formation in macaque tooth roots. Int J Osteoarch 3:199–206.

Dean MC. 1995. The nature and periodicity of incremental lines in primate dentine and their relationship to periradicular bands in OH 16 (*Homo habilis*). In: J Moggi-Cecchi, editor. Aspects of Dental Biology; Paleontology, Anthropology and Evolution. Florence: International Institute for the Study of Man. pp. 239–265.

Dean MC. 1998a. A comparative study of cross striation spacings in cuspal enamel and of four methods of estimating the time taken to grow molar cuspal enamel in *Pan*, *Pongo*, and *Homo*. J Hum Evol 35:449–462.

Dean MC. 1998b. Comparative observations on the spacing of short-period (von Ebner's) lines in dentine. Arch Oral Biol, 43:1009–1021.

Dean MC. 1999. Hominoid tooth growth: using incremental lines in dentine as markers of growth in modern human and fossil primate teeth. In: Hoppa RD, FitzGerald CM, editors. Human Growth in the Past: Studies from Bones and Teeth. Cambridge: Cambridge University Press. pp. 111–127.

Dean MC, Beynon AD. 1991. Histological reconstruction of crown formation times and initial root formation times in a modern human child. Am J Phys Anthropol 86:215–228.

Dean MC, Scandrett AE. 1995. Rates of dentine mineralization in permanent human teeth. Int J Osteoarch 5:349–358.

Dean MC, Scandrett AE. 1996. The relation between enamel cross striations and long-period incremental markings in dentine in human teeth. Arch Oral Biol 41:233–241.

Dirks W. 1998. Histological reconstruction of dental development and age at death in a juvenile gibbon (*Hylobates lar*). J Hum Evol 35:411–425.

Eli I, Sarnat H, Talmi E. 1989. Effect of the birth process on the neonatal line in primary tooth enamel. Pediatr Dent 11:220–223

FitzGerald CM. 1996. Tooth crown formation and the variation of enamel microstructural growth markers in modern humans. Ph.D. Thesis. University of Cambridge.

FitzGerald CM. 1998. Do enamel microstructures have regular time dependency? Conclusions from the literature and a large-scale study. J Hum Evol 35:371–386.

FitzGerald CM, Saunders SR, Macchiarelli R, Bondioli L. (1999). Large scale histological assessment of deciduous crown formation. In: Mayhall JT, Heikkinen T, editors. Proceedings of the 11th International Symposium of Dental Morphology, Aug 26–30, 1998, Oulu, Finland.

Fukuhara T. 1959. Comparative anatomical studies of the growth lines in the enamel of mammalian teeth. Acta Anat Nipp 34:322–332.

Fujita T. 1939. Neue Festsellungen über Retzius'schen Parallelstreifung des Zahnschmelzes. Anat Anz 87:350–355.

Goodman AH, Armelagos GJ, Rose JC. 1984. The chronological distribution of enamel hypoplasias from prehistoric Dickson Mounds populations. Am J Phys Anthropol 65:259–266.

Goodman AH, Rose JC. 1990. Assessment of systemic physiological perturbations from dental enamel hypoplasias and associated histological structures. Yrbk Phys Anthropol 33:59–110.

Goodman AH, Rose JC. 1991. Dental enamel hypoplasias as indicators of nutritional status. In: Larsen C, Kelley M, editors. Advances in Dental Anthropology. New York: Alan R Liss. pp. 279–293.

Grine FE. 1986. Effects of different etching agents on bovid tooth enamel. S Afr J Sci 82:265–270.

Gustafson G. 1950. Age determination on teeth. Odontologisk Tidskrift 67:361–472.

Gustafson A. 1955. The similarity between contralateral pairs teeth. Odontologisk Tidskrift 63:245–248.

Hillson S. 1986. Teeth. Cambridge: Cambridge University Press.

Hillson SW. 1992. Dental enamel growth, perikymata, and hypoplasia in ancient tooth crowns. J R Soc Med 85:460–466.

Hillson S. 1996. Dental Anthropology. Cambridge: Cambridge University Press.

Hillson S, Bond S. 1997. Relationship of enamel hypoplasia to the pattern of tooth crown growth: a discussion. Am J Phys Anthropol 104:89–104.

Hoppa RD, FitzGerald CM. 1999. From head to toe: integrating studies from bones and teeth in biological anthropology. In: Hoppa RD, FitzGerald CM, editors. Human Growth in the Past: Studies from Bones and Teeth. Cambridge: Cambridge University Press. pp. 1–31.

Huda TF, Bowman JE. 1995. Age determination from dental microstructure in juveniles. Am J Phys Anthropol 92(2):135–150.

Johanson G. 1971. Age determination from human teeth. Odontologisk Revy 22:1–126.

Lucy D, Pollard AM. 1995. Further comments on the estimation of error associated with the Gustafson dental age estimation method. J Forensic Sci 40:222–227.

Lucy D, Pollard AM, Roberts CA. 1994. A comparison of three dental techniques for estimating age at death in humans. J Archaeol Sci 22:151–156.

Mann A. 1975. Paleodemographic Aspects of the South African Australopithecines. Pennsylvania: University of Pennsylvania Publications in Anthropology.

Mann A, Lampl M, Monge JM. 1987. Maturational patterns in early hominids. Nature 328:673–675.

Marks MK, Rose JC, Davenport WD Jr. 1996. Technical note: thin section procedure for enamel histology. Am J Phys Anthropol 99: 493–498.

Massler M, Schour I. 1946. The appositional life span of the enamel and dentine-forming cells. J Dent Res 25:145–150.

Miller CS, Dove SB, Cottone JA. 1988. Failure of use of cemental annulations in teeth to determine the age of humans. J Forensic Sci 33:137–143.

Moorrees CFA, Fanning EA, Hunt EE. 1963a. Formation and resorption of three deciduous teeth in children. Am J Phys Anthropol 21: 205–213.

Moorrees CFA, Fanning EA, Hunt EE. 1963b. Age variation of formation stages for 10 permanent teeth. J Dent Res 42:1490–1502.

Newman HN, Poole DGF. 1974. Observations with scanning and transmission electron microscopy on the structure of human surface enamel. Arch Oral Biol 19:1135–1143.

Newman HN, Poole DGF. 1993. Dental enamel growth. J R Soc Med 86:61.

Okada M. 1943. Hard tissues of animal body— highly interesting details of Nippon studies in periodic patterns of hard tissue are described. Shanghai Evening Post Medical Edition September 1943, 15–31.

Osborn JW. 1990. A three-dimensional model to describe the relation between prism directions, parazones, and diazones, and the Hunter-

Schreger bands in human tooth enamel. Arch Oral Biol 35:869–878.

Risnes S. 1986. Enamel apposition rate and the prism periodicity in human teeth. Scandinavian J Dent Res 94:394–404.

Risnes S. 1990. Structural characteristics of staircase-type Retzius lines in human dental enamel analyzed by scanning electron microscopy. Anat Rec 226:135–146.

Risnes S. 1998. Growth tracks in dental enamel. J Hum Evol 35:331–350.

Rosenberg GD, Simmons DJ. 1980a. Rhythmic dentinogenesis in the rabbit incisor: allometric aspects. Calcif Tissue Int 32:45–53.

Rosenberg GD, Simmons DJ. 1980b. Rhythmic dentinogenesis in the rabbit incisor: circadian, ultradian, and infradian periods. Calcif Tissue Int 32:29–44.

Schenk RK, Otah AJ, Hermann N. 1984. Preparation of calcified tissues for light microscopy. In: Dickson GR, editor. Methods of Calcified Tissue Preparation. Amsterdam: Elsevier. pp. 1–56.

Scheving LE, Pauly JE. 1974. Circadian rhythms; some examples and comments upon clinical application. Chronobiologica 1:3–21

Schmidt WT, Keil A. 1971. Polarizing Microscopy of Dental Tissues. Oxford: Pergamon Press.

Schour I. 1936. The neonatal line in the enamel and dentine of the human deciduous teeth and first permanent molar. J Am Dent Assoc 23: 1946–1955.

Schour I, Hoffman MM. 1939. The rate of apposition of enamel and dentine in man and other animals. J Dent Res 18:161–175

Schour I, Massler M. 1941. The development of the human dentition. J Am Dent Assoc 28: 1153–1160.

Schour I, Massler M. 1944. Development of the Human Dentition. Chart. Second edition. American Dental Association, Chicago.

Schour I, Poncher HG. 1937. Rate of apposition of enamel and dentine, measured by the effect of acute fluorosis. American Journal of Diseases of Childhood 54:737–756

Shellis RP. 1984. Variations in growth of the enamel crown in human teeth and a possible relationship between growth and enamel structure. Arch Oral Biol 29:697–705.

Shellis RP. 1998. Utilization of periodic markings in enamel to obtain information on tooth growth. J Hum Evol 35:387–400.

Shinoda H. 1984. Faithful records of biological rhythms in dental hard tissues. Chemistry Today 162:34–40.

Simpson SW. 1999. Reconstructing patterns of growth disruption from enamel microstructure. In: Hoppa RD, FitzGerald CM, editors. Human Growth in the Past: Studies from Bones and Teeth. Cambridge: Cambridge University Press. pp. 241–263.

Skinner M, Anderson GS. 1991. Individualization and enamel histology: a case report in forensic anthropology. J Forensic Sci 36:939–948.

Smith BH. 1991. Standards of human tooth formation and dental age assessment. In: Kelley M, Larsen CS, editors. Advances in Dental Anthropology. New York: Alan R. Liss. pp. 143–168.

Stott GG, Sis RF, Levy BM. 1982. Cemental annulation as an age criterion in forensic dentistry. J Dent Res 61:814–817.

Takiguchi H. 1966. Chronological relationship of human tooth crown formation. Nihon University Dental Journal 40:391–397.

Ten Cate AR. 1989. Oral Histology: Development, Structure, and Function. St. Louis: The C.V. Mosby Co.

Walker PL, Cook DC, Lambert PM. 1997. Skeletal evidence for child abuse: a physical anthropological perspective. J Forensic Sci 42:196–207.

Warshawsky H. 1988. The Teeth. In: Weiss L, editor. Cell and Tissue Biology. Baltimore: Urban and Schwarzenberg. pp. 598–641.

Weber D, Eisenmann D. 1971. Microscopy of the neonatal line in developing human enamel. Am J Anat 132:375–392.

Whittaker DK, Richards D. 1978. Scanning electron microscopy of the neonatal line in human enamel. Arch Oral Biol 23:45–50.

Wilson DF, Schroff FR. 1970. The nature of the striae of Retzius as seen with the optical microscope. Aust Dent J 15:162–171.

CHAPTER 7

HISTOMORPHOMETRY OF HUMAN CORTICAL BONE: APPLICATIONS TO AGE ESTIMATION

ALEXANDER G. ROBLING AND SAM D. STOUT

INTRODUCTION

Quantitative bone histology (histomorphometry) has been used to estimate age at death for nearly a century, the first published report appearing in 1911 (Balthazard and Lebrun, 1911). Bone histomorphometry offers a powerful tool to the skeletal biologist, and its application to age estimation in modern, historic, and prehistoric populations has been met with encouraging results. These successes can be further enhanced by incorporating several factors that have been observed to affect the accuracy of histological age estimates—sex and population variability; adequate sampling techniques, including reference sample composition, choice of skeletal element, and topographic sampling procedure; and the effects of pathological conditions and the biomechanical loading environment. Indeed, proper use of histomorphometric age estimation techniques requires an understanding of the effect of these intrinsic and extrinsic factors on derived age estimates. This chapter reviews the physiological basis for histomorphometric age estimation techniques, the histomorphology of cortical bone and its relation to age estimation, some factors known to affect derived estimates,

and, finally, considers future directions in the field. Appendix A provides worked examples of two techniques commonly used for histomorphometric age estimation and includes labeled schematic diagrams for both examples. Appendix B profiles selected age estimation techniques.

THE PHYSIOLOGICAL BASIS FOR HISTOMORPHOMETRIC AGE ESTIMATION TECHNIQUES: BONE MODELING AND REMODELING

Development of the adult skeleton is achieved by growth, modeling, and remodeling. Growth and modeling are two processes that work in concert in the normal growing individual and thus will be considered together. In long bones, growth increases bone length and diameter (both internal and external) as specified by the genetic program of the organism. This baseline architecture is modified by the modeling process, which sculpts the bone's size, shape, and curvature to optimally sustain the mechanical loads typically borne by that bone. The separate effects of growth and modeling are apparent in the limb bones of paralyzed, growing children and animals, which usually lack significant bone curvature, develop subnormal cortical thickness, and exhibit a roughly circular cross section. Modeling adjusts bone

Biological Anthropology of the Human Skeleton, Edited by M. Anne Katzenberg and Shelley R. Saunders.
ISBN 0-471-31616-4   Copyright © 2000 by Wiley-Liss, Inc.

architecture and mass via modeling drifts, which add bone to some surfaces and remove it from others. Modeling drifts move bone through tissue space (Fig. 7.1) and can simultaneously increase or decrease the cross section's size by selectively inhibiting or promoting cellular activity at the resorptive and appositional surfaces accordingly. In the normal developing skeleton, growth and modeling result in the production of organized, parallel sheets of primary lamellar bone—circumferential and endosteal lamellae—typically visible in diaphyseal cross sections (Fig. 7.2A). Some circumferential and endosteal lamellae deposited early in the developmental period are removed or "modeled out" as the bone drifts. Thus, the

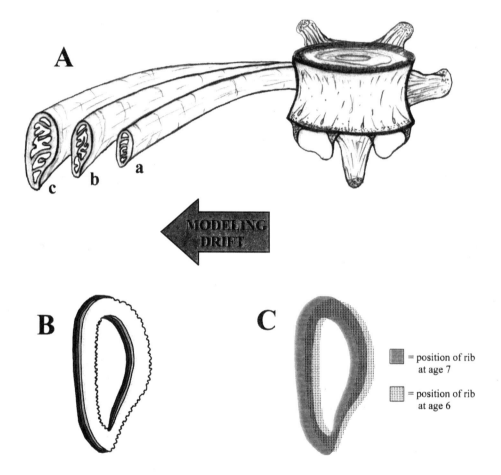

Figure 7.1 (A) During development, modeling drifts in the middle third of the sixth rib remove bone from the internally facing surfaces and deposit bone on the externally facing surfaces. As the rib drifts laterally, the formation surfaces outpace the resorptive surfaces, and the rib gains cross-sectional area. Note that none of the tissue present in the young rib (a) is present in the adult rib (c); it has been completely "modeled out." (B) Enlarged view of the drifting rib cortex (trabeculae have been removed for clarity). The younger bone (lamellae) is darker, and the older bone is lighter. The cross section thus comprises a mosaic of different aged lamellae. (C) The same drifting rib cortex illustrated in (B). The stippled region represents the size and position of the rib cortex at time 1 (arbitrarily designated as age 6 in the figure). A year later (shaded silhouette), some of the cortex that was present at age 6 is still present (region exhibiting both stippling *and* shading). However, nearly half of the cortical bone present at age 7 did not exist in the same rib just one year earlier. Bone modeling is a dynamic process in the growing skeleton that regularly and rapidly alters the size, shape, relative position, and age of bone tissue.

A

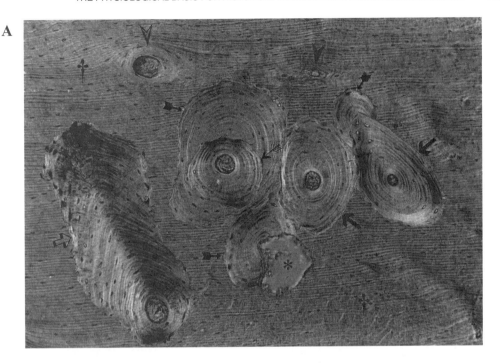

B

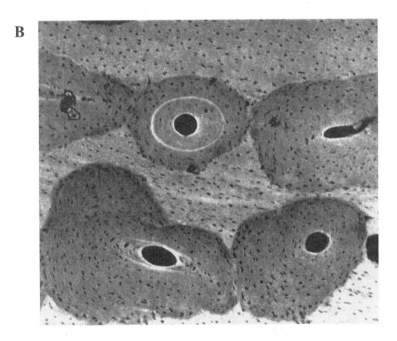

Figure 7.2   (A) Undecalcified cross section of a tibial diaphysis illustrating cortical histomorphology. Cross (†) = circumferential (primary) lamellar bone. Solid arrow (→) = type I (common) osteons. Feathered arrow (➹) = type II osteon. Darts (➹) = osteon fragments. Asterisk (*) = resorptive bay. Open arrow (⇨) = drifting osteon. Open point (≻) = primary osteon. Closed point (➤) = primary vascular canal (non-Haversian canal). (B) Micro-radiograph from an ulnar diaphysis illustrating a double-zonal osteon (center). Note that the arrest line (lighter ring) follows the contours of the centripetal lamellae and osteocyte lacunae.

adult cortex comprises a collection of lamellae exhibiting an array of different ages. Their mean age, however, is always less than the individual's chronological age. The circumferential and endosteal lamellae deposited during modeling provide the canvas upon which discrete units of cortical *re*modeling leave their mark (see below).

Once skeletal maturity is reached, modeling is reduced to a trivial level compared to that which occurs during development. Renewed modeling in the adult skeleton can occur, however, in some disease states and in cases where the mechanical loading environment has been altered radically. These observations are relevant to those using histomorphometric techniques to estimate age because renewed adult modeling, in the absence of a concurrent increase in remodeling, will decrease the mean tissue age and ultimately result in age estimates lower than actual age.

Unlike modeling, which involves either resorption or formation (but not both) at a locus, bone *re*modeling always follows an activation→ resorption→ formation sequence at a locus (Fig. 7.3). Remodeling removes and replaces discrete, measurable "packets" of bone. These packets, or bone structural units (BSUs), form the basis for most histomorphometric age estimation techniques. Within the cortex of bone, BSUs comprise secondary osteons.

Bone is remodeled by a complex arrangement of cells, collectively called the basic multicellular unit (BMU). Intracortical BMUs tunnel through long bone diaphyses in a nearly longitudinal orientation (Hert et al., 1994). The leading region of the BMU is lined with osteoclasts—specialized cells capable of bone resorption. The diameter of the tunnel excavated by osteoclasts, which typically reaches roughly 250–300 μm, defines the cross-sectional size of the osteon that will form in its wake. A histological section that transects the resorptive phase of a BMU (the cutting cone) will exhibit a cavity with rough, scalloped edges (Howship's lacunae), known as a resorptive bay (Figs. 7.2a and 7.3). Howship's lacunae are

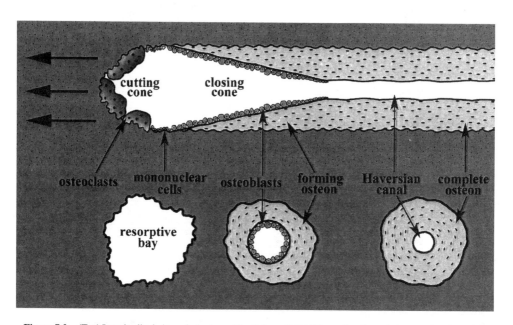

Figure 7.3 (Top) Longitudinal view of a basic multicellular unit (BMU) moving through tissue space from right to left. (Bottom) Schematic illustrations of an evolving osteon corresponding to selected transverse sections of the longitudinal system depicted above. (Redrawn after Stout, 1989.)

characteristic of all actively resorbing bone surfaces.

Following closely behind the osteoclasts is a group of mononuclear cells. The exact function of these cells remains unclear (Eriksen and Langdahl, 1995). Mononuclear cells line the resorptive bay during the reversal phase (the period between resorption and formation). It is likely that they smooth off the scalloped periphery of the resorptive bay in preparation for the deposition of a reversal line—a thin, mineral-deficient, sulfur-rich layer of matrix that separates an osteon from surrounding interstitial lamellae (Schaffler et al., 1987). An appreciation of reversal lines is particularly important in applying histomorphometric age estimation techniques because their presence can be used to differentiate secondary osteons (a product of remodeling) from primary osteons (a product of modeling).

Behind the mononuclear cells, rows of osteoblasts adhere to the reversal zone and deposit layers of osteoid (unmineralized bone matrix) centripetally. The size of the remodeling space constricts as more concentric osteonal lamellae are deposited and mineralized. At a specified point, deposition ceases leaving a Haversian canal in the center.

CORTICAL BONE HISTOMORPHOLOGY AND AGE ESTIMATION

Several types of osteons exist in compact bone. Many methods employ different osteon types as variables, thus, an understanding of their morphology and the ability to distinguish among different osteon types are necessary in applying such methods.

During modeling, some blood vessels in the periosteum become incorporated into the circumferential lamellae being deposited, producing primary vascular channels in the cortex. In some primary vascular channels (non-Haversian canals) a few rudimentary concentric lamellae are deposited around the periphery of

the channel, thus producing a primary osteon with a central non-Haversian canal. Others do not deposit lamellae, and they are simply non-Haversian canals (Fig. 7.2a). Note that primary channels with and without concentric lamellae exhibit non-Haversian canals. As bone remodels, fewer non-Haversian canals are present in the cortex. Several researchers have made use of the association between age and the prevalence of non-Haversian canals/primary osteons by incorporating their frequency into age-predicting equations (e.g., Ericksen 1991; Fangwu 1983; Kerley 1965).

Several varieties of secondary osteons exist in cortical bone. The existence of a reversal line at their periphery distinguishes secondary osteons (including all subtypes) from primary osteons. Common secondary osteons (also called type I) are formed by BMUs as described in the previous section (Figs. 7.2 and 7.3). Their number tends to increase with age, and many existing methods employ the number of type I osteons in a specified area or per unit area as an age-predicting variable (see Appendix B). One must pay particular attention to the definition of secondary osteons (and of all other structures[1]) provided in the method intended for use. Table 7.1 provides examples of five different sets of criteria for counting a structure as a secondary osteon. Proper use of a method requires strict adherence to the definitions.

As age increases, the cortex becomes crowded with secondary osteons. As a result, new osteons remove portions of older ones, thus creating osteon fragments. The number of osteon fragments is also positively correlated with age, an observation many researchers have incorporated into their age estimation methods. Some methods (e.g., Stout and Paine, 1992) combine the density (number per mm^2) of intact and fragmentary osteons to form a new variable, the osteon

---

[1]Thompson (1979), for example, includes primary osteons in his Haversian canal counts.

population density (OPD). OPD increases with advancing age until an asymptote is reached—a point at which subsequent osteon creations remove all evidence of previous ones. When the cortex reaches asymptote, OPD can not increase further. The asymptote imposes obvious limitations on histological methods, the ramifications of which are discussed below.

Other age estimation variables derived from type I osteons include mean number of lamellae per osteon (Singh and Gunberg, 1970); mean osteon area (Iwamoto and Konishi, 1982; Narasaki, 1990; Thompson, 1979; Yoshino et al., 1994) and perimeter (Narasaki, 1990; Thompson 1979); and mean Haversian canal area (Singh and Gunberg, 1970; Thompson, 1979; Yoshino, et al. 1994), diameter (Balthazard and Lebrun, 1911; Iwamoto and Konishi, 1982; Rother et al., 1978; Samson and Branigan, 1987), perimeter (Narasaki, 1990; Thompson, 1979), and population density (Samson and Branigan, 1987). Reported associations with age exhibited by some of these variables (and others described below) vary and are still open to question (Table 7.2).

Type II (embedded) osteons are smaller versions of type I osteons that form by radial remodeling of a preexisting Haversian canal (Jaworski et al., 1972; Richman et al., 1979). The completed type II osteon appears as a small Haversian system—complete with a reversal line and concentric lamellae—embedded completely within a larger, parent osteon (Fig. 7.2a). Some authors (Ericksen, 1991; Yoshino et al., 1994) report that the number of type II osteons/mm^2 increases with age, a factor they have incorporated into their age-predicting equations. Richman et al. (1979), however, report no significant association with age.

Double-zonal osteons exhibit a hypercalcified ring within their concentric lamellae, demarcating a point during the formation phase where matrix elaboration temporarily ceased (Fig. 7.2b). Double-zonal osteons typically exhibit two "zones" of similar radiopacity on microradiographs, separated by the hypercalcified ring (arrest line) (Pankovich et al., 1974). They can be distinguished from type II osteons by their lack of an internal reversal line, and by the parallel contours of lamellae and osteocyte lacunae between the inner and outer zones. The observation by Yoshino et al. (1994) that the number of double-zonal osteons/mm^2 decreases with age has been incorporated into their predicting equations. Pankovich et al. (1974), however, report an increase with age, and Stout and Simmons (1979) report no change.

Drifting osteons form from BMUs that simultaneously travel longitudinally and transversely through the cortex, a process that

TABLE 7.1   Variation in Secondary Osteon Definitions Used by Different Authors

Author(s)	Criteria used to include a BSU in secondary osteon counts:
Kerley (1965:162)	Exhibits 80% or more of its original lamellar area and has an intact Haversian canal.
Wu et al. (1970:218)	Completely unremodeled (entire lamellar area intact, regardless of their age.
Ortner (1975:29)	Must have a Haversian canal of normal size.
Stout (1986:297)	Exhibits a Haversian canal at least 90% unencroached upon.
Ericksen (1991:174)	Exhibits a completely intact Haversian canal; Volkmann's canals also counted.

BSU, bone structural unit.

TABLE 7.2 Variation in Reports of Association between Histomorphological Features and Age[a]

Microstructural variable	Increases with age	Decreases with age	No change
Osteon size		Yoshino et al. (1994)[h] Jowsey (1966)[r] Currey (1964)[f]	Jowsey (1966)[f] Pfeiffer (1988)[f,r]
Haversian canal size	Yoshino et al. (1994)[h] Jowsey (1968)[f] Bocquet-Appel et al. (1980)[f]	Singh and Gunberg (1970)[m,f,t]	Jowsey (1966)[r] Currey(1964)[f]
Type II osteon population density	Yoshino et al. (1994)[h] Ericksen (1991)[f]		Richman et al. (1979)[f]
Double Zonal osteon population density	Pankovich et al. (1974)[r]	Yoshino et al. (1994)[h]	Stout and Simmons (1979)[h]

[a]other, less equivocal relations (e.g., osteon population density and age) are not included. Superscripts denote bone(s) examined: [f]mandible, [f]femur, [h]humerus, [r]rib, [t]tibia.

results in a transversely elongated osteon exhibiting a hemicyclic lamellar "tail" (Robling and Stout, 1999) (Fig 7.2a). Despite their documented association with age (Coutelier, 1976; Sedlin et al., 1963), drifting osteons have not been incorporated in published age estimation techniques.

An alternative method that avoids distinguishing among the different types of osteons and their frequency was first proposed by Ahlqvist and Damsten (1969), who measured the percentage of the microscopic field occupied by remodeled bone, that is, by bone of any secondary osteon subtype. This approach purports to reduce interobserver error associated with counting the number of specific microstructures in a given field (see Lynnerup et al., 1998). Several subsequent methods have used percent remodeled bone as a variable in their age estimation equations (e.g., Uytterschaut 1985, 1993). Ericksen (1991) and Cool et al. (1995) use a variation of this approach by quantifying the percentage of bone occupied by the different microstructures (osteonal bone, fragmental bone, unremodeled bone).

Several methods have incorporated other, nonhistological variables, such as sternal rib end morphology (Stout et al., 1994), cortical thickness, volume, weight, and density (Thompson, 1979). The prevalence of these

and other variables discussed above is tabulated in Appendix B.

EFFECTS OF INTRINSIC AND EXTRINSIC VARIABILITY ON HISTOMORPHOMETRIC AGE ESTIMATES

A number of factors besides age are known to affect cortical bone remodeling, and, consequently, histological age estimates (Frost, 1987). Those factors most relevant to bioanthropology and related fields are discussed below.

Sex-Related Variation

Differences in the rate at which cortical bone is remodeled in postmenopausal women and in men of the same age have been known for some time (e.g., Heaney et al., 1978a, 1978b; Oursler et al., 1996). There is an increase in bone remodeling in women immediately after the onset of menopause (Parfitt, 1979). What is less clear, however, is (1) whether this geriatric sex difference has an appreciable effect on the overall accuracy of age estimates derived from pooled-sex equations, and (2) whether differences exist in males and females of younger (premenopausal) ages. The data addressing these issues are equivocal. Kerley (1965) found no significant sex difference in his sample of 126 lower limb bones, nor did Stout and colleagues (Stout and Paine, 1992; Stout et al., 1994, 1996) in their samples of ribs and clavicles. Ahlqvist and Damsten (1969), and later, Uytterschaut (1985, 1993), did not investigate sex differences, citing Kerley's conclusion that they do not exist. Singh and Gunberg (1970) began their study with a sample of 52 males and 7 females, but subsequently dropped the females from the reference sample for use as an independent test sample. The male-based predicting equations produced errors "within experimental and measurement error and [were] not significant" when tested on the 7 females (1970:376). Yoshino et al. (1994), Iwamoto and Konishi (1982), and Samson and Branigan (1987) also used reference samples comprised solely of males.

Thompson (1979) appears to be the first author to present sex-specific predicting equations. He later (1981) tested their use on a series of 54 autopsy specimens, and, despite the lower standard errors obtained for males in his original article, he obtained better results for females in the autopsy series. The pooled-sex equations were not tested. Ericksen (1991) found that sex-specific equations gave better results than those based on pooled sexes. She notes that females accumulate intact osteons until the sixth decade of life, compared to the tenth decade in males. Sex differences in fragmentary osteon accumulation were also noted.

In addition to the rate at which osteons are created, male–female differences in osteon size could also have an effect on age estimates. For example, female Pecos Indians exhibit greater mean femoral osteon area (0.041 mm^2) than their male counterparts (0.034 mm^2) (Burr et al., 1990). This difference could potentially produce greater age estimates in males than in females of the same age, because an average square millimeter of cortex can accommodate fewer large osteons than small osteons. The packing arrangement, however, would also have an effect on both the observed OPD and percent remodeled bone

(Frost, 1987). Additionally, Burr and colleagues note that osteons appear to increase in size with advancing age among females, while in males they decrease. Exactly the opposite conclusion was reached by Broulik and colleagues (1982) in a modern sample. The apparently conflicting results could be due to population differences, or to the sampling location (Broulik et al., sampled cortex from the ilium rather than from a long bone). Recent data on osteon size in samples from twentieth-century South Africans, nineteenth-century Canadian settlers, and eighteenth-century English suggest that no significant sex differences exist in osteon size in the femoral midshaft or in the sternal third of the sixth rib (Pfeiffer, 1998).

Skeletal modeling differences between males and females could also affect age estimates derived from pooled-sex equations, particularly at the younger (18–22 years) age range. The well-documented differences in maturation rates and in the timing of growth cessation (e.g., epiphyseal union) between males and females (e.g., Tanner, 1978) could reflect differing ages at which the adult cortex is completed by modeling. If females complete their adult cortex at an earlier age, that is, they have a greater effective age of adult compacta, then the mean tissue age—and consequently the amount of time osteons would have had to accumulate in the cortex—would differ between a young man and woman of the same chronological age. At present, there are no data available that address sex differences in effective age of adult compacta, but future research could elucidate them and their effect, if any, on histological age estimates.

Physical Activity

Studies of animal models have demonstrated that intracortical bone remodeling can accelerate as a result of increased mechanical loading (Bouvier and Hylander, 1981; Hert et al., 1972; Lieberman, 1997). It is likely that skeletal strain levels, distributions, and frequencies experienced by past populations were variable from population to population, and different from those experienced by industrialized, modern populations. Technological developments, landscape topography, and food procurement strategies all contribute to the strain milieu experienced by the skeleton. Ruff (Chapter 3) presents data indicating that past populations practicing different subsistence economies often exhibit differences in the gross geometry of their long bones that may be strain related. These differences in gross geometry are also manifested intracortically (Burr et al., 1990). Age estimates in highly physically active populations that are based on regression equations from more sedentary (modern) individuals, therefore, could exhibit significant bias.

For example, in an analysis of two Late Woodland ossuaries from southern Maryland, Ubelaker (1974) found markedly different age estimates using Ahlqvist and Damsten's (1969) method and methods based on the gross metamorphosis of the pubis. He notes that individuals comprising Ahlqvist and Damsten's reference sample (modern Finns) may have been less physically active than individuals from the ossuaries, and that this difference may account for the greater histological age estimates in the Indian samples. Additionally, Walker et al. (1994) have shown that OPD in the midshaft femur correlates more strongly with the cross section's bending rigidity (a hypothesized indicator of physical activity) than with age among individuals of 50 years and older.

Severe disuse also can have profound effects on bone remodeling. Animals with artificially induced limb impairments exhibit a dramatic increase in bone turnover immediately after onset of disuse (Uhthoff and Jaworski, 1978). However, severe disuse states often can be recognized in skeletal remains by grossly visible atrophy of the cortex.

In addition to its effect on remodeling, physical activity level also appears to affect modeling. Lieberman (1996) has shown that, in

pigs, increased exercise promotes modeling throughout the skeleton, not just in those bones being loaded. Consequently, in physically active individuals or populations, mean tissue age could be less than age-matched individuals from a more sedentary population. Histomorphometric age estimates in the former population could be lower than actual age because secondary osteons would have had less time to accumulate in the cortex and because older osteons would be removed by subsequent modeling drifts. The interaction between lower mean tissue age and increased remodeling resulting from a more physically active lifestyle is at present, unclear.

Population Variation

Many organs in the human body exhibit substantial interpopulational variation in metabolism (e.g., melanin production by the integument), and the skeleton appears to be among them. It is this attribute, coupled with the fact that bone microstructure provides a record of past metabolic events, that makes histological investigations of past and present skeletal populations so fruitful. However, population-level differences in bone remodeling dynamics can potentially lead to complications in age estimates when equations based on one population are applied to others. Some examples of population differences in bone remodeling follow:

Weinstein and Bell (1988) found that African Americans exhibit lower trabecular bone turnover rates than U.S. whites, an observation later confirmed in cortical bone by Cho (1997) in a series of historic African-American skeletons from Missouri. Curiously, black Africans exhibit bone turnover rates more similar to whites than to African Americans (Schnitzler, 1993). However, both African Americans and black Africans show (compared to U.S. whites) decreased susceptibility to osteoporotic fracture (Farmer et al., 1984; Solomon, 1979), a puzzling finding that could reflect greater bone quality in blacks than in whites.

Ericksen and Stix (1991) tested Ericksen's wedge age estimation technique on a series of interred nineteenth century African-American skeletons from Philadelphia. Their results compared favorably to macroscopic age estimates. Interestingly, the majority of individuals whose age estimates fell outside one standard error were *over*aged by the histological method, a surprising result given the slower turnover noted for African Americans. The inclusion of a significant number of blacks (from the Dominican Republic) in Ericksen's reference sample may partially account for the overestimates, whereas Cho's (1997) application of largely white-based equations (Stout and Paine, 1992) to the Missouri African-American sample could explain the resulting underestimates. It should also be noted that Cho (1997) had exact age at death data from burial markers, whereas Ericksen's histological estimates could be compared only to macroscopically estimated ages (see Aiello and Molleson, 1993; Pfeiffer, 1980).

Eskimos, on the other hand, appear to exhibit greater bone turnover rates than U.S. whites. Thompson and Gunness-Hey (1981) reported that their sample of femoral cores from a series of nineteenth-century Eskimo femora exhibited greater osteon densities than cores from modern (autopsy and cadaver) U.S. whites. When Thompson and Cowen (1984) estimated age in two Eskimo mummies using pubic morphology and Thompson's (1979) histological technique, they found that histological age estimates exceeded mean macroscopic estimates in both individuals. Eskimos also appear to exhibit greater turnover than other Native American populations, including Arikara and Pueblo Indians (Ericksen, 1973; Richman et al., 1979). Thompson and Gunness-Hey conclude that population-specific equations are required to overcome genetic differences in bone remodeling, a recommendation supported by the poor age estimates they obtained using Thompson's (U.S. white-based) technique on the large Eskimo sample.

Despite Kerley's success in applying his method (Kerley, 1965) to skeletal remains from different populations (interred Indian skeletons from Kentucky, Florida, Virginia, and the Aleutian and Philippine islands), Ubelaker (1977, 1986) found that Kerley's method produced errors averaging 11 years when applied to a modern sample of black and mulatto femora from the Dominican Republic. Fangwu (1983) applied Kerley's method to a sample of 35 modern Chinese femora. He found that the 42% of the individuals' ages were correctly estimated to within ±5 years, 25% were between ±5 and ±10 years, and the remaining 33% produced estimates with errors greater than ±10 years. Aiello and Molleson (1993) tested Kerley's method on a series of eighteenth- and nineteenth-century skeletons of known age from London. Although Kerley's method was biased, underestimating true age in most (70%) of the individuals, 65% of the estimates were reasonably accurate, producing age estimates within 10 years of actual age.

Pathological Conditions

A number of pathological conditions can affect bone modeling and remodeling, and, consequently, histological age estimates can be affected. Metabolic disturbances are manifest in the skeleton via a number of pathways. For example, osteogenesis imperfecta (OGIM), an inherited condition that results in abnormally brittle bones, is associated with an increase in the number of osteons created per year (activation frequency). This would have the effect of overestimating true age in individuals with OGIM. However, OGIM is also associated with sustained modeling in adulthood. Consequently, mean tissue age in adults with OGIM is less than that in age-matched normals. The lower mean tissue age has a profound effect on observed osteon populations: despite an accelerated activation frequency, individuals with OGIM exhibit subnormal OPDs (Wu et al., 1970). Thus histological age estimates in individuals with OGIM could be biased toward a younger age.

Hyperparathyroidism (HP), on the other hand, is associated with an increase in activation frequency, with no known effect on bone modeling. Individuals suffering from HP usually exhibit greater osteon counts than age-matched normals, thus histological age estimates can be affected. HP (and especially secondary HP) is a particularly relevant condition when studying bone remodeling in extinct populations, because many groups are known to have suffered from dietary stresses. An inadequate supply of dietary calcium or a reduction in the body's ability to absorb calcium from the gut (e.g., vitamin D deficiency) can result in low levels of serum calcium—a factor known to trigger excessive release of parathyroid hormone and subsequently increase osteoclast differentiation, that is, increase the number of active BMUs. Cook et al. (1988) have presented data supporting a diagnosis of hyperparathyroidism in a 50- to 60-year-old female excavated from a Roman period site in central Egypt.

A number of local noxious stimuli can affect age estimates by increasing the remodeling rate locally. Frost (1983) has called this factor the "regional acceleratory phenomenon" (RAP). Fractures, bone infections, local circulatory complications, and a number of other factors can result in RAP. The effects of RAP are local, thus they may not be detectable from biopsies at distant sites. The effect of RAP on histomorphometrics—and on derived age estimates—can go unchecked if a small tissue sample from a RAP-affected area is analyzed. This risk can be reduced by reading a large number of fields distributed throughout a cortical cross section. Some of the age estimation techniques that employ a small sample of tissue (e.g., core or wedge) have been criticized by Stout (1989, 1992) on exactly these grounds.

Some ways to evaluate whether a pathological condition may be affecting an age estimate follow:

1. Scan the cross section for any signs of abnormal histomorphology, including abnormal modeling drifts, and the presence of woven bone. The latter condition can be pathognomic of several metabolic disorders, including Paget's disease, renal osteodystrophy, or OGIM.

2. Consider the cortical thickness from which the thin section comes. High turnover rates on the endosteum can result in reduced cortical thickness, a common symptom of osteoporosis-related disorders.

3. If possible, analyze a sample of trabecular bone (preferably from the ilium) from the same individual. Because of its much greater surface-area-to-volume ratio, trabecular bone usually exhibits the effects of systemic metabolic bone disease more rapidly and to a greater extent than cortical bone. Abnormal values of trabecular bone volume, surface density, mean BSU wall thickness, and total resorptive surface can be diagnostic of certain disease states. These static parameters are all measurable in well-preserved archaeological remains (Cook et al., 1988), and reference values for age-matched normal individuals are available in the literature (Lips et al., 1978; Merz and Schenk, 1970). Moreover, needle biopsy can be used to remove small bone cores (e.g., from the ilium) with very little damage to the specimen (Weinstein et al., 1981). Age estimates should be suspect when trabecular parameters deviate substantially from age-matched normal values.

Undoubtedly, individuals affected with conditions known to alter histomorphometry have made their way into many samples from which predicting equations have been generated. Ericksen (1991) purposefully included individuals in her reference sample that were diagnosed with pathological conditions known to affect bone remodeling, such as diabetes and chronic renal disease. Her aim was to produce age estimation equations that included conditions that are likely to be encountered in unidentified individuals. Thompson (1979) provides specific equations for a pathological subset of his sample. However, given that pathological conditions can either accelerate (e.g., hyperparathyroidism) or retard (e.g., diabetes) remodeling rates, the utility of these equations is questionable.

Research Methods

The importance of reading an adequate amount of cross-sectional area has been known for at least 30 years: "Two serial cross sections of rib with only 10 mm^2 cortical area each may exhibit several hundred percent difference in bone formation, whereas two serial cross sections of the femur of the same patient, with more than 300 mm^2 cortical area each, will differ by less than 5%" (Wu et al., 1970:216). Thus the amount of cortical area read per individual is a paramount concern in accurately quantifying the remodeling history from a region of bone.

Sampling area is a difficult issue to deal with in histological investigations of archaeological or fossil bone because permission to remove complete cross sections is rarely granted. These considerations have lead to the development of techniques that do not require complete cross sections, and leave the original specimen largely intact. Thompson's (1979) method requires only a small (0.4 cm in diameter) core of bone. Ericksen's (1991) method involves removal of a small wedge (1 cm in transverse width) of bone from the anterior cortex, providing a larger cross-sectional area than that obtained by Thompson's technique. The sampling technique that provides the greatest amount of cross-sectional area yet leaves the original specimen intact is described in Aiello and Molleson (1993). At the femoral midshaft, they made two parallel transverse cuts, starting from the anterior surface, extending approximately three quarters of the way through the bone. Using a chisel, they removed a C-shaped block, from which

sections—exhibiting all but the posterior quadrant—were prepared. The original shape, length, and most of the diaphysis of the femur were thus retained for future morphological study. This sampling technique is recommended when complete cross sections cannot be removed.

The distribution of histological structures in a typical long-bone cross section is not uniform, a fact that has been known for some time. Jowsey (1966) showed that the regions of bone near the marrow cavity are more heavily remodeled than more peripheral (subperiosteal) regions. Drusini (1987) reported on the great variability in osteon density around the periphery of the femoral cortex (see also Pfeiffer et al., 1995). Thus, it is imperative that the exact topographic sampling location described in a particular method is followed precisely. This caveat can impose severe limitations on a method in archaeological investigations, for example, if the region or quadrant of bone necessary to apply a particular method is missing. More commonly, significant wear on the periosteal surface caused by taphonomic processes removes subperiosteal bone (of an unknowable depth) from the remains. The vast majority of age estimation methods are based on the subperiosteal cortex (see Appendix B), so the application of methods based on the subperiosteal cortex to remains exhibiting significant wear can produce erroneously high age estimates. Pfeiffer (1992) and Ericksen (1997) encountered this very problem when attempting to estimate age at death in samples of interred nineteenth-century Canadians and Preceramic Chileans, respectively.

In order to circumvent the influence of significant periosteal wear on age estimates, Stout and colleagues (Stout, 1986; Stout and Paine, 1992; Stout et al., 1994, 1996) have incorporated into their methods a topographic sampling procedure where every other field in the entire section is read. This procedure results in a "checkerboard" sampling pattern, which has the advantage of not relying on any one region of the cross section for histomorphometrics.

Though this procedure works well for bones with minimal cross-sectional area (e.g., rib, clavicle), it may be impractical in larger bones (e.g., femur, tibia).

For larger bones, age estimation methods that sample the endosteal region of the cortex would be of particular use in archaeological contexts. Such a strategy avoids complications introduced by significant periosteal wear—a factor which appears to be the rule rather than the exception in many archaeological collections. Hauser et al. (1980) presented age estimation equations based on the circa-medullary (endosteal) region and on the subperiosteal region of the femur and tibia. Correlation between the circa-medullary histomorphometry and age was *greater* than that between the subperiosteal histomorphometry and age—a result challenging the observation that the deeper cortex does not reflect age changes as accurately as the peripheral cortex (Aiello and Molleson, 1993; Kerley, 1965). Further support for the use of the endosteal region in age-estimation methods is presented in Pfeiffer et al. (1995), who found that fields at or near the endosteum were similar to those located subperiosteally, but both locations were significantly different from fields in between the subperiosteal and endosteal fields. Given their utility in archaeological material, age estimation techniques that employ endosteal regions of the cortex warrant further investigation.

Additionally, statistical methods used in producing age-predicting equations can have a significant effect on age estimates. Most methods present equations derived from the "classical" regression model, in which the quantified histological variable (e.g., OPD) is the dependent variable and is regressed onto age at death, the independent variable. Rogers and Stout (1998) report that classical regression can reduce bias and provide more accurate age estimates for histological methods derived from samples for which correlation coefficients are moderate, that is, $r \approx .82$. Inverse regression was found to provide better results when correlation is high ($r \geq .82$) or low

($r \leq .65$). These observations are based on a limited set of data, and further research is needed to confirm their utility in other existing and new methods.

CONCLUSIONS: FUTURE DIRECTIONS AND CONSIDERATIONS IN HISTOLOGICAL AGE ESTIMATION

It is clear from the preceding discussion that a number of factors—both physiological and methodological—are germane to the proper use of histomorphometric age estimation techniques. Advances in bone biology and histology made over the past thirty years have identified many factors that have known effects on bone remodeling dynamics. Knowledge of their effects were, for the most part, not available to Kerley and other early pioneers of histological age estimation methods. Today, efforts should focus on finding ways to account for some of the variation in age estimates resulting from these influences, that is, differences in physical activity levels, sex, genetic differences, and states of health. We suggest some guidelines and potentially fruitful areas of investigation for those endeavoring to develop new age estimation methods, and some issues to consider for consumers of existing and forthcoming methods.

1. The composition of the reference sample used in any new method should be reported in as much detail as possible, including total n, the n for each sex, age ranges and mean ages for each sex, and the ethnic composition of the sample. Given that the age range and distribution of the reference sample can bias considerably the age estimates produced for other samples (Lazenby, 1984; Masset, 1976), a complete description of the reference sample should be provided so those using the method are aware of potential biases they may encounter. Additionally, given the histomorphomet-

ric variability in sampling location (Drusini, 1987, 1996, Iwaniec, 1977; Pfeiffer et al., 1995), the exact topographic sampling technique should be described and illustrated. A brief review of Appendix B reveals some sample-reporting deficiencies among several methods currently in use.

2. If ethnically heterogeneous reference samples are used, some indication of the influence of the subgroups on the method should be reported. For example, reporting mean residual scores for different subgroups will give the reader some indication of potential biases, and their expected direction, if the method is applied to individuals from a particular population.

3. Examining sections from multiple skeletal elements is recommended for several reasons:

   A) Biomechanical factors affecting bone remodeling appear to be local, usually affecting only those bones being strained (Bouvier and Hylander, 1981; Tommerup et al., 1993). By sampling more than one bone—preferably including bones from both the axial and appendicular regions—the risk of arriving at an age estimate substantially altered by excessively vigorous or trivial physical activity is reduced.

   B) Regional acceleratory phenomenon is also a locally acting phenomenon. Multiple-site sampling also reduces the risk of RAP having a severe effect on an age estimate.

   C) Several authors (e.g., Lazenby, 1984; Martin et al., 1981; Walker et al., 1994; Willows, 1991) have discussed the inability of histological methods to produce accurate age estimates among individuals of 50 years and older. Most of the deficiencies can be attributed to the fact that the cortex reaches asymptote in later years.

That bones vary in their baseline remodeling rates (Marotti, 1976) could be used to circumvent the problem associated with the remodeling asymptote. Some slow-turnover bones (e.g., tibia, metatarsals) may reach asymptote at a later age than other, more rapid-turnover bones (e.g., femur, rib), though this remains to be confirmed. Using bones with low and high turnover rates in conjunction should allow more accurate age estimates in samples that include individuals of young and advanced ages.

4. In addition to devising age estimation methods that employ microstructural data from multiple skeletal sites, we also recommend exploring techniques that incorporate both microscopic and macroscopic variables into one method (e.g., Stout et al., 1994). Studies that have compared microscopic and macroscopic age estimates show that their combined use is usually better than either alone (Aiello and Molleson, 1993; Dudar et al., 1993).

5. Studies of topographic variation in histomorphometry have the potential to overcome curator-imposed limitations on tissue sampling (Pfeiffer et al., 1995). For example, Iwaniec (1997) determined that 95% of the variation in OPD in the anterior quadrant of the femur is accounted for by two 1- mm wide columns that span from periosteum to endosteum. This discovery significantly reduces the number of fields required to accurately quantify bone turnover in the anterior cortex. However, these results apply only to the anterior quadrant; studies on the remaining three quadrants are needed. Thus it might be possible to remove three or four bone cores from the appropriate cortical locations, and accurately quantify bone turnover in the

entire cross section (most of which could remain in the intact bone). Iwaniec (1997) further reports that in the pig, only 50% of the midshaft femoral cross section need be read to account for over 90% of the variation in the entire cross section. This area of research warrants further investigation, particularly in humans.

6. As discussed earlier, it has become clear that mechanical loading has profound effects on cortical bone microstructure. In order to augment some of the differences in age estimates attributable to physical activity, it may be necessary to include in the analysis other variables, such as cortical thickness or normalized second moments of area, that can potentially account for some of the variability associated with physical activity differences (see Ruff, Chapter 3).

7. Both inverse and classical regression should be explored in the development of new age estimation methods. This step has the potential to substantially reduce bias and increase the accuracy of estimates derived from the resulting prediction equations.

8. Lastly, differences in mean tissue age can introduce substantial error into histological age estimates. Investigations of sex and population differences in skeletal maturation and mean tissue age would be particularly enlightening for the bone palaeohistologist, in both age estimations and other investigations (e.g., remodeling rates). Research in this direction has already begun and appears promising (Stout and Lueck, 1995).

REFERENCES

Ahlqvist J, Damsten O. 1969. A modification of Kerley's method for the microscopic determination of age in human bone. J Forensic Sci 14:205–212.

Aiello LC, Molleson T. 1993. Are microscopic ageing techniques more accurate than macroscopic ageing techniques? J Archaeol Sci 20:689–704.

Balthazard, Lebrun. 1911. Les canaux de Havers de l'os humain aux différents ages. Ann Hyg Pub Med Lég 15:144–152.

Bocquet-Appel JP, de Almeida Tavers de Rocha MA, Xavier de Morais MH. 1980. Peut-on estimer l'âge au décès à l'aide du remaniement osseux? Biometrie Humaine 15:51–56.

Bouvier M, Hylander WL. 1981. Effect of bone strain on cortical bone structure in macaques (*Macaca mulatta*). J Morphol 167:1–12.

Bouvier M, Ubelaker DH. 1977. A comparison of two methods for the microscopic determination of age at death. Am J Phys Anthropol 46: 391–394.

Broulik P, Kragstrup J, Mosekilde L, Melsen F. 1982. Osteon cross-sectional size in the iliac crest: variation in normals and patients with osteoporosis, hyperparathyroidism, acromegaly, hypothyroidism and treated epilepsia. Acta Pathol Microbiol Immunol Scand [A] 90:339–344.

Burr DB, Ruff CB, Thompson DD. 1990. Patterns of skeletal histologic change through time: comparison of an archaic Native American population with modern populations. Anat Rec 226: 307–313.

Cera F, Drusini A. 1985. Analisi critica e sperimentale dei metodi di determinazione dell'eta attraverso le microstrutture ossee. Quaderni di Anatomia Pratica 41:105–121.

Cho H. 1997. Population-specific histological age estimating method: a comparison of European-American and African-American rib samples. Master's Thesis, University of Missouri, Columbia.

Cook M, Molto E, Anderson C. 1988. Possible case of hyperparathyroidism in a Roman period skeleton from the Dakhleh Oasis, Egypt, diagnosed using bone histomorphometry. Am J Phys Anthropol 75:23–30.

Cool SM, Hendrikz JK, Wood WB. 1995. Microscopic age changes in the human occipital bone. J Forensic Sci 40:789–796.

Coutelier L. 1976. Le remaniement interne de l'os compact chez l'enfant. Bull Ass Anat Nancy 60:95–110.

Currey JD. 1964. Some effects of ageing in human Haversian systems. J Anat 98:69–75.

Deslypere P, Baert H. 1958. Assessment of age by the measurement of the haversian canals of human bones. J Forensic Med 5:195–199.

Drusini A. 1987. Refinements of two methods for the histomorphometric determination of age in human bone. Z Morphol Anthropol 77:167–176.

Drusini A. 1996. Sampling location in cortical bone histology. Am J Phys Anthropol 100:609–610.

Drusini A, Businaro F. 1990. Skeletal age determination by mandibular histomorphometry. Int J Anthropol 5:235–243.

Dudar JC, Pfeiffer S, Saunders SR. 1993. Evaluation of morphological and histological adult skeletal age-at-death estimation techniques using ribs. J Forensic Sci 38:677–685.

Ericksen MF. 1973. Age-related bone remodeling in three aboriginal American populations. Ph.D. Dissertation. George Washington University, Washington D.C.

Ericksen MF. 1991. Histologic estimation of age at death using the anterior cortex of the femur. Am J Phys Anthropol 84:171–179.

Ericksen MF. 1997. Comparison of two methods of estimating age at death in a Chilean Preceramic population. Int J Osteoarch 7:65–70.

Eriksen EF, Langdahl B. 1995.. Bone remodeling and its consequences for bone structure. In: Odgaard A, Weinans H, editors. Bone Structure and Remodeling. New Jersey: World Scientific. pp. 25–36.

Ericksen MF, Stix AI. 1991. Histologic examination of age of the First African Baptist Church adults. Am J Phys Anthropol 85:247–252.

Fangwu Z. 1983. Preliminary study on determination of bone age by microscopic method. Acta Anthropol Sinica 2:142–151.

Farmer ME, White LR, Brody JA, Bailey KR. 1984. Race and sex differences in hip fracture incidence. Am J Public Health 74:1374–1380.

Frost HM. 1983. The regional acceleratory phenomenon: a review. Henry Ford Hosp Med J 31:3–9.

Frost HM. 1987. Secondary osteon populations: an algorithm for determining mean bone tissue age. Yrbk Phys Anthropol 30:221–238.

Hauser R, Barres D, Durigon M, Derobert L. 1980. Identification par l'histomorphometrie du femur et du tibia. Acta Med Leg Soc 30:91–97.

Heaney RP, Recker RR, Saville PD. 1978a. Menopausal changes in calcium balance performance. J Lab Clin Med 92:953–963.

Heaney RP, Recker RR, Saville PD. 1978b. Menopausal changes in bone remodeling. J Lab Clin Med 92:964–970.

Hert J, Fiala P, Petrtyl M. 1994. Osteon orientation of the diaphysis of the long bones in man. Bone 15:269–277.

Hert J, Pribylová E, Lišková M. 1972. Reaction of bone to mechanical stimuli. Part 3: microstructure of compact bone of rabbit tibia after intermittent loading. Acta Anat 82:218–230.

Iwamoto S, Konishi M. 1982. Study on the age-related changes of the compact bone and the age estimation: 3. Determination of the age limitation. Med J Kinki Univ 7:33–40.

Iwamoto S, Oonuki E, Konishi M. 1978. Study on the age-related changes of the compact bone and the age estimation: 2. On the humerus. Acta Medica Kinki Univ 3:203–208.

Iwaniec UT. 1997. Effects of acidity on cortical bone remodeling: a histomorphometric assessment. Ph.D. Dissertation. University of Wisconsin, Madison.

Jaworski ZF, Meunier P, Frost HM. 1972. Observations on two types of resorption cavities in human lamellar cortical bone. Clin Orthop 83:279–285.

Jowsey J. 1966. Studies of Haversian systems in man and some animals. J Anat 100:857–864.

Jowsey J. 1968. Age and species differences in bone. Cornell Vet 56(suppl):74–94.

Kerley ER. 1965. The microscopic determination of age in human bone. Am J Phys Anthropol 23:149–164.

Kerley ER, Ubelaker DH. 1978. Revisions in the microscopic method of estimating age at death in human cortical bone. Am J Phys Anthropol 49:545–546.

Kimura K. 1992. Estimation of age at death from second metacarpals. Z Morph Anthropol 79:169–181.

Lazenby RA. 1984. Inherent deficiencies in cortical bone microstructural age estimation techniques. Ossa 9–11:95–103.

Lieberman DE. 1996. How and why humans grow thin skulls: experimental evidence for systemic cortical robusticity. Am J Phys Anthropol 101:217–236.

Lieberman DE. 1997. Making behavioral and phylogenetic inferences from hominid fossils: considering the developmental influences of mechanical forces. Ann Rev Anthropol 26:185–210.

Lips P, Courpron P, Meunier PJ. 1978. Mean wall thickness of trabecular bone packets in the human iliac crest: changes with age. Calcif Tissue Res 26:13–17.

Lynnerup N, Thomsen JL, Frohlich B. 1998. Intra- and inter-observer variation in histological criteria used in age at death determination based on femoral cortical bone. Forensic Sci Int 91:219–230.

Marotti G. 1976. Map of bone formation rate values recorded throughout the skeleton of the dog. In: Jaworski ZFG, editor. Proceedings of the First Workshop on Bone Morphometry. Ottawa: University of Ottawa Press. pp. 202–207.

Martin DL, Goodman AH, Armelagos GJ. 1981. On the use of microstructural bone for age determination. Curr Anthropol 22:437.

Masset C. 1976. Sur quelques fâcheuses methodes de determination de l'âge des squelettes. Bull Mem Soc Anthropol (Paris) 13:329–336.

Merz WA, Schenk RK. 1970. Quantitative structural analysis of human cancellous bone. Acta Anat (Basel) 75:54–66.

Narasaki S. 1990. Estimation of age at death by femoral osteon remodeling: application of Thompson's core technique to modern Japanese. J Anthropol Soc Nippon 98:29–38.

Ortner DJ. 1975. Aging effects on osteon remodeling. Calcif Tissue Res 18:27–36.

Oursler MJ, Kassem M, Turner R, Riggs BL, Spelsberg TC. 1996. Regulation of bone cell function by gonadal steroids. In: Marcus R, Feldman D, Kelsey J, editors. Osteoporosis. New York: Academic Press. pp. 237–260.

Pankovich AM, Simmons DJ, Kulkarni VV. 1974. Zonal osteons in cortical bone. Clin Orthop 100:356–363.

Parfitt AM. 1979. Quantum concept of bone remodeling and turnover: implications for the pathogenesis of osteoporosis. Calcif Tissue Int 28:1–5.

Pfeiffer S. 1980. Bone-remodeling age estimates compared with estimates by other techniques. Curr Anthropol 21:793–794.

Pfeiffer S. 1992. Cortical bone age estimates from historically known adults. Z Morphol Anthropol 79:1–10.

Pfeiffer S. 1998. Variability in osteon size in recent human populations. Am J Phys Anthropol 106:219–227.

Pfeiffer S, Lazenby R, Chiang J. 1995. Brief communication: cortical remodeling data are affected by sampling location. Am J Phys Anthropol 96:89–92.

Richman EA, Ortner DJ, Schulter-Ellis FP. 1979. Differences in intracortical bone remodeling in three aboriginal American populations: possible dietary factors. Calcif Tissue Int 28:209–214.

Robling AG, Stout SD. 1999. Morphology of the drifting osteon. Cells Tissues Organs. 164:192–204.

Rogers NL, Stout SD. 1998. Selecting a calibration method to reduce bias in histological aging methods. Am J Phys Anthropol 26(suppl):191. (abstract).

Rother VP, Krüger G, Mechlitt J, Hunger H. 1978. Histomorphometrische sowie regressions—und faktor—analytische Untersuchungen von Altersveränderungen des Humerus. Anat Anz 144:346–365.

Samson C, Branigan K. 1987. A new method of estimating age at death from fragmentary and weathered bone. In: Boddington A, Garland AN, Janaway RC, editors. Death Decay and Reconstruction Approaches to Archaeology and Forensic Science. Manchester: Manchester University Press. pp. 101–108.

Schaffler MB, Burr DB, Frederickson RG. 1987. Morphology of the osteonal cement line in human bone. Anat Rec 217:223–228.

Schnitzler CM. 1993. Bone quality: a determinant for certain risk factors for bone fragility. Calcif Tissue Int 53(suppl 1):S27–S31.

Sedlin ED, Frost HM, Villanueva AR. 1963. Age changes in resorption in the human rib cortex. J Gerontol 18:345–349.

Singh IJ, Gunberg DL. 1970. Estimation of age at death in human males from quantitative histology of bone fragments. Am J Phys Anthropol 33:373–381.

Solomon L. 1979. Bone density in ageing Caucasian and African populations. Lancet 2:1326–1330.

Stout SD. 1986. The use of bone histomorphometry in skeletal identification: the case of Francisco Pizarro. J Forensic Sci 31:296–300.

Stout SD. 1989. Histomorphometric analysis of human skeletal remains. In: İşcan MY, Kennedy KAR, editors. Reconstruction of Life from the Skeleton. New York: Alan R. Liss. pp. 41–52.

Stout SD. 1992. Methods of determining age at death using bone microstructure. In: Saunders SR, Katzenberg MA, editors. Skeletal Biology of Past Peoples: Research Methods. New York: Wiley-Liss, Inc. pp. 21–35.

Stout SD, Dietze WH, İşcan MY, Loth SR. 1994. Estimation of age at death using cortical histomorphometry of the sternal end of the fourth rib. J Forensic Sci 39:778–784.

Stout SD, Gehlert SJ. 1980. The relative accuracy and reliability of histological aging methods. Forensic Sci Int 15:181–190.

Stout SD, Lueck R. 1995. Bone remodeling rates and skeletal maturation in three archaeological skeletal populations. Am J Phys Anthropol 98:161–171.

Stout SD, Paine RR. 1992. Brief communication: histological age estimation using rib and clavicle. Am J Phys Anthropol 87:111–115.

Stout SD, Porro MA, Perotti B. 1996. Brief communication: a test and correction of the clavicle method of Stout and Paine for histological age estimation of skeletal remains. Am J Phys Anthropol 100:139–142.

Stout SD, Simmons DJ. 1979. Use of histology in ancient bone research. Yrbk Phys Anthropol 44:263–270.

Tanner JM. 1978. Fetus into Man: Physical Growth from Conception to Maturity. Cambridge, MA: Harvard University Press.

Thompson DD. 1979. The core technique in the determination of age at death of skeletons. J Forensic Sci 24:902–915.

Thompson DD. 1981. Microscopic determination of age at death in an autopsy series. J Forensic Sci 26:470–475.

Thompson DD. 1984. Age at death and bone biology of the Barrow mummies. Arctic Anthropol 21:83–88.

Thompson DD, Cowen KS. 1984. Age at death and bone biology of the Barrow mummies. Arctic Anthropol 21:83–88.

Thompson DD, Galvin CA. 1983. Estimation of age at death by tibial osteon remodeling in an autopsy series. Forensic Sci Int 22:203–211.

Thompson DD, Gunness-Hey M. 1981. Bone mineral-osteon analysis of Yupik-Inupiaq skeletons. Am J Phys Anthropol 55:1–7.

Thompson DD, Salter EM, Laughlin WS. 1981. Bone core analysis of Baffin Island skeletons. Arctic Anthropol 17:87–96.

Tommerup LJ, Raab DM, Crenshaw TD, Smith EL. 1993. Does weight-bearing exercise affect non-weight-bearing bone? J Bone Miner Res 8:1053–1058.

Ubelaker DH. 1974. Reconstruction of demographic profiles from ossuary skeletal samples. A case study from the tidewater Potomac. Smithsonian Contributions to Anthropology No. 18. Washington: Smithsonian Institution Press.

Ubelaker DH. 1977. Problems with the microscopic determination of age at death. Paper presented at the 1977 Meeting of the American Academy of Forensic Sciences.

Ubelaker DH. 1986. Estimation of age at death from histology of human bone. In: Zimmerman MR, Angel JL, editors. Dating and Age Determination of Biological Materials. London: Croom Helm. pp. 240–247.

Uhthoff HK, Jaworski ZFG. 1978. Bone loss in response to long-term immobilisation. J Bone Joint Surg 60B:420–429.

Uytterschaut HT. 1985. Determination of skeletal age by histological methods. Z Morphol Anthropol 75:331–340.

Uytterschaut HT. 1993. Human bone remodeling and aging. In: Grupe G, Garland AN, editors. Histology of Ancient Human Bone: Methods and Diagnosis. New York: Springer-Verlag. pp. 95–109.

Walker RA, Lovejoy CO, Meindl RS. 1994. Histomorphological and geometric properties of human femoral cortex in individuals over 50: implications for histomorphological determination of age-at-death. Am J Hum Biol 6:659–667.

Weinstein RS, Bell NH. 1988. Diminished rates of bone formation in normal black adults. N Engl J Med 319:1698–1701.

Weinstein RS, Simmons DJ, Lovejoy CO. 1981. Ancient bone disease in a Peruvian mummy revealed by quantitative skeletal histomorphometry. Am J Phys Anthropol 54:321–326.

Willows ND. 1991. A comparison of two methods for estimating age at death from bone microstructure. Master's Thesis. University of Calgary, Alberta, Canada.

Wu K, Schubeck KE, Frost HM, Villanueva A. 1970. Haversian bone formation rates determined by a new method in a mastodon, and in human diabetes mellitus and osteoporosis. Calcif Tissue Res 6:204–219.

Yoshino M, Imaizumi K, Miyasaka S, Seta S. 1994. Histological estimation of age at death using microradiographs of humeral compact bone. Forensic Sci Int 64:191–198.

APPENDIX A: WORKED EXAMPLES OF TWO AGE ESTIMATION METHODS

I. Kerley (1965) and Kerley and Ubelaker (1978) method for the femur.

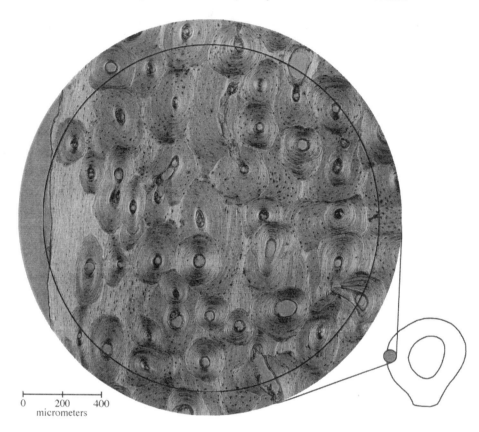

The black ring represents the field of view at 100×. The visible area has been expanded to allow structures traversing the periphery of the field—which were included in Kerley's counts—to be seen and counted. This is accomplished in practice by moving the stage controller back and forth slightly at each field. Four microscopic fields, one at each of the four subperiosteal fields along the anatomical axes, are read per section. Results for the lateral field illustrated in the photomicrograph (above) are highlighted in the table below. Results from the remaining three fields (not illustrated) are also tabulated below.

The field diameter = 1.68 mm, therefore the field size = 2.22 mm^2. To correct for differences in field size between Kerley's microscope and yours, divide your field size into Kerley's original field size of 2.06 mm^2. The quotient is a correction factor by which the sums of each variable (e.g., osteons, osteon fragments) are multiplied. In this example, the correction factor = 2.06 mm^2 ÷ 2.22 mm^2 = 0.93. To calculate age at death, insert the corrected sums (Σ_{corr}) into their respective predicting formulae (see equations below) and apply to the profile chart provided in Kerley (1965), or simply average the two estimates as recommended in Stout and Gehlert (1980).

Cortex	Osteons	Fragments
Anterior	22	9
Medial	39	15
Lateral	38	22
Posterior	27	13
Σ	126	59
Σ_{corr}	117.18	54.87

Variable	Formula	Estimated Age
Osteons:	Age = $2.28 + 0.187X + 0.00226X^2$ =	55.23
Fragments:	Age = $5.241 + 0.509X + 0.017X^2 - 0.00015X^3$ =	59.57

*Mean estimated age = 57.40

*Actual age at death from death certificate = 55 years.

II. Stout and Paine (1992) method for the rib.

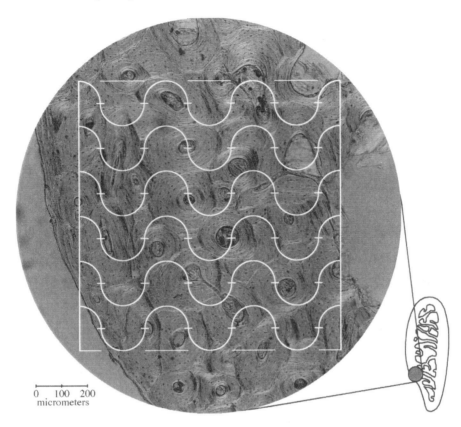

0   100   200
micrometers

The superimposed grid is a Merz counting reticule containing 36 intersections or "hits." Structures exhibiting approximately one-half or more of their area within the grid are included in the count. Every other field in the section is read, so the total number of fields read will depend on the cross-sectional size of the rib. The field illustrated in the photomicrograph is 1 of 11 fields read for this particular section, and is recorded as field 7 in the table below. Results from the remaining 10 fields (not illustrated) are also tabulated below.

The distance between intersections (hits) = 170 μm (or 0.17 mm); therefore one hit represents $(0.17 \text{ mm})^2$ or 0.0289 mm^2 of bone area. The area read equals 252 hits $\times$ 0.0289 mm^2 per hit = 7.28 mm^2. Osteon population density (OPD) is the population of intact ostens (P_1) plus the population of osteon fragments (P_1) divided by the area read.

In this example, OPD = 178 ÷ 7.28 mm^2 = 24.45/mm^2.

To calculate age at death, insert rib OPD into Stout and Paine (1992) rib formula and solve for age:

$$\ln(\text{age}) = 2.343 + 0.050877 \times \text{OPD}_{rib} = 3.59$$
$$e^{3.59} = 36.1$$

Estimated age* = 36.1 years.

*Actual age at death from death certificate = 38 years.

Field	Hits	P_i	P_f
1	17	12	3
2	29	13	8
3	14	5	3
4	18	7	6
5	36	15	8
6	33	19	8
7	36	18	10
8	36	15	11
9	12	3	3
10	14	4	4
11	7	2	1
Σ	252	113	65

III. Schematic illustrations of counted structures (shaded) from the previous two examples. Counted intact osteons are labeled with numbers, osteon fragments are labeled with letters.

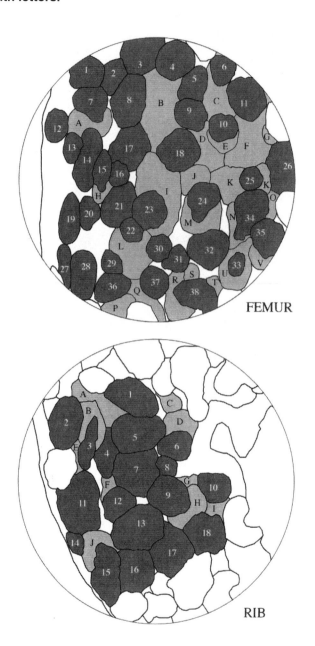

FEMUR

RIB

APPENDIX B: PROFILE OF SELECTED AGE ESTIMATION

Bone	Method	Sample Parameters: (N); Age Range {x̄}, Sex [♂:♀:?] and Ethnic Composition	Specimen Sampling Technique	Variables Used in Analysis	Reported Accuracy	Comments; [references for test of method]
Occipital	Cool et al., 1995	(17); 21–70 {46.8} [17:0:0] Australian whites		Fractional Volume of: 1. Primary osteons 2. Secondary osteons 3. Secondary osteon fragments 4. Unremodeled lamellar bone	$r^2 = .10$ (secondary osteons) $r^2 = .44$ (osteon fragments) $r^2 = .32$ (lamellar bone)	Both outer and inner tables of cortex were investigated. Authors concluded that the method is not recommended for age estimation because of low correlation of variables with age, even when subjected to multivariate analysis.
Second Metacarpal	Kimura, 1992	(227); 30–98 {68} [114:113:0] Modern Japanese		1. Cortical bone density 2. Cortical thickness 3. Total number of osteons and osteon fragments in section 4. Total osteon density [OPD]	S.E.E. = 9.99–14.82 (for total sample); 5.51–8.64 (for 30- to 65-year-old group); 5.64–7.68 (for 66- to 98-year-old group).	Microradiographs used. Complete cross section is sampled. Excellent sample size. Author found much better results when sample was analyzed separately in two groups (ages 30–65 and 66–98).
Mandible	Singh and Gunberg, 1970	(52); 39–87 {64} [52:0:0] Cadavers from U.S.; no ethnic data provided		1. Total number of osteons in two microscopic fields 2. Mean number of lamellae per osteon 3. Mean Haversian canal diameter	S.E.E. = 2.55–3.83 95% of sample within ±5 yrs. 67% of sample within ±3 yrs.	Authors found the mandible provided the greatest accuracy of the three bones they investigated. The sample of sections analyzed included both decalcified (33) and undecalcified (19) preparations. Equations based on males only.
	Drusini and Businaro, 1990	(50); 18–97 {35.3} [32:18:0] Modern Italians?		1. Mean number of secondary osteons per mm² 2. Mean number of secondary osteon fragments per mm²	S.E.E. = 6.42–11.45 for pooled sex; 6.84–13.19 for males; 5.14–7.09 for females.	Singh and Gunberg's sampling technique is followed; but only undecalcified sections are used. Much better topographical sampling of the section than Singh and Gunberg.
Fibula	Kerley, 1965; Kerley and Ubelaker, 1978	(25); 0–83 {34.5} [19:5:1] American whites and African Americans; distribution in sample not provided		Number of (1) intact osteons, (2) osteon fragments, (3) non-Haversian canals, (4) % unremodeled bone in a 2.06 mm² field	S.E.E. = 5.27–10.85 for single variables. Accuracy is increased when overlap of age range from all variables is used.	Of the three lower limb bones Kerley analyzed, the fibula provided the most accurate age estimates. In osteopenic fibulae (e.g., from the elderly), the diameter of the microscopic field can exceed the thickness of the cortex. [Cera and Drusini, 1985; Stout and Gehlert, 1980.]
Ulna	Thompson, 1979	(31); ?–? {68.8} [?:?:?] New England whites		19 variables analyzed. See original article for description.	S.E.E. = 7.9–10.6	Core technique minimizes destruction to specimen. Size of area read may increase risk of sampling an atypical field.

ªPredicting equations are not provided in the table. In order to use a method properly, the original article in which the formulae are presented must be consulted.

Bone	Reference	Sample	Diagram	Variables	S.E.E.	Comments
Femur	Kerley, 1965; Kerley and Ubelaker, 1978	(67); 0–95 {41.6} [43:17:7] American whites and African Americans; distribution in sample not provided		Number of (1) Intact osteons, (2) Osteon fragments, (3) Non-Haversian canals, and (4) percent unremodeled bone in a 2.06 mm² field	S.E.E. = 9.4–13.9 for single variables. Accuracy is increased when overlap of age range from all variables is used.	Widely used technique. Several authors have expressed difficulty in consistently identifying microstructures. [Aiello and Molleson, 1993; Bouvier and Ubelaker, 1977; Cera and Drusini, 1985; Stout and Gehlert, 1980; Ubelaker, 1986; Willows, 1991; Walker et al., 1994]
	Ahlqvist and Damsten, 1969	(20); ?–? {55} [?:?:?] Autopsy specimens; no ethnic data provided		Percent remodeled bone in 1 mm² square field	S.E.E. = 6.71	Small sample size. Variable employed appears less subjective than others (e.g., counting different microstructures). [Bouvier and Ubelaker, 1977; Stout and Gehlert, 1980; Uytterschaut, 1993]
	Singh and Gunberg, 1970	(33); 39–87 {62.3} [33:0:0] Cadavers from U.S.; no ethnic data provided		1. Total number of osteons in two microscopic fields 2. Mean number of lamellae per osteon 3. Mean Haversian canal diameter	S.E.E. = 3.24–5.01	Decalcified sections were used in study sample (possible shrinkage). Authors caution that results for femur are preliminary and should be interpreted conservatively (due to small sample size). Equations based on males only (no sex differences reported).
	Thompson, 1979	(116); 30–97 {71.7} [64:52:0] New England whites		19 variables analyzed. See original article for description.	S.E.E. = 7.1–8.6 for pooled sex; 6.4–8.3 for males; 7.2–9.4 for females.	Core technique minimizes destruction to specimen. Size of area read may increase risk of sampling an atypical field. [Cera and Drusini, 1985; Pfeiffer, 1992; Thompson, 1981; Willows, 1991]
	Ericksen, 1991	(328); 14–97 {62.8} [174:154:0] 251 U.S. whites, 12 U.S. oriental, 1 U.S. blacks, 6 Chilean hispanics, 58 Domin. Repub. blacks		Density of (1) osteons, (2) type II osteons, (3) fragments, (4) resorption spaces, and (5) non-Haversian canals. Also, mean % (6) unremodeled, (7) osteonal, and (8) fragmented bone.	S.E.E. = 10.1–12.2 for pooled sex; 10.1–12.0 for males; 10.0–11.6 for females.	Excellent sample size; ethnic mixture of sample is favorable for applying predicting equations to individuals or populations of unknown origin. Sampling technique is a good compromise between destruction of original specimen and adequate size of tissue sample. [Ericksen, 1997; Ericksen and Stix, 1991]
	Fangwu, 1983	(35); 5–86 {39.1} [29:6:0] Modern Chinese		Number of intact osteons, osteon fragments, and non-Haversian canals in 100X field, and mean thickness of outer circumferential lamellae	80% of sample within ±5 yrs. 90% of sample within ±10 yrs.	This technique applies Kerley's research design to the femora of modern Chinese. Resulting equations are more accurate on modern Chinese than are Kerley's formulae.
	Hauser et al, 1980	(96); 21–87 {?} [?:?:?] Modern Europeans		1. Population density of osteons 2. Mean minimum diameter of Haversian canals 3. Percentage of surface occupied by Haversian canals	S.E.E. = 10.7–11.4	Separate formulae provided for the subperiosteal region and endocortical region. Endocortical formulae could be useful in archaeological cases where periosteal surface is worn (e.g. Ericksen, 1997; Pfeiffer, 1992).

			Variables	S.E.E.	Comments
Femur (cont'd)	Cera and Drusini, 1985; Drusini, 1987	(20); 19–50 {28.8} [?:?:?] Modern Italians	Number of secondary osteons per mm²	S.E.E. = 3.92	Small sample size. Large portion of the cortex sampled. Osteon fragments are not included in this method, as they are in Drusini's later (e.g., Drusini and Businaro, 1990) methods.
	Samson and Branigan, 1987	(58); 16–91 {?} [31:27:0] English whites	1. Number of Haversian canals per mm² 2. Mean Haversian canal diameter 3. Mean cortical thickness excluding linea aspera	S.E.E. = 6 for males; 16 for females	A potentially useful approach for poorly preserved bones. Method purports to allow for age at death determination, but prediction equations are not provided. Criteria used to accept or reject Haversian canals for measurements and counts were decided upon by the authors, but not reported. Good topographic sampling. [Aiello and Molleson, 1993]
	Narasaki, 1990	(52); 43–98 {77.5} [28:24:0] Modern Japanese	Core (1) thickness and (2) weight; (3) intact osteonal bone area; Mean secondary osteon: (4) density, (5) area, (6) σ of area (7) perimeter, (8) σ of perimeter	S.E.E. = 9.28 (for males); 9.95 (for females)	This study applies Thompson's core technique and 6 of his 19 variables (plus two new ones) to modern Japanese.
Tibia	Kerley, 1965; Kerley and Ubelaker, 1978	(33); 0–85 {?} [24:8:1] American whites and African Americans; distribution in sample not provided	Number of (1) intact osteons, (2) osteon fragments, (3) non-Haversian canals, (4) % un-remodeled bone in a 2.06 mm² field	S.E.E. = 6.69–13.62 for single variables. Accuracy is increased when overlap of age range from all variables is used.	Several authors have expressed difficulty in consistently identifying microstructures. [Cera and Drusini, 1985; Stout and Gehlert, 1980]
	Singh and Gunberg, 1970	(33); 39–87 {62.3} [33:0:0] Cadavers from U.S.; no ethnic data provided	1. Total number of osteons in two microscopic fields 2. Mean number of lamellae per osteon 3. Mean Haversian canal diameter	S.E.E. = 3.02–4.59	Decalcified sections were used in study sample (possible shrinkage). Authors caution that results for tibia are preliminary and should be interpreted conservatively (due to small sample size). Equations based on males only (no sex differences reported).
	Thompson and Galvin, 1983	(53); 17–53 {30.2} [48:5:0] 41 U.S. whites, 12 U.S. blacks	(1) Core weight, (2) cortical bone density and (3) thickness, (4) secondary osteon number, (5) area, and (6) perimeter, and (7) Haversian canal area and (8) perimeter	11 test cases resulted in mean difference between actual and estimated age of 6.45 years.	Thompson's original (1979) method for the tibia produced poor results among individuals below 55. The new method (based primarily on osteon number instead of size) produces more accurate age estimates.
	Hauser et al., 1980	(31); 18–88 {?} [?:?:?] Modern Europeans	1. Population density of osteons 2. Mean minimum diameter of Haversian canals 3. Percentage of surface occupied by Haversian canals	S.E.E. = 13.5–16.0	Small sample size; large standard error. Separate formulae provided for the subperiosteal region and endocortical region. Endocortical formulae could be useful in archaeological cases where periosteal surface is worn (e.g., Ericksen, 1997; Pfeiffer, 1992).

Bone	Reference	Sample	Diagram	Variables	Accuracy	Comments
Tibia (cont'd)	Uytterschaut, 1985, 1993	(20); 17–92 {54} [?:?:?] Cadavers from the Netherlands; no ethnic data provided		Percent remodeled bone in 1 mm² square field	S.E.E. = 6.29	This technique applies Ahlqvist and Damsten's research design for the femur to the tibia. Small sample size may contribute to the relatively low S.E.E.
	Balthazard and Lebrun, 1911	(65); 0–84 {39.2} [?:?:?] ? ? ? ?		Mean diameter of (100–200) Haversian canals in anterior tibial cortex	67% of sample within ±5 years	First published method for estimating age from bone microstructure. Deslypere and Baert (1958) found poor results using this method on an independent test sample.
	Thompson, 1979	(31); ?–? {67.9} [?:?:?] New England whites		19 variables analyzed. See original article for description.	S.E.E. = 6.2–9.5	Core technique minimizes destruction to specimen. Size of area read may increase risk of sampling an atypical field. Thompson later (1981) discourages use of humeral cores for age estimations because of inaccuracy.
Humerus	Yoshino et al., 1994	(40); 23–80 {47.6} [40:0:0] Modern Japanese		Density of (1) secondary, (2) type II, (3) double-zonal, and (4) low-density osteons, (5) fragments, and (6) resorption spaces. Also, mean (7 & 8) and total (9 & 10) Haversian canal and osteon area	S.E.E. = 6.1–8.8	Microradiographs are necessary to accurately distinguish different types of osteons. Sections can be removed by Ericksen's wedge technique with minimal damage to the original specimen.
	Iwamoto et al., 1978	(42); 41–102 {69.1} [42:0:0] Modern Japanese		1. Osteons / mm² 2. Osteon size 3. Haversian canal diameter 4. Interstitial lamellae / mm²	95% of estimates within ±11.7 years	Reference sample comprises only older individuals (none below 40 years). Variables are somewhat confusing (e.g., interstitial lamellae per mm² = number of fragments? number of circumferential lamellae?).
	Rother et al., 1978	(70); 20–81 {?} [42:28:0] Modern Germans		Diameter of (1) Haversian canals and (2) osteons; (3) osteocyte, (4) Haversian canal, and (5) Volkmann's canal density; (6) % osteonal and interstitial bone	S.E.E. = 8.5–9.7 years	Authors found greater accuracy when macroscopic variables were entered into the regressions. They also present results from a factor analysis on the histological variables.
Sixth Rib	Stout and Paine, 1992	(40); 13–62 {28.6} [32:7:1] 32 U.S. whites, 4 U.S. blacks, 4 ?		Sum of intact and fragmentary osteons per mm² (OPD)	Mean absolute difference between estimates and actual age = 3.9 years	Two sections per bone sampled. Good topographic sampling technique. Better results were obtained using a formula combining clavicle and rib OPD. [Dudar et al., 1993]

Fourth Rib	Stout et al., 1996	(59); 11–88 {39.2} [?:?:?] U.S. whites (autopsy)		Sum of intact and fragmentary osteons per mm² (OPD) (also sternal rib phase)	S.E.E. = 10.43 for rib histology alone; 7.18 for combined rib histology and sternal rib end phase	Reference sample combines both historic (1800s) and modern (autopsy) specimens. This method exploits the available information (gross morphology and microstructure) to increase accuracy of age estimates.
Clavicle	Stout et al., 1996	(123); 13–75 {34.0} [73:49:1] 32 U.S. whites; 4 U.S. blacks; 4 ? (autopsy); 83 19th cent. Swiss		Sum of intact and fragmentary osteons per mm² (OPD)	r² = 8.5	Supersedes Stout and Paine (1992) method for clavicle. Good sample size and topographic sampling technique. Age estimates using this method are less affected by periosteal wear than others that sample only the subperiosteal cortex.

PART III

PREHISTORIC HEALTH AND DISEASE

CHAPTER 8

PALEOPATHOLOGICAL DESCRIPTION AND DIAGNOSIS

NANCY C. LOVELL

INTRODUCTION

The underlying principle of paleopathology (literally, the study of ancient suffering[1]) is that many kinds of illness and injury leave their mark on bone. Paleopathology has a time span of interest that covers many millions of years. Evidence of fractures and arthritis in dinosaurs and injury and illness in fossilized plants demonstrates that trauma and disease are not solely afflictions of contemporary human society. In the study of archaeological human skeletons, paleopathology is particularly important in prehistoric contexts from which no written records of health or of medical practices remain. As a discipline, paleopathology is approximately two hundred years old. It aims to reconstruct the history and geography of diseases, to illuminate the interaction between disease and cultural processes, to document the evolution of diseases over time, and to understand the effect of disease processes on bone growth and development. These aims are restricted, however, by the fact that, in spite of excellent preservation and meticulous excavation of skeletons, rarely are we able to determine how the individual died. Although many kinds of illness and injury do leave their mark on bone, many others, especially those that are leading causes of death today, such as heart attacks and acute gastrointestinal and respiratory infections, do not. Thus, paleopathological investigation is generally confined to trauma and chronic conditions (those of slow progress and long duration), including chronic infections, arthritis, and dental disease. As such, pathological lesions in the skeleton may tell us much about morbidity but tend to tell us little about mortality patterns in antiquity, such as those caused by epidemic diseases that had such a devastating impact historically (e.g., influenza and smallpox). Furthermore, it is likely that the frequency of some conditions in antiquity is seriously underestimated since in not all infected individuals will the disease spread to the skeleton. It has been estimated, for example, that the skeleton is involved in fewer than 10% of patients with tuberculosis (Aufderheide and Rodriguez-Martin, 1998). Additionally, even with chronic conditions the individual may die of soft tissue disease before the skeleton becomes involved. Finally, we may never know for certain what disease was involved since the pathogen is rarely preserved, only its effects.

Fortunately, there are other sources of paleopathological data in addition to the skeleton. Skeletal and dental remains are primary sources of data, as are mummified remains, which provide data on soft tissue pathology

---

[1]One of the most common errors in paleopathological description and classification is referring to pathological lesions or conditions as "pathologies," since "logos" means "the science of" (from the Greek).

Biological Anthropology of the Human Skeleton, Edited by M. Anne Katzenberg and Shelley R. Saunders.
ISBN 0-471-31616-4   Copyright © 2000 by Wiley-Liss, Inc.

(e.g., heart disease), and preserved fecal remains and latrine residues, which are primary sources of information on ancient parasitic diseases. Preserved kidney stones and gallstones also are considered primary sources of paleopathological data. Secondary sources of data include documents such as early medical histories and papyri, nonliterary art forms (e.g., some Peruvian ceramics and Egyptian tomb paintings), and artifacts such as splints and other therapeutic devices. A knowledge of the physical and sociocultural environmental context for the remains provides a tertiary source of data, for this context provides information about the conditions (such as heat and humidity or high population density) that are necessary for the existence of certain pathological conditions (such as fungal infections and influenza epidemics). This chapter provides a review of the development and current status of methods used to obtain paleopathological data from primary sources, especially archaeological skeletal remains but also, to a lesser extent, mummified soft tissue remains (see Hillson, Chapter 9, regarding dental pathology).

HISTORICAL DEVELOPMENT OF PALEOPATHOLOGY

The origin of the term *paleopathology* has been the subject of much debate, credit alternatively being given to Ruffer (e.g., Goldstein, 1963) and Schufeldt (e.g., Brier, 1994; Waldron, 1994). Regardless of the identity of its originator, its inception is agreed to have occurred more than one hundred years ago and its etymology to be derived from the Greek *paleos* (ancient), *pathos* (suffering), and *logos* (study). Paleopathology thus has come to mean the study of diseases in antiquity. Recent reviews of the history of the discipline (e.g., Angel, 1981; Armelagos, 1997; Aufderheide and Rodriguez-Martin, 1998; Buikstra and Cook, 1980; Ubelaker, 1982) usually have identified three or four chronological periods that characterize the development of this field.

The early periods were mainly descriptive, with pathological lesions treated primarily as interesting anomalies. The early 1900s witnessed a burgeoning interest in the ancient evidence for disease. Sir Marc Armand Ruffer, for example, wrote numerous papers on the soft tissue pathology of Egyptian mummies while a professor of bacteriology at Cairo Medical School. And at roughly the same time the first extensive study of skeletal remains in the Old World was carried out by Sir Grafton Elliot Smith, a British anatomist teaching in Cairo, who examined an estimated ten thousand skeletons excavated during the first archaeological survey of Nubia. The Americans entered the paleopathological arena in the 1920s and 1930s when Roy Moodie published his monumental work on paleopathology, which included evidence for disease and trauma in nonhuman vertebrates and plants, a review of pre-Columbian pathology in the Americas, and an historical account of Ruffer's work on ancient Egyptians (Moodie, 1923). Hooton is usually credited with introducing a new dimension to paleopathological inquiry, that of the population approach (Hooton, 1930). This early work on the skeletal populations from Pecos Pueblo is considered particularly important because Hooton evaluated the influence of ecology (especially diet) and culture on disease expression, a perspective that subsequently was more fully elaborated by Angel (e.g., Angel, 1966). In the latter part of this century, progress in paleopathology can be attributed to improved technology leading to increased diagnostic accuracy, more realistic disease classifications, and the explicit examination of disease in a biocultural context. These can be readily recognized in the key literature of the period, such as the synthetic and illustrative work of the 1960s (e.g., Brothwell and Sandison, 1967; Jarcho, 1966; Wells, 1964), the subsequent detailed aids to diagnosis and interpretation based on clinical pathology (e.g., Ortner and Putschar, 1981; Steinbock, 1976), the problem-oriented, biocultural approach to disease in antiquity (e.g.,

Armelagos and McArdle, 1975; Cohen and Armelagos, 1984), and the most recent reviews and syntheses (e.g., Aufderheide and Rodriguez-Martin, 1998; Rothschild and Martin, 1993).

Clearly indicative of the continuing professional interest in paleopathology and the expansion of the discipline is the growth of the Paleopathology Association from an original group of five in 1973 to more than 500 members in over 40 countries some 25 years later. Collaboration among specialists can lead to creative and vital new explorations and interpretations, with one example being taken from the study of the arthritides: on one hand, rheumatologists can identify joint space narrowing, one of the symptoms of arthritis, on radiographic images while osteologists cannot directly observe this phenomenon in dry bone specimens. On the other hand, however, osteologists can observe some of the earliest bony changes of arthritis in dry bone well before these changes lead to sufficient alterations of normal bone density to be detected on radiographs.

DESCRIPTION AND DOCUMENTATION

There are four diagnostic criteria in paleopathology: (1) the appearance of pathological lesions, (2) the location of the lesions within a skeletal element, (3) the skeletal distribution of the lesions in an individual, and (4) the distribution of lesions in a population. This section focuses on the methods necessary for the proper description and documentation of the appearance of lesions as a necessary first step toward diagnosis, and is organized around the three primary levels of analysis that form the basis of contemporary scientific study of tissue abnormality: macroscopic, microscopic, and biochemical. Following Ortner (1994), description is the process that helps us answer the question, "What is the abnormality?" Proper lesion description and documentation should seek to improve the accuracy and precision of diagnosis without going further than the data allow.

Macroscopic Analysis

The macroscopic analysis of archaeological human remains includes visual observation, radiography, and endoscopy. Visual observation is generally the first method employed when examining archaeological remains for pathological lesions. In many cases it may be the only method required, while in some circumstances it may be the only method available. Radiography has proven to be a valuable adjunct to visual observation because it can, in essence, see "inside" bodies and bodily structures. Similarly, endoscopy permits the visualization of hidden internal structures and has proven to be of great value in the paleopathological examination of mummies.

Visual Observation

The most important first step is to describe what is observed, before attempting a diagnosis. Bony reactions to trauma and disease often can be noted and described relatively easily, but determining what caused the reaction (i.e., making a diagnosis) may not be possible. Although a basic classification, such as "trauma," "arthritis," or "infection" can usually be attempted, with more than 200 different types of arthritis and a similar variety of specific and nonspecific infections recognized by clinicians it is clear that a more definitive diagnosis is often impossible. Many researchers have stressed the need for careful description (e.g., Mann and Murphy, 1990; Rothschild and Martin, 1993; Steinbock, 1976) but none as forcefully as Ortner (e.g., Ortner, 1991, 1992, 1994; and see also Ortner and Putschar, 1981). Accurate and comprehensive descriptions of pathological lesions are necessary for accurate diagnoses and also permit other researchers to evaluate proposed diagnoses. Photographic documentation is also considered crucial (e.g., Fig. 8.1), particularly in cases of tenuous diagnosis or identification of rare conditions. While there is not yet a universally accepted list of terminology, there have been several protocols for lesion description advocated in recent years

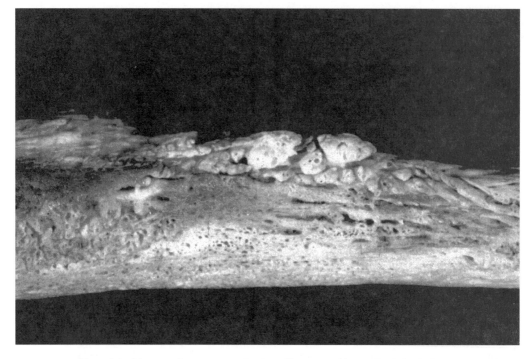

Figure 8.1 Macroscopic appearance of periosteal bone apposition on the shaft of a fibula.

(e.g., Buikstra and Ubelaker, 1994; Thillaud, 1992). Table 8.1, although not exhaustive, lists some recommended descriptive terms for macroscopic observation of pathological lesions, which are used to answer the following questions:

- What does the abnormality look like?
- Was the abnormality formed by a proliferative process, a resorptive one, or a combination of the two?
- At what speed did the process occur?
- Is the lesion forming, healing, or healed?

Smooth and dense proliferative lesions indicate that the process was chronic and the lesion slowly formed, while porous fiber bone forms more rapidly, and projecting spicules of bone typically indicate very rapid and aggressive processes of formation. The speed of resorptive processes can be determined similarly from the characteristics of the lesion: lesions with well-defined margins that are lined with compact bone indicate a slow, chronic process, while the absence of compact bone indicates a more rapid process, and lesions with poorly defined margins represent the most rapid and aggressive process.

Radiography

An important adjunct to visual observation of pathological lesions is their radiographic imaging. Most of us are familiar with the medical and dental uses of X-rays (more correctly, radiographs) to illustrate broken bones or the presence of impacted wisdom teeth, but many students of paleopathology may not know that the first application of projection radiography to archaeological mummified remains took place more than one hundred years ago. Radiographs were made of a mummified child and cat (König, 1896), a mummified bird (Holland, 1896), a Peruvian mummy and other artifacts (Culin, 1898), and an Egyptian mummy

(Petrie, 1898) very shortly after Roentgen first published X-ray images of his wife's hand (Roentgen, 1896). Radiography is a transmission imaging technique. Radiation (in the form of X-ray energy photons) is emitted from a source and transmitted through an object. The object attenuates the X-rays through processes of absorption and scatter and produces a pattern of transmitted X-rays that is imaged by a detector.

Projection Radiography

In projection radiography, radiation is produced by an X-ray tube and radiographic film (in conventional film-screen systems) is used to detect the transmitted X-rays (e.g., Fig. 8.2). Projection radiography has several features that distinguish it from other imaging techniques: the image produced is life-sized; appears as a "negative" on conventional radiographic film, and superimposes the three-dimensional structure of the object onto a two-dimensional film, so that information about depth is lost. The technique is nondestructive and inflicts no

damage on inanimate objects such as archaeological human remains, even though X-rays penetrate matter and are more or less "absorbed" in the process.

The thickness and composition of tissues that the X-rays pass through determine the density of the optical image that results, with denser objects absorbing relatively more X-rays compared to less dense objects, producing variations in opacity on the radiographic film. Other features of image quality include contrast and definition. Contrast, or density difference, arises from variation in the intensity of the X-ray beam and from the characteristics of the screen-film system being used. Low contrast ("wide latitude") systems are needed when radiographing the chest of a living person, for example, since there is a wide range of densities inherent in the different soft tissues, hard tissues, body fluids, and air spaces. In bone radiology, however, the range of densities to be imaged is much reduced, and high-contrast films are recommended. The contrast of a radiographic image also can be enhanced

TABLE 8.1   **Examples of Recommended Descriptive Terms for Pathological Lesions**

Types of lesions	
"Holes"	Cleft, crack, gap, groove, hole, perforation, pit
"Bumps"	Ridge, buildup, deposit, layer, plateau, sheet, spicules
Volume deformation	Articular, diaphyseal, epiphyseal
Surface deformation	

Lesion attributes	
Border, edge, margin	Blunt, ragged, sharp, clearly defined, poorly defined
Bottom, floor, side, wall	Smooth, compact, pitted, porous
Contour	Intact, broken, punched out, collapsed, flat, raised, lobulated, stellate, straight, curved, angular, bent, bowed, undulating, elevated, depressed, projecting, overlapping
Surface	Coarse, fine, discolored, built-up, eroded, worn, lytic, eburnated, effaced
Volume	Narrow, wide, widened, thick, thin, prominent, increased, decreased, localized, generalized, focal, multifocal, diffuse, disseminated
Number	Single, multiple
Consistency	Regular, irregular, homogeneous, heterogeneous, heavy, light, dense, atrophic, robust, fragile, delicate
Measured size	In mm or mm^2

(Adapted from Buikstra and Ubelaker, 1994, and Thillaud, 1992.)

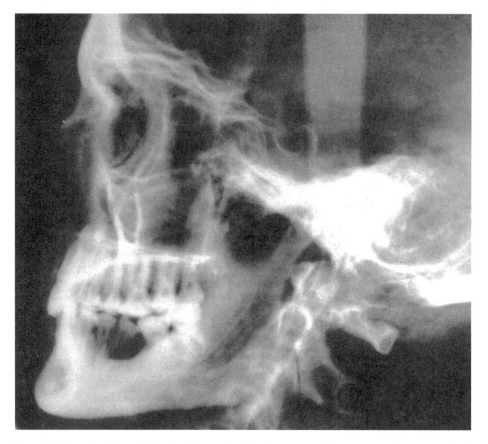

Figure 8.2 Lateral radiograph of the head of an ancient Egyptian mummy. Antemortem tooth loss can be clearly detected on the mandible.

by increasing the exposure time. Long exposure times are ill-advised for safety reasons when the subject is living, but this restriction is not necessary with ancient remains. Most medical X-ray detectors combine radiographic film in a cassette with one or more intensifying screens, in what is called a screen-film system. Screens are designed to improve sensitivity of the film so that exposure times to living subjects can be reduced. They vary in composition and hence in their ability to intensify the image, but generally they result in loss of resolution, or clarity of detail in the image (what is typically described as definition or sharpness). Definition is further influenced by the size of the X-ray source (smaller being better) and by geometry, such as the distance between the X-ray source and the object and between the object and the film. The orientation of any feature of interest on or within the object, relative to the X-ray beam trajectory, is also important. Since the center of the X-ray beam is usually perpendicular to the film, it should pass through the middle of the feature in order to minimize distortion. Distortion is also a problem with objects that are thick and irregular in shape, since the resulting scattering of X-rays leads to blurring of detail and image distortion.

A special type of photographic film is most commonly used to detect and record a radiographic image. It is available in a variety of sizes, from small dental films to larger sheets. Film in sheet form is usually exposed in a rigid medical-industrial cassette. The front or top of the cassette is radiolucent and faces the X-ray source; the object is placed between the source and the cassette (film) so that it absorbs X-rays according to density and the X-rays that are not absorbed expose the film. Lead sheets of 1-mm thickness or more are often used to sequentially protect different areas of the cassette so that several exposures can be made on the same film, in order to save money as well as film processing time. Because lead of this thickness prevents the transmission of X-rays to the film, small letters are often placed beside bones to indicate whether they are from the right or left side of the body, and lead numbers or identification plates can be used for record-keeping purposes.

Traditional radiographic practice requires the use of a light-tight photographic darkroom, equipped with, among other things, a clean, temperature-controlled water supply. In the darkroom, unexposed film is loaded safely into cassettes and then exposed film is removed from cassettes and subject to wet chemical processing, washing, fixing, etc. Many modern radiology centers, however, use what are commonly referred to as daylight systems. These mechanisms load fresh film into one end of the cassette and eject the exposed film into the processor without the cassette ever being opened, thus obviating the need for a darkroom. Furthermore, the processing units for these systems are fast and automated.

Many paleopathological studies have relied on medical and dental radiographic centers for imaging, and this is often the most convenient approach if the bones or remains to be examined are located near a hospital or clinic, are transportable, and few in number. Alternatively, portable radiographic units have proven invaluable in field settings (e.g., Notman and Beattie, 1996) as well as in some museums. A radiographic survey of mummies undertaken at the Egyptian Museum in Cairo relied on a portable radiographic machine with which some six or eight images could be taken before the film was rushed to a nearby hotel, where a makeshift darkroom was employed to process the film (Harris and Weeks, 1973). Similarly, a portable veterinary X-ray machine was used by Lukacs and co-workers at Harappa (Dales,

1990). Portable systems that rely on battery packs and Polaroid instant film provide reverse density images but are particularly useful in field situations where electricity and darkroom facilities are not readily available.

Xeroradiography

Mention must be made of the wealth of xeroradiographic images of mummies that exist archivally and in many publications of the last two decades (e.g., Cockburn et al., 1975; Davis, 1997; Rideout, 1977). Xeroradiography was once touted as a superior radiographic technique due to its improved edge enhancement (particularly with overlapping structures, such as the wrappings and coffin surrounding a mummy) and its ability to include objects of widely varying density in the same radiograph. Improved film systems and digital imaging technology now obtain the same results with a lower radiation dose to living subjects, however, and thus xeroradiography has been supplanted to the extent that Xerox no longer supports it.

Computed Tomography

In projection radiography, the problem of lack of depth information is usually dealt with by repositioning the object on the film cassette to produce a set of images that are taken from different angles. Computed tomography (CT) scanning,[2] however, accomplishes this automatically by measuring the simultaneous transmission of X-rays through an object in different directions. The resulting transmission data are computed to construct a cross-sectional image in electronic form, which can then be used as digital information or converted to a pictorial display (see Bushberg et al., 1994; Ross, 1979; for details). Developed in the early 1970s, the most common application of CT scanning in paleopathology is in the analysis of mummies (e.g., Harwood-Nash, 1979; Lewin et al., 1990), the first attempt at which is usu-

---

[2]CT was previously known as CAT scanning, and variably defined as computer-aided tomography, computer-assisted tomography, and computed axial tomography.

ally attributed to Lewin and Harwood-Nash in 1977 (Lewin, 1991).

The technique continues to be refined and improvements in diagnostic precision over a period of 15 years are well illustrated by the examination of an Egyptian mummy at the University of Alberta in 1981 and again in 1996. In the later investigation the additional capability of tissue density measurements made it possible to rule out a previously suggested diagnosis of cancer in the right fibula in favor of embalming artifact: the "lesion" in question turned out to have a density that was incompatible with bone but consistent with the embalming resin that could be observed to have pooled in the fabric wrappings around the legs and feet (Fig. 8.3).

Although there are various kinds of CT systems in use today, CT scanning is time- and resource-consuming and expensive, and port-

able equipment is uncommon. Thus, while it may be the preferred imaging technique for complex three-dimensional objects such as mummies, it is not likely to replace conventional projection radiography as the most widely used means of imaging the internal structures of archaeological human remains.

Magnetic Resonance Imaging

Magnetic resonance imaging (MRI) is unsuitable for examining bone or dried soft tissue, but would seem to have potential application to well-hydrated soft tissues (e.g., Hauswirth et al., 1991) and to frozen tissues, once thawed (Notman and Aufderheide, 1995). The technique depends primarily upon the presence of protons; as part of hydrogen atoms these are abundant in the living human body, roughly 70% of which is water. MRI is preferred over CT and projection radiography in certain clini-

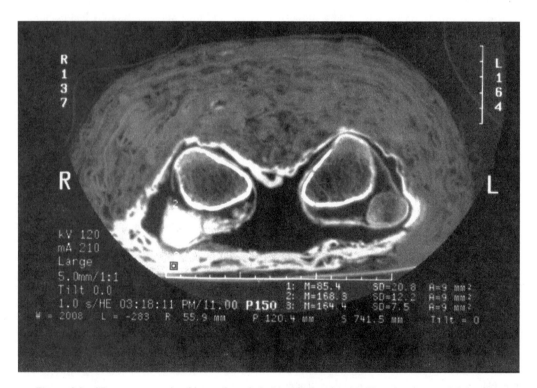

Figure 8.3 CT scan cross-sectional image through the lower limbs of ancient Egyptian mummy. Fabric wrappings are clearly visible, and the pooling of resin under the body and around the right fibula is clearly demonstrated. Density values (#1, 2, and 3) at the right fibula indicate that the opacity on the anterior surface of the fibula is due to resin artifact.

cal applications (especially neurological examinations) because of its sensitivity to soft tissue differences and its ability to capture real-time physiological activities (e.g., blood flow). Because it uses non-ionizing, radio-frequency radiation, exposure times of a minute or more are possible without risk to living patients.

The physics of the technique are complex, but, simply put, the protons and neutrons of the nucleus of an atom have a magnetic field associated with their nuclear spin and charge. The method consists of placing the body in a strong magnetic field to align the nuclear spins, adding a radio-frequency signal to alter the alignment, and measuring the signal that is given off as the spins revert to their original orientation. The resulting signals are mathematically manipulated to produce a two-dimensional image. MRI differs from projection radiography and CT imaging in three main ways: (1) the latter two modalities use X-ray energy radiation while the former uses radio-frequency radiation; (2) the latter produce images based on the differential transmission of energy according to density while the former produces images based on the differential absorption and re-emission of energy according to the nuclei present and their environment (i.e., according to the type of tissue, such as cerebrospinal fluid, white matter, fat, vitreous humor, etc.); and (3) the methods use different detection and data processing systems. For more detailed information on MRI and other imaging techniques, the reader is referred to Bushberg and colleagues (1994).

Endoscopy

Endoscopic examination relies on the insertion of a narrow tube through a body orifice or incision to permit the visualization of structures within the body, as well as the removal of tissue for subsequent microscopic analysis. While the basics of this technique of internal examination may have been developed by the Greeks (Tapp et al., 1984), endoscopy has been applied routinely to mummified human remains for little more than 15 years (e.g., Notman et al., 1986;

Tapp, 1984). The modern endoscopic apparatus employs a wide range of working lengths and diameters but is characterized by a flexible tube, the direction of which can be controlled by the operator, fiber optic-produced illumination at the probing end of the endoscope, and biopsy capability. Virtually nondestructive, endoscopy has proven to be of great value in the paleopathological examination of mummies by documenting the presence of parasites, such as *Strongyloides* and *Ecchinococcus,* as well as the lesions of diseases such as pneumoconiosis and atherosclerosis in antiquity (e.g., Sandison, 1962; Tapp and Wildsmith, 1992; Tapp et al., 1975, 1984).

Microscopic Analysis

While macroscopic analysis is the first step in the examination of pathological conditions in human remains, microscopic analysis provides a clearer picture of cellular activities in response to trauma or disease. The principles behind the modern light microscope date to the sixteenth century and the development of the first crude compound microscope (Rochow and Rochow, 1978), but the history of microscopic analysis of archaeological bone and soft tissue covers only slightly more than a century. While Sir Marc Armand Ruffer is usually credited with perfecting the technique of rehydrating mummified soft tissues for microscopic analysis (Ruffer, 1909), and Shattock examined microscopic sections of the aorta of an Egyptian pharaoh at roughly the same time (Shattock, 1909), Janos Czermak apparently identified arteriosclerosis in an Egyptian mummy several decades earlier (Strouhal and Vyhnanek, 1979).

The first histological examination of thin sections of human bone may be attributed to Weber (1927; cited in Schultz, 1997), but the technique has fallen in and out of favor many times since. It is clear, however, that the use of microscopic analysis to clarify, confirm, or refute the nature of lesions that have been identified macroscopically is of tremendous importance in paleopathology. For example,

Rogers and Kanis (1992) used histomorphometric data to confirm a diagnosis of metabolic bone disease that was suspected on the basis of visual observation and radiographic imaging and, further, to determine that the nature of the bony lesions was consistent with Paget's disease. Similarly, microscopic analysis demonstrated that several cases of porosis of the orbital roof were due to inflammatory processes, refuting a diagnosis of anemia based on macroscopic findings (Wapler and Schultz, 1996).

The microscopic analysis of bony response to disease rests on understanding of bone cells and their functions (for detailed reviews, see Bergman et al., 1996; Cormack, 1993; and Eriksen et al., 1994). The activities of bone cells vary by virtue of the maturity of the bone, the speed of bone deposition, and the effect of disease or injury. The advantage of microscopy in paleopathological investigations is that the results of these activities can be clearly detected. Three types of bone cells, osteoblasts, osteocytes, and osteoclasts, are responsible for bone production, maintenance, and resorption, respectively. Osteoblasts are small, single nucleated cells that produce the organic matrix of bone, osteoid, which consists primarily of collagen. The inorganic matrix of bone consists of mineral crystals (mainly hydroxyapatite) that infuse the osteoid and cling to collagen fibers in the manner of scales, imparting rigidity (Marks and Hermey, 1996; Ott, 1996). The initial mineralization of newly deposited osteoid occurs within a few days and accounts for up to 75% of mineralization. As the osteoid is forming, some osteoblasts become incorporated in the matrix and change, functionally, from bone-producing cells to bone-maintaining cells, or osteocytes. Osteocytes play a large role in the body's mineral metabolism: they pick up hormonal signals that indicate the need to resorb calcium or phosphate from the surrounding bone to maintain appropriate levels of calcium in the circulation, and can respond to these signals in minutes (see Vaughan, 1981, for a review of biomineralization). Osteoclasts, which are bone-resorbing cells, release en-

zymes such as collagenase and acid phosphatase to break down protein and dissolve bone mineral. Osteoclasts work much more slowly than do osteocytes. Thus, their resorption activities are more involved in structural remodeling than in mineral metabolism. They are large, multinucleated cells and can be readily distinguished from other bone cells under high-power magnification. Imbalances in cellular function that result from disease have predictable results. For example, bone resorption in osteoporosis is normal but bone formation has slowed down so that eventually there is too much resorption; cancellous bone (e.g., in vertebral bodies) is most greatly affected. The opposite imbalance occurs in hyperparathyroidism, where the activity of osteoclasts is stimulated but bone formation is normal; the outcome, however, is also too much resorption. Osteopetrosis, in contrast, is characterized by normal bone resorption but overformation.

Remodeling of bone occurs in several modes: during growth; during maturation of cortical bone (i.e., the production of secondary osteons); during maturation of cancellous bone (which is primarily degenerative, as trabeculae in marrow spaces are resorbed by osteoclasts when marrow production reduces with age); as a consequence of increases or decreases in functional stresses on the bone; and as a response to disease and injury (see Robling and Stout, Chapter 7, Pfeiffer, Chapter 10; also see Bilezikian et al., 1996; Martin and Burr, 1989). Histologically, these modes of remodeling result in two varieties of bone: primary (immature, or non-Haversian) and secondary (mature, or Haversian). The structural components of these two types of bone are similar, but their formation processes differ. Primary bone is highly vascularized and, as woven bone, is the first bone tissue to form in the growth of the skeleton and in the repair process. It forms rapidly, and collagen fibers are haphazardly arranged to form a fibrous or woven bone matrix in which numerous blood vessels become entrapped. As bone is deposited around each blood vessel a feature called a primary osteon is formed. Osteons consist of 15 to 20 sheets of bone in which the collagen fibers are arranged parallel to each other, the sheets being arranged in concentric tubes around a blood vessel. Not all mature bone is organized into osteons; some appears as large sheets of circumferential lamellae on the periosteal and endosteal surfaces of long bones. As bone matures and remodels, secondary bone is formed by the replacement of primary bone tissue by secondary osteons (also known as Haversian systems) in a process by which osteoclasts tunnel through the primary bone and are followed by osteoblasts that deposit osteoid (which is subsequently mineralized). This is a comparatively slow process that continues throughout life. The two types of osteons can be readily distinguished histologically: secondary osteons are distributed nonrandomly, are regular in appearance, large in size, and demarcated by a cement line.

A comprehensive review of microscopic analyses of archaeological human bone is that of Grupe and Garland (1993), and a superb compilation of illustrations of microscopic images has been produced by Schultz (1986). Additional examples of the contributions of microscopy to paleopathology can be found in Ascenzi (1986), Garland (1993), and Schultz (1993). Pfeiffer (Chapter 10) provides detailed information on the preparation of bone for microscopic analysis. Robling and Stout (Chapter 7) discuss bone remodeling as it applies to the determination of age at death. For the student of paleopathology, it is important to understand the differences in the kinds of information that can be provided by different microscopic techniques.

Transmitted Light Microscopy

The most common microscopic technique applied to archaeological human remains is transmitted light microscopy. It is essentially a destructive technique that uses thin sections of bone mounted on glass slides, onto which light is focused from below. The examination of bone thin sections ranges from $20\times$ to $200\times$ magnification. At this power the primary changes in bone that can be detected include the differentiation between woven and lamellar bone, an increase in mineralized bone mass (i.e., sclerosis), and/or a decrease in mineralized bone mass (i.e., rarefaction). Some of the many applications of transmitted light microscopy to paleopathology include the study of osteoporosis (Martin and Armelagos, 1985), biparietal thinning (Bianco and Ascenzi, 1993), and generalized osteopenia and localized reactive bone lesions (Cockburn et al., 1998).

The standard method of transmitted light microscopy is bright field inspection, in which light passes through the objective aperture of the microscope and illuminates the background against which the image is seen (Fig. 8.4). Dark field microscopy increases the contrast of the object against the background by limiting the light that passes through the objective. The object image is seen in brilliant white against a black background, but has the disadvantage of producing a certain amount of glare so that the object may appear as little more than a silhouette, obscuring detail. Polarized light is generally considered more useful than ordinary light for obtaining a detailed picture of cell and tissue structure in transparent specimens by revealing the birefringence of long molecules, such as those characteristic of collagen fibers. Ordinary waves of light traveling away from the light source are scattered and traveling in many directions or planes whereas in polarized light the vibrations are partially or completely suppressed in certain directions. For example, "plane-polarized" light is light in which there is only one vibration direction. The result is an image that is displayed in bright and dark areas. No modification is necessary to the mounted thin section but the microscope is fitted with a polarizer below the substage condenser and an analyzer in the body tube above the objective.

Fluorescence microscopy, in which the image is formed by fluorescence emitted from the object, can be used to detect the presence of certain compounds in archaeological bone. Such applications are limited, however, since only a few compounds have the natural ability to fluoresce. The technique uses a specialized

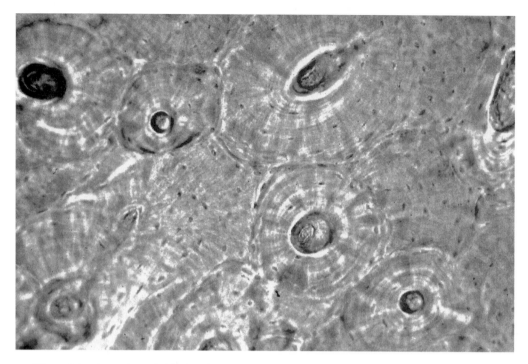

Figure 8.4 Osteons in cortical bone as imaged by transmitted light microscopy, bright field inspection (100×
magnification).

light source as well as purified reagents and
other supplies because slides, cover slips, embedding media and fixatives may all fluoresce
to some degree, causing image artifacts. Several paleopathological studies have used fluorescence microscopy to identify naturally
occurring antibiotics in archaeological bone
(e.g., Bassett et al., 1980; Cook et al., 1989;
Hummert and van Gerven, 1982). The observed fluorescence "labels" have been interpreted as resulting from the ingestion of
tetracycline-like compounds that developed
naturally in stored grain.

Stains may be employed in the microscopic
examination of bone. The introduction of a
coloring agent to improve contrast in mammalian tissues is credited to Leeuwenhoek in
the early eighteenth century, but the modern
development of dyes and their applications
dates to the latter half of the nineteenth century. The purpose of staining is to dye poorly
contrasted specimens in one or more colors so
that the contrast between chemically different
parts of the specimen (and between the specimen and its mounting medium) is increased.
Histological staining relies on dyes and proteins, and the fundamental process involved is
the chemical bonding between the carboxyl
groups of the dyes and the amino groups of the
proteins. Dyes are aromatic organic compounds that are based on the structure of ben-
zene and appear colored because they absorb
radiation in the visible region of the electro-
magnetic spectrum. For example, acid fuchsin
dye absorbs blue-green light and the color that
is detected by the human eye is transmitted
light in the red region (in this case, usually vi-
olet or magenta). Dyes can be classified in
several ways, such as by their origin (natural
or synthetic), chemical grouping, or ability to
differentiate nuclear features or cytoplasmic
structures. When classified according to their
behavior, stains are usually classified as general stains, specific stains, or histochemical
reagents. General stains color all the tissue in
different shades, while specific stains are

those that selectively color only certain tissue components. Histochemical stains are based on antibody-antigen reactions; antibodies are linked with a dye so that when they are applied to tissue they stain the antigen if it is present. Staining methods commonly used in microscopic examination often combine several dyes. For example, Goldner's method is particularly well suited to the examination of osteoblastic and osteoclastic activity in metabolic bone disease; it combines five dyes with two types of acid plus distilled water. Most dyes or stains are available commercially, but their application should be left to trained histologists. Details of stains and their applications are beyond the scope of this chapter, but the interested reader can find more information in textbooks of histology, such as Bancroft and Stevens (1996), or the standard reference for histochemists, *Conn's Biological Stains* (Lillie, 1977).

Methods for the microscopic examination of mummified soft tissues are similar to those used for bone but require special techniques for reconstitution and fixation of the tissue, which is stained with an agent appropriate for the type of tissue and for the detection of pathogens or tissue abnormalities. For example, "fatty plaques" in blood vessels (atherosclerosis) can be demonstrated by the application of Sudan IV or Scarlet R stains. Unfortunately, whether intentionally or accidentally mummified, soft tissues are often degraded and may be difficult to stain. Haematoxylin, for example, is a stain with a great affinity for cell nuclei but does not work well on mummified tissues. Other stains may produce a different color pattern than expected, perhaps due to reaction with postmortem contaminants (Tapp, 1992). In spite of these difficulties, it has been possible to identify a number of pathological conditions in mummified human remains, including smallpox, pneumoconiosis, pulmonary anthracosis, schistosomiasis, and infection with intestinal parasites such as tapeworm and *Ascaris* sp. in ancient Egyptians (Cockburn et al., 1998; Millet et al., 1998; Ruffer, 1911a, 1911b; Tapp, 1986).

Transmission Electron Microscopy

The transmission electron microscope (TEM) also uses thin sections of tissue, but a beam of electrons is directed through the section to produce an image. This method has made it possible to identify certain tissue structures, such as cell nuclei, that could not be prepared satisfactorily by staining for viewing with the light microscope. Furthermore, because the wavelength of electrons is much smaller than that of light, the resolution of TEM images is many orders of magnitude better than that of images obtained from a light microscope. The modern TEM can routinely obtain magnifications of $300,000\times$ and greater, and can reveal the finest details of structure, as small as individual atoms. Cell structure and morphology are commonly determined with TEM, and specialized preparative techniques make it possible to identify antigens or other cell components in modern tissues. When applied to mummified soft tissues, for example, TEM has identified viral agents (Fornaciari and Marchetti, 1986; Lewin, 1967, 1984).

Microradiography

Microradiography detects differences in mineral density in the bone section and has obvious applications to the study of metabolic bone disease, such as osteoporosis, so that the quality of bone, in addition to its quantity and architecture, can be assessed. Thin sections of bone are used to make contact radiographs, which are then examined under a microscope. The method has specific X-ray energy requirements in order to optimize imaging capabilities and must be undertaken at an appropriate facility. Illustrations of mineral distribution in thin sections taken from pathological bone can be seen in Heuck (1993).

Stereomicroscopy

Stereobinocular or dissecting microscopes have a relatively great depth of field which enables them to be used in the examination of uneven surfaces of bones and teeth, and, because they can be used with a long working distance between the objective and the stage, the object under examination can be easily manipulated during observation. They do not require that the specimen be sectioned, although in some cases the structural components of bone and teeth can be more easily observed if the specimen is first sectioned and polished and then chemically etched. Stereobinocular microscopes are commonly used to examine a variety of biological materials, minerals, sand grains, etc., and usually have a range of from $40\times$ to $400\times$ magnification. Because stereomicroscopes use reflected light they require intense light sources (commonly tungsten-halogen), which are commonly available as flexible fiber-optic lamps. In paleopathology, this type of microscopy can be used to show the varied topographic features of a lesion.

Scanning Electron Microscopy

Scanning electron microscopy (SEM) is specially designed to scan the object in a raster pattern. Signals at discrete and uniform intervals are received from the object by a sensor and displayed on a screen or stored for further processing. The image is built up serially. Like reflected light microscopy, SEM makes it possible to examine the surface features of bone microstructures with three-dimensional resolution, but with the use of electrons a higher magnification without loss of detail (up to as much as $40,000\times$) is possible. The combination of high resolution, great range of magnification, and high depth of field makes the SEM well suited to the study of bone and tooth surfaces. Features such as microfractures and the scalloped edges of Howship's lacunae, which are the visible remains of bone destruction by osteoclasts (Fig. 8.5), may be readily imaged (e.g., Boyde et al., 1986; Chappard et al., 1984; Krempien and Klimpel, 1981; Ortner, 1994; Roberts and Wakely, 1992; Schultz, 1986, 1993; Sela, 1977; Wakely et al., 1991).

Scanning electron microscopy should be considered a destructive technique. Although the equipment used for SEM varies, usually only very small samples of bone or teeth, per-

haps only 1 cm^2, can be accommodated. In addition, the method requires that a nonremovable coating, usually gold or carbon, be applied to the sample in order to reduce the charging effects that appear when nonconductive materials, such as bone, are analyzed. Samples may be further damaged if they are very porous, since this technique requires that the specimen be placed under vacuum. Thus, where possible, it is usually advantageous to make a replica of the specimen of interest (described in Bromage, 1987) in order to avoid damage and to examine surfaces when the original specimen is too valuable for coating or is too large to fit in the SEM specimen chamber. Replicas may also be used to record the progression of surface defects under experimental conditions.

Scanning Probe Microscopy

Scanning probe microscopy is a method of analysis that has been developed within the last 20 years. It includes scanning tunneling microscopy (STM) and atomic force microscopy (AFM). In both of these, a very sharp probe is used to map the surface of a sample. STM relies on the relationship between tunneling electrons and the distance between an electrically conductive tip and the sample surface. AFM brings the tip of a stylus into direct contact with the surface and then measures the atomic forces of interaction (primarily van der Waals forces) between the scanning tip and sample's surface atoms. Both techniques generate three-dimensional data by calculating the position of the probe as it is scanned across a surface, and a computer constructs surface topographs from the data. Instead of focused beams of light or electrons to see the surface of a sample, scanning probe microscopes are said to "feel" the sample. AFM is considered particularly useful for examining the structure of biological samples because of its ability to image nonconductive materials, and to image under atmospheric pressure and room temperature. AFM combines the vertical resolution of a transmission

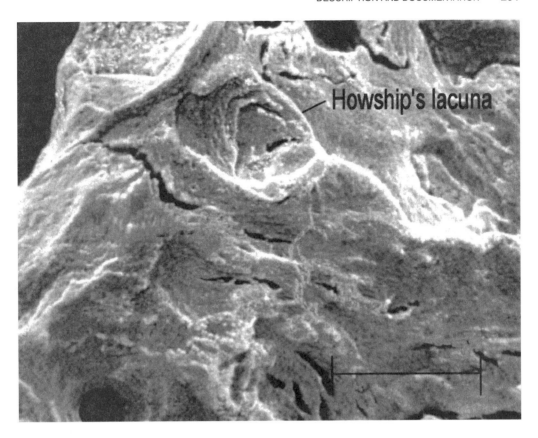

Figure 8.5   SEM photograph showing a Howship's lacuna. The scale bar in the bottom right of the photograph represents 20μm.

electron microscope (its vertical range is more than 5 μm) and the field of view of a scanning electron microscope (its field of view is larger than 125 μm). It is possible to compare AFM images with features seen in the light microscope. It also is possible to determine which features on a sample surface are of similar chemical composition. Samples in a variety of shapes and sizes, such as microtomed blocks up to 1.5-in thick, can be accommodated in custom-designed adapters, and, unlike SEM, samples do not require coating. In spite of its potential, AFM has not yet been embraced by paleopathological researchers, no doubt due to the specialized nature of equipment, its limited availability, and the cost of analysis. As the technique becomes more accessible, however, it will likely play an important role in the imaging of paleopathological lesions.

Biochemical Analysis

Biochemical analysis can be applied to samples of specific lesions, although the majority of investigations, especially earlier studies, have addressed systemic conditions. Since their applications to archaeological human remains were first noted in the early 1970s, chemical methods of analysis have been applied to a number of diagnostic problems in paleopathology. Described here are the principles and applications of three approaches: elemental and isotopic analyses, paleoserology and histochemistry, and the study of ancient DNA. These approaches are described in greater detail elsewhere in this volume so this discussion focuses on applications to pale-opathology (see Katzenberg, Chapter 11; Sandford and Weaver, Chapter 12; and Stone, Chapter 13).

Elemental and Isotopic Analysis

Elemental Analysis

The essential trace elements (e.g., iron and zinc) are under homeostatic control through a regulatory system that involves absorption, storage, and excretion, and their deficiency or toxicity can occur because of malnutrition and disease, changes in hormonal, physiological, and metabolic systems, or exposure via inges-tion or exposure. A few trace elements (e.g., iron, copper) are found in the organic matrix of bone, but most investigations concern the ele-ments present in the inorganic fraction. Al-though the vast majority of scholarly work on the elemental compositions of ancient human bone has addressed questions of dietary recon-struction, such as the amount of meat in prehis-toric human diets, the link between trace elements and disease has been the subject of much investigation in the biomedical literature and has been described as highly promising for the study of the cause of some pathological conditions that afflict the archaeological skele-ton (Armelagos et al., 1989; Oster, 1988), for the assessment of nutritional status as linked to health (Klepinger, 1993), and for the examina-tion of health and cultural practices of past populations that were exposed to toxic ele-ments such as lead (Aufderheide, 1989; Auf-derheide et al., 1988; Jambor and Smrčka, 1993). Regrettably, the effects of diagenetic changes in bone have severely restricted these applications. The concept of diagenesis has been the focus of considerable discussion in the past decade and much of the literature con-cerns postmortem alterations of elemental pro-files in the inorganic fraction of buried bone, such as the addition to bone of elements found in the soil and/or the leaching of elements from

bone. The mechanisms of diagenesis are com-plex and beyond the scope of this paper, but the reader is referred to Ezzo (1994) and Sandford (1992, 1993) for detailed discussions. Details of methods of elemental analysis can be found in Sandford (1992, Sandford and Weaver, Chapter 12) and Aufderheide (1989).

As has been so cogently argued by Ezzo (1994), a fundamental understanding of hu-man physiology is necessary for investiga-tions of the chemical responses of skeletal tissues to trauma and disease. For example, although iron levels in bone have been used in investigations of prehistoric anemia (e.g., For-naciari et al., 1981), very little iron is actually incorporated into bone and there is no evi-dence to document a relationship between iron levels in bone and overall iron status in the living (measured in various ways, but typ-ically reflecting serum levels of iron). Pub-lished values for iron in modern human bone vary widely (e.g., Bowen, 1979), further com-plicating the construction of a predictive model for pathologically low levels of iron in archaeological bone. In contrast to the low concentration of iron in bone, nearly 30% of the body's zinc is contained in the skeleton (Hambidge et al., 1986; Miller, 1983). Zinc's role in tissue growth and development appears to be well established (reviewed in Miller, 1983) and conventional wisdom holds that el-evated levels of zinc would accompany sites of bone deposition in cases of fracture healing and response to inflammatory or other patho-logical conditions. Alternatively, it has been proposed that it may be possible to identify zinc deficiency as an etiological factor in cases of retarded skeletal growth (Klepinger, 1993; but see Ezzo, 1994). Zinc concentra-tions in bone have been found to vary widely (O'Connor et al., 1980; Underwood, 1977), however, including within single bones of an individual (Lovell, unpublished data), even though bone zinc is not substantially changed by disease or diet (Miller, 1983). The extent of zinc deficiency in modern human popula-tions is largely unknown, in part because ex-isting biochemical measures do not provide definitive indications of zinc status. Thus, the detection of elevated or deficient zinc in archaeological bone is compromised not only by diagenesis but also by the lack of a clear understanding of the physiology and measurement of zinc. The level of zinc in hair provides some indication of zinc status under experimental conditions (Miller, 1983) and would seem to warrant further study.

Even more concentrated in the skeleton is lead. Approximately 95% of the body's lead burden is stored in the skeleton and appears to represent lifetime lead exposure (Aufderheide, 1989), suggesting that bone tissue may be a valuable source of data for the investigation of lead exposure in ancient and historic times. Unfortunately, the effects of diagenesis on lead concentrations in archaeological bone are as yet unclear, although it has been demonstrated that certain burial conditions (such as within a lead coffin) are responsible for profound contamination (Waldron, 1983; Whittaker and Stack, 1984). Furthermore, the range of bone lead values varies widely within individuals and within bones (reviewed in Aufderheide, 1989), illustrating the complex mechanisms of lead metabolism. However, there are several applications of lead analysis that are informed by the cultural and physical environments of the individuals or populations being studied. For example, through the study of lead toxicity in historical human remains it has been possible to assess the development of lead technology, to identify status differences and occupational activities, and to measure changes in lead exposure over time. Aufderheide and co-workers have documented status differences in skeletal lead levels that appear to be linked to the use of pewter vessels by wealthy plantation owners and managers during the American colonial period, as well as toxic lead levels among slaves on a sugar plantation due to lead contamination during sugar processing and rum distillation as well as from rum consumption (Aufderheide, 1989; Aufderheide et al., 1988). Lead poisoning also has been implicated in the ill-fated Sir John Franklin arctic expedition, through the analysis of tissues obtained from the frozen bodies of several of Franklin's crew and of lead-soldered tin containers for food (Keenleyside et al., 1996; Kowal et al., 1991). In another example, elemental analysis confirmed elevated levels of iron in lung tissue that showed macroscopic evidence of pulmonary bleeding (Nerlich et al., 1995).

Isotopic Analysis

In contrast to the postmortem diagenetic alteration of elemental concentrations in bone mineral, the chemical characteristics of collagen are very stable and therefore the postmortem composition of collagen can be assumed to represent that during life, unless the bone has been heated by cooking or cremation, or is poorly preserved. While a wealth of literature is devoted to paleodietary aspects of stable isotopes in bone (reviewed in Ambrose, 1993; Katzenberg, 1992, Chapter 11; Katzenberg and Harrison, 1997; Pate, 1994; Schoeninger and Moore, 1992; Schwarcz and Schoeninger, 1991), comparatively little work has been undertaken in the realm of the links between disease processes that affect bone and the consequent effects on isotopic values. A recent study has revealed that recently deposited bone is sometimes distinct from older bone on the basis of variation in the ratios of stable isotopes of nitrogen (Katzenberg and Lovell, 1999) and suggests that additional research in this area may be very helpful in improving our understanding of protein metabolism in response to injury and disease.

Other proteins, such as collagen from tooth dentin and skin, and keratin from hair, can be sampled for stable isotope analysis, but of these only hair has been subjected to fairly rigorous experimentation and validation. The interpretation of carbon isotope data from the hair of naturally preserved mummies from ancient Nubia identified ingestion of a seasonally restricted food item, and, since a majority of the individuals from this cemetery sample apparently consumed this food in the months just prior to death, this provides information on the season of death in which more people died (White, 1993) and has implications for paleopathological studies of biological frailty and fitness.

Paleoserology and Histochemistry

In the early 1970s Aiden Cockburn theorized that serum-derived proteins (i.e., antibodies) that were present in the body at the time of death could provide information on infectious diseases in antiquity if they could be recovered from ancient remains (Reyman et al., 1998). While early studies met with limited success, the typing of blood and other tissue (Hart et al., 1977; Henry, 1980) suggested that the application of immunological techniques to the investigation of ancient disease had much potential. Indeed, many histochemical and immunohistochemical stains have successfully detected a variety of substances in mummified soft tissue, including iron and antigens of malaria and cancer (Miller et al., 1994; Tapp, 1984).

Since mummified remains are rarer than skeletons and often are restricted to small, usually elite segments of a past population (e.g., dynastic Egyptian mummies), population studies would be more appropriately based on the recovery of proteins from bone. However, although the survival of proteins such as collagen in ancient bone is well documented, difficulties in identifying specific noncollagenous proteins in degraded bone have served to limit interest in this avenue of research among paleopathologists. The most successful applications so far appear to be restricted to the identification of organic residues, such as serum albumin, as either human or nonhuman (e.g., Newman et al., 1998). Some success has been reported for the identification of one of the immunoglobulins (IgG) from archaeological bone (Barraco, 1980; Cattaneo et al., 1992, 1994; Tuross, 1991). Several major types of antibodies, or immunoglobulins, can be distinguished in an individual, but IgG is present in the highest concentration and is thought to be the most important in resistance to infection. While IgG may take two weeks to appear in the blood after an antigen

enters the body, levels of IgG rise quickly upon re-exposure to the antigen. In theory, IgG-secreting cells store the immunologic history of an individual and thus, in the case of archaeological tissues, an individual need not have been infected at the time of death in order to provoke a antigen-antibody reaction.

The method most commonly used for the detection of antibodies in archaeological bone is inhibition enzyme-linked immunosorbent assay (ELISA). Simply put, ELISA is an assay in which the material being tested for antibody is added to material that is coated with known antigen. The presence of antibody bound to the antigen can be determined by the addition of immunoglobulin-specific antibody, to which is linked an enzyme and its substrate (the two of which serve as the indicator system). In positive tests the enzyme remains part of the antigen-antibody complex and reacts with the substrate when it is added. In inhibition tests, scores are based on the degree of color inhibition in the reaction. Samples of approximately 10 gm, usually cancellous bone, are pulverized and subjected to a multistep chemical extraction procedure.Methodological details are described by Cattaneo and co-workers (1992, 1994). Rothschild recommends the use of an immunofluorescence technique instead of ELISA and reports that this method revealed the presence of treponemal antigen in the skeleton of a Pleistocene bear (Rothschild, 1992; Rothschild and Turnbull, 1987). The extent or problems with cross-reactivity and contamination when dealing with highly degraded proteins is as yet undetermined, however, and it remains to be seen how successful immunological detection methods can be when applied to the diagnosis of specific diseases in ancient bone. Ascenzi and co-workers were unable to identify thalassemia, apparently due to the insensitivity of the method they employed (Ascenzi et al., 1985), and there have been surprisingly few published accounts of immunological detection of ancient diseases given the claim that immunofluorescence is a viable technique (Rothschild, 1992). It seems likely that many researchers have instead embraced ancient DNA analysis, which became more attractive after 1987 due to technical improvements.

Ancient DNA Analysis

DNA contains an individual's inherited genetic information and is present in all cells of the body. Thus, there has been tremendous interest in the potential of ancient DNA (aDNA), preserved in human bone and soft tissue, for investigating the history and geography of genetic relationships among ancient peoples (for a review and methodological details, see Stone, Chapter 13). For paleopathology, the analysis of aDNA has an obvious application to the study of genetic diseases, such as sickle cell anemia and other diseases with known genetic markers. Should a method for identifying the aDNA genome for sickle cell anemia be established, it may be possible to screen skeletal populations for the sickle cell trait and to investigate the correlation of skeletal lesions of porotic hyperostosis with individuals possessing the genetic marker.

Potentially the most rewarding application of aDNA is the direct identification of pathogenic microorganisms or their protein products, or the detection of human defenses to specific pathogens. The extraction and identification from bone or soft tissue of pathogenic aDNA is made difficult, however, by the fact that some disease-producing organisms are closely related to each other and/or to soil-dwelling organisms. Thus, probes that identify the DNA of a disease-causing agent must be specific to that agent. To date, the pathogen most commonly claimed to be identified in archaeological bone and soft tissue is *Mycobacterium tuberculosis* (Baron et al., 1996; Braun et al., 1998; Salo et al., 1994; Spigelman and Lemma, 1993; Taylor et al., 1996) although *M. leprae* and bacterial DNA typical of the human colon (*Clostridium*) apparently also have been detected (Rafi et al., 1994; but see Blondiaux, 1995; Ubaldi et al., 1998). It has been argued that the analysis of aDNA will be

a tremendous boon for the study of ancient diseases that have no, or limited, skeletal involvement and hence cannot be easily studied using conventional methods. Thus, skeletal evidence for a disease is not a precondition for identification of the aDNA of its causative pathogen. Studies proceed, however, from the assumption that the DNA of ancient infecting microorganisms will be resident in the bones of ancient sufferers even in the absence of skeletal involvement by the disease, and the pathophysiology of these diseases has not always been fully explicated. For example, it is one thing to identify aDNA of *M. tuberculosis* in a preserved pulmonary lesion, another to identify it in a bony lesion whose appearance is consistent with infection with *M. tuberculosis,* and quite another to identify it through a speculative, exploratory screening of normal-looking bone. While aDNA analysis for the purpose of reconstructing genetic relationships can utilize any tissue because all of one's body cells contain the same, personal, DNA, it has not been clearly demonstrated that the cellular remains of pathogenic organisms are preserved in, for example, vascular tunnels in dry bone. Currently there are very few tests of the detection of aDNA from disease-causing agents through the extraction and identification of such DNA from various sites in the skeleton of an individual known to have been infected with the disease. The comparison of aDNA obtained from the teeth of individuals alleged to have died of the plague to aDNA from negative controls apparently recognized the presence of ancient plague in the historically identified victims (Drancourt et al., 1998), and some studies claim to have authenticated results by analyzing aDNA taken from dry bones that showed gross evidence of the disease of interest (e.g., Braun et al., 1998; Crubezy et al., 1998; Spiegelman and Lemma, 1993; Taylor et al., 1996). Unfortunately, a number of inconsistencies in the results of many of these studies (e.g., the detection of unexpected multiple polymerase chain reaction (PCR) products; the unexplained absence of the pathogenic DNA in bone that displays gross lesions suggestive of the disease, and modifications to the expected sequence) indicate that this type of analysis is still far from maturity.

PSEUDOPATHOLOGY

While the methods of analysis described above can provide valuable information on the appearance and nature of pathological lesions, an important part of paleopathological investigation is the observer's ability to distinguish between pathological, or abnormal, features and those that are not caused by injury or disease. Nonpathological, or pseudopathological, features that are commonly misidentified tend to be those that represent normal variation in morphology or those that result from postdepositional taphonomic changes to the remains.

Vascular depressions on the surfaces of bones are often misinterpreted as antemortem cut marks, while foramina may be misidentified as lytic lesions of infection, as may small depressions, usually called Pacchionian or arachnoid depressions, that occur normally on the endocranial surface in older individuals. A wealth of nonmetric traits (also called epigenetic traits or discontinuous traits), such as the persistence in adults of the metopic suture, have been recognized as normal morphological variants and may have identifiable genetic associations (for a comprehensive summary of nonmetric traits of the cranium, the reader is referred to Hauser and De Stefano, 1989), but these are sometimes thought to be pathological features by the inexperienced. In addition, many students have little experience with subadult skeletal material and hence are unfamiliar with the appearance of rapidly remodeling bone surfaces. The repair of bone incorporates the same three processes that characterize growth and maturation: the removal of (damaged) bone tissue by osteoclasts; the deposition of new bone, and the maturational remodeling of that new bone. Thus, the recognition of normal immature bone in subadult remains is crucial for paleopathology since it may otherwise be mis-

taken for the woven bone that is associated with the early stages of disease or injury repair.

Postdeposition changes that can be confused with pathological lesions include the marks of roots, insects, rodents, or carnivores, as well as the effects of weathering and mechanical or chemically erosive soil conditions (e.g., warping, cortical spalling, and color changes). Examples of these can be found in the *Standards* volume, edited by Buikstra and Ubelaker (1994) and several papers in the *Forensic Taphonomy* volume, edited by Haglund and Sorg (1997). In all of these cases, radiographic or microscopic analysis will usually differentiate pathological lesions from pseudopathological artifact when visual observation is inadequate. Microscopic examination of bone tissue has detected the presence of fungi, algae, and bacteria, as well as the physical remains of roots and insects, as postmortem contaminants (Schultz, 1986, 1997). Biochemical analyses are also subject to "pseudo" pathological results, particularly due to postmortem effects, commonly referred to as diagenesis. Details of the processes of diagenesis and their detection are beyond the scope of this paper, but are fully described by Sandford (1992; Sandford and Weaver, Chapter 12), and Stone (Chapter 13).

DIAGNOSIS

While description and documentation help us determine the nature of an abnormality, diagnosis seeks to determine how that abnormality relates to normal bone tissue and to other abnormalities. Diagnosis thus requires that the first criterion, the accurate and precise description and documentation of lesions, be followed by examination of the presence of lesions within a bone, within an individual, and within a population. Once these data have been collected, their patterning can be compared to reference standards (e.g., Ortner and Putschar, 1981). As part of attempts to determine the diagnosis of a condition, often it is the case that the appearance of paleopathological lesions is compared to the appearance of clinically documented cases of trauma or disease. However, as pointed out by Ragsdale (1996, 1997), modern examples found in textbooks of orthopedic pathology and radiology represent conditions that have been intercepted in an individual at a point short of their full course. Autopsy specimens are more likely to represent advanced cases, but these may have been modified by surgical or pharmacologic therapy. Similarly, patterns of disease and trauma in modern populations may not be entirely applicable to past populations due to changes in physical and sociocultural environments, as well as possible medical intervention. Ragsdale therefore advocates comparison, where possible, with untreated cases, such as may be available from historical sources or developing countries.

Patterns of Lesions Within a Bone

The first phase of paleopathological investigation, description, and documentation involves recording the pattern of lesions within a bone and within an individual. Table 8.2 lists recommended observations for identifying the patterns of lesions on a bone, which are based on the following questions:

- Which bone is involved?
- Where on the bone is the abnormality located, and how much of the bone is affected?
- What is the distribution of the lesions on the bone?

The importance of these questions is due to the fact that some conditions are characterized by a pathological process that is very selective. In leprosy, for example, involvement of the

TABLE 8.2 Recommended Data to Be Recorded for Patterns of Lesions on an Affected Bone

Identity of bone	By proper anatomical name
Section of bone	Proximal epiphysis
	Distal epiphysis
	Proximal articular surface
	Distal articular surface
	Both proximal and distal articular surfaces
	Proximal third of shaft
	Middle third of shaft
	Distal third of shaft
	Proximal two-thirds of shaft
	Distal two-thirds of shaft
	Total shaft
Aspect of bone	Superior
	Inferior
	Both superior and inferior
	Medial
	Lateral
	Both medial and lateral
	Posterior
	Anterior
	Circumferential
Distribution on bone	Discrete
	Multifocal
	Diffuse

infracranial bones favors the subarticular bone in the epiphysis, a region that is highly vascularized, over the bone shaft. In contrast, treponemal infections usually spare the epiphyseal region (Ortner and Putschar, 1981). The location of a fracture on a bone may help identify the mechanism of trauma (Lovell, 1997).

Patterns of Lesions Within an Individual

As with patterns within a bone, standard questions regarding the distribution of pathological lesions within an individual can be asked:

- If a paired bone, which side is involved? Or does the condition appear bilaterally?
- Are there similar lesions elsewhere on the skeleton?
- Are there different lesions on the skeleton that may indicate a predisposing or complicating condition?

A variety of conditions have the potential to affect the entire skeletal system, such as metabolic bone disease and the blood-borne spread of infectious pathogens, while various forms of arthritis will affect certain bones preferentially. The pattern of these lesions may be crucial in differential diagnosis, such as the case of rheumatoid arthritis, in which lesions are usually bilateral, multi-joint, and symmetrical, and target the metacarpo-phalangeal joints and the proximal interphalangeal articulations. The differential diagnosis of many diseases is aided by visualization of the patterning of lesions, as illustrated in Figure 8.6, where the distribution of skeletal lesions within an individual are compared for two treponemal diseases.

In other cases, one condition may be superimposed on another, such as when crush fractures of the vertebral body occur secondary to osteoporosis. Similarly, osteoarthritis at a joint may be a complication of a long bone fracture if the limb's biomechanics are altered. It is also possible, however, for one or more unrelated conditions to be expressed in the remains and it should not be assumed that lesions are associated.

Patterns of Lesions Within a Population

Paleoepidemiology is the term used when referring to the study of patterns of trauma or disease in which the population, rather than the individual, is the unit of analysis. Paleoepidemiological studies focus on how the pathological condition is related to age, sex, occupation, social status, or other variables, as well as how the condition is distributed geographically and over time. For example, females are more affected by rheumatoid arthritis than males by a factor of 3:1. While many of the statistics and approaches are borrowed from contemporary epidemiology, one key distinction is that frequencies of a condition in an archaeological population are measured as the prevalence (usually expressed as a percentage of the total size of the population), but usually cannot be measured as the incidence; incidence is the rate at which new cases of a disease occur in a defined population at risk, over a specified unit of time (e.g., the number of new cases of chicken pox per 1000 elementary school children in the city of Edmonton during the month of January). Except for some historical samples, the period of time from which a skeletal sample is drawn is almost always imprecisely known.

Usually the attempt of population prevalence studies is to extrapolate the frequency of the condition from the skeletal sample to the past living population, and to calculate age-, sex-, and/or status-specific prevalences. However, it has been shown that these rates are reasonable approximations only for those conditions that do not shorten life span, such as arthritis (Waldron, 1991, 1994). Furthermore, the researcher must employ caution when assessing the representativeness of the skeletal sample, since, for example, systematic overestimation of the prevalence of leprosy in a population would result if a leper cemetery were sampled.

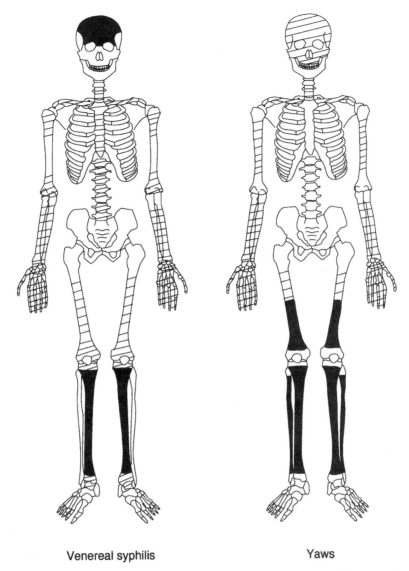

Venereal syphilis   Yaws

Figure 8.6 Distribution of lesions in an individual, comparing the pattern of venereal syphilis to that of yaws. The black indicates most frequent sites while the diagonal lines indicate less frequent site . (After Steinbock, 1976.)

Missing values are among the most common problems encountered by paleopathologists who are trying to reconstruct population frequencies. If one is calculating the frequency of distal tibia fractures in a population, one can express the frequency as the number of individuals with a tibia fracture out of the total sample. However, if not all individuals had both tibiae preserved for observation then one could be either under- or overestimating the prevalence of fractures, depending upon whether the "missing" tibiae were fractured or not. Thus, it is usually recommended that a range be calculated, the lowest frequency resulting from the assumption that none of the missing tibiae were fractured and the highest frequency resulting from the assumption that all of the missing tibiae were fractured. Clearly, it is vital that not only must lesions be scored as present or absent on observable skeletal elements, but that missing or damaged bones and articular surfaces are tallied as "unobservable."

Other problems plague paleoepidemiological studies. In the past decade there has been heated debate about the validity of paleopathological interpretations of health and disease in antiquity due to apparent shortcomings in the nature of the underlying sample—the age estimation of older adults (see Jackes, Chapter 15), the sex determination of subadults (see Saunders, Chapter 5), and the inherent limits of skeletal samples (see, e.g., Boddington, 1987; Cohen, 1997; Lukacs, 1994; Milner et al., Chapter 16; Waldron, 1994; Wood et al., 1992). For example, the infant mortality rate may be of particular interest to many researchers due to its association with infectious disease, but it is impossible to calculate unless the number of live births is known. Alternatively, it may be that subtle links between diseases and environmental causes or lifestyles affected a large segment of the population and had a major impact on public health, but inherent biases, assumptions, and methodological weaknesses of paleoepidemiology may render us incapable of recognizing such weak associations. Large effects can usually be discerned, but the distinction between a small effect and no effect may be impossible to detect. In contrast, confounding factors are often hidden variables in the populations being studied, and these can generate an association that may be real but is not what we think it is. For example, it may appear that males in a sample are more affected by osteoarthritis than are females, but if the subsample of males consists of older individuals than does the female subsample then the effect may be due to age, not sex. The fundamental question should be: What are the limitations of the data? One important criterion for the validity of an association is that there is both a strong association and also a highly plausible biological or sociocultural mechanism for it. Meta-analysis is a technique for combining studies that do not show unambiguous results to see if their results tend in the same direction. Weak associations may therefore be considered convincing because they show up repeatedly, but only if the studies used different research designs, methodologies, and samples and still came up with the same results. Consistent results, then, even if demonstrating a weak association, may be fodder for further investigation.

CONCLUSIONS, CAVEATS, AND FUTURE DIRECTIONS

As aids to diagnosis, a variety of macroscopic, microscopic, and biochemical methods of analysis are employed by paleopathologists to describe the nature of tissue responses to trauma and disease. These methods, however, are not equally accessible or amenable to use by nontechnical personnel. Visual observation and transmitted light and stereobinocular microscopy are the most commonly employed techniques and may be considered the most valid since they have developed over a century or more and much is now known about their advantages and limitations. They are relatively inexpensive and easy to use, and require comparatively modest sample preparation and observer training. Currently, biochemical methods of analysis have the greatest shortcomings, due to the short span of their development and hence our incomplete understanding of both the physiological and diagenetic processes that affect them. Significant advances in the application of these methods to paleopathology depend on insuring that students receive sufficient training in biochemistry and geochemistry to fully understand these new techniques. If we consider that it took some 15 to 20 years after their first applications for the extent of problems with elemental analyses of archaeological bone to be widely recognized, then the next decade of research is likely to produce much new knowledge about the strengths and weaknesses of aDNA analysis. Until that time, the results obtained by such "cutting-edge" techniques should be viewed with caution. This does not mean that visual, macroscopic observation is inherently better than the alternatives, but rather that paleopathologists should not assume that technology will render our current uncertainties about diagnosis superfluous. Indeed, while great technological advances have been made in recent decades, tests undertaken during workshops of the Paleopathology Association have demonstrated that paleopathologists usually can correctly classify pathological lesions only according to the primary descriptive type, not to the diagnostic category of disease, and that the greatest accuracy is obtained by researchers with the most experience (Miller et al., 1996). Special attention to accurate and precise description, then, remains one of the key requirements of paleopathological investigation, although our diagnostic capabilities are poised to improve through the application of aDNA and other new analytical techniques.

Beyond description and diagnosis, advances also have been made in the construction of research designs as investigators attempt to forge new approaches to the aims of paleopathology. Once a probable diagnosis has been identified, it is the interpopulational distribution of the pathological condition according to time, space, and technology that becomes important for the interpretation of health and disease in a biocultural context. Progress has been made, incrementally, in the reconstruction of the history and geography of diseases (e.g., syphilis), the illumination of the interaction between disease and cultural processes (e.g., paleopathology at the origins of agriculture), the documentation of the evolution of diseases over time (e.g., tuberculosis), and the understanding of the effect of disease processes on bone growth and development (e.g., osteoporosis), but what is "new" in paleopathology during the past decade? Several developments are readily apparent. One of these is the analysis of pathological conditions in free-ranging nonhuman primates and the consideration of these conditions in behavioral, socioecological, and evolutionary contexts (e.g., DeGusta and Milton, 1998; DeRousseau, 1988; Jurmain, 1989, 1997; Kilgore, 1989; Lovell, 1990a, 1990b, 1991; Lovell et al., in press; Rothschild and Woods, 1989, 1991; Stoner, 1995; Sumner et al., 1989). Another is the interpretation of

"musculoskeletal stress markers" as indicators of behavior (e.g., Hawkey and Merbs, 1995; Kennedy, 1989; Lai and Lovell, 1992; Lovell and Dublenko, 1999; Steen and Lane, 1998; Stirland 1991, 1998). Certainly, the former example illustrates the opportunities that exist for paleopathologists to explore the roles of disease and injury as selective factors, while the latter example demonstrates the importance of understanding normal bone remodeling and biomechanical adaptation in our study of tissue responses to disease and injury. Given the growing interest in the study of diseases in antiquity, we can hope that the future will bring wider agreement on data collection protocols, improved diagnostic ability, and the explicit incorporation of theory in research designs. While paleopathological interpretations build upon a foundation of description and documentation and incremental increases in our knowledge base, it is crucial also to step back and consider the larger role of disease and injury as factors in human biological and sociocultural evolution if we wish our work to have relevance outside our scientific community.

REFERENCES

Ambrose SH. 1993. Isotopic analysis of paleodiets: methodological and interpretive considerations. In: Sandford MK, editor. Investigations of Ancient Human Tissue: Chemical Analyses in Anthropology. Langhorne: Gordon and Breach. pp. 59–130.

Angel JL. 1966. Porotic hyperostosis, anemias, malarias, and marshes in the prehistoric eastern Mediterranean. Science 153:760–763.

Angel JL. 1981. History and development of paleopathology. Am J Phys Anthropol 56:509–515.

Armelagos GJ. 1997. Paleopathology. In: Spencer F, editor. History of Physical Anthropology, Vol. 2. New York: Garland, pp. 790–796.

Armelagos GJ, Brenton B, Alcorn M, Martin D, van Gerven DP. 1989. Factors affecting elemental and isotopic variation in prehistoric human skeletons. In: Price TD, editor. The Chemistry of Prehistoric Human Bone. New York: Cambridge University Press. pp. 230–244.

Armelagos, GJ, McArdle A. 1975. Population, disease and evolution. Am Antiq 40:1–10, Memoir 30.

Ascenzi A. 1986. Microscopy and ultramicroscopy in palaeopathology. In: Hermann B, editor. Innovative Trends in Prehistoric Anthropology. Mitt Berliner Ges Anthropol Ethnol Urgesch 7:149–156.

Ascenzi A, Brunori M, Citro G, Zito R. 1985. Immunological detection of hemoglobin in bones of ancient Roman times and of Iron and Eneolitic Ages. Proc Natl Acad Sci USA 82:7170–7172.

Aufderheide AC. 1989. Chemical analysis of skeletal remains. In: İşcan MY, Kennedy KAR, editors. Reconstruction of Life from the Skeleton. New York: Alan R. Liss. pp. 237–260.

Aufderheide AC, Rodriguez-Martin C. 1998. The Cambridge Encyclopedia of Human Paleopathology. Cambridge: Cambridge University Press. 478 pp.

Aufderheide AC, Wittmers LE Jr, Rapp G Jr, Wallgren J. 1988. Anthropological applications of skeletal lead analysis. Am Anthropol 90: 931–936.

Bancroft JD, Stevens A, editors. 1996. Theory and Practice of Histological Techniques. 4th ed. New York: Churchill Livingstone. 766 pp.

Baron H, Hummel S, Hermann B. 1996. *Mycobacterium tuberculosis* complex DNA in ancient human bone. J Archaeol Sci 23:667–671.

Barraco RA. 1980. Paleobiochemistry. In: Cockburn A, Cockburn E, editors. Mummies, Disease, and Ancient Cultures. New York: Cambridge University Press. pp. 312–326.

Bassett EJ, Keith M, Armelagos G, Martin D, Villaneuva A. 1980. Tetracycline-labeled human bone from ancient Sudanese Nubia (AD 350). Science 209:1532–1534.

Bergman RA, Afifi AK, Heidger PM Jr. 1996. Histology. Philadelphia: Saunders. 342 pp.

Bianco P, Ascenzi A. 1993. Palaeohistology of human bone remains: a critical evaluation and an example of its use. In: Grupe G, Garland AN, editors. Histology of Ancient Human Bone. Berlin: Springer-Verlag. pp. 157–170.

Bilezikian JP, Raisz LC, Roan GA, editors. 1996. Principles of Bone Biology. San Diego: Academic Press. 1398 pp.

Blondiaux J. 1995. 'DNA of *Mycobacterium leprae* detected by PCR in ancient bone' by Rafi et al. Int J Osteoarchaeol 5:299.

Boddington A. 1987. From bones to population: the problem of numbers. In Boddington A, Garland AN, Janaway RC, editors. Death, Decay and Reconstruction. Manchester: Manchester University Press. pp. 180–197.

Bowen HJM. 1979. Environmental Chemistry of the Elements. London: Academic Press. 333 pp.

Boyde A, Maconnachie E, Reid SA, Delling G, Mundy GR. 1986. Scanning electron microscopy in bone pathology: review of methods, potential, and applications. Scan Elec Microsc 4:1537–1554.

Braun M, Cook DC, Pfeiffer S. 1998. DNA from *Mycobacterium tuberculosis* complex identified in North American, pre-Columbian human skeletal remains. J Archaeol Sci 25:271–277.

Brier B. 1994. Egyptian Mummies. New York: William Morrow. 352 pp.

Bromage T. 1987. The scanning electron microscope/replica technique and recent applications to the study of fossil bone. Scan Elec Microsc 1:607–613.

Brothwell D, Sandison AT, editors. 1967. Diseases in Antiquity: A Survey of the Diseases, Injuries and Surgery of Early Populations. Springfield, Ill.: Charles C. Thomas. 766 pp.

Buikstra JE, Cook DC. 1980. Palaeopathology: An American Account. Ann Rev Anthropol 9:433–470.

Buikstra JE, Ubelaker DH. 1994. Standards for Data Collection from Human Skeletal Remains. Res Ser No. 44. Fayetteville: Arkansas Archaeological Survey. 206 pp.

Bushberg JT, Siebert JA, Leidholdt EM Jr, Boone JM. 1994. The Essential Physics of Medical Imaging. Baltimore: Williams and Wilkins. 742 pp.

Cattaneo C, Gelsthorpe K, Phillips P, Sokol RJ. 1992. Detection of blood proteins in ancient human bone using ELISA: a comparative study of the survival of IgG and albumin. Int J Osteoarchaeol 2:103–107.

Cattaneo C, Gelsthorpe K, Sokol RJ. 1994. Immunological detection of albumin in ancient human cremations using ELISA and monoclonal antibodies. J Archaeol Sci 21:565–571.

Chappard D, Alexandre C, Laborier JC, Roberts JM, Riffat G. 1984. Paget's disease of bone: a scanning electron microscope study. J Submicrosc Cytol 16:341–348.

Cockburn TA, Barraco RA, Peck WH, Reyman TA. 1975. Autopsy of an Egyptian mummy. Science 187:1155–1160.

Cockburn TA, Barraco RA, Peck WH, Reyman TA. 1998. A classic mummy: PUM II. In: Cockburn A, Cockburn E, Reyman TA, editors. Mummies, Disease and Ancient Cultures, 2nd ed. Cambridge: Cambridge University Press. pp. 69–90.

Cohen MN. 1997. Does paleopathology measure community health? A rebuttal of "The Osteological Paradox" and its implication for world history. In: Paine RR, editor. Integrating Archaeological Demography: Multidisciplinary Approaches to Prehistoric Populations. Cen Archaeol Inves Occ Paper No. 24. Carbondale: Southern Illinois University. pp. 242–260.

Cohen MN, Armelagos GJ, editors. 1984. Paleopathology at the Origins of Agriculture. Orlando: Academic Press. 615 pp.

Cook M, Molto E, Anderson C. 1989. Fluorochrome labeling in Roman period skeletons from Dakhleh Oasis in Egypt. Am J Phys Anthropol 80:137–143.

Cormack D. 1993. Essential Histology. Philadelphia: Lippincott. 430 pp.

Crubezy E, Ludes B, Pveda JD, Clayton J, Cruau RB, Montagnon D. 1998. Identification of *Mycobacterium* DNA in an Egyptian Pott's disease of 5,400 years old. Comptes Rendus Acad Sci Serie III, Sci Vie 321:941–951.

Culin S. 1898. An archaeological application of the Roentgen rays. Bull No 4, Free Mus Sci Art. Philadelphia: University of Pennsylvania. pp. 183.

Dales GF. 1990. Excavations at Harappa—1988. Pakistan Archaeol 24:68–176.

Davis R. 1997. Clinical radiography and archaeohuman remains. In: Lang J, Middleton A, editors. Radiography of Cultural Material. Oxford: Butterworth-Heinemann. pp. 117–135.

DeGusta D, Milton K. 1998. Skeletal pathologies in a population of *Aloutta palliata*: behavioral, ecological, and evolutionary implications. Int J Primatol 19:615–650.

DeRousseau CJ. 1988. Osteoarthritis in rhesus monkeys and gibbons: a locomotor model of joint degeneration. Vol. 25, Contributions to Primatology. Basel: Karger.

Drancourt M, Aboudharam G, Signoli M, Dutour O, Raoult D. 1998. Detection of 400-year old *Yersinia pestis* DNA in human dental pulp: an approach to the diagnosis of ancient septicemia. Proc Nat Acad Sci USA 95:12637–12640.

Eriksen EF, Axelrod DW, Melsen F. 1994. Bone Histomorphometry. New York: Raven Press. 74 pp.

Ezzo JA. 1994. Putting the "chemistry" back into archaeological bone chemistry analysis: modeling potential paleodietary indicators. J Anthropol Archaeol 13:1–34.

Fornaciari G, Mallegni F, Bertino D, Nuti V. 1981. Cribra orbitalia and elemental bone iron in the Punics of Carthage. Ossa 8:63–77.

Fornaciari G, Marchetti A. 1986. Intact smallpox virus particles in an Italian mummy of the XVI century: an immuno-electron microscope study. Paleopathol News 56:7–12.

Garland AN. 1993. An introduction to the histology of exhumed mineralized tissue. In: Grupe G, Garland AN, editors. Histology of Ancient Human Bone. Berlin: Springer-Verlag. pp. 1–16.

Goldstein MS. 1963. Human paleopathology. J Nat Med Assoc 55:100–106.

Grupe G, Garland AN. 1993. Histology of Ancient Human Bone. Berlin: Springer-Verlag. 223 pp.

Haglund WD, Sorg MH, editors. 1997. Forensic Taphonomy: The Postmortem Fate of Human Remains. Boca Raton: CRC Press. 636 pp.

Hambidge KM, Casey CL, Krebs NF. 1986. Zinc. In: Mertz W, editor. Trace Elements in Human and Animal Nutrition. Vol 2. 5th ed. Orlando: Academic Press. pp. 1–137.

Harris JE, Weeks KR. 1973. X-raying the Pharaohs. New York: Scribner's. 195 pp.

Hart GD, Kvas I, Soots ML. 1977. Blood group testing: autopsy of an Egyptian mummy. Can Med Assoc J 117:461–473.

Harwood-Nash D. 1979. Computed tomography of ancient mummies. J Comput Assist Tomogr 3:768–773.

Hauser G, De Stefano GF. 1989. Epigenetic Variants of the Human Skull. Stuttgart: Schweizerbart. 301 pp.

Hauswirth WW, Dickel CD, Doran GH, Laipis PJ, Dickel DN. 1991. 8000-year-old brain tissue from the Windover site: anatomical, cellular, and molecular analysis. In: Ortner DJ, Aufderheide AC, editors. Human Paleopathology. Washington: Smithsonian Institution. pp. 60–72.

Hawkey DE, Merbs CF. 1995. Activity-induced musculoskeletal stress markers (MSM) and subsistence strategy changes among ancient Hudson (sic) Bay Eskimos. Int J Osteoarchaeol 5:324–338.

Henry RL. 1980. Paleoserology. In: Cockburn A, Cockburn E, editors. Mummies, Disease, and Ancient Cultures. New York: Cambridge University Press. pp. 327–334.

Heuck FW. 1993. Comparative histological and microradiographic investigations of human bone. In: Grupe G, Garland AN, editors. Histology of Ancient Human Bone. Berlin: Springer-Verlag. pp. 125–136.

Holland T. 1896. X-rays in 1896. (Reprint.) Liverpool Med-Chir J (1937) 45:61.

Hooton EA. 1930. The Indians of Pecos Pueblo: A Study of Their Skeletal Remains. New Haven: Yale University Press. 391 pp.

Hummert JR, van Gerven DP. 1982. Tetracycline-labeled human bone from a medieval population in Nubia's Batn El Hajar (AD 550–1450). Hum Biol 54:355–371.

Jambor J, Smrčka V. 1993. Tin in human bones. Przeglad Antropologiczny (Poznan) 56:151–156.

Jarcho S, editor. 1966. Human Palaeopathology. New Haven: Yale University Press. 182 pp.

Jurmain R. 1989. Trauma, degenerative disease, and other pathologies among the Gombe chimpanzees. Am J Phys Anthropol 80:229–237.

Jurmain R. 1997. Skeletal evidence of trauma in African apes, with special reference to the Gombe chimpanzees. Primates 38:1–14.

Katzenberg MA. 1992. Advances in stable isotope analysis of prehistoric bones. In: Saunders SR, Katzenberg MA, editors. Skeletal Biology of Past Peoples: Research Methods. New York: Wiley-Liss. pp. 105–119.

Katzenberg MA, Harrison RG. 1997. What's in a bone? Recent advances in archaeological bone chemistry. J. Archaeol Res 5:265–293.

Katzenberg MA, Lovell NC. 1999. Stable isotope variation in pathological bone. Int J Osteoarchaeol 9:316–324.

Keenleyside A, Song X, Chettle DR, Webber CE. 1996. The lead content of human bones from the 1845 Franklin expedition. J Archaeol Sci 23:461–465.

Kennedy KAR. 1989. Skeletal markers of occupational stress. In: İşcan MY, Kennedy KARK, editors. Reconstruction of Life from the Skeleton. New York: Alan R. Liss. pp. 129–160.

Kilgore L. 1989. Dental pathologies in ten free-ranging chimpanzees from Gombe National Park, Tanzania. Am J Phys Anthropol 80: 219–227.

Klepinger LL. 1993. Culture, health and chemistry: a technological approach to discovery. In: Sandford MK, editor. Investigations of Ancient Human Tissue. Langhorne: Gordon and Breach. pp. 292–320.

König W. 1896. Photographien mit Rontgen-Strahlen, aufgenommen im Physikalischen Verein. Frankfurt: JA Barth.

Kowal W, Beattie OB, Baadsgaard J, Krahn PM. 1991. Source identification of lead found in tissues of sailors from the Franklin Arctic Expedition of 1845. J Archaeol Sci 18:193–203.

Krempien B, Klimpel F. 1981. Scanning electron microscopical studies of resorbing surfaces. In: Jee WSS, Parfitt AM, editors. Bone Histomorphometry. Paris: Armour Montagu. pp. 45–51.

Lai P, Lovell NC. 1992. Skeletal markers of occupational stress in the fur trade: a case study from a Hudson's Bay Company Fur Trade Post. Int J Osteoarchaeol 2:221–234.

Lewin PK. 1967. Palaeo-electron microscopy of mummified tissue. Nature 213:416–417.

Lewin PK. 1984. "Mummy" riddles unraveled. Microsc Soc Canada Bull 12:4–8.

Lewin PK. 1991. Technological innovations and discoveries in the investigation of ancient preserved man. In: Ortner DJ, Aufderheide AC, editors. Human Paleopathology. Washington: Smithsonian Institution. pp. 90–91.

Lewin PK, Trodagis JE, Stevens JK. 1990. Three-dimensional reconstruction from serial X-ray tomography of an Egyptian mummified head. Clin Anat 3:215–218.

Lillie RD. 1977. HJ Conn's Biological Stains, 9th ed. Baltimore: Williams and Wilkins. 692 pp.

Lovell NC. 1990a. Illness and Injury in Great Apes: a skeletal analysis. Washington: Smithsonian Institution. 273 pp.

Lovell NC. 1990b. Skeletal and dental pathology of free-ranging mountain gorillas. Am J Phys Anthropol 81:399–412.

Lovell NC. 1991. An evolutionary framework for assessing illness and injury in nonhuman primates. Yrbk Phys Anthropol 34:117–155.

Lovell NC. 1997. Trauma analysis in paleopathology. Yrbk Phys Anthropol 40:139–170.

Lovell NC. 1999. Unpublished ms. on file with the author.

Lovell NC, Dublenko AA. 1999. Further aspects of fur trade life depicted in the skeleton. Int J Osteoarchaeol 9:248–256.

Lovell NC, Jurmain RD, Kilgore L. Skeletal Evidence of Probable Treponemal Infection in Free-ranging African Apes. Primates (in press)

Lukacs JR. 1994. The osteological paradox and the Indus Civilization: problems inferring health from human skeletons at Harappa. In: Kenoyer JM, editor. From Sumer to Meluhha: Contributions to the Archaeology of South and West Asia in Memory of George F. Dales, Jr. Archaeol Rpts Vol 3. Madison: University of Wisconsin. pp. 143–155.

Mann RW, Murphy SP. 1990. Regional Atlas of Bone Disease: A Guide to Pathologic and Normal Variation in the Human Skeleton. Springfield, Ill.: Charles C. Thomas. 208 pp.

Marks SC Jr, Hermey DC. 1996. The structure and development of bone. In: Bilezikian JP, Raisz LC, Rodan GA, editors. Principles of Bone Biology. San Diego: Academic Press. pp. 3–14.

Martin DL, Armelagos GJ. 1985. Skeletal remodeling and mineralization of indicators of health: an example from prehistoric Sudanese Nubia. J Hum Evol 14:527–537.

Martin RB, Burr DB. 1989. Structure, function and adaptation of compact bone. New York: Raven Press. 275 pp.

Miller E, Ragsdale BD, Ortner DJ. 1996. Accuracy in dry bone diagnosis: a comment on paleopathological methods. Int J Osteoarchaeol 6:221–229.

Miller RL, Ikram S, Armelagos GJ. 1994. Diagnosis of *Plasmodium falciparum* in mummies using the rapid manual Para Site TM-F test. Trans R Soc Trop Med Hyg 88:31–52.

Miller WJ. 1983. Zinc in animal and human health. In Rose J, editor. Trace Elements in Health. London: Butterworth. pp. 182–192.

Millett NB, Hart GD, Reyman TA, Zimmerman MR, Lewin PK. 1998. ROM I: Mummification for the common people. In: Cockburn A, Cockburn E, Reyman TA, editors. Mummies, Disease and Ancient Cultures, 2nd ed. Cambridge: Cambridge University Press. pp. 91–105.

Moodie RL. 1923. Paleopathology: An Introduction to the Study of Ancient Evidences of Disease. Urbana: University of Illinois Press. 567 pp.

Nerlich A, Parsche F, Wiest I, Schramel P, Loehrs U. 1995. Extensive pulmonary haemorrhage in an Egyptian mummy. Virchows Archiv 427:423–429.

Newman ME, Byrne G, Ceri H, Dimnik LS, Bridges PJ. 1998. Immunological and DNA analysis of blood residues from a surgeon's kit used in the American Civil War. J Archaeol Sci 25:553–557.

Notman DNH, Aufderheide AC. 1995. Experimental mummification and computed imaging. In: Proceeding of the First World Congress on Mummy Studies, Vol. 2. Santa Cruz de Tenerife: Museo Arqueológico y Ethnografico de Tenerife. pp. 821–828.

Notman DNH, Beattie O. 1996. The palaeoimaging and forensic anthropology of frozen sailors from the Franklin Arctic expedition mass disaster (1845–1848): a detailed presentation of two radiological surveys. In: Splindler K, Wilfing H, Rastbichler-Zissernig E, zur Nedden D, Nothdurfter H, editors. Human Mummies: A Global Survey of Their Status and the Techniques of Conversation, Vol. 3: The Man in the Ice. Vienna: Springer-Verlag. pp. 93–106.

Notman DNH, Tashijian J, Aufderheide AC, Cass OW, Shane OC III, Berquist TH, Gray JE, Gedguados E. 1986. Modern imaging and endoscopic biopsy techniques in Egyptian mummies. Am J Roentgenol 146:93–96.

O'Connor BH, Kerriga GC, Taylor KR, Morris PD, Wright CR. 1980. Levels and temporal trends of trace element concentrations in vertebral bone. Arch Environ Health 35:21–28.

Ortner DJ. 1991. Theoretical and methodological issues in paleopathology. In: Ortner DJ, Aufderheide AC, editors. Human Paleopathology: Current Syntheses and Future Options. Washington: Smithsonian Institution. pp. 5–12.

Ortner DJ. 1992. Skeletal paleopathology: probabilities, possibilities, and impossibilities. In: Verano JW, Ubelaker DH, editors. Disease and Demography in the Americas. Washington: Smithsonian Institution. pp. 5–15.

Ortner DJ. 1994. Descriptive methodology in pale-opathology. In: Owsley DW, Jantz RJ, editors. Skeletal Biology in the Great Plains. Washington: Smithsonian Institution. pp. 73–80.

Ortner DJ, Putschar WGJ. 1981. Identification of Pathological Conditions in Human Skeletal Remains. Contributions to Anthropology No. 28. Washington: Smithsonian. 479 p.

Oster O. 1988. The diagnosis of disease by elemental analysis. In: Grupe G, Hermann B, editors. Trace Elements in Environmental History. Heidelberg: Springer-Verlag. pp. 151–166.

Ott SM. 1996. Theoretical and methodological approach. In: Bilezikian JP, Raisz LC, Rodan GA (eds.), Principles of Bone Biology. San Diego: Academic Press, pp. 231–241.

Pate FD. 1994. Bone chemistry and paleodiet. J Archaeol Method Theory 1:161–209.

Petrie WMF. 1898. Deshasheh. London: Egypt Exploration Fund. 51 pp.

Rafi A, Spigelman M, Stanford J, Lemma E, Donohue H, Zias J. 1994. DNA of *Mycobacterium leprae* detected by PCR in ancient bone. Int J Osteoarchaeol 4:287–290.

Ragsdale BD. 1996. The irrelevance of contemporary orthopedic pathology to specimens from antiquity. Paleopathol News 95:6–10.

Ragsdale BD. 1997. The irrelevance of contemporary orthopedic pathology to specimens from antiquity (concluded). Paleopathol News 99:5–9.

Reyman TA, Nielsen H, Thuesen I, Notman DNH, Reinhard KJ, Tapp E, Waldron T. 1998. New investigative techniques. In: Cockburn A, Cockburn E, Reyman TA, editors. Mummies, Disease and Ancient Cultures. 2nd ed. Cambridge: Cambridge University Press. pp. 353–394.

Rideout DM. 1977. Radiologic examination: autopsy of an Egyptian mummy. Can Med Assoc J 117:463.

Roberts C, Wakely J. 1992. Microscopical findings associated with the diagnosis of osteoporosis in palaeopathology. Int J Osteoarchaeol 2:23–30.

Rochow TG, Rochow EG. 1978. An Introduction to Microscopy by Means of Light, Electrons, X-rays, or Ultrasound. New York: Plenum. 367 pp.

Roentgen WC. 1896. On a new kind of rays. Nature 53:274–276.

Rogers J, Kanis JA. 1992. Paleohistology of Paget's disease in two medieval skeletons. Am J Phys Anthropol 89:325–331.

Ross RJ. 1979. Computed tomography. In: Early PJ, Razzak MA, Sodee DB, editors. Textbook of Nuclear Medicine Technology, 3rd ed. St. Louis: Mosby. pp. 571–583.

Rothschild BM. 1992. Advances in detecting disease in earlier populations. In: Saunders SR, Katzenberg MA, editors. Skeletal Biology of Past Peoples: Research Methods. New York: Wiley-Liss. pp. 131–151.

Rothschild BM, Martin LD. 1993. Paleopathology: Disease in the Fossil Record. Boca Raton: CRC Press. 396 pp.

Rothschild BM, Turnbull W. 1987. Treponemal infection in a Pleistocene bear. Nature 329:61–62.

Rothschild BM, Woods RJ. 1989. Spondyloarthropathy in gorillas. Semin Arthritis Rheum 18:267–276.

Rothschild BM, Woods RJ. 1991. Reactive erosive arthritis in chimpanzees. Am J Primatol 25:49–56.

Ruffer MA. 1909. Note on the histology of Egyptian mummies. Br Med J 1:11.

Ruffer MA. 1911a. On arterial lesions found in Egyptian mummies. J Path Bacteriol 15:453–462.

Ruffer MA. 1911b. Note on an eruption resembling that of variola in the skin of a mummy of the Twentieth Dynasty (1200–1100 BC). J Path Bacteriol 15:1–3.

Salo WL, Aufderheide AC, Buikstra JE, Holcomb TA. 1994. Identification of *Mycobacterium tuberculosis* DNA in a pre-Columbian Peruvian mummy. Proc Nat Acad Sci USA 91:2091–2094.

Sandford MK. 1992. A reconsideration of trace element analysis in prehistoric bone. In: Saunders SR, Katzenberg MA, editors. Skeletal Biology of Past Peoples: Research Methods. New York: Wiley-Liss. pp. 79–103.

Sandford MK. 1993. Understanding the biogenic-diagenetic continuum: interpreting elemental concentrations of archaeological bone. In: Sandford MK, editor. Investigations of Ancient Human Tissue. Langhorne: Gordon and Breach. pp. 3–57.

Sandison TA. 1962. Degenerative vascular disease in the Egyptian mummy. Med Hist 6:77–81.

Schoeninger MJ, Moore K. 1992. Bone Stable Isotope Studies in Archaeology. J World Prehist 6:247–296.

Schultz M. 1986. Die mikroskopische Untersuchung prähistorischer Skeletfunde: Anwendung und Aussagemöglichkeiten der differential-diagnostischen Untersuchung in der Paläopathologie. Archäeologie und Museum, vol. 6, Liestal, Switzerland: Amt für Museen und Archäologie BL. 139 pp.

Schultz M. 1993. Initial stages of systemic bone disease. In: Grupe G, Garland AN, editors. Histology of Ancient Human Bone. Berlin: Springer-Verlag. pp. 185–203.

Schultz M. 1997. Microscopic investigation of excavated skeletal remains: a contribution to paleopathology and forensic medicine. In: Haglund WD, Sorg MH, editors. Forensic Taphonomy: The Postmortem Fate of Human Remains. Boca Raton: CRC Press. pp. 201–222.

Schwarcz HP, Schoeninger MJ. 1991. Stable isotope analyses in human nutritional ecology. Yrbk Phys Anthropol 34:283–321.

Sela J. 1977. Bone remodeling in pathologic conditions: a scanning electron microscopic study. Calcif Tiss Res 23:229–234.

Shattock SG. 1909. Microscopic sections of the aorta of King Mernephtah. Lancet 179:319.

Spigelman M, Lemma E. 1993. The use of the polymerase chain reaction (PCR) to detect *Mycobacterium tuberculosis* in ancient skeletons. Int J Osteoarchaeol 3:137–143.

Steen SL, Lane RW. 1998. Evaluation of habitual activities among two Alaskan Eskimo populations based on musculoskeletal stress markers. Int J Osteoarchaeol 8:341–353.

Steinbock RT. 1976. Paleopathological Diagnosis and Interpretation. Springfield, Ill.: Charles C. Thomas. 423 pp.

Stirland AJ. 1991. Diagnosis of occupationally related paleopathology: can it be done? In: Ortner DJ, Aufderheide AC, editors. Human Paleopathology. Washington: Smithsonian Institution. pp. 40–47.

Stirland AJ. 1998. Musculoskeletal evidence for activity: problems of evaluation. Int J Osteoarchaeol 8:354–362.

Stoner KE. 1995. Dental pathology in *Pongo satyrus borneensis*. Am J Phys Anthropol 98:307–321.

Strouhal E, Vyhnanek L. 1979. Egyptian mummies in Czechslovak collections. Acta Musei Nationalis Pragae 35B:1–195.

Sumner DR, Morbeck ME, Lobick JJ. 1989. Apparent age-related bone loss among adult female Gombe chimpanzees. Am J Phys Anthropol 79:225–246.

Tapp E. 1984. Disease and the Manchester mummies: the pathologist's role. In: David AR, Tapp E, editors. Evidence Embalmed: Modern Medicine and the Mummies of Ancient Egypt. Manchester: Manchester University Press. pp. 78–95.

Tapp E. 1986. Histology and histopathology of Manchester mummies. In: David AR, editor. Science in Egyptology. Manchester: Manchester University Press. pp. 347–350.

Tapp E. 1992. The histological examination of mummified tissue. In David AR, Tapp E, editors. The Mummy's Tale. New York: St. Martin's Press. pp. 121–131.

Tapp EA, Curry A, Anfield CC. 1975. Sand pneumoconiosis in an Egyptian mummy. Br Med J 2:276.

Tapp E, Wildsmith K. 1992. The autopsy and endoscopy of the Leeds mummy. In: David AR, Tapp E, editors. The Mummy's Tale. New York: St. Martin's Press. pp. 132–153.

Tapp E, Stanworth P, Wildsmith K. 1984. The endoscope in mummy research. In: David AR, Tapp E, editors. Evidence Embalmed: Modern Medicine and the Mummies of Ancient Egypt. Manchester: Manchester University Press. pp. 65–77.

Taylor GM, Crossey M, Saldanha J, Waldron T. 1996. DNA from *Mycobacterium tuberculosis* identified in mediaeval human skeletal remains using polymerase chain reaction. J Archaeol Sci 23:789–798.

Thillaud PL. 1992. Retrospective diagnosis in paleopathology. Paleopathol News 80(suppl):1–4.

Tuross N. 1991. Recovery of bone and serum proteins from human skeletal tissue: IgG, osteonectin, and albumin. In: Ortner DJ, Aufderheide AC, editors. Human Paleopathology: Current Syntheses and Future Options. Washington: Smithsonian Institution. pp. 51–54.

Ubaldi M, Luciana S, Marota I, Fornaciari G, Cano RJ, Rollo F. 1998. Sequence analysis of bacterial DNA in the colon of an Andean mummy. Am J Phys Anthropol 107:285–295.

Ubelaker DH. 1982. The development of American paleopathology. In: Spencer F, editor. A History of American Physical Anthropology, 1930–1980. Orlando: Academic Press. pp. 337–356.

Underwood EJ. 1977. Trace Elements in Human and Animal Nutrition. 4th ed. New York: Academic Press. 545 pp.

Vaughan J. 1981. The Physiology of Bone. 3rd ed. Oxford: Clarendon Press. 265 pp.

Wakely J, Manchester K, Roberts C. 1991. Scanning electron microscopy of rib lesions. Int J Osteoarchaeol 1:185–189.

Waldron HA. 1983. On the post-mortem accumulation of lead by skeletal tissues. J Archaeol Sci 10:35–40.

Waldon T. 1991. Rate for the job. Measures of disease frequency in palaeopathology. Int J Osteoarchaeol 1:17–25.

Waldron T. 1994. Counting the Dead: The Epidemiology of Skeletal Populations. Chichester, UK: John Wiley and Sons. 109 pp.

Wapler U, Schultz M. 1996. A method of histological research applied to archaeological bone material: the example of cribra orbitalia. Bull Mem Soc d'Anthropol Paris 8:421–431.

Wells C. 1964. Bones, Bodies and Disease. London: Thames and Hudson. 288 pp.

White CD. 1993. Isotopic determination of seasonality in diet and death from Nubian mummy hair. J Archaeol Sci 20:657–666.

Whittaker DK, Stack MV. 1985. The lead, cadmium and zinc content of some Romano-British teeth. Archaeometry 26:37–42.

Wood JW, Milner GR, Harpending HC, Weiss KM. 1992. The osteological paradox: problems of inferring prehistoric health from skeletal samples. Curr Anthropol 33:343–370.

CHAPTER 9

DENTAL PATHOLOGY

SIMON HILLSON

INTRODUCTION

The diseases and injuries of teeth and jaws are among the most common conditions seen in human remains. Many of them occur so frequently that they can be practically regarded as normal. Among the most frequent are dental defects, preserved lifelong, resulting from disturbances to the formation of teeth during childhood. Other conditions reflect the uses to which the teeth are put during life, such as anomalous or exceptionally heavy tooth wear, fracturing or chipping, or the way in which the bone of the jaws remodels around their roots. The long-term presence of microorganisms in dental plaque deposits in the mouth gives rise to a range of conditions such as dental caries and periodontal disease, which cause damage to the tissues of the teeth and loss of supporting bone in the jaws. Plaque-related disease is in turn strongly related to the progress of dental wear, and to the remodeling of the jaws taking place independently, in response to changing mechanical forces. All these processes are therefore best seen as an integrated whole (Fig. 9.1), and their pattern of progression within a population is strongly indicative of the nature of the diet and the mode of subsistence. The linkages are complex, however, and it is important to recognize that the different dental conditions include a variety of lesions and defects,

often interacting in contrasting ways. There are several different categories of dental caries and loss of supporting bone, just as there are several different types of tooth wear with contrasting implications for the life history of the teeth. Recording systems for use in the study of human remains need to reflect these differences, even at the expense of complexity.

DEFECTS OF DENTAL DEVELOPMENT IN THE ENAMEL OF THE TOOTH CROWN

The development (Smith, 1991) of permanent tooth *crowns* (roots continue to form after crowns are completed) takes place in three phases:

- Incisors, canines, and first molars are initiated during the first year after birth (or just before birth) and completed between 3 and 7 years.
- Premolars and second molars start formation during the second and third years after birth and are completed between 4 and 8 years.
- Third molars are initiated any time between 7 and 12 years, and completed sometime between 10 and 18 years of age.

A whole range of factors (Goodman and Rose, 1990; Hillson, 1996; Pindborg, 1982) may disrupt crown development during this

Biological Anthropology of the Human Skeleton, Edited by M. Anne Katzenberg and Shelley R. Saunders.
ISBN 0-471-31616-4   Copyright © 2000 by Wiley-Liss, Inc.

period, including dietary deficiency, childhood fevers, and major infections such as congenital syphilis. Each disruption is expressed as enamel defects (Fig. 9.2) in all the crowns that were being formed at the time of the episode so, in theory, the pattern of defects (which is preserved into adulthood) provides a detailed record of growth disturbance. This, together with the generalized nature of growth-disturbing factors that can cause such defects, makes them ideal indicators when fitting Selyean stress models to interpretation of human remains in archaeology (Goodman and Rose, 1990; Goodman et al., 1988). Care needs to be taken, however, because the mechanisms by which the defects are created are complex, poorly understood, and vary depending upon which particular part of the tooth crown is being formed at the time (Hillson, 1992a, 1992c; Hillson and Bond, 1997). The defects are best studied in relation to the microscopic pattern of growth layering preserved within the enamel.

The most prominent expression of growth layering, seen in microscope sections under low magnifications (around 10×), is a concentric pattern of lines radiating out from the enamel underlying the cusp tips (see Fitz-Gerald and Rose, Chapter 6). They are called the brown striae of Retzius, and each represents the momentary position of the enamel-forming front at a particular point in development. In the deeper part of the enamel jacket that coats the tooth crown, the brown striae are often poorly defined and irregular, but where they angle up to meet the crown surface they become sharply defined and regularly spaced at 20–40 μm (or one quarter the diameter of a human hair) apart. At the point where each brown stria reaches the surface, there is a groove running around the circumference of the crown side. This gives a rippled or wavelike appearance to the crown side when seen under modest magnification, and the grooves are collectively known as perikymata (Greek *peri-* "around", *kymata* "waves"). They vary in spacing from about 150μm (a little wider than a hair) at the cusps, down to 30 μm or less at the base of the crown, largely (but not

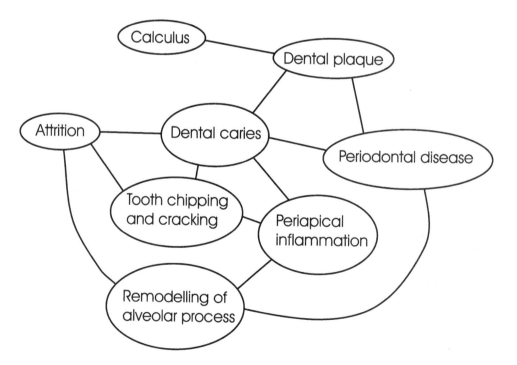

Figure 9.1   Interrelationships of different dental conditions.

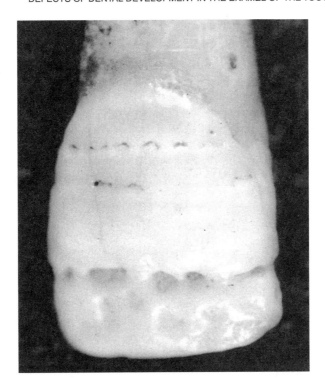

Figure 9.2   An upper first incisor from a British medieval site, showing different forms of enamel hypoplasia. There are pitted defects, furrow-form defects, and combinations of the two.

entirely) as a result of the changing angle at which the brown striae meet the surface. The brown striae are superimposed over an even finer set of incremental structures, the prism cross striations, which represent a 24-hour growth rhythm. Where both they and the brown striae are sharply defined and regular, there seems to be a constant number of cross striations between neighboring striae throughout the enamel of each tooth for one individual. This number varies between 7 and 11 between individuals and represents some fundamental, but little understood, rhythm in enamel matrix formation. The cross striations themselves form the basis of a detailed chronology of dental development.

The defects seen at the crown surface most commonly take the form of furrows, steps, or pits arranged circumferentially in bands around the crown side (Berten, 1895; Hillson and Bond, 1997). They parallel the perikymata

and are thus clearly both episodic and developmental in origin. It is important to distinguish them from the much rarer inherited enamel defects, usually affecting most teeth in both permanent and deciduous dentitions in a similar way (and so not attributable to particular periods of disturbance), and collectively known as amelogenesis imperfecta (Bäckmann, 1989; Cook, 1980; Shields, 1983; Winter and Brook, 1975; Witkop, 1957). For this reason, the phrase "developmental defects of enamel (DDE)" is often used (Commission on Oral Health, 1982), although frequently "enamel hypoplasia" is used with the same meaning. Various types have long been recognized (Fig. 9.2). By far the most common are furrow-form defects, formed partly by a disruption to the even spacing of perikymata and ranging from microscopic furrows that involve just one pair of perikymata up to defects that can be seen with the naked eye and involve 20 or more perikymata. These large furrow defects are often called LEH or "linear enamel hypoplasia" in anthropological literature (Goodman and Rose, 1990). There is a considerable body of clinical literature linking them with medical histories involving dietary deficiency (Eliot et al., 1934; Goodman et al., 1991; Infante and Gillespie, 1974; Sweeney et al., 1971), fevers, infectious disease (Lindemann, 1958; Pindborg, 1982; Sarnat and Schour, 1941), and a whole host of other childhood conditions. Much less commonly, whole layers of enamel matrix are missing, exposing the plane of a brown stria curving down into the crown, or even the underlying dentine. Such plane-form defects are usually bounded by a prominent step running around the crown, marking the resumption of normal enamel matrix formation. It is usually assumed that they represent a more marked growth disturbance than the furrow-form defects, but there is no direct evidence for this. In between, there are the pitted defects where the exposure of a brown stria plane is more intermittent, with normal enamel matrix in between. Such pits may decorate the edge of a full plane-form defect, or they may accentuate a furrow-form defect. Occasionally a band of pits may occur on its own.

Enamel hypoplasia contributes to the study of human remains in several ways. Firstly, the pattern of defects may allow isolated teeth from a commingled burial to be matched. Secondly, the prevalence of defects may suggest the importance of childhood infectious diseases and/or dietary deficiency in the health of an ancient community. The sequence of defects, if this can be determined from their position in the sequence of tooth crown development, would give a unique record of the seasonality of such conditions, and their distribution with age. The difficulty, however, lies in devising a simple system for recording the presence of the defects, their size, and their timing. They vary in size from a microscopic disruption at a single perikyma groove to a pronounced deformity of the whole crown (Hillson and Bond, 1997). For the most common furrow-form defects, the size and prominence

has more to do with the period of time over which growth was disturbed, and where the defect is situated on which tooth crown, than it has to do with the severity of the disruption. The only way to resolve these questions satisfactorily is to study the furrow defects under a microscope, as part of the whole sequence of layered growth. For plane-form or pit-form defects there is still a problem because they are very difficult to relate to the sequence of crown development shown at the surface by the perikymata. It has been common to measure the size and position of furrow-, plane-, and pit-form defects using calipers, and then to estimate timing and duration from a table that assumes linear growth in crown height, calculated on the basis of an average final crown height and standard ages for the start and completion of crown formation, all drawn from the literature (Goodman et al., 1980; Goodman and Rose, 1990; Swärdstedt, 1966). Usually a single tooth class, the canine, is selected. This is regarded as a standard approach (Buikstra and Ubelaker, 1994), but it has formidable difficulties (Hillson, 1992c, 1996; Hillson and Bond, 1997). Firstly, although the size of a growing tooth germ (measured by weight or the height of its axis from base to tip) has a relationship with age up to 5 years or so, this relationship does not follow a simple straight line for permanent teeth (Liversidge et al., 1993). Furthermore, the growth of the crown surface is even less linear. The first 20 to 50% of crown growth is hidden under the cusp tips (see FitzGerald and Rose, Chapter 6), while the crown surface is strongly curved and grows more rapidly at the base of the cusps than near the cervix. Use of the canine may minimize the latter difficulty, because the middle part of its tall crown sides has a fairly constant extension rate, but there are still too many assumptions made. Unworn crown height varies over several millimeters (Woelfl, 1990) even within one collection of dentitions and, where most teeth are heavily worn, it is impossible to check. Wear and abrasion, in any case, make hypoplasia difficult to study—modern teeth are so heavily abraded by tooth brushing that they are often almost useless for comparative purposes. In fact, the heavy occlusal wear of archaeological teeth is preferable, because at least the cervix and protected interproximal/approximal parts of the crown can still be studied, and it is possible to find equivalent parts of other teeth that can continue the sequence. In addition to all the above, the size and prominence of furrow-form defects vary with their position on the tooth crown (this may be ascertained by comparing the effects of the same period of growth disturbance on different teeth), and with the angle of view and orientation of lighting. Matters are even worse for plane- or pit-form defects, where the size is unlikely to bear any relationship whatever to the duration of the growth disturbance.

As a basic record, the Fédération Dentaire Internationale DDE Index (Commission on Oral Health, 1982) is well defined in many ways, and has been recognized as a standard (Buikstra and Ubelaker, 1994; Hillson, 1986). The main difficulty with the DDE Index, and any other scoring system, is that the minimum size of defect to be recorded as hypoplasia has not been defined. It is difficult to see how consistency can be maintained when defects vary

in a continuous series, from those that are microscopic up to those that can be seen clearly at a distance of some yards (Hillson and Bond, 1997). If detailed defect sequences are required, then there is little alternative to a microscope and the histological approach (Dean and Beynon, 1991; Hillson, 1992a). Microscopic studies of crown surfaces supported, in an ideal world, by sections and cross-striation counts are time consuming and are most successful when applied to teeth showing little wear, from children in their late infancy to early teens. The most useful preliminary record is one that describes the type of defects, where they occur, on which teeth, and confirms their existence by matching them between the parts of different tooth crowns that form at a similar age (Table 9.1). Measurements add little to this, and the most detailed record to take away from a museum or field laboratory is a good quality dental impression. At the time of writing, the highest resolution impression material for this work is Coltène President (Coltène/Whaledent Inc., Mahweh, NJ) (Beynon, 1987; Hillson, 1992b). In most cases, it is best just to take impressions of the labial-buccal surfaces of all teeth present. These can be stored in bags

TABLE 9.1   Stages of Crown Formation for Different Teeth[a]

	First molars	Upper and lower first incisors	Lower second incisors	Canines	Upper second incisors	Premolars and second molars	Third molars
A	Occlusal	Occlusal					
B	Intermediate	Intermediate	Occlusal				
C	Cervical	Intermediate	Intermediate	Occlusal			
D		Cervical	Cervical	Intermediate	Occlusal	Occlusal	
E				Intermediate	Cervical	Intermediate	
F				Cervical		Cervical	
G							Occlusal
H							Cervical

[a]Lines may be drawn across the table to represent the matching occurrences of hypoplastic defects between the crown *surfaces* of different tooth classes (note that upper second incisors have different timings from lower second incisors). The different stages have deliberately not been given ages, but stage A begins around 1 year or a few months more after birth (the upper first incisors follow a few months behind the lowers). Stage C finishes with completion of the first molar crown at very roughly 3 years of age, similarly D at 4–5 years, E about 5 years, and F at approximately 6–8 years.

(After Hillson, 1996.)

or envelopes and, in the laboratory, used to cast epoxy resin replicas which can be examined either by light microscopy or in the scanning electron microscope (see Fitzgerald and Rose, Chapter 6). In order to build a defect/perikyma groove sequence for teeth in which some of the occlusal layers are worn away, counts are taken back from the last increment formed at the cemento-enamel junction of each tooth (Hillson, 1992a, 1993). The repeat interval of cross striations between pairs of brown striae (and thus perikyma grooves) is unknown without sectioning, but relative timings of defects can be reckoned in terms of percentage total counts of perikyma grooves between, say, the end of first molar crown formation and end of second molar crown formation.

One particular form of hypoplasia is associated with congenital syphilis. Three characteristic defects have been defined for more than one hundred years—Hutchinson's incisors, Moon's molar, and mulberry molars (Hillson et al., 1998; Jacobi et al., 1992). A mulberry molar is a plane-form defect (initiated a few weeks after birth) surrounding the cusps of permanent first molars, leaving the cusps themselves as small nodules set into the normal-sized occlusal area. These nodules usually break away, and the occlusal surface is rapidly worn or develops a carious lesion, so they are seen clearly only in children. The defect overlaps the possible range of general hypoplasia, but its position and sharpness are at least distinctive. By contrast, a Moon's molar (also permanent first molars only) shows no clear hypoplastic defect and is normal in appearance in every way except that the cusp tips are abnormally close together, compared with the main bulge of the crown side. The mechanism by which this morphological anomaly is formed has not yet been investigated (Hillson et al., 1998). In Hutchinson's incisors, the central one of the usual three mamelons (small cusplets along the incisal edge) is little developed. This leads to a notch, and a drawing-in of the incisal edge so that the labial outline of the incisor crown is more oval than normal. The notch wears away rapidly, so that the evidence is again lost in early adulthood. The disruption is probably confined to a few weeks or so after birth, and the defect is outside the wider range of hypoplasia because of its position.

TOOTH WEAR: CHIPPING AND FRACTURES

Many collections of archaeological human remains show evidence of rapid tooth wear, both on the occlusal surfaces and at the contact points between teeth in the same jaw (Fig. 9.3). The rate, pattern, and orientation of wear seem to be strongly related to the nature of subsistence and, for example, hunter-gatherer groups and early agricultural groups have markedly contrasting wear. Loss of crown height due to this wear, together with decreased length of the crowns along the tooth row, causes remodeling of the bone and other supporting tissues in the jaws and results in a progressive upward and sideways migration of the teeth and their sockets throughout life (Fig 9.7). This is known as continuous eruption. As more and more of the roots are exposed, then the nature of mechanical forces acting on the jaws changes, further initiating remodeling of the bone. In many past populations, wear was rapid enough to progress down the roots during older adulthood, and eventually teeth were lost through lack of bony support. Heavy tooth wear populations were also typically subject to dental fractures, from minor chipping to major cracks and breaks, which exposed the dental pulp to infection. In addition, many such groups show evidence of abnormal abrasion, apparently due to the use of teeth for preparing food or in the manufacture of artefacts. All these factors have a profound effect on the development of dental disease.

Tooth-on-tooth wear that creates wear facets on both teeth involved is described as attrition. The important features to record from a dental pathology point of view are: (1) the exposure of new sites for initiation of dental caries, or the modification of existing sites, (2) the progressive loss of crown height in relation to con-

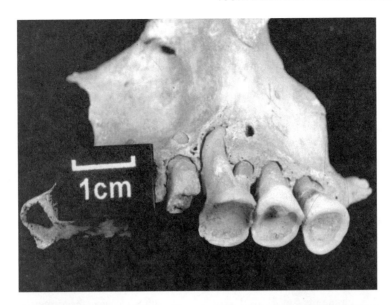

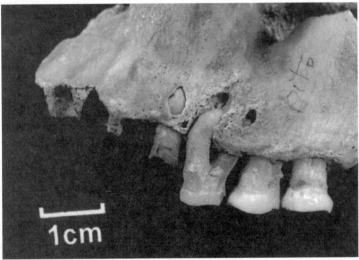

Figure 9.3 Two views of a left upper jaw from an Anglo-Saxon site in Winchester, England. The central part of the occlusal surface in the molars has been worn away to expose the softer dentine, leaving a higher rim of the harder enamel. Approximal attrition has broken through the mesial and distal sides of this rim in the first molar, and has thinned it on these sides in the second molar. The second premolar was fractured during life, and subsequently became worn. There is no clear evidence of bone loss from periodontal disease, but remodeling of the alveolar process has led to thinning of the buccal plate. This is particularly evident over the sockets of the incisors, canines, and premolars, which bulge outward. The first molar is loose and has dropped down slightly in the lower picture to reveal an opening into the smooth-walled cavity of a periapical granuloma around the apex of its disto-buccal root. The wafer-thin opening suggests that the granuloma has been exposed by a fenestration due to the buccal plate thinning, and not by the sinus of an abscess. There is no sign of an open pulp chamber or root canal on the worn occlusal surface of this tooth, so it may be that a fine crack allowed the pulp to be infected. In the fractured second premolar there is also no evidence of root canal exposure or periapical inflammation, and the fenestration that exposes the root surface must again be due to general remodeling of the buccal plate. The exposed root surfaces are roughened and bulbous, suggesting hypercementosis. Eroded remnants of supragingival calculus are visible on the roots of the molars. (This specimen is in the collection of the Natural History Museum, London, and has been photographed with their permission.)

tinuous eruption, and (3) the distribution and orientation of wear facets in relation to remodeling of the alveolar process as it responds to forces acting on the dentition. Occlusal attrition is usually recorded by scoring the pattern of dentine exposed as the wear progresses. The most frequently used system is that of Smith (1984), and this is the recognized standard (Buikstra and Ubelaker, 1994). The similar method of Molnar (1971) has some advantages for the study of dental pathology, in that it also records the exposure of secondary dentine and the shape and orientation of wear facets. Both of these are satisfactory in relation to the study of dental caries. A detailed method defined by Scott (1979) is confined to the molars, and is therefore too limiting in this context. It is difficult to define measurements for occlusal wear, although attempts have been made to measure the reduction in crown height (Molnar et al., 1983; Tomenchuk and Mayhall, 1979; Walker et al., 1991). The difficulty here is that the height of unworn crowns is variable within any population, and it is hard to interpret results because of this. In addition, many archaeological teeth are so worn that the crown is missing altogether down one side. In relation to studies of continuous eruption versus root exposure due to periodontal disease, it might be more appropriate to measure the height of the occlusal facet in relation to the crest of the alveolar process. This can be done simply using a graduated periodontal probe at the same time as measuring the root exposure. In the mandible, another suggestion is to measure the height of both the occlusal facet and the alveolar crest in relation to the inferior alveolar canal (Fig. 9.7), in an attempt to find an independent landmark on which to base the dimension (Whittaker, 1986; Whittaker et al., 1987, 1990). This makes it possible to see if the occlusal plane has changed its position with increasing wear,

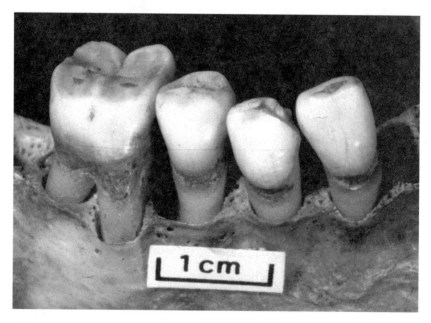

Figure 9.4 Lower first molar, premolars, and canine of a post-medieval jaw from London. On either side, the empty sockets denote teeth that have been lost postmortem. Alveolar bone (lining the socket) has been lost around the roots of the molar and, most noticeably in this view, around the second premolar to create a deep crater between it and the molar. This is the classic appearance of bone loss due to periodontal disease. The crests of the interdental plates between other teeth are much less affected, but are still somewhat porous. Along the cemento-enamel junction (CEJ) of all four teeth is a lesion that looks very much like root surface caries but, in archaeological material like this, it is important to consider possible diagenetic effects.

and the few studies that have been done in this way suggest that the rate of continuous eruption approximately matches the rate of wear (in heavy wear populations) so that the occlusal plane remains in about the same position with respect to the body of the mandible. Such measurements require X rays that include the whole mandibular body, and there is the further difficulty that the inferior alveolar canal varies in position between individuals, relative to the boundaries of the body as a whole, so that it is not entirely a homologous reference point. Still other measurements have been devised to record the angle of occlusal wear facets (Smith, 1984, 1986; Walker et al., 1991), and these have shown that there may be differences between hunter-gatherers and agriculturalists in the progression of angular changes in relation to stage of molar wear.

Wear between neighboring teeth in the same jaw is known as approximal, interproximal, or interstitial attrition (Wolpoff, 1970). The rate of approximal attrition, relative to occlusal attrition, is particularly high in hunter-gatherer groups when compared with early agriculturalists (Hinton, 1982). It is rather more difficult to record, but the edge of approximal attrition facets is a common site for the initiation of dental caries. One method is to measure the buccal-lingual length of the facet, as exposed at the edge of the occlusal facet, with a pair of needle-point calipers. This has proved useful in studies of the pattern of wear, but from the dental pathology viewpoint it is more appropriate to record the exposure of dentine in the wear facet, the extension of wear down to the cervical margin of the tooth, and the eventual loss of approximal contact between teeth due to the combined results of heavy occlusal and approximal wear. For a detailed study, therefore, it makes sense to record both the length of the facet and a simple score for its appearance (see Appendix).

Wear that results from contact with objects other than teeth is known as abrasion. General abrasion occurs in all teeth with increasing age, especially on the buccal/labial and lingual surfaces (Hillson, 1996; Scott and Wyckoff,

1949). Today, toothbrush abrasion is seen in almost all teeth as a very glossy polish to the crown surface. As the roots become exposed with increasing age, the softer cement and dentine may be abraded more rapidly, to undercut the enamel (Soames and Southam, 1993). The very heavy abrasion seen today results from the use of toothpastes containing abrasives, and nothing like it is seen in most archaeological or museum collections. However, one particular feature of European jaws from the eighteenth and nineteenth centuries (and of other populations that have used pipes) is clay pipe facets—semicircular notches worn usually in the canines and premolars by holding the pipe stem (Kvaal and Derry, 1996). Some assemblages of Native American remains from the Northwest also have a characteristic pattern of very heavy abrasion on the labial/buccal surfaces of teeth. These relate to the wearing of labrets; plugs of stone, bone, or ivory fitted into openings into the lips and cheeks (Cybulski, 1994; Milner and Larsen, 1991). Labret facets are readily identifiable as flat areas on the labial/buccal surfaces of incisors, canines, and premolars, usually in the lower jaw, but there may be more general polishing or more limited grooving of a single tooth. Wear of this type presumably went slowly enough for secondary dentine deposition in the pulp chamber to repair the damage, because cases of pulp exposure and periapical inflammation are not recorded. The same is true of deliberate tooth mutilation by cutting, drilling, or filling, as is seen particularly in human remains from Central and South America (Milner and Larsen, 1991; Romero, 1970). Many different patterns are known, often involving deep penetration into the crown, and some ethnographic accounts suggest that the cuts were made in small increments, with long intervals between operations (as is currently on display in the Odontological Museum of the Royal College of Surgeons, London) that must have allowed reparative secondary dentine to build up slowly in the pulp chamber. Restorative procedures in dental surgery, starting mainly in the nineteenth century are, in effect, also a form of abrasion. An important branch of dental studies is the matching of jaws with dental records in identification for forensic purposes (Clark, 1992; Cottone and Standish, 1981; and see Ubelaker, Chapter 2).

Another range of common abrasions results from causes more difficult to identify. One of these is heavy scratching, particularly of the labial surface of incisors, and especially in hunter-gatherer groups (Bermúdez de Castro et al., 1988; Fox, 1992; Fox and Frayer, 1997; Fox and Pérez-Pérez, 1994; Frayer and Russell, 1987). It is usually assumed that these represent the cutting of objects held between the teeth, but there are various forms and orientations of marks that imply a variety of causes. Another such feature is so-called approximal grooving—broad grooves running from buccal to lingual along the cervical margin of cheek teeth (Bermúdez de Castro et al., 1997; Brown, 1991; Brown and Molnar, 1990; Formicola, 1991; Frayer, 1991; Milner and Larsen, 1991; Ubelaker et al., 1969). These are now quite commonly recognized in a range of archaeological and fossil material. Suggested causes include use of toothpicks and the stripping of tendon fibers between the teeth to produce sewing threads, but this is still a subject of considerable debate. Other grooves may be seen, particularly on the occlusal wear facets of incisor, canine, or premolar teeth (Larsen, 1985; Molleson, 1994). It is assumed that these result from the holding of fibers or yarn when processing materials or weaving artifacts.

A number of standard terms are recognized in the study of abrasions, but the only recording system is that of Romero (Romero, 1958, 1970) for classifying tooth mutilation. In general studies, good photographs and descriptions are the main requirements along with, perhaps, dental impressions.

Fractures of the teeth and jaws are also common in archaeological assemblages. Teeth often show chipping around the edges of occlusal attrition facets, especially in molars (Milner and Larsen, 1991; Pedersen, 1947; Turner and Cadien, 1969), and there are sometimes major breaks, which can be distinguished from post-mortem damage by the presence of wear on the exposed surface (Fig 9.3). These may open the pulp chamber to infection. It is also possible for teeth to be cracked, and there may be little surface sign that this has taken place. Sometimes an apparently intact tooth has associated periapical inflammation (Fig. 9.3), and one possible explanation is that a fine crack has exposed the pulp chamber (Alexandersen, 1967; Pedersen, 1938). Heavy wear on crowns may predispose them to cracking and more serious breaks. Still other fractures may occur in the roots (Pindborg, 1970), with little sign at the surface even in living people. Fractures of the bone of the mandibular body, or alveolar process in the maxilla, are sometimes seen in archaeological collections. Such fractures tend to track down the socket of a tooth, as a line of weakness. Not only does this involve the teeth in the processes of inflammation and repair, it also commonly makes the fracture a compound one in which the wound penetrates to the surface and is thus exposed to infection. Cracking and chipping of the teeth themselves can be recorded by simple coding, supported by photographs and description.

PLAQUE-RELATED DISEASES

Dental plaque deposits form on the surfaces of all teeth. They consist of large colonies of microorganisms and associated extracellular material, and collections of human remains show abundant evidence for the presence of plaque, in the form of mineralized plaque, known as dental calculus or tartar (Figs. 9.3 and 9.6). Long-standing accumulations of microorganisms and their extracellular products next to the gums provoke an immune response. This follows a well-established pattern through life, and episodes of inflammation alternate with periods of recovery, leading to a cumulative loss of support for the affected tooth and remodeling of the bone of the jaw, resulting in a progressive reduction in height of the alveolar process and eventual loss of teeth (Figure 9.4). The extracellular products of plaque microorganisms also affect the surfaces of the teeth themselves. Organic acids form as by-products of plaque physiology, and result in localized demineralization of the tooth surface, to produce the characteristic lesions of dental caries (Figure 9.5). A cavity may develop and ultimately this may penetrate the pulp and expose it to an infection, which may result in inflammation of the tissues around the apex of the root. The nature and age-related development of dental caries lesions are indicative of the diet and, particularly, its carbohydrate component.

Dental Calculus

The presence of dental calculus indicates long-standing plaque accumulations, but it is difficult to deduce anything further because the factors that initiate mineralization are little understood. Two types of calculus are recognized: supragingival and subgingival. The irregular claylike deposits often seen on the surface of crowns (and sometimes roots) are all supragingival calculus. They can be so large that they overhang the gums, but do not appear to have any direct role in irritating the periodontal tissues, except in providing an extended surface on which living plaque can accumulate. At a population level, there is a slight inverse relationship between calculus and caries prevalence (Manji et al., 1989b), which is understandable in that the first is a mineralization phenomenon whereas the second is mostly a demineralization phenomenon. The relationship is not at all strong, however, and in an individual jaw it is common to see both carious cavities and supragingival calculus deposits (Thylstrup et al., 1989). Sometimes they are found on the same teeth (Jones and Boyde, 1987). Both are long-term conditions, and the lesions could represent different phases of plaque biochemistry, but the development of caries relates to very local biochemical changes, which may continue even underneath a calculus deposit.

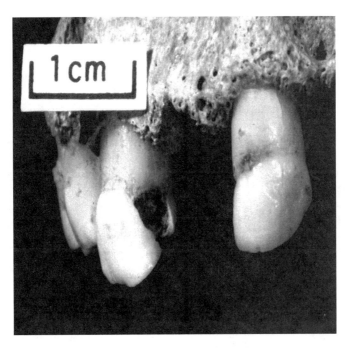

Figure 9.5 Gross approximal caries that has destroyed the mesial side of an upper incisor in an early medieval skull from London. The lesion may well have been initiated at the contact point but has advanced so far that it is not possible to be sure.

Subgingival calculus is a much thinner, less obvious, layer coating the surface of the roots in a periodontal pocket. There is usually an area of exposed root, bare of subgingival calculus, around the cervix of tooth marking the opening into the pocket where the gingival cuff (border of the gums) rested. A subgingival deposit frequently has a more strongly pigmented apical border, but this can only be used to infer the minimum size of the pocket as the deeper parts of the pocket may not be underlain by calculus (Richardson et al., 1990).

Should calculus be recorded? It is certainly difficult to deduce much from its presence. In any case, great care needs to be taken when recording archaeological material and museum specimens, because the supragingival deposits can easily be dislodged to leave only a vestige on the crown side. On the other hand, calculus is relatively quick and simple to record. Most anthropologists use Brothwell's (1981) three-stage score for supragingival deposits, and a graduated probe can be used to measure the maximum length of root covered by subgingival deposits (Powell and Garnick, 1978).

Microscopic investigation of calculus demonstrates the plaque architecture and the forms of microorganisms, preserved as voids within the mineralized matrix, and it is possible to distinguish between supragingival and subgingival deposits (Bercy and Frank, 1980; Friskopp, 1983; Friskopp and Hammarstrom, 1980). Ideally, tooth and calculus are resin impregnated and sectioned together, producing a flat surface suitable for backscattered electron microscopy or confocal light microscopy (Boyde and Jones, 1983; Jones, 1987). The biochemistry of calculus is complex and not well understood. One potentially useful aspect is that calculus is an effective preserver of DNA (see Stone, Chapter 13). Human cheek cells are incorporated into plaque and subsequently mineralized, and it is possible to determine the sex of the owner of a tooth by DNA extraction from calculus and PCR amplification of appropriate sequences on the X and Y chromosomes (Ka-

wano et al., 1995). Removal of small calculus samples would be relatively simple and non-destructive.

Dental Caries

Dental caries is a progressive demineralization of the enamel, cementum, and dentine of the tooth by organic acids, which are produced through the fermentation of dietary carbohydrates by some plaque bacteria. During the present century, sugars have been established as the main factor in caries rates (Navia, 1994; Rugg-Gunn, 1993; Sheiham, 1983). This was shown in a particularly striking way by the decrease in caries rate amongst children as a result of sugar rationing in Japan, Norway, and the Island of Jersey during World War II. Sucrose is often regarded as the sugar mainly responsible for caries, but this is probably because it is eaten in greatest quantity. There is little difference in cariogenicity between fructose, glucose, lactose, and sucrose. It should be noted, however, that it is possible for an individual to develop caries even if they do not eat sugar (Rugg-Gunn, 1993). Starches seem generally to have a low cariogenicity relative to sugars, but they do cause caries, and a mixture of starches and sugars is as cariogenic, weight for weight, as pure sugar. The role of dietary proteins and fats is currently not well understood, but milk products seem to have a protective effect (Bowen and Pearson, 1993; Mundorff-Shrestha et al., 1994), and the caries rate was very low among recent Inuit who ate almost entirely animal-based foods, with little or no carbohydrates (Mayhall, 1970; Pedersen, 1966). On an archaeological time scale, caries was not common up until the adoption of agriculture (Larsen, 1995, 1997; Larsen et al., 1991), presumably due to the addition of fermentable carbohydrates from cultivated crops. From that point onward, there was a steady rise in caries with, in Britain and North America, a sharp rise during the nineteenth century accompanied by a change in the pattern of lesions that may be related to an increase in sugar consumption (Corbett and Moore, 1976; Moore and Corbett, 1971, 1973, 1975; Hillson, 1996; Saunders et al., 1997; Sledzik and Moore-Jansen, 1991; Sutter, 1995). Caries, along with dental attrition and stable isotope studies (see Katzenberg, Chapter 11), thus has considerable potential for identifying dietary changes in the archaeological record.

Recording and interpretation of dental caries statistics need to keep in mind the nature of the disease. In most cases, it is very slowly progressive, with alternating phases of stability and activity over many years (Pine and ten Bosch, 1996). Not all lesions recorded will currently be active and, even if most of the crown is destroyed, the tooth is not necessarily just about to be lost. In fact, the main cause of tooth loss in caries is deliberate extraction to treat tooth pain. When modern clinical studies record teeth as "missing due to caries" they mean that a painful tooth, that might have had a clear cavity in it, was previously extracted (Manji et al., 1989a). Sensitivity and pain result from an acute inflammation of the pulp and periapical tissues, but such inflammation does not produce the type of bone resorption that would cause a tooth to be lost without human intervention. Nevertheless, tooth extraction is one of the oldest surgical procedures, and would quite possibly have been available to many people in the ancient past. The slowly progressive nature of caries leads to a pattern of development strongly related to age (Thylstrup and Fejerskov, 1994). It is therefore essential to divide a collection of jaws into different age groups when preparing caries statistics. It is also necessary to recognize that carious lesions fall into several different categories, in relation to their site of initiation on the tooth surface. These categories have contrasting etiologies, and develop in different ways with increasing age, so that they also need to be kept separate. Typically, the average rate of caries (the word *prevalence* has deliberately not been used—see below) in a population is due to a few individuals with a high caries experience, balanced by the bulk of the population who have relatively little experience of caries. This is a difficult situation for

archaeology, where collections are often small, and affected by taphonomic factors including variable preservation and uneven recovery. Not only does the potential for differential survival of particular age groups need to be considered, but also caries rates in males versus females, and in the different parts of the dentition. In almost all clinical studies of caries, females show higher rates than males, and there frequently seems to be a bias against the burial and survival of female remains in archaeology (Larsen, 1997; Thylstrup and Fejerskov, 1994). Similarly, whereas caries is usually symmetrical between left and right sides, there are considerable differences between upper and lower teeth, and between incisors, canines, premolars, and molars. This means that such factors as relative survival of upper and lower jaws, and the frequent loss of single-rooted teeth (incisors, canines, lower premolars), will greatly affect caries statistics in archaeological and museum assemblages. Separate statistics are needed for each category, and this increases the complexity of recording, but there is no alternative.

Carious lesions (Figs. 9.4, 9.5 and 9.6) can be divided into two main forms (Thylstrup and Fejerskov, 1994): coronal caries and root surface caries. The root surface lesions are initiated along the cemento-enamel junction (CEJ) at the base of the crown, or on the cement of the root, as they are exposed in adults by periodontal disease. They appear to be initiated only on root surfaces exposed above the margin of the gingivae (gums) and not inside periodontal pockets (Thylstrup and Fejerskov, 1994). Coronal lesions may be initiated at any age, in the enamel surface of the crown, or in dentine exposed by wear. Two important sites of initiation in modern populations are in the occlusal fissures and fossae of molars (occlusal caries), and the protected sides of the crown just below the contact points between neighboring teeth (approximal or interproximal caries). In the more worn teeth of many archaeological collections, other coronal sites appear to have been created (or modified) in wear facets, or damage by chipping (Hillson,

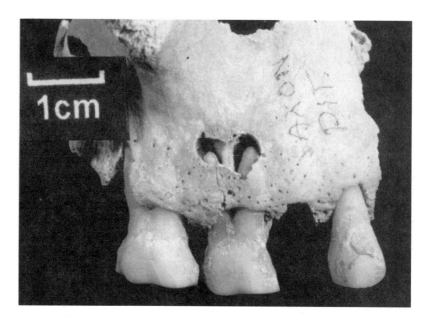

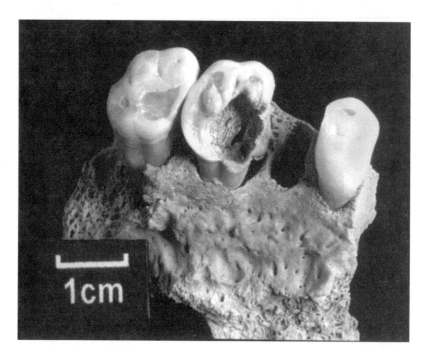

Figure 9.6 Two views of part of the right upper jaw from an Anglo-Saxon skull from Winchester, England. The lower view shows a gross gross lesion (so large that it cannot reliably be distinguished as coronal in origin), which has exposed the open root canal of the upper first molar. The second premolar next to it has been lost postmortem. The upper view shows the buccal side of the same specimen. The thinned buccal plate of the alveolar process has broken away (the sharp broken edge is clearly visible) to reveal the smooth cavities of two periapical granulomata around the apices of the buccal roots of the molar. There are eroded remnants of supragingival calculus on the crown and roots of the first molar and first premolar. (This specimen is in the collection of the Natural History Museum, London, and has been photographed with their kind permission.)

1996). From its original site of initiation (Thylstrup and Fejerskov, 1994), a lesion may progress from a white or brown spot into a cavity, which may in turn grow into the dentine, and ultimately penetrate the secondary dentine defenses of the pulp to expose the soft tissues of the pulp to infection. Untreated, this sequence seems in most cases to take many years. There are relatively few clinical studies of the development of caries in a living population where dental treatment is very limited (the so-called natural history of caries). What evidence there is (Baelum et al., 1993; Manji et al., 1988, 1989a, 1989b, 1990, 1991; Matthesen et al., 1990) suggests a lifelong development, with occlusal and approximal caries dominating in children and young adults, and these forms being replaced gradually by dentine caries and pulp exposure, loss of teeth (presumably through both extraction and periodontal disease), and root surface caries. This sequence is shown in caries statistics for the population as a whole, but reflects mostly the contribution of a relatively small, caries-prone, group of individuals.

Caries is more common in women than men, and shows a stronger age-related development (Larsen, 1997; Thylstrup and Fejerskov, 1994). Cheek teeth are more strongly affected by caries than canines and incisors, and upper teeth more than lower. The populations studied in this way are predominantly rural agriculturalists, but although studies in the 1940s and 1950s of recent hunter-gatherer groups suggest an equally age-related development, the nature and pattern of caries was greatly different. Among the Australian Aboriginal people (Barrett, 1953; Campbell, 1925; Campbell and Barrett, 1953; Campbell and Gray, 1936; Cran, 1959; Moody, 1960) and !Kung Bushmen (du Plessis, 1986; van Reenen, 1964, 1966) carious lesions of any type were rare in children and young adults, and caries was predominantly a disease of older adults associated with advanced wear, abrasions, and chipping of teeth. Until recently, East Greenland Inuit (Pedersen, 1938, 1947, 1966) ate no carbohydrates at all, and experienced almost no caries. It is not surprising that archaeological collections show a range of lesion types and distributions, reflecting the nature of the diet. Some, such as archaic Native Americans (Larsen, 1995, 1997) or Upper Palaeolithic/Mesolithic European material (Brothwell, 1963; Lubell et al., 1994), have heavy wear but very little evidence of caries and conform well to the hunter-gatherer model. Others, such as eighteenth century Londoners (Molleson and Cox, 1993), have slight wear and a pattern of caries similar to recent times. Still others, such as British Anglo-Saxon or Native American agriculturalists (Larsen, 1995, 1997), may have heavy wear in association with coronal caries in many adults.

Most modern studies of living people use the DMF score (a simple count of decayed, missing, or filled teeth) to summarize an individual's experiences of caries, and the mean DMF score to represent a caries index for the population (Thylstrup and Fejerskov, 1994). There are many difficulties with this approach, even in living populations, particularly when the study includes all age groups. Mean DMF score is not *prevalence* (Waldron, 1994) in epidemiological terms (the number of individuals affected divided by the overall number in the population), but is instead the average number of teeth per individual affected. It implicitly assumes that all populations have the same average starting number of teeth, that all missing teeth were lost due to a similar balance of caries and other factors, and that equivalent proportions of males and females, and different age groups, are present in the study groups. The latter assumption could be built into the selection of groups for modern clinical studies, although it makes for difficulties in comparing different studies, but it is an insuperable problem with archaeological collections where there is much less scope for control of selection. The other two assumptions are equally problematic, particularly when groups with widely differing diets and patterns of subsistence are compared. For archaeological and museum material, there is the added difficulty that many teeth are missing postmortem, simply because they have fallen out of the jaws, with no evidence whether or not they were carious.

However widespread they may be in the clinical literature, DMF scores are therefore not appropriate for archaeology. The most commonly used alternative is the percentage of teeth with caries out of the total in the collection (Hillson, in press). This takes some account of postmortem tooth loss, and has the advantage of allowing even isolated teeth to be used. It ignores, however, the varied survival of different tooth classes, which must have a profound effect on apparent caries rate because of the greatly differing susceptibilities of anterior and cheek teeth. The inclusion of isolated teeth makes it difficult to distinguish between males and females and, in its most common usage, the percentage of teeth does not distinguish between different age groups or types of carious lesions. For these reasons, the basic overall percentage is also inappropriate for archaeological material.

Various modifications have been proposed (Costa, 1980; Lukacs, 1995), but the fundamental development has been the work of Corbett and Moore (1976; Moore and Corbett, 1971, 1973, 1975), who recorded separate percentages for different lesion categories, different tooth classes, and different age groups. For each lesion category, they calculated the percentage out of the number of "teeth at risk" of developing that type of lesion, because these teeth retained the appropriate initiation sites (for example, only counting premolars and molars for occlusal fissure caries). They also introduced a separate category of "gross caries," where the lesion had removed so much of the crown that its original site of initiation could not be determined with any certainty. Their procedure has been proposed as the standard (Buikstra and Ubelaker, 1994) for presentation of caries statistics in anthropology, and it can be developed in a number of ways.

For this approach, the initiation site is the basic unit of recording rather than the tooth. In every tooth, for each individual, separate records are kept for the presence of occlusal fissures, enamel just below the approximal contact points, and cemento-enamel junction or exposed root surface. These are recorded as normal, bearing a white or stained spot (possibly a carious lesion), or bearing a clear cavity, and whether or not this cavity exposes dentine or the pulp chamber. Where the expected initiation site is missing or obscured for any reason (breakage, wear, calculus, or even a gross carious lesion), it is counted as absent because its status as a site of caries initiation is unknown. Gross caries is recorded as the combination of sites in which it might have been initiated—gross occlusal/approximal, gross coronal/CEJ, gross gross (when none of the crown is left to tell whether it was initiated there or in the roots). Both occlusal and approximal attrition have to be recorded, with the additional initiation sites that they open up through exposure of dentine. The scoring methods of Smith or Molnar (above) are suitable, although a new score needs to be added to describe the nature of these lesion sites. For interpreting root surface caries, it is useful to have some record of the exposure of root surfaces. In a modern clinical study, the exposure of roots by gingival recession would be noted (Fejerskov et al., 1993; Luan et al., 1989), but this is not possible in archaeological material because the position of the gingival margin cannot be reconstructed. Subgingival calculus deposits merely indicate the presence of a periodontal pocket, and it is not thought that carious lesions are initiated within such pockets. Where there is a band free of subgingival calculus at the cervix of the tooth, however, this may indicate the position of the gingival margin. The simplest way to keep a general record of root exposure in dry bone specimens is to take measurements from the cemento-enamel junction to the crest of the alveolar process with a graduated probe (Watson, 1986), without taking into account intra-bony defects (below). It needs to be made clear, however, that this does not correspond to the level of gingival attachment and such measurements can only be used on a comparative basis. In clinical radiography, 2 to 3 mm would be regarded as a normal value (Whaites, 1992), so this could be used as a cutoff point when tabulating root exposure against root surface caries.

Finally, some consideration needs to be given to antemortem tooth loss. This is important because, in a population where caries is common, the most heavily affected teeth are those that are lost due to extraction. The difficulty is that the cause of antemortem tooth loss cannot reliably be determined, and caries cannot be assumed. Postmortem and antemortem tooth loss, and potential factors that might initiate tooth loss, therefore need to be recorded as separate categories, in such a way that alternative causes can be assessed. For this reason, it is important that congenital absence of teeth, impaction, trauma, alveolar bone loss, and periapical bone loss are all recorded. These will be present, in any case, in any detailed dental study.

Diagnosis of caries is also a problem, although archaeology presents both advantages and added difficulties. Archaeological teeth are fully exposed and dry, may be rocked to one side in their sockets to show the approximal area, can be brightly lit from any direction, examined under a microscope, and X-rayed without restriction. They may, however, be subject to diagenetic changes that mimic caries (Fig. 9.4) (Poole and Tratman, 1978), and the patient cannot be asked a question for a history such as, "Did the tooth hurt or was it wobbly before you lost it?" Examination is by eye, with the aid of a low-power stereomicroscope and routine X rays, as used in trials of clinical methods on isolated teeth in the laboratory (Ekstrand et al., 1995). A sharp dental probe or explorer is unlikely to improve the diagnosis, and may indeed scratch delicate specimens (Penning et al., 1992). If a critical diagnosis must be confirmed, even at the expense of the specimen, relatively nondestructive sections may be made by impregnating a tooth in methylmethacrylate resin, cutting it open with a slow-speed saw, and then examining the polished surface for signs of dentine involvement and secondary dentine reaction in the pulp chamber using backscattered electron imaging in the scanning electron microscope or confocal light microscopy (Jones, 1987; Jones and Boyde, 1987). The methylmethacrylate can be removed in acetone, and only a thin layer at the center of the tooth is lost.

In diagnosis, the main difficulty is in recognizing the early stages of coronal caries, in which there is only a small opaque white (or brown) spot in the translucent enamel, with no evidence of a cavity or even surface roughness. Many clinical studies do not record such "incipient caries" because of the difficulty in attaining consistency between observers (Burt, 1997; Lussi, 1996). More recently it has been suggested that there are fewer interobserver problems than had been thought, and the exclusion of the incipient stage must underestimate caries considerably (Ismail, 1997). Where white or brown spots are recorded, it is probably best to note them as a separate category rather than including them in the overall caries statistics. Further difficulty arises in occlusal caries, where the initiation site may be very deep in the fissures (Ekstrand et al., 1995; Penning et al., 1992; Tveit et al., 1994). The lesion may progress to a cavity with little sign at the surface, and X rays are of limited use because of the convoluted nature of the (much more radiopaque) enamel in this part of the crown, so that they only record the lesion when the underlying dentine is significantly demineralized (Espelid et al., 1994). Nevertheless, a combination of microscope examination and X ray catches the majority of developing lesions in the fissures (Lussi, 1996). Most "stained fissure" lesions or minor cavities in the occlusal surface are accompanied by underlying dentine caries (Ekstrand et al., 1995).

A number of factors may predispose a tooth to caries. One of the best known relationships is between caries and enamel hypoplasia, where the defects act as lines of weakness through the enamel. The demineralization of dental caries occurs selectively along such lines, and may potentially reach the dentine faster than in sound enamel. Individuals with hypoplasia are therefore more likely to have dental caries (Mellanby, 1927). If hypoplasia is recorded in occlusal, mid-crown, and cervical parts of the crown as described above, this can be linked to the position of lesions on the crown.

Fluoride also needs to be considered, but poses much more difficult questions. The presence of fluoride ions in the hydroxyapatite crystal lattice of the enamel has an important inhibiting effect on caries, and fluoridation of the water supply together with fluoride additives in toothpaste are probably the main reasons for the reduction in dental caries in Europe and North America over recent years (Thylstrup and Fejerskov, 1994). High levels of fluoride during growth cause hypomineralized and hypoplastic defects in the enamel, but it is difficult to use these as an index of fluoridation (Fejerskov et al., 1988; Lukacs et al., 1985). Nor is it possible to use measurements of fluorine in the enamel, because the element is highly mobile in the soil and, indeed, gradually accumulates in buried bones and teeth. The best approach may be to consider present-day water analyses from the region, and assess the potential water supply for the people whose remains are being studied.

Bone Loss from the Alveolar Process

The alveolar process is a site of very active bone turnover and remodeling at all ages. Within the arch of the process in both jaws, the sockets (or alveolae) migrate slowly to allow changes in the position of the teeth in response to the developing occlusion and progress of wear. Even after the initial eruption of permanent teeth during childhood and young adulthood, they continue to erupt gradually throughout life (Fig. 9.7). Part of this is due to deposition of cement at the apex of the roots, but this is generally only a thin layer (although, see the discussion of hypercementosis below) and a more important factor seems to be the remodeling of the alveolar process, with migration of the sockets upward. Even where there is no bone loss due to periodontal disease, the cervical part of the root is progressively exposed with increasing age while the sockets become shallower. At the same time, the alveolar process stays at approximately the same height so that, in populations where there is little tooth wear, facial height increases with age (Whittaker et al., 1990).

There is some evidence to suggest that the rate of remodeling may adapt to the rate of wear, and that rapidly wearing teeth are accompanied by a more rapid rate of continuous eruption, which maintains the occlusal surfaces (and face as a whole) at a similar height through life (Whittaker et al., 1982, 1985). In addition to vertical migration of the sockets, there is mesial migration in response to approximal wear between teeth. Such "mesial drift" is a particular feature of the rapidly wearing dentitions of hunter-gatherers (Begg, 1954; Corruccini, 1991; Kaul and Corruccini, 1992). Another common feature in such dentitions is that teeth, together with their sockets, may become progressively inclined as the alveolar process remodels around them. As this takes place, the buccal/labial plate of cortical bone is often thinned so that there is a depression between the positions of each pair of sockets (Fig. 9.3). The combined socket and buccal plate may become so thin that an aperture exposes the root in dry bone specimens. If the aperture appears around the apex of the root, it is known as a fenestration, but if it simply extends as a notch down from the cervix it is called a dehiscence (Clarke and Hirsch, 1991; Muller and Perizonius, 1980). These are usually covered by soft tissue during life, although there may be a large area of exposed root surface in some cases. It is assumed that all these features relate to the forces (MacPhee and Cowley, 1975) acting upon the teeth. They may simply be the body's response to such forces, and may occur independently from any inflammatory processes, although in many cases the two probably influence one another.

One final factor that seems also to be common in the heavily worn teeth of hunter-gatherers is excessive deposition of cement around the apex and lower half of the roots (so-called hypercementosis, Figure 9.3). The grow-

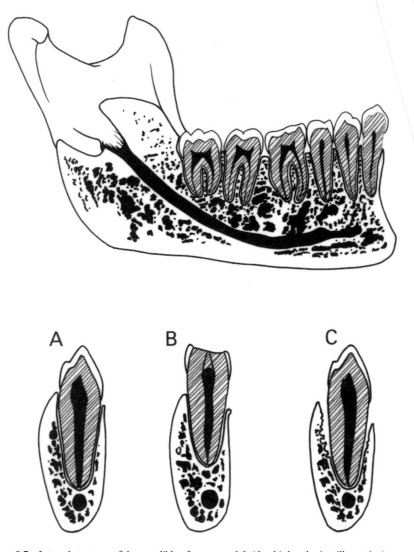

Figure 9.7   Internal structure of the mandible of a young adult (the third molar is still erupting), seen as a section along the mandibular body and showing the inferior alveolar canal as well as the interdental walls of bone between tooth sockets. Smaller diagrams A, B, and C are all transverse sections of the mandibular body at the position of a premolar. A is the form expected in a young adult, with little worn teeth and no evidence of periodontal disease. B is an older adult, in which there has been occlusal attrition and continuous eruption of the teeth so that the roots are exposed, and the apex is further away from the inferior alveolar canal, but the height of the body has not been diminished. C is a young adult in which periodontal disease has caused loss of the alveolar bone that lines the tooth socket. (Outlines of sections based upon diagrams in Brescia NJ. 1961. *Applied Dental Anatomy.* St. Louis: Mosby.)

ing mass of cement requires bone to be remodeled around it, and this may also be a factor in exposing the apical region of the root. Hypercementosis is found among older individuals in most populations (Soames and Southam, 1993), and it shows some relationship with the

forces acting on the teeth and to the presence of periapical inflammation.

Bone may also be lost from the alveolar process (Clarke and Hirsch, 1991; Hildebolt and Molnar, 1991) due to inflammation of the supporting tissues of the teeth (known as the

periodontal ssues). Two distinct types of
bone loss seen. One is the preferential removal of alveolar bone proper (Figs. 9.4
and 9.7 he lining of the sockets—in a narrow tr extending down from the tooth
cerv Kerr, 1991; Soames and Southam,
199 his relates to the condition known as
p ntal disease, which involves inflam-
of the gums and supporting tissues.
ther form of bone loss (Figs. 9.3 and
is concentrated around the apex of the
ts (Dias and Tayles, 1997), and relates to
-called periapical inflammation originating
infections of the pulp. Both forms are very
common in archaeological specimens, and
they may be so extensive that they are hard
to distinguish from one another. They may
also be difficult to distinguish from the general remodeling of the alveolar process described above.

Periodontal Disease

The microorganisms present in dental plaque
produce a variety of antigens that trigger an
immune response in the supporting tissues of
the teeth (Lehner, 1992; MacPhee and Cowley,
1975; Marsh and Martin, 1992; Schluger et al.,
1990). In most people's mouths there are at
least some areas of low-level inflammation in
the gums at all times. With long-standing
plaque deposits, there are intermittent local es-
calations of this inflammatory reaction in particular areas of the mouth. This higher level of
inflammatory response involves the underlying tissues, and disrupts the periodontal ligament that binds the roots into their sockets.
The continuity of fibers linking the cement of
the root surface with the alveolar bone of the
socket is broken, starting at the cervical part of
the root and extending gradually down toward
the apex. A so-called periodontal pocket forms
down the side of the root, and subgingival
plaque accumulates within it. Once the connection with the root is broken, the alveolar
bone is resorbed, and this is what causes the
characteristic pattern of bone loss. The condition as a whole is called periodontal disease
and, in its most common form, it is episodic in

nature, with intervals of inflammation alternating with periods of relative normality during adult life.

The loss of alveolar bone therefore progresses gradually, and eventually reaches the
point at which the tooth becomes unstable. This
mobility of teeth is characteristic of periodontal disease, and is the prelude to the eventual
loss of the teeth. Once the teeth have gone, the
dental plaque, the source of irritation, is also
lost and the lesion heals over. The underlying
bone develops a smooth surface, with no sign
that tooth sockets were ever there, and the alveolar process is greatly reduced in height. Periodontal disease particularly affects the molars,
and it is quite common to find mandibles in
which the anterior teeth are still present in a
high "prow" of bone, whereas the cheek tooth
area is much lower and smoothed over. This
pattern strongly suggests that periodontal disease had a major part in the loss of the teeth,
but it must be remembered that dental caries is
also common in populations with periodontal
disease, and molars are particularly affected by
it, so that teeth may also have been extracted
for this reason.

The initial phase of bone loss in periodontal
disease is a trenchlike removal of alveolar
bone around the cervix of a tooth. This tooth
loss may be monitored by examining the interdental walls (Fig. 9.4) that separate neighboring sockets (Kerr, 1991). In effect, these walls
are the combined alveolar bone of the sides of
the sockets, with the trabecular bone in between (Fig 9.7). The tops of these plates normally bulge up between incisors, or run level
between cheek teeth, and have a relatively
smooth cortical bone surface. When affected
by inflammation in the overlying soft tissues,
this surface becomes porotic. With a deeper
involvement of supporting tissues, the normal
contour of the plate is disrupted to create a
concave top with a sharp, ragged texture. Further development of the disease is marked by
increased loss of bone at the top of the interdental walls, making a deep, steep-sided
"intra-bony" defect. Phases of active inflammation are marked by the sharp, ragged tex-

ture, whereas quiescent phases are marked by a smoother but still porotic texture.

As more alveolar bone is lost, the surrounding trabecular bone and buccal and lingual cortical plates are also remodeled. This creates a more general reduction in the height of the alveolar process and, depending upon how many teeth are involved, may create a relatively regular outline ("horizontal bone loss") or a strongly irregular one. Karn et al. (1984) devised a classification to describe irregular defects. Alveolar bone is not necessarily lost equally around all sides of the roots, so they distinguished a "crater," which involved just one side, a "trench," which involved two or three sides (Fig. 9.4) and a "moat," involving all four sides. When both alveolar bone and outer cortical bone plates were lost, they distinguished a "ramp" with margins at different levels and a "plane" with margins all at a similar level. Thus, irregular defects may be used to suggest the presence of periodontal disease, particularly the crater, trench, and moat forms. Diagnosis of periodontal disease, however, is difficult even in the living, because no one feature is pathognomonic (uniquely diagnostic). In dry bone specimens there is also the difficulty of distinguishing the remodeling of the alveolar process, which relates to tooth wear, occlusal forces, and continuous eruption, and has nothing to do with periodontal disease. Where a large proportion of the alveolar process has been lost, it is additionally difficult to distinguish the defects of periapical inflammation.

Periapical Inflammation

When dental caries, attrition, and fracturing expose the pulp, microorganisms from the mouth enter and cause an inflammation of the pulp, or pulpitis (Dias and Tayles, 1997; Soames and Southam, 1993; Wood and Goaz, 1997). Sometimes this causes short bouts of sharp pain and is described as acute pulpitis, or it may cause longer bouts of dull pain and is described as chronic pulpitis. Some patients have no history of tooth/jaw pain. Indeed, the symptoms experienced may bear little relationship to the size or type of lesion in the pulp. A number of de-

fense mechanisms come into play, including deposition of secondary dentine, and the rate of progression of the lesion, which varies between individuals or even between different roots of a single molar. It is possible for the inflammation to resolve, but, with its narrow connection to the vascular system through the root apex, the ability of the pulp to heal is limited and the usual end result is that the tooth dies, right down the root canal to the apical foramen. This allows the products of inflammation, bacterial toxins, or perhaps bacteria themselves, to emerge from the foramen and initiate an inflammatory response in the tissues around the apex of the root (periapical inflammation). The response may cause severe pain from even the lightest pressure on the tooth, and is described as acute periapical periodontitis. In such cases, inflammatory exudate has accumulated in the periodontal ligament and, being noncompressible, may cause the tooth to protrude slightly. In some cases, pus is formed and the lesion becomes an acute abscess—even more painful. The pus drains through spaces in the bone, usually without causing changes detectable by radiography, and the inflammation resolves. Sometimes there is an area of diffuse bone loss (Goaz and White, 1994), which is reversed once the acute phase subsides.

Acute periapical lesions may pass into a more chronic phase of inflammation (or alternate with one), in which granulation tissue is produced around the apex of the root (a periapical granuloma). Chronic periapical periodontitis of this kind is usually symptomless, although there are often intervals when the tooth is sensitive to pressure. It is also possible for pulpitis to progress into a chronic periapical lesion without going through an acute phase. As the small mass of granulation tissue grows, bone is resorbed around the apex of the root, to create a smooth-walled chamber up to 3 mm or so in diameter (Dias and Tayles, 1997). This is detected in dental X rays as a radiolucency, which may be the first sign of the lesion. In dry bone specimens, such chambers may not be visible on the surface but, if remodeling has made the buccal plate of the alveolar process thin enough, they are often seen through a small opening—in effect a fenestration (Figs. 9.3 and 9.6). This can be enlarged in archaeological or museum specimens because the edges of such openings are thin and fragile.

A periapical granuloma may remain in this state for some considerable time without the patient being aware of it. It may, however, develop in two ways, making it more noticeable. One is the development of an apical periodontal cyst (also called a radicular cyst). This is a replacement of the granulation tissue by a fluid and results in progressive growth of the bone cavity. Differential diagnosis in dry bone specimens is only possible from the size of the cavity because, in both granuloma and cyst, the lining of the cavity is smooth. Most granulomata are small, less than 2 or 3 mm in diameter, and most cysts are larger than that although many remain less than 5 mm (Goaz and White, 1994). Looking at dry bone specimens, Dias and Tayles (1997) identified such cavities as granulomata when the diameter (measured from the side of the root) was 3 mm or less, and as cysts when larger. Radiology textbooks (Goaz and White, 1994; Whaites, 1992) use a 15 mm diameter as the dividing line for interpreting radiolucencies in X rays. The outer "shell" of a cyst may be very thin and can bulge outside the surface of the alveolar process, but it is frequently broken through in dry bone specimens. Periodontal (radicular) cysts are by far the most frequent type of cyst and are almost always associated with permanent teeth of adults, especially the upper anterior teeth. They may remain in the jaw after the tooth around which they were initiated has been extracted. It should be noted, however, that a variety of other cysts with very different origins may be found (Soames and Southam, 1993).

The other way in which a periapical granuloma may develop is through the accumulation of pus (a periapical abscess). In acute cases, this produces symptoms of pain, swelling of the gums, and sensitivity of the tooth to pressure, but here the pus usually migrates through the spaces in the alveolar process without leaving a clear track, and the lesion usually heals once the pus has discharged. Chronic cases result in an intermittent discharge of pus through a well-defined channel (commonly called a sinus or fistula) in the buccal plate of the alveolar process or, in some cases, through the lingual plate, into the nose or the maxillary sinus. Apart from this noxious discharge, a chronic periapical abscess is usually pain-free, and accounts of recent Australian aboriginals (Moody, 1960) suggest that they might well have been common amongst older people in the absence of dental treatment. In dry bone specimens, an abscess of this type can be difficult to distinguish from a granuloma, because the sinus takes the path of least resistance, which is often through the much-thinned buccal plate of the alveolar process. Where there is an opening of this kind, there may be no particular grounds for suggesting that it is an abscess sinus rather than the "window" of a granuloma exposed by remodeling, unless there is a clear tubelike hole with substantial walls instead of an edge of irregular, waferlike remnants of thinned cortical bone. At the apical end of the sinus in a chronic abscess, there may be a small cavity with rough walls (Dias and Tayles, 1997). Slightly roughened walls in a better defined cavity may be an acute abscess that developed in a granuloma or cyst. Larger areas of bone loss within a jaw (usually the cheek tooth area of the mandible), possibly associated with a sequestrum of dead bone, multiple sinuses, or cloacae, and subperiosteal new bone formation (involucrum) at the surface, are defined as osteomyelitis. They may originate in a periapical infection or compound fracture and are distinguished from a localized periapical abscess by their involvement of the marrow spaces of the bone (Goaz and White, 1994; Soames and Southam, 1993).

A periapical granuloma may be associated with hypercementosis. Even when not associated with inflammation of this kind, hypercementosis is accompanied by loss of bone around the apex of the root in order to accommodate its increased bulk. This may create a fenestration, but a granuloma is distinguished by the cavity that leaves a gap between the root and the alveolar bone of the socket.

Chronic periapical inflammation causes bone loss mostly at the apex but, unless this area of loss becomes very large or is located at the side of the root, leaves the crest of the alveolar process intact. Mechanically, therefore, it usually has less effect on the stability of a tooth than does periodontal disease. Loosening of teeth is not commonly associated with gross caries, pulpitis, or periapical inflammation, and bone loss around the apex is unlikely to lead on its own to tooth loss. There is a widespread idea that dental caries might be a major cause of antemortem tooth loss in ancient populations, but it is hard to see how this might work unless the teeth were deliberately extracted to treat acute pulpitis, or periapical bone loss became combined with loss from the crest of the alveolar process due to periodontal disease. It is also possible that the migration of the tooth sockets through the jaw, as part of the process of continuous eruption, might bring a small zone of periapical bone loss closer to the alveolar crest, and more general remodeling around it might seriously weaken support for the tooth. Another point of potential confusion is that the apical foramen may not be the only opening of a root canal. Some teeth have the so-called lateral canal emerging as a tiny foramen part way down the side of a root, and it is perfectly possible for a granuloma to be initiated around one of these without involving the root apex (Clarke, 1990; Clarke and Hirsch, 1991). The cavity of the granuloma is much closer to the crest of the alveolar process than one at the apex and, in such cases, may become exposed by remodeling to contribute to the loss of tooth support. Clarke and Hirsch (1991) have suggested that such "alveolar defects of pulpal origin" have been underestimated as a potential cause of tooth loss.

The main requirement for a comprehensive study of periapical inflammation is appropriate X rays (Goaz and White, 1994; Whaites, 1992). While many archaeological specimens display ample surface evidence, there are cases with apparent pulp exposure that show no such signs of periapical inflammation and have a granuloma deep inside. It can also be difficult to examine the walls of a chamber inside the alveolar process, even when there is an aperture open to the outside. Bright lights and a low-power stereomicroscope help, and it may be possible to withdraw the tooth slightly from the socket. No appropriate recording systems have been defined and it would seem best to make notes, with detailed photographs and X rays, including the evidence for pulp exposure (carious cavity, wear facet, or tooth fracture), size of radiolucency or visible chamber (radius measured from the side of the root), the texture of its wall, nature of any opening (bearing in mind that it may have been widened by postmortem damage), and the presence of any local resorption or new bone formation around it. Other important details might include general remodeling of the alveolar process, which might tend to expose granulomata, or evidence for alveolar bone loss relating to periodontal disease. Where the height of the process has been considerably reduced, it may be very difficult to determine the most important contributing cause.

The Place of Dental Palaeopathology in Archaeology

Few archaeologists would even dream about justifying a cemetery excavation on the basis of dental palaeopathology. This author is probably biased, but maybe they should. At a site where the artifactual finds are unexceptional and the bones fragmentary, the dental pathology may be the most exciting finding. However, teeth have a variable pattern of recovery in excavations and survival in storage and this may strongly affect the results. When a jaw is lifted from the ground, it needs to be checked by a knowledgeable eye to make sure that the full surviving set of teeth is lifted with it. Sifting the soil from around the jaws (with a relatively fine mesh) is another good idea, and any washing should automatically take place over a 1 mm sieve. Teeth do not always *look* particularly like teeth, especially when they are not fully formed, are heavily worn, or if a gross carious lesion has removed most of the crown. In such cases it can also be difficult to identify their type and position, even for a specialist. Errors at this point may have an important effect on the results of a palaeopathological study. Cleaning needs to be fairly gentle, with the minimum of soaking and no rough scrubbing, and teeth need to be allowed to dry slowly or they may split along natural lines of weakness. In a similar vein, the air in most storage areas is a little too dry for teeth and there is progressive damage over the years (the recommended relative humidity is 50–65%), particularly affecting dentine (the problem is even more intense for elephant and hippopotamus tusks). The anterior teeth sometimes fall out and may easily become lost, so it is wise to bag and label any loose teeth separately within the box (pierce small holes in plastic bags to keep the air circulating). The traditional skull box holds the lower jaw in occlusion, under the skull, and has probably contributed more to the damage of important dental pathology specimens than any other factor because the tooth crowns are crushed and chipped. It is better to bag or wrap the lower jaw separately within the box or, at the very least, provide a pad between the jaws. Crumpled-up acid-free tissue paper is a good way to stop loose bones rattling about.

For the future, some of the most pressing concerns involve methodology. Because of the way enamel hypoplasia is presented through the dentition, it is difficult to record in any simple, routine way that is likely to be consistent among all observers and that makes it possible to fit the defects into a framework of growth chronology. It seems likely that further development will involve the use of microscopy and the measurement of incremental structures on the crown surface, and some progress has been made already, but there are still awkward issues to resolve. These include the treatment of partially abraded teeth, where the general form of defects can be seen but little detail of incremental structures can be made out, the definition of the level of growth disruption that constitutes a recordable defect, and how to relate pit-form and plane-form defects to the sequence of tooth crown formation. All of this will involve a lot of careful histological work, particularly on thin sections of teeth, where the defects at the surface can be related directly to the sequence of development mapped out inside the crown. There is great potential for gaining from the study of enamel hypoplasia knowledge of what it was like to grow up in past human communities, but there are many pitfalls and it requires a very careful approach.

For the plaque-related diseases, the challenge is to view the dental records of museum and site collections in relation to the modern clinical knowledge of the natural history of these conditions. To do this, appropriate records need to be made and bioarchaeologists need to be very clear-sighted about what factors may influence the statistics they compile. An archaeological collection is very different from a sample of living patients in a clinical study, and it can be difficult to keep this in view at all times. Biological age estimates must be recognized, and different sexes and age groups need to be distinguished. In particular, tooth wear was a major factor in caries development in past populations and, if wear is used for age estimation, this produces a circular argument. The relationship between caries and wear is inadequately addressed in modern clinical studies, and this should be a priority for archaeologists because it seems to be a fundamental part of changing dental function with the adoption of agriculture.

Another priority in archaeology should be to ensure that records distinguish between the different types of carious lesions, and between different classes of teeth, in a consistent way. This is important for interpretation, not only because the different types have contrasting causes, but also because their rates vary between tooth classes and are therefore strongly affected by differential preservation. This chapter concludes with an appendix that lists some suggestions for the way in which recording might be extended. Many will no doubt feel that it is complicated, but it is important to realize that many past studies have not recorded caries in enough detail to make the data interpretable. Even if the level of detail is increased, there are still issues of diagnosis that need to be addressed. Researchers need to be clear about what they are recording. There is in any case clinical discussion of the level of lesions to record, and archaeology has the additional problems of diagenetic change, which commonly produces dark stains and erosions of its own. This is an area where careful work is still required because, if observers differ in what they record and false lesions are not recognized, the caries statistics will be worth nothing. The future challenge to bioarchaeology is therefore to produce basic records, statistical analyses, and interpretations of dental disease that, while they cannot be compared directly with modern clinical studies because of the different nature of the collection of dentitions studied, can at least stand beside them under rigorous scrutiny.

Providing that care is taken so that the surviving specimens of teeth and jaws really do represent what was preserved in the ground, the distribution of dental disease is a valuable source of evidence for the activities and subsistence of a past population. In a society with limited artifactual technology, the dentition is an important piece of equipment, used for making objects and handling materials, as well as for preparing food and eating it. Even emotional state can have an effect—abnormally heavy wear is now common among stressed-out young business people who habitually hold their jaws clamped together. The advent of arable agriculture and the type of staple crop grown, its consistency, and carbohydrate and protein content all leave their mark as a clear horizon in the frequency and type of dental caries and periodontal disease, as well as the pattern of tooth wear. Dental pathology should have a central place in many discussions of change in subsistence and technology. It fits well with evidence derived from the analysis of stable isotopes, artifactual evidence for the gathering, production, and processing of food and the remains of food animals and plants.

APPENDIX: SUGGESTED SCORING SYSTEMS FOR CARIES AND PERIODONTAL DISEASE

The following detailed system is proposed in Hillson (in press), as an extension of the standard methods recommended elsewhere (Buikstra and Ubelaker, 1994). Experience in the field and the museum has shown that it is better to record pathology on paper rather than directly into a database, because this is more secure (allowing for dust, mistakes, theft, power supply fluctuations, etc.) and enables nonstandard features both to be drawn and described in words. Some kind of recording sheet helps. It is, however, sensible to transfer the scores and measurements to a computer database regularly, otherwise the task becomes overwhelming. The database can have a field for each of the categories below, so that each tooth has one record that is identified by a code for the individual and an FDI code for the tooth (Fédération Dentaire Internationale, 1971; Hillson, 1996). This makes it possible to extract information either by tooth type or by individual.

The scores in the list below are numbered to match across different categories, so some of the numbers are missing in particular categories where the scores do not match in this way (e.g., "Presence/Absence of Tooth," below). To the list below, it will be necessary to add general information such as an identification code and aging and sexing data. It is far better to record all the original data, such as measurements, pubic symphysis scores, and so on, rather than a simple diagnosis of male/female and age. The age/sex diagnosis is vital for interpreting the pathological data, but is a matter of opinion and should be capable of being questioned.

Presence/Absence of Tooth, and Score for Gross Gross Caries

Use the following scores for gross gross caries and to record presence or absence of a tooth:

BLANK = missing postmortem and jaw with socket also missing

0 = tooth present, without gross gross caries

7 = gross gross carious cavity, involving the loss of so much of the tooth that it is not possible to determine whether the lesion was initiated in the crown or root

8 = gross gross carious cavity, defined as in 7 above, in which there is a clear opening into an exposed pulp chamber or root canal

10 = tooth missing, leaving an empty socket in the jaw without any sign of remodeling (postmortem tooth loss)

11 = tooth missing, leaving an empty cavity in which there are signs of remodeling, but the bone is not fully remodeled to a level contour

12 = tooth missing, with full remodeling of the jaw to leave a level contour

13 = no evidence that the tooth has ever erupted (due to young age, impaction, or agenesis)

14 = tooth partly erupted (crypt communicating with crest of alveolar process, or tooth not yet in wear)

15 = anomalous eruption, so that the tooth has not reached its normal position in the tooth row.

Supragingival Calculus

Refer to the Brothwell (1981) score. Where the level of the gingival margin has been lowered, there may be supragingival calculus on the root as well as the crown, and Brothwell's maximum score of 3 can be applied.

Occlusal Surface Caries in Premolars and Molars

Scores for the fissure system, groove and fossa sites in the occlusal surface follow. Count the whole occlusal fissure system of each premolar or molar as one site when any part of it remains and can be seen unobscured. Score the most developed lesion, if there is more than one.

BLANK = sites missing for any reason, or fully obscured

0 = sites present but enamel is translucent and with a smooth surface

1 = white or stained opaque area in enamel of fissure/groove/fossa with smooth and glossy or matte surface

2 = white or stained opaque area with associated roughening or slight surface destruction

3 = small cavity where there is no clear evidence that it penetrates to the dentine

5 = larger cavity that clearly penetrates the dentine

6 = large cavity that was clearly initiated in a fissure/groove/fossa site within the occlusal surface (it does *not* involve the contact areas), within the floor of which is the open pulp chamber or open root canals

7 = gross coronal caries involving the occlusal crown surface *and* a contact area or pit

8 = gross coronal caries, defined as in score 7 above, within the floor of which is the open pulp chamber or open root canals

Caries in Pit Sites of Molars and Upper Incisors

Score each discrete pit present. Not all dentitions have them, but there is often one buccal pit on molars and sometimes a lingual pit tucked in above the lingual tubercle of upper incisors (rarely canines). It would be uncommon for there to be more than one pit site per tooth, but it can happen.

BLANK = pit site not present or not visible (for any reason)

0 = site or sites present but enamel is translucent and with a smooth surface

1 = white or stained opaque area in enamel of pit with smooth and glossy or matte surface

2 = white or stained opaque area with associated roughening or slight surface destruction

3 = small cavity where there is no clear evidence that it penetrates to the dentine

5 = larger cavity that clearly penetrates the dentine

6 = large cavity that was clearly initiated in a pit site, within the floor of which is the open pulp chamber or open root canals

7 = gross coronal caries involving a pit and the occlusal crown surface (see "Occlusal Sur-

face Caries in Premolars and Molars" scores of 6 and 7 above)

8 = gross coronal caries, defined as in score 7, within the floor of which is the open pulp chamber or open root canals

Occlusal Attrition Score

The Smith (1984) system is simplest to use.

BLANK = occlusal surface not present, or obscured, for any reason

1–8 = Smith attrition stage

10 = tooth fractured, leaving a surface that shows some wear

Occlusal Attrition Facet Dentine Caries and Pulp Exposure

Count whole facet as one site, and record the most severe lesion if there is more than one.

BLANK = worn dentine surface either not yet exposed, missing, or obscured (for whatever reason)

0 = dentine exposed in occlusal attrition facet but without any stained areas or cavitation

4 = stained area of dentine and/or enamel that may or may not be a carious lesion

5 = clear cavity in dentine

6 = pulp chamber, exposed in the attrition facet, that is stained or appears to have been modified by the development of a cavity

8 = exposed pump chamber in which there is no sign of either staining or irregular formation of a cavity

Occlusal Attrition Facet Enamel Edge Chipping and Caries

This category may only be important in some collections—particularly hunter-gatherer groups. Count the enamel rim of the attrition facet as one site, because there may be many small areas of chipping around it.

BLANK = worn enamel rim not yet exposed at any point on the perimeter of the occlusal surface, missing or obscured (for whatever reason)

0 = enamel rim of occlusal attrition facet exposed at any point, but intact with no chipping

1 = chipping that appears to be postmortem in origin

2 = chipping that appears to be antemortem but is not affected by caries

3 = chipping associated with carious lesion

7 = gross carious lesion (scores 7 or 8 in "Occlusal Surface Caries," "Occlusal Attrition Facet Caries," "Pit Caries," "Contact Area Caries") involving the enamel rim of the occlusal facet but not clearly associated with any chipping

8 = gross carious lesion as defined in score 7, involving the enamel rim, within the floor of which is the open pulp chamber or open root canals

Approximal Attrition Facet Measurement

In the occlusal plane, the maximum buccolingual breadth of the facet (measured in millimeters with needle-point calipers). See Hinton (1982). Enter separate measurement for mesial and distal sides of each tooth.

Mesial and Distal Approximal Attrition Score

Enter separate score for mesial and distal sides of each tooth.

BLANK = contact point missing (for whatever reason)

0 = no attrition facet around contact point

1 = approximal attrition facet confined to the enamel

2 = approximal attrition facet exposing dentine at its center

3 = approximal attrition facet exposes dentine all the way down to the cemento-enamel junction (CEJ)

4 = occlusal attrition has proceeded down into the roots of the teeth so that there is no longer any contact between neighboring teeth

Mesial and Distal Contact Area Caries

Enter separate score for mesial and distal sides of each tooth.

BLANK = contact area missing or not visible (for any reason)

0 = contact area present but enamel is translucent with a smooth surface (and any exposed dentine is unstained and not cavitated)

1 = white or stained opaque area in enamel with smooth glossy or matte surface (or stained patch in dentine)

2 = white or stained opaque area of enamel with associated roughening or slight surface destruction

3 = small enamel cavity where there is no clear evidence that it penetrates to the dentine

4 = discoloration in exposed dentine of an approximal attrition facet

5 = larger enamel cavity that clearly penetrates the dentine (or clear cavity in dentine of approximal attrition facet)

6 = large cavity, clearly initiated in the contact area or approximal attrition facet, within the floor of which is the open pulp chamber or open root canals

7 = gross cavity in the contact area or approximal attrition facet that involves neighboring occlusal sites ("Occlusal Surface Caries," "Occlusal Attrition Facet Caries" above) and/or root surface sites (below)

8 = gross cavity, defined as in score 7, within the floor of which is the open pulp chamber or open root canals

Buccal/Labial and Lingual Enamel Smooth Surface Caries Site

This is a single site, just above the margin of the gingivae in life. Count as present only when it is clearly separate from the CEJ and score only if the lesion clearly does not involve the CEJ, the fissure system, a pit, or any worn occlusal attrition facet. This is rare in archaeological material.

BLANK = site not present or not visible (for any reason)

0 = site present but enamel is translucent with a smooth surface

1 = white or stained opaque area in enamel with smooth and glossy or matte surface

2 = white or stained opaque area with associated roughening or slight destruction of the enamel surface

3 = small enamel cavity where there is no clear evidence that it penetrates to the dentine

5 = larger cavity that clearly penetrates the dentine

6 = large cavity that has exposed the open pulp chamber, still without involving the CEJ

7 = gross cavity that involves neighboring occlusal sites and/or root surface sites

8 = gross cavity, defined as in score 7, within the floor of which is the open pulp chamber or open root canals

Root Surface Caries

Count one site per buccal/labial, lingual, mesial, or distal surface of each tooth, and score separately for each. The site may run into other root surface sites.

BLANK = no part of root surface or CEJ preserved, or at least not visible if present

0 = root surface/CEJ present and visible with no evidence of staining or cavitation

1 = area of darker staining along CEJ or on root surface

5 = shallow cavity (stained or unstained) following the line of the CEJ, or confined to the surface of the root

6 = cavity involving the CEJ or root surface alone, within the floor of which is the open pulp chamber or open root canals

7 = gross cavity, including the CEJ or root surface, that involves the neighboring contact area site, occlusal sites, or occlusal attrition facet sites (above)

8 = gross cavity, defined as in score 7, within the floor of which is the open pulp chamber or open root canals

Root Exposure on Buccal/Labial, Lingual, Mesial, and Distal Sides

Maximum vertical measurement (to the nearest millimeter) from the CEJ to the alveolar bone lining socket, using a graduated periodontal probe, made separately for each side of the root. If there is an "intra-bony" defect (crater, trench, or moat in the terms of Karn and colleagues [1984]), do not take the measurement down into the defect. Do not take the measurement if there is evidence that the alveolar process has been damaged postmortem. The presence on the root surface of subgingival calculus in association with specifically alveolar bone loss, or supragingival calculus where there has been more general bone loss, can confirm that the roots were exposed antemortem. If wear has proceeded down into the root, take the maximum exposure, either to the occlusal wear facet or to the CEJ (if present), whichever is the greatest.

Subgingival Calculus on Buccal/Labial, Lingual, Mesial, and Distal Sides

Maximum extent (measured to the nearest millimeter) of subgingival calculus deposit, down the long axis of the root from the CEJ, separately for each side of the root. There is usually a calculus-free space along the CEJ, but this is irregular and it is simplest to ignore it.

General Remodeling of the Buccal and Lingual Plates

There are no published standards for describing the thinning of the buccal and lingual cortical plates of the alveolar process, which forms part of the process of remodeling for continuous eruption and occlusal adaptation. The changes are usually more common in the buccal plate than the lingual plate.

Thinning of the Buccal Plate

The main surface manifestation of buccal plate thinning is that pronounced grooves develop on the surface of the alveolar process, between the

roots. In advanced cases, the whole outline of the roots can be clearly made out through the thin "skin" of bone. Some roots are in any case particularly prominent, most notably the upper canines, followed by the upper incisors, but the level of prominence becomes much greater. At the same time, the bone around the cervix of the tooth shows wafer thin against the root, rather than making a stout edge.

Dehiscence

A dehiscence is a V-shaped opening in the alveolar process, extending down a root from the cervix of the tooth (Clarke and Hirsch, 1991; Muller and Perizonius, 1980). It may be deep or shallow, narrow or wide. The margins are usually wafer thin. A dehiscence is believed to represent part of the process of remodeling in adaptation to changing occlusion and functional load (MacPhee and Cowley, 1975). Care must be taken to distinguish it from postmortem damage (look for a sharp edge with a different color), and from irregular defects of periodontal disease (look for involvement of the alveolar bone in the socket either side).

Fenestration

A fenestration is similar to a dehiscence, but is a circumscribed opening, further down the root (Clarke and Hirsch, 1991; Muller and Perizonius, 1980). It may expose a granuloma, and it is important to distinguish it from the sinus of an abscess (defined below).

Hypercementosis

Hypercementosis is common in heavy wear populations, where the alveolar process is usually strongly remodeled in later life. The irregular swelling of the apical half of the roots is accommodated by resorption, and they may be exposed in a fenestration or dehiscence. Hypercementosis can also be detected in X rays as a swollen and irregular root.

Marginal Lipping

Many archaeological collections of jaws show a ridge along the buccal margin of the crest of the alveolar process, in the cheek tooth region of the mandible. This may become quite sharp and prominent. It is accentuated by the alveolar bone loss of periodontal disease, but is thought to be more an adaptation to changing occlusion and the functional loads placed on the jaw (Clarke and Hirsch, 1991; Newman and Levers, 1979).

Periapical Bone Loss

Various descriptive terms can be used, and it is important to distinguish between the different ways in which an area of bone loss is exposed to view. Both direct observation and X-ray interpretation are ideally used.

Visible Periapical Cavity

Defined as a cavity around the apex of a root, or roots in multirooted teeth. Occasionally seen at the side of a root, where there is a lateral canal and foramen.

Visibility
- visible through an opening in the thinned buccal or lingual wall of the alveolar process (that is, not a clear sinus)
- seen through a sinus
- seen upon extracting the tooth from its socket
- seen through a postmortem break in the bone (look for a line of different colored bone along the break)

Location
- most granulomata are at the apex of one or more roots of a tooth
- some occur in relation to a lateral canal part way up the root
- others may be up toward the cervical part of the root (Clarke and Hirsch, 1991)

Size
- less than 3-mm diameter (make allowance for root apex protruding into cavity)

- more than 3-mm diameter
- more than 15-mm diameter

Wall of Cavity
- smooth and well demarcated
- slightly roughened
- clearly roughened, with a ragged margin

Sinus
Defined as a well-demarcated tube or opening, with substantial walls, that is clearly cutting through the bone cortex rather than representing a thinning of the cortical plate—most apertures around the apex are probably not a sinus but a fenestration. Care needs to be taken to recognize an opening made or enlarged by postmortem damage. A sinus may have new bone deposition around its point of emergence, which can be

- through the buccal/labial or lingual plate of the alveolar process
- through the angle of the palatine process of the maxilla into the floor of the nose
- into the maxillary sinus
- onto the buccal or lingual aspect of the mandibular body

Interpretation
Following the diagnostic criteria of Dias and Tayles (1997), a periapical granuloma is a small cavity (<3 mm) with smooth walls, a cyst is a larger cavity of the same type, an acute abscess developing in a granuloma or cyst shows as a slight roughening of the wall, and a chronic abscess is a small cavity with rougher, more ill-defined walls and a sinus, while a larger cavity of this type is identified as chronic osteomyelitis (it may also have multiple cloacae, sequestra, and involucrum).

Periapical Radiolucency

The following terminology is from Whaites (1992) and Goaz and White (1994). Care needs to be taken because the size and prominence of the radiolucency depends to some extent on the projection of the image, and the presence of other spaces such as the maxillary sinus.

Normal

The root and apex are outlined by a narrow radiolucent band that represents the space occupied in life by the periodontal ligament. This may be narrower in archaeological specimens because the ligament is no longer in position. Outside the ligament space is a thin, clearly demarcated line of radiopacity (called the lamina dura) marking the position of the alveolar bone lining the socket. Between adjacent sockets, and within the body of the alveolar process, an irregular, dense granular texture of radiopacity is created by the trabeculae (particularly large trabeculae may sometimes be visible individually, especially in the mandible).

Ligament Space

In living patients, the edema of acute inflammation within the ligament causes the space to increase as the tooth protrudes out of the socket. Clearly, in archaeological specimens, this is not a useful consideration.

Lamina Dura

As bone is resorbed, there is local loss of the radiopaque line of the lamina, and this may be apparent without a wider area of radiolucency.

Radiolucency

Within the trabecular texture surrounding the lamina dura, there may be a radiolucency of varying size and shape. It may be circular to pear-shaped, and centered on the apex of a root (occasionally the side), or more widespread. It may be diffuse, without clear margins, or sharply defined with a clear radiopaque line around the margin.

Sclerosis

Thickening of trabeculae and deposition of isolated areas of denser bone are seen as patches of radiopacity. Sometimes, individual trabeculae may be made out, and the area of opacity as a whole may be diffuse or clearly defined. It may occur right next to the lamina dura of the

apex or root side, or around the edge of a radiolucency. Occasionally, sclerotic patches occur adjacent to teeth that do not have any evidence of pulp exposure—the cause is unknown.

Secondary Dentine

There is no difference in opacity between primary and secondary dentine, but the pulp chamber/root canal size is reduced, starting at its root (infilling of the horns or diverticles), followed by more general reduction in width. The chamber/canal may appear to be infilled completely, but there may still be a thread of living pulp running down the root, so it cannot be assumed necessarily that the tooth is dead.

Interpretation

Well-defined circular or pear-shaped radiolucencies centered on a root apex are most likely to be granulomata or radicular cysts and, of these, granulomata are very much the most common cause. It is not possible to distinguish cysts from granulomata radiographically (Wood and Goaz, 1997) because they do not differ in overall appearance and overlap considerably in the diameter of the radiolucency. Cysts, however, do tend to be larger, and a radiolucency that is 16 mm or more in diameter is more likely to be a cyst than a granuloma. Sclerosis is taken to be evidence of chronicity of the infection. A periapical abscess may not give rise to any radiographic features, but they are present in about 2% of radiolucencies. In such situations it is usually considered that a granuloma or cyst was present before the abscess developed. In chronic abscesses, the border of the radiolucency may become poorly defined. Osteomyelitis (involving the marrow spaces of the bone) is almost always confined to the cheek tooth area of the mandible, and is seen as a much larger, diffuse, ragged radiolucency with a "moth-eaten" appearance.

Deformities of the Alveolar Process

Use letter scores (C, T, R, P, CR, and RC) from Karn et al. (1984). See Hillson (1996).

Approximal Wall Defect Score

Use number scores from Kerr (1991). See Hillson (1996).

Presentation of Caries Rates

Caries percentages should be calculated separately for each site (or combination of sites in the case of gross caries), and for each tooth type (left and right sides can be combined). Males and females and different age groups need to be tabulated separately. The tables are big, because separate percentages also need to be presented for opacities/stains, cavities, dentine penetration, and pulp exposure. A minimum list of categories could then include:

1. Occlusal caries as a percentage of fissure and fossa occlusal sites surviving.

2. Occlusal attrition facet caries as a percentage of facets present.

3. Pit caries as a percentage of pit sites preserved.

4. Smooth surface caries as a percentage of sites preserved (combine buccal and lingual figures).

5. Contact area caries as a percentage of contact area sites surviving (combine mesial and distal figures).

6. Root surface caries as a percentage of root surface sites preserved (combine mesial, distal, buccal, and lingual figures). Tabulate root surface exposure separately.

7. Gross occlusal caries as a percentage of occlusal crown surfaces surviving (worn or unworn, one per tooth).

8. Gross occlusal/contact area caries as a percentage of the number of mesial or distal crown elements surviving (two per tooth).

9. Gross root surface/contact area caries as a percentage of the number of mesial or distal tooth elements surviving (two per tooth).

10. Gross root surface/contact area/occlusal caries as a percentage of the number of mesial or distal tooth elements surviving (two per tooth).

11. Gross gross caries as a percentage of teeth surviving.

REFERENCES

Alexandersen V. 1967. The pathology of the jaws and temporomandibular joint. In: Brothwell DR, Sandison AT, editors. Diseases in Antiquity. Springfield, Ill.: Charles C. Thomas. pp. 551–595.

Bäckmann B. 1989. Amelogenesis Imperfecta. An Epidemiologic, Genetic, Morphologic and Clinical Study. University of Umeä, Sweden: Departments of Pedodontics and Oral Pathology.

Baelum V, Luan W-M, Chen X, Fejerskov O. 1993. Predictors of tooth loss over 10 years in adult and elderly Chinese. Community Dent Oral Epidemiol 25:204–210.

Barrett MJ. 1953. Dental observations on Australian Aborigines: Yuendumu, Central Australia, 1951–52. Aust J Dentistry 57:127–138.

Begg PR. 1954. Stone Age man's dentition. Am J Orthod 40:298–312, 373–383, 462–475, 517–531.

Bercy P, Frank RM. 1980. Microscopie electronique a balayage de la plaque dentaire et du tartre a la surface du cement humain. J Biol Buccale 8:299–313.

Bermúdez de Castro JM, Arusaga JL, Perez P-J. 1997. Interproximal grooving in the Atapuerca-SH hominid dentitions. Am J Phys Anthropol 102:369–376.

Bermúdez de Castro JM, Bromage TG, Jalvo YF. 1988. Buccal striations on fossil human anterior teeth: evidence of handedness in the middle and early Upper Pleistocene. J Hum Evol 17:403–412.

Berten J. 1895. Hydopolasie des Schmelzes (Congenitale Schmelzdefecte; Erosionen). Deutsche Monatsschrift für Zahnheilkunde 13:425–439, 483–498, 533–548, 587–606.

Beynon AD. 1987. Replication techniques for studying microstructure in fossil enamel. Scanning Microsc 1:663–669.

Bowen WH, Pearson SK. 1993. Effect of milk on cariogenesis. Caries Res 27:461–466.

Boyde A, Jones SJ. 1983. Backscattered electron imaging of dental tissues. Anat Embryol 15:145–150.

Brothwell DR. 1963. The macroscopic dental pathology of some earlier human populations. In: Brothwell DR, editor. Dental Anthropology. London: Pergamon Press. pp. 272–287.

Brothwell DR. 1981. Digging Up Bones. London: British Museum and Oxford University Press.

Brown T. 1991. Interproximal grooving: different appearances, different etiologies, reply to Dr. Formicola. Am J Phys Anthropol 86:86–87.

Brown T, Molnar S. 1990. Interproximal grooving and task activity in Australia. Am J Phys Anthropol 81:545–553.

Buikstra JE, Ubelaker DH, editors. 1994. Standards for data collection from human skeletal remains. Fayetteville: Arkansas Archeological Survey.

Burt BA. 1997. How useful are cross-sectional data from surveys of dental caries. Community Dent Oral Epidemiol 25:36–41.

Campbell TD. 1925. Dentition and palate of the Australian Aboriginal. Adelaide: University of Adelaide.

Campbell TD, Barrett MJ. 1953. Dental observations on Australian Aborigines: a changing environment and pattern. Aust Dent J 57:1–6.

Campbell TD, Gray JH. 1936. Observations on the teeth of Australian Aborigines. Aust J Dentistry 40:290–295.

Clark DH, editor. 1992. Practical Forensic Odontology. Oxford: Wright.

Clarke NG. 1990. Periodontal defects of pulpal origin: evidence in early man. Am J Phys Anthropol 82:371–376.

Clarke NG, Hirsch RS. 1991. Physiological, pulpal, and periodontal factors influencing alveolar bone. In: Kelley MA, Larsen CS, editors. Advances in Dental Anthropology. New York: Wiley-Liss. pp. 241–266.

Commission on Oral Health. 1982. An epidemiological index of developmental defects of dental enamel (DDE Index). Int Dent J 32:159–167.

Cook DC. 1980. Hereditary enamel hypoplasia in a prehistoric Indian child. J Dental Res 59:1522.

Corbett ME, Moore WJ. 1976. Distribution of dental caries in ancient British populations: IV. The 19th century. Caries Res 10:401–414.

Corruccini RS. 1991. Anthropological aspects of profacial and occlusal variations and anomalies. In: Kelley MA, Larsen CS, editors. Advances in Dental Anthropology. New York: Wiley-Liss. pp. 295–323.

Costa RL. 1980. Incidence of caries and abscesses in archeological Eskimo skeletal samples from Point Hope and Kodiak Island, Alaska. Am J Phys Anthropol 52:501–514.

Cottone JA, Standish SM, editors. 1981. Outline of Forensic Dentistry. Chicago: Year Book Medical Publishers.

Cran JA. 1959. The relationship of diet to dental caries. Aust Dent J 4:182–190.

Cybulski JS. 1994. Culture change, demographic history, and health and disease on the Northwest Coast. In: Larsen CS, Milner GR, editors. In the Wake of Contact. Biological Responses to Conquest. New York: Wiley-Liss. pp. 75–86.

Dean MC, Beynon AD. 1991. Histological reconstruction of crown formation times and initial root formation times in a modern human child. Am J Phys Anthropol 86:215–228.

Dias G, Tayles N. 1997. "Abscess cavity"—a misnomer. Int J Osteoarchaeol 7:548–554.

du Plessis JB. 1986. Prevalence of dental caries in !Kung Bushmen of Bushmanland. J Dent Assoc S Afr 41:535–537.

Ekstrand KR, Kuzmina I, Bjørndal L, Thylstrup A. 1995. Relationship between external and histologic features of progressive stages of caries in the occlusal fossa. Caries Res 29:243–250.

Eliot MM, Souther SP, Anderson BG, Arnim SS. 1934. A study of the teeth of a group of school children previously examined for rickets. Am J Dis Children 48:713.

Espelid I, Tveit AB, Fjelltveit A. 1994. Variations among dentists in radiographic detection of occlusal caries. Caries Res 28:169–175.

Fédération Dentaire Internationale 1975. Two-digit system of designating teeth. Int Dent J 21: 104–106.

Fejerskov O, Baelum V, Østergaard ES. 1993. Root caries in Scandinavia in the 1980's and future trends to be expected in dental caries experience in adults. Adv Dent Res 7:4–14.

Fejerskov O, Manji F, Baelum V. 1988. Dental Fluorosis—A Handbook for Health Workers. Copenhagen: Munksgaard.

Formicola V. 1991. Interproximal grooving: different appearances, different etiologies. Am J Phys Anthropol 86:85–86; discussion 86–87.

Fox CL. 1992. Information obtained from the microscopic examination of cultural striations in human dentition. Int J Osteoarchaeol 2:155–169.

Fox CL, Frayer DW. 1997. Non-dietary marks in the anterior dentition of the Krapina neanderthals. Int J Osteoarchaeol 7:133–149.

Fox CL, Pérez-Pérez A. 1994. Cutmarks and *postmortem* striations in fossil human teeth. Hum Evol 9:165–172.

Frayer DW. 1991. On the etiology of interproximal grooves. Am J Phys Anthropol 85:299–304.

Frayer DW, Russell MD. 1987. Artificial grooves on the Krapina neanderthal teeth. Am J Phys Anthropol 74:393–405.

Friskopp J. 1983. Ultrastructure of nondecalcified supragingival and subgingival calculus. J Periodont 54:542–550.

Friskopp J, Hammarstrom L. 1980. A comparative, scanning electron microscopic study of supragingival and subgingival calculus. J Periodont 51:553–562.

Goaz PW, White SC. 1994. Oral Radiology. Principles and Interpretation. St. Louis: C. V. Mosby.

Goodman AH, Armelagos GJ, Rose JC. 1980. Enamel hypoplasias as indicators of stress in three prehistoric populations from Illinois. Hum Biol 52:515–528.

Goodman AH, Martinez C, Chavez A. 1991. Nutritional supplementation and the development of linear enamel hypoplasias in children from Tezonteopan, Mexico. Am J Clin Nutr 53:773–781.

Goodman AH, Rose JC. 1990. Assessment of systemic physiological perturbations from dental enamel hypoplasias and associated histological structures. Yrbk Phys Anthropol 33:59–110.

Goodman AH, Thomas RB, Swedlund AC, Armelagos GJ. 1988. Biocultural perspectives of stress in prehistoric, historical and contemporary population research. Yrbk Phys Anthropol 31:169–202.

Hildebolt CF, Molnar S. 1991. Measurement and description of periodontal disease in anthropological studies. In: Kelley MA, Larsen CS, editors. Advances in Dental Anthropology. New York: Wiley-Liss. pp. 225–240.

Hillson SW. 1986. Teeth. Cambridge: Cambridge University Press.

Hillson SW. 1992a. Dental enamel growth, perikymata and hypoplasia in ancient tooth crowns. J R Soc Med 85:460–466.

Hillson SW. 1992b. Impression and replica methods for studying hypoplasia and perikymata on human tooth crown surfaces from archaeological sites. Int J Osteoarchaeol 2:65–78.

Hillson SW. 1992c. Studies of growth in dental tissues. In: Lukacs JR, editor. Culture, Ecology and Dental Anthropology. Delhi: Kamla-Raj Enterprises. pp. 7–23.

Hillson SW. 1993. Histological studies of ancient tooth crown surfaces. In: Davies WV, Walker R, editors. Biological Anthropology and Study of Ancient Egypt. London: British Museum Press, pp. 24–53.

Hillson SW. 1996. Dental Anthropology. Cambridge: Cambridge University Press.

Hillson SW. (in press) Recording dental caries in archaeological human remains. Int J Osteoarch.

Hillson SW, Bond S. 1997. Relationship of enamel hypoplasia to the pattern of tooth crown growth: a discussion. Am J Phys Anthropol 104:89–104.

Hillson SW, Grigson C, Bond S. 1998. The dental defects of congenital syphilis. Am J Phys Anthropol 107:25–40.

Hinton RJ. 1982. Differences in interproximal and occlusal tooth wear among prehistoric Tennessee Indians: implications for masticatory function. Am J Phys Anthropol 57:103–115.

Infante PF, Gillespie GM. 1974. An epidemiologic study of linear enamel hypoplasia of deciduous anterior teeth in Guatemalan children. Arch Oral Biol 19:1055–1061.

Ismail AI. 1997. Clinical diagnosis of precavitated carious lesions. Community Dent Oral Epidemiol 25:13–23.

Jacobi KP, Collins Cook D, Corruccini RS, Handler JS. 1992. Congenital syphilis in the past: slaves at Newton Plantation, Barbados, West Indies. Am J Phys Anthropol 89:145–158.

Jones SJ. 1987. The root surface: an illustrated review of some scanning electron microscope studies. Scanning Microsc 1:2003–2018.

Jones SJ, Boyde A. 1987. Scanning microscopic observations on dental caries. Scanning Microsc 1:1991–2002.

Karn KW, Shockett HP, Moffitt WC, Gray JL. 1984. Topographic classification of deformities of the alveolar process. J Periodont 55:336–340.

Kaul SS, Corruccini RS. 1992. Dental arch length reduction through interproximal attrition in modern Australian Aboriginies. In: Lukacs JR, editor. Culture, Ecology and Dental Anthropology. Delhi: Kamla-Raj Enterprises. pp. 195–200.

Kawano S, Tsukamoto T, Ohtaguro H, Tustsumi H, Takahashi T, Miura I, Mukoyama R, Aboshi H, Komuro T. 1995. Sex determination from dental calculus by polymerase chain reaction (PCR) (In Japanese). Nippon Hoigaku Zasshi 49:193–198.

Kerr NW. 1991. Prevalence and natural history of periodontal disease in Scotland—the mediaeval period (900–1600 AD). J Periodont Res 26:346–354.

Kvaal SI, Derry TK. 1996. Tell-tale teeth: abrasion from the traditional clay pipe. Endeavour 20:28–30.

Larsen CS. 1985. Dental modifications and tool use in the western Great Basin. Am J Phys Anthropol 67:393–402.

Larsen CS. 1995. Biological changes in human populations with agriculture. Annu Rev Anthropol 24:185–213.

Larsen CS. 1997. Bioarchaeology. Cambridge: Cambridge University Press.

Larsen CS, Shavit R, Griffin MC. 1991. Dental caries evidence for dietary change: an archaeological context. In: Kelley MA, Larsen CS, editors. Advances in Dental Anthropology. New York: Wiley-Liss. pp. 179–202.

Lehner T. 1992. Immunology of Oral Diseases. Oxford: Blackwell Scientific Publications.

Lindemann G. 1958. Prevalence of enamel hypoplasia among children that had previously suffered from gastrointestinal disease. Odontologisk Tidskrift 66:101–126.

Liversidge HM, Dean MC, Molleson TI. 1993. Increasing human tooth length between birth and 5.4 years. Am J Phys Anthropol 90:307–313.

Luan W-M, Baelum V, Chen X, Fejerskov O. 1989. Dental caries in adult and elderly Chinese. J Dent Res 68:1171–1776.

Lubell D, Jackes M, Schwarcz H, Knyf M, Meiklejohn C. 1994. The Mesolithic-Neolithic transition in Portugal: isotopic and dental evidence of diet. J Archaeol Sci 21:201–216.

Lukacs JR. 1995. The "caries correction factor": a new method of calibrating dental caries rates to compensate for antemortem loss of teeth. Int J Osteoarchaeol 5:151–156.

Lukacs JR, Retief DH, Jarrige J-F. 1985. Dental disease in prehistoric Baluchistan. National Geographic Research Spring 1985:184–197.

Lussi A. 1996. Impact of including or excluding cavitated lesions when evaluating methods for the diagnosis of occlusal caries. Caries Res 30:389–393.

MacPhee T, Cowley G. 1975. Essentials of Periodontology and Periodontics. Oxford: Blackwell Scientific Publications.

Manji F, Fejerskov O, Baelum V. 1988. Tooth mortality in an adult rural population in Kenya. J Dent Res 67:496–500.

Manji F, Fejerskov O, Baelum V. 1989a. Pattern of dental caries in an adult rural population. Caries Res 23:55–62.

Manji F, Fejerskov O, Baelum V. 1990. Dental caries in developing countries in relation to the appropriate use of fluoride. J Dent Res 69:733–741.

Manji F, Fejerskov O, Baelum V, Luan W-M, Chen X. 1991. The epidemiological features of dental caries in African and Chinese populations: implications for risk assessment. In: Johnson NW, editor. Volume 1. Dental Caries. Markers of High and Low Risk Groups and Individuals. Cambridge: Cambridge University Press. pp. 62–99.

Manji F, Fejerskov O, Baelum V, Nagelkerke N. 1989b. Dental calculus and caries experience in 14–65 year olds with no access to dental care. In: ten Cate JM, editor. Recent Advances in the Study of Dental Calculus. Oxford: IRL Press at Oxford University Press. pp. 223–234.

Marsh P, Martin M. 1992. Oral Microbiology. London: Chapman & Hall.

Matthesen M, Baelum V, Aarslev I, Fejerskov O. 1990. Dental health of children and adults in Guinea-Bissau, West Africa, in 1986. Community Dent Health 7:123–133.

Mayhall JT. 1970. The effect of culture change upon the Eskimo dentition. Arctic Anthropol 7:117.

Mellanby M. 1927. The structure of human teeth. Br Dent J 48:737–751.

Milner GR, Larsen CS. 1991. Teeth as artifacts of human behavior: intentional mutilation and accidental modification. In: Kelley MA, Larsen CS, editors. Advances in Dental Anthropology. New York: Wiley-Liss. pp. 357–378.

Molleson T. 1994. The eloquent bones of Abu Hureyra. Sci Am August 1994:60–65.

Molleson T, Cox M, editors. 1993. The people of Spitalfields: the Middling Sort. York: Council for British Archaeology.

Molnar S. 1971. Human tooth wear, tooth function and cultural variability. Am J Phys Anthropol 34:175–190.

Molnar S, McKee JK, Molnar I. 1983. Measurements of tooth wear among Australian Aborigines. I. Serial loss of the enamel crown. Am J Phys Anthropol 61:51–65.

Moody JEH. 1960. The dental and periodontal conditions of aborigines at settlements in Arnhem Land and adjacent areas. In: Mountford CR, editor. Records of the American-Australian Scientific Expedition to Arnhem Land: Anthropology and Nutrition. Melbourne: Melbourne University Press. pp. 60–71.

Moore WJ, Corbett ME. 1971. Distribution of dental caries in ancient British populations. I. Anglo-Saxon period. Caries Res 5:151–168.

Moore WJ, Corbett ME. 1973. Distribution of dental caries in ancient British populations. II. Iron Age, Romano-British and medieval periods. Caries Res 7:139–153.

Moore WJ, Corbett ME. 1975. Distribution of dental caries in ancient British populations. III. The 17th century. Caries Res 9:163–175.

Muller D, Perizonius WRK. 1980. The scoring of defects of the alveolar process in human crania. J Hum Evol 9:113–116.

Mundorff-Shrestha SA, Featherstone JDB, Eisenberg AD, Cowles E, Curzon MEJ, Espeland MA, Shields CP. 1994. Cariogenic potential of foods. II. Relationship of food composition, plaque microbial counts, and salivary perameters to caries in the rat model. Caries Res 28:106–115.

Navia JM. 1994. Carbohydrates and dental health. Am J Clin Nutr 59:719s–727s.

Newman HN, Levers BGH. 1979. Tooth eruption and function in an early Anglo-Saxon population. J Roy Soc Med 72:341–350.

Pedersen PO. 1938. Investigations into the dental conditions of about 3000 ancient and modern Greenlanders. Dental Record 58:191–198.

Pedersen PO. 1947. Dental investigations of Greenland Eskimos. Proc Roy Soc Med 40: 726–732.

Pedersen PO. 1966. Nutritional aspects of dental caries. Odontologisk Revy 17:91–100.

Penning C, van Amerongen JP, Seef RE, ten Cate JM. 1992. Validity of probing for fissure caries diagnosis. Caries Res 26:445–449.

Pindborg JJ. 1970. Pathology of the Dental Hard Tissues. Philadelphia: W. B. Saunders.

Pindborg JJ. 1982. Aetiology of developmental enamel defects not related to fluorosis. Int Dent J 32:123–134.

Pine CM, ten Bosch JJ. 1996. Dynamics of and diagnostic methods for detecting small carious lesions. Caries Res 30:381–388.

Poole DFG, Tratman EK. 1978. Post-mortem changes on human teeth from late upper Palaeolithic/Mesolithic occupants of an English limestone cave. Arch Oral Biol 23:1115–1120.

Powell B, Garnick JJ. 1978. The use of extracted teeth to evaluate clinical measurements of periodontal disease. J Periodont 49:621–624.

Richardson AC, Chadroff B, Bowers GM. 1990. The apical location of calculus within the intrabony defect. J Periodont 61:118–122.

Romero J. 1958. Mutilaciones dentarias prehispanicas de Mexico y America en general. Mexico: Instituto Nacional de Antropologia e Historia.

Romero J. 1970. Dental mutilation, trephination, and cranial deformation. In: Stewart TD, editor. Physical Anthropology. Austin, Texas: University of Texas Press. pp. 50–67.

Rugg-Gunn AJ. 1993. Nutrition and Dental Caries. Oxford: Oxford University Press.

Sarnat BG, Schour I. 1941. Enamel hypoplasia (chronologic enamel aplasia) in relation to systemic disease: a chronologic, morphologic and etiologic classification. J Am Dent Assoc 28:1989–2000.

Saunders SR, DeVito C, Katzenberg MA. 1997. Dental caries in nineteenth century Upper Canada. Am J Phys Anthropol 104:71–87.

Schluger S, Yuodelis R, Page RC, Johnson RH. 1990. Periodontal Diseases. Basic Phenomena, Clinical Management, and Occlusal and Restorative Interrelationships. Philadelphia: Lea & Febiger.

Scott DB, Wyckoff RWG. 1949. Studies of tooth surface structure by optical and electron microscopy. J Am Dent Assoc 39:275–282.

Scott EC. 1979. Dental wear scoring technique. Am J Phys Anthropol 51:213–218.

Sheiham A. 1983. Sugars in dental decay. Lancet 1:282–284.

Shields ED. 1983. A new classification of heritable human enamel defects and a discussion of dentin defects. Birth Defects: Original Article Series 19:107–127.

Sledzik PS, Moore-Jansen PH. 1991. Dental disease in nineteenth century military skeletal samples. In: Kelley MA, Larsen CS, editors. Advances in Dental Anthropology. New York: Wiley-Liss. pp. 215–224.

Smith BH. 1984. Patterns of molar wear in hunter-gatherers and agriculturalists. Am J Phys Anthropol 63:39–56.

Smith BH. 1986. Development and evolution of the helicoidal plane of dental occlusion. Am J Phys Anthropol 69:21–35.

Smith BH. 1991. Standards of human tooth formation and dental age assessment. In: Kelley MA, Larsen CS, editors. Advances in Dental Anthropology. New York: Wiley-Liss. pp. 143–168.

Soames JV, Southam JC. 1993. Oral Pathology. Oxford: Oxford University Press.

Sutter RC. 1995. Dental pathologies among inmates of the Monroe County Poorhouse. In: Grauer AL, editor. Bodies of Evidence: Reconstructing History Through Skeletal Analysis. New York: Wiley-Liss. pp. 185–196.

Swärdstedt T. 1966. Odontological aspects of a medieval population in the province of Jämtland/ Mid Sweden. Akademisk Avhandling som med vederbörligt tillstand av Odontologiska Fakulteten vid Lunds Universitet för vinnande av Odontologie Doktorgraqd offentilgen försvarasi Tandläkarhöskolans Aula, Malmö, 9 December, 1966, Lund, Sweden.

Sweeney EA, Saffir AJ, Leon Rd. 1971. Linear hypoplasia of deciduous incisor teeth in malnourished children. Am J Clin Nutr 24:29–31.

Thylstrup A, Chironga L, Carvalho Jd, Ekstrand KR. 1989. The occurrence of dental calculus in occlusal fissures as an indication of caries activity. In: ten Cate JM, editor. Recent Advances in the Study of Dental Calculus. Oxford: IRL Press at Oxford University Press. pp. 211–222.

Thylstrup A, Fejerskov O. 1994. Textbook of Clinical Cariology. Copenhagen: Munksgaard.

Tomenchuk J, Mayhall JT. 1979. A correlation of tooth wear and age among modern Igloolik Eskimos. Am J Phys Anthropol 51:67–78.

Turner CG II, Cadien JD. 1969. Dental chipping in Aleuts, Eskimos and Indians. Am J Phys Anthropol 31:303–310.

Tveit AB, Espelid I, Fjelltveit A. 1994. Clinical diagnosis of occlusal dentin caries. Caries Res 28:368–372.

Ubelaker DH, Phenice TW, Bass WM. 1969. Artificial interproximal grooving of the teeth in American Indians. Am J Phys Anthropol 30: 145–149.

van Reenen JF. 1964. Dentition, jaws and palate of the Kalahari Bushman. J Dent Assoc S Afr 19:1–16, 38–44, 67–80.

van Reenen JF. 1966. Dental features of a low-caries primitive population. J Dent Res 45:703–713.

Waldron HA. 1994. Counting the Dead. Chichester: John Wiley.

Walker PL, Dean G, Shapiro P. 1991. Estimating age from tooth wear in archaeological populations. In: Kelley MA, Larsen CS, editors. Advances in Dental Anthropology. New York: Wiley-Liss. pp. 169–178.

Watson PJC. 1986. A study of the pattern of alveolar recession. In: Cruwys E, Foley RA, editors. Teeth and Anthropology. Oxford: British Archaeological Reports. pp. 123–132.

Whaites E. 1992. Essentials of Dental Radiography and Radiology. Edinburgh: Churchill Livingstone.

Whittaker DK. 1986. Occlusal and approximal wear in Romano-British skulls. In: Cruwys E, Foley RA, editors. Teeth and Anthropology. Oxford: British Archaeological Reports. pp. 177–188.

Whittaker DK, Griffiths S, Robson A, Roger Davies P, Thomas G, Molleson T. 1990. Continuing tooth eruption and alveolar crest height in an eighteenth-century population from Spitalfields, east London. Arch Oral Biol 35:81–85.

Whittaker DK, Molleson T, Daniel AT, Williams JT, Rose P, Resteghini R. 1985. Quantitative assessment of tooth wear, alveolar-crest height and continuing eruption in a Romano-British population. Arch Oral Biology 30:493–501.

Whittaker DK, Parker JH, Jenkins C. 1982. Tooth attrition and continuing eruption in a Romano-British population. Arch Oral Biol 27:405–409.

Whittaker DK, Ryan S, Weeks K, Murphy WM. 1987. Patterns of approximal wear in cheek teeth of a Romano-British population. Am J Phys Anthropol 73:389–396.

Winter GB, Brook AH. 1975. Enamel hypoplasia and anomalies of the enamel. Dent Clin North Am 19:3–24.

Witkop CJ. 1957. Hereditary defects in enamel and dentin. Acta Genet Statist Med 7:236–239.

Woelfl JB. 1990. Dental Anatomy: Its Relevance to Dentistry. Philadelphia: Lea & Febiger.

Wolpoff MH. 1970. Interstitial wear. Am J Phys Anthropol 34:205–228.

Wood NK, Goaz PW. 1997. Differential Diagnosis of Oral and Maxillofacial Lesions, 5th ed. St. Louis: Mosby.

CHAPTER 10

PALAEOHISTOLOGY: HEALTH AND DISEASE

SUSAN PFEIFFER

INTRODUCTION

We study the remains of past populations because we want to know who the people were and how they lived. Human skeletal remains yield information that can form the basis of satisfyingly specific interpretations of past lives. However, if we wish to learn as much as we can about the biological and mechanical processes that gave the bones their distinctive shapes and sizes, we might do well to study the tissue of which the bones are made, as well as the bones themselves. This concept is not new. In 1955, Weinmann and Sicher organized their text, *Bone and Bones,* around this distinction. Still, tissue-based research remains relatively uncommon within biological anthropology. We can learn from both gross bone morphology and the structure of the bone tissue at the microscopic level, termed *bone histomorphology.* For example, the robustness of a long bone is one indicator of how that bone responded to activity patterns and diet during life, but the size and organization of the histological structures within the bone tissue may help us interpret those lifestyle variables more accurately. This chapter will summarize how anthropologically oriented histomorphology is done, what factors impinge on its success, and where the research may be going.

Biological Anthropology of the Human Skeleton, Edited by M. Anne Katzenberg and Shelley R. Saunders.
ISBN 0-471-31616-4   Copyright © 2000 by Wiley-Liss, Inc.

BONE TISSUE BACKGROUND

Human skeletons are comprised of three gross types of bone tissue: compact (cortical), spongy (cancellous), and subchondral (Shipman et al., 1985). Cortical bone, the major component of long bone shafts and the external surface of bones, has few pores and spaces, and appears compact to the unaided eye. Cancellous bone, found in long bone marrow spaces and the bones of the trunk, is comprised of small platelike or rodlike elements called trabeculae. This term is derived from the Latin word for little beams. Subchondral bone occurs at the articular surfaces. In life it is covered by hyaline cartilage; as dry bone it is smooth and highly vascularized. All components of the skeleton perform two crucial life functions: mechanical and homeostatic. The skeleton supports the mass and movement of the soft tissues and it acts as a reservoir for calcium and other minerals. To act effectively, the bone undergoes processes of modeling and remodeling throughout life. Most of the modeling, or macroarchitectural shaping, occurs during growth. Most of the remodeling, or internal bone turnover, occurs during adulthood. The focus of this chapter will be on remodeling. Throughout the average skeleton, there are estimated to be about 1.5 million sites of remodeling (Gallagher 1991).

Descriptions of the microscopic structure of cortical and cancellous bone can be found in both biologically and anthropologically oriented literature (for the latter, see Schwartz,

1995; Steele and Bramlett, 1988; Ubelaker, 1989; White, 1991). The key features of interest here are lamellar bone (the term referring to layers, each of which is composed of collagen fibrils oriented in one plane and hydroxyapatite crystals within and between the fibrils), osteons (lamellar bone organized concentrically around vascular canals, osteons being classified as primary or secondary), and Haversian canals (the name for the vascular structures). Sometimes osteons are known as Haversian systems and cortical remodeling is called Haversian remodeling, named after Clopton Havers who described the porous nature of bone in 1691 (Martin and Burr, 1989).

All secondary bone tissue structures are the product of the A-R-F sequence of bone remodeling: activation, resorption, and formation. These stages are enacted by the basic multicellular unit (BMU) (Frost, 1969), also known as the bone remodeling unit, BRU (Eriksen et al., 1994). The BMU produces a bone structural unit (BSU), like a secondary osteon. In human cortical bone, the resorption process lasts more than 30 days and the formation period lasts 90 days or more (Eriksen et al., 1994). Cancel-

lous bone remodels slightly faster. The lifetime of a BSU is between 3 and 20 years, depending on the local remodeling rate (Gallagher, 1991). Thus, remodeling is not a speedy process and cannot be expected to reflect brief, transient life events. Studies of biochemical markers in adult humans suggest that bone remodeling is not the primary mode of maintaining serum mineral concentrations. It may be that hormonal factors strongly influence the BMU at some points, such as puberty (Schiessl et al., 1998), while biomechanical factors are dominant during other periods. Referring to the more responsive cancellous bone, Ott (1996) estimates that at any one time, approximately 20% of the bone surface is undergoing remodeling, and at any one surface location, remodeling will occur about every 2 to 4 years.

PALAEOHISTOMORPHOLOGY

The clinical study of histomorphology and the measurement of the tissue structures (histomorphometry) focus on contributing to the analysis of metabolic bone disease (Eriksen

TABLE 10.1   A Summary of the Effects for Various Metabolic Bone Conditions on Histomorphological Traits That Can Be Measured on Archaeologically Derived Cortical Bone

Condition	Cortical Width	Porosity	Mineral Apposition Rate
Primary parathyroidism	↓	↑	↓
Acromegaly	↑	—	↑
Glucocorticoids	↓	—	↓
Anticonvulsant drugs	↓	↑	—
Immobilization	↓↓	—	↓
Postmenopausal osteoporosis	↓	—	↑↓
Thyrotoxicosis	—	↑↑	↑
Paget's disease	↑↑	↓	↑
Alcoholism	↓	—	↓
Other conditions affecting bone: renal osteodistrophy, cancers, AIDS, and more.	—	—	—

(Information from Weinstein, 1992.)

Direction of the arrows indicates whether the trait can be expected to increase/accelerate (an upward arrow) or decrease/decelerate (a downward arrow). Two arrows going the same way indicate a particularly strong effect; opposite directions indicate unpredictability.

et al., 1994; Parfitt, 1992). Tissue, normally from an iliac crest biopsy, is studied to assess the activity of the BMU, which may show a number of patterns of imbalance between resorption and depositional activities. Because cancellous bone is more metabolically active and is a much more common site of osteopenic fracture, it is the focus of most clinical attention (Ott, 1996). When adjusting to a stressor, bone tissue can only respond by resorption or deposition. The balance between these two factors determines net gain or loss of tissue. The nonspecificity of bone changes is apparent from the diversity of bone responses to disease factors, summarized in Table 10.1.

When scrutiny of bone tissue structures is extended to past human populations, the same clinically accepted terminology and definitions should be applied (Parfitt et al., 1997). A glance at this literature, however, will show that the clinical field is not transferable to the archaeological setting in a wholesale fashion. The extent to which histomorphometric parameters can be quantified in an archaeologically derived bone tissue is ill-defined, except of course that the cells responsible for bone formation and deposition are gone. Even the fundamental distinction of depositional and resorptive surfaces is confounded by these cells' absence, since an apparently resorptive bone surface may have been covered by a layer of osteoblasts (bone formation cells), with death intervening before the mineralization stage was reached (Mosekilde, 1990). The density and juxtaposition of the trabeculae that comprise cancellous bone can be altered by postmortem damage. Therefore most palaeo-histological studies have noted the size, position, and special characteristics of structures within cortical bone. The emphasis has been on static rather than dynamic measures (cf. Stout and Lueck, 1995) because the still ill-defined variability in the former has an influence on the latter.

There are advantages to studying human bone biology through archaeologically derived specimens (Grupe and Garland, 1993; Martin, 1991; Schultz, 1997a, 1997b). The skeletons of earlier human populations often show a more balanced mortality profile, including juveniles and young adults. Causes of death are very frequently acute and we assume that long-term medication with substances that would alter bone metabolism is improbable. Sample sizes can be large, and sometimes sex and age at death are available from cemetery records. With due care given to choice of sample and hypothesis, intriguing patterns can be seen.

While histological study of very ancient specimens is uncommon, conditions sometimes permit microscopy, as with images of an unspecified long bone fragment from the paleoanthropological site of Swartkrans (Schultz, 1986), the remarkably well-preserved complete femoral cross section from Broken Hill (Goldman, 1996), and the early exploration of ancient human histology with the femora from Trinil (Day and Molleson, 1973; Dubois, 1937). Histological analysis of the pathological long bones of a *Homo erectus* woman from approximately 1.6 millions years ago, KNM-ER 1808, suggests that she suffered from vitamin A poisoning. This was likely caused by eating the liver of a large predator, like a lion or leopard (Walker et al., 1982). This observation reinforces other lines of evidence that *Homo erectus* was oriented toward reliance on meat.

METHODS

Most of the research into cortical bone structure relies on thin sections and transmitted light microscopy. Reflected light microscopy, backscatter electron imaging microscopy and confocal microscopy may also be used for special applications, but preparation for transmitted light microscopy will be the focus here. Preparing archaeologically derived bone tissue normally combines biological approaches (dehydrating, de-greasing) and geological approaches (embedding, cutting, polishing). There is good news and bad news inherent in the preparation of thin sections. The good news is that the tissue can often be prepared with minimal exposure to chemicals and no complex staining protocols.

The bad news is that the effects of diagenesis (discussed below) are unpredictable, and they often lead to poor results, even from well-prepared thin sections.

The anatomical site must be chosen with care, with attention to what comparative information is available as well as practical considerations. Many past studies of cortical remodeling have focused on histology of the femoral midshaft, sectioned perpendicular to the long axis. While this region is often well preserved, its use necessitates sampling from literally thousands of osteons, whose distribution is not random (Pfeiffer et al., 1995). There is also a curatorial argument that sampling destroys the integrity of the femur. Smaller skeletal elements, like ribs and metacarpals, may be easier to procure and are easier to prepare. Some research questions will require samples from different bones of the same skeleton. When tissue is removed for histology, the original anatomical orientation should be noted. For example, if an anterior wedge of a femur is used (obtained by making one horizontal and one oblique saw cut), the most anterior aspect should be marked. Colored nail polish works well for this. Depending on the condition of the bone tissue, it may be beneficial to process it through graded alcohols for dehydration and some de-greasing effect, or de-grease it in vapors of trichloroethylene (take precautions to avoid skin or respiratory exposure). If you have access to an archaeological faunal laboratory, a veterinary or human anatomy laboratory, talk with the technicians about the removal of grease from bone. There are many techniques, sometimes developed through trial and error, and your local informants may be happy to accommodate your small-scale needs for gentle de-greasing.

Once a sample of cortical tissue is obtained, it can be prepared for microscopy using automated systems (found in many departments of geology) or it can be prepared by hand with only a diamond-blade wafering saw (or cut-off saw) and human energy (a.k.a. "elbow grease"). Whatever level of technology is available, the sample should be embedded in a material that will keep the periosteal surface from breaking away. The multistage embedding processes of medical histology, which truly pervade the bone tissue (e.g., methylmethacrylate), do provide a satisfactory product, but the much simpler epoxy-type products from geological suppliers such as Buehler Ltd. (41 Waukegan Rd., Lake Bluff, IL 60044) and Struhers (Valhøjs Alle 176, DK-2610, Rodøvre, København, Danmark) work almost as well, are much faster and less toxic. Use of a vacuum chamber for evacuating air bubbles during the curing process can greatly improve the quality of the product.

Once embedded, the section is cut in a planar fashion, ground to an appropriate thinness (no more than 100μm), polished, and mounted on a glass slide. There are several ways to approach these steps, depending on the equipment available (cf. Grupe and Garland, 1993; Schenk et al., 1984; Schultz, 1986; Schwartz, 1995; Ubelaker, 1989). The published procedures tend not to mention a matter that has caused distress in my laboratory over the years: During cutting, grinding, and polishing, water is used as a lubricant. Because the bone absorbs water and the embedding medium does not, the bone tends to buckle as it becomes thin enough to flex. Therefore, specimens should be placed under pressure to keep them flat between processing steps. This sensitivity to humidity, combined with some residual greasiness, means that the bone may lift off the slide at some point after preparation. These problems are especially vexing when the tissue sample is large, like a complete femoral cross section. The tension can crack the glass slide.

Diagenesis

The term *diagenesis* is defined by the Oxford English Dictionary as, "transformation by dissolution and recombination of elements." If used as a key word, it can lead the reader into a confusion of literature. Diagenetic processes have long been a concern to geologists, so that the minerological and sedimentological specializations have different definitions for the term. In the archaeological literature, it has come to mean postdepositional changes to materials of archaeological interest, both chemical and structural, including weathering. As such, it does not correspond neatly to the geological usages of the term. The focus here will be on structural changes to bone in the postmortem environment.

A bone can appear grossly unaltered, yet yield cloudy, incomplete, or structurally altered histological images. The bone tissue may have yielded satisfactory chemical indicators such as light stable isotope values, carbon to nitrogen (C:N) ratios, or even amino acid profiles (see Katzenberg, Chapter 11), yet it may not show good histological preservation (Pfeiffer, 1989, 1995; Pfeiffer and Varney, in press). The alterations may be caused by dynamics of physical chemistry (ground water ionic ex-change and mineral deposition), by postmorten biological activity (bacteria, fungi, and proto-zoa), or by combinations of factors (Figs. 10.1 and 10.2). A number of bacteria have been identified that break down collagen (Child et al., 1993). In organic soils or contexts that deter water drainage, like coffins and crypts, both physical and biological change is probable.

It is difficult to predict from the gross appearance of a bone whether the tissue will prove to be diagenetically altered at the microscopic level. Still, some generalizations can be made. Histological preservation is likely to be poor if the burial environment has been moist, and/or if the bone is easy to cut, "chalky," and yields no smell of grease. The presence of purple (or any other color) fungus within the cortex is a bad sign. Desert conditions, shell middens, and proximity

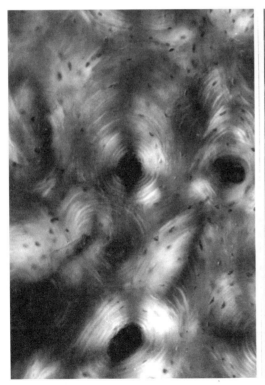 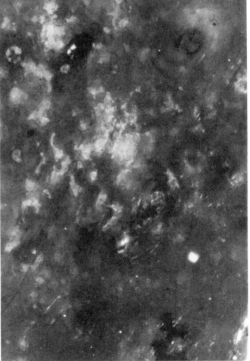

Figure 10.1 Photomicrographs of two femoral midshaft thin sections, viewed under polarized light, from burials near Lake Erie. The well-preserved material (left), approximately 3000 years old, comes from well-drained gravels and was buried with copper artifacts (Sartori site, Late Archaic [Donaldson and Wortner, 1995]). The cloudy material (right), about 700 years old, comes from organic soils in a settlement area, Sandusky Bay (Pearson site, Late Woodland [Stothers and Abel, 1989]).

to copper artifacts tend to yield well-preserved bone. Coffins foster diagenesis. Well-preserved bone is relatively easy to prepare for microscopy, but if diagenetic alteration has occurred there is very little that can be done to improve the histological view. Because diagenetically altered bone does not transmit light as well as normal bone, it appears to be "too thick." While making the section thinner may improve light transmission marginally, frequently one ends up polishing the section until there is nothing left.

Design Considerations

If possible, research protocols should accommodate diagenesis by allowing the measurement of those structures that are visible rather than a complete census of all structures that once existed in a bone cross section. The sizes of cortical structures like osteons and Haversian canals can be quite variable, and are not normally distributed (Fig. 10.3) (Pfeiffer, 1998). Therefore, it is necessary to assess a large number of structures to get a true sense of their central tendency. A measure of the dispersion of those values must be retained in subsequent analyses and the data may need to be transformed prior to statistical analysis. Measures of variance like the standard deviation tend to be much higher within a bone section than between people in a sample, so statistically based comparisons must incorporate that variance.

Thinking of an osteon as a roughly circular structure that is analogous in shape to a long bone shaft viewed transversely, total osteon area (On.Ar) is equivalent to total cross-

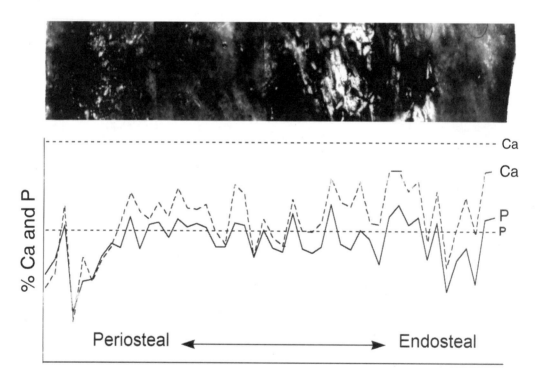

Figure 10.2   The upper part of the figure is a collage made from photomicrographs of a femoral thin section showing poor histological preservation (Ball site, southern Ontario, about 500 BP [Knight and Melbye, 1983]). Moving from the periosteal surface (left), there is a fungal ingrowth, cloudiness that reflects collagen breakdown, a well-preserved segment, then more cloudiness. Below the photo is a plot of calcium (Ca) and phosphorus (P), quantified along this axis via electron microprobe. Both elements fluctuate beyond the expected range (indicated by the horizontal dotted lines), with calcium depleted throughout. There is little correspondence between histology and chemistry, except that the organic debris periosteally appears as reduced Ca and P.

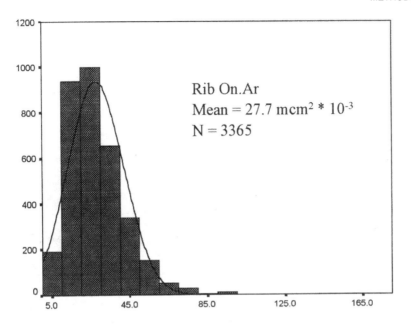

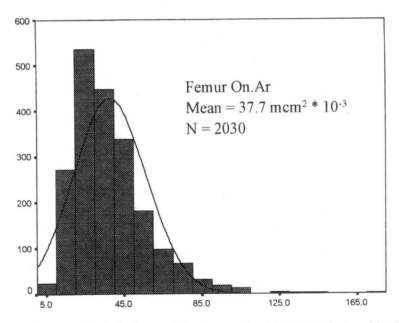

Figure 10.3 Histograms of On.Ar for femora and ribs, demonstrating their leptokurtotic, skewed distributions. (Samples described in Pfeiffer, 1998.)

sectional area, Haversian canal area (H.Ar) is equivalent to medullary area. To avoid osteons that have been cut obliquely, only osteons with maximum diameters that are less than twice their minimum diameters should be included.

Osteons from all parts of the cortex—the periosteal, mid-cortex, and endosteal envelopes—should be included.

Treating the mean value from a bone sample as an adequate representation and working only with the measure of dispersion between samples can lead to type I errors, that is, seeing differences between subsets where none truly occur. Furthermore, the structures are not randomly distributed throughout a bone's cross section. In a study of nine complete femoral midshaft cross sections, we found that biomechanically defined axes showed less variability than anatomically defined axes (Pfeiffer et al., 1995). This suggests that there is merit in using bones with small cross sections, where evaluation of all well-preserved histological features is a reasonable goal. Ribs, metacarpals, and metatarsals fit these criteria, and can supply supplementary information on age at death and bone strength (especially second metacarpals, cf. Fox et al., 1986). For a discussion of age estimation from ribs, see Robling and Stout, Chapter 7; for an example of work using the metatarsal see Turban-Just and Grupe (1995).

CONTRIBUTIONS

Normal Range of Variation

The basic unit of organization in mature human cortical bone is the secondary osteon. This structure is comprised of concentric circles surrounding a hole that accommodated the Haversian canal when it is cut perpendicular to its long axis. It is distinguished from the primary osteon, which supplies blood to the circumferential lamellar bone of youth, by its completely encircling lamellae (Martin and Burr, 1989). All subsequent discussion of osteons in this chapter refers to secondary osteons.

The maximum diameter of an osteon is marked by a dense reversal line, that point in the osteon's formation at which resorption ceased and deposition began. The maximum size of an osteon is thus determined by the resorption process. The diameter of the Haversian canal is determined by the point in the osteon's formation at which in-filling ceased. Therefore, total osteon area should reflect the vigor of the resorptive component of the BMU and Haversian canal area should reflect the vigor of the depositional component.

While many mature mammals form cortical osteons, the human pattern is to some degree unique, making it possible in forensic situations to differentiate human bone from nonhuman bone using histological criteria (Enlow and Brown, 1956, 1957, 1958; Foote, 1916, Harsanyi, 1993; Ubelaker, 1989). Among those species whose cortical bone has osteons, human osteons are rounder, less "plexiform" in shape, and they overlap one another in a seemingly random manner. Humans may even be distinguishable from other primates, although there has been little study done. The different cortical remodeling pattern seen in macaques has been explored in the context of their use as models in biomedical research (Burr, 1992). In humans, the proportion of osteonal to nonosteonal bone becomes greater with age (see Robling and Stout, Chapter 7), but the patterning of the remodeling associated with osteon formation is not predictable with much accuracy. The dynamic interaction of mechanical and metabolic factors, which we presume dictates the action of the BMU, remains to be fully understood.

Human osteons are different sizes in bones from different parts of the body, and some past human populations had distinctly smaller osteons compared to recent humans. Focusing on the two key variables of total osteon area (On.Ar) and Haversian canal area (H.Ar), there are within-bone, between-bone, and between-person sources of variation. These patterns can be seen in a study of known age and sex individuals from three quite disparate samples: eighteenth-century Huguenots in England (Spitalfields, $n = 20$), nineteenth-century British settlers in Canada (St. Thomas', $n = 21$), and twentieth-century South African cadavers (University of Cape Town, $n = 30$) (Pfeiffer, 1998). It is clear that rib osteons are usually about three-quarters the size of femur osteons. It seems probable that other bones of the body would have characteristic osteon sizes as well, were they to be studied. Some studies have found males to have larger osteons than females (Pfeiffer, 1998), while other studies have noted the opposite (Abbott et al., 1996; Dupras and Pfeiffer, 1996; Mulhern and Van Gerven, 1997).

No statistically significant sex differences have been found in studies that incorporate within-bone variability, so it seems likely that there is not a consistent sex difference. Similarly, when studied in this fashion age does not appear to have an influence on On.Ar.

Haversian canal sizes are more variable than On.Ar (Table 10.2), as we might expect since death may intervene during the osteon filling process or a condition of ill health may cause incomplete filling of the osteons. Within a bone section, the variance may be substantially greater than the mean. That is, the coefficient of variation may exceed 100. Nevertheless, statistically significant population differences can be found. Intriguingly, rib H.Ar values from Spitalfields (the eighteenth-century Londoners) are very small (Dupras and Pfeiffer, 1996; Pfeiffer, 1998). The H.Ar values from the femora of these same people are not distinctive. Dupras (1995), in a study of 58 Spitalfields adults of known age (aged 20–50 years, including the 20 studied by Pfeiffer), found that H.Ar values increased with age significantly among females. Some studies of known-age recent samples have reported an increase in Haversian canal size with age (Singh and Gunberg, 1970; Thompson, 1980) while others have not (Pfeiffer, 1998). In general, it appears that the more recent a sample's origin is, the larger H.Ar will be (Table 10.2). Perhaps this reflects the tendency for more recent humans

TABLE 10.2   Recent Human Osteon Sizes, Haversian Canal Sizes

Sample	Number of Persons	Osteon Area (On.Ar)	Haversian Canal Area (H.Ar)	Source
Femur				
Moderns, 60 yr or less	11	—	4.5	Currey, 1964
Moderns, 50–59 yr	11	—	m (4):4.1 f (7):6.3	Thompson, 1980
"Modern Men"		41.0	—	Evans, 1976
Pecos Pueblo[b]	55	m: 35.3 f: 41.0	m: 2.3 f: 2.3	Burr et al., 1990
Medieval Nubian males	24	40	2	Mulhern and Van Gerven, 1997
Medieval Nubian females	19	36	2	Mulhern and Van Gerven, 1997
Spitalfields males	11	46.5	4.1	Pfeiffer, 1998
Spitalfields females	9	43.1	3.4	Pfeiffer, 1998
St. Thomas' males	14	39.2	3.1	Pfeiffer, 1998
St. Thomas' females	7	35.7	3.2	Pfeiffer, 1998
Rib				
Ledders[b]	31	33	—	Stout, 1976
Gibson[b]	30	35	—	Stout, 1976
Spitalfields males	24	30.3	1.4	Dupras, 1995
Spitalfields females	29	31.7	1.4	Dupras, 1995
St. Thomas' males	14	30.7	3.4	Pfeiffer, 1998
St. Thomas' females	7	32.3	3.3	Pfeiffer, 1998
Cape Town males	16	28.9	1.9	Pfeiffer, 1998
Cape Town females	14	27.9	1.9	Pfeiffer, 1998

[a]Units are $(mm^2)(10^3)$; this can also be expressed as $(mcm^2)(10^{-3})$.

[b]Prehistoric Amerindian samples.

to live with chronic conditions that affect bone metabolism. Alternately, it may reflect our increased sedentariness.

While we do not know what variables may explain the differences between samples, these data demonstrate that population differences exist among recent humans. It is intriguing that there were no significant differences found among "racial" subsections of the South African cadavers, while there are differences between eighteenth-century Europeans and later European-origin people. This suggests that environmental factors may be contributing more to the variance in On.Ar and H.Ar than genetic factors. Differences in methodology preclude statistically based comparisons, and authors may not define the variables in exactly the same way. Nevertheless, a gross comparison suggests that within a specified bone (the femur) osteon size is more consistent across human samples than Haversian canal size. This introduces the possibility that osteon area is guided more strongly by genetically based developmental canalization and Haversian canal area is more sensitive to shorter-term homeostatic variables.

More Ancient Patterns

Even more intriguing is the pattern seen in some Late Pleistocene humans. Tiny long bone fragments from the well-known sites of Shanidar, Tabun, Skhūl, Broken Hill (Abbott et al., 1996), and Border Cave (Pfeiffer and Zehr, 1996) have been carefully collected and prepared as thin sections. While these fragments represent varying locations from varying long bones (mostly femora, one tibia, one humerus), and so do not provide the basis for a tightly controlled comparison, some individuals have osteons that are substantially smaller than expected. Of the 11 specimens compared to date, nine fall below the 50th percentile for recent femoral On.Ar. One specimen, the femur of Skhūl 3, falls below the 5th percentile (Pfeiffer, 1998). Therefore, there appears to be a strong trend toward smaller osteons in the Late Pleistocene.

As with variability among recent humans, the reasons for smaller osteons in the Late Pleistocene remain elusive. Because both anatomically modern and Neanderthal specimens show low On.Ar values, once again it appears that environmental factors may be especially important. Are they tied to whole body robusticity? Did increased strain stimulate frequent and rapid remodeling? A small study of femora from nineteenth-century British settlers to Canada ($n = 21$) demonstrated an absence of statistical relationship between On.Ar and biomechanical variables like cross-sectional area, percent cortical area, and polar moment of area (Pfeiffer and Zehr, 1995). Assuming that the cross-sectional mass of bone tissue is strongly influenced by loading factors, the microscopic structure of the tissue should not be subject to consistently increased or decreased strains. Are the small osteons a function of some metabolic difference? Or is there a developmentally determined set point, as there appears to be in the different bones within the body? More data, from both ancient and recent humans, should tell the tale.

Activity-Related Indicators

Histological study confirms the observations of biomechanical studies, that loading stimulates bone remodeling. In a study of a young man from the turn of the twentieth century who used a peg leg, Lazenby and Pfeiffer (1993) documented increased bone remodeling within the femur from the amputated leg such that osteon density yielded an age of 68 years, while the femur from the intact leg yielded an accurate age in the early 20s.

More subtle, normal adjustments to loading also occur. Termed continuing periosteal apposition, this ongoing bone deposition continues into old age, presumably as a compensation for resorption at the medullary surface (Lazenby, 1990a, 1990b). Ruff and Hayes (1988) argue that males show greater rates of periosteal bone apposition, and that the location of new bone is related to strain. Lazenby's data confirm the latter observation. Thus, activity patterns appear to influence this phenomenon. Because it is difficult to measure, histological confirmation of continuing periosteal apposition is important. Evidence that increased total area of the femoral midshaft preceded increased medullary area in middle-aged twentieth-century Australian men (Feik et al., 1996) illustrates how incomplete our understanding of this phenomenon is. Studies of archaeologically derived bone could be very useful.

Health-Related Indicators

Certain diseases lead to modification of bone tissue such that histological quantification can contribute to diagnosis (Bell, 1990), but case studies are relatively rare. Conditions studied to date include Paget's disease (Aaron et al., 1992; Bell and Jones, 1991), fluorosis (Boivin and Meunier, 1993), rickets (Capasso et al., 1995), hypervitaminosis A (Walker et al., 1982), tumors (Schultz, 1992), osteoporosis (Roberts and Wakely, 1992), tuberculosis (Wakely et al., 1991), and syphilis (Schultz, 1993a). The need for more clearly defined histological criteria of differential diagnosis is generally recognized (Schultz, 1993a, 1993b). To link with the modern clinical literature, the paleohistologist often must anticipate what something would look like histologically when the case studies are described radiologically. It has proven difficult to find and prepare sections of bone tissue from individuals who had a particular condition in life, especially when that condition is transient or nonfatal, like chronic sinusitis, for example.

Because reproductive variables are so important to understanding human evolution, and because pregnancy and lactation affect calcium balance, it would be helpful if there were markers of these phenomena in human cortical bone. Experimental evidence indicates that female mammals accommodate calcium demands during pregnancy without significant net bone loss, but they may lose some bone during lactation, at least transiently (Miller and Bowman, 1998; Sowers, 1996). Cancellous

(metaphyseal) bone is the most active component. While some studies have noted sex differences in the size of osteons and Haversian canals (Martin and Armelagos, 1985; Mulhern and Van Gerven, 1997), no consistent marker or patterning has emerged. It is, of course, difficult to differentiate sex differences due to reproduction from those that may reflect habitual differences in activity patterns. Given the slowness of the cortical remodeling process, brief changes to a person's metabolic status are not likely to register.

It has been suggested that physiological stress can cause intermittent deposition of bone tissue, which in turn can lead to a zonal osteon. A zonal osteon exhibits an abrupt change in mineral density, suggestive of an arrest in growth analogous to a Harris (growth arrest) line on a radiograph. A visually similar structure, the type II osteon, is the result of resorption and subsequent formation being initiated and completed within an osteon resulting in a reversal line within an osteon (Ortner, 1970; Stout, 1989). While the type II osteon can be differentiated from the zonal osteon by its absence of smooth lamellae at the boundary between inner and outer osteons, in practice these two structures are easily confused. The proportion of zonal osteons may correlate positively with chronological age (Pankovich et al., 1974; Pfeiffer and Zehr, 1996; Yoshino, 1994). They have also been studied as possible chronic stress indicators, with variable success. Martin and Armelagos (1985) as well Hartnady (1997) have asserted their value, while Trivers and Armelagos (1997) have found no correlation between zonal osteons and other skeletal indicators of ill health. Type II osteons have been associated with dietary stress (Richman et al., 1979), but a recent re-study of the samples used by these researchers failed to reproduce their results (Iwaniec, 1997). This outcome may be best explained by the difficulty in differentiating these structures and replicating methods, especially if researchers are using different microscopy approaches. If this is so, careful standardization may yield useful results in future.

FUTURE DIRECTIONS

Future progress in paleohistology is contingent on a number of factors. Research would be expedited if the preparation of thin sections could be seen as the transformation of material rather than the destruction of material. At the least, we may hope that curatorial institutions will not simply institute "no sampling" policies without serious consideration of the information at issue. The use of smaller bone elements, like the rib and metacarpal, will expedite lab work and minimize the disruption of curated materials. Archaeological workers must be made aware that these elements have value beyond that of constituting a handy, expendable sample for radiocarbon dating.

For research to proceed efficiently, we need to understand—or at least be able to predict—diagenesis. It is possible that certain methods of microscopy may lend themselves to bone that has been altered in certain ways. For example, backscatter electron microscopy may work better than transmitted light when collagen content is low.

Anthropologically oriented researchers need to document the characteristics of bone in a manner consistent with clinically oriented histomorphological research, and to link in to those research questions. While the histomorphometric parameters of human cancellous bone are well characterized in the clinical literature, cortical bone has not been the focus of much normative study. This may change as clinical researchers evaluate the pervasive effects of antiosteopenic drugs. Archaeologically derived materials, with their broad mortality spectrum and absence of medication regimens, may offer useful information. However, the clinical field appears to be moving toward noninvasive, biochemical markers of bone activity (Garnero and Delmas, 1996), so our common ground may be limited.

We also need to think about which of the clinically important features of cancellous bone might yield the clearest information about past populations, and then set about measuring archaeologically derived bone with es-

tablished methods. For example, Agarwal and Grynpas (1996) have hypothesized that senile osteoporosis was rare, or perhaps did not exist, in prehistory. They base their argument on the lack of reporting of osteoporotic fractures from prehistoric skeletal samples. The fractures associated with osteoporosis are difficult to quantify. Compression fractures of the vertebrae are highly variable in their manifestation, and may be caused by factors other than systemic bone loss. Fractures of the femoral neck may occur soon before death so that the healing that signals a break as antemortem may be absent. Because fractures are not an inevitable outcome of reduced bone mass and because they are difficult to quantify, hypotheses about prehistoric osteoporosis would best be tested not through fracture frequencies but through bone density measurements.

Our access to juvenile skeletal material puts paleohistology in a good position to contribute information to our understanding of the attainment of peak bone mass during growth and maturation. For example, the suggestion by Schiessl and colleagues (1998) that hormone levels at puberty stimulate bone modeling, modulated by lean body mass, could be effectively explored through archaeologically derived samples, looking for patterns of cortical bone deposition to be linked to body size and maturation.

Histological patterns of human cortical bone appear to be somewhat distinctive among mammals, and they appear to vary temporally and spatially. We do not yet know what factors determine this variability. As more biological anthropologists establish a level of comfort with tissue-based research, the answers may come quickly. This will benefit our understanding of the past and our management of present health issues.

REFERENCES

Aaron JE, Rogers J, Kanis JA. 1992. Paleohistology of Paget's disease in two medieval skeletons. Am J Phys Anthropol 89:325–331.

Abbott S, Trinkaus E, Burr DB. 1996. Dynamic bone remodeling in later Pleistocene fossil hominids. Am J Phys Anthropol 99:585–601.

Agarwal SC, Grynpas MD. 1996. Bone quantity and quality in past populations. Anat Rec 246:423–432.

Bell L. 1990. Paleopathology and diagenesis: an SEM evaluation of structural changes using backscattered electron imaging. J Archaeol Sci 17:85–102.

Bell LS, Jones SJ. 1991. Macroscopic and microscopic evaluation of archaeological pathological bone: backscattered electron imaging of putative Pagetic bone. Int J Osteoarchaeol 1:179–184.

Boivin G, Meunier PJ. 1993. Histomorphometric methods applied to bone. In: Grupe G, Garland AN, editors. Histology of Ancient Human Bone: Methods and Diagnosis. Berlin: Springer-Verlag. pp. 137–156.

Burr DB. 1992. Estimated intracortical bone turnover in the femur of growing macaques: implications for their use as models in skeletal pathology. Anat Rec 232:180–189.

Burr DB, Ruff CB, Thompson DD. 1990. Patterns of skeletal histologic change through time: comparison of an archaic Native American population with modern populations. Anat Rec 226: 307–313.

Capasso L, Metoni C, di Tota G. 1995. Changes due to rickets: preliminary histological observations on paleopathological samples. Gazetta Medica Italiana Archivio per le Scienze Mediche 154: 91–95.

Child AM, Gillard RD, Pollard AM. 1993. Microbially-induced promotion of amino acid racemization in bone: isolation of the microorganisms and the detection of their enzymes. J Archaeol Sci 20:159–168.

Currey JD. 1964. Some effects of ageing in human Haversian systems. J Anat 98:69–75.

Day MH, Molleson TI. 1973. The Trinil femora. In: Day MH, editor. Human Evolution. London: Taylor and Francis. pp. 127–154.

Donaldson WS, Wortner S. 1995. The Hind Site and the Glacial Kame burial complex in Ontario. J Ont Archaeol Soc 59:5–95.

Dubois E. 1937. The osteone arrangement of the thigh-bone compacta of man identical with that, first found, of Pithecanthropus. K ned Akad Wet 40:864–870.

Dupras TL. 1995. Sexual Dimorphism at Gross and Histological Levels in Human Ribs. Can Soc Forensi Sci J 29:221–232.

Enlow DH, Brown SO. 1956. A comparative histological study of fossil and recent bone tissues. Part 1. Texas J Sci 8:405–443.

Enlow DH, Brown SO. 1957. A comparative histological study of fossil and recent bone tissues. Part 2. Texas J Sci 9:186–214.

Enlow DH, Brown SO. 1958. A comparative histological study of fossil and recent bone tissues. Part 3. Texas J Sci 10:187–230.

Eriksen EF, Aselrod DW, Melsen F. 1994. Bone Histomorphometry. New York: Raven Press.

Evans FG. 1976. Mechanical properties and histology of cortical bone from younger and older men. Anatomical Record 185:1–12.

Feik S, Thomas C, Clement J. 1996. Age trends in remodeling of the femoral midshaft differ between the sexes. J Orthopaed Res 14:590–597.

Foote JS. 1916. A contribution to the Comparative Histology of the Femur. Washington: Smithsonian Institution.

Fox KM, Tobin JD, Plato CC. 1986. Longitudinal study of bone loss in the second metacarpal. Calcif Tissue Int 39:218–225.

Frost HM. 1969. Tetracycline-based histological analysis of bone remodeling. Calcif Tissue Res 3:211–237.

Gallagher JA. 1991. Bone remodeling, human. In: Encyclopedia of Human Biology Vol. 1. San Diego: Academic Press. pp. 811–823.

Garnero P, Delmas PD. 1996. Measurements of biochemical markers: methods and limitations. In: Bilezikian JP, Raisz LG, Rodan GA, editors. Principles of Bone Biology. San Diego: Academic Press. pp. 1277–1292.

Goldman HM. 1996. A histological analysis of a mid-shaft femoral section of an archaic *Homo sapiens* from Broken Hill. Am J Phys Anthropol S22:114.

Grupe G, Garland AN, editors. 1993. Histology of Ancient Human Bone: Methods and Diagnosis. Berlin: Springer-Verlag.

Harsanyi L. 1993. Differential diagnosis of human and animal bone. In: Grupe G, Garland AN, editors. Histology of Ancient Human Bone: Methods and Diagnosis. Berlin: Springer-Verlag. pp. 79–94.

Hartnady P. 1997. Alteration of bone microstructure in skeletal tuberculosis. Am J Phys Anthropol S24:44–47.

Iwaniec UT. 1997. Effects of Dietary Acidity on Cortical Bone Remodeling: A Histomorphometric Assessment. Ph.D. Dissertation, University of Wisconsin–Madison.

Knight D, Melbye J. 1983. Burial patterns at the Ball site. Ontario Archaeol 40:37–48.

Lazenby RA. 1990a. Continuing periosteal apposition I: documentation, hypotheses, and interpretation. Am J Phys Anthropol 82:451–472.

Lazenby RA. 1990b. Continuing periosteal apposition II: the significance of peak bone mass, strain equilibrium, and age-related activity differentials for mechanical compensation in human tubular bones. Am J Phys Anthropol 82:473–484.

Lazenby RA, Pfeiffer S. 1993. Effects of a nineteenth century below-knee amputation and prosthesis on femoral morphology. Int J Osteoarchaeol 3:19–28.

Martin DL. 1991. Bone histology and paleopathology: methodological considerations. In: Ortner DJ, Aufderheide AC, editors. Human Paleopathology: Current Syntheses and Future Options. Washington: Smithsonian Institution Press. pp. 55–59.

Martin DL, Armelagos G. 1985. Skeletal remodeling and mineralization as indicators of health: an example from prehistoric Sudanese Nubia. J Hum Evol 14:527–537.

Martin RB, Burr DB. 1989. Structure, Function and Adaptation of Compact Bone. New York: Raven Press.

Miller SC, Bowman BM. 1998. Comparison of bone loss during normal lactation with estrogen deficiency osteopenia and immobilization osteopenia. Anat Rec 251:265–274.

Mosekilde L. 1990. Consequences of the remodelling process for vertebral trabecular bone structure: a scanning electron microscope study (uncoupling of unloaded structures). Bone and Mineral 10:13–35.

Mulhern DM, Van Gerven DP. 1997. Patterns of femoral bone remodeling dynamics in a medieval Nubian population. Am J Phys Anthropol 104:133–146.

Ortner DJ. 1970. The effects of aging and disease on the micromorphometry of human compact bone.

Ph.D. Dissertation. University of Kansas. Ann Arbor: University Microfilms International.

Ott SM. 1996. Theoretical and methodological approach. In: Bilezikian JP, Raisz LG, Rodan GA, editors. Principles of Bone Biology. San Diego: Academic Press. pp. 231–241.

Pankovich AM, Simmons DJ, Kudarni VV. 1974. Zonal osteons in cortical bone. Clin Ortho Rel Res 100:356–363.

Parfitt AM. 1992. The physiologic and pathogenetic significance of bone histomorphometric data. In: Coe FL, Favus MJ, editors. Disorders of Bone and Mineral Metabolism. New York: Raven Press. pp. 475–489.

Parfitt AM, Drezner MK, Glorieux FH, Kanis JA, Malluche H, Meunier PJ, Ott SM, Recker RR. 1987. Bone histomorphometry: standardization of nomenclature, symbols, and units. J Bone Min Res 2:595–610.

Pfeiffer S. 1989. Characterization of archaeological bone decomposition in a sample of known length of interment. Am J Phys Anthropol 78:283 (abstract).

Pfeiffer S. 1995. An exploration of possible relationships between structural and chemical decomposition of bone. Proceedings of the I World Congress on Mummy Studies, Museo Arqueologico y Etnografico doe Tenerife, Islas Canarias (Spain). pp. 549–558.

Pfeiffer S. 1998. Variability in osteon size in recent human populations. Am J Phys Anthropol 106:219–227.

Pfeiffer S, Lazenby R, Chiang J. 1995. Brief communication: cortical remodeling data are affected by sampling location. Am J Phys Anthropol 96:89–92.

Pfeiffer S, Varney TL. (in press) Quantifying histological and chemical preservation in archaeological bone. In: Ambrose SH, Katzenberg MA, editors. Close to the Bone: Biogeochemical Approaches to Paleodietary Analysis in Archaeology. New York: Plenum Press.

Pfeiffer S, Zehr M. 1995. Variability and correlations of osteon size in modern humans. Am J Phys Anthropol S20:170–171.

Pfeiffer S, Zehr M. 1996. A morphological and histological study of the human humerus from Border Cave. J Hum Evol 31:49–59.

Richman EA, Ortner DJ, Schulter-Ellis FP. 1979. Differences in intracortical bone remodeling in three aboriginal American populations: possible dietary factors. Calcif Tissue Int 28:209–214.

Roberts C, Wakely J. 1992. Microscopical findings associated with the diagnosis of osteoporosis in paleopathology. Int J Osteoarchaeol 2:23–30.

Ruff CB, Hayes WC. 1988. Sex differences in age-related remodeling of the femur and tibia. J Ortho Res 6:886–896.

Schenk RK, Olah AJ, Herrman W. 1984. Preparation of calcified tissues for light microscopy. In: Dickson GR, editor. Methods of Calcified Tissue Preparation. New York: Elsevier Science Publishers. pp. 1–56.

Schiessl H, Frost HM, Jee WSS. 1998. Estrogen and bone-muscle strength and mass relationships. Bone 22:1–6.

Schultz M. 1986. Die mikroskopiche Untersuchung prahistorischer Skeletfunde: Anwendung und Aussagemoglichkeiten der differentialdiagnostischen Untersuchung in der Palaopathologie. Archaologie und Museum: Liestal.

Schultz M. 1992. The Microscopic Investigation of Bone Tumours Found in Archaeological Skeletal Materials. In: Cockburn E, editor. Papers of the Ninth European Members Meeting of the Paleopathology Society, Barcelon, Spain. (Abstract).

Schultz M. 1993a. A new approach to diagnosing syphilis in ancient bones by histopathology. In: Cockburn E, editor. Papers of the Twentieth Annual Meeting of the Paleopathology Association, Toronto, Ontario. (Abstract).

Schultz M. 1993b. Microscopic investigation of archaeological skeletal remains—a convincing necessity for differential diagnosis in paleopathology. Am J Phys Anthropol S16:175.

Schultz M. 1997a. Microscopic structure of bone. In: Haglund WD, Sorg MH, editors. Forensic Taphonomy: The Postmortem Fate of Human Remains. Boca Raton: CRC Press. pp. 187–199.

Schultz M. 1997b. Microscopic investigation of excavated skeletal remains: a contribution to paleopathology and forensic medicine. In: Haglund AH, Sorg M, editors. Forensic Taphonomy: The Postmortem Fate of Human Remains. Boca Raton: CRC Press. pp. 201–222.

Schwartz JH. 1995. Skeleton Keys: An Introduction to Human Skeletal Morphology, Development, and Analysis. New York: Oxford University Press.

Shipman P, Walker A, Bichell D. 1985. The Human Skeleton. Cambridge: Harvard University Press.

Singh IJ, Gunberg DL. 1970. Estimation of age at death in human males from quantitative histology of bone fragments. Am J Phys Anthropol 33:373–381.

Sowers M. 1996. Pregnancy and lactation as risk factors for subsequent bone loss and osteoporosis. J Bone Mineral Res 11:1052–1060.

Steele DG, Bramblett CA. 1988. The Anatomy and Biology of the Human Skeleton. College Station: Texas A&M University Press.

Stothers D, Abel TJ. 1989. The position of the "Pearson complex" in the late prehistory of Ohio. Archeol E N Am 17:109–141.

Stout SD. 1976. Histomorphometric Analysis of Archaeological Bone. Ph.D. Dissertation, Washington University, St. Louis.

Stout SD. 1989. Histomorphometric analysis of human skeletal remains. In: Íscan Y, Kennedy K, editors. Reconstruction of Life from the Skeleton. New York: Wiley-Liss.

Stout SD, Lueck R. 1995. Bone remodeling rates and skeletal maturation in three archaeological skeletal populations. Am J Phys Anthropol 98:161–171.

Thompson DD. 1980. Age changes in bone mineralization, cortical thickness and Haversian canal area. Calcif Tissue Int 31:5–11.

Trivers K, Armelagos G. 1997. Double zonal osteons and HDI bodies in bone remodeling and modeling in ancient Nubia. Am J Phys Anthropol S24:229–230.

Turban-Just S, Grupe G. 1995. Postmortem-Rekonstruktion von Stoffwechselraten mittels Histomorphometrie bondengelagerter menschlicher Knochenkompakta. Anthropol Anz 53:1–25.

Ubelaker DH. 1989. Human Skeletal Remains: Excavation, Analysis, Interpretation. Washington: Taraxacum Press.

Wakely J, Manchester K, Roberts C. 1991. Scanning electron microscopy of rib lesions. Int J Osteoarchaeol 1:191–198.

Walker A, Zimmerman MR, Leakey REF. 1982. A possible case of hypervitaminosis A in *Homo erectus*. Nature 296:248–250.

Weinmann JP, Sicher H. 1955. Bone and Bones: Fundamentals of Bone Biology. St. Louis: Mosby.

Weinstein RS. 1992. Clinical use of bone biopsy. In: Coe FL, Favus MJ, editors. Disorders of Bone and Mineral Metabolism. New York: Raven Press. pp. 455–473.

White TD. 1991. Human Osteology. San Diego: Academic Press.

Yoshino ME. 1994. Histological estimation of age at death using microradiographs of humeral compact bone. Forensic Sci Int 64:191–198.

PART IV

CHEMICAL AND GENETIC ANALYSES OF HARD TISSUES

CHAPTER 11

STABLE ISOTOPE ANALYSIS: A TOOL FOR STUDYING PAST DIET, DEMOGRAPHY, AND LIFE HISTORY

M. ANNE KATZENBERG

INTRODUCTION

Detailed study of the human skeleton ranges from observations of morphological features, such as those that distinguish males from females, to microscopic structure and minor variations in the chemical composition of components of skeletal tissues. This chapter is about chemical variation and its application to studies of diet, demography, and life history. Bones and teeth provide direct evidence of past diets, including infant diets. Knowledge gained from bone chemistry relates to other evidence for diet and, in turn, the interaction of nutrition and disease. Understanding infant diets and the duration of nursing relates to demographic variables such as birth spacing and population growth. While stable isotope analysis may be viewed as a fairly technical research specialty, the results of such analyses make a significant contribution to the reconstruction of past human life.

Uses of Stable Isotope Analysis in Skeletal Biology

The routine use of stable carbon isotopes in skeletal studies in the 1990s is very different from the excitement generated by the first ap-

Biological Anthropology of the Human Skeleton, Edited by M. Anne Katzenberg and Shelley R. Saunders.
ISBN 0-471-31616-4 Copyright © 2000 by Wiley-Liss, Inc.

plications of stable carbon isotopes to human paleodiet reconstruction. The idea that one could determine whether or not prehistoric peoples of North America consumed corn (maize) by performing chemical tests on their bones seemed like science fiction to most archaeologists and physical anthropologists in the mid-1970s when it was first attempted (Vogel and van der Merwe, 1977). Today, stable carbon isotope analysis is part of a suite of technical specialties performed on remains from archaeological sites. In addition to studying stable carbon and nitrogen isotopes in preserved protein, it is now possible to study stable isotopes of carbon, oxygen, and strontium from the mineral portion of bones and teeth. This chapter provides some background to the use of stable isotopes in bioarchaeological studies. It includes technical information on how such analyses are performed, a sampling of applications, problems, and finally, promises for the future. This is not intended to be a review of the now vast literature on methods and applications of stable isotope analysis in studies of past peoples. Such literature reviews are available elsewhere (Katzenberg and Harrison, 1997; Pate, 1994; Schoeninger and Moore, 1992; Schwarcz and Schoeninger, 1991). However the various discussions may serve to guide the reader to the relevant literature if more detailed information is desired.

Developments in Stable Isotope Analysis

From the perspective of the archaeologist, the first stable isotope studies of past diet were carried out in the 1970s (DeNiro and Epstein, 1978, 1981; van der Merwe and Vogel, 1978; Vogel and van der Merwe, 1977). However, studies of stable isotopes began in the early years of the twentieth century in the laboratories of chemists and physicists. Following the discovery of stable isotopes in 1913, improvements in instrumentation and intensive study resulted in the identification of most of the stable isotopes by the mid-1930s. The first commercial mass spectrometer was used to analyze petroleum in 1942 (Gross, 1979). Throughout the 1950s and 1960s mass spectrometers and the applications of stable isotope studies advanced very rapidly in chemistry, biology, and geochemistry. Efforts were directed toward understanding variation in the relative abundances of stable isotopes of the various elements. For example, geochemists explored oxygen isotope variation and its potential for studies of past climate (reviewed by Luz and Kolodny, 1989). Major advances in understanding stable isotope variation in the biosphere and geosphere occurred during the 1950s and 1960s. Botanists and geochemists explored stable carbon isotope variation in plants (Craig, 1954; Smith and Epstein, 1971), and researchers in radiocarbon dating laboratories shared their interest (Bender, 1968; Hall, 1967; Lowdon, 1969) since this variation is relevant to radiocarbon dating methods.

Along with advances in understanding the processes that cause variation in stable isotope abundance ratios in different substances, there have been major advances in instrumentation. While improvements in resolution, detection, and overall design of mass spectrometers have occurred throughout the twentieth century, advances in the last ten years have had an enormous impact on the use of stable isotope methods due to the ability to run more samples at a much lower cost. Stable isotope analysis used to be a time-consuming and, therefore,

expensive method. Preparation of samples, isolation of gasses containing specific elements of interest, and the actual analysis and corrections to standards were very laborious processes. Only a small number of samples per day could be analyzed and analyses required constant attention by laboratory personnel. In the late 1980s new instrumentation was developed that simplifies sample preparation, automates introduction of samples into the system, requires much smaller samples, is much faster, and, therefore, is much less expensive. This has opened up many more applications of stable isotope analysis, most notably in ecological research (Barrie et al., 1989; Griffiths, 1998; Rundel et al., 1989). It has also made it possible for many more samples to be analyzed in archaeological studies. Instead of selecting a few human bones for analysis, researchers now routinely analyze nonhuman faunal bone and either prehistoric or modern plants to compare potential foods with human stable isotope data. These newer methods have allowed researchers to analyze many more human samples, revealing previously unknown variation within populations. Stable isotope methods have now been applied to studies of demography, residence patterns, and disease in addition to studies of diet. While newer instruments simplify analyses, it is imperative to have trained personnel in reputable laboratories running the instruments to insure accuracy and precision.

History of Applications to Analysis of Past Peoples

The realization that stable isotopes of carbon could be used to investigate past diets can be traced to two different but related fields of study (reviewed by van der Merwe, 1982). Scientists working to determine ^{14}C dates on ancient organic remains noted variation in dates derived from some human skeletal remains. It was also noted that maize from archaeological sites gave anomalous dates relative to wood charcoal (Bender, 1968; Hall,

1967). This coincided with research on different biochemical pathways of photosynthesis among plants (Smith and Epstein, 1971). Maize fixes carbon by a different pathway and, as a result, contains more ^{13}C relative to ^{12}C than most other plants from temperate regions. Since samples for radiocarbon dating were assumed to have the same carbon isotope composition as the standard, those samples containing relatively more ^{13}C, such as maize cobs and kernels, gave erroneous dates. In addition to its use in differentiating human consumption of plants with different photosynthetic pathways, carbon isotopes have been shown to differentiate marine- from terrestrial-based diets in humans (Chisholm et al., 1982; Tauber, 1981).

Carbon was the first element for which stable isotope variation was used in archaeology, which follows from archaeologists' familiarity with radiocarbon. Once the potential of studying stable carbon isotopes in preserved protein was generally understood, interest in other elements such as nitrogen, oxygen, and sulfur flourished. Each of these has been studied extensively in geological and ecological systems as well. In fact, archaeologists are relative latecomers to the study of stable isotope variation of the elements, with the exception of carbon.

The second element to be used in paleodiet research was nitrogen. DeNiro and Epstein studied both carbon (1978) and nitrogen (1981) in several species using controlled feeding experiments. Shortly after that, DeNiro, working with two postdoctoral researchers, explored trophic level and regional variation in nitrogen isotopes (Schoeninger and DeNiro, 1984) and trophic level variation and dietary differences in east Africa (Ambrose and DeNiro, 1987).

Carbon and nitrogen stable isotopes are the most commonly studied in human remains. More recently, oxygen and strontium isotopes have been studied in bone and in tooth enamel. Principles of oxygen and strontium isotopes and their applications to reconstructing human life will be discussed in a later section.

BASIC CONCEPTS OF STABLE ISOTOPE VARIATION

Isotopes are atoms of the same element with the same number of protons, but different numbers of neutrons. Since the atomic mass is determined by the number of protons and neutrons, isotopes of an element vary in their masses. Table 11.1 shows some of the chemical elements that have several isotopes and the abundances of those isotopes. In contrast to unstable (radioactive) isotopes, stable isotopes do not decay over time. For example, ^{14}C in a dead organism decays to ^{14}N whereas the amounts of ^{12}C and ^{13}C in the same organism will remain constant.

In chemical reactions, such as the conversion of CO_2 into glucose by plants, the relative amounts of ^{12}C and ^{13}C differ in plant tissue relative to CO_2. This variation is due to the fact that isotopes vary in mass and therefore have slightly different chemical and physical properties. Isotopes with higher mass (heavier isotopes) such as ^{13}C usually react slightly more slowly than lighter isotopes such as ^{12}C. The resulting difference in the isotope ratio of the carbon in the plant tissues as compared to the carbon in atmospheric CO_2 is termed "fractionation." Two terms that are frequently confused in isotope studies are "isotope effect" and "fractionation." Isotope effects are physical phenomena that occur during chemical reactions and these effects result in fractionation. More detailed discussions of isotope effects and fractionation can be found in textbooks such as that by Hoefs (1997) and in a brief article by Hayes (1982).

Tissues Used in Stable Isotope Studies

The first tissue to be used in archaeological stable isotope studies of human paleodiet was the collagen of bone. Methods for isolating collagen had already been developed in radiocarbon dating laboratories since collagen was used in dating. Information on isolating colla-

TABLE 11.1 Average Terrestrial Abundances of Stable Isotopes of Elements Used in Analyses of Ancient Human Tissues

Element	Isotope	Abundance (%)
Hydrogen	^{1}H	99.985
	^{2}H	0.015
Carbon	^{12}C	98.89
	^{13}C	1.11
Nitrogen	^{14}N	99.63
	^{15}N	0.37
Oxygen	^{16}O	99.759
	^{17}O	0.037
	^{18}O	0.204
Sulfur	^{32}S	95.00
	^{33}S	0.76
	^{34}S	4.22
	^{36}S	0.014
Strontium	^{84}Sr	0.56
	^{86}Sr	9.86
	^{87}Sr	7.02
	^{88}Sr	82.56

Extracted from Table 1.1 Ehleringer and Rundel, 1989.

gen from bones and teeth is provided by Ambrose (1990), who critically reviews the various methods available. Bone is composed of an organic matrix of the structural protein, collagen, which is studded with crystals of calcium phosphate, largely in the form of hydroxyapatite. Dry bone is approximately 70% inorganic and 30% organic by weight. Most of the organic portion (85–90%) is collagen. The remainder includes noncollagenous proteins, proteoglycans and lipids (Triffit, 1980). Because of the intimate structural relationship between collagen and hydroxyapatite, collagen may survive for thousands of years (Tuross et al., 1980), and protein that is probably degraded collagen has even been recovered from dinosaur fossils (Wyckoff, 1980). The detection of postmortem degradation of collagen is an active area of research (e.g., Child, 1995; Schoeninger et al., 1989).

Because collagen does degrade over time and at varying rates depending on the burial environment, researchers have sought other sources of carbon that are representative of lifetime carbon intake. Another biological source of carbon in bones and teeth is in the form of carbonate (CO_3), which occurs in the mineral portion of bone. Bone mineral is largely composed of hydroxyapatite, $Ca_{10}(PO_4)OH_2$. However there are a number of ions that can substitute for the constituent ions of the hydroxyapatite crystals (see Sandford and Weaver, Chapter 12). Well-known from the trace element literature are the substitutions of Sr^{++} (strontium) or Pb^{++} (lead) for Ca^{++}. Another common substitution is CO_3^- for $PO_4^=$ (LeGeros et al., 1967). Sullivan and Krueger (1981) proposed using the carbon in bone mineral for stable carbon isotope studies in fossil bone, when collagen was too badly degraded to be used. This proposal was challenged by Schoeninger and DeNiro (1982) and a debate in the literature followed (reviewed by Krueger, 1991; Lee-Thorp and van der Merwe, 1991). The challenge centered on whether bone carbonate was altered in the postmortem environment by exchange between constituents of buried bone and carbonates in sediments such that the carbon isotope ratios would not reflect lifetime carbon deposition. These concerns have been addressed by Lee-Thorp (1989), who developed preparation methods to remove the more soluble carbonates, which are those most likely to be diagenetic in origin. More recent debate has centered on the use of carbonate in tooth enamel versus dentin and bone (Koch et al., 1997). There are two compelling reasons to pursue the use of carbonate in biological apatite as a source of carbon isotope ratios. It allows stable isotope studies to be applied to much older materials where it is no longer possible to isolate collagen (e.g., Lee-Thorp et al., 1989; Sponheimer and Lee-Thorp, 1999), and carbon from biological apatite records slightly different dietary information than does collagen.

The idea that the carbon in the carbonate of bones and teeth comes from different dietary components than the carbon in collagen was first proposed by Krueger and Sullivan (1984). Ambrose and Norr (1993) and Tieszen and Fagre (1993), in two separate controlled feeding experiments, demonstrated that Krueger and Sullivan were correct in suggesting that collagen carbon comes mainly from ingested protein in the diet while the carbon in biological apatite reflects whole diet. The reason is that collagen is composed of a mix of essential and nonessential amino acids. The essential amino acids come from ingested protein. The nonessential amino acids may come from ingested protein, or may be formed from other dietary sources and breakdown products within the body. Carbonate in bone is formed from dissolved bicarbonate in the blood and this comes from dietary carbohydrate, lipid, and protein. Therefore, the carbon in biological apatite provides a picture of the total diet while collagen is more reflective of dietary protein.

The mineral portion of bone is also the source of oxygen and strontium used in isotope studies. Oxygen isotopes are most often isolated from PO_4 (Luz and Kolodny, 1989; Stuart-Williams and Schwarcz, 1997) and have been used in paleoclimate and more recently, paleodemographic studies. Strontium is a common trace element in bone where it substitutes for calcium. Strontium isotopes have been used in paleodiet and residence studies (Ericson, 1985, 1989; Ezzo et al., 1997; Price et al., 1994a, 1994b; Sealy et al., 1991, 1995).

Methods for Isolating Specific Components for Stable Isotope Analysis

Specific instructions for isolating various components of bone can be found in the sources cited throughout this section. It is important to understand the chemical principals of each method. There is a wide range of variation in postmortem environments, duration of interment, and therefore the preservation of hard tissues. It is sometimes necessary to vary the methods for poorly preserved bone samples. For example, by weakening the acid solution, the process of dissolving the bone mineral is less harsh and proceeds more slowly. Sometimes postmortem alteration is so extensive that specific analyses are not possible.

Collagen

Most researchers use one of three methods for isolating collagen from bones and teeth (primarily dentin). Sealy (1986) describes a simple method in which small chunks of bone (1–3 g in total) are decalcified in one molar hydrochloric acid. An additional soak in sodium hydroxide may follow in order to remove decayed organic matter from the burial environment. The remaining collagen is freeze-dried.

Another method, described by Tuross and colleagues (1989) makes use of EDTA (ethylenediaminetetraacetic acid), a sodium salt, to separate collagen from noncollagenous proteins and bone mineral. A third method was originally described by Longin (1971) and later modified by Schoeninger and DeNiro (1984), and by Brown and colleagues (1988). Powdered bone is demineralized in hydrochloric acid for a short period of time (around 18 min). This is followed by a slow hydrolysis in weakly acidic hot water. This method is preferable for poorly preserved bone, however the risk is that one may obtain other organic matter in addition to collagen.

Several researchers have compared methods and their yields (Chisholm et al., 1983; Schoeninger et al., 1989). Boutton and colleagues (1984) and Katzenberg (1989; Katzenberg et al., 1995) have demonstrated that some collagen is lost when demineralized bone is soaked in sodium hydroxide, but that the other material removed in the soak contains humic contaminants (decayed organic matter) that may skew $\delta^{13}C$ values. For example, Katzenberg and colleagues (1995) demonstrated that the residue removed during the sodium hydroxide soak of prehistoric human bones from southern Ohio had a much lighter $\delta^{13}C$ than the collagen, indicating that the residue contained decayed C_3 plant remains.

In all of these procedures, the objective is to isolate collagen from bone mineral and any organic matter introduced in the postmortem environment. With advances in the field, several researchers have focused their attention on isolating individual amino acids, initially for accelerator radiocarbon dating (Stafford et al., 1991). Stable isotope values vary among the different amino acids so preferential loss of certain amino acids due to diagenesis can alter the overall $\delta^{13}C$ (Hare and Estep, 1982). There is also interest in isolating the indispensable (essential) amino acids from collagen for stable isotope analysis for dietary reconstruction (Hare et al., 1991). Since these amino acids come from dietary protein and are incorporated into human proteins such as collagen, they provide a more direct tracer than collagen as a whole, which is made up of both dispensable and indispensable amino acids. Methods used for such study are much more complex than those for simply isolating collagen and are described by Stafford and colleagues (1991) and Hare and colleagues (1991). There is considerable promise in pursuing these methods, particularly with the development of GC/C/IRMS (gas chromatography/combustion/isotope ratio mass spectrometry) (Macko et al., 1997). This method allows the researcher to isolate specific organic compounds and then to introduce them into the mass spectrometer. Students interested in graduate study in this area are well advised to become familiar with the principles and methods of biochemistry.

Biological Apatite

A method for isolating the carbonate fraction of bone mineral was developed by Lee-Thorp (1989; Lee-Thorp et al., 1989; Lee-Thorp and van der Merwe, 1991). Ground bone is soaked in sodium hypochlorite in order to remove organic material. Carbonate adsorbed from the burial environment is removed with one molar acetic acid. Samples are then reacted with phosphoric acid to release the structural carbonate. CO_2 is collected by cryogenic distillation. Specific steps are described in the references cited above and by Tieszen and Fagre (1993) and Ambrose and Norr (1993).

Oxygen isotope measurements in bone make use of the oxygen in phosphate, which is less affected by diagenetic processes than carbonate. Stuart-Williams (1996; Stuart-Williams and Schwarcz, 1995, 1997) has developed a method of isolating organic phosphate from bone that is simpler and safer than previous procedures.

Strontium substitutes for calcium in the hydroxyapatite crystals of bone mineral. Two different methods of isolating bone mineral for analysis of strontium isotopes have been described in the recent literature. The method used by Sealy and colleagues (1995) and by Sillen and colleagues (1998) makes use of Sillen's (1986) solubility profile method. Bone or tooth powder is washed in acetic acid and sodium acetate buffer solution repeatedly, saving each wash. The various washes are analyzed by ICP (inductively coupled plasma emission spectrometry). The first few washes presumably contain recently deposited contaminants from the burial environment and show variation in trace element concentrations. Later washes tend to show less variation in the concentration of strontium and other trace elements. It is these later washes, which are thought to contain the biologically deposited strontium, that are used for strontium isotope analysis by mass spectrometry.

A second method of preparation for strontium isotope analysis, described by Price and colleagues (1994a) begins with mechanical cleaning of the outer surface of bone, followed by an overnight soak in one normal acetic acid. The acid removes soluble carbonates and the portion of bone most likely to contain elements from the burial environment. The residue is then wet ashed in nitric acid in preparation for mass spectrometry. Both methods attempt to isolate bone mineral that has not been diagenetically altered and while Sillen's method is more conservative it is also more labor intensive. Sillen and Sealy (1995) have demonstrated that the solubility profile method does not result in any recrystallization of bone mineral, unlike methods that employ dry ashing (heating to high temperature to destroy the organic component). Price and colleagues (1994a, 1994b) use wet ashing (destroying the organic component with nitric acid). It would be useful to compare strontium isotope results from a number of samples prepared using the preparation methods described by Sillen and those described by Price and colleagues.

Lipids

Methods for treating lipids from bone samples depend on whether one intends to remove the lipids so that only protein or carbonate is analyzed, or whether one wants to determine the $\delta^{13}C$ of lipid. Lipids have lighter (more negative $\delta^{13}C$ than bone collagen. Therefore it is necessary to remove lipids from bone samples prior to analysis. This is particularly important when analyzing bones of recent origin for comparative purposes. Liden and colleagues (1995) discuss methods of removing lipids. The most commonly used method involves soaking the bone in a mixture of chloroform and methanol (Bligh and Dyer, 1959; Folch et al., 1957) following demineralization. The residue must be rinsed carefully since these are organic solvents that may contaminate the sample. Bone may also be soaked in diethyl ether prior to demineralization followed by the normal sodium hydroxide soak following demineralization (Ambrose and Norr, 1993). These methods will effectively eliminate lipids from collagen preparations. Bligh and Dyer (1959) describe a method for extracting and purifying lipid from biological materials. Recent work by Evershed and colleagues (Evershed, 1993; Stott and Evershed, 1996) on characterization of lipid extracts from ancient materials shows promise for refining paleodiet studies by allowing $\delta^{13}C$ determinations on lipids.

Mass Spectrometry

Stable isotope abundance ratios are measured in isotope ratio mass spectrometers (IRMSs), which should not be confused with organic mass spectrometers, which are used to characterize complex organic molecules. Isotope ratio mass spectrometers are composed of four components: an inlet system, an ion source, a mass analyzer, and a series of ion detectors (Fig. 11.1). For most of the elements of interest (H, O, N, C) the sample is introduced to the mass spectrometer as a gas (H_2, CO_2, N_2, and CO_2, respectively). Until recently, most stable isotope work done with collagen or carbonate required combustion of the sample in sealed tubes. After combustion, the resultant CO_2 and H_2O were separated offline before the CO_2 was let into the mass spectrometer. Modern instruments now interface combustion furnaces and gas analyzers with mass spectrometers to simplify and ease the conversion of the sample into the requisite gaseous form. In such a setup, collagen is weighed into tin sample holders, which are then placed into an automated sample tray. The revolving tray drops samples into the furnace where N_2, CO_2, and H_2O are produced. These gases, carried by helium carrier gas, are separated before being swept into the mass spectrometer. (For a detailed presentation of continuous-flow stable isotope analysis, see Barrie et al., 1989; Barrie and Prosser, 1996).

Once in the mass spectrometer, the gas of interest is let into the second component of the mass spectrometer, the ion source. In the ion source, some of the gas molecules are ionized by electron bombardment, allowing them to be controlled and focused into a beam. The ion

DOUBLE COLLECTOR STABLE ISOTOPE MASS SPECTROMETER

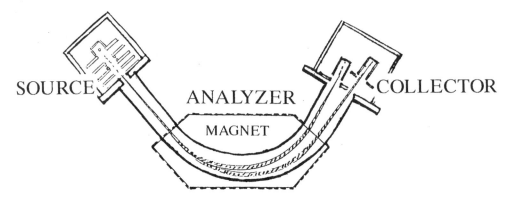

Figure 11.1 Diagram showing three of the four components of the mass spectrometer: gas is introduced into the source, where molecules are ionized then accelerated; the resulting ion beam is directed into the mass analyzer, where ions of different masses are separated; ion collectors measure intensities of the separated ion beams. (Courtesy of H.R. Krouse.)

beam is then directed, via a flight tube, into the mass analyzer zone of the mass spectrometer. As the name suggests, the mass analyzer separates the ion beam into several smaller beams by passing it between the poles of a magnet. This is completely analogous to the separation of white light into its constituent wavelengths through a prism. The separation of one ion beam into several beams according to mass results in the desired "mass spectrum." The beam intensities of the respective ion beams can then be measured in the ion collector section of the instrument. The relative intensities of the individual isotope ion beams are then reported as isotope ratios, for example, $^{13}CO_2$:$^{12}CO_2$. In order to report a meaningful value, the mass spectrometer alternately analyzes aliquots of the unknown sample and a known standard gas, thereby providing a ratio of the stable isotopes in the sample relative to that same ratio in the standard.

Because the element of interest cannot always be converted into an easily handled gas, it is sometimes necessary to introduce the sample in solid form. For strontium isotope analysis, the sample is deposited directly on a filament near the ion source where it is heated to evapo-

ration and ionized under vacuum. A different ion source is required for this analysis. Many labs will have separate instruments for analyzing gases and solids.

It is helpful to know enough about mass spectrometry to be able to discuss one's needs with various laboratory personnel at the beginning of a research project. It is important to be able to understand problems that may arise when the data have been collected. Considerations include the general composition of the sample and the range of expected results. For example, departures from the expected range of carbon to nitrogen in bones and teeth may signal poor preservation or contamination. It is necessary to have some idea of the range of isotope compositions expected since the standards used should bracket the expected values.

Mass spectrometers are analytical instruments that have many uses in chemistry, geochemistry, and ecology. Instruments vary in their setup depending on the needs of the researcher. A laboratory may be set up to perform analyses on certain types of samples and may specialize in certain elements. Laboratories carrying out ecological research are most

TABLE 11.2 **Primary (International) and Reference Standards for Selected Elements**

Element	Primary Standard	Other Reference Standards
Hydrogen	Vienna standard mean ocean water (VSMOW)	V-GISP, V-SLAP, NBS-30
Oxygen	Standard mean ocean water (VSMOW)	NBS 19, 20, 18, 28, 30, V-GISP, V-SLAP
Carbon	PeeDee belemnite (VPDB)	NBS 18, 19, 20, 21
Nitrogen	Atmospheric nitrogen (air)	
Sulfur	Canyon Diablo meteorite troilite (VCDT)	

(From Hoefs, 1997, and Coplen, 1994.)

likely to be able to accommodate most analyses of interest to the archaeologist and physical anthropologist.

Standards, Precision, and Accuracy

Stable isotope abundance ratios are determined relative to the ratios of those same isotopes in standard materials. The mass spectrometer compares the stable isotope abundance ratio in the sample to the stable isotope ratio in a standard. Thus the reported value uses the following notation:

$$\delta \text{ in } \text{\textperthousand} = \frac{R_{(sample)} - R_{(standard)}}{R_{(standard)}} \times 1000$$

Where R = the ratio of the number of heavier to lighter isotopes, so that for carbon isotopes, the equation is:

$$\delta^{13}C\text{\textperthousand } PDB = \frac{^{13}C/^{12}C_{sample} - ^{13}C/^{12}C_{standard}}{^{13}C/^{12}C_{standard}} \times 1000$$

The ‰ (permille sign) means "per thousand" since the ratio is multiplied by 1000.

There are international standards available through the National Bureau of Standards (NBS) and the International Atomic Energy Agency, Vienna (IAEA). The circulation of these standards among laboratories allows comparison of results from different researchers working in different laboratories. However due to the cost, individual laboratories normally also have internal standards. These are substances whose isotopic ratio is well characterized relative to an international

standard and which are run routinely with batches of unknowns to check for consistency in the instrument. Internal and reference standards are reported relative to a primary reference standard for a particular element, which by definition has a δ value of 0. Absolute isotope abundances of some primary reference standards are available in textbooks such as that of Hoefs (1997). Primary and other reference standards for elements discussed in this chapter are listed in Table 11.2.

The sensitivity of mass spectrometers varies and it is important to know the precision of the instrument used before making interpretations from the data. Most light isotope mass spectrometers can measure $\delta^{13}C$ values with a precision of ±0.1‰ and ^{15}N values with a precision of ±0.2‰. Newer models have improved sensitivity, although some newer continuous flow systems that simultaneously measure more than one element in a sample sacrifice precision for speed and economy of sample size. Precision should be determined for individual instruments using multiple analyses of samples with similar composition to those of interest.

APPLICATION OF STABLE ISOTOPE ANALYSIS TO SELECTED PROBLEMS IN SKELETAL BIOLOGY

In recent years there have been numerous review articles published on stable isotope applications in anthropology and archaeology. The field has moved very quickly and has shifted directions in terms of research questions and materials analyzed. As stated earlier in this chapter, these shifts largely parallel improvements in instrumentation and requirements for much smaller samples. Katzenberg and Harrison (1997) discuss these changes and review the literature since 1989. Other reviews, which include basic concepts in stable isotope studies, have been prepared by Schwarcz and Schoeninger (1991), Schoeninger and Moore (1992), and Pate (1994). Collections of papers from two seminars that focused on stable isotope applications to paleodiet studies have been prepared more recently (Ambrose and Katzenberg, in press; Bocherens et al., 1999). Initially, most applications of stable isotope analysis to human remains were concerned with reconstructing diet. More recently other research questions have been addressed with stable isotope methods. These questions include determining the duration of breast-feeding, effects of disease processes, and determination of residence and migration patterns. The following sections highlight some of these recent applications in addition to more traditional approaches to paleodiet studies.

Paleodiet

C_3 and C_4 Plants

Maize is one of several tropical grasses that fixes carbon by a different photosynthetic pathway (referred to as the Hatch-Slack or C_4 pathway) than most plants found in temperate regions. C_4 plants, which also include sorghum, millet, and sugar cane, adapt to heat and aridity by minimizing the amount of time that the leaf pores (stomata) are open, thereby minimizing water loss. These plants discriminate less against the heavier isotope, ^{13}C, than do temperate plant species, which utilize the C_3 (Calvin) photosynthetic pathway. Atmospheric CO_2 has a $\delta^{13}C$ value of $-7‰$. C_4 plants range from -9 to $-14‰$ while C_3 plants range from -20 to $-35‰$ (Deines, 1980). The nonoverlapping ranges of C_3 and C_4 plants provide the basis for using stable isotopes of carbon in preserved human tissue for revealing diet. A number of studies have been carried out to determine the difference between the $\delta^{13}C$ of

the diet and the $\delta^{13}C$ value of various body tissues (Ambrose and Norr, 1993; Lyon and Baxter, 1978; Tieszen and Fagre, 1993; Vogel, 1978). Bone collagen $\delta^{13}C$ is approximately 5‰ greater than $\delta^{13}C$ of the diet. This is the basis for the expression, "You are what you eat +5‰." Interestingly, this number was first suggested by van der Merwe and Vogel (1978) based on measurements of free-ranging large mammals and their diets, then was confirmed experimentally by Ambrose (1997).

Following the demonstration that carbon stable isotopes in bone collagen could be used to document the consumption of C_4 plants such as maize against a background of C_3 plants (van der Merwe and Vogel, 1978; Vogel and van der Merwe, 1977), a number of other researchers applied these same principles to other regions where maize was the major introduced cultigen (e.g., Buikstra and Milner, 1991; Katzenberg et al., 1995; Larsen et al., 1992; Schurr and Redmond, 1991; Schwarcz et al., 1985). The method works very nicely in eastern North America where maize is the predominant, and in some places the only, C_4 plant consumed in any quantity. Follow-up studies took into consideration the fact that if the animals exploited by human groups consumed C_4 plants, then their tissues would be enriched in the heavier isotope and this would show up in human bone collagen carbon (Katzenberg, 1989).

Marine- Versus Terrestrial-Based Diets

The method also works well in coastal areas where it is possible to test hypotheses about the relative importance of marine and terrestrial foods in the diet (Blake et al., 1992; Chisholm et al., 1982; Hayden et al., 1987; Keegan and DeNiro, 1988; Lubell et al., 1994; Norr, 1991; Tauber, 1981; Walker and DeNiro, 1986). The main source of carbon for marine organisms is dissolved carbonate, which has a $\delta^{13}C$ value of 0‰ while the main source of carbon for terrestrial organisms is atmospheric CO_2, which has a ^{13}C value of $-7‰$. Tauber (1981) and Chisholm and colleagues (1982, 1983) demonstrated that this 7‰ difference is reflected in mammals, including humans, feeding from these two different ecosystems.

There are a number of regions of archaeological interest that were avoided initially because it did not appear that stable isotopes could provide any additional information. For example, application of stable isotope methods came somewhat later to the American Southwest, where there are a number of C_4 and CAM plants (a third photosynthetic pathway with values intermediate to C_3 and C_4 plants) in addition to human exploitation of animals who consume C_4 plants. Nevertheless, researchers did tackle this more complex region (Decker and Tieszen, 1989; Katzenberg and Kelley, 1991; Matson and Chisholm, 1991; Spielmann et al., 1990) with useful results in terms of documenting the intensity of maize use. The addition of nitrogen stable isotopes helps to sort out some of the information that is not discernable with stable carbon isotopes alone.

Nitrogen Isotopes and Diet

Trophic Level Distinctions

At the same time that DeNiro and Epstein demonstrated that carbon isotope ratios of diet are reflected in the tissues of an animal, they carried out a study of the relationship of diet and tissues for stable isotopes of nitrogen (1981). Nitrogen isotopes vary depending on trophic level. Atmospheric nitrogen (N_2) is the primary standard and its value is set at 0‰. Some plants (legumes) have a symbiotic relationship with bacteria of the genus *Rhizobium*. The bacteria live in the roots and are able to fix nitrogen (combine it with other elements such as hydrogen or oxygen) thereby making it available to the plant (Brill, 1977). Other plants must get their nitrogen from decomposed organic matter, which breaks down to compounds such as ammonia (NH_2) or nitrate (NO_3). Legumes have $\delta^{15}N$ values closer to that of atmospheric nitrogen while nonleguminous plants have higher $\delta^{15}N$ values. Herbivore $\delta^{15}N$ values are approximately 3‰ higher than the $\delta^{15}N$ of their diet; thus herbivores consuming legumes will have lower

$\delta^{15}N$ values than those consuming nonleguminous plants. Carnivore tissues are again enriched in the heavier isotope resulting in $\delta^{15}N$ values approximately 3‰ higher than their diet. This principle of enrichment through successively higher trophic levels, which was first pointed out by Minagawa and Wada (1984) and Schoeninger and DeNiro (1984), provides the basis for using stable nitrogen isotopes to infer trophic level. Ideally, a range of animals and plants from the environment under study is analyzed and humans are viewed relative to the other organisms in their environment. An example is provided in Figure 11.2, which shows carbon and nitrogen stable isotope ratios for humans from several prehistoric sites in New Mexico relative to other mammals from the region (from Katzenberg and Kelley, 1991). Humans have the highest $\delta^{15}N$ and $\delta^{13}C$ values. In this region, humans consumed maize as well as animals that fed on C_4 plants. The figure indicates that both jackrabbits and bison consumed some C_4 plants. Humans are approximately 3‰ higher than deer, antelope, and bison for $\delta^{15}N$. The elevated $\delta^{15}N$ for deer and antelope relative to cottontail may reflect consumption of some legumes by cottontail, but may also be related to habitat. Cottontail and deer prefer forested habitats while antelope and jackrabbit are adapted to open range habitat. Heaton and colleagues (1986) and Ambrose (1991) have demonstrated that $\delta^{15}N$ is sensitive to climate and is elevated in arid regions. For this reason, Ambrose (1991) suggests that species from different ecosystems cannot be directly compared without considering the isotopic composition of the local food web.

Freshwater Resources

Initially, it was assumed that freshwater fish had carbon isotope values similar to those of terrestrial C_3-consuming organisms. Little was known about nitrogen isotope values in freshwater systems. In 1989, Katzenberg explored this question by analyzing bones of freshwater fish from archaeological sites

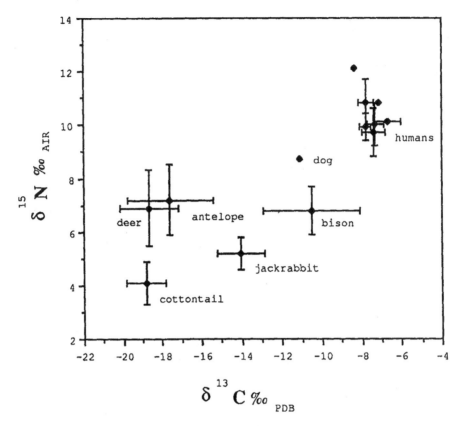

Figure 11.2 $\delta^{13}C$ and $\delta^{15}N$ values (mean ± one standard deviation) for collagen from human and faunal bone samples from sites in the Sierra Blanca region of New Mexico, dating from A.D. 800 to A.D. 1400. (Reproduced from Katzenberg and Kelley [1991] with permission of the publisher.)

around the Great Lakes. It was discovered that freshwater fish exhibit a trophic level effect, which results in higher $\delta^{15}N$ in carnivorous fish and slightly elevated $\delta^{13}C$. Thus it is possible to estimate reliance on fish in regions like the Great Lakes where they are an abundant resource. This is particularly significant since fish are frequently underrepresented in the zooarchaeological record due to cultural practices and, in earlier excavations, due to methods of recovery.

Freshwater fish also exhibit more variation in $\delta^{13}C$ than had been assumed. A number of studies of freshwater ecosystems by ecologists have provided the background to understanding the sources of this variation (France, 1995; Hecky and Hesslein, 1995; Kiyashko et al., 1991; Zohary et al., 1994). Freshwater plants

have numerous sources of carbon, unlike terrestrial plants whose source is atmospheric CO_2. In freshwater ecosystems, carbon comes from atmospheric CO_2, CO_2 in the water, bicarbonate and carbonate from rocks and soils, and organic carbon as waste and decomposition products from plants and animals living in the water (Zohary et al., 1994). The result is that fish living in different habitats within freshwater lakes display widely varying $\delta^{13}C$. This is illustrated in Figure 11.3, which shows a reconstruction of the stable isotope ecology of the region around Lake Baikal, Siberia (from Katzenberg and Weber, 1999). The $\delta^{13}C$ of fish bones ranges from -14.2 to $-24.6‰$ with heavier $\delta^{13}C$ in species inhabiting the shallow waters and lighter $\delta^{13}C$ for fish inhabiting the deeper, open waters of the lake

(Katzenberg and Weber, 1999). The heavier $\delta^{13}C$ for some fish explains the observed variation in human bone collagen $\delta^{13}C$ from the region. This is an important finding since there are no C_4 plants in the area.

Figure 11.3 also illustrates the trophic level effect in $\delta^{15}N$ in both terrestrial and freshwater organisms. Large terrestrial herbivores have $\delta^{15}N$ around 4 to 5‰. Humans from a large number of sites in the region range from 10.1 to 14.4‰. Fish and the freshwater seals of Lake Baikal vary according to their trophic position. Carp (*Caras a.*) are bottom-feeders and have the lightest $\delta^{15}N$. Lenok (*Branchimystax l.*) are highest in the littoral food web and have heavier $\delta^{15}N$. Seals (*Phoca s.*) occupy the highest position in the freshwater food web with $\delta^{15}N$ around 14‰.

Nitrogen Isotopes and Water Stress

Environmental variation in $\delta^{15}N$ of plants has been demonstrated in coastal versus inland regions and in arid versus wetter regions (Heaton, 1987; Shearer et al., 1983; Virginia and Delwiche, 1982). Heaton and colleagues (1986) and Sealy and colleagues (1987) have also shown that $\delta^{15}N$ varies in animals of the same species from arid versus wetter regions. Sealy and coworkers (1987) point out the importance of recognizing reasons for elevated $\delta^{15}N$ in arid regions when those regions are also in close proximity to coastal resources, as is the case on the southern cape of Africa. Incorrect dietary interpretations for human samples can result if higher $\delta^{15}N$ is attributed to the use of marine resources without recognizing that the same $\delta^{15}N$ might result from consump-

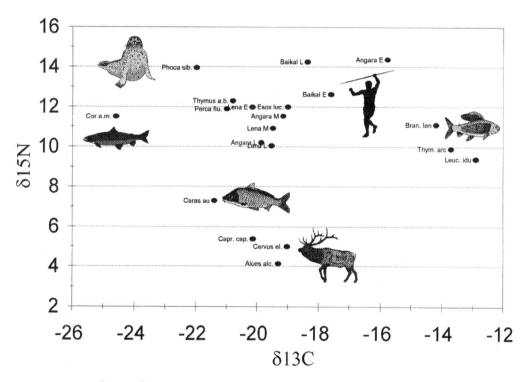

Figure 11.3 $\delta^{13}C$ and $\delta^{15}N$ values (means) for collagen from human and faunal bone samples from sites from the western shore of Lake Baikal, the Angara River Valley, and the Upper Lena River valley, Siberia, dating from the Early Neolithic (5800–4900 B.C.) to the Early Bronze Age (3400–1700 B.C.). Fish bones are from modern specimens. Mean values for human bones are plotted by site and location (e.g., Baikal E refers to Early Neolithic Lake Baikal site; Lena M refers to Middle Neolithic Lena valley site, and Angara L refers to Early Bronze Aga Angara valley site). (Reprinted from Katzenberg and Weber [1999] with permission.)

tion of water-stressed terrestrial animals. Ambrose (1991) has explored the physiological basis for $\delta^{15}N$ variation in mammals living in arid regions. Ambrose and DeNiro (1986) proposed a model based on varying nitrogen loss in urea, which is excreted in urine. Urea is depleted in ^{15}N relative to diet. Under conditions of water stress, more urea is excreted relative to the total volume of urine and therefore more of the lighter isotope, ^{14}N, is lost. Therefore, more ^{15}N is retained in the body where it is available for tissue synthesis. The result is that tissue $\delta^{15}N$ will increase under prolonged water stress conditions.

Nitrogen Isotopes and Protein Stress

Another cause of elevated $\delta^{15}N$, relative to expectations from diet, is protein stress. This is related to the model above in that insufficient protein intake results in the breakdown and re-utilization of existing tissues in the body that are already enriched in ^{15}N due to preferential excretion of ^{14}N. Hobson and colleagues, in two different studies on birds (1992, 1993), have found that under conditions of nutritional stress, new protein is synthesized from the products of catabolism of existing protein. Katzenberg and Lovell (1999) have presented evidence that suggests this may be detected in humans. They compared $\delta^{13}C$ and $\delta^{15}N$ in normal versus pathological segments of bones from individuals of known medical history. One individual, who died of AIDS and experienced some new bone deposition due to osteomyelitis, showed elevated $\delta^{15}N$ in the diseased segment relative to the two unaffected segments of bone. This suggests that the recently deposited bone collagen was synthesized, at least in part, from amino acids liberated from the catabolism of existing proteins in the body. White and Armelagos (1997) reported elevated $\delta^{15}N$ in bones from individuals with osteoporosis from an arid region of Sudan. They discuss water stress as a possible factor to explain the nitrogen isotope data, but it is possible that protein stress was also a factor. The use of stable isotopes to address questions in paleopathology is a relatively new area

of inquiry that promises to add to our understanding of disease processes as well as to our understanding of stable isotope variation in metabolism.

Infant Feeding and Weaning Studies

One of the big questions that carries through many approaches to studying past peoples from their skeletal and cultural remains is the timing and rate of population growth. Buikstra and colleagues (1986) presented an interesting hypothesis that draws together the adoption of agriculture, the development of thin-walled ceramic vessels, and, therefore, the ability to prepare cereal pap as a weaning food. The result would be earlier weaning (defined here as the introduction of non-milk foods rather than the complete cessation of breast-feeding) and therefore decreased interbirth intervals, increased population growth, and larger population size. This is based on the fact that nursing suppresses ovulation so that supplementing mother's milk with cereal gruel will result in a shorter period of infertility following childbirth. The hypothesis that weaning occurs sooner in agricultural societies was tested by Fogel and colleagues (1989, 1997) in a study that included stable nitrogen isotopes from fingernails of nursing mothers and their infants. They found a trophic level increase in $\delta^{15}N$ (+2.4‰ on average) of infant protein beginning shortly after birth (around three months) and decreasing when supplemental foods were introduced. By three to five months after nursing ceased, fingernail $\delta^{15}N$ for mothers and babies was the same. Fogel and colleagues (1989, 1997) then analyzed bone collagen from pre-agricultural and agricultural sites to see if the latter children were weaned at an earlier age. In both groups, $\delta^{15}N$ decreased at 18 to 20 months of age. This study demonstrated that the trophic level effect of increased $\delta^{15}N$ is reflected in protein, including bone collagen, and that there is the potential to apply this method to skeletal samples.

Others have applied this method and have attempted to refine estimates of the duration of nursing in the past (reviewed by Katzenberg et al., 1996; Schurr, 1998). For example, Herring and colleagues (1998) studied the process of weaning (introduction of non-breast milk foods and the gradual cessation of breast-feeding) in a nineteenth-century skeletal sample from Ontario by using stable nitrogen isotopes, parish records, census data, and skeletal evidence. The sample is from an Anglican church cemetery. (See Saunders, Chapter 5, for additional background information on the cemetery). A large number of skeletons of infants and young children were included in the sample, and parish records as well as the regional censuses could be consulted in order to obtain multiple sources of mortality data. Careful age determination of the individuals allowed the construction of a mortality profile, which could be compared with the parish records. Since mortality increases as infants are weaned, due to exposure to infectious agents and loss of passive immunity, it was possible to compare mortality with the nitrogen isotope evidence for weaning. The combined data show that non-breast milk foods were introduced around the age of 5 months, as indicated by increasing mortality, and that milk continued to be the major source of protein until around 14 months, as indicated by decreasing $\delta^{15}N$.

A potential problem with using stable isotopes of nitrogen in this way is that the subjects under study died in infancy and early childhood of unknown causes. Since $\delta^{15}N$ may be elevated in situations of nutritional stress, it may not be possible to separate the trophic effect of breast-feeding from cause of death in some cases. This possibility has been examined but it is not yet clear that it is a serious problem (Katzenberg, 1999).

One way to avoid the problem of analyzing bones from individuals who died in infancy or early childhood is to analyze tissues that were formed early in postnatal development that can be isolated from older children and adults. The permanent tooth crowns are formed between the ages of three months (incisors) and seven years (second premolars and second molars) (Hillson, 1996). The third molar crown forms

later but is highly variable. Analysis of nitrogen isotopes in dentin collagen and oxygen and carbon isotopes in enamel apatite can provide information about nursing and weaning for individuals who survived into at least late childhood. This approach has been followed by Wright and Schwarcz (1998). They analyzed stable isotopes of carbon and oxygen from the carbonate in tooth enamel. Oxygen isotope measurements are normally done on the phosphate of bones and teeth since phosphate is less likely to undergo diagenetic change than is carbonate. Wright and Schwarcz (1998) point out that the procedure for isolating phosphate is more complex than that for isolating carbonate, and that tooth enamel is less likely to be affected by diagenetic processes than bone mineral. The principle of using stable isotopes of carbon and oxygen is as follows: Carbon isotopes reflect the introduction of weaning foods, which, in the Americas, are usually maize-based gruel. Therefore $\delta^{13}C$ is expected to increase as this C_4-based weaning food is introduced into the diet. Oxygen isotopes reflect water source. Body water has a higher $\delta^{18}O$ than ingested water because more ^{16}O relative to ^{18}O is lost in expired water vapor. Since breast milk incorporates body water, it is enriched in the heavier isotope in comparison to other water sources for the infant. Therefore as the infant is weaned, $\delta^{18}O$ should decrease and breast-fed infants should have higher $\delta^{18}O$ than infants who are not breast-fed. Wright and Schwarz (1998) compared $\delta^{13}C$ and $\delta^{18}O$ in enamel carbonate from tooth crowns formed at different ages and showed that, as expected, $\delta^{13}C$ increases with age while $\delta^{18}O$ decreases with age. Attempts to refine the method by looking at specific sections of individual teeth are underway (Wright, 1999).

RESIDENCE AND MIGRATION STUDIES

From the preceding information it is obvious that some of the principles regarding stable isotope variation may be used to indicate place of residence. Stable carbon isotope abundance ratios vary based on diet while stable nitrogen isotope abundance ratios vary due to diet and habitat. Oxygen isotope abundance ratios vary due to climate and water source. In general, $\delta^{18}O$ decreases with increasing latitude, increasing distance from the coast, and increasing altitude. This is because more of the heavy isotope, ^{18}O, falls in precipitation (Dansgaard, 1964). Other variables that affect the $\delta^{18}O$ of human bone phosphate include humidity and the plants and animals consumed (Luz and Kolodny, 1989). Comparisons of stable isotope ratios in tissues laid down early in life and those that turn over throughout life may be used to determine whether individuals have moved. An elegant example of this type of study is that of Sealy and colleagues (1995), who compared enamel, dentin, and bone from five individuals from the southern Cape of Africa. Two individuals are prehistoric Khoisan hunter-gatherers, and three others date to the historic period. Of the historic burials, two were thought to be males of European ancestry and one was thought to be a female who was brought to the Cape as a slave. Enamel, dentin, and bone were analyzed for stable isotopes of carbon, nitrogen, and strontium. The prehistoric individuals have similar isotope values for all tissues analyzed. However two of the historic individuals show significant variation in stable isotope values for the different tissues, indicating that they moved between childhood and several years prior to death.

The use of stable oxygen isotopes to identify the geographical origin of prehistoric peoples has been carried out on prehistoric human bones from Mexico (White et al., 1998) and historic soldiers from northeastern North America (Schwarcz et al., 1991). The method becomes problematic in more recent peoples because our food and water comes from many sources (e.g., Perrier water from France is quite popular in North America, as is New Zealand lamb). However in people who were unlikely to move frequently, and who had fairly monotonous diets, oxygen isotope analysis is a useful indicator of residence.

Strontium isotopes are also useful in residence and migration studies since their variation is tied to local geology. Strontium isotopes vary depending on the underlying bedrock that gives rise to soils, and also vary between people feeding on marine versus terrestrial resources (Sealy et al., 1991). In addition to the study described above by Sealy and colleagues (1995), strontium isotopes have been used in studies of residence at the Grasshopper Pueblo in Arizona (Ezzo et al., 1997; Price et al., 1994a) and in a Bell Beaker sample from Bavaria (Price et al., 1994b). The potential of using strontium isotopes for residence studies was first pointed out by Ericson (1985). Because of the strontium isotope differences between marine and terrestrial foods they can also be used in paleodiet studies (Sealy et al., 1991).

A DAY WITHOUT STABLE ISOTOPES: WHAT HAS THEIR USE ADDED TO OUR KNOWLEDGE?

The use of stable isotope methods to address archaeological questions now dates back over 20 years. Some cynics say, "We already knew people ate corn. Why do we need expensive and complicated analyses to tell us that?" The presence of a food item in an archaeological assemblage does not necessarily imply that it was locally produced, or that it was eaten. Differential preservation of food remains may confuse interpretations of the relative importance of particular foods. Charred maize cobs and kernels may be well preserved in comparison to other plants and this has resulted in situations where the importance of maize was overestimated, as shown by stable isotope analyses. The use of nitrogen isotopes has allowed researchers to have a clearer picture of the importance of freshwater fish in the diets of inland populations. Collectively, the use of stable isotopes for dietary reconstruction refines estimates of the relative importance of various foods and therefore leads to more accurate interpretations of the effects of changing diet on health and demography. It is also the only means currently available of detecting sex and age differences in diet within past human groups. The use of nitrogen as well as carbon and oxygen isotopes to estimate the duration of breast-feeding also ties into demographic reconstruction. Residence and migration studies help explain population interaction and movement in the past.

With advances in instrumentation and the increasing use of stable isotopes in ecological studies, there has been a very fruitful exchange of information between bioarchaeologists and ecologists. This is illustrated in the example of the Lake Baikal study by Katzenberg and Weber (1999) where much of the information on stable carbon isotope values for freshwater fish was obtained from ecological studies. The exchange has also been beneficial in the other direction in that ecological studies have benefited from the extensive stable isotope ecology reconstructions carried out by archaeologists such as Ambrose, working in East Africa (1986, 1991; Ambrose and DeNiro, 1986) and Sealy, working in southern Africa (1986; Sealy et al., 1987; Sealy and van der Merwe, 1988).

There are still problems to be solved, but many of the problems identified in 1989, in an important paper by Sillen and colleagues titled "Chemistry and Paleodietary Research: No More Easy Answers," have seen significant progress. Controlled feeding studies carried out by Ambrose and Norr (1993; Ambrose, in press) and by Tieszen and Fagre (1993) have addressed questions about $\delta^{13}C$ differences in collagen and bone carbonate. Research has become more sophisticated in terms of understanding the underlying biochemical processes that affect stable isotopes. Examples include Ambrose's work on nitrogen isotopes and water stress (1991), Fogel and colleagues' (1997) insights into protein stress and amino acid metabolism, and Evershed's research on stable isotopes in lipids (1993; Stott and Evershed, 1996).

Remaining problems include ethical issues and the limitations on the information that may be provided by stable isotopes. Ethical is-

sues center on the fact that stable isotope analysis is destructive. Even though methods have increasingly been improved and refined so as to require as little as less than a gram of bone, some legislation completely prohibits any destructive analyses of human remains. These issues are discussed by Walker (Chapter 1) and are not unique to stable isotope analysis. Even when destructive analyses are permitted on skeletal samples one must be careful to consider the long-term integrity of collections. Are there other ways to obtain the information? Is the method likely to be successful and informative?

It is also important to be aware of limitations on the information that may be provided. This is particularly the case with paleodiet studies where consumption of several different combinations of foods with varying emphasis on each one may result in the same stable isotope ratios. Use of multiple elements and familiarity with other archaeological sources of dietary information can go a long way toward unraveling this problem. Recent developments using GC/IRMS in which specific amino acids, or other specific biomolecules, are isolated and analyzed can also help to solve this problem.

The future of stable isotope analysis will include many of the applications that have become routine over the last 20 years, but the field is also moving forward very quickly. It is increasingly important for individuals wishing to pursue this area of study to have training in chemistry and biochemistry, since the level of sophistication has increased substantially. This is true of both the methods for isolating specific components in bone samples as well as the interpretation of the results. Indeed many recent advances have been made by individuals with backgrounds in biochemistry, geochemistry, and ecology who have become interested in archaeological applications. At the same time, some of the most fruitful collaborations have been between individuals trained in the physical sciences and those trained in archaeology and physical anthropology.

ACKNOWLEDGMENTS

I wish to express my appreciation to the Killam Foundation for granting me a Killam Resident Fellowship at the University of Calgary during the fall term, 1998, for the purpose of preparing this chapter and working on this book. I am also grateful to Steve Taylor and Roy Krouse, Department of Physics, University of Calgary, for providing useful comments on some sections of this chapter, and to my colleagues Shelley Saunders and Susan Pfeiffer for reading and commenting on the complete chapter. Thanks also to my graduate students Sandra Garvie-Lok, Tamara Varney, and Roman Harrison, who read and commented on the chapter.

REFERENCES

Ambrose SH. 1986. Stable carbon and nitrogen isotope analysis of human and animal diet in Africa. J Human Evol 15:707–731.

Ambrose SH. 1990. Preparation and characterization of bone and tooth collagen for isotopic analysis. J Archaeol Sci 17:431–451.

Ambrose SH. 1991. Effects of diet, climate and physiology on nitrogen isotope abundances in terrestrial foodwebs. J Archaeol Sci 18:293–317.

Ambrose SH. 1997. Results of 24 controlled diet experiments on carbon isotopes of bone collagen and carbonate: implications for diet reconstruction. Paper presented at the Fifth Advanced Seminar on Paleodiet, Valbonne, France, 1–5 September 1997.

Ambrose SH. in press. Controlled diet and climate experiments on nitrogen isotope ratios of rats. In: Ambrose SH, Katzenberg MA, editors. Close to the Bone: Biogeochemical Approaches to Paleodietary Analyses in Archaeology. New York: Plenum Press.

Ambrose SH, DeNiro MJ. 1986. Reconstruction of African human diet using bone collagen carbon and nitrogen isotope ratios. Nature 319:321–324.

Ambrose SH, DeNiro MJ. 1987. Bone nitrogen isotope composition and climate. Nature 325:201.

Ambrose SH, Katzenberg MA, editors. in press. Close to the Bone: Biogeochemical Approaches to Paleodietary Analyses in Archaeology. New York: Plenum Press.

Ambrose SH, Norr L. 1993. Experimental evidence for the relationship of the carbon isotope ratios of whole diet and dietary protein to those of bone collagen and carbonate. In: Lambert JB, Grupe G, editors. Prehistoric Human Bone: Archaeology at the Molecular Level. Berlin: Springer-Verlag, pp. 1–37.

Barrie A, Davies JE, Park AJ, Workman CT. 1989. Continuous-flow stable isotope analysis for biologists. Spectroscopy 4(7):42–52.

Barrie A, Prosser SJ. 1996. Automated analysis of light-element stable isotopes by isotope ratio mass spectrometry. In: Boutton TW, Yamasaki S, editors. Mass Spectrometry of Soils. New York: Marcel Dekker. pp. 1–46.

Bender MM. 1968. Mass spectrometric studies of carbon 13 variations in corn and other grasses. Radiocarbon 10(2):468–472.

Blake M, Chisholm BS, Clark JE, Voorhies B, Love MW. 1992. Prehistoric subsistence in the Soconusco region. Curr Anthropol 33(1):83–94.

Bligh EG, Dyer WJ. 1959. A rapid method of total lipid extraction and purification. Can J Biochem Physiol 37:911–917.

Bocherens H, van Klinken GJ, Pollard AM. 1999. Special Issue: Proceedings of the 5th Advanced Seminar on Paleodiet, Centre de Recherches Archéologiques, Valbonne, 1–5 September 1997. J Arch Sci 26.

Boutton TW, Klein PD, Lynnott MJ, Price JE, Tieszen LL. 1984. Stable carbon isotope ratios as indicators of prehistoric human diet. In: Turnlund JR, Johnson PE, editors. Stable Isotopes in Nutrition. Washington: American Chemical Society. pp. 191–204.

Brill W. 1977. Biological Nitrogen Fixation. Scientific Am 236:68–74.

Brown TA, Nelson DE, Vogel JS, Southon JR. 1988. Improved collagen extraction by modified Longin method. Radiocarbon 30(2):171–177.

Buikstra JE, Konigsberg LW, Bullington J. 1986. Fertility and the development of agriculture in the prehistoric midwest. Am Antiq 51:528–546.

Buikstra JE, Milner GR. 1991. Isotopic and archaeological interpretations of diet in the central Mississippi valley. J Archaeol Sci 18:319–329.

Child AM. 1995. Towards an understanding of the microbial decomposition of archaeological bone in the burial environment. J Archaeol Sci 22:165–174.

Chisholm BS, Nelson DE, Hobson KA, Schwarcz HP, Knyf M. 1983. Carbon isotope measurement techniques for bone collagen: notes for the archaeologist. J Archaeol Sci 10:355–360.

Chisholm BS, Nelson DE, Schwarcz HP. 1982. Stable carbon isotope ratios as a measure of marine versus terrestrial protein in ancient diets. Science 216:1131–1132.

Coplen TB. 1994. Reporting of stable hydrogen, carbon, and oxygen isotopic abundances. Pure Appl Chem 66(2):273–276.

Craig H. 1954. Carbon 13 in plants and the relationships between carbon 13 and carbon 14 variations in nature. J Geol 62(2):115–149.

Dansgaard W. 1964. Stable isotopes in precipitation. Tellus 16:436–468.

Decker KW, Tieszen LL. 1989. Isotopic reconstruction of Mesa Verde diet from Basketmaer III to Pueblo III. Kiva 55(1):33–47.

Deines P. 1980. The isotopic composition of reduced organic carbon. In: Fritz P, Fontes JC, editors. Handbook of Environmental Isotope Geochemistry. Amsterdam: Elsevier. pp. 329–406.

DeNiro MJ, Epstein S. 1978. Influence of diet on the distribution of carbon isotopes in animals. Geochim Cosmochim Acta 42:495–506.

DeNiro MJ, Epstein S. 1981. Influence of diet on the distribution of nitrogen isotopes in animals. Geochim Cosmochim Acta 45:341–351.

Ehleringer JR, Rundel PW. 1989. Stable isotopes: history, units, and instrumentation. In: Rundel PW, Ehleringer JR, Nagy KA, editors. Stable Isotopes in Ecological Research. New York: Springer-Verlag. pp. 1–15.

Ericson JE. 1985. Strontium isotope characterization in the study of prehistoric human ecology. J Hum Evol 14:503–514.

Ericson JE. 1989. Some problems and potentials of strontium isotope analysis for human and animal ecology. In: Rundel PW, Ehleringer JR, Nagy KA, editors. Stable Isotopes in Ecological Research. New York: Springer-Verlag. pp. 252–259.

Evershed RP. 1993. Biomolecular archaeology and lipids. World Archaeol 25(1):74–93.

Ezzo JA, Johnson CM, Price TD. 1997. Analytical perspectives on prehistoric migration: a case study from east-central Arizona. J Archaeol Sci 24:447–466.

Fogel ML, Tuross N, Johnson BJ, Miller GH. 1997. Biogeochemical record of ancient humans. Organic Geochem 27(5/6):275–287.

Fogel ML, Tuross N, Owsley DW. 1989. Nitrogen isotope tracers of human lactation in modern and archaeological populations. Carnegie Institution, Annual Report of the Director; Geophysical Laboratory. pp. 111–117.

Folch J, Lees M, Stanley GHS. 1957. A simple method for the isolation and purification of total lipids from animal tissues. J Biol Chem 226:497–509.

France R. 1995. Differentiation between littoral and pelagic food webs in lakes using stable carbon isotopes. Limnol Oceanogr 40(7):1310–1313.

Griffiths H, editor. 1998. Stable Isotopes: Integration of Biological, Ecological and Geochemical Processes. Environmental Plant Biology Series. Oxford, U.K.: BIOS Scientific Publishers, Ltd.

Gross ML. 1979. Mass Spectrometry. In: Bauer HH, Christian GD, O'Reilly JE, editors. Instrumetal Analysis. Boston: Allyn and Bacon. pp. 443–486.

Hall RL. 1967. Those late corn dates: isotopic fractionation as a source of error in Carbon-14 dates. Michigan Archaeol 13(3):171–180.

Hare PE, Estep M. 1982. Carbon and nitrogen isotopic composition of amino acids in modern and fossil collagens. Carnegie Institute Washington Yearbook 82:410–414.

Hare PE, Fogel ML, Stafford TW Jr, Mitchell AD, Hoering TC. 1991. The isotopic composition of carbon and nitrogen in individual amino acids isolated from modern and fossil proteins. J Archaeol Sci 18:227–292.

Hayden B, Chisholm B, Schwarcz HP. 1987. Fishing and foraging: marine resources in the Upper Paleolithic of France. In: Soffer O, editor. The Pleistocene Old World: Regional Perspectives. New York: Plenum Press, pp. 279–291.

Hayes JM. 1982. Fractionation, et al.: an introduction to isotopic measurements and terminology. Spectra 8(4):3–8.

Heaton THE. 1987. 1987. The 15N/14N ratios of plants in South Africa and Namibia: relationship to climate and coastal/saline environments. Oecologia 74:236–246.

Heaton THE, Vogel JC, Chevallerie G, Collett G. 1986. Climatic influence on the isotopic composition of bone nitrogen. Nature 322:822–823.

Hecky RE, Hesslein RH. 1995. Contributions of benthic algae to lake food webs as revealed by stable isotope analysis. J N Am Benthol Soc 14(4):631–653.

Herring DA, Saunders SR, Katzenberg MA. 1998. Investigating the weaning process in past populations. Am J Phys Anthropol 105:425–439.

Hillson S. 1996. Dental Anthropology. Cambridge: Cambridge University Press.

Hobson KA, Alisauskas RT, Clark RG. 1993. Stable-nitrogen isotope enrichment in avian tissues due to fasting and nutritional stress: implications for isotopic analyses of diet. Condor 95:388–394.

Hobson KA, Clark RG. 1992. Assessing avian diets using stable isotopes. II: factors influencing diet-tissue fractionation. Condor 94:187–195.

Hoefs J. 1997. Stable Isotope Geochemistry, 4th ed. Berlin: Springer-Verlag.

Katzenberg MA. 1989. Stable isotope analysis of archaeological faunal remains from southern Ontario. J Archaeol Sci 16:319–329.

Katzenberg MA. 1999. A re-examination of factors contributing to elevated stable nitrogen isotope values in infants and young children (abstract). Am J Phys Anthropol (suppl) 28:165.

Katzenberg MA, Harrison RG. 1997. What's in a bone? Recent advances in archaeological bone chemistry. J Archaeol Res 5(3):265–293.

Katzenberg MA, Herring DA, Saunders SR. 1996. Weaning and infant mortality: evaluating the skeletal evidence. Yrbk Phys Anthropol 39:177–199.

Katzenberg MA, Kelley JH. 1991. Stable isotope analysis of prehistoric bone from the Sierra Blanca region of New Mexico. Mogollon V: Proceedings of the 1988 Mogollon Conference Las Cruces, N.M.: COAS Publishing and Research. pp. 207–219.

Katzenberg MA, Lovell NC. 1999. Stable isotope variation in pathological bone. Int J Osteoarchaeol 9:316–324.

Katzenberg MA, Schwarcz HP, Knyf M, Melbye FJ. 1995. Stable isotope evidence for maize horticulture and paleodiet in southern Ontario, Canada. Am Antiq 60(2):335–350.

Katzenberg MA, Weber A. 1999. Stable isotope ecology and paleodiet in the Lake Baikal region of Siberia. J Archaeol Sci 26(6):651–65.

Keegan WF, DeNiro MJ. 1988. Stable carbon- and nitrogen-isotope ratios of bone collagen used to study coral-reef and terrestrial components of prehistoric Bahamian diet. Am Antiq 53: 320–336.

Kiyashko SI, Mamontov AM, Chernyaev MZ. 1991. Food web analysis of Lake Baikal fish by ratios of stable carbon isotopes. Dok Biol Sci 318: 274–276.

Koch PL, Tuross N, Fogel ML. 1997. The effects of sample treatment and diagenesis on the isotopic integrity of carbonate in biogenic hydroxylapatite. J Archaeol Sci 24(5):417–429.

Krueger HW. 1991. Exchange of carbon with biological apatite. J Archaeol Sci 18:355–361.

Krueger HW, Sullivan CH. 1984. Models for carbon isotope fractionation between diet and bone. In: Turnlund JE, Johnson PE, editors. Stable Isotopes in Nutrition. American Chemical Society Symposium Series 258. pp. 205–222.

Larsen CS, Schoeninger MJ, van der Merwe NJ, Moore KM, Lee-Thorp JA. 1992. Carbon and nitrogen stable isotopic signatures of human dietary change in the Georgia Bight. Am J Phys Anthropol 89(2):197–214.

Lee-Thorp JA. 1989. Stable carbon isotopes in deep time: the diets of fossil fauna and hominids. Unpublished doctoral dissertation, University of Cape Town, South Africa.

Lee-Thorp JA, Sealy JC, van der Merwe MJ. 1989. Stable carbon isotope ratio differences between bone collagen and bone apatite, and their relationship to diet. J Archaeol Sci 16:585–599.

Lee-Thorpe JA, van der Merwe NJ. 1991. Aspects of the chemistry of modern and fossil biological apatites. J Archaeol Sci 18:343–354.

LeGeros RZ, Trautz OR, LeGeros JP, Klein E. 1967. Apatite crystallites: effects of carbonate on morphology. Science 155:1409–1411.

Liden K, Takahashi C, Nelson DE. 1995. The effects of lipids in stable carbon isotope analysis and the effects of NaOH treatment on the composition of extracted bone collagen. J Archaeol Sci 22: 321–326.

Longin R. 1971. New method of collagen extraction for radiocarbon dating. Nature 230:241–242.

Lowdon JA. 1969. Isotopic fractionation in corn. Radiocarbon 11(2):391–393.

Lubell D, Jackes M, Schwarcz H, Knyf M, Meiklejohn C. 1994. The Mesolithic-Neolithic transition in Portugal: isotopic and dental evidence of diet. J Archaeol Sci 21:201–216.

Luz B, Kolodny Y. 1989. Oxygen isotope variation in bone phosphate. Appl Geochem 4:317–323.

Lyon TDB, Baxter MS. 1978. Stable carbon isotopes in human tissues. Nature 48:187–191.

Macko SA, Uhle ME, Engel MH, Andrusevich V. 1997. Stable nitrogen isotope analysis of amino acid enantiomers by gas chromatography/combustion/isotope ratio mass spectrometry. Anal Chem 69:926–929.

Matson RG, Chisholm B. 1991. Basketmaker II subsistence: carbon isotopes and other dietary indicators from Cedar Mesa, Utah. Am Antiq 56(3):444–459.

Minagawa M, Wada E. 1984. Stepwise enrichment of 15N along food chains: further evidence and the relation between δ15N and animal age. Geochim Cosmochim Acta 48:1135–1140.

Norr LC. 1991. Nutritional consequences of prehistoric subsistence strategies in lower Central America. Unpublished doctoral dissertation. University of Illinois at Urbana–Champaign, Urbana, Illinois.

Pate FD. 1994. Bone Chemistry and Paleodiet. J Archaeol Method Theory 1(2):161–209.

Price TD, Johnson CM, Ezzo JA, Ericson J, Burton JH. 1994a. Residential mobility in the prehistoric southwest United States: a preliminary study using strontium isotope analysis. J Archaeol Sci 21:315–330.

Price TD, Grupe G, Schroter P. 1994b. Reconstruction of migration patterns in the Bell Beaker period by stable strontium isotope analysis. Appl Geochem 9:413–417.

Rundel PW, Ehleringer JR, Nagy KA. 1989. Stable Isotopes in Ecological Research. Ecological Studies: Analysis and Synthesis No. 68. New York: Springer-Verlag.

Schoeninger MJ, DeNiro MJ. 1982. Carbon isotope ratios of apatite from fossil bone cannot be used to reconstruct diets of animals. Nature 297(5867):577–578.

Schoeninger MJ, DeNiro MJ. 1984. Nitrogen and carbon isotopic composition of bone collagen from marine and terrestrial animals. Geochim Cosmochim Acta 48:625–639.

Schoeninger MJ, Moore K. 1992. Bone stable isotope studies in archaeology. J World Prehistory 6(2):247–296.

Schoeninger MJ, Moore KM, Murray ML, Kingston JD. 1989. Detection of bone preservation in archaeological and fossil samples. Appl Geochem 4:281–292.

Schurr MR. 1998. Using stable nitrogen-isotopes to study weaning behavior in past populations. World Archaeol 30(2):327–342.

Schurr MR, Redmond BG. 1991. Stable isotope analysis of incipient maize horticulturists from the Gard Island 2 Site. Midcontinental J Archaeol 16(1):69–84.

Schwarcz JP, Gibbs L, Knyf M. 1991. Oxygen isotope analysis as an indicator of place of origin. In: Pfeiffer S, Williamson RF, editors. Snake Hill: An Investigation of a Military Cemetery from the War of 1812. Toronto: Dundurn Press. pp. 263–268.

Schwarcz HP, Melbye FJ, Katzenberg MA, Knyf M. 1985. Stable isotopes in human skeletons of southern Ontario: reconstructing paleodiet. J Archaeol Sci 12:187–206.

Schwarcz HP, Schoeninger MJ. 1991. Stable isotope analyses in human nutritional ecology. Yrbk Phys Anthropol 34:283–322.

Sealy JC. 1986. Stable carbon isotopes and prehistoric diets in the southwestern Cape Province South Africa. Oxford: BAR International Series 293.

Sealy JC, Armstrong R, Schrire C. 1995. Beyond lifetime averages: tracing life histories through isotopic analysis of different calcified tissues from archaeological human skeletons. Antiquity 69(263):290–300.

Sealy JC, van der Merwe NJ. 1988. Social, spatial and chronological patterning in marine food use as determined by δ13C measurements of Holocene human skeletons from the southwestern Cape, South Africa. World Archaeol 20(1):87–102.

Sealy JC, van der Merwe NJ, Lee Thorp JA, Lanham JL. 1987. Nitrogen isotopic ecology in southern Africa: implications for environmental and dietary tracing. Geochim Cosmochim Acta 51:2707–2717.

Sealy JC, van der Merwe NJ, Sillen A, Kruger FJ, Krueger HW. 1991. $^{87}Sr/^{86}Sr$ as a dietary indicator in modern and archaeological bone. J Archaeol Sci 18:399–416.

Shearer G, Kohl DH, Virginia RA, Bryan BA, Skeeters JL, Nilsen ET, Sharifi MR, Rundel PW. 1983. Estimates of N_2-fixation from variation in the natural abundance of ^{15}N in Sonoran desert ecosystems. Oecologia 56:365–373.

Sillen A. 1986. Biogenic and diagenetic Sr/Ca in Plio-Pleistocene fossils of the Omo Shangura Formation. Paleobiology 12:311–323.

Sillen A, Hall G, Richardson S, Armstrong R. 1998. ^{87}Sr/^{86}Sr ratios in modern and fossil food-webs of the Sterkfontein Valley: implications for early hominid habitat preference. Geochim Cosmochim Acta 62(14):2463–2473.

Sillen A, Sealy JC. 1995. Diagenesis of strontium in fossil bone: a reconsideration of Nelson et al. (1986). J Archaeol Sci 22:313–320.

Sillen A, Sealy JC, van der Merwe NJ. 1989. Chemistry and paleodietary research: no more easy answers. Am Antiquity 54:504–512.

Smith BN, Epstein S. 1971. Two categories of ^{13}C/^{12}C ratios for higher plants. Plant Physiol 47:380–384.

Spielmann KA, Schoeninger MJ, Moore K. 1990. Plains-Pueblo interdependence and human diet at Pecos Pueblo, New Mexico. Am Antiq 55(4):745–765.

Sponheimer M, Lee-Thorp JA. 1999. Isotopic evidence for the diet of an early hominid, *Australopithecus africanus*. Science 283:368–370.

Stafford TW Jr, Hare PE, Currie L, Jull AJT, Donahue DJ. 1991. Accelerator radiocarbon dating at the molecular level. J Archaeol Sci 18:35–72.

Stott AW, Evershed RP. 1996. δ^{13}C analysis of cholesterol preserved in archaeological bones and teeth. Anal Chem 68:4402–4408.

Stuart-Williams HLQ. 1996. Analysis of the variation of oxygen isotopic composition of mammalian bone phosphate. Unpublished doctoral dissertation, McMaster University.

Stuart-Williams HLQ, Schwarcz HP. 1995. Oxygen isotopic analysis of silver orthophosphate using a reaction with bromine. Geochim Cosmochim Acta 59(18):3837–3841.

Stuart-Williams HLQ, Schwarcz HP. 1997. Oxygen isotopic determination of climatic variation using phosphate from beaver bone, tooth enamel, and dentine. Geochim Cosmochim Acta 61: 2539–2550.

Sullivan CH, Krueger HW. 1981. Carbon isotope analysis in separate chemical phases in modern and fossil bone. Nature 292:333–335.

Tauber H. 1981. 13C evidence for dietary habits of prehistoric man in Denmark. Nature 292: 332–333.

Taylor HP, O'Neil JR, Kaplan IR, editors. 1991. Samuel Epstein: scientist, teacher and friend. In:

Stable Isotope Geochemistry: A Tribute to Samuel Epstein. Special Publication No. 3. San Antonio, Texas: The Geochemical Society. pp. xiii–xvi.

Tieszen LL, Fagre T. 1993. Effect of diet quality and composition on the isotopic composition of respiratory CO_2, bone collagen, bioapatite and soft tissues. In: Lambert JB, Grupe G, editors. Prehistoric Human Bone: Archaeology at the Molecular Level. Berlin: Springer-Verlag. pp. 121–155.

Triffit JT. 1980. The organic matrix of bone tissue. In: Urist MR, editor. Fundamental and Clinical Bone Physiology. Philadelphia: J.B. Lippincott. pp. 45–82.

Tuross N, Behrensmeyer AK, Eanes ED, Fisher LW, Hare PE. 1989. Molecular preservation and crystallographic alterations in a weathering sequence of wildebeest bones. Appl Geochem 4:261–270.

Tuross N, Eyre DR, Holtrop ME, Glimcher MJ, Hare PE. 1980. Collagen in fossil bones. In: Hare PE, Hoering TC, King K Jr, editors. Biogeochemistry of Amino Acids. New York: John Wiley & Sons. pp. 53–63.

van der Merwe NJ. 1982. Carbon isotopes, photosynthesis, and archaeology. Am Sci 70:596–606.

van der Merwe NJ, Vogel JC. 1978. 13C content of human collagen as a measure of prehistoric diet in Woodland North America. Nature 276:815–816.

Virginia RA, Delwiche CC. 1982. Natural ^{15}N abundance of presumed N_2-fixing and non-N_2-fixing plants from selected ecosystems. Oecologia 54:317–325.

Vogel JC. 1978. Isotopic assessment of the dietary habits of ungulates. S Afr J Sci 74:298–301.

Vogel JC, van der Merwe NJ. 1977. Isotopic evidence for early maize cultivation in New York State. Am Antiq 42(2):238–242.

Walker PL, DeNiro MJ. 1986. Stable nitrogen and carbon isotope ratios in bone collagen as indices of prehistoric dietary dependence on marine and terrestrial resources in southern California. Am J Phys Anthropol 71:51–61.

White CD, Armelagos GJ. 1997. Osteopenia and stable isotope ratios in bone collagen of Nubian female mummies. Am J Phys Anthropol 103(2): 185–199.

White CD, Spence MW, Stuart-Williams HLQ, Schwarcz HP. 1998. Oxygen isotopes and the identification of geographical origins: The Valley of Oaxaca versus the Valley of Mexico. J Archaeol Sci 25:643–655.

Wright LE. 1999. Stable isotopic analysis of enamel microsamples: examining childhood dietary change at Kaminaljuyu, Guatemala. (abstract). Am J Phys Anthropol (suppl) 28:281–282.

Wright LE, Schwarcz HP. 1998. Stable carbon and oxygen isotopes in human tooth enamel: identifying breastfeeding and weaning in prehistory. Am J Phys Anthropol 106(1):1–18.

Wyckoff RWG. 1980. Collagen in fossil bones. In: Hare PE, Hoering T, King CK Jr, editors. Biogeochemistry of Amino Acids. New York: John Wiley & Sons. pp. 17–22.

Zohary T, Erez J, Gophen M, Berman-Frank I, Stiller M. 1994. Seasonality of stable carbon isotopes within the pelagic food web of Lake Kinneret. Limnol Oceanogr 39(5):1030–1043.

CHAPTER 12

TRACE ELEMENT RESEARCH IN ANTHROPOLOGY: NEW PERSPECTIVES AND CHALLENGES

MARY K. SANDFORD AND DAVID S. WEAVER

INTRODUCTION

Research in skeletal biology took on radically new dimensions during the 1970s with the introduction of trace element analysis to the discipline (Brown, 1973; Gilbert, 1975, 1977). At that time, researchers enthusiastically described the potential of trace element analysis of human bone for reconstructing prehistoric diets using both multielemental approaches (Gilbert, 1975, 1977) as well as those focused more specifically on the determination of concentrations of strontium (Sr) and calcium (Ca) (Brown, 1973).

During this "inaugural period" of elemental analysis in anthropology, a virtually unbridled optimism predominated. Although elemental analysis was attempted chiefly as an adjunct tool for performing dietary discrimination and evaluating temporal changes in dietary patterns, other potential uses of elemental analyses were being recognized and discussed. These included "studies of dietary stress, disease states, growth and development of individuals, sex differences, age statuses, social class distinctions and subsistence economy" (Blakely, 1977:6). Within the larger contexts of burgeoning interest in the "new archaeol-

ogy," as well as mounting biocultural and paleoepidemiological investigations, bone chemistry studies, in general, and trace element analysis, in particular, were believed at the time to represent something of a breakthrough (Buikstra and Cook, 1980; reviewed in Sandford, 1992, 1993:3–7).

More than two decades since its inception, activity in elemental analysis continues, although the face of and prognosis for this research specialization are radically different. Simply stated, there are tremendous limitations and complications involving elemental analyses of archaeological tissue. Indeed, the field has been so transformed that vastly new demands, limitations, and expectations are imposed on those who would use the approach and attempt to further its development in our discipline.

The first inklings that elemental analysis is considerably more complicated than was initially suspected arose near the close of the inaugural period when Lambert and coworkers (1979) first systematically investigated the effects of diagenesis, or postmortem alteration in biogenic signals. Such developments helped to spark an "intermediate period" in elemental analysis. During this period, some investigators tested additional applications of elemental analyses and, in some instances, proposed new strategies for confronting the challenges of diagenetic change (Edward et al., 1984;

Biological Anthropology of the Human Skeleton, Edited by M. Anne Katzenberg and Shelley R. Saunders.
ISBN 0-471-31616-4   Copyright © 2000 by Wiley-Liss, Inc.

Katzenberg, 1984; Schoeninger 1979, 1981; Sillen, 1981). Still others explored additional uses of elemental analyses, including investigations of physiological status (Blakely, 1989; Sillen and Smith, 1984), nutritional disorders (Fornaciari et al., 1983; Sandford et al., 1983), and elemental toxicity (Aufderheide et al., 1981, 1985, 1988). The somewhat mixed results of such studies may well have encouraged more confidence in elemental analysis than truly was warranted.

Toward the end of the intermediate period, some investigators were already applying systematic approaches to understand and, where possible, correct diagenetic change in the field and laboratory (Klepinger et al., 1986; Pate and Hutton, 1988; Sillen, 1986). Several influential papers, marking the terminus of this period, clearly articulated the profound difficulties that were hindering successful implementation of elemental analysis in anthropology (see especially Buikstra et al., 1989; Sillen, 1989; Sillen et al., 1989). Buikstra and coworkers (1989), for example, emphasized the need to know the chemical composition of ancient dietary components when framing expectations or offering interpretations regarding past elemental concentrations. Moreover, those same researchers became the first to apply principal components analyses to "discover the kinds and directions of relationships among various trace elements and between trace elements and carbon isotopes" (1989:191). As described further below, because elemental concentrations of archaeological bone represent a host of ante- and postmortem processes, multivariate statistical techniques are requisite to unraveling such complexities and for identifying the myriad chemical interactions among the elements.

A classic paper, "Chemistry and Paleodietary Research: No More Easy Answers" by Sillen and co-authors (1989), also delineated the major challenges facing bone chemistry research and helped set the course for future research involving elemental analysis. Their critique included recommendations for additional experimental work to test some of the most basic assumptions of elemental analysis

and greater emphasis on developing methods for recognizing and circumventing diagenetic change.

The call for more rigorous and critical perspectives involving elemental analysis had a substantial impact on subsequent research. Most important, such criticisms (Buikstra et al., 1989; Sillen et al., 1989) stimulated greater use of experimental approaches in the laboratory and field in the "modern period." The investigation of diagenetic activity became the focus of most such work and, by the mid-1990s, had emerged as a research specialization in its own right (Hedges and Millard, 1995; Hedges et al., 1995). In addition to such fundamental attempts to model and characterize diagenesis, many researchers (see especially Baraybar, 1999; Baraybar and de la Rua, 1997; Edward and Benfer, 1993; Farnum and Sandford, 1997; Hedges et al., 1995) now employ a multifaceted approach to detect the intensity, nature, and direction of diagenetic change.

Apart from investigations of diagenesis, others in the modern period are applying experimental methods toward the understanding of elemental deposition in bone. In particular, relationships between dietary constituents and elemental bone concentrations have been explored using animal protocols (Klepinger, 1990; Lambert and Weydert-Homeyer, 1993a, 1993b) and quantitative modeling (Burton and Wright, 1995). Additional advancements during the modern period include the further application of multivariate statistical methods to elemental data, including principal components analysis and multidimensional scaling (Farnum and Sandford, 1997; Sandford and Kissling, 1994). Also in this period some researchers have underscored the importance of understanding skeletal and elemental physiology and biochemistry as requisite to proper application of elemental analysis (Aufderheide, 1989; Ezzo, 1994a, 1994b; Pate, 1994; Sandford, 1993).

As should be apparent from the proceeding discussion, the modern period of trace element analysis has been one of tremendous change.

Some critics have demanded greater scientific rigor in the field, along with the testing of some of the most basic assumptions of elemental analysis (see especially Ezzo, 1994a, 1994b; Radosevich, 1993). Indeed, questions concerning the capacity of bone to reflect dietary information have led some researchers to advocate the use of strontium (Sr), calcium (Ca), and barium (Ba) for paleodietary reconstruction and the abandonment, at least temporarily, of the multielement approach (Baraybar, 1999; Ezzo, 1994a:22).

From within this context, the chief goal of the present chapter is to provide an assessment of the current status of elemental analysis in anthropology, emphasizing developments in the modern period (see also Katzenberg and Harrison, 1997; Pate, 1994). To this end, we take a historical perspective, focusing on the interpretive and methodological complications that unfolded soon after the advent of elemental analysis in anthropology. We identify the applications of this technique that appear the most viable, emphasizing the uses of Ba, Sr, and lead (Pb), while exploring the feasibility of the multielement approach. In this context, we address issues related to biogenic and diagenetic processes, as well as sampling, instrumentation, and the statistical evaluation of elemental data. Finally, we identify some similarities with developments in other research specializations in skeletal biology, including paleopathology. Such comparisons across research areas afford identification of common, underlying problems and provide a framework for making recommendations for future research and training.

BONE CHEMISTRY

Understanding bone microstructure and physiology is essential for interpretation of elemental concentrations for several reasons (see also Sandford, 1993:18–19). First, several major and trace elements, including calcium, phosphorus (P), zinc (Zn), copper (Cu), and manganese (Mn), play fundamental roles in maintaining skeletal structure and in processes such as growth, modeling, and remodeling (Peretz, 1996). Second, some of the variables that influence skeletal processes, including dietary, immunological, and/or hormonal factors, may also affect elemental concentrations. Third, and from a practical perspective, evaluation of bone histology is often useful for evaluating diagenetic change (Farnum and Sandford, 1997; Hedges et al., 1995; Schoeninger et al., 1989).

Given the important relationships between elemental concentrations and function of the skeletal system, it is encouraging that more researchers are incorporating information about skeletal physiology in their discussion of trace elements (Ezzo, 1994a; Pate, 1994). The importance of understanding, using, and conveying the most recent information about bone physiology in accurate and complete terms must be underscored, however. The complex nature of the skeleton as an organ system has been described in overly simplistic terms. Favus (1999) provides a helpful discussion of bone physiology and Ott (1996) describes the tight coupling and participation of both osteoclasts and osteoblasts in the cycle of remodeling.

Structurally, bone is composed of an organic phase and an inorganic mineral phase. The former accounts for approximately 23% of the dry weight of bone, while the later makes up approximately 77% (Recker, 1992). Although a few trace elements (e.g., iron (Fe) and Cu, Spadaro et al., 1970a, 1970b) are found chiefly in the organic phase, almost all of the trace elements are found in the inorganic phase of bone. The most abundant mineral component of the inorganic phase is calcium phosphate, in the form of poorly crystalline hydroxyapatite (Glimcher, 1992; Neuman and Neuman, 1958; Sillen, 1989:213).

Although there are important reasons to think the correspondence is far from perfect, hydroxyapatite crystals in bone mostly represent the proportions of various trace minerals in the diet. Stoichiometric variations (i.e., other elements substituting for calcium, phosphorus, or hydrogen) in hydroxyapatite are largely due to the phenomenon of heteroionic exchange whereby various ions are incorporated into bone by displacing its normal chemical constituents (Neuman, 1980; Neuman and Neuman, 1958). Specific ion exchanges are regulated by a number of factors, ranging from thermodynamic forces to developmental changes in individual hydroxyapatite crystals (Buikstra et al., 1989; McLean and Urist, 1955:35–39; Neuman and Neuman, 1958: 61; Wing and Brown, 1979). Ion exchanges that may take place during crystal development include the substitution of Sr^{++}, Pb^{++}, Mg^{++} (magnesium ion) and Na^{++} (sodium ion) for Ca^{++}, the replacement of hydroxyl ions (OH^-) by fluoride (F^-) and chloride (Cl^-) ions, and the exchange of phosphate PO_4^- by carbonate CO_3^- ions (McLean and Urist, 1955:35; Posner, 1969:765). In general, more mature hydroxyapatite crystals are more stable against exchange than are newly formed crystals (McLean and Urist, 1955).

Variation in both the structure and chemical composition of inorganic bone indicates both the need for mineral homeostasis in the individual and the mineral content of the diet. Unfortunately for trace mineral studies in bone, the same qualities of hydroxyapatite that allow for in vivo mineral exchange make the crystals susceptible to postmortem diaganetic effects. Distinguishing between in vivo effects and diagenetic effects therefore is crucial to useful and informative trace element analysis and interpretation and has been a central preoccupation for trace element work since the recognition of diagenesis as a confounding factor in studies.

BIOGENIC PROCESSES

Throughout the course of a life, elements move in and out of skeletal tissue through biogenic processes. Homeostatic mechanisms, acting in concert with dietary intakes and environmental exposures, are among the biogenic factors that influence skeletal elemental concentrations (Parker and Toots, 1980). Metabolic processes,

including absorption, excretion, pregnancy, lactation, and growth, may affect elemental levels though direct or indirect means.

Some researchers have argued that it is advantageous for anthropologists to focus on nonessential elements such as Sr and Ba since they are not governed by the "tight homeostatic regulation" as are essential elements (Ezzo, 1994a:8). However, *all* elements are affected to varying degrees by biogenic processes, including interactions with essential elements and other dietary constituents (see discussion in Lambert and Weydert-Homeyer, 1993b:286). Indeed the basis for the use of Sr as a dietary indicator rests to a significant extent on its relationships and physiochemical interactions with Ca, an essential major element. An understanding of biogenic mechanisms and processes is critical, therefore, to the interpretation of all elemental concentrations, whether essential or nonessential.

Classification and Functions of Elements

Alternative schemes have been advanced for categorizing the elements found in the human body (Frieden, 1972; Pais and Jones, 1997; Schroeder, 1973; Schutte, 1964; Underwood, 1977). Traditionally, major elements refer to those that are found in relatively large amounts in higher animals and human beings and include carbon (C), hydrogen (H), nitrogen (N), calcium (Ca), phosphorus (P), oxygen (O), potassium (K), sulfur (S), chlorine (Cl), sodium (Na), and magnesium (Mg) (Schutte, 1964). These elements all perform a variety of essential functions, and they all play critical roles in maintaining the structural integrity of organisms.

Trace elements have been classified in a variety of ways, with some variation as to which elements are considered "essential" (see Pais and Jones, 1997, for a recent review). Pais and Jones (1997:57–58) recognize the following elements as being essential for normal development and function among animals and humans: iron (Fe), zinc (Zn), copper (Cu), manganese

(Mn), cobalt (Co), molybdenum (Mo), chromium (Cr), selenium (Se), iodine (I), and fluorine (F). Essential trace elements function primarily in catalytic reactions are often associated with specific enzymes either as metalloenzymes or metal-activated enzymes (Prasad, 1978; Reinhold, 1975; Sandford, 1993; Schutte, 1964; Underwood, 1977).

The nature of toxic trace elements is more difficult; virtually all trace elements are toxic if taken up in excessive quantities over relatively long periods of time (Aufderheide, 1989; Pais and Jones, 1997; Underwood, 1977). Usual practice considers toxic elements those that have toxic consequences at rather low levels such as lead (Pb), mercury (Hg), and cadmium (Cd) (Underwood, 1977:2)

Elemental Intakes

Chemical elements are distributed differentially both within and between the myriad sources of food exploited by human populations. The initial anthropological trace element studies were founded on this observation, as they sought to determine the relative proportions of animal and plant resources in prehistoric diets (see Brown, 1973; Gilbert, 1975; Sandford 1993:5–11). It was proposed that by comparing concentrations of specific elements, paleonutritionists could reconstruct the relative contributions of food types or staples to prehistoric diets.

Attempts to use trace element analysis in this manner have proven extremely problematic, however. Apart from dietary considerations, other factors may have significant impacts on the elemental concentrations in tissues. Trace elements can be introduced into food or drink through utensils or containers. Lead from lead-based or pewter food and drink containers (Aufderheide, 1989) and iron in cooking pots (Baumslag and Petering, 1976; Bothwell and Finch, 1962; Underwood, 1977) have had clear effects on Pb and Fe levels in tissue. Environmental levels in soil and water also may make substantial contributions to elemental intake (Pais and Jones, 1997).

Soil element concentrations influence dietary intakes by both direct and indirect mechanisms. Soil pH and interactions with other elements in soil affect the bioavailability of elements (Mertz, 1996; Pais and Jones, 1997: 49). Soil contamination of food also may introduce significant amounts of elements into the diet, as exemplified by the introduction of soil Fe during cultivation, processing, and storage of the local cereal *teff* in Ethiopia (Fritz, 1972; Underwood, 1997).

Elemental Homeostasis, Absorption, and Excretion

Once consumed, elemental amounts are affected by other processes that ultimately produce observed tissue concentrations (see Saltman et al., 1984). Absorption and excretion, as well as processes governing storage and mobilization of elements, play important roles in maintaining mineral homeostasis. The manner, location, and degree of absorption are highly variable and are influenced by the age, sex, health, and nutritional status of a person. In addition, dietary components and chemicals can profoundly alter element absorption and use and thus affect the bioavailability of the elements. Antagonistic or synergistic interactions between elements and between elements and other chemicals can substantially affect element uptake. For example, Zn antagonists include Ca, Cu, Fe, Cd, and Cr (Cunnane, 1988), and high dietary P and Ca deter Sr absorption (Cabrera et al., 1999:661). Other compounds can interact with minerals, preventing or reducing their absorption, as is the case for phytate binding of Zn, Fe, and Mg (Fairweather-Tate, 1992; Halsted et al., 1972; Mills, 1992). Chemical synergism in enhancing absorption is known for Fe and ascorbic acid and ethanol (Fairweather-Tate, 1992; Kent et al., 1990; O'Dell, 1985) and vitamin A, Mg, and N maintain synergistic interactions with Zn (Cunnane, 1988:115–118).

Excretion also plays an essential role in maintaining mineral homeostasis, serving in the case of Mg (Aikawa, 1981) and Mn (Leach,

1976) as the primary mechanism for maintaining internal concentration of these minerals. Primary excretion of minerals occurs in the feces, and lesser amounts of excretion take place as biliary and pancreatic secretions, urine, and sweat (Mertz, 1985).

While elemental intake, absorption, and excretion are of the utmost importance in predicting and interpreting tissue concentrations, physiological states such as stress, growth, weaning, and pregnancy and lactation also affect elemental absorption, excretion, and use (Chesney et al., 1992; Farnum, 1996; Garner and Anderson, 1996; Sillen and Smith, 1984). For example, pregnant and lactating females have enhanced intestinal absorption of both Ca and Sr, although discrimination against Sr in favor of Ca by the placenta and mammary glands during uptake are believed to underlie the higher skeletal Sr and lower skeletal Ca in such women (Chesney et al., 1992). Changes in element concentrations may indicate weaning (Farnum, 1996, Sillen and Smith, 1984), or gestational stores in very young infants (Radosevich, 1989; Sandford et al., 1988).

Strangely, in spite of intriguing observations and unanswered questions, the effects of dietary intakes and physiological processes on skeletal element concentrations remain among the least explored areas of anthropological trace element research. Lambert and Weydert-Homeyer (1993a, 1993b) contributed to the understanding of diet and elemental bone concentrations in their analyses of femora and humeri of laboratory rats fed controlled diets. Of the 10 elements analyzed, the researchers found few direct and significant correlations between elemental levels in the diet and elemental concentrations. Such findings are not unexpected, given the complexity of the biogenic processes that are responsible for the deposition of elements in bone. For example, bone concentrations of Ca and P were not altered by gross dietary levels; however, increased dietary fiber was associated with significantly lower bone Ca levels, and higher Sr and Ba concentrations. Similarly, direct relationships between bone Zn and dietary Zn were not documented. Rather, bone Zn demonstrated its strongest positive correlation with dietary protein, although such associations were restricted to high casein and peanut diets. Diets high in meat or fish failed to produce high Zn concentrations in bone, possibly due to antagonistic interactions with P. In contrast, bone levels of Fe and K correlated highly with their dietary concentrations. Where feasible, additional studies of this nature could help to further unravel the complexities of elemental uptake and deposition in bone. While such investigations may suggest hypothetical relationships with or explanations for elemental bone concentrations in our own species, the possibility of species-specific differences also should be considered.

DIAGENETIC PROCESSES

As adapted by anthropologists, the term *diagenesis* refers specifically to postmortem alterations in the chemical constituents of bone following deposition in soil. As skeletal material enters soil, the homeostatic relationship that once existed between this tissue and the living, physiological environment is supplanted by an equally dynamic interaction between bone and various geochemical forces. In this postdepositional milieu, bone can either gain or lose chemical constituents.

Diagenetic changes of inorganic bone are attributable to several mechanisms (Parker and Toots, 1980:199; Pate and Hutton, 1988:730; Sillen, 1989). First, minerals such as calcite ($CaCO_3$), barite ($BaSO_4$), and Fe and Mn oxides may be precipitated as separate "void-filling" mineral phases in the small cracks and pores of bone. In addition, soluble ions present in soils may be exchanged for those that normally occupy lattice positions in skeletal hydroxyapatite. Finally, diagenesis may promote recrystallization and growth of apatite crystals and biogenic apatite may serve as the foundation for crystals of diagenetic derivation (Sillen, 1989:221–223).

Diagenesis is furthered during crystal precipitation by ionic substitution. As in ionic exchange (which takes place after precipitation), various actions (Sr^{++}, Ba^{++}, Pb^{++}, for example) and anions (F^-, CO_3^-, for example) are substituted for those normally found in biogenic apatite (Parker and Toots, 1980:199; Price, 1989:134; Sillen, 1989:221–222). The incorporation of such changes may bring about greater crystallinity and closer stoichiometric agreement (as measured by Ca/P ratios) than is typical of skeletal hydroxyapatite (Sillen, 1989).

Following Von Endt and Ortner (1984), such diagenetic processes are influenced by "extrinsic" and "intrinsic" forces. More recently, the mechanisms that drive diagenetic changes, as well as the factors that determine the intensity and rate of such processes, have been studied through innovative theoretical and experimental approaches (Hedges and Millard, 1995; Hedges et al., 1995).

Extrinsic variables that temper postmortem modifications include characteristics of the soil and geochemical environment (Parker and Toots 1980:198–199). Such factors include soil pH (Gilbert, 1975:148–150; Gordon and Buikstra, 1981), temperature (Hare, 1980; Von Endt and Ortner, 1984), microorganisms (Child, 1995; Grupe and Piepenbrink, 1988; White and Hannus, 1983), groundwater (Hedges and Millard, 1995), precipitation (Hare, 1980), and soil texture, hydrology, mineralogy, and organic content (Buikstra et al., 1989:172; Hedges and Millard, 1995; Newesely, 1988:3–4; Pate and Hutton, 1988:730; Radosevich, 1993).

Intrinsic forces stem largely from the chemical characteristics of bone in contributing to the nature and extent of diagenetic change. Such factors include the size, microscopic structure (histology), porosity, and biochemistry of bone (Grupe, 1988; Hedges and Millard, 1995; Hedges et al., 1995; Von Endt and Ortner, 1984). Hedges and coworkers (1995) found that among intrinsic aspects of diagenesis, including measures of histological integrity, collagen loss, increased crystallinity,

and changes in porosity, pore size emerged as the best indicator of diagenetic activity and that the other parameters were not clearly associated with each other and showed substantial intrasite variation.

Diagenesis of bone mineral is related to and further affected by the breakdown of soft tissues, through the processes of autolysis and putrefaction (Pate, 1994:183) as well as the organic component of bone (Hare, 1980; Sillen, 1989; Von Endt and Ortner, 1984). The breakdown of both soft tissue and the organic portion of bone are enhanced by microbial activity (Grupe and Piepenbrink, 1988; Grupe et al., 1993; Pate, 1994; White and Hannus, 1983). The myriad factors that can contribute to diagenesis render it a highly variable process. The specific modes and mechanisms of diagenesis may vary over time and space although such changes may not be uniform or easy to predict (see Ezzo, 1992; Hedges et al., 1995; Klepinger et al., 1986; Radosevich, 1989, 1993; Runia, 1987, 1988). For example, elements that initially enter bone as contaminants may later leach out and vice-versa (Edward, 1987; Edward and Benfer, 1993; Parker and Toots, 1980). Diagenetic activity may even vary at different locations along a single bone from an individual (Farnum and Sandford, 1997).

Despite the inherent variability of diagenesis, some generalizations are possible and important to emphasize. First, all elements are vulnerable to diagenesis, although some elements such as Sr, Ca, and Ba may be less susceptible than others to diagenetic activity (but see discussions in Pate, 1994:184–186; Sillen, 1992:498–499). Second, bone that is more porous and less dense, such as bone from infants and juveniles, may be predisposed to diagenetic change (Baraybar, 1999; Buikstra et al., 1989; Gordon and Buikstra, 1981; Grupe, 1988; Lambert et al., 1979, 1982; Radosevich, 1993). Similarly, cancellous bone appears to have a greater propensity for diagenesis than cortical bone (Lambert et al., 1982). Finally, diagenetic changes do not necessarily obviate the interpretation of biogenic signatures (Byrne and Parris, 1987; Ezzo, 1992; Ezzo et al., 1995; Kyle, 1986; Radosevich, 1993; Sandford, 1984; Sandford and Kissling, 1994; Sandford et al., 1988). Indeed, diagenetic enrichment may, in some instances, augment or accentuate differences that were originally due to physiology.

During the intermediate and modern periods, anthropological trace element researchers developed a much greater understanding of the complexity and variability of diagenesis. This recognition has led to the implementation of many strategies to recognize and counter diagenesis. Such tactics are presented following a discussion of the applications of elemental analysis for paleodietary reconstruction.

ANTHROPOLOGICAL APPLICATIONS OF TRACE ELEMENT ANALYSIS

Strontium and Barium

Among the most promising applications of trace element analysis in anthropology are those that involve three alkaline earth elements, the major element Ca and Sr, and Ba, and are based on the observations of Elias and co-workers (1982) relating to the biopurification of calcium at different trophic levels. The use of skeletal Sr and Ca concentrations in paleodietary reconstruction relates to the principle that organisms take up Sr in quantities that vary inversely to their position on the trophic pyramid (Katzenberg, 1984; Sandford, 1993; Sillen, 1992; Sillen and Kavanagh, 1982). Therefore, herbivores should display higher Sr concentrations than those of carnivores, while omnivores (including humans) should contain intermediate levels.

Several developments in the intermediate and modern periods qualified and extended our understanding of the theoretical bases for Sr analyses and Sr/Ca ratios in bone. Sillen (1992) discussed these developments in reporting his use of Sr/Ca ratios to characterize the trophic position of fossilized faunal remains from Swartkrans. In particular, he emphasized the potential for Sr concentrations to vary between

food webs due to differences in geology and soil composition. Also, Sr/Ca ratios vary within trophic levels. For example, roots and seeds are associated with higher Sr/Ca ratios than leaves. Such observations underscore the need to conduct systematic studies of local food webs, including analyses of representative faunal and floral remains. As discussed above, the laboratory studies involving animal protocols (Lambert and Weydert-Homeyer (1993a, 1993b) also have provided valuable information about associations between dietary fiber and Sr/Ca.

A study by Burton and Wright (1995) helped to clarify relationships between bone Sr and hypothesized diets. By applying quantitative modeling to five different diets, they demonstrated that bone Sr is particularly sensitive to dietary components that are high in Ca. Thus, seemingly minor dietary practices and food items, including the addition of culinary ash to corn, can make a substantial contribution to Sr concentrations. Burton and Wright concluded that while bone Sr levels consistently reflect average Sr/Ca ratios, Sr is not a simple indicator of trophic level position.

More recently, applications involving the use of Ba in conjunction with Sr have increased (Burton and Price, 1990, 1991; Ezzo, 1992; Ezzo et al., 1995; Farnum and Sandford, 1997; Gilbert et al., 1994). Elias and co-workers (1982) made the initial observation that Ba is internally discriminated against in favor of Ca in a manner inversely related to an organism's trophic level. Gilbert and co-workers (1994:173) report a ratio of 10:5:1 for the differential intestinal uptake of Ca, Sr, and Ba. Therefore, Ba/Ca ratios are even more reduced at higher trophic levels than Ba/Sr. In addition, Ba is much less abundant in seawater and, consequently, in more marine resources than Sr.

Burton and Price (1990, 1991) conducted the first systematic evaluations of Ba as a dietary discriminator in archaeological human bone using samples from 14 inland and coastal sites from North and South America. They differentiated diets derived chiefly from marine as opposed to terrestrial resources, finding that log Ba/Sr ratios for marine-based diets ranged from –1.3 to –1.8, while diets derived mainly from terrestrial foods ranged from 0 to –0.4

Gilbert and co-workers (1994), working with material from the southwestern Cape of South Africa, determined log Ba/Sr and log Ba/Ca ratios from a host of contemporary indigenous marine and terrestrial resources as well as from a small sample of archaeological human bones. While Ba was of virtually no use in discerning dietary patterns within terrestrial food webs in their study, log Ba/Sr and log Ba/Ca clearly separated marine and terrestrial foods.

In a similar vein, an investigation of human bones from the Tutu site on the island of St. Thomas (Farnum and Sandford, 1997) explored the utility of Ba, Sr, and Ca concentrations for dietary reconstruction and diachronic dietary changes. Overall, log Ba and log Sr levels, as well as log Ba/Sr ratios, fell in the middle of the scales defined by Burton and Price (1990), and were consistent with a diet consisting of mixed terrestrial and marine resources. When log Ba and log Sr concentrations were compared over two time periods the later time period results suggested an increased reliance on marine resources. The latter observation is supported by independent analyses of fauna from the site (Wing et al., 1995).

Promising results relating elemental data from human bones to weaning, pregnancy, and lactation were generated by Farnum (1996) in her study of the Paloma site in Peru. She found that Sr and Zn were successful in predicting weaning age (estimated between two to three years of age), but not in estimating the age ranges associated with parity. The estimated age of weaning concurred with other lines of evidence, including paleodemographic data and some nonspecific indicators of stress.

Although Ba, Sr, and Ca show great promise for reconstructing past diets, their ability to act as dietary discriminators may be hindered by such factors as the large standard deviations in femoral Ba concentrations (Farnum and Sandford, 1997; Lambert et al., 1984), and regional variation in geological fac-

tors (Gilbert et al., 1994). Finally, all three elements are subject to diagenetic alteration.

Multielement Analyses

As first conceptualized, multielement studies focus on a broader array of analyzed elements for purposes of dietary discrimination. This approach was applied initially to skeletal material from Dickson Mounds (Gilbert 1975, 1977, 1985) in an attempt to document the change from hunting-gathering to agricultural subsistence by contrasting levels of elements that are presumably more abundant in vegetation with those that are more prevalent in animal resources. Zinc emerged as the most promising dietary discriminator, demonstrating significantly higher levels in the hunting and gathering population and appearing to have been less subject to diagenesis.

Lambert and co-workers (1979) used the multielement approach to try to recognize and, where possible, circumvent diagenetic effects as those efforts unfolded during their subsequent investigations (Lambert et al., 1982, 1983, 1984, 1985, 1989). Buikstra and co-workers (1989) identified several key issues in the use of elemental analysis by anthropologists and modeled, through their own analysis, a more problem-oriented approach to elemental investigations in our field. First, they called for exploration of the elemental content of prehistoric food items, such as nuts and maize, and an evaluation of our assumptions regarding these foodstuffs. Second, they encouraged future investigators to frame specific expectations or hypotheses about elemental concentrations of skeletal samples prior to conducting such analyses. Finally, they discussed the importance of using appropriate statistical techniques for analyzing complex elemental data and introduced principal components analysis for elemental investigations.

The multielement approach has grown steadily since the inaugural period and has been widely applied to studies of past populations throughout the Old and New Worlds (Baraybar and de la Rua, 1997; Edward, 1987; Edward and Benfer, 1993; Edward et al., 1984; Farnum,

1996; Farnum and Sandford, 1997; Farnum et al., 1995; Francalacci and Tarli, 1988; Grupe 1988; Klepinger et al., 1986; Kyle, 1986; Sandford et al., 1988). However, the nature and foci of multielement studies are changing in several substantive ways. First, most such studies reflect an increasing awareness of diagenesis and the need for greater statistical rigor. For example, the frequent inclusion of several independent diagnostic methods into a single research design is commonplace in contemporary elemental studies (Baraybar, 1999; Baraybar and de la Rua, 1997; Byrne and Parris, 1987; Edward and Benfer, 1993; Farnum and Sandford, 1997; Kyle, 1986). Second, multielement studies are adopting a more problem-oriented approach, aimed at testing specific hypotheses about dietary change, burial customs, and diagenetic change. Third, an increased focus on diagenesis, together with emphasis on the need to test basic assumptions about trace elements, has led to growing skepticism concerning the use of many elements, including Zn, as paleodietary indicators (see especially Baraybar, 1999; Ezzo, 1994b; Ezzo et al., 1995). Some researchers are retaining the multielement approach chiefly to screen for diagenetic activity, while focusing on Sr, Ba, and Ca as potential dietary indicators. Thus, the aforementioned trends are even more apparent when multielement studies are coupled with those more specifically focused on Sr and/or Ba (Ezzo, 1992; Ezzo et al., 1995; Price, 1989; Radosevich, 1989; Runia, 1987).

In contemplating the future of multielement analysis, it is clear that basic assumptions must be tested and the usefulness of most individual elements as dietary indicators must be demonstrated through additional laboratory and problem-oriented field studies. On the other hand, multielement approaches must be used in many instances to discern relevant patterns of elemental interaction in both bone and soil.

Trace Elements and Skeletal Pathology

Investigations of elemental concentrations in relation to a particular disorder or disease in a past population have been extremely limited. A small number of researchers (Edward and Benfer, 1993; Fornaciari et al., 1983; Zaino, 1968), have investigated Fe status and skeletal conditions in past populations. The results have been mixed, as might be expected given the complex relationships between Fe, skeletal conditions, and diagenesis.

Lead has been the focus of most investigations of trace elements and pathology (Aufderheide, 1989; Aufderheide et al., 1981, 1985, 1988; Ghazi and Reinhard, 1994; Jarcho, 1964; Keenleyside et al., 1996; Kowal et al., 1989; Reinhard and Ghazi, 1992; Waldron HA, 1981, 1983; Waldron T, 1987). Anthropological applications of skeletal Pb analyses have been much more thoroughly explored than any other single element (see especially Aufderheide, 1989; Aufderheide et al., 1988) with the exception of Sr. Most, though not all such studies (see Gonzalez-Reimers et al., 1999) have been used as evidence for Pb toxicity in the past.

Efforts by Aufderheide and co-workers (1981, 1985, 1988) are particularly noteworthy. In a study of lead content in colonial American human remains, they confirmed the past importance of pewter utensils and food containers and demonstrated the utility of such analyses to delineate socioeconomic differences within populations and the occupational categories of specific individuals.

Waldron and Waldron (Waldron HA, 1981, 1983; Waldron T 1987) have similarly analyzed skeletons from the United Kingdom and documented excessive Pb intakes, probably from containers and water pipes, among Romano-British and medieval populations. Unfortunately, Pb, like other elements, is subject to diagenetic change and Waldron (1981) found that bones buried in lead coffins had accumulated Pb on their external and internal surfaces, a pattern typical of diagenetic contamination.

Finally, Pb analyses of historic skeletons from North America, together with other forms of documentation, have yielded some intriguing examples of possible lead toxicity. For example, historic records and bone chemistry data suggest that members of the Franklin Arctic expedition suffered from accidental Pb poisoning due to exposure of toxic quantities of the element from canned foods sealed with Pb solder (Keenleyside et al., 1996; Kowal et al., 1989).

METHODOLOGY

The methodological stages of elemental analyses follow procedures established in analytical chemistry and include (1) sampling, (2) sample preparation, (3) determination and quantification of chemical contents, and (4) evaluation and interpretation (Goffer, 1980:22).

Because of the chemical heterogeneity of bone, and possible age- and/or sex-specific physiological differences, sampling requires special considerations. For most anthropological elemental analyses, cortical bone is far superior to trabecular bone in that it is less susceptible to diagenesis, shows less intraindividual variation, and, due to its slower turnover compared to cancellous bone, may represent a larger portion of a person's lifetime (Edward and Benfer, 1993; Edward et al., 1984; Farnum et al., 1995; Gilbert, 1975:138, 1985:350–351; Grupe, 1988; Harritt and Radosevich, 1992; Lambert et al., 1982, 1989). Representative cortical cross sections with intact periosteal and endosteal surfaces should be obtained for most elemental investigations. The actual amount needed for analysis depends largely on the specific instrumentation to be used, and the reader is referred to instrumentation-specific protocols below. Because of significant heterogeneities in cortical tissue, however, some researchers (Klepinger et al., 1986) advise grinding and blending approximately 5 g of bone to secure a representative sample.

In most instances, an approximately 3–4 cm long section, taken from the mid-diaphyseal region of the femur or tibia should be more than adequate and afford the retention of adequate bone for histological, electron microprobe (EMP), and other related studies, if desired. Cross sections are usually extracted for elemental investigations using various types of saws, chisels, or neurosurgical or trephining bits (Aufderheide et al., 1981; Edward and Benfer, 1993; Grupe, 1988; Radosevich, 1993). To avoid possible contamination, blades and cutting implements can be rinsed between uses with nitric and hydrochloric acid solutions as well as distilled-deionized water.

Following extraction, bone samples are prepared for analysis in a manner appropriate to the instrumentation. Subsequent steps include cleaning, drying, and pulverizing samples. Of particular importance are some steps, taken during cleaning, that are aimed at minimizing diagenetic effects. For example, many investigators physically abrade the superficial periosteal and endosteal surfaces (Edward and Benfer, 1993; Edward et al., 1984; Farnum and Sandford, 1997; Farnum et al., 1995; Lambert et al., 1989; Price et al., 1992). This procedure may remove surface contaminants and help free the sample of soil particles, spongy bone, or occasional fragments of preserved soft tissue (Edward and Benfer, 1993). In addition, special washing procedures may be modified somewhat if the organic phase of bone is extremely well-preserved (Edward, 1987; Edward and Benfer, 1993).

Finally, chemical cleaning methods demonstrate great promise and are becoming more widely practiced (Gilbert et al., 1994; Price et al., 1992; Sealy and Sillen, 1988; Sillen, 1989, 1992; Sillen et al., 1989). The use of solubility profiles is particularly important in this regard (Sillen, 1986). Protocols for this technique involve the use of sequential acetic acid/sodium acetate buffer washes to isolate mineral components with different solubilities. Attempts to identify the mineral phases most representative of biogenic levels are made using adjunct techniques including inductively coupled plasma emission spectroscopy (ICP) and atomic absorption spectrometry (AAS). Strontium/calcium ratios and other chemical parameters are determined to assist in the determination of different chemical phases.

In addition, and depending on the technique, ashing and digesting samples may also be performed (Lambert et al., 1979:117). Researchers using neutron activation analysis

(NAA) may elect not to dry ash samples, as recent investigations by Edward and co-workers (1990) have demonstrated that concentrations of several elements may be seriously affected by ashing. Instrumentation-specific considerations relating to the preparation and analysis of archaeological human bone can be found in the following sources: AAS (Lambert et al., 1979; Sealy and Sillen, 1988; Szpunar et al., 1978), NAA (Edward and Benfer, 1993; Farnum and Sandford, 1997; Farnum et al., 1995; Radosevich, 1993), ICP (Baraybar and de la Rua, 1997; Ezzo et al., 1995; Klepinger et al., 1986), X-ray fluorescence (XRF) (Katzenberg, 1984; Kyle, 1986).

Analytical Instrumentation

The most frequently used techniques for quantitative elemental analyses of archaeological bone are AAS, NAA, ICP, and XRF. Selection of the most appropriate instrumentation includes pragmatic considerations related to cost, time, requisite skill, and accessibility (Vandecasteele and Block, 1993). For the theoretical foundations of these types of instrumentation, along with discussion of their advantages and disadvantages for anthropological studies, see Aufderheide (1989), Gilbert (1985), Goffer (1980), Hamilton (1979), and Vandecasteele and Block (1993).

The most frequently used technique in anthropological elemental research is AAS, with most researchers preferring to use electrothermal as opposed to flame-generated sources of heat (Aufderheide, 1989:241; Gilbert, 1977:94). AAS is a particularly popular choice for investigations focusing on Sr, Ca, and Ba due to its high sensitivity for these elements (Brown, 1973; Gilbert et al., 1994; Schoeninger, 1979, 1982; Sealy and Sillen, 1988; Sillen, 1981, 1988, 1992). In addition to its high sensitivity for many elements, the instrumentation is readily accessible on most college campuses and is relatively inexpensive and easy to use. The primary disadvantage of AAS is that it analyzes only one element at a time, a factor that should be considered if multielement studies are contemplated.

Because of its sensitivity and/or capability for simultaneous analysis of numerous elements, ICP is being used increasingly for elemental analyses of archaeological bone (Baraybar and de la Rua, 1997; Byrne and Parris, 1987; Ezzo et al., 1995; Francalacci and Tarli, 1988; Klepinger et al., 1986; Price, 1989; Runia, 1987). Although increasing in use, this instrumentation is still less widely available than AAS and initial equipment costs are quite high (Aufderheide, 1989:244).

Two nondestructive methods, which provide a means of reanalyzing the same samples, represent the remaining quantitative techniques used by anthropologists in elemental investigations. The first method, NAA, holds the major advantages of analyzing numerous elements simultaneously coupled with the relative ease of sample preparation (Goffer 1980:74–75; Vandecasteele and Block, 1993:300–318). Unfortunately, sample analysis can be quite costly. Discussions of NAA and useful points about sample preparation and analysis are provided in Edward and Benfer (1993), Farnum and Sandford (1997), Farnum et al. (1995), Hancock et al. (1987, 1989), and Radosevich (1993).

Last, quantitative analysis of bone samples may also be accomplished by X-ray fluorescence spectrometry (XRF) (Goffer, 1980: 45–47; Hamilton, 1979:314–331). Katzenberg (1984:56) and Kyle (1986) provide useful details concerning preparation and analysis of bone samples by this technique.

Recognizing and Confronting Diagenesis

In recent years, experimental and theoretical designs involving field, laboratory, and statistical techniques have enhanced our understanding and recognition of diagenesis (Ezzo, 1992; Farnum and Sandford, 1997; Hedges and Millard, 1995; Hedges et al., 1995; Klepinger et al., 1986; Pate and Hutton, 1988; Radosevich, 1993; Sandford and Kissling, 1994; Sillen, 1989; Sillen et al., 1989). Most researchers now routinely employ several different techniques for diagnosing diagenetic activity (Baraybar, 1999; Baraybar and de la Rua, 1997; Buikstra et al., 1989; Edward, 1987; Edward and Benfer, 1993; Farnum, 1996; Farnum and Sandford, 1997; Radosevich, 1993).

Soil analysis is mandatory. The oldest and most frequently used techniques for assessing diagenesis involve chemical analyses of soil and are based on some basic assumptions derived from concentration gradient theory (see discussions in Edward, 1987; Edward and Benfer, 1993; Farnum, 1996; Farnum and Sandford, 1997; Farnum et al., 1995; Klepinger, 1984:79; Lambert et al., 1979:119; Radosevich, 1989, 1993). The results of some investigations have cast doubts on some of these assumptions (see discussions in Edward and Benfer, 1993; Hedges et al., 1995; Klepinger, 1984:79; Lambert et al., 1984, 1985).

Several additional factors should be considered in soil analysis. Samples should be taken from a variety of contexts at a given site to provide greater characterization of the geochemical environment (see Farnum, 1996; Farnum and Sandford, 1997; Sandford et al., 1988). Second, as recognized by Pate and Hutton (1988:729), soil analyses for bulk elemental abundances may be less useful than analyses for soluble and exchangeable ions because a majority of the inorganic chemical reactions of the soil entail ions in solution. Ionic exchange processes as significant diagenetic forces in varied environments are discussed by Baraybar and de la Rua (1997), Edward and Benfer (1993), Farnum (1996), and Farnum and Sandford (1997). Farnum (1996:19) points out the inherent bias in assuming that the ionic solubility of archaeological soil samples is reflective of past environmental conditions.

Because soil analyses are not sufficient for interpreting diagenetic processes, they should be used in combination with other techniques, including histological studies of the bone (Baraybar and de la Rua, 1997; Hanson and Buikstra, 1987; Hedges et al., 1995; Schoeninger et al., 1989; White and Hannus, 1983). Hedges and co-workers (1995) argue that histological degradation proceeds independently

of other diagenetic parameters, including increased porosity of bone, and their findings argue persuasively for the use of multiple techniques for evaluating diagenetic change.

The electron microprobe (EMP) in conjunction with the scanning electron microscope (SEM) can provide valuable information about the histological integrity and the distribution of elements within bone. First employed by Gilbert (1975), the technique has been adapted by a number of subsequent researchers with varying degrees of success (Farnum and Sandford, 1997; Klepinger et al., 1986; Lambert et al., 1983, 1984; Parker and Toots, 1980; Radosevich, 1989, 1993). Using SEM X-ray mapping in connection with EMP, several investigators have demonstrated concentration gradients in the distribution of diagenetic elements, such that contaminants typically accumulate along the periosteal and endosteal cortical surfaces (Lambert et al., 1983; Radosevich, 1993: 298). Farnum and Sandford (1997) used energy-dispersive X-ray microanalysis (EDS) to examine the histological distribution of elements in bone from the pre-Columbian Caribbean Tutu site and showed that diagenetic or reprecipitated Ca, Co, Cl, and S in some samples was concentrated most heavily around Haversian canals. Failure to find such heterogeneity in elemental distributions of SEM maps is not necessarily indicative of the absence of diagenesis (Klepinger et al., 1986:329; Lambert et al., 1983). Even the presence of well-preserved histological structures in no way precludes the possibility of diagenetic activity (Radosevich, 1993).

X-ray diffraction (XRD) spectrometry, another specialized form of instrumentation, has become widely used in documenting diagenesis (Baraybar, 1999; Baraybar and de la Rua, 1997; Hedges et al., 1995; Kyle, 1986; Pate and Hutton, 1991; Schoeninger, 1981, 1982; Sillen, 1989:213–217). For example, Baraybar and de la Rua (1997) employed XRD to confirm significant contamination of bone samples by calcium carbonate—the diagenetic pattern that was suspected due to the abundance of the compound in the postdepositional environment of the funerary cave.

Exciting new approaches for detecting diagenetic activity are under development. Lee and coworkers (1995) have conducted a promising pilot study involving the application of solid state nuclear magnetic resonance spectroscopy (NMR) in investigating diagenetic change. Other innovative techniques for characterizing the nature of diagenetically altered bone include infrared spectroscopy and Fourier transform infrared spectroscopy (FTIR) (Wright and Schwarcz, 1996). The refinement and further development of innovative technology toward the detection of diagenetic change are important in this increasingly specialized area of study.

Additional methods for detecting diagenesis can be categorized as comparative skeletal studies, where the elemental concentrations of excavated skeletal material are typically examined against baseline levels documented for other bones, species, or human populations. While most comparative skeletal studies evaluate mean differences in elemental concentrations, intra-bone comparisons are typically based on correlations between the elements themselves and are viewed in conjunction with soil analyses (Edward, 1987; Edward and Benfer, 1993; Edward et al., 1984; Katzenberg, 1984; Kyle, 1986). An extension of this approach involves the recognition and interpretation of patterns of multielemental interaction (Buikstra et al., 1989; Farnum and Sandford, 1997; Sandford and Kissling, 1994).

Inter-bone comparisons most often involve comparisons between different types of bones, such as femora and ribs (Edward, 1987; Edward and Benfer, 1993; Lambert et al., 1982). While this technique may be an appropriate adjunct to other, more direct methods for assessing diagenesis (see Edward, 1987; Edward and Benfer, 1993), it is not advisable to rely solely on information derived from this method due to questions concerning bone turnover and/or sex- and age-specific physiological differences.

Interspecies comparisons, in which elemental constituents of human bone are compared to those of fauna representing different dietary patterns, are of greater applicability (Baraybar and de la Rua, 1997; Byrne and Parris, 1987; Ezzo, 1992; Gilbert et al., 1994; Katzenberg, 1984; Kyle, 1986; Radosevich, 1989, 1993; Runia, 1987; Schoeninger, 1981; Sillen, 1981, 1992). Faunal analyses serve a dual function: diagenetic activity is suspected when elemental levels deviate from values predicted on the basis of trophic level and presumed dietary patterns, while biogenic concentrations of fauna facilitate reconstruction of prehistoric human diets (Buikstra et al., 1989:176). Inherent difficulties in the application of interspecies comparisons include recovery of sufficient representative material and dietary variability among animal species (see Buikstra et al., 1989; Runia, 1987, 1988; Sillen et al., 1989).

The paucity of comparative, baseline data from prehistoric and modern human populations is recognized as a significant problem in anthropological trace element research (Price, 1989:248). Some data from contemporary populations were used in the earliest anthropological studies (see Gilbert, 1975; Lambert et al., 1979). More recently, new data have been generated and, in some cases, used to cast doubt on elemental analyses of archaeological bone (Hancock et al., 1987, 1989). The applicability of modern, comparative data is limited, however, by the lack of documentation of dietary and physiological factors (but see Byrne and Parris, 1987). Comparative archaeological data, while more abundant, present similar limitations. Moreover, researchers working with comparative data must consider that many variables, including subtle differences in the elemental compositions of soil and ground water (Radosevich, 1989; Runia, 1988; Sillen et al., 1989) may lead to substantial interpopulational differences in biological and diagnetic deposition.

Statistical Evaluation and Interpretation

Analysis and interpretation of elemental data are complicated by many potential sources of biogenic and diagenetic influences. These considerations, coupled with the inherent complexities of the statistical distributions of elemental concentrations, underlie the need for statistical analyses that are both rigorous and appropriate. Despite the importance of using proper statistical techniques in elemental analyses, there have been surprisingly few discussions of such methods in the trace element literature. Attention was first focused on such concerns by Klepinger (1984:76) who noted that elemental data often are non-normally distributed and recommended using nonparametric statistical methods. For the most part, however, the statistical techniques that were initially employed by anthropologists engaged in trace element research were relatively unsophisticated and descriptive in nature, thus limiting our ability to discern complex patterns presented by elemental data.

It was thus an important milestone when Buikstra and colleagues (1989:188–207) used principal components analyses in conjunction with their investigations of trace element and carbon isotopes in human bone from the lower Illinois Valley. The greatest advantage of principal components analysis is the ability to weigh concomitantly the impact of factors stemming from diet, diagenesis, physiology, and elemental interactions (Baraybar and de la Rua, 1997; Sandford and Kissling, 1994). More recently, both metric (Sandford and Kissling, 1994) and nonmetric (Farnum and Sandford, 1997) multidimensional scaling techniques have been used as pattern recognition techniques in elemental analyses. Finally, Sandford and Kissling (1995) have developed a statistical method with the potential for assessing and, ultimately, correcting for the effects of diagenetic change. This method uses a spatial analysis technique, based on an empirical Bayes estimator, to examine microgeographic variation in elemental concentrations.

CONCLUSIONS

The history of elemental analysis in anthropology, while quite brief, has been most tumultuous. Contemporary trace element research differs in both substance and tone from the atmosphere that surrounded its introduction to our discipline. As we have seen, most contemporary elemental analyses for purposes of dietary reconstruction are more problem-oriented and complex than the initial studies in the field. Generally, predictions and hypotheses about elemental concentrations are stated a priori and based on independent data. Such procedures represent a radical departure from the early days of elemental analysis where expectations regarding elemental concentrations were stated in the broadest possible terms. Moreover, contemporary studies are accompanied by advanced techniques for evaluating the nature and severity of diagenesis, identifying patterns in elemental interaction, and interpreting elemental concentrations. Researchers typically are incorporating several independent strategies for assessing diagenetic change in a single study while growing increasingly reliant on multivariate statistical techniques. Like the study of diagenetic change, statistical techniques used in elemental analysis have grown increasingly complex and sophisticated. This again underscores that specialized training and interdisciplinary collaboration will be needed to propel elemental investigations of archaeological samples forward.

Investigations aimed at paleodietary objectives are developing in the context of other, more specialized avenues of research. The study of both biogenic and diagenetic processes is progressing along several critical lines. First, some investigators are focusing on the determination of baseline concentrations of elements for humans and other species (Beck Jensen et al., 1996; Glab and Szostek, 1995; Hancock et al., 1993). While some studies are being conducted with specific paleodietary objectives in mind, others are taking place in connection with biomedical research. In addition, associations between dietary regimens and elemental concentrations are being established slowly through experimental models (Klepinger 1990; Lambert and Weydert-Homeyer, 1993a, 1993b). While such studies are critical for testing and verifying some of the most fundamental underlying assumptions of elemental analysis, their applicability to humans must be carefully weighed. Ezzo (1994a, 1994b) has pointed out, for example, that our assumptions relating to the ability of bone to reflect dietary zinc have not been adequately substantiated, while other researchers have called attention to the uncritical acceptance of various other assumptions (Buikstra et al., 1989; Radosevich, 1993; Sandford and Kissling, 1994; Sillen et al., 1989).

Future investigators will continue to test some of the assumptions of the technique, while performing basic experimental research that will help to illuminate the biogenic and diagenetic processes that are responsible for elemental concentrations. In this regard, a potentially important but largely untouched area lies at the interfaces of skeletal physiology, pathology, and elemental metabolism. Although a number of elements play essential roles in bone growth and remodeling (Peretz, 1996), studies of associations between elemental concentrations, skeletal pathology, growth, and histology remain largely unexplored.

In reflecting on the historical development of elemental analysis in anthropology, there are some interesting and instructive relationships with the larger fields of skeletal biology and paleopathology. As we have seen, the development of paleopathology and, in particular, the growth of paleoepidemiology, encouraged and hastened the rise of elemental analysis in anthropology (Sandford, 1993). Specifically, interest in the interaction between diet and disease and in the impact of dietary changes on disease rates encouraged attempts to reconstruct prehistoric diets through all means, including elemental analysis. While the population- and problem-based approaches of paleoepidemiology represent a vast advance over the diagnostic/clinical model applied by the founders of the field, both paleopathology and elemental analyses would be strengthened by synthesizing the findings of basic research in skeletal physiology with perspectives from the diagnostic/clinical and paleoepidemiological models (Sandford, 1998; Sandford et al.,

1998). This can only be achieved, however, through genuine interdisciplinary collaborations and more specialized, up-to-date training of our students in skeletal physiology and histology. Similarly, the new practitioners of elemental analysis must be willing and able to receive adequate training in and form research collaborations with scientists in such other fields as chemistry, statistics, and geology.

Issues surrounding interdisciplinary collaborations and the formal education of our students are seldom consciously and intentionally addressed in our discipline. One of the most basic lessons shown by the development of elemental analysis in anthropology is that there is an acute need to revisit the basics of scientific processes, methods, and investigation with our students in our classrooms and laboratories (Sandford, 1998). It is only by taking these steps that the field of elemental analysis in anthropology will be assured of a future.

ACKNOWLEDGMENTS

We thank Julie Farnum for her comments and suggestions on an earlier draft of this chapter. We would like to thank Shelley Saunders and Annie Katzenberg for the opportunity to contribute to this volume.

REFERENCES

Aikawa JK. 1981. Magnesium: Its Biological Significance. Boca Raton: CRC Press.

Aufderheide AC. 1989. Chemical analysis of skeletal remains. In: İşcan MY, Kennedy KAR, editors. Reconstruction of Life from the Skeleton. New York: Alan R. Liss. pp. 237–260.

Aufderheide AC, Angel JL, Kelley JO, Outlaw AC, Outlaw MA, Rapp G Jr, Wittmers LE. 1985. Lead in bone III: prediction of social content in four colonial American populations (Catoctin Furnace, College Landing, Governor's Land and Irene Mound). Am J Phys Anthropol 66:353–361.

Aufderheide AC, Neiman FD, Wittmers LE Jr, Rapp G. 1981. Lead in bones II: skeletal lead content as an indicator of lifetime lead ingestion and the social correlates in an archaeological population. Am J Phys Anthropol 55:285–291.

Aufderheide AC, Wittmers LE, Rapp G, Wallgren J. 1988. Anthropological applications of skeletal lead analysis. Am Anthropol 90:932–936.

Baraybar JP. 1999. Diet and death in a fog oasis site in central coastal Peru: a trace element study of Tomb 1 Malache 22. J Archaeol Sci 26:471–482.

Baraybar JP, de la Rua C. 1997. Reconstruction of diet with trace elements of bone at the Chalcolithic site of Pico Ramos, Basque Country, Spain. J Archaeol Sci 24:355–364.

Baumslag N, Petering AG. 1976. Trace metal studies in Bushmen hair. Arch Environ Health 31: 254–257.

Beck Jensen J-E, Larsen MM, Kringholm B, Pritzl G, Sorensen OH. 1996. Measurement of trace elements in bone by ICP-MS. In: Neve J, Chappuis P, Lamand M, editors. Therapuetic Uses of Elements. New York: Plenum Press. pp. 297–301.

Blakely RI. 1977. Introduction: changing strategies for the biological anthropologist. In: Blakely RI, editor. Biocultural Adaptations in Prehistoric America. Athens: University of Georgia Press. pp. 1–9.

Blakely RI. 1989. Bone strontium in pregnant and lactating females from archaeological samples. Am J Phys Anthropol 80:173–185.

Bothwell TH, Finch CA. 1962. Iron Metabolism. Boston: Little, Brown and Co.

Brown A. 1973. bone strontium content as a dietary indicator in human skeletal populations. Ph.D. Dissertation, University of Michigan. Ann Arbor: University Microfilms, Publication No. 7415. p. 677.

Buikstra JE, Cook DC. 1980. Paleopathology: an American account. Ann Rev Anthropol 9: 433–470.

Buikstra JE, Frankenberg S, Lambert JB, Xue L. 1989. Multiple elements: multiple expectations. In: Price TD, editor. The Chemistry of Prehistoric Human Bone. Cambridge: Cambridge University Press. pp. 155–210.

Burton JH, Price TD. 1990. The ratio of barium to strontium as a paleodietary indicator of consumption of marine resources. J Archaeol Sci 17:547–557.

Burton JH, Price TD. 1991 Paleodietary applications of barium in bone. In: Pernicka E, Wagner GA,

editors. Proceedings of the 27th International Symposium on Archaeometry. Basel: Berkhauser Verlag AG. pp. 787–795.

Burton, JH, Wright, LE. 1995. Nonlinearity in the relationship between bone Sr/Ca and diet: paleodietary implications. Am J Phys Anthropol 96:273–282.

Byrne KB, Parris DC. 1987. Reconstruction of the diet of the Middle Woodland Amerindian population at Abbott Farm by bone trace-element analysis. Am J. Phys Anthropol 74:373–384.

Cabrera WE, Schrooten I, De Broe ME, D'Haese PC. 1999. Strontium and bone. J Bone Min Res 14:661–668.

Chesney RW, Specer BL, Mimouni F, McKay CP. 1992. Mineral metabolism during pregnancy and lactation. In: Coe FL, Fauvus MJ, editors. Disorders of bone and mineral metabolism. New York: Raven Press. pp. 383–393.

Child AM. 1995. Towards an understanding of the microbial decomposition of archaeological bone in the burial environment. J Archaeol Sci 22:165–174.

Cunnane SC. 1988. Zinc: Clinical and Biological Significance. Boca Raton: CRC Press.

Edward J. 1987. Studies of human bone from the Preceramic Amerindian site at Paloma, Peru by neutron activation analysis. Ph.D. Dissertation, University of Missouri.

Edward JB, Benfer RA. 1993. The effects of diagenesis on the Paloma skeletal material. In: Sandford MK, editor. Investigations of Ancient Human Tissue: Chemical Analyses in Anthropology. Langhorne: Gordon and Breach. pp. 183–268.

Edward JB, Benfer RA, Morris JS. 1990. The effects of dry ashing on the composition of human and animal bone. Biol Trace Elem Res 25:219–231.

Edward J, Fossey JM, Yaffee L. 1984. Analysis by neutron activation of human bone from the Hellenistic cemetery at Asine, Greece. J Field Archaeol 11:37–46.

Elias RW, Hirao Y, Patterson CC. 1982. The circumvention of the natural biopurification of calcium along nutrient pathways by atmospheric inputs of industrial lead. Geochimica et Cosmochimica Acta 46:2561–2580.

Ezzo JA. 1992. A test of diet versus diagenesis at Ventana Cave, Arizona. J Archaeol Sci 19:23–37.

Ezzo JA. 1994a. Putting the "chemistry" back into archaeological bone chemistry analysis: modeling potential paleodietary indicators. J Anthropol Archaeol 13:1–34.

Ezzo JA. 1994b. Zinc as a paleodietary indicator: an issue of theoretical validity in bone-chemistry analysis. Am Antiq 59:606–621.

Ezzo JA, Larsen CS, Burton JH. 1995. Elemental signatures of human diets from the Georgia Bight. Am J Phys Anthropol 98:471–481.

Fairweather-Tait SJ. 1992. The metabolism of iron and its bioavailability in foods. In: Widdowson EM, Mathers JC, editors. The Contribution of Nutrition to Human and Animal Health. Cambridge: Cambridge University Press. pp. 151–161.

Farnum JF. 1996. Multi-method approaches to diet and health reconstruction and estimations of ages of pregnancies and weaning for Paloma, Peru using Sr, Zn, and non-specific indicators of stress. M.A. Thesis, University of Missouri.

Farnum JF, Glascock MD, Sandford MK, Gerritsen S. 1995. Trace elements in ancient and human bone and associated soil using NAA. J Radioanal Nucl Chem 196(2):267–274.

Farnum JF, Sandford MK. 1997. Trace element analysis of the Tutu skeletal remains. Report Submitted to the Office of Planning and Natural Resources, Division of Archaeology and Historic Preservation, Government of the United States Virgin Islands.

Favus MJ. 1999. Primer on the metabolic diseases and disorders of mineral metabolism. Philadelphia: Lippincott Williams & Wilkins.

Fornaciari G, Mallegni F, Bertini D, Nuti Y. 1983. Cribra orbitalia and elemental bone iron in the Punics of Carthage. Ossa 8:63–77.

Francalacci P, Tarli SB. 1988. Mulielementary analysis of trace elements and preliminary results on stable isotopes in two Italian prehistoric sites. Methodological aspects In: Grupe G, Herrmann B, editors. Trace Elements in Environmental History. Heidelberg: Springer-Verlag. pp. 41–52.

Frieden E. 1972. The chemical elements of life. In: Human Nutrition: Readings from Scientific American. San Francisco: WH Freeman. pp. 148–155.

Fritz JC. 1972. Iron and associated trace mineral problems in man and animals. In: Cannon HL, Hopps HC, editors. Geochemical Environment in Relation to Health and Disease. Geo Soc Am 140:25–32.

Frost HM. 1985. The "new bone": some anthropological potentials. Yrbk of Phys Anthropol 28:211–226.

Garner SC, Anderson JJB. 1996. Calcium and bone metabolism during pregnancy. In: Anderson JJB, Garner SC, editors. Calcium and Phosphorus in Health and Disease. Boca Raton: CRC Press. pp. 237–246.

Ghazi AM, Reinhard KJ. 1994. Further evidence of lead contamination of Omaha skeletons. Am J Phys Anthropol 95:427–434.

Gilbert C, Sealy J, Sillen A. 1994. An investigation of barium, calcium, and strontium as paleodietary indicators in the southwestern Cape, South Africa. J Archaeol Sci 21:173–184.

Gilbert RI. 1975. Trace element analysis of three skeletal Amerindian populations at Dickson Mounds. Ph.D. Dissertation, University of Massachusetts. Ann Arbor, MI: University Microfilms, Publication No. 76-5854.

Gilbert RI. 1977. Applications of trace element research to problems in archaeology. In: Blakely RL, editor. Biocultural Adaptations in Prehistoric America. Athens: University of Georgia Press, pp. 85–100.

Gilbert RI. 1985. Stress, paleonutrition, and trace elements. In: Gilbert RI, Mielke JH, editors. The Analysis of Prehistoric Diets. Orlando: Academic Press. pp. 339–358.

Glab H, Szostek K. 1995. Variability of trace element content in permanent teeth of Macaca mulatta—two different populations. Folia Primatol 64:215–217.

Glimcher JM. 1992. The nature of the mineral component of bone and mechanism of calcification. In: Coe FL, Fauvus JM, editors. Disorders of Bone and Mineral Metabolism. New York: Raven Press. pp. 265–263.

Goffer Z. 1980. Archaeological Chemistry: A Source Book on the Applications of Chemistry to Archaeology. New York: John Wiley & Sons.

Gonzalez-Reimers E, Arnay-De-La-Rosa M, Velasco-Vazquez J, Galindo-Martin L, Delgado-Ureta E, Santolaria-Fernandex F. 1999. Bone lead in the prehistoric population of Gran Canaria. Am J Hum Bio 11:405–410.

Gordon CC, Buikstra JE. 1981. Soil pH, bone preservation and sampling bias at mortuary sites. Am Antiq 46:566–571.

Grupe G. 1988. Impact of the choice of bone samples on trace element data in excavated human skeletons. J Archaeol Sci 15:123–129.

Grupe G, Piepenbrink H. 1988. Trace element contaminations in excavated bones by micro-organisms. In: Grupe G, Herrmann B, editors. Trace Elements in Environmental History. Heidelberg: Springer-Verlag. pp. 103–112.

Grupe G, Dreses-Werringloer U, Parsche F. 1993. Initial stages of bone decomposition: causes and consequences. In: Lambert JB, Grupe G, editors. Prehistoric Human Bone—Archaeology at the Molecular Level. Heidelberg: Springer-Verlag. pp. 257–274.

Halsted JA, Ronaghy HA, Abadi P, Haghshenass M, Amirhakemi GH, Barakat RH, Reinhold TC. 1972. Zinc deficiency in man: the Shiraz experiment. Am J Med 53:277–284.

Hamilton EI. 1979. The chemical elements and man: measurements, perspectives, applications. Springfield, Ill: Charles C. Thomas.

Hancock RGV, Grynpas MD, Akesson K, Obrant KB, Turnquist J, Kessler MJ. 1993. Baselines and variabilities of major and trace elements in bone. In: Lambert JB, Grupe G, editors. Prehistoric Human Bone: Archaeology at the Molecular Level. Berlin: Springer-Verlag. pp. 189–202.

Hancock RGV, Grynpas MD, Alpert B. 1987. Are archaeological bones similar to modern bones? An INAA assessment. J Radioanal Nuclear Chem 110:283–291.

Hancock RGV, Grynpas MD, Pritzker KPH. 1989. The abuse of bone analyses for archaeological dietary studies. Archaeometry 31:169–179.

Hanson DB, Buikstra JE. 1987. Histomorphological alteration in buried human bone from the Lower Illinois valley: implications for paleodietary research. J Archaeol Sci 14:549–563.

Hare PE. 1980. Organic geochemistry of bone and its relation to the survival of bone in the natural environment. In: Behrensmeyer AK, Hill AP, editors. Fossils in the Making. Chicago: University of Chicago Press. pp. 208–219.

Harritt RK, Radosevich SC. 1992. Results of instrument neutron-activation trace-element analysis of human remains from the Naknek region, southwest Alaska. Am Antiq 57:288–299.

Hedges REM, Millard AR. 1995. Bones and groundwater: towards the modeling of diagenetic processes. J Archaeol Sci 22:155–164.

Hedges FEM, Millard AR, Pike AWG. 1995. Measurements and relationships of diagenetic alteration of bone from three archaeological sites. J Archaeol Sci 22:201–209.

Jarcho S. 1964. Lead in the bones of prehistoric lead-glaze potters. Am Antiq 30:94–96.

Katzenberg MA. 1984. Chemical analysis of prehistoric human bone from five temporally distinct populations in Southern Ontario. National Museum of Man, Mercury Series. Archaeological Survey of Canada, Paper 129.

Katzenberg MA, Harrison RG. 1997. What's in a bone? Recent advances in archaeological bone chemistry. J Archaeol Res 5:265–293.

Keenleyside A, Song X, Chettle DR, Webber CE. 1996. The lead content of human bones from the 1845 Franklin Expedition. J Archaeol Sci 23:461–465.

Kent S, Weinberg ED, Stuart-Macadam P. 1990. Dietary and prophylactic iron supplements: helpful or harmful. Human Nature 1:53–79.

Klepinger LL. 1984. Nutritional assessment from bone. Annu Rev Anthropol 13:75–96.

Klepinger LL. 1990. Magnesium ingestion and bone magnesium concentrations in paleodietary research: cautionary evidence from an animal model. J Archaeol Sci 17:513–517.

Klepinger LL, Kuhn JK, Williams WS. 1986. An elemental analysis of archaeological bone from Sicily as a test of predictability of diagenetic change. Am J Phys Anthropol 70:325–331.

Kowal WA, Krahn P, Beattie OB. 1989. Lead levels in human tissues from the Franklin Forensic Project. Internat J Environ Analyt Chem 35: 119–126.

Kyle JH. 1986. Effect of post-burial contamination on the concentrations of major and minor elements in human bones and teeth. J Archaeol Sci 13:403–416.

Lambert JB, Simpson SV, Buikstra JE, Hanson D. 1983. Electron microprobe analysis of elemental distribution in excavated human femurs. Am J Phys Anthropol 62:409–423.

Lambert JB, Simpson SV, Szpunar CB, Buikstra JE. 1984. Copper and barium as dietary discriminants: the effects of diagenesis. Archaeometry 26:131–138.

Lambert JB, Simpson SV, Weiner SG, Buikstra JE. 1985. Induced metal ion exchange in excavated human bone. J Archaeol Sci 12:85–92.

Lambert JB, Szpunar CB, Buikstra JE. 1979. Chemical analysis of excavated human bone from middle and late Woodland sites. Archaeometry 21:403–416.

Lambert JB, Vlasak SM, Thometz AC, Buikstra JE. 1982. A comparative study of the chemical analysis of ribs and femurs in Woodland populations. Am J Phys Anthropol 59:289–294.

Lambert JB, Weydert-Homeyer. 1993a. Dietary inferences from element analysis of bone. In: Lambert JB, Grupe G, editors. Prehistoric Human Bone: Archaeology at the Molecular Level. Berlin: Springer-Verlag. pp. 217–228.

Lambert JB, Weydert-Homeyer. 1993b. The fundamental relationship between ancient diet and the inorganic constituents of bone as derived from feeding experiments. Archaeometry 35: 279–294.

Lambert JB, Xue L, Buikstra JE. 1989. Physical removal of contaminative inorganic material from buried human bone. J Archaeol Sci 16:427–436.

Leach RM. 1976. Metabolism and function of manganese. In: Prasad AS, editor. Trace Elements in Human Health and Disease. Vol. II. New York: Academic Press. pp. 235–247.

Lee AP, Klinowski J, Marseglia EA. 1995. Application of nuclear magnetic resonance spectroscopy to bone diagenesis. J Archaeol Sci 22:257–262.

McLean FC, Urist MR. 1955. Bone: An Introduction to the Physiology of Skeletal Tissue. Chicago: University of Chicago Press.

Mertz W. 1985. Metabolism and metabolic effects of trace elements. In: Chandra RK, editor. Trace Elements in Nutrition of Children. New York: Raven Press. pp. 107–119.

Mertz W. 1996. Risk assessment for essential trace elements in humans. In: Neve J, Chappuis P, Lamand M, editors. Therapeutic Uses of Trace Elements. New York: Plenum press. pp. 1–15.

Mills CF. 1992. Trace element investigations in man and animals. In: Widdowson EM, Mathers JC, editors. The Contribution of Nutrition to Human and Animal Health. Cambridge: Cambridge University Press. pp. 162–173.

Neuman WF. 1980. Bone mineral and calcification mechanisms. In: Urist MR, editor. Fundamental and Clinical Bone Physiology. Philadelphia: JB Lippincott. pp. 83–107.

Neuman WF, Neuman MW. 1958. The Chemical Dynamics of Bone Mineral. Chicago: University of Chicago Press.

Newesely H. 1988. Chemical stability of hydroxyapatite under different conditions. In: Grupe G, Herrmann B, editors. Trace Elements in Environmental History. Heidelberg: Springer-Verlag. pp. 1–16.

O'Dell BK. 1985. Bioavailability of and interactions among trace elements. In: Chandra RK, editor. Trace Elements in Nutrition of Children. New York: Raven Press. pp. 41–62.

Ott SM. 1996. Theoretical and methodological approach. In: Bilezikian JP, Raosz LG, Rodan GA, editors. Principles of Bone Biology. San Diego: Academic Press. pp. 231–242.

Pais I, Jones JB. 1997. The Handbook of Trace Elements. Boca Raton: St. Lucie Press.

Parker RB, Toots H. 1980. Trace elements in bones as paleobiological indicators. In: Behrensmeyer AK, Hill AP, editors. Fossils in the Making. Chicago: University of Chicago Press. pp. 197–207.

Pate FD. 1994. Bone chemistry and paleodiet. J Archaeol Meth The 1:161–209.

Pate FD, Hutton JT. 1988. The use of soil chemistry data to address post-mortem diagenesis in bone mineral. J Archaeol Sci 15:729–739.

Pte FD, Hutton JT, Gould RA, Pretty GL. 1991. Alterations of in vivo elemental dietary signatures in archaeological bone: evidence from the Roonka Flat Dune, South Australia. Archaeol Oceania 26:58–69.

Peretz A. 1996. Trace elements and bone metabolism. In: Neve J, Chappuis P, Lamand M, editors. Therapeutic Uses of Trace Elements. New York: Plenum Press, pp. 271–276.

Posner AS. 1969. Crystal chemistry of bone mineral. Phys Rev 49:760–792.

Prasad AS. 1978. Trace Elements and Iron in Human Metabolism. New York: Plenum Press.

Price TC. 1989. Multielement studies of diagenesis in prehistoric bone. In: Price TD, editor. The

Chemistry of Prehistoric Human Bone. Cambridge University Press. pp. 126–154.

Price TD, Blitz J, Burton J, Ezzo JA. 1992. Diagenesis in prehistoric bone: problems and solutions. J Arch Sci 19:513–529.

Radosevich SC. 1989. Diet or diagenesis? An evaluation of the trace element analysis of bone. Ph.D. Dissertation, University of Oregon.

Radosevich SC. 1993. The six deadly sins of trace element analysis: a case of wishful thinking in science. In: Sandford MK, editor, Investigations of Ancient Human Tissue: Chemical Analyses in Anthropology. Langhorne: Gordon and Breach. pp. 219–240.

Recker RR. 1992. Embryology, anatomy and microstructure of bone. In: Coe FL, Fauvus MJ, editors. Disorders of Bone and Mineral Metabolism. New York: Raven Press. pp. 219–240.

Reinhard KJ, Ghazi AM. 1992. Evaluation of lead concentrations in 18th century Omaha Indian skeletons. Am J Phys Anthropol 89:183–195.

Reinhold JG. 1975. Trace elements—a selective survey. Clin Chem 21:476–500.

Runia LT. 1987. Analysis of bone from the Bronze Age site Bovenkarspel—Het Valkje, The Netherlands: a preliminary report. Archaeometry 29:221–232.

Runia L. 1988. Discrimination factors on different trophic levels in relation to the trace element content in human bones. In: Grupe G, Herrmann B, editors. Trace Elements in Environmental History. Heidelberg: Springer-Verlag. pp. 53–66.

Saltman P, Hegenauer J, Strause L. 1984. For the want of a nail . . . trace elements in health and disease. In: Rennert OM, Chan WY, editors. Metabolism of Trace Metals in Man. Boca Raton: CRC Press. pp. 1–16.

Sandford MK. 1984: Diet, disease, and nutritional stress: an elemental analysis of human hair from Kulubnarti, a medieval Sudanese Nubian population. Ph.D. Dissertation, University of Colorado. Ann Arbor, MI: University Microfilms, Publication No. DA 8428681.

Sandford MK. 1992. A reconsideration of trace element analysis in prehistoric bone. In: Saunders SR, Katzenberg MA, editors. Skeletal Biology of Past Peoples: Research Methods. New York: Wiley-Liss, Inc. pp. 79–103.

Sandford MK. 1993. Understanding the biogenic-diagenetic continuum: interpreting elemental concentrations of archaeological bone. In: Sandford MK, editor. Investigations of Ancient Human Tissue: Chemical Analyses in Anthropology. Langhorne: Gordon and Breach. pp. 3–57.

Sandford MK. 1998. Elemental analyses and paleopathology at the new millennium: back to the basics. Paper presented at the Annual Meeting of the Southeastern Archaeological Conference, Greenville, South Carolina.

Sandford MK, Kissling GE. 1994. Multivariate analyses of elemental hair concentrations from a Medieval Nubian population. Am J Phys Anthropol 95:41–52.

Sandford MK, Kissling GE. 1995. The chemistry of mummified hair: new approaches to interpretation. Paper presented at a symposium on Medicine and Diet: The Mummy's Perspective at the Second World Congress on Mummy Studies, Cartegena, Colombia.

Sandford MK, Repke DB, Earle AL. 1988. Elemental analysis of human bone from Carthage: a pilot study. In: Humphrey JH, editor. The Circus and a Byzantine Cemetery at Carthage, Vol. I. Ann Arbor: University of Michigan Press. pp. 285–296.

Sandford MK, Van Gerven DP, Meglen RR. 1983. Elemental hair analysis: new evidence on the etiology of cribra orbitaria in Sudanese Nubia. Hum Biol 55:831–844.

Sandford MK, Weaver DS, Bogdan G. 1998. Paleopathology: future directions and challenges. Paper presented at the Annual Meeting of the American Anthropological Association, Philadelphia, Pennsylvania.

Schoeninger MJ. 1979. Diet and status at Chalcatzingo: some empirical and technical aspects of strontium analysis. Am J Phys Anthropol 51:295–310.

Schoeninger MJ. 1981. The agricultural "revolution": Its effect on human diet in prehistoric Ivan and Israel. Paleorient 7:73–92.

Schoeninger MJ. 1982. Diet and the evolution of modern human form in the Middle East. Am J Phys Anthropol 58:37–52.

Schoeninger MJ, Moore KM, Murray ML, Kingston JD. 1989. Detection of bone preservation in archaeological and fossil samples. App Geochem 4:281–292.

Schroeder HA. 1973. The Trace Elements and Man. Old Greenwich, Conn.: Devin-Adair.

Schutte KM. 1964. The Biology of Trace Elements. Philadelphia: J.B. Lippincott.

Sealy JC, Sillen A. 1988. Sr and Sr/Ca in marine and terrestrial foodwebs in the southwest Cape, South Africa. J Archaeol Sci 15:425–438.

Sillen A. 1981. Strontium and diet at Hayonim Cave. Am J Phys Anthropol 56:131–137.

Sillen A. 1986. Biogenic and diagenetic Sr/Ca in Plio-Pleistocene fossils of the Momo Shangura Formation. Paleobiology 12:311–323.

Sillen A. 1988. Elemental and isotopic analyses of mammalian fauna from southern Africa and their implications for paleodietary research. Am J Phys Anthropol 76:49–60.

Sillen A. 1989. Diagenesis of the inorganic phase of cortical bone. In: Price TD, editor. The Chemistry of Prehistoric Bone. Cambridge: Cambridge University Press. pp. 211–229.

Sillen A. 1992. Strontium-calcium ratios (Sr/Ca) of *Australopithecus robustus* and associated fauna from Swartkrans. J Hum Evol 23:495–516.

Sillen A, Kavanagh M. 1982. Strontium and pale-odietary research: a review. Yrbk Phys Anthropol 25:67–90.

Sillen A, Sealy JC, van der Merwe NJ. 1989. Chemistry and paleodietary research: no more easy answers. Am Antiq 54:504–512.

Sillen A, Smith P. 1984. Sr/Ca ratios in juvenile skeletons portray weaning practices in a medieval Arab population. J Archaeol Sci 11: 237–245.

Spadaro JA, Becker RO, Bachman CH. 1970a. The distribution of trace metal ions in bone and tendon. Calcif Tissue Res 6:49–54.

Spadaro JA, Becker RO, Bachman CH. 1970b. Size specific metal complexing sites in native collagen. Nature 225:1134–1136.

Szpunar CB, Lambert JB, Buikstra JE. 1978. Analysis of excavated bone by atomic absorption. Am J Phys Anthropol 48:199–202.

Underwood EJ. 1977. The Trace Elements in Human and Animal Nutrition. 4th ed. New York: Academic Press.

Vandecasteele C, Block CB. 1993. Modern Methods for Trace Element Determination. West Sussex: John Wiley & Sons.

Von Endt DW, Ortner DJ. 1984. Experimental effects of bone size and temperature on bone diagenesis. J Archaeol Sci 11:247–253.

Waldron HA. 1981. Postmortem absorption of lead by the skeleton. Am J Phys Anthropol 55: 395–398.

Waldron HA. 1983. On the post-mortem accumulation of lead by skeletal tissues. J Archaeol Sci 10:35–40.

Waldron T. 1987. The potential of analysis of chemical constituents of bone. In: Boddington A, Garland AN, Janaway RC, editors. Death, Decay, and Reconstruction: Approaches to Archaeology and Forensic Science. Manchester: Manchester University Press. pp. 149–159.

White EM, Hannus LA. 1983. Chemical weathering of bone in archaeological sites. Am Antiq 48:316–322.

Wing E, Brown AB. 1979. Paleonutrition. New York: Academic Press.

Wing ES, deFrance S, Kozuch L. 1995. Faunal remains from the Tutu Archaeological Village, St. Thomas, USVI. A Report Submitted to the Office of Planning and Natural Resources, Division of Archaeology and Historic Preservation, Government of the United States Virgin Islands.

Wright LE, Schwarcz H. 1996. Infrared and isotopic evidence for diagenesis of bone apatite at Dos Pilas, Guatemala: paleodietary implications. J Archaeol Sci 23:933–944.

Zaino EC. 1968. Elemental bone iron in the Anasazi Indians. Am J Phys Anthropol 29:433–435.

CHAPTER 13

ANCIENT DNA FROM SKELETAL REMAINS

ANNE C. STONE

INTRODUCTION

Molecular archaeology, the study of DNA from archaeological remains, is a new and exciting field that uses techniques from molecular biology to address anthropological questions. The analysis of DNA from ancient bone and other tissue is feasible because of advances in molecular genetics during the last fifteen years. The first experiments to determine whether DNA survived in ancient material used dried tissue, such as skin from a 2400-year-old Egyptian mummy (Pääbo, 1985a). A few years later, DNA was extracted from human bone (Hagelberg et al., 1989). The initial research was aimed primarily at successfully extracting the DNA, examining its state of preservation, and demonstrating its authenticity. To date, the results of ancient DNA investigations have been applied to questions in physical anthropology, archaeology, evolutionary biology, and forensic science. These data have shed some light on the sex of individuals, relationships between individuals within a cemetery, origins of migrant populations, history of animal and plant domestication, and phylogenetic relationships between modern and extinct species, including Neanderthals and modern humans. Although the results generated thus far are limited, ancient DNA research holds great promise in address-

ing archaeological questions; however, the technical difficulties and problems with contamination make it slow, and at times frustrating, work. This chapter discusses the technical requirements and difficulties of working with degraded DNA and reviews the literature concerning the analysis of ancient DNA from humans. The state of current research and future prospects are also discussed.

METHODS

Ancient DNA can be extracted from the cellular remains of soft tissues (preserved in water, frozen, or dried), bone, tooth roots, coprolites, seeds, and other plant materials. Typically, the first step in the extraction procedure is to prepare the sample by removing any surface contamination from previous handling of the material. This is particularly important for human remains, which may have been handled by numerous excavators, archaeologists, and osteologists, as well as the laboratory workers. Surface contamination can be removed by cutting or grinding away the exposed layers, irradiating the surface with ultraviolet (UV) light, or soaking the material in a hydrochloric acid or bleach solution. Acid or bleach should not be used in cases where it can penetrate deeply into the material. After a bone or tooth root sample is cleaned, it is ground to dust in a bone mill or other grinder, while soft tissue samples are cut into fine pieces. This increases the surface area of the material, enhancing the release

Biological Anthropology of the Human Skeleton, Edited by M. Anne Katzenberg and Shelley R. Saunders.
ISBN 0-471-31616-4   Copyright © 2000 by Wiley-Liss, Inc.

of the DNA from the material during the extraction.

Two principle techniques have been used to extract DNA from ancient remains. The first is a proteinase K digestion followed by a phenol/chloroform extraction. The proteinase K digestion works to break up the proteins in the tissue in order to release the DNA, while the extraction separates the DNA from the proteins in the solution. This method is standard in biology and results in a high yield of DNA. For bone, some investigators precede the phenol/chloroform method with a soak in ethylenediaminetetraacetic acid (EDTA) buffer to decalcify the bone sample (e.g., Hagelberg and Clegg, 1991). One problem, however, with the phenol/chloroform protocol for ancient DNA work has been the co-extraction of inhibitors that make it difficult to copy and analyze the DNA. The other primary method, the silica/guanidine isothiocyanate technique (Höss and Pääbo, 1993), has the advantage of removing the inhibitors. In addition, it is a fairly simple

and fast method, but the DNA yield may not be as high. Other methods for extracting DNA from ancient remains include using silica-based spin columns (Cano and Poinar, 1993; Yang et al., 1998), cetyltrimethylammonium (CTAB) buffer (Yang et al., 1997), chelex (Faerman et al., 1995; Poinar et al., 1993), or using a combination of the two primary methods (Krings et al., 1997). Extractions using chelex have the disadvantage of causing degradation in the DNA over time, and, therefore, the DNA must be used quickly in any analyses. Chelex is a resin that binds to impurities but not to DNA, which can then be recovered from the solution.

After extraction, the polymerase chain reaction (PCR) is used to copy the DNA fragment of interest millions of times so that there is sufficient DNA for analysis. PCR copies, or amplifies, the fragment using a three-step process of DNA denaturation, primer annealing, and DNA extension (Fig. 13.1a). First, the DNA is heated to separate (or denature) the double he-

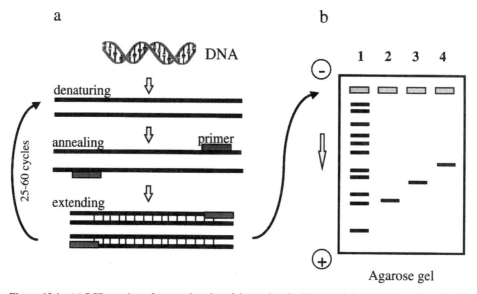

Figure 13.1 (a) PCR consists of repeated cycles of denaturing the DNA at high temperature, annealing the primers to the single stranded DNA at a lower temperature, and extending the DNA using Taq polymerase at approximately 72°C. (b) After PCR, a portion of the products is loaded in the wells of an agarose gel. A current is applied causing the slightly negatively charged DNA to migrate toward the positive pole. The DNA fragments migrate according to size with small fragments (lane 2) migrating faster than larger fragments (lane 4). A "ladder" with DNA fragments of known size is used as a reference (lane 1).

lix structure into single strands. The temperature is then decreased to let primers stick (or anneal) to the DNA. Primers are short single-stranded fragments of DNA (usually 15 to 25 base pairs long) that are complementary to a portion of the sequence of interest and which define the segment of DNA to be amplified. Last, the temperature is increased to approximately 72°C to enhance the activity of the Taq polymerase, an enzyme that positions itself next to the primer and begins adding complementary bases to extend the DNA molecule. This cycle of denaturation, annealing, and extension is then repeated 25 to 40 times during PCR. Although initially only a small amount (maybe only a few molecules) of DNA is present, PCR increases the amount of a specific DNA fragment exponentially so that, following PCR, millions of copies are present. After PCR, a few microliters of the PCR products, as well as a size standard, are loaded into an agarose gel (Fig. 13.1b). An electric current is then applied, causing the slightly negatively charged DNA to migrate toward the positive pole. As the DNA migrates through the gel, large fragments move slowly while smaller fragments move more quickly; thus, the DNA is separated by size. The DNA is then visualized with ethidium bromide or some other type of stain on a UV light table. After PCR, the DNA can be analyzed by cutting the DNA with restriction enzymes that cleave the DNA at sequence specific sites, or by directly sequencing the DNA to determine the order of nucleotide bases.

Damage to the DNA and the low number of starting molecules (often less than 1% of the original amount) make PCR amplification of ancient DNA difficult (Handt et al., 1994b; Höss et al., 1996b; Pääbo, 1989). Some solutions to these difficulties include examining DNA fragments less than 200 base pairs (bp) in length, increasing the number of PCR cycles, and using a hot start PCR (Chou et al., 1992). For a hot start PCR, the Taq polymerase is separated physically or chemically from the other reagents, in particular the primers, so that unspecific priming at low temperatures cannot specific priming at low temperatures cannot

occur. Once the initial denaturing temperature of 94°C is reached, the Taq polymerase is released to mix with the other PCR reagents. Some researchers have also attempted to use enzymes to repair such damage as cross-linking, where the DNA molecule chemically links to other DNA molecules or to itself, and oxidative lesions, where DNA damage is caused by exposure to oxygen (Poinar et al., 1998; Rogan and Salvo, 1990).

The original environment and the treatment of samples after they are discovered also affect the preservation of ancient DNA. In general, samples recovered from environments with cooler temperatures, neutral or slightly alkaline pH, and dry conditions are best for DNA preservation, although samples found in wet anoxic conditions (Hagelberg and Clegg, 1991; Lawlor et al. 1991; Pääbo et al., 1988) or frozen in permafrost (Hagelberg et al., 1994b; Höss et al., 1994) have also yielded DNA. Differing microenvironments, even within the same burial or excavation site, may cause varying success for DNA analysis (Hagelberg and Clegg, 1991; Stone and Stoneking, 1999). To date, the oldest samples that have yielded reliable DNA results are from cave or permafrost environments (Hagelberg et al., 1994b; Hänni et al., 1994; Höss et al., 1994, 1996a; Krings et al., 1997; Yang et al., 1996). The source of the material used in the extraction can also affect the amount of DNA recovered. Typically, the quality and quantity of DNA isolated from an individual is better from tooth roots than bone, and better from bone than from soft tissue (O'Rourke et al., 1996). In mummified soft tissue, DNA is usually best preserved in peripheral tissues that are more likely to desiccate rapidly, thus escaping extensive degradation from lytic enzymes (Pääbo, 1985b; Pääbo et al., 1989). This difference in preservation between hard and soft tissues may be the result of hydroxyapatite content. Hydroxyapatite forms the framework for bones and teeth, where it is particularly dense. It binds DNA and thus may protect it from subsequent degradation. Other environmental factors include substances that can co-extract with the DNA to inhibit PCR and make DNA analysis difficult. Fulvic acids, which are breakdown products of organic soils, and Maillard reaction products, which are produced during the initial decay of organic matter (Poinar et al., 1998; Tuross, 1994), fall into this category.

The methods used to preserve a sample after excavation can also influence the amount of DNA recovered (Cooper, 1993; Thuesen and Engberg, 1990), with some preservatives such as formaldehyde, gamma radiation, and tanning agents destroying or degrading the remaining DNA. In addition, surface coatings of glue or varnish may introduce contaminants from the preparator, from previous samples that were treated with the varnish, or from the preservative itself (if it was of animal or plant origin) (Cooper, 1993; Krings et al., 1997). Solutions to these problems include using bovine serum albumin (BSA) in the PCR to bind some interfering molecules, removing surface treatments, modifying the extraction method as noted above, and withholding preservative treatment during or after excavation for samples that will be subject to DNA analysis.

Depending on the conditions of preservation both in and out of the ground, and after pushing the limits of molecular technology, the success rate of retrieving DNA from ancient remains at a given site ranges from 0 to 90%. Success also depends on the genetic locus examined. Most ancient DNA research has targeted mitochondrial DNA (mtDNA). Unlike nuclear DNA, mtDNA is circular and approximately 16,500 base pairs in length. It is maternally inherited, does not recombine, and has a higher mutation rate. MtDNA is present in almost 1000 copies per cell. The high copy number means that mtDNA is more likely to survive over time than nuclear DNA. Nevertheless, several studies have examined nuclear DNA loci, including Y chromosome sequences, for sex identification and short tandem repeat (STR) loci (discussed below) for determining relatedness between individuals. Finally, a few studies have investigated bacterial DNA or genetic disease loci from individuals with pathological lesions suspected to result from a particular disease.

Regardless of the protocols used to extract and analyze ancient human DNA, or the locus examined, the greatest concern is contamination. Several precautions must be taken in order to assure the authenticity of the results (Handt et al., 1994a, 1996; Richards et al., 1995; Stoneking, 1995). First, equipment and reagents that are used only for ancient DNA work are necessary. In addition, the work should be performed in a laboratory that is completely separate from the main laboratory where modern DNA and post-PCR products are analyzed and stored. The reagents also must be tested for contamination by including a "blank" tube without any DNA in each extraction and PCR. All results must be confirmed by multiple independent extractions and analyses. Finally, the results should make phylogenetic sense (i.e., the sequences should not match the investigator or belong to a cow when you are expecting a horse sequence). The care necessary to work with ancient DNA and the need for multiple independent analyses of materials makes this research slow, expensive, and sometimes very frustrating. Thus, the questions asked and the probability of actually getting sufficient data to answer the questions should be carefully considered before undertaking a project.

EARLY WORK IN "MOLECULAR ARCHAEOLOGY"

Early research focused primarily on demonstrating the feasibility of obtaining authentic ancient DNA from different tissues. Initial success came in 1984 when DNA was extracted, cloned, and sequenced from the dried muscle of a quagga (Higuchi et al., 1984). The quagga, an extinct member of the horse family, had an mtDNA sequence that was similar to the sequence of the mountain zebra (Higuchi et al., 1984, 1987). DNA from a 2400-year-old mummy of a child was the first to be examined from an ancient human (Pääbo, 1985b). After cloning the DNA, one clone was found to contain two Alu repeats, which are found throughout the nuclear component of the human genome. One of these repeats was sequenced to verify its identity. The sequence revealed that the DNA did not appear to be significantly modified after death since it was very similar to Alu sequences from modern humans. The presence of Alu and mtDNA sequences was also demonstrated in an 8000-year-old human brain found at the Windover Pond site (Doran et al., 1986; Pääbo, 1986). Pääbo's (1986) research also indicated the presence of DNA in the remains of Egyptian and Peruvian mummified tissue ranging in age from 400–5000 B.P. Several of these studies employed the technique of cloning, where fragments of DNA are inserted into bacteria. The bacteria then reproduce and in the process copy the inserted DNA. Although cloning is a long-standing method of copying DNA fragments, persuading the bacteria to take up DNA that is old and damaged proved to be very difficult (Pääbo, 1986). The advent of PCR (Saiki et al., 1988) greatly simplified the process of copying DNA. PCR is much faster, has a lower error rate during replication, and can start with a much smaller amount of DNA.

The arrival of PCR revolutionized molecular biology and essentially made the field of "molecular archaeology" possible. In the first ancient DNA research to take advantage of this new technique, Pääbo and colleagues (1988) examined mtDNA extracted from a 7000-year-old brain found in a peat bog at Little Salt Spring, Florida. They noted that most of the DNA from the brain appeared to be degraded into small fragments, generally 50–200 bp in size, and that attempts to amplify larger fragments using PCR failed. Two small regions of mtDNA containing markers characteristic of Native Americans were successfully amplified and sequenced. This revealed that the individual did not possess a 9 bp deletion in region V or a Hinc II restriction site loss at nucleotide 13,259. These markers respectively characterize group B and C mtDNA lineages found in both Asia and the New World (Wallace et al.,

1985; Wrischnik et al., 1987). In modern Native Americans these markers distinguish two of the four primary mtDNA lineages. Group B lineages are present in frequencies ranging from 0% in the Dogrib and Haida to 67.4% in the Aymara and 71.4% in the Atacamenos, while group C lineages are present in frequencies ranging from 0% in the Ngobe, Haida, and Navajo to 54.2% in the Yanomama (Bailliet et al., 1994; Kolman et al., 1995; Merriwether et al., 1995; Torroni et al., 1992, 1993).

PCR was first used to amplify nuclear DNA from the soft tissue remains of one individual recovered from the Windover Pond site (Lawlor et al., 1991). Sequences were obtained from the β_2-microglobulin gene and from HLA class I genes. The β_2-microglobulin sequence was identical to that found in modern humans, while 14 different sequences were identified from the HLA genes. HLA genes code for immune system components that recognize pathogens, and thus are important for disease resistance. The HLA sequences recovered included nine sequences that matched or were similar to alleles found in modern humans and five chimeras or erroneous DNA sequences made up of fragments originating from more than one gene. Such chimeras are probably formed during PCR when the Taq polymerase stalls at a damaged site and "jumps" from one fragment to another with an identical or similar sequence. In a later study (Hauswirth et al., 1994), HLA class I alleles were examined in 14 additional individuals using a dot blot approach. For the dot blot method used in this study, the PCR products were fixed to a membrane (one "dot" of PCR product for each sample) and then probed using radioactively labelled allele-specific DNA fragments that matched four of the alleles found in the first study. If the allele-specific probe could bind to the DNA from a particular sample, that "dot" would appear dark on X-ray film. Another nuclear locus, the APO-A2 locus, and mtDNA sequences were also examined in these individuals.

In 1989, DNA was first recovered from ancient bone (Hagelberg et al., 1989). The samples ranged in age from 300–5,500 years B.P. and included individuals from England and the Middle East. Several mtDNA fragments were examined, and Hagelberg and co-workers (1989) noted that DNA presence appeared to correlate more with bone preservation than age. A year later, DNA was extracted from the pulp cavity of teeth ranging in age from 3 months to 20 years (Ginther et al., 1992). These samples included teeth from a murder victim whose skeleton was found in a shallow grave. MtDNA sequence results showed a match between the victim and a woman whose son had been reported missing. These initial studies set the stage for ancient DNA research in past populations and demonstrated the potential of ancient DNA research for forensic applications.

USING ANCIENT DNA TO ADDRESS ARCHAEOLOGICAL QUESTIONS

Ancient DNA can be used to examine many different questions of anthropological interest, and these questions can focus on an individual or on an entire community or region. At the level of the individual, DNA can identify biological sex or the cause of a skeletal disorder, and, in some special cases, can provide evolutionary information about our species. DNA can also be used to identify the species classification of plant and animal remains or to determine the identity of a person recovered in a forensic investigation. At the level of the population, DNA can address questions about the migration of individuals into an area or about the biological relationships between individuals within a cemetery. Such analyses, however, typically require more sizable samples (a minimum of 20 to 50 samples that provide actual data) and the examination of multiple genetic markers. Larger sample sizes are necessary to provide a clear idea of how reliable a genetic marker is in a given population for answering a particular question. For example, if two people share a genetic polymorphism, or allele, that is rare in that population, they are

more likely to be closely related than two individuals who share a common polymorphism. Multiple markers allow the examination of both maternal and paternal genetic histories and are needed to provide evidence of close relationship such as a parent-child or sibling relationship that is statistically supported. To date, however, most research has focused on one or two markers and fairly small samples because of the difficulty of successfully amplifying a given marker from ancient samples, the cost of the research, and the time required.

MITOCHONDRIAL DNA

As noted previously, mtDNA sequences are the most commonly examined DNA from ancient remains, although only a few studies have included large samples of individuals. MtDNA analyses have focused on the two hypervariable segments of the control region, a noncoding "spacer" region where one of two origins of replication is located, on restriction sites located throughout the mitochondrial genome, and on a 9-bp deletion found in some populations in a small noncoding segment between the cytochrome oxidase subunit II (COII) gene and a gene coding for a lysine tRNA. These studies have analyzed ancient DNA data using methods from both population genetics and archaeology to address questions about migration, ancient allele frequencies, and cemetery organization. It should be remembered, however, that all of the genes and noncoding regions in the mtDNA genome are linked and can be considered one locus. Linked loci are passed as a unit from parent to child (i.e., they do not recombine to form new associations). Most of the questions mentioned above will require many unlinked loci to answer them with statistical confidence.

From an archaeological perspective, a migration into a previously uninhabited area can be fairly easy to document while the movement of new peoples into a previously occupied area may be difficult to distinguish from the movement of new trade items or ideas. In both cases, the source of the migrant population and the numbers involved are of interest and can be estimated using ancient DNA data. Hagelberg and colleagues (Hagelberg and Clegg, 1993; Hagelberg et al., 1994a) tested 50 prehistoric skeletons for mtDNA markers in order to investigate the initial colonization of Polynesia. Two hypotheses for the peopling of the Pacific were examined. The first proposes that people from Southeast Asia associated with the Lapita cultural complex moved rapidly through Melanesia and onward into Polynesia, while the second hypothesis suggests that indigenous Melanesians settled the far reaches of the Pacific. The investigators examined a 9-bp deletion found in the mtDNA genome of many modern Asian populations and present in virtually all modern Polynesians. In addition, a 228-bp portion of the hypervariable region I (HVI) of the mtDNA control region was amplified. The 9-bp deletion marker was successfully identified in 33 ancient individuals from throughout the Island Pacific (including Easter

Island, New Britain, New Zealand, Yap, and Fiji) ranging in age from 200 to 2700 B.P. (Fig. 13.2). The ancient Polynesian samples, like modern Polynesians, have a very high frequency of the 9-bp deletion (16 of 16) (Hagelberg and Clegg, 1993; Hagelberg et al., 1994a). The 9-bp deletion in Polynesians was also associated with particular hypervariable region mutations. In ancient samples from Melanesia and the central Pacific, however, the 9-bp deletion, as well as the associated hypervariable region sequence changes, was not common (1 out of 11 individuals) (Hagelberg and Clegg, 1993).

These results suggest that the earliest migrants to the central Pacific who were associated with the Lapita culture did not possess the limited number of mtDNA lineages characteristic of modern Polynesians. Hagelberg and Clegg (1993) concluded that genetic bottleneck and founder effects during the settlement of Polynesia likely resulted in the restriction of mtDNA lineages, although they noted that a

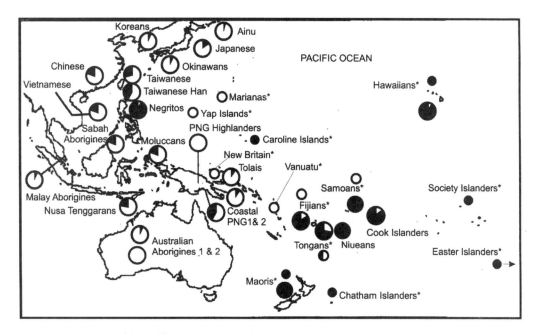

Figure 13.2   Map of the Pacific, southeast Asia and Australia showing the frequency of the 9 bp deletion (shaded portion of the circle) in modern (large circles) and in ancient populations (small circles). Modern population data is from Redd et al. (1995). Ancient DNA data is from Hagelberg and colleagues (Hagelberg and Clegg, 1993; Hagelberg et al., 1994a), and the populations with ancient DNA data are also marked by an asterisk.

larger sample would be helpful to support these data.

Oota and colleagues (1995) examined mtDNA sequences from individuals excavated from the 2000-year-old Takuta-Nishibun site in Japan in order to investigate the genetic history of the Yayoi people, and to explore associations between burial style and genetic relationships. The Yayoi people appear morphologically and culturally different from the preceding Jomon people and may have migrated more recently to Japan from mainland Asia (see Pietrusewsky, Chapter 14, for another approach to population relationships in Asia and the Pacific). At Takuta-Nishibun, the Yayoi buried their dead either in large earthenware jars or directly in the earth. A total of 112 skeletons were excavated from the cemetery, and 35 individuals (9 buried in jars and 26 direct burials) were included in DNA analysis.

Sequences from both hypervariable segments (HVI and HVII) of the mtDNA control region were investigated in the Takuta-Nishibun population. For HVI, sequences were recovered from 14 of 35 individuals (40%), while 26 individuals (74%) yielded DNA data for HVII. Oota et al. (1995) compared these date with mtDNA data from modern Japanese, including the Ainu, as well as from two ancient Yayoi and five ancient Jomon published previously (Horai et al., 1991; Kurosaki et al., 1993). Their results indicate that the level of mtDNA nucleotide diversity in the Takuta-Nishibun population (0.013) is similar to that found in the modern Japanese population (0.016). When the style of burial of the 26 individuals with HVII mtDNA data was examined, a significant correlation was found between individuals buried in jars and particular mtDNA sequences. Oota and colleagues (1995) suggest that either kinship dictated style of burial at the site or that these two types of burial were used during different times and the genetic composition of the community changed.

More recently, Oota and co-workers (1999) obtained mtDNA sequences from 24 individuals from the 2000-year-old Yixi site in northeastern China in order to investigate their relationship both to modern Asian populations and to ancient Japanese populations. In particular, the genetic relationship to the ancient Yayoi of Japan, who migrated from the Eurasian mainland to Japan approximately 2300 years ago, was explored. A total of 58 samples (42 teeth and 16 bone) from the Yixi site were tested using primers specific to mtDNA hypervariable regions I and II. Fragments of HVI were sequenced from 23 individuals, while 16 individuals yielded results for HVII. These authors reported that the mtDNA results from the Yixi sample suggest that they are less similar to the ancient Yayoi and more closely related to the modern Taiwanese Han. They noted, however, that the Yixi shared some mtDNA sequences with several Asian populations, including the ancient Yayoi and Jomon.

In the New World, the genetic history of a prehistoric population and the association between DNA types and cemetery organization were investigated in a 700-year-old Native American community from central Illinois, the Norris Farms site (Stone and Stoneking, 1993; 1998). From a burial population of approximately 270 individuals, 152 were selected for DNA analysis. Four markers, based on three restriction sites and the 9-bp deletion, that define the four major Native American mtDNA haplogroups (groups A–D) were examined. A haplogroup is a group of lineages that share particular linked mutations. In the Norris Farms population, the mtDNA haplogroup was successfully identified in 108 people (71%) using these markers, and all four major groups of lineages were found. In addition, six individuals had mtDNA types that did not appear to belong to one of these haplogroups. Sequence analysis of a 353-bp segment of HVI was also performed in 52 (34%) of the 108 individuals for whom the mtDNA haplogroup was successfully defined. These individuals included members of the four primary clusters as well as those who did not appear to fall into one of these groups, in roughly proportional numbers to the presence of these groups in the cemetery. Twenty-three lineages were retrieved (Stone and Stoneking, 1998) with characteristic HVI mutations that were concordant with the haplogroup designation in each individual. Two additional lineages were recovered that were determined to be the result of contamination from modern sources, and thus not included in further analyses.

The data were used to examine pre-Columbian mtDNA diversity, to investigate the genetic history of the peopling of the New World, and to detect patterns of spatial organization in the Norris Farms cemetery. Because the large population changes following European contact may distort our view of Native American genetic history, ancient DNA can provide a window into the levels of precontact genetic diversity. According to Stone and Stoneking (1993, 1998), mtDNA diversity in the Norris Farms community was high and similar to the level of diversity found in modern aboriginal populations, as would be expected from their geographic location. They also suggested that other than a possible reduction in the number of rare lineages in many populations, it does not appear that European contact significantly modified patterns of Native American mtDNA variation.

Phylogenetic analyses of the mtDNA HVI sequences from the Norris Farms population, modern Native Americans, and Mongolians were used to investigate the genetic history of the initial colonization of the Americas. These analyses show that the lineages within each haplogroup cluster together, although statistical support is low, and that the lineage that falls outside of the four primary haplogroups found in Native Americans typically groups with particular Nuu-Chah-Nulth and Mongolian lineages (Stone and Stoneking, 1998). The Nuu-Chah-Nulth are Native Americans from the northwest coast of North America, while Mongolia is in central Asia. Pair-wise comparisons of the mtDNA data were used to investigate the diversity within haplogroups and estimate the timing of their expansion in the New World (Stone and Stoneking, 1998). These analyses provide expansion dates of 23,000–37,000 years B.P. using the mutation

rate of 10.3% per site per million years (11,000–19,000 years using a very fast rate of 20.5% per site per million years). Population expansion is also supported by Tajima's test (Tajima, 1989), which examines whether a particular DNA sequence is evolving at a neutral or steady rate, undisturbed by selection, expansion, or other perturbation. These data are in agreement with times estimated by others (Bonatto and Salzano, 1997a, 1997b; Forster et al., 1996) for the diversification of mtDNA lineages in the New World and suggest a pre-Clovis colonization of the Americas (sometime before the traditionally accepted date of 12,000 years ago), although these data do not rule out a late colonization.

The spatial patterning of mtDNA lineages in the Norris Farms cemetery was also investigated to determine whether maternally related individuals were more likely to be interred near each other (Fig. 13.3) (Stone and Stoneking, 1993). Such a pattern was not found, although several graves contained multiple individuals with the same mtDNA haplogroup (Stone, 1996; Stone and Stoneking, 1993). Initial results from Norris Farms showed that one haplogroup was only present in males, suggesting that these individuals could represent maternally related males who immigrated into the community, possibly to offset losses from violent conflict (Stone and Stoneking, 1993). Subsequent research, however, found this haplogroup in females as well (Stone, 1996; Stone and Stoneking, 1998). Further research will combine archaeological, osteological, and DNA data in a mortuary analysis of the Norris Farms cemetery (in preparation).

Several other researchers have also assessed mtDNA diversity in ancient Native American populations from large samples in order to investigate population history. Parr and colleagues (1996) examined haplogroup markers in 47 prehistoric Fremont skeletons from Utah. The remains, dating from A.D. 252 to A.D. 1296, were excavated from the Great Salt Lake wetland. Of the 47 people sampled, the haplogroup could be identified for 30 (64%), while DNA from two individuals did not fall into one of the four

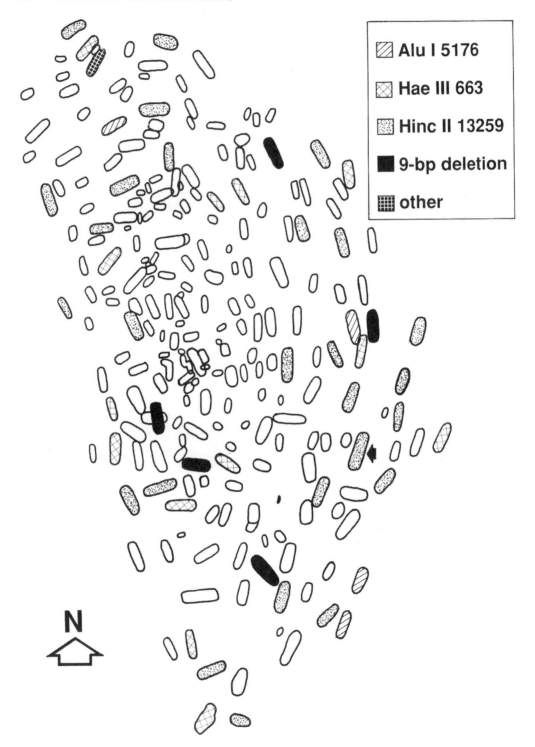

Figure 13.3 Spatial patterning of mtDNA lineages in the Norris Farms Cemetery (Stone and Stoneking, 1993). Outlines indicate the position of burials, and the arrow indicates a burial found with two individuals, each with the Hinc II-13259 marker (haplogroup C).

major haplogroups. These authors found that haplogroup A lineages were not present in the sample, while group B lineages were most common (73%). The Fremont culture disappears from the archaeological record after approximately A.D. 1300. A new tradition identified as Paiute-Shoshoni then appears. This chain of events has been hypothesized to indicate a replacement of the Fremont by Numic-speaking migrants during the fourteenth century. In modern Numic-speaking Shoshone and Paiute populations of the Great Basin, the frequency of the 9-bp deletion (group B) is lower, reaching 14.3% (Lorenz and Smith, 1994), and Parr and colleagues (1996) suggested that this provides evidence that Numic speakers did replace the Fremont populations. They noted, however, that genetic drift can obscure relationships through time and, therefore, the analysis of additional loci and samples is necessary.

Seventy-five individuals were surveyed from four South American populations, the Kaweskar, Yamana, and Selknam of Tierra del Fuego and the Aonikenk of Patagonia, for the major Native American haplogroup markers (Lalueza et al., 1997). Marker analysis was successful in 60 individuals (80%) and indicated that all mtDNA lineages sampled in these populations belonged to haplogroups C or D. DNA from one Selknam did not possess any of the characteristic marker changes. HVI sequences were obtained from two people, and characteristic HVI mutations were found in agreement with the marker analysis for those individuals. According to the authors (Fox, 1996a, 1996b; Lalueza et al., 1997), the absence of haplogroup A and B lineages suggests a common genetic origin of these populations rather than a concurrent loss of these types through random genetic drift.

In special cases, small samples can also provide answers to archaeological questions. Stone and Stoneking (1996) analyzed mtDNA sequences from an 8000-year-old skeleton found in a high-altitude cave in Colorado. The results indicated that haplogroup B, thought by some to have been brought to the New World by late migrants from the north or from Poly-

nesia, was indeed present in early Native Americans. More recently, mtDNA was successfully extracted from the Neanderthal type specimen, a skeleton found in 1856 in the Neander Valley of Germany (Krings et al., 1997). Although the exact age of this skeleton is unknown, classic Neanderthal morphological features indicate an age of 35,000–100,000 years, making it, at present, the oldest hominid skeleton discovered with preserved DNA. A 357-bp segment of the HVI was sequenced, and comparisons with over one thousand modern human sequences from around the world indicated an average of about 27 differences between them and the Neanderthal sequence. The average number of differences between any two modern humans was eight. Using population genetic methods, the age of the common ancestor of modern human and Neanderthal mtDNA sequences was estimated to be 550,000–690,000 years ago, almost four times the age of the common ancestor of modern human mtDNA sequences. Since the Neanderthal sequence appeared to fall outside the range of modern human variation and since European mtDNA types did not appear to be more closely related to the Neanderthal sequence, Krings and colleagues (1997) suggested that Neanderthals became extinct without contributing mtDNA to modern humans.

NUCLEAR DNA

Although nuclear DNA is more difficult to recover from skeletal remains, the large number of different genetic loci that can be examined provides the opportunity to address the questions mentioned above as well as to reveal kinship relationships, identify the sex of an individual, and distinguish disease-causing alleles.

Short Tandem Repeats

The biological relationship of two individuals can be established with a high degree of certainty using multiple, highly polymorphic loci. Many short tandem repeat (STR) sequences are commonly used for this purpose in modern forensic cases. STRs consist of sequences of two to five bases that are tandemly repeated, sometimes hundreds of times, in a region of nuclear DNA. Hagelberg et al. (1991) used six STR loci to compare DNA from the skeletal remains of a murder victim with DNA from her presumptive parents. The DNA results suggested with high statistical confidence that the remains did belong to the missing daughter. Only a few archaeological studies have examined STR loci.

Kurosaki and co-workers (1993) used 10 STR loci to examine kinship in two sets of remains from the Hirohata and Hanaura sites in Japan. These sites are approximately 1500 and 2000 years old respectively. The individuals examined at each site were thought to be related based on archaeological data. From the Hirohata site, two males from the same tomb were compared at nine loci and the data are consistent with kinship between these individuals. Although their results appear to corroborate the archaeological data, Kurosaki and colleagues (1993) are cautious in defining the degree of kinship since the frequencies of these STR alleles is unknown in this ancient population. At the Hanaura site, two females found buried side-by-side in a hillside were hypothesized to be mother and daughter. Alleles in three of the seven STR loci examined in these individuals do not match, thus ruling out a parent-child relationship. A comparison of their mtDNA sequences also precluded a kinship relationship on the maternal side, such as maternal aunt and niece.

Zierdt and colleagues (1996) examined a pentanucleotide repeat locus (VWA31/A) in a sizable sample from a medieval burial site at Weingarten, Germany. DNA was extracted from bone and/or tooth samples of 200 individuals, and the STR was successfully amplified in 76 (38%). The success rate was higher in DNA extracted from teeth (36%) than in DNA extracted from bone (22.2%). In some samples with low amounts of DNA, only one allele was amplified during one PCR, indicating homozygosity, but in a subsequent PCR, two alleles

were found, indicating heterozygosity. These results underscore the need for multiple PCR tests of the same sample to ensure accurate results. Zierdt and co-workers (1996) noted that such allele dropout might be the cause of the apparent deficiency of heterozygotes in this population. Although additional loci are necessary for kinship analyses, these results illustrate the difficulty of investigating nuclear loci in a large sample from an ancient population.

Sex Identification

Molecular methods identifying the sex of an individual are particularly useful for juvenile and fragmentary remains where sex determination is not possible by traditional morphological techniques. Methods of sex identification using DNA focus on either repetitive DNA sequences that are chromosome specific (Kogan et al., 1987; Witt and Erickson, 1989) or single-copy genes found on both the X and Y chromosomes (Aasen and Medrano, 1990; Cui et al., 1994; Ebensperger et al., 1989; Nakahori et al., 1991a). Analysis of ancient DNA for sex identification (see Brown, 1998, for another review) has adapted some of these forensic methods developed for degraded DNA and primarily focused on repetitive sequences (Honda et al., 1990; Hummel and Herrmann, 1991) or the amelogenin gene (Faerman et al., 1995; Gill et al., 1994; Stone et al., 1996).

Repetitive sequences on the Y chromosome that have been examined include the DYZ1 and DYZ2 repeat sequences, which are found at the ends of the chromosome, and alpha satellite sequences, which are long repetitive DNA sequences that are found in the region around the centromere. DXZ3 repeat sequences from the X chromosome have also been examined (Ovchinnikov et al., 1998). The sequences of these repeats are chromosome specific and each is present in hundreds of copies. Because of the high copy number, repeat sequences should be much easier to amplify in ancient remains than single copy sequences. However, one major flaw in this system exists: while the presence of a product after PCR amplification of a Y-specific repeat sequence indicates that an individual is male, the absence of a product does not necessarily indicate that an individual is female. PCR amplification failure may simply be the result of low quantity or quality DNA or of PCR inhibition by other components in the sample.

The amplification of both X and Y chromosome sequences with one set of primers solves the dilemma revealed by repeat sequence analysis for sex identification. Examining these sequences with one set of primers is accomplished by amplifying a fragment of a gene found on both chromosomes that has slight sequence differences on the X and Y chromosomes that allow the source of the fragment to be identified. One such gene is the amelogenin gene, which is involved in enamel formation and has sequences on the X and Y chromosome that are approximately 90% homologous (Nakahori et al., 1991b). Two types of methods have been employed in the study of ancient DNA to identify the X and Y copies of the

amelogenin gene after PCR (Fig. 13.4). The first type of method uses a size difference between the X and Y fragments that are amplified (Faerman et al., 1995; Sullivan et al., 1993) while the second uses sequence specific probes (Stone et al., 1996).

Although the amelogenin systems may not be as sensitive to degraded, low-quantity DNA as using the X or Y chromosome repeats, it is easily apparent whether the reaction fails or works. Several researchers have noted, however, that the small amount of ancient DNA that is the starting material for PCR may only include a few molecules (or even a single molecule) of DNA from the region of interest, and, thus, sometimes only the X or the Y copy may be amplified during a particular PCR (Faerman et al., 1995; Lassen et al., 1996; Stone et al., 1996). This problem is referred to as allele dropout and is solved by performing multiple PCR experiments. For example, assuming that both X and Y copies are equally likely to be amplified, the Y chromosome copy of the

a

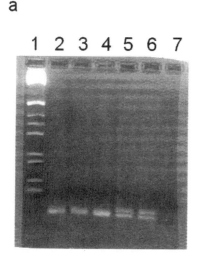

b

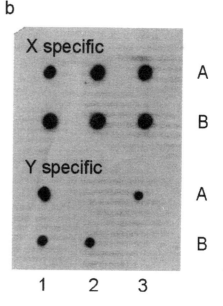

Figure 13.4 (*a*) Results of PCR amplification using the Sullivan et al. (1993) method. Lane 1: 1 kb ladder, lanes 2–4: one band is present, indicating that these individuals are female, lanes 5 and 6: two bands are present indicating that these individuals are male, lane 7: PCR blank. (*b*) Sex identification results generated using the Stone et al. (1996) method. Dot blots of PCR products were probed with X-specific and Y-specific oligonucleotides. A1 and A2 are the male and female controls, respectively. A3, B1 and B2 are males while B3 is female.

fragment should be detected after four successful PCR attempts with a 94% probability if it is present. This assumption may not be true where the copies differ by size since smaller fragments are more easily amplified from ancient DNA (Handt et al., 1994a). Faerman and colleagues (1995) reported that their size-based method was more likely to amplify the smaller Y chromosome copy when low amounts of DNA are present. Using the size-based method of Sullivan and colleagues (1993), Lassen and colleagues (1996) found 2 individuals in 13 where only the smaller-sized, female-specific product was amplified while amplification of the Y-specific repeats indicated that these individuals were male.

Molecular sex identification tests have been used in anthropological research to indicate the sex of juveniles and fragmentary remains, and to compare molecular results with morphological and archaeological indicators of sex. At the Norris Farms cemetery, 46 individuals were tested using the sequence-specific probe method of Stone and colleagues (1996). The sex of 21 (46%) individuals was identified, while PCR amplification was not successful in 25 samples (Stone and Stoneking, 1999; Stone et al., 1996). In adults with clear morphological indicators of sex, the DNA results were in agreement with the morphology with the exception of one individual where the difficulty of PCR amplification indicated insufficient DNA for successful molecular analysis (Stone et al., 1996).

Ovchinnikov and colleagues (1998) also found agreement between molecular, morphological, and archaeological indicators of sex at a medieval cemetery from north Russia. Of 24 individuals tested, the sex of 6 (25%) was determined using the fragment-size method of Sullivan and colleagues (1993), while X and Y chromosome repeat sequences were successfully used in 19 (79%) individuals, including one child. For the six samples that could be examined using both molecular methods, the results were in agreement.

Lassen and colleagues (1997) examined 120 neonates recovered from a Swiss cemetery in use from the early Middle Ages through the nineteenth century. The sex of 75 (62%) of the 120 neonates was successfully identified using the fragment-size method of Sullivan and colleagues (1993). Morphological results, which are less accurate in juveniles, suggested an excess of female infants buried in the cemetery, while molecular data did not. Faerman and co-workers (1997) examined the sex of 43 neonates found in a sewer beneath a Roman bathhouse in Ashkelon on the coast of Israel. Nineteen (44%) samples produced results while the remainder did not amplify successfully. These data indicated the majority were males (14 out of 19 infants), which these authors suggested may be the unwanted children of women working in the bathhouse.

Genetic Diseases

Several genetic disorders, such as thalassemia, dwarfism, and Gaucher's disease, result in skeletal changes that can be identified in ancient populations (Ortner and Putschar, 1981). The genetic mutations that cause many of these disorders have been discovered and can be examined in past peoples. Filon and colleagues (1995) examined DNA from the skeletal remains of a child excavated from a Phoenician cemetery, approximately 3800 years old, in Israel. The child died at the age of eight with skeletal pathology indicating severe anemia. Anemia can be caused by genetic and environmental conditions, including malnutrition, sickle cell anemia, and thalassemia. A 232-bp segment of the β-globin gene, a component of hemoglobin, was examined and the child was found to be homozygous for a mutation that causes a null phenotype (i.e., no β-globin to be produced). This mutation is found at a frequency of 2–10% in modern populations living in the eastern Mediterranean region. Most people with this particular form of thalassemia require blood transfusions from early childhood (when fetal hemoglobin is replaced by adult hemoglobin) to survive. The ancient child, however, lived to the age of eight and haplotype analysis of the DNA sequence suggests that the child had elevated levels of fetal hemoglobin enhancing survival (Filon et al., 1995).

DETECTION OF PATHOGENS

Using DNA to diagnose pathogenic diseases in prehistoric skeletons is intriguing because it provides the opportunity to look at the evolution of a disease-causing agent, to investigate the history of the spread of a disease around the world, and to identify the causative agent in cases where several agents may result in similar morphological changes in the skeleton. Sequence information from ancient pathogens can help in the understanding of why some strains of a virus or bacteria are more virulent than others. Pathogens such as the flu, tuberculosis, and the plague have had large effects on human populations, and ancient DNA analysis can add further insight into what may have been significant forces of natural selection in humans.

Ancient DNA techniques also allow researchers to reexamine old archived medical specimens, which may reveal that a newly discovered pathogen was the cause of disease in someone in the past and, thus, that this pathogen has been affecting people for some time. For example, pathogenic DNA was first recovered from archived paraffin-embedded tissues approximately 40 years old. The results indicated that the samples were positive for human papilloma virus (Shibata et al., 1988). More recently, sequences from the 1918 flu virus, which was particularly virulent, were obtained from preserved samples from a U.S. serviceman who died during the epidemic (Taubenberger et al., 1997). The researchers hope to obtain sufficient sequence information to compare this strain to other flu strains and understand why it was so deadly.

DNA from pathogenic agents is probably the most difficult type to recover from ancient skeletal and mummified remains since the total amount of viral or bacterial DNA present is likely to be small even in a heavily infected in-

dividual. Despite this difficulty, Salo and colleagues (1994) were able to recover tuberculosis DNA from a lung lesion in a 1000-year-old mummy from Peru. A small (123-bp) fragment of an insertion element present in several copies in the genome of *Mycobacterium tuberculosis* was amplified. These results indicate that tuberculosis was present in the New World prior to European contact. Molecular analysis was subsequently used to confirm the presence of tuberculosis in a 12-year-old girl from Chile who died approximately 900 years ago (Arriaza et al., 1995).

(Drancourt et al., 1998) recovered DNA sequences from *Yersinia pestis,* the causative agent of bubonic plaque, from unerupted teeth of four out of five individuals tested who died during the plague epidemics of 1590 and 1722 in France. These individuals were interred in mass graves. According to historical information, these graves were used to bury people who had died at a plague quarantine hospital. In addition, teeth from seven individuals that were not thought to have died from plague were also tested. These individuals dated from the medieval period in France. All of the teeth (11 of 11) yielded results for a 110-bp fragment of the human β-globin gene, indicating that DNA was indeed preserved in all of the samples (although one of the five plague individuals was not tested at this locus).

Two loci specific to *Y. pestis* were then tested: a 133-bp fragment of rpoB, the RNA polymerase β-subunit-encoding gene, and a 300-bp segment of pla, the plasminogen activator-encoding gene that is associated with virulence. Two individuals from the mass grave in Lambesc and four medieval period individuals were tested for the rpoB fragment. After two rounds of PCR, rpoB amplified only in the suspected plague victims, and sequence analysis of the rpoB fragment indicated that it was identical to the 6/69 M biotype, orientalis strain of *Y. pestis.* All of the samples were tested for the pla gene. Two individuals from the Marseille mass grave and two individuals from the Lambesc mass grave gave positive results after one round of PCR, while none of the medieval samples amplified. Sequencing yielded a 160-bp fragment that matched the KIM5 strain of *Y. pestis*.

OTHER SAMPLES

In addition to contributing data about the people themselves, ancient DNA can provide information about their environment. Ancient DNA has been used to examine plants found with the Iceman (Rollo et al., 1994), to learn about the history of wheat, corn, and cattle domestication (Bailey et al., 1996; Brown and Brown, 1992; Goloubinoff et al, 1993), and to identify the source of paints and parchment (Reese et al., 1996). Since ancient DNA analysis is destructive, common animal bones can also serve as test material to investigate the preservation of DNA in more rare material from the same archaeological context.

CONCLUSIONS AND FUTURE PROSPECTS

Ancient DNA research has moved past the initial stage of excitement about the presence of the DNA and has been applied successfully to several questions of anthropological interest. Several problems, however, continue to plague the field. Of these, contamination is the greatest problem, requiring great care in prevention as well as time and expense to repeat experiments in order to ensure authenticity. In particular, the repetition of experiments using independent extractions is necessary to verify previous results and, for nuclear loci, to ensure that allele dropout has not occurred. Samples that are extremely old, rare, or likely to produce particularly controversial results should be examined in more than one laboratory.

Experimental design also warrants greater attention. The significant challenges of working with ancient DNA and the expense of such work require careful thought about the hypotheses to be examined and whether ancient DNA data can realistically test those hypothe-

ses. For example, if claims are made about such issues as familial kinship between individuals in a cemetery, the relatedness of two populations separated by time or distance, or the relationship between a disease agent and a modern pathogen, several questions come to mind: Are a sufficient number of loci being examined in a large enough sample? Are these loci highly variable in modern populations and, thus, could they be expected to be powerful in statistical analyses? Could genetic drift or natural selection have large effects on these loci? Do sequence data from the loci investigated in disease agents provide enough information to distinguish different strains or identify the level of virulence?

Given the difficulty and expense of ancient DNA work, comparisons between the different techniques used for analyses would also be helpful. For example, a number of different DNA extraction methods are currently being used, and it is unclear which removes inhibition and yet recovers the most DNA (both nuclear and mitochondrial). Several protocols for sex identification have been employed in ancient DNA analyses, but these have also not been rigorously compared. Future analysis of ancient pathogens would benefit from the use of samples with historical documentation, such as the samples used in Drancourt and colleagues study of *Y. pestis* or old samples from medical school collections, to confirm the ability to amplify a specific pathogen before ancient samples from individuals who died of unknown causes are tested.

Future research has the potential to provide new and exciting perspectives on prehistoric societies by focusing on multiple genetic markers in sizable samples that are clearly defined chronologically and spatially in an archaeological context. This could allow the examination of the social organization of a population as reflected by their mortuary practices and by the arrangement of graves of nuclear family members and other kin. For example, in communities where burials are located within household compounds, the kinship structure of households could be investigated to distinguish different extended family or nuclear family arrangements. Hypotheses about population movements might also be examined. These could include significant migrations that may have occurred over a large geographic region, such as the proposed migration of farmers out of the Middle East and into Europe, as well as small-scale migrations of foreign laborers into a larger population.

As noted above, ancient DNA can contribute more information about the history and evolution of disease agents in humans. For example, the strains of tuberculosis found in the New World prior to contact could be compared to the strains found in the Old World. Questions about the origins of diseases such as syphilis could also be addressed.

Ancient DNA data may also answer questions about the people who initially colonized different parts of the world, and these data could potentially shed more light on the debate about modern human origins. In particular, the history of the peopling of large areas such as northeast Asia and the New World as well as the Pacific could be further investigated. More recent colonizations of less hospitable regions such as the far north or far south might also be examined. Finally, DNA data from more Neanderthals as well as from Cro-Magnon individuals would help in the analysis of the biological relationship between these groups. Thus, despite the challenges, "molecular archaeology" promises to continue to be a lively and informative field.

REFERENCES

Aasen E, Medrano JF. 1990. Amplification of the ZFY and ZFX genes for sex identification in humans, cattle, sheep and goats. Biotechnology 8:1279–1281.

Arriaza BT, Salo W, Aufderheide AC, Holcomb TA. 1995. Pre-Columbian tuberculosis in northern Chile: molecular and skeletal evidence. Am J Phys Anthropol 98:37–45.

Bailey JF, Richards MB, Macaulay VA, Colson IB, James IT, Bradley DG, Hedges REM, Sykes BC.

1996. Ancient DNA suggests a recent expansion of European cattle from a diverse wild progenitor species. Proc R Soc Lond B Biol Sci 263:1467–1473.

Bailliet G, Rothhammer F, Carnese FR, Bravi CM, Bianchi NO. 1994. Founder mitochondrial haplotypes in Amerindian populations. Am J Hum Genet 55:27–33.

Bonatto S, Salzano FM. 1997a. Diversity and age of the four major mtDNA haplogroups, and their implications for the peopling of the New World. Am J Hum Genet 61:1413–1423.

Bonatto SL, Salzano FM. 1997b. A single and early migration for the peopling of the Americas supported by mitochondrial DNA sequence data. Proc Natl Acad Sci USA 94:1866–1871.

Brown KA. 1998. Gender and sex—What can ancient DNA tell us? Ancient Biomolecules 2:3–15.

Brown TA, Brown KA. 1992. Ancient DNA and the archaeologist. Antiquity 66:10–23.

Cano RJ, Poinar HN. 1993. Rapid isolation of DNA from fossil and museum specimens suitable for PCR. Biotechniques 15:432–436.

Chou Q, Russell M, Birch DE, Raymond J, Bloch W. 1992. Prevention of pre-PCR mis-priming and primer dimerization improves low-copy-number amplifications. Nucleic Acids Res 20:1717–1723.

Cooper A. 1993. DNA from museum specimens. In: Herrmann B, Hummel S, editors. Ancient DNA. New York: Springer-Verlag. pp. 149–165.

Cui K-H, Warnes GM, Jeffrey R, Matthews CD. 1994. Sex determination of preimplantation embryos by human testis-determining-gene amplification. Lancet 343:79–82.

Doran GH, Dickel DN Jr, Ballinger WE Jr, Agee OF, Laipis PJ, Hauswirth WW. 1986. Anatomical, cellular and molecular analysis of 8,000-yr-old human brain tissue from the Windover archaeological site. Nature 323:803–806.

Drancourt M, Aboudharam G, Signoli M, Dutour O, Raoult D. 1998. Detection of 400-year-old *Yersinia pestis* DNA in human dental pulp: an approach to the diagnosis of ancient septicemia. Proc Natl Acad Sci USA 95:12637–12640.

Ebensperger C, Studer R, Epplen JT. 1989. Specific amplification of the ZFY gene to screen sex in man. Hum Genet 82:289–290.

Faerman M, Filon D, Kahila G, Greenblatt CL, Smith P, Oppenheim A. 1995. Sex identification of archaeological human remains based on amplification of the X and Y amelogenin alleles. Gene 167:327–332.

Faerman M, Kahila G, Smith P, Greenblatt C, Stager L, Filon D, Oppenheim A. 1997. DNA analysis reveals the sex of infanticide victims. Nature 385:212–213.

Filon D, Faerman M, Smith P, Oppenheim A. 1995. Sequence analysis reveals a β-thalassaemia mutation in the DNA of skeletal remains from the archaeological site of Akhziv, Israel. Nat Genet 9:365–368.

Forster P, Harding R, Torroni A, Bandelt H-J. 1996. Origin and evolution of Native American mtDNA variation: a reappraisal. Am J Hum Genet 59:935–945.

Fox CL. 1996a. Analysis of ancient mitochondrial DNA from extinct aborigines from Tierra del Fuego-Patagonia. Ancient Biomolecules 1:43–54.

Fox CL. 1996b. Mitochondrial DNA haplogroups in four tribes from Tierra del Fuego-Patagonia: inferences about the peopling of the Americas. Hum Biol 68:855–871.

Gill P, Ivanov PL, Kimpton C, Piercy R, Benson N, Tully G, Evett I, Hagelberg E, Sullivan K. 1994. Identification of the remains of the Romanov family by DNA analysis. Nat Genet 6:130–135.

Ginther C, Issel-Tarver L, King M-C. 1992. Identifying individuals by sequencing mitochondrial DNA from teeth. Nat Genet 2:135–138.

Goloubinoff P, Pääbo S, Wilson AC. 1993. Evolution of maize inferred from sequence diversity of an Adh2 gene segment from archaeological specimens. Proc Natl Acad Sci USA 90:1997–2001.

Hagelberg E, Clegg JB. 1991. Isolation and characterization of DNA from archaeological bone. Proc R Soc Lond Biol Sci 244:45–50.

Hagelberg E, Clegg JB. 1993. Genetic polymorphisms in prehistoric Pacific Islanders determined by analysis of ancient bone DNA. Proc R Soc Lond Biol Sci 252:163–170.

Hagelberg E, Gray IC, Jeffreys AJ. 1991. Identification of the skeletal remains of a murder victim by DNA analysis. Nature 352:427–429.

Hagelberg E, Quevedo S, Turbon D, Clegg JB. 1994a. DNA from ancient Easter Islanders. Nature 369:25–26.

Hagelberg E, Sykes B, Hedges R. 1989. Ancient bone DNA amplified. Nature 342:485.

Hagelberg E, Thomas MG, Cook CE Jr, Sher AV, Baryshnikov GF, Lister AM. 1994b. DNA from ancient mammoth bones. Nature 370:333–334.

Handt O, Höss M, Krings M, Pääbo S. 1994a. Ancient DNA: methodological challenges. Experientia 50:524–529.

Handt O, Krings M, Ward RH, Pääbo S. 1996. The retrieval of ancient human DNA sequences. Am J Hum Genet 59:368–376.

Handt O, Richards M, Trommsdorff M, Kilger C, Simanainen J, Georgiev O, Bauer K, Stone A, Hedges R, Schaffner W, Utermann G, Sykes B, Pääbo S. 1994b. Molecular genetic analyses of the Tyrolean Ice Man. Science 264:1775–1778.

Hänni C, Laudet V, Stehelin D, Taberlet P. 1994. Tracking the origins of the cave bear (*Ursus spelaeus*) by mitochondrial DNA sequencing. Proc Natl Acad Sci USA 91:12336–12340.

Hauswirth WW, Dickel CD, Rowold DJ, Hauswirth MA. 1994. Inter- and intrapopulation studies of ancient humans. Experientia 50:585–591.

Higuchi R, Bowman B, Freiberger M, Ryder OA, Wilson AC. 1984. DNA sequences from the quagga, an extinct member of the horse family. Nature 312:282–284.

Higuchi RG, Wrischnik LA, Oakes E, George M, Tong B, Wilson A. 1987. Mitochondrial DNA of the extinct quagga: relatedness and extent of postmortem change. J Mol Evol 25:283–287.

Honda K, Harihara S, Nakamura T, Hirai M, Misawa S. 1990. Sex identification by analysis of DNA extracted from hard tissues. Japan Forensics J 44:293–301.

Horai S, Kondo R, Murayama K, Hayashi S, Koike H, Nakai N. 1991. Phylogenetic affiliation of ancient and contemporary humans inferred from mitochondrial DNA. Phil Trans R Soc Lond B Biol Sci 333:409–417.

Höss M, Dilling A, Currant A, Pääbo S. 1996a. Molecular phylogeny of the extinct ground sloth *Mylodon darwinii*. Proc Natl Acad Sci USA 93:181–185.

Höss M, Jaruga P, Zastawny TH, Dizdaroglu M, Pääbo S. 1996b. DNA damage and DNA sequence retrieval from ancient tissues. Nucleic Acids Res 24:1304–1037.

Höss M, Pääbo S. 1993. DNA extraction from Pleistocene bones by a silica-based purification method. Nucleic Acids Res 21:3913–3914.

Höss M, Pääbo S, Vereshchagin NK. 1994. Mammoth DNA sequences. Nature 370:333.

Hummel S, Herrmann B. 1991. Y-chromosome-specific DNA amplified in ancient human bone. Naturwissenschaften 78:266–267.

Kogan SC, Doherty M, Gitschier J. 1987. An improved method for prenatal diagnosis of genetic diseases by analysis of amplified DNA sequences. N Engl J Med 317:985–990.

Kolman CJ, Bermingham E, Cooke R, Ward RH, Arias TD, Guionneau-Sinclair F. 1995. Reduced mtDNA diversity in the Ngöbé Amerinds of Panama. Genetics 140:275–283.

Krings M, Stone A, Schmitz RW, Krainitzki H, Stoneking M, Pääbo S. 1997. Neandertal DNA sequences and the origin of modern humans. Cell 90:19–30.

Kurosaki K, Matsushita T, Ueda S. 1993. Individual identification from ancient human remains. Am J Hum Genet 53:638–643.

Lalueza C, Pérez-Pérez A, Prats E, Cornudella L, Turbón D. 1997. Lack of founding Amerindian mitochondrial DNA lineages in extinct aborigines from Tierra del Fuego-Patagonia. Hum Mol Genet 6:41–46.

Lassen C, Hummel S, Herrmann B. 1996. PCR based sex identification of ancient human bones by amplification of X- and Y-chromosomal sequences: a comparison. Ancient Biomolecules 1:25–33.

Lassen C, Hummel S, Herrman B. 1997. Molekulare Geschlechtsbestimmung an Skelettresten früh-und neugeborener Individualen des Gräberfeldes Aegerten, Schweiz. Anthropologischer Anzeiger 55:183–191.

Lawlor DA, Dickel CD, Hauswirth WW, Parham P. 1991. Ancient HLA genes from 7,500-year-old archaeological remains. Nature 349:785–788.

Lorenz JG, Smith DG. 1994. Distribution on the 9-bp mitochondrial DNA region V deletion among North American Indians. Hum Biol 66:777–788.

Merriwether DA, Rothhammer F, Ferrell RE. 1995. Distribution of the four founding lineage haplotypes in Native Americans suggests a single wave of migration for the New World. Am J Phys Anthropol 98:411–430.

Nakahori Y, Hamano K, Iwaya M, Nakagome Y. 1991a. Sex identification by polymerase chain reaction using X-Y homologous primer. Am J Med Genet 39:472–473.

Nakahori Y, Takenaka O, Nakagome Y. 1991b. A human X-Y homologous region encodes "Amelogenin." Genomics 9:264–269.

Oota H, Saitou N, Matsushita T, Ueda S. 1995. A genetic study of 2,000-year-old human remains from Japan using mitochondrial DNA sequences. Am J Phys Anthropol 98:133–145.

Oota H, Saitou N, Matsushita T, Ueda S. 1999. Molecular genetic analysis of remains of a 2,000-year-old human population in China—and its relevance for the origin of the modern Japanese population. Am J Hum Genet 64: 250–258.

O'Rourke DH, Carlyle SW, Parr RL. 1996. Ancient DNA: methods, progress and perspectives. Am J Hum Biol 8:557–571.

Ortner DJ, Putschar WGJ. 1981. Identification of Pathological Conditions in Human Skeletal Remains. Washington: Smithsonian Institution Press.

Ovchinnikov IV, Ovtchinnikova OI, Druzina EB, Buzihilova AP, Makarov NA. 1998. Molecular genetic sex determination of medieval human remains from North Russia: comparison with archaeological and anthropological criteria. Anthropologischer Anzeiger 56:7–15.

Pääbo S. 1985a. Molecular cloning of ancient Egyptian mummy DNA. Nature 314:644–645.

Pääbo S. 1985b. Preservation of DNA in ancient Egyptian mummies. J Archaeol Sci 12:411–417.

Pääbo S. 1986. Molecular genetic investigations of ancient human remains. Cold Spring Harb Symp Quant Biol LI pp. 441–446.

Pääbo S. 1989. Ancient DNA: extraction, characterization, molecular cloning, and enzymatic amplification. Proc Natl Acad Sci USA 86:1939–1943.

Pääbo S, Gifford JA, Wilson AC. 1988. Mitochondrial DNA sequences from a 7000-year-old brain. Nucleic Acids Res 16:9775–9787.

Pääbo S, Higuchi RG, Wilson AC. 1989. Ancient DNA and the polymerase chain reaction: the emerging field of molecular archaeology. J Biol Chem 264:9709–9712.

Parr RL, Carlyle SW, O'Rourke D. 1996. Ancient DNA analysis of Fremont Amerindians of the Great Salt Lake wetlands. Am J Phys Anthropol 99:507–518.

Poinar GOJ, Poinar HN, Cano RJ. 1993. DNA from amber inclusions. I: B Herrmann, S Hummel, editors. Ancient DNA. New York: Springer-Verlag. pp. 92–103.

Poinar H, Hofreiter M, Spaulding WG, Martin PS, Stankiewicz BA, Bland H, Evershed RP, Possnert G, Pääbo S. 1998. Molecular coproscopy: dung and diet of the extinct ground sloth *Nothrotheriops shastensis*. Science 281:402–406.

Redd AJ, Takezaki N, Sherry ST, McGarvey ST, Sofro ASM, Stoneking M. 1995. Evolutionary history of the COII/tRNA^{Lys} intergenic 9 base pair deletion in human mitochondrial DNAs from the Pacific. Mol Biol Evol 12:604–615.

Reese RL, Hyman M, Rowe MW, Derr JN, Davis SK. 1996. Ancient DNA from Texas pictographs. J Archaeol Sci 23:269–277.

Richards MB, Sykes BC, Hedges REM. 1995. Authenticating DNA extracted from ancient skeletal remains. J Archaeol Sci 22:291–299.

Rogan PK, Salvo JJ. 1990. Molecular genetics of pre-Columbian South American mummies. UCLA Symposium in Molecular Evolution pp. 223–234.

Rollo F, Asci W, Antonini S, Marota I, Ubaldi M. 1994. Molecular ecology of a Neolithic meadow: the DNA of the grass remains from the archaeological site of the Tyrolean Iceman. Experientia 50:576–584.

Saiki RK, Gelfand DH, Stoffel S, Scharf SJ, Higuchi R, Horn GT, Mullis KB, Erlich HA. 1988. Primer-directed enzymatic amplification of DNA with a thermostable DNA polymerase. Science 239:487–491.

Salo WL, Aufderheide AC, Buikstra J, Holcomb TA. 1994. Identification of *Mycobacterium tuberculosis* DNA in a pre-Columbian Peruvian mummy. Proc Natl Acad Sci USA 91:2091–2094.

Shibata D, Martin WJ, Arnheim N. 1988. Analysis of DNA sequences in forty-year-old paraffin-embedded thin-tissue sections: a bridge between molecular biology and classical histology. Cancer Res 48:4564–4566.

Stone AC. 1996. Genetic and mortuary analyses of a prehistoric Native American community. Ph.D. Dissertation. Pennsylvania State University, University Park.

Stone A, Milner G, Pääbo S, Stoneking M. 1996. Sex determination of ancient human skeletons using DNA. Am J Phys Anthropol 99:231–238.

Stone A, Stoneking M. 1993. Ancient DNA from a pre-Columbian Amerindian population. Am J Phys Anthropol 92:463–471.

Stone A, Stoneking M. 1996. Genetic analyses of an 8000 year-old Native American skeleton. Ancient Biomolecules 1:83–87.

Stone AC, Stoneking M. 1998. MtDNA analysis of a prehistoric Oneota population: implications for the peopling of the New World. Am J Hum Genet 62:1153–1170.

Stone AC, Stoneking M. 1999. Analysis of ancient DNA from a prehistoric Amerindian cemetery. Phil Trans R Soc Lond B Biol Sci 354(1379): 153–159.

Stoneking M. 1995. Ancient DNA: how do you know when you have it and what can you do with it? Am J Hum Genet 57:1259–1262.

Sullivan KM, Mannucci A, Kimpton CP, Gill P. 1993. A rapid and quantitative DNA sex test: fluorescence-based PCR analysis of X-Y homologous gene amelogenin. Biotechniques 15:636–641.

Tajima F. 1989. Statistical method for testing the neutral mutation hypothesis by DNA polymorphism. Genetics 123:585–595.

Taubenberger JK, Reid AH, Kraft AE, Bijwaard KE, Fanning TG. 1997. Initial genetic characterization of the 1918 "Spanish" influenza virus. Science 275:1793–1796.

Thuesen I, Engberg J. 1990. Recovery and analysis of human genetic material from mummified tissue and bone. J Archaeol Sci 17:679–689.

Torroni A, Schurr TG, Cabell MF, Brown MD, Neel JV, Larsen M, Smith DG, Vullo CM, Wallace DC. 1993. Asian affinities and continental radiation of the four founding Native Americans mtDNAs. Am J Hum Genet 53:563–590.

Torroni A, Schurr TG, Yang C-C, Szathmary E, Williams RC, Schanfield MS, Troup GA, Knowler WC, Lawrence DN, Weiss KM, Wallace DC. 1992. Native American mitochondrial DNA analysis indicates that the Amerindian and the Nadene populations were founded by two independent migrations. Genetics 130:153–162.

Tuross N. 1994. The biochemistry of ancient DNA in bone. Experientia 50:530–535.

Wallace DC, Garrison K, Knowler WC. 1985. Dramatic founder effects in Amerindian mitochondrial DNAs. Am J Phys Anthropol 68: 149–155.

Witt M, Erickson RP. 1989. A rapid method for detection of Y-chromosomal DNA from dried blood specimens by the polymerase chain reaction. Hum Genet 82:271–274.

Wrischnik LA, Higuchi RG, Stoneking M, Erlich HA, Arnheim N, Wilson AC. 1987. Length mutations in human mitochondrial DNA: direct sequencing of enzymatically amplified DNA. Nucleic Acids Res 15:529–542.

Yang DY, Eng B, Waye JS, Dudar JC, Saunders SR. 1998. Improved DNA extraction from ancient bones using silica-based spin columns. Am J Phys Anthropol 105:539–543.

Yang H, Golenberg EM, Shoshani J. 1996. Phylogenetic resolution within the Elephantidae using fossil DNA sequence from the American mastidon (*Mammut americanum*) as an outgroup. Proc Natl Acad Sci USA 93:1190–1194.

Yang H, Golenberg EM, Shoshani J. 1997. Proboscidean DNA from museum and fossil specimens: an assessment of ancient DNA extraction and amplification techniques. Biochem Genet 35:165–179.

Zierdt H, Hummel S, Herrmann B. 1996. Amplification of human short tandem repeats from medieval teeth and bone samples. Hum Biol 68:185–199.

PART V

QUANTITATIVE METHODS AND
POPULATION STUDIES

CHAPTER 14

METRIC ANALYSIS OF SKELETAL REMAINS: METHODS AND APPLICATIONS

MICHAEL PIETRUSEWSKY

INTRODUCTION

Despite the recent trend among skeletal biologists to examine more diverse topics such as health, paleopathology, paleoepidemiology, and paleodemography, statistical analysis of metric data continues to attract attention in the discipline. Measurement of living humans (anthropometry) and their skeletal remains (osteometry) can be traced to anthropology's initial stages and represents one of the discipline's most notable contributions to science. A great deal of this early attention to measurement and description focused on investigations of human population structure and past biological relationships, including the assignment of unknown specimens to reference groups. Interest in these areas, so-called biodistance studies, continues to the present as witnessed by the number of publications over the past three decades (e.g., Heathcote, 1986; Hemphill, 1998; Howells, 1973, 1989, 1995; Jantz, 1973; Konigsberg and Blangero, 1993; Pietrusewsky, 1990, 1994, 1997; Relethford, 1994; Relethford and Lees, 1982; Rightmire, 1970, 1972, 1976; Sciulli, 1990; Sokal et al., 1987; and many others).

In recent years, several convincing arguments have been made supporting the use of measurements, especially craniometry, as sources of taxonomic information (see e.g., Howells, 1973, 1989, 1995; Van Vark and Howells, 1984). The precision and repeatability of measurements, the conservative nature of continuous variation, the direct link with the past, and the demonstration of a heritability component for this category of biological variation (e.g., Sjøvold, 1984) provide the theoretical foundation for metric analysis. Perhaps most important, from a statistical and mathematical point of view, is the continuous (and correlated) nature of measurements, which makes them highly suited for applying multivariate statistical procedures. The focus of this chapter is the analysis of metric, or quantitative, data using multivariate statistical procedures, methods that have emerged as the most appropriate and advanced for investigating metric data. Although the methods to be discussed are based on rather complex and sometimes intimidating mathematical statistical theory, the present discussion is nontechnical and largely devoid of mathematical formulae and detailed statistical discourse. Although familiarity with such theory facilitates the use of these methods, this chapter will focus on the application and interpretation of results primarily generated by computer statistical packages, a strategy that will hopefully encourage others to use these methods. Further, because of the popularity of the skull in investigating population structure and past relationships, the

Biological Anthropology of the Human Skeleton, Edited by M. Anne Katzenberg and Shelley R. Saunders.
ISBN 0-471-31616-4   Copyright © 2000 by Wiley-Liss, Inc.

examples selected to illustrate some of these methods will use craniometric data. The use of multivariate statistics in skeletal biology, including biodistance analyses, has been reviewed by Buikstra et al. (1990). More recently, Larsen (1997) has provided an excellent summary and synthesis of specific studies in skeletal biology that make extensive use of biodistance measures using metric as well as nonmetric data. Several recent publications further summarize the use of multivariate statistics in biological anthropology (e.g., Feldesman, 1997; Van Vark, 1995; Van Vark and Schaafsma, 1992).

Traditionally, the variables used in metric analyses have been simple distances and angles (linear dimensions) defined by craniometric landmarks. These variables are measured directly on the specimen using hand-held calipers. Recent alternatives to landmark measurements include coordinate points (Dean, 1995), surface contouring (e.g., moiré fringe patterns), holography, methods that capture images through the use of digitizing pads, video-based systems, and three-dimensional imaging techniques such as those utilized in morphometric studies (Read, 1990; Rohlf, 1990; Rohlf and Bookstein, 1990). This chapter will focus exclusively on the application of multivariate statistical procedures using traditional craniometric landmark data. Richtsmeier and colleagues (1992) have recently reviewed comparable methods for analyzing three-dimensional landmark coordinate data in morphometric analyses (see Mayhall, Chapter 4, for a discussion of moiré). While these technical developments in recording three-dimensional objects are the wave of the future, traditional measurement methods are still practical for geographically dispersed study samples and provide the foundation for student instruction.

Despite the development of mathematical theory, which underlies multivariate statistical methods, in the early decades of the present century, the analysis of metric data using these procedures was slow to gain widespread usage. Much of the initial reluctance can be attributed to the often extensive and tedious computations involved. A variety of historical, political, and scientific reasons, in the mid-twentieth century, further diverted attention away from the study of skulls, including the use of measurements, to other areas of interest in the field (Lahr, 1996:xv). General applications of these methods had to wait for the appearance of mainframe computers, commencing in the late 1960s and early 1970s, and then personal computers, which have become available only in recent years. The use of these methods continues to the present.

METRIC ANALYSIS: UNIVARIATE APPROACH

The use of measurements in physical anthropology and skeletal biology has considerable antiquity. Cranial morphology, including craniometry, has been an integral part of this long history. The ubiquitous cranial index and its attendant labels, brachycranic, dolichocranic, and mesocranic, which were used to express cranial vault shape, are synonymous with early physical anthropology and its attempt to reconstruct human racial history. As W.W. Howells (in Lahr, 1996:viii) has stated, "When Anders Retzius, a century and a half ago, invented the cranial index, he gave us an answer for which there was no question."

These early, often very industrious, efforts in physical anthropology, now regarded as exercises in typological racial classification, resulted in massive compilations of descriptive information on human populations, which, including their use as classificatory devices, are now of dubious value. Individuals, or their skeletal remains, were assigned (typed) to groups on the basis of a number of observable qualitative and/or quantitative features. The approach was largely visual where combinations of observed features determined group membership. More mathematical approaches to this problem followed some time later.

Given this early concern with quantification, it is not surprising that the fields of physical anthropology and mathematical statistics have shared, at least in their formative stages, a mutually beneficial relationship (Howells, 1984). For example, early statisticians, such as Karl Pearson, used skeletal measurements to develop new statistical procedures. These earliest analytical methods were predominantly restricted to descriptive, or univariate, statistics such as measures of central tendency, dispersion, and variance. As emphasized by Howells (1969:312), univariate statistics are the statistics of measurements—not individuals or populations. While comparisons between populations might proceed one measurement at a time, or possibly two at a time as in the case of an index or bivariate plot, the statistics of populations and the treatment of individual specimens in the context of their parent population had to await the introduction of multivariate statistical procedures by Fisher (1936), Hotelling (1933), Mahalanobis et al. (1949), and Rao (1948, 1952), among others, beginning in the third decade of the twentieth century.

MULTIVARIATE STATISTICS

Multivariate statistical procedures comprise a family of related mathematical procedures that allow the simultaneous analysis of multiple variables (i.e., measurements or nonmetric traits) recorded for individuals or objects from one or more groups. More rigorous definitions require that all variables must be random and interrelated and that their different effects cannot be interpreted individually in a meaningful way (Hair et al., 1998). Multivariate statistical procedures are expressly well suited for investigating interrelationships among the variables, examining group differences, and making other inferences of the variables and groups selected.

By definition, measurements, which represent distance or quantity, have continuous distributions and phenotypes. Theoretically, metric traits (e.g., maximum cranial length) can assume any value between any two fixed points that fall along, or define, a continuum. Nonmetric data have discontinuous (qualitative) phenotypes and are expressed by certain fixed numerical values, or they express some character state (e.g., the presence or absence of metopic suture). The distinction between these two kinds of data, continuous and discontinuous, is important in selecting the appropriate multivariate statistical procedure.

Another important concept in multivariate analysis is the variate, here defined as a linear combination of weighted variables represented by a single value. These values are generated by a specific multivariate statistical procedure such as discriminant analysis or factor analysis.

Some of the multivariate techniques may be considered extensions of univariate techniques; others, like factor analysis, discriminant analysis, and generalized distance, require more complicated statistical procedures that resolve the entire data matrix using matrix algebra. The data for a single group usually take the form of a data matrix consisting of **N** rows of observations (number of individuals) and **P** variables (number of measurements), which are arranged in columns. Reading the rows, an individual becomes a vector of its scores on **P** traits while the vector of measurements is read by examining the scores for **N** individuals in the columns. The mean vector (or centroid) is the mean of each of the variables. Univariate statistical techniques are concerned with mean vectors and variance, while multivariate statistics must consider the entire matrix of numbers that requires a consideration of covariance (and correlation) of each possible pair of variables in the matrix.

The primary purpose of multivariate analysis is to investigate relationships among the transformed variables. By reducing the information contained in the original measurements to a smaller number of uncorrelated (orthogonal) variables, or scales, multivariate procedures overcame one of the greatest obstacles posed in earlier attempts to devise a distance statistic—for example, Pearson's Coefficient of Racial Likeness (Pearson, 1926) and Penrose's Size and Shape statistic (Penrose, 1954)—

namely that of correcting for the correlation among measurements and the repeated influence of size in individual measurements. Finally, these secondary, transformed, variables allowed individuals and/or populations to be located in multivariate space. The mathematical basis of multivariate statistical methods rely on the matrices of variation and covariation. These methods allow individual specimens to become vectors of their measurements, which, in turn, allows them to be located in multivariate space defined by the newly created transformed variables. This appropriateness of multivariate analyses in handling populations is succinctly stated by Howells (1973:3–4):

> [M]ethods of multivariate analysis . . . allow a skull to be treated as a unit, i.e., as a configuration of the information contained in all its measurements. Next, they allow populations to be treated as configurations of such units, taking account of their variation in shape because they in turn are handled as whole configurations of individual dimensions. Finally, the relations and differences between all the populations being considered are set forth in terms of their several individual multivariate ranges of variation. Thus it is possible to see the range of the whole species in such complete and objective informational terms. That is the importance of multivariate statistics: they fit the model of populations looked on not as centroids or means, but as swarms of the varying individuals who compose them; and the differentiation of these swarms from one another constitutes a statement of the degree and nature of the difference between the populations. Although the information is ultimately limited by the measurements selected to describe the skull, their relationships and their relative taxonomic significance are not otherwise biased by the worker.

These refinements in technique have made multivariate methods theoretically the most soundly based for analyzing metric variation. The procedures adopted depend on the questions being asked but traditionally, differences (or distances) between human groups and classification (grouping analysis) have been the

two principal concerns in physical anthropology. Skeletal biologists have addressed similar issues, usually from an archaeological and/or bioarchaeological perspective, including studies that investigate the processes of evolution (e.g., selection, drift, gene flow, and the effects of geography), and whether differences in population structure can be attributed to internal versus external (i.e., introduced) influences. Other studies in skeletal biology have been designed to examine more specific issues such as the identification of population (ethnic) boundaries, postmarital residence patterns, familial and kin relationships, cemetery formation, evidence for social stratification, and the presence of intrusive individuals and/or evidence of admixture with different groups (Buikstra et al., 1990; Konigsberg and Buikstra, 1995; Larsen, 1997; Williams-Blangero et al., 1990). Other potential uses of this family of statistical procedures include the identification of individual crania for repatriation claims and forensic applications.

ASSUMPTIONS OF MULTIVARIATE DATA

Several physical anthropologists have cautioned against the inappropriate and "blind" use of multivariate statistical procedures (e.g., Kowalski, 1972; Rhoads, 1984; Van Vark, 1976; Van Vark and van der Sman, 1982). In an attempt to prevent possible misuses of these procedures, careful scrutiny of the data and the assumptions underlying multivariate data are recommended.

All multivariate statistical procedures have a number of underlying statistical and conceptual assumptions that require evaluation if statistical inferences are to be made (e.g., Campbell, 1978; Corruccini, 1975; Kowalski, 1972; Van Vark and Pasveer, 1994:231). Among the assumptions, multivariate normality and equality of covariances (or within-group variances) are perhaps the most critical. Adherence to the mathematical conditions of multivariate analyses, including adequate sample sizes, however, helps alleviate most of the assumption violations.

Multivariate procedures require sufficiently large sample sizes. As a general rule, some (e.g., Corruccini, 1975; McHenry and Corruccini, 1975) have suggested that the sample size should exceed the number of variables used. Others (e.g., Lachenbruch and Goldstein, 1979:70) suggest that there should be at least three times as many individuals for each sample as there are measurements (variables). Aside from these and other more general guidelines, there is lack of unanimous agreement on what constitutes a "sufficiently" large sample. Howells (1973, 1989, 1995), who maintains that samples should be relatively large and comparable in size, ultimately selected 50 to 55 specimens of each sex in his multivariate analyses. Opinions vary on the effects of unequal sample size, especially with regard to the covariance matrix. As a general precaution, however, it is advised that sample sizes be kept uniform.

Multivariate normality of the data refers to the shape of the distribution of each metric variable and each combination of metric variables. Ideally, the distribution should be normal, but opinions vary as to the adversity of the effects of non-normal distributions in influencing the results of multivariate analyses. Maintaining equal and sufficiently large samples would appear to satisfy this condition. Reyment (1990) discusses some of the more robust techniques that control for non-normality. There are also distribution-free inferential techniques such as jackknife and bootstrap analyses, based on resampling, that do not require normally distributed data.

Perhaps the most critical assumption of the multivariate conditions is homogeneity of the covariance (variance-covariance) matrix (Campbell, 1978), an assumption that may never be completely satisfied (Van Vark and Schaafsma, 1992:236). If the covariance matrices of individual groups (these represent the deviation between one variable and its mean times the deviation between a second variable and its mean, etc.) are unequal, the results of multivariate analyses can be adversely affected. Main-

taining large and approximately equal sample sizes should, at least on mathematical and statistical grounds, reduce the likelihood of violating the homogeneity covariance assumption.

However daunting these assumptions may appear, potential users, including those with little or no background in mathematics and/or statistics, should not be unduly dissuaded from applying these methods. Statistical tests for normality and equivalence of covariances, and their remedies, are available in most multivariate statistical packages. Choosing samples with care, maintaining equal and large sample sizes, careful scrutiny of the data, and the possible preselection of variables using discriminant analysis as prescribed by some (Van Vark and Schaafsma, 1992), help to avoid violating these underlying assumptions.

CLASSICAL MULTIVARIATE STATISTICAL METHODS

The statistical procedures most commonly used by skeletal biologists and physical anthropologists include factor analysis, principal components analysis, discriminant function analysis, and generalized distance. The latter two multivariate procedures are designed to handle two or more groups, while principal components analysis, factor analysis, and related techniques are for investigating underlying patterns in a single group. Various clustering methods, and multidimensional scaling techniques, provide a useful means of visualizing the results of multivariate procedures. Some of the newest approaches include the use of digitizing nodes to produce three-dimensional images as well as other uses of coordinate geometry that generate a multitude of measurements in place of the traditional caliper-generated ones.

Principal Components Analysis

Factor analysis and related procedures such as principal components analysis (PCA), by focusing on the interrelationship (covariation) among a large number of variables of a single sample, seek to identify common underlying patterns of variation through an inspection of their shared underlying factors, or axes. Unlike discriminant function analysis, PCA does not employ any criterion for maximizing differences among the groups. Individual specimens can be scored or located on these new axes, or factors. Examples that use factor analysis and PCA in physical anthropology include studies by Howells (1957, 1972, 1973) and Brown (1973).

Discriminant (Canonical Analysis)

The major purpose of discriminant analysis is to maximize differences between two groups. The mathematical basis (Goldstein and Dillon, 1978) for this procedure is to weight and combine, in a linear manner, two or more discriminating variables in such a way that the intercorrelations of the variables are considered and the ratio of between-group variance to the within-group (total) variance is maximized (Tatsuoka, 1970). This concept can then be extended to include more than two groups, in which case the procedure is commonly referred to as multiple discriminant function, or canonical variate analysis. The resulting transformed variables, known as discriminant functions, or canonical variates, possess the important property of being orthogonal (uncorrelated, or independent). Individuals and/or groups can then be placed in a multidimensional space, thus providing a means of visualizing these interrelationships. The total number of functions is one less than the number of groups entered, or one less than the original number of measurements if that is less. Typically, the first few transformed variables account for the preponderance of the variation among groups. The remaining functions, usually ranked in decreasing importance, are responsible for the residual variation. Although originally designed to assign an unknown specimen to one or more groups, discriminant analysis is now widely used as a measure of group separation (Campbell, 1978).

The original measurements selected in computing the linear classification functions can be chosen in a stepwise manner (stepwise discriminant function analysis) such that, at each step, the measurement that adds the most to the separation of the groups is entered into the discriminant function in advance of the others (Dixon and Brown, 1979:711). The technique further identifies which of the measurements (variables) are most responsible for the observed differentiation. One useful aspect of the latter procedure is that it allows for the selection of a subset of measurements for use in subsequent distance analyses (Heathcote, 1994; Rightmire, 1970). In the examples to be presented in this chapter, the interpretation of the discriminant functions and patterns of group separation is based on an inspection of standardized canonical, or discriminant, coefficients. At the end of the stepping process, each individual specimen is classified into one of the original groups based on the several discriminant scores it receives. The probability of group membership can be mathematically evaluated through the calculation of posterior probabilities and/or typicality probabilities. The former assume that the unknown belongs to one of the groups included in the function while that latter evaluate how likely the unknown belongs to any, or none, of the groups based on the average variability of all the groups in the analysis (Tatsuoka, 1971: 228–232; Van Vark and Schaafsma, 1992: 244–246). The results are presented in the form of a classification matrix. The classification results provide a further check on how well the groups are, or are not, differentiated from one another. The "correct" and "incorrect" classifications provide a general guide for assessing the homogeneity or heterogeneity of each group. Most major computer packages provide cross-validation procedures (e.g., jackknife methods) to check discriminant results and the probability that an individual belonging to a specified group has been misclassified. In order to insure that the results are externally as well as internally valid, the final stage of discriminant analysis typically involves the validation of the discriminant function results. One such technique, as will be demonstrated in the examples in this chapter, is the jackknife classification method in which the discriminant function is re-estimated on multiple subsets of the original samples. In these examples each case is reclassified into a group (its own or any other one included in the analysis) according to the classification functions computed from all data except the individual case being classified.

Some of the earliest and best known examples that utilize discriminant function analysis in skeletal biology are concerned with assigning an unknown individual to a given reference group for determining race (Giles and Elliot, 1962) and sex (Giles and Elliot, 1963). In these early examples discriminant functions (or equations with weights for a number of measurements of an individual, which are multiplied to provide a single score) are computed from the measurements of two defined groups (e.g., male and female) such that the differences between the two groups are maximized (F-ratios are maximized) while the deviation of individual cases from their respective means remains minimal. Once a discriminant function has been computed between two groups, an unknown specimen can be assigned to one or the other. There have been many other applications, before and since, including, most notably, the assignment of unknown human or nonhuman primate fossils (e.g., Albrecht, 1992; Campbell, 1984; Howells, 1966; Rightmire, 1979; Van Vark, 1995).

A number of statistical packages, with a variety of multivariate procedures designed for mainframe and personal computers such as BMDP (Dixon, 1990a, 1990b; Dixon and Brown, 1979), SAS (1990a, 1990b), SSPS (1990a, 1990b, 1992, 1993), SYSTAT (1992a, 1992b), and NTSYS (Rohlf, 1993) are now available. Further, several specialized programs written for personal computers, such as CRANID2 (Wright, 1992a, 1992b) and FORDISC2 (Ousley and Jantz, 1996), which have modified and/or improved these procedures are available commercially.

Similar procedures, although not available to the general public, have been introduced by Van der Sluis and colleagues (1985) and Howells (1995). The former method, POSCON, recently used by Van Vark and Schaafsma (1992), is similar to CRANID2 in that both use principal components analysis rather than discriminant function analysis, and the database provided by Howells (1989), to assign an unknown skull to a group. POSCON uses Euclidean distances (explained in the next section) between the unknown skull and the group centroids for classification, while CRANID2 examines the Euclidean distances (space) of all the individuals of the reference groups and determines the identity of the unknown skull by reading the list of the 50 nearest individuals. Howells (1995) uses methods similar to both of these (DISPOP and POPKIN), but these are based on discriminant function analysis.

Mahalanobis' Generalized Distance and Euclidean Distance

Although several different distance measures are available, the most commonly used one is Euclidean distance, which can be represented geometrically (hence the name) as the length of the hypotenuse of a right angle, which is calculated by the formula: $\sqrt{(X_2 - X_1)^2 + (Y_2 - Y_1)^2}$ where X_1Y_1 and X_2Y_2 represent the respective coordinates of two points plotted on two variables, X and Y. This concept may then be extended to more than two variables. Mahalanobis' distance (D^2) uses the squared (i.e., the sum of squared distances without taking the square root in the above formula) Euclidean distance.

Mahalanobis' generalized distance, or D^2 (Mahalanobis, 1930, 1936; Mahalanobis et al., 1949; Rao 1948, 1952), remains the classic, if only realistic (Reyment et al., 1984) measure of biological distance for analyzing metric data. The immense popularity of the D^2 statistic as a measure of distance stems from its theoretical soundness. Generalized distance is computed by maximizing the difference between pairs of groups by maximizing the between-group variance to the pooled within-group variance. This involves an inversion of the pooled correlation (within-group variance-covariance) matrix. The usual assumptions of equivalence of covariance matrices, normal distribution of variables, and large sample sizes are usually satisfied by pooling sample covariance matrices and avoiding small and extremely uneven sample sizes. Sneath and Sokal (1973), as well as Gower (1972), provide the mathematical basis for computing D^2.

Through this procedure, the original variables are transformed to a new (uncorrelated) set of variables whose correlation with the remaining variables has been removed. D^2 represents the summed squared difference between the transformed mean values of any two groups compared. The failure to correct for this correlation was a major flaw with earlier proposed distance statistics such as Pearson's C.R.L. (Pearson, 1926) and Penrose's Size and Shape statistic (Penrose, 1947, 1954). A further attraction of generalized distance is that its values do not change if the number and kinds of measurements differ (Van Vark and Schaafsma, 1992:238).

Statistical testing of the significance of the derived distances was first introduced by Hotelling (1933). The method described in Rao (1952:245), one used by Talbot and Mulhall (1962) and recently reiterated by Buranarugsa and Leach (1993:17), is the one used in the examples presented in this chapter: The quantity, $(n_i n_j / n_i + n_j) D^2_{ij}$, is distributed as chi-square with p degrees of freedom (n_i = sample size of group i; n_j = sample size of group j; D^2_{ij} = square of the generalized distance between groups i and j; and p = number of variables employed). Nonsignificance of D^2 generally indicates that the differences are too small for detection of group differences and/or that the sample sizes are too small.

Because a single quantitative value, which measures dissimilarity between pairs of groups is obtained, a further attraction of the generalized distance statistic is that various methods for clustering groups based on these numbers

can be applied. Mahalanobis' generalized distance is computed in discriminant function analysis programs available in most computer statistical packages.

Other Ordination Methods (Q-Mode and R-Mode Analyses)

Other ways of portraying relationships between individual specimens or groups that utilize multivariate results are canonical plots, metric multidimensional scaling (Torgerson, 1952), and principal coordinate analysis (Gower, 1966). The latter two procedures are most often used in association with factor analysis and Q-mode principal component analysis.

Q-mode and R-mode analyses represent two related multivariate techniques, which represent the inverse of principal components analysis and related procedures. R-mode analysis focuses on relationships between variables, while Q-mode methods analyze relationships between individuals. The principal aim of Q-mode analysis is a graphical visualization of the interrelationships between individuals of a sample and the identification of clusters (Reyment, 1990:125). Several researchers have recently adopted Q-mode analysis for analyzing skeletal metric data (Hanihara, 1996; Howells, 1989).

Alternatives to these methods include the use of Chernoff "faces" (Chernoff, 1973, 1978), Fourier transformations, and boxplots, etc., which some researchers have adopted (e.g., Brown, 1996; Wilson, 1984). Most of the applications in skeletal biology, however, utilize distance matrices or some measure of similarity, or dissimilarity.

Finally, group means, or centroids, can be plotted for the first few canonical variates, or functions, in multiple discriminant function analysis or canonical variate analysis to represent intergroup relationships. Although the procedures are mathematically unrelated, there is substantial agreement between tree construction procedures, discussed in the next section, and these other methods of representing multivariate results.

CLUSTER ANALYSIS AND CLUSTERING ALGORITHMS

Cluster analyses are often regarded as one group of related multivariate procedures, which differ from the other procedures discussed in this chapter in that they do not actually estimate a variate but rather use one that has already been specified (e.g., D^2). Again, these techniques involve the simultaneous utilization of many variables whose purpose is to group individuals (or objects) on the basis of characteristics they possess (Hair et al., 1998). The results of cluster analysis are typically depicted as a treelike structure, or dendrogram, which has become a popular and convenient way to graphically illustrate and summarize multivariate data (Everitt and Dunn, 1992). Wilmink and Uytterschaut (1984) provide the historical and theoretical background for the use of cluster analysis in physical anthropology. Gower (1967, 1972) provides good comparisons of several methods of cluster analysis.

While clustering is not phylogeny (the determination of ancestor-descendant relationships) (Howells, 1984), dendrograms like those based on Mahalanobis' distances, have implications for the latter and are routinely used in interpreting past relationships. The theoretical and methodological background for the majority of these techniques derives from classical numerical taxonomy (Sneath and Sokal, 1973). The latter includes those numerical (quantitative) methods for grouping usually based on overall morphological (phenetic) similarity where each character, when assigned some numerical value, is considered to have equal weight. These methods typically allow the selection of the largest number of traits possible. Numerical, or phenetic, taxonomy represents one of the two major approaches to systematic biological classification. The other is phylogenetic systematics, or cladistics, in which evolutionary history is inferred from branching patterns of phylogeny that require the careful weighting of only a few traits.

The most commonly used clustering methods comprise a family of procedures known as the hierarchical (either agglomerative or divisive) clustering techniques. Agglomerative clustering techniques commence by placing each object (or group) in a single cluster. In subsequent steps, the two most similar clusters are combined into a new (aggregate) cluster, a process that continues until all groups are combined into a single cluster. In the opposite clustering procedure, hierarchical divisive methods, the process begins by placing all groups into a single cluster that is then divided into two clusters that contain the most dissimilar groups. Since clusters at any stage are obtained by the combination (or division) of two clusters from the previous stage, these methods lead to a hierarchal structure for the diagram. Different options are available (e.g., single lineage, complete linkage, or group average) depending on how distance, or similarity, of the clusters is measured.

One of the most commonly used agglomerative clustering techniques is UPGMA, or the Unweighted Pair-Group Method arithmetic average algorithm, which measures similarity as the average distance between all cases in one cluster to all cases in another. That is, the average distance between all cases in the resulting cluster is as small as possible and the distance between two clusters is taken as the average between all possible pairs of cases in the cluster. For those interested in phylogenetic tree reconstruction, this method assumes a constant rate of evolution.

An alternative clustering algorithm, the Neighbor-Joining (NJ) method (Saitou and Nei, 1987; Saitou et al., 1991), used initially to construct trees from genetic data, is growing in popularity among some skeletal biologists. This algorithm, also known as the method of minimum evolution, is conceptually related to cluster analysis but differs from UPGMA in that it does not assume that all the lineages have diverged equal amounts, thus removing the assumption of constant rates of evolution. Recent computer simulations (Saitou and Imanishi, 1989; Saitou and Nei, 1987) have suggested that the NJ method yields more accurate trees than the UPGMA method and thus produces a truer phylogenetic tree, at least when gene frequency data are used. The NTSYS-pc computer software program by Rohlf (1993) provides one of the most comprehensive selections of clustering algorithms of interest to skeletal biologists.

RESEARCH DESIGN

Regardless of the intrinsic problems in defining human groups, biologically and statistically, selection and definition of these groups is a necessary preliminary step to data analysis. Most of the multivariate statistical procedures reviewed in this chapter require that individual specimens be assigned to groups a priori. The skeletal series encountered most frequently in skeletal biology represent aggregates of individuals found in a specified area at a given time, or some subgrouping of individuals below the species level. As is often the case in skeletal biology, archaeological human remains may easily represent individuals who lived and died at different times and/or have different ancestries. In many instances, the "series" represents a collection of skulls housed in museums documented as having been collected from a specific village, island, or region. In ideal circumstances, exact provenance of the specimens may be available, but quite often in these situations completeness, preservation, and the number of specimens available are frequently problematic.

Two basic underlying theoretical assumptions in distance studies using morphological data are that morphometric similarity implies genetic similarity and that the more similar two groups are, the more closely related they must be relative to groups that exhibit greater differences. Despite the demonstration of significant heritability components for both metric and nonmetric traits, morphological traits (including measurements) are also subject to nongenetic influences. Environment and/or allometry rather than gene flow, migration, genetic drift, and other isolating factors may be responsible, or at least contribute, to the results obtained in biodistance analysis. However, there is some consensus (see, e.g., Van Vark and Schaafsma, 1992:241) that biological relatedness as measured by biological distances based on metric data reflects genetic similarity overall. Konigsberg and Ousley's (1995) finding of a correlation between anthropometric and quantitative genetic analyses strengthens this assertion.

Of the two basic approaches to the analysis of metric data in studies of population structure outlined by Relethford and Lees (1982), model-bound and model-free, the latter approach appears to be the one most frequently adopted in studies in physical anthropology and skeletal biology. Multivariate statistical methods, such as measures of biological distances and discriminant functions, have frequently been used in anthropology as exploratory tools for summarizing data on patterns of variability and overall similarities among groups (often accompanied by comparisons with other types of data) and for reconstructing the evolutionary histories of these groups, regardless of cause. Model-bound approaches, while methodologically appealing because they incorporate measures of population similarity directly into models of population structure to estimate one or more parameters (e.g., admixture, genetic drift, gene flow) like the methods used to analyze living populations, have been used less frequently in metric studies of past populations.

The approach used in the examples illustrated in this chapter is model-free. Mahalanobis' generalized distance and discriminant function analysis are used to investigate patterns of craniometric variation, which, in turn, are used to reconstruct the evolutionary histories and possible origins of the groups, regardless of cause.

APPLICATIONS: TWO EXAMPLES

Two examples, which focus on the population history of early historic and prehistoric Japan, will be used to illustrate some of the methods discussed in this chapter (Pietrusewsky, 1996).

Two multivariate statistical procedures, stepwise discriminant function analysis and Mahalanobis' generalized distance, are applied to cranial measurements for assessing biological relatedness among the modern and early inhabitants of Japan and neighboring regions. In the first example, 10 male Japanese cranial series, representing prehistoric to modern times, are compared. In the second example, these comparisons are extended to include 43 additional comparative cranial series from the surrounding regions of East Asia, Southeast Asia, Australia, and the Pacific. The data were recorded and analyzed by Pietrusewsky (1990, 1992, 1994, 1995, 1997) and Pietrusewsky and colleagues (1992).

Preparation of Data

Variable selection

Although the need in craniometric analysis to improvise new measurements continues (see, e.g., Howells, 1973), many of the measurements currently used by skeletal biologists can be traced to early international conventions (e.g., Frankfort Agreement of 1882) and attempts to standardize technique so that all measurements could be replicated (e.g., Broca, 1875; Martin and Saller, 1957; Vallois, 1965; etc.). These traditional measurements require detailed definitions, including landmark definitions and instrumentation (e.g., spreading, sliding, or coordinate calipers), information that is available in several recent publications (Bräuer, 1988; Buikstra and Ubelaker, 1994; Moore-Jansen et al., 1994). Although there are exceptions (e.g., Van Vark and Pasveer, 1994:233), for most multivariate analyses it is generally preferable to begin with as many variables as possible from which subsets of variables may be selected. Which measurements are ultimately selected for analysis depends on the research questions being addressed.

Errors

The reliability (i.e., the extent to which a metric variable is reproducible over time) of metric data hinges on precision (freedom from measurement error at the individual level) as well as the dependability of the variable, or its freedom from short-term random influences (Marks et al., 1989). The latter, which are generally beyond the control of the individual observer, probably are of minor concern compared to error introduced at the observer level. The recognition of climatic influences on cranial measurements (Utermhole et al., 1983), however, would seem to argue for proper storage of specimens.

Certainly, the precision of measurements can be greatly enhanced with the standardization of the technique and calibration of the measuring equipment. Other sources of possible error (and imprecision) may be attributed to reading, recording, and data entry errors. If more than a single observer is involved, the possible sources of error may be greatly compounded. In the case of a single observer, the approach is to focus on intraobserver, or within-observer, reliability and replication. For intraobserver error, access to the original material offers the best solution. Interobserver (more than one observer) error is more a concern in reliability studies. A variety of statistical techniques (from basic descriptive statistics to the analysis of variance and correlation coefficients, etc.) are available for assessing the degree of error (Utermhole and Zegura, 1982). While the potential for interobserver error would seem to argue against the combining of data from different observer, a recent study (Willis, 1999) that uses data recorded by several independent researchers spanning a considerable period of time concluded that interobserver error, at least among those measurements found to be common, was not a major concern. This finding should be of some comfort to future researchers contemplating metric analyses but who are otherwise denied access to skeletal remains.

Missing Data

Most multivariate procedures require complete sets of data, which often means that missing measurements, a frequent occurrence in studies involving archeological human remains, must be supplied by estimation. A common solution to this problem is to replace the missing observation with its regressed value (Howells, 1973; Van Vark and Pasveer, 1994). Various statistical packages such as BMDP (Dixon, 1990a, 1990b; Dixon and Brown, 1979), contain suitable regression analysis programs for such purposes. These procedures, however, should only be used when a few of the measurements are missing either per individual or per variable, which means that only complete or nearly complete specimens can be ultimately utilized in multivariate statistical analyses. More details on missing observations and general guidelines for dealing with them are described by Howells (1973:33–35), Van Vark (1985, 1995), Van Vark and Pasveer (1994) and Van Vark and Schaafsma (1992).

Removal of the Size-Based Component (Z-Scores and C-Scores)

A fairly common concern in morphometric analyses is to determine the relative contribution of size and shape in distance measures. Size is defined as the magnitude of a vector of measurements on an organism, while shape is a function of relative proportion normalized by size (Corruccini, 1987:289,290). Many researchers regard shape rather than size as being of greater importance when the taxonomic units in question are above the deme or subspecies level and thus warranting the removal of the size-based component (Corruccini, 1973:743). Several researchers (e.g., Brace and Hunt, 1990; Brace and Tracer, 1992; Brace et al., 1990; Howells, 1989) have advocated the use of C-scores as a way to compensate, at least partially, for the unequal influence that size differences may exert on the patterns of variation.

Although the use of C-scores theoretically compensates for size differences and hence their unequal influence on the patterns of variation, others (e.g., Green 1990; Pietrusewsky, 1994, 1995) have demonstrated that removal of this size-based component has little or no effect on the interpretation of patterns of craniometric variation. Accordingly, C-score measures are not used in the examples provided.

Cranial Series and Measurements

The 10 cranial sites used in the first example represent prehistoric Jomon, Ainu, and modern Japanese since the Yayoi Period (Table 14.1). These 10 human cranial series represent a broad temporal, spatial, and archaeological sampling of ancient and near contemporary inhabitants of the Japanese Islands beginning with some of the archipelago's earliest inhabitants, the Jomon. The Ainu represent a distinct separate aboriginal group inhabiting Hokkaido and Sakhalin Islands and perhaps elsewhere in the past. The Yayoi Period is archaeologically characterized as the time when intensive rice agriculture was practiced, possibly coinciding with a major influx of new immigrants from the neighboring Asiatic mainland. The Kofun, Kamakura, and Edo series represent later archaeological periods. Three of the series (Kanto, Tohoku, and Kyushu) represent near modern non-Ainu Japanese from two of the main Japanese Islands. The approximate locations of these and the comparative cranial series used in the second example are shown in Figure 14.1. Additional information for the 43 comparative series has been presented elsewhere (Pietrusewsky, 1996).

The 29 standard cranial measurements included in these analyses are defined in Table 14.2. The number of measurements represents the greatest number of variables comparable to all the series. Missing measurements, which were minimal, were replaced with regressed values obtained through stepwise regression analysis using the computer program, PAM, of the BMDP statistical package (Dixon and Brown, 1979).

First Example (10 Japanese Groups, 29 Cranial Measurements)

Stepwise Discriminant Function Analysis

The computer program, BMDP-7M (Dixon and Brown, 1979), written for a mainframe computer, was used to perform stepwise discriminant function analysis using 10 Japanese cranial series and 29 cranial measurements.

TABLE 14.1 Ten Male Japanese Cranial Series

Sample (abbrev.)	No. of Crania	Location[a] and number	Remarks
Kanto Japanese (KAN)	50	CHB-50	A dissecting room population of modern Japanese from the Kanto District of eastern Honshu. The majority of the individuals were born during the Meiji period (1868–1911) and died well before 1940.
Tohoku Japanese (TOH)	53	SEN-53	Dissecting room specimens of modern Japanese from the Tohoku District in northern Honshu Island.
Kyushu Japanese (KYU)	51	KYU-51	Modern Japanese which derive mostly from Fukuoka Prefecture in Kyushu Island. Other specimens are from Yamaguchi, Saga, Nagasaki, and adjoining prefectures.
Edo (EDO)	55	NSM-52	The specimens are from the Joshinji (Tokyo) site and date to the Edo Period or approximately the seventeenth to mid-nineteenth centuries.
Kamakura (KAM)	52	NSM-9;TKO-43	Specimens are from the medieval mass burial sites of Zaimokuza and Gokurakuji in the city of Kamakura, believed to be victims of a war that occurred in 1333.
Kofun (KOF)	62	KYO-5;KYU-53; NSM-4	The Kofun Period of Japan follows the Yayoi period. The traditional dates for the Kofun Period are the fourth to seventh century A.D.
Yayoi (YAY)	62	KYU-62	A combined sample of Yayoi specimens from Doigahama (39), Yoshimohama (14), and Nakanohama (2) sites in Yamaguchi Prefecture. Others (7) are from Koura, Shimane Prefecture, in southern Honshu Island. The dates for the Yayoi Period of Japan are approximately 300 B.C. to A.D. 300.
Jomon (JOM)	51	TKO-16;NSM-19 KYO-15;SAP-1	All specimens represent Late to Latest [ca 2000 B.C. to 300 B.C.] Jomon sites on Honshu Island. The largest series are Ebishima (11) in Iwate Prefecture in Tohoku District and Tsukumo (12), Okayama Prefecture in the Chugoku District.
Ainu (AIN)	50	SAP-18 TKM-5 TKO-27	These skeletons were collected by Koganei in 1888–1889 from abandoned Ainu cemeteries in Hokkaido (Koganei 1893–1894).
Ryukyu Islands (RYU)	62	KYU-34;KYO-18 TKO-10	Specimens are from the Sakishima (13), Okinawa (13), and Amami (30) groups, respectively, of the Ryukyu Islands. Six more are identified only as Ryukyu Island.

[a]CHB = Chiba University School of Medicine, Chiba; KYO = Laboratory of Physical Anthropology, Faculty of Science, Kyoto University, Kyoto; KYU = Department of Anatomy, Faculty of Medicine, Kyushu University, Fukuoka; NSM = National Science Museum, Tokyo; SAP = Department of Anatomy, Sapporo Medical College, Sapporo; SEN = Department of Anatomy, School of Medicine, Tohoku University, Sendai; TKM = Medical Museum, University Museum, University of Tokyo; TKO = University Museum, University of Tokyo, Tokyo.

A summary of the measurements, ranked according to the F-values (tests of equality of group means using classical one-way analysis of variance) received in the final step of discriminant function analysis (Table 14.2) provides an indication of the discriminatory power of the original variables. The maximum breadth of the cranium, bimaxillary breadth, basion-nasion length, and nasal height are ranked highest (i.e., they contribute the most to the discrimination produced) in this analysis.

Eigenvalues, which represent the amount of variance accounted for by each function or variate, here expressed as the percentage of total dispersion, and level of significance (tested by Bartlett's criterion) for the first nine canonical variates is presented in Table 14.3. These latter provide an indication of the proportion of dispersion accounted for by each corresponding transformed, or canonical, variate. In this analysis, the first three canonical variates account for 72.8% of the total variation in this analysis. The first six eigenvalues are significant at the 1% level, indicating significant heterogeneity for these canonical variates, or axes.

Canonical coefficients, those values by which an individual's measurements may be multiplied to obtain its score, for 29 measurements for the first three canonical variates are given in Table 14.4. Orbital breadth, cranial vault length, bimaxillary subtense, and nasal breadth (those variables with the highest coefficients regardless of sign) are the most important variables in producing group separation in the first canonical variate. This first variate may, therefore, be defined essentially as a cranial vault length, orbital and nasal breadth, and subnasal projection discriminator. Dimensions of upper facial breadth (biorbital breadth and bifrontal breadth), height of the nasal aperture, and cranial base length (basion-nasion) are most responsible for group separation produced in the second canonical variate. Length of the maxillo-alveolar arch, biorbital breadth, and cheek height are primarily responsible for the discrimination produced in the third canonical variate.

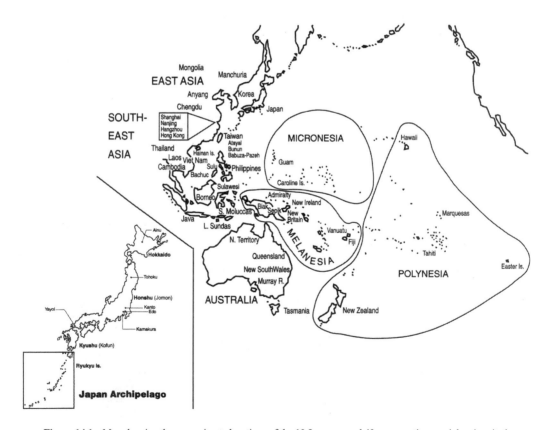

Figure 14.1 Map showing the approximate locations of the 10 Japanese and 43 comparative cranial series cited in the examples.

TABLE 14.2   Summary Ranking of Cranial Measurements According to F-Values Received in the Final Step of Discriminant Function Analysis (10 Male Groups, 29 Measurements)

Step No.	Measurement	F-Value	$\text{d.f.}_B/\text{d.f.}_W$[a]	p[b]
1	Maximum cranial breadth (M^d-8)	12.412	9/537	*
2	Bimaxillary breadth (M-46)	10.916	9/536	*
3	Basion-nasion length (M-5)	6.667	9/535	*
4	Nasal height (M-55)	8.607	9/534	*
5	Orbital breadth (M-51a)	5.013	9/533	*
6	Mastoid height (H^e-MDL)	4.896	9/532	*
7	Inferior malar length (H-IML)	4.831	9/531	*
8	Bijugal breadth [M-45(1)]	4.578	9/530	*
9	Minimum cranial breadth (M-14)	5.017	9/529	*
10	Alveolar length (M-60)	3.550	9/528	*
11	Nasio-occipital length (M-1d)	3.219	9/527	*
12	Bimaxillary subtense (H-SSS)	2.972	9/526	*
13	Lambda-opisthion chord (M-31)	3.172	9/525	*
14	Bregma-lambda chord (M-30)	3.171	9/524	*
15	Biauricular breadth (M-11b)	2.997	9/523	*
16	Biorbital breadth (H-EKB)	2.415	9/522	*
17	Bifrontal breadth (M-43)	3.079	9/521	*
18	Bistephanic breadth (H-STB)	2.444	9/520	*
19	Minimum frontal breadth (M-9)	2.579	9/519	*
20	Maximum frontal breadth (M-10)	2.140	9/518	n.s.[c]
21	Nasal breadth (M-54)	1.990	9/517	n.s.
22	Cheek height [M-40(4)]	1.980	9/516	n.s.
23	Basion-bregma height (M-17)	2.019	9/515	n.s.
24	Orbital height (M-52)	1.632	9/514	n.s.
25	Maximum cranial length (M-11)	1.474	9/513	n.s.
26	Mastoid width (H-MDB)	1.353	9/512	n.s.
27	Alveolar breadth (M-61)	1.234	9/511	n.s.
28	Nasion-bregma chord (M-29)	1.086	9/510	n.s.
29	Biasterionic breadth (M-12)	0.934	9/509	n.s.

[a]$\text{d.f.}_B/\text{d.f.}_W$ = degrees of freedom between/degrees of freedom within
[b]$p \leq .01$; [c]n.s. = not significant   [d]M = Martin & Saller (1957)   [e]H = Howells (1973)

A summary of the group classification results, based on posterior probabilities (Table 14.5), indicate that the Jomon, Ainu, and Kanto are among the series having the best classification results (i.e., the greatest number of cases correctly classified to their own group). The poorest classification results are found for the Edo, Ryukyu, Kamakura, Kyushu, and Tohoku series. Four Jomon specimens are classified as Ainu and four more as Kofun. Two of the Jomon specimens are classified as Yayoi and two more are classified as Ryukyu. Ten of the Edo Period specimens are

classified as modern Kyushu. The largest number of misclassifications among the Ryukyu series are reassignments (seven each) to the Kamakura and Yayoi series.

Jackknifed classification results (Table 14.6), a common cross-validation procedure used in multiple discriminant analysis where cases are classified without using these misclassified individuals in computing the classification function, reveal a higher percentage of misclassifications. However, as found in the previous set of results, Jomon and Ainu, respectively, have the highest proportion of correct assignments and Edo, Kamakura, Ryukyu, and Kyushu, respectively, have the poorest classification results. Thirteen of the cases originally classified as Kamakura were reclassified as Ryukyu and nine additional cases were assigned to the Kofun series. Ten of the Ryukyu specimens are reclassified as Yayoi and nine as Kamakura. These results reiterate the relative cranial morphological homogeneity of the prehistoric Jomon and modern Ainu series and the generally more heterogeneous modern Japanese, Kamakura, and Ryukyu Island cranial series. Further, the mutual misclassifications between Kamakura and Ryukyu, Kamakura and Kofun, and the Ryukyu and Yayoi series underscores the mutual morphological closeness of these series.

When the group means are plotted on the first two canonical variates (Figure 14.2), three distinct clusters are apparent. The Edo Period cranial series clusters with three near modern cranial series from Kyushu, Tohoku, and Kanto. The near modern Ryukyu Islanders and Yayoi, Kofun, and Kamakura form a second cluster. Jomon and Ainu occupy an isolated third cluster. A plot of the means for these same groups on the first three canonical variates (Figure 14.2) reiterates this tripartite divisioning. The closeness of the spikes for the Kofun and Yayoi,

and the Kamakura and Ryukyu series, respectively, in this figure, indicates a close affinity among these series. The spikes for Edo, Tohoku, Kyushu, and Kanto further suggest a morphological closeness for these four groups. Jomon and Ainu are each represented by isolated spikes in this representation.

Mahalanobis' Generalized Distance

Mahalanobis' distances and tests of significance using 29 measurements for 10 male groups are presented in Table 14.7. The majority of these distances are significant at either the 1% or 5% level. The five nonsignificant distances are invariably the smallest distances in this analysis, implying no significant dissimilarity between these groups. The smallest distances are those between Ryukyu-Kamakura (1.413), Kyushu-Edo (1.560), Tohoku-Edo (1.738), Yayoi-Kofun (1.802), and Kyushu-Tohoku (2.423). The largest distances, implying the greatest dissimilarities, are generally those between either the Jomon or Ainu series and the remaining series. Equally large distances were found between Kanto and all nonmodern cranial series. Applying the UPGMA clustering technique results in the dendrogram shown in Figure 14.3. As seen in the previous canonical plots, three distinct clusters are indicated in this

TABLE 14.3   Eigenvalues, Percentage of Total Dispersion, Cumulative Percentage of Dispersion, and Level of Significance for the First Nine Canonical Variates (10 Groups, 29 Measurements)

Canonical Variate	Eigenvalue	% Dispersion	Cumulative % Dispersion	d.f.[a]	p[b]
1	0.71578	33.9	33.9	37	*
2	0.53538	25.4	59.3	35	*
3	0.28544	13.5	72.8	33	*
4	0.18466	8.7	81.5	31	*
5	0.12963	6.2	87.7	29	*
6	0.11870	5.6	93.3	27	*
7	0.07164	3.4	96.7	25	n.s.
8	0.03898	1.8	98.5	23	n.s.
9	0.03115	1.5	100.0	21	n.s.

[a]d.f. = degrees of freedom = $(p + q - 2) + (p + q - 4)$

[b]$p < 0.01$ when eigenvalues are tested for significance according to criterion $[N - \frac{1}{2}(p + q)] \log_e (\lambda + 1)$, where N = total number of crania, p = number of variables, q = number of groups, λ = eigenvalue, all of which are distributed approximately as chi-square (Rao 1952:323), n.s. = not significant.

TABLE 14.4   **Canonical Coefficients of 29 Cranial Measurements for the First Three Canonical Variates (10 Groups, 29 Measurements)**

Variable	Canonical Variate 1	Canonical Variate 2	Canonical Variate 3
Maximum cranial length	0.11644	−0.07036	−0.06712
Nasio-occipital length	−0.12613	0.01813	0.01356
Basion-nasion length	−0.01188	−0.11102	−0.02558
Basion-bregma height	0.05275	−0.02705	−0.01491
Maximum cranial breadth	−0.03601	−0.09954	0.05843
Maximum frontal breadth	−0.00070	−0.08260	0.01578
Minimum frontal breadth	0.04654	−0.05293	0.01734
Bistephanic breadth	−0.05876	0.05771	−0.01446
Biauricular breadth	−0.02162	0.09180	0.05629
Minimum cranial breadth	0.09494	−0.00471	0.06801
Biasterionic breadth	−0.00946	−0.00617	0.00375
Nasal height	0.04238	0.12091	0.05211
Nasal breadth	−0.12020	0.02160	0.00563
Orbital height	0.04101	0.06021	0.00135
Orbital breadth	−0.17227	−0.10538	−0.01841
Bijugal breadth	−0.09406	−0.04955	0.00129
Alveolar length	−0.04227	0.05638	0.15945
Alveolar breadth	0.04348	0.02110	0.00720
Mastoid height	0.10088	−0.03412	0.04786
Mastoid breadth	−0.05378	−0.02423	−0.00098
Bimaxillary breadth	−0.09053	0.08237	−0.07071
Bifrontal breadth	−0.00204	0.13228	−0.05451
Biorbital breadth	0.07789	−0.13547	0.14259
Malar length, inferior	0.07059	0.10639	−0.05168
Cheek height	−0.04722	0.10720	0.12677
Nasion-bregma chord	−0.00110	0.04677	−0.03879
Bregma-lambda chord	−0.04498	0.04652	−0.00085
Lambda-opisthion chord	0.01983	−0.00412	0.01826
Bimaxillary subtense	0.12351	0.01623	0.02976

diagram. The four modern Japanese series form a single cluster. A second cluster includes the Kamakura, Ryukyu, Kofun, and Yayoi series. The tightest cluster in this diagram is one between Kamakura and Ryukyu. The last and most isolated cluster to join is the one that forms between the Ainu and Jomon series.

Second Example (53 Male Groups, 29 Measurements)

In the second example, stepwise discriminant function analysis and Mahalanobis' generalized distance are applied to the same 29 mea-surements recorded in 2518 male crania repre-senting 53 groups from Japan, East Asia, Southeast Asia, Australia, and the Pacific.

Stepwise Discriminant Function Analysis

A summary ranking of the 29 cranial measure-ments according to F-values received in the fi-nal step of discriminant function analysis (Table 14.8), indicates that alveolar length, maximum cranial breadth, basion-nasion length, and minimum cranial breadth are among the most important discriminating vari-ables in this analysis.

Eigenvalues, percentage of dispersion, and the level of significance for the first 10 canonical variates (Table 14.9) indicate that the first three canonical variates account for 61.6% of the total variation produced.

Canonical coefficients for 29 cranial measurements for the first three canonical variates (Table 14.10) indicate biorbital breadth, nasio-occipital length, alveolar length, bimaxillary subtense, maximum cranial length, and

TABLE 14.5 Summary of Classification Results from Discriminant Function Analysis (Number of Cases Classified into Groups) 10 Groups, 29 Measurements

Group	KAN	EDO	KAM	KOF	YAY	TOH	KYU	AIN	RYU	JOM
Kanto	33	3		1	2	4	1	1	2	3
Edo	5	17	3	3	5	5	10	5	1	1
Kamakura	3	3	24	5	2	3	3	1	7	1
Kofun		5	6	31	6	3	2	2	3	4
Yayoi	4	3	5	5	33	2	1	2	5	2
Tohoku	6	5		2	2	26	3	4	4	1
Kyushu	4	4	4	3	2	4	25	1	3	1
Ainu	3	1	3	1		1	3	34	1	3
Ryukyu	2	2	7	4	7	1	4	3	28	4
Jomon			1	4	2	1	1	4	2	36
Total Cases Orig. Assign	50	55	52	62	62	53	51	50	62	51
No. Correctly Assign.	33	17	24	31	33	26	25	34	28	36
% Correct Assign.	66.0	30.9	46.2	50.0	53.2	49.1	49.0	68.0	45.2	70.6

TABLE 14.6 Summary of Jackknifed Classification Results from Discriminant Function Analysis (Number of Cases Classified into Groups) 10 Groups, 29 Measurements

Group	KAN	EDO	KAM	KOF	YAY	TOH	KYU	AIN	RYU	JOM
Kanto	19	5	1	1	2	6	8	1	4	3
Edo	7	13	4	3	5	5	10	5	1	2
Kamakura	3	3	13	9	2	3	3	2	13	1
Kofun	0	5	7	21	8	3	2	4	4	8
Yayoi	4	4	7	9	23	4	1	2	5	3
Tohoku	7	5	3	3	2	18	2	6	5	2
Kyushu	8	5	6	3	2	4	14	3	5	1
Ainu	3	3	2	2	1	1	3	25	4	6
Ryukyu	2	3	9	7	10	2	6	3	16	4
Jomon	1	0	2	4	3	1	2	6	3	29
Total Cases Orig. Assign	50	55	52	62	62	53	51	50	62	51
No. Correctly Assign.	19	13	13	21	23	18	14	25	16	29
% Correct Assign.	38	23.6	25	33.9	32.1	34.0	27.5	50.0	25.8	56.9

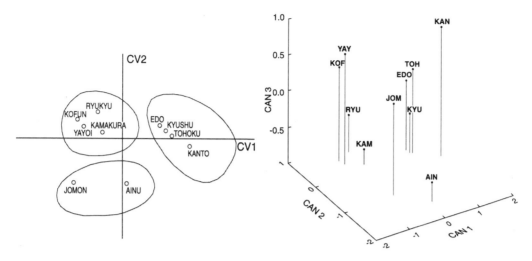

Figure 14.2 Plots of 10 male Japanese group means on the first two (on left) and first three (on right) canonical variates using 29 cranial measurements. The abbreviations used in the latter are explained in Table 14.1.

cheek height are among the most important variables producing separation in the first canonical variate. This canonical variate, although difficult to characterize, discriminates primarily on the basis of upper facial breadth, vault length, subnasal projection, and the length of the hard palate. With the exception of basion-nasion length, the second canonical variate is primarily a breadth discriminator. Basion-nasion length, nasal breadth, alveolar breadth, bijugal breadth, and minimum cranial breadth are among the variables responsible for group separation in the second variate. Dimensions of the nasal aperture, bifrontal breadth, inferior length of zygomatic bone, and nasio-occipital length, are primarily responsible for group separation in the third canonical variate.

A summary of the classification results, regular and the more rigorous jackknife procedure (Table 14.11), reveal that the groups with the highest percentage of "correct" classifications (i.e., the specimens are reclassified to their originally assigned groups) include Mongolia, Easter Island, Bunun, Babuza-Pazeh, Hawaii, and Tasmania. Groups with the poorest classification results (i.e., the fewest specimens are returned to their originally as-

signed groups) include Edo, Hangzhou, Lesser Sundas, Sulawesi, and Shanghai.

When the 53 group means are plotted on the first two canonical variates (Fig. 14.4) several major constellations are evident. The cranial series representing Australia and Melanesia, Polynesia (and Guam), Southeast Asia, China and Northern Asia, and the Japanese Archipelago, respectively, fall out into separate groupings. Adding a third axis to this representation (Fig. 14.5), reiterates this separation.

Mahalanobis' Generalized Distance

Applying Mahalanobis' generalized distance to the same 29 cranial measurements recorded in the same 53 male groups, results in a matrix of 2756 distances (Table 14.12). Inspection of variance ratios for these distances indicates only 27 have nonsignificant values. As was the case in the first example, the nonsignificant distances are generally the smallest distances, or the groups having the smallest sample sizes. Six of the smallest distances in this analysis are associated with the Korean series. Among the Japanese cranial series, several nonsignificant distances, including Edo-Tohoku (1.762), Edo-Kyushu (1.412), Tohoku-Kyushu (2.210),

Kamakura-Ryukyu (1.445), and Kofun-Yayoi (1.635), are noteworthy. Additional nonsignificant distances are those among several of the Southeast Asian series, such as those between Sulawesi, Borneo, and the Philippines and some of the other Southeast Asian groups.

The dendrogram that results when UP-GMA clustering algorithm is applied to these distances is shown in Figure 14.6. The major separation in this diagram is one between Australo-Melanesian and a second large cluster containing all the Asian (including Polynesian) groups. Mongolia remains an extreme outgroup of the latter division. The Ainu and Jonom cluster connects with other Japanese series before connecting with any of

TABLE 14.7   Mahalanobis' Generalized Distances (Upper Half) and Variance Ratios (Lower Half) for 10 Japanese Groups Using 29 Cranial Measurements

Group	KAN	EDO	KAM	KOF	YAY	TOH	KYU	AIN	RYU	JOM
Kanto		2.658	6.782	7.323	6.633	2.959	3.004	6.774	6.542	8.292
Edo	1.75[a]		3.530	4.084	4.137	1.738	1.560	4.991	3.197	7.694
Kamakura	4.29[b]	2.39[b]		2.753	3.217	3.766	2.886	4.662	1.413	5.538
Kofun	5.21[b]	3.11[b]	2.01[b]		1.802	5.122	4.492	7.101	2.490	5.265
Yayoi	4.72[b]	3.15[b]	2.35[b]	1.48[c]		4.661	5.652	6.323	2.431	5.457
Tohoku	1.90[a]	1.19[c]	2.48[b]	3.80[b]	3.45[b]		2.423	5.700	4.274	7.597
Kyushu	1.88[a]	1.04[c]	1.85[a]	3.24[b]	4.08[b]	1.58[c]		5.114	3.262	7.587
Ainu	4.17[b]	3.28[b]	2.95[b]	5.05[b]	4.50[b]	3.66[b]	3.19[b]		6.666	4.857
Ryukyu	4.65[b]	2.43[b]	1.03[c]	2.05[b]	2.00[b]	3.17[b]	2.35[b]	4.74[b]		6.334
Jomon	5.18[b]	5.13[b]	3.55[b]	3.80[b]	3.94[b]	4.94[b]	4.80[b]	3.03[b]	4.57[b]	

[a]= significant at 5% level

[b]= significant at 1% level

[c]= not significant

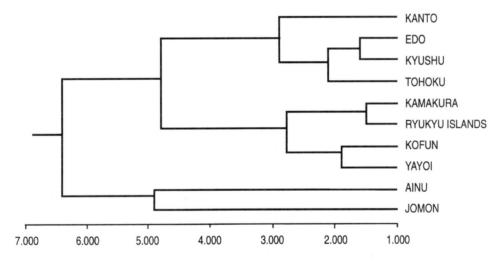

Figure 14.3   Diagram of relationship based on a cluster analysis (UPGMA) of Mahalanobis' generalized distances using 29 cranial measurements recorded in 10 male Japanese groups.

TABLE 14.8   Summary Ranking of Cranial Measurements According to F-Values Received in the Final Step of Discriminant Function Analysis (53 Male Groups, 29 Measurements)

Step No.	Measurement	F-Value	d.f.$_B$/d.f.$_W$[a]	p[b]
1	Alveolar length	37.619	52/2464	*
2	Maximum cranial breadth	30.586	52/2463	*
3	Basion-nasion length	19.722	52/2462	*
4	Minimum cranial breadth	17.562	52/2461	*
5	Nasal height	14.959	52/2460	*
6	Orbital breadth	14.693	52/2459	*
7	Nasio-occipital length	12.422	52/2458	*
8	Basion-bregma height	12.443	52/2457	*
9	Bimaxillary subtense	10.679	52/2456	*
10	Malar length, inferior	10.411	52/2455	*
11	Nasal breadth	9.726	52/2454	*
12	Biauricular breadth	9.847	52/2453	*
13	Maximum cranial breadth	9.029	52/2452	*
14	Bimaxillary breadth	7.627	52/2451	*
15	Bifrontal breadth	7.495	52/2450	*
16	Bijugal breadth	8.291	52/2449	*
17	Alveolar breadth	7.015	52/2448	*
18	Biorbital breadth	6.982	52/2447	*
19	Nasion-bregma chord	6.478	52/2446	*
20	Cheek height	5.599	52/2445	*
21	Orbital height	5.677	52/2444	*
22	Lambda-opisthion chord	5.309	52/2443	*
23	Bistephanic breadth	5.038	52/2442	*
24	Maximum frontal breadth	6.308	52/2441	*
25	Mastoid height	4.064	52/2440	*
26	Bregma-lambda chord	3.798	52/2439	*
27	Biasterionic breadth	3.183	52/2438	*
28	Mastoid width	3.025	52/2437	*
29	Minimal frontal breadth	2.936	52/2436	*

[a] d.f.$_B$/d.f.$_W$ = degrees of freedom between/degrees of freedom within
[b] $p \leq .01$

the other Asian series in this analysis. The internal ordering of the Japanese cranial series, including the Ainu and Jomon series, is identical to that found in the first example. These latter, in turn, form a cluster, with a subcluster of northeast Asian series that includes Taiwan and Hainan Chinese, Korea, bronze age Chinese, and a single Taiwan Aboriginal group (Atayal). Ultimately, these northeast Asian series, and all the Japanese series, cluster with the remaining Chinese series and one from Manchuria. The cluster containing the Southeast Asian series is well separated from these latter.

Discussion of Results

The results presented in these examples allow some tentative conclusions regarding the biological relationships of Japan's inhabitants, early and more recent, and their relationship to the surrounding regions.

The demonstration of two distinctly different morphological groups within Japan, one represented by the prehistoric Jomon and modern Ainu and the second that includes Japanese cranial series since the Yayoi/Kofun times, is a finding similar to the results presented by other researchers (see, e.g., Hanihara, 1991). The former grouping, which pairs prehistoric Jomon (people who inhabited the archipelago for approximately 10,000 years beginning in ca. 12,000 years B.P.) and the modern Ainu, is also supported by numerous lines of evidence, including genetic and skeletal data (e.g., Brace and Hunt, 1990; Brace and Tracer, 1992; Brace et al., 1989; Dodo 1986; Dodo and Ishida, 1990; Hanihara, 1985; Hanihara, 1993; Hanihara et al., 1993; Howells, 1966, 1986; Kozintsev, 1990; Matusumura, 1989; Mizoguchi, 1986; Omoto et al., 1996; Ossenberg, 1986, 1992; Turner, 1976, 1987, 1990; Yamaguchi, 1982, 1985, 1992; etc.). The association of cranial series representing the Yayoi (ca. 300 B.C.–A.D. 300) and Kofun (fourth through seventh centuries A.D.) periods and the more modern Japanese suggests a later immigration and displacement, at least in part, of the indigenous Jomon and their descendants.

One association found in the results presented here that is more problematic is the close connection between the present-day inhabitants of the Ryukyu Islands and the medieval series from Kamakura, an ancient capital located in the Kanto Plains of present-day eastern Honshu Island, which in turn are most similar to both Yayoi and Kofun series. This association suggests that these groups have either shared a common origin or that the Ryukyu Islanders experienced an almost complete replacement by this later group of immigrants. Using a limited number of craniofacial and tooth measurements, Brace and colleagues (Brace and Hunt, 1990; Brace and Tracer, 1992; Brace et al., 1989) as well as Hanihara (1991) using cranial and dental morphology, have argued for a connection between the Kamakura and the Ainu (Samurai), a view that is not supported by the results of this new analysis. Similarly, a connection between Jomon and Ainu and the inhabitants of the Ryukyu Islands, based on classic genetic marker data (Omoto and Saitou, 1997) and cranial/dental morphology (Hanihara, 1991) finds no support in the results presented in this example.

TABLE 14.9   Eigenvalues, Percentage of Total Dispersion, Cumulative Percentage of Dispersion, and Level of Significance for the First 23 Canonical Variates (53 Groups, 29 Measurements)

Canonical Variate	Eigenvalue	% Dispersion	Cumulative % Dispersion	d.f.[a]	p[b]
1	3.33551	40.7	40.7	80	*
2	0.91664	11.2	51.9	78	*
3	0.79834	9.7	61.6	76	*
4	0.56514	6.9	68.5	74	*
5	0.45781	5.6	74.1	72	*
6	0.31865	3.9	78.0	70	*
7	0.26598	3.3	81.3	68	*
8	0.22331	2.7	84.0	66	*
9	0.19404	2.4	86.4	64	*
10	0.16333	2.0	88.4	62	*

[a]d.f. = degrees of freedom = $(p + q - 2) + (p + q - 4)$

[b]$p < 0.01$ when eigenvalues are tested for significance according to criterion $[N - \frac{1}{2}(p + q)] \log_e (\lambda + 1)$, where N = total number of crania, p = number of variables, q = number of groups, λ = eigenvalue, all of which are distributed approximately as chi-square (Rao 1952:323).

TABLE 14.10   Canonical Coefficients of 29 Cranial Measurements for the First Three Canonical Variates (53 Groups, 29 Measurements)

Variable	Canonical Variate 1	Canonical Variate 2	Canonical Variate 3
Maximum cranial length	−0.10718	0.04171	0.04168
Nasio-occipital length	0.13274	−0.07601	0.11272
Basion-nasion length	0.03546	−0.12441	0.03742
Basion-bregma height	0.01919	0.00454	−0.02025
Maximum cranial breadth	0.04901	0.04315	−0.01181
Maximum frontal breadth	−0.01305	0.06819	0.01249
Minimum frontal breadth	−0.04149	0.00556	0.00762
Bistephanic breadth	0.03930	−0.05624	−0.01253
Biauricular breadth	0.01141	−0.06737	−0.01251
Minimum cranial breadth	0.09231	0.10769	0.05988
Biasterionic breadth	−0.02871	0.02508	0.02740
Nasal height	−0.00506	0.00188	−0.13429
Nasal breadth	−0.04136	0.11527	−0.13649
Orbital height	0.03707	−0.02128	−0.10531
Orbital breadth	−0.05968	−0.07521	−0.04373
Bijugal breadth	0.03786	−0.10928	0.01447
Alveolar length	−0.12170	−0.00389	−0.00148
Alveolar breadth	−0.02140	0.11295	0.04689
Mastoid height	−0.01648	−0.04575	−0.04246
Mastoid breadth	0.03888	−0.03638	0.00548
Bimaxillary breadth	0.06133	0.03026	−0.02193
Bifrontal breadth	0.04519	0.06695	0.12474
Biorbital breadth	−0.14816	0.01707	−0.06356
Malar length, inferior	−0.08780	0.07578	−0.11614
Cheek height	0.10138	−0.03780	−0.09124
Nasion-bregma chord	−0.04133	−0.04126	−0.07574
Bregma-lambda chord	−0.01134	0.01853	−0.03462
Lambda-opisthion chord	0.00161	−0.02418	−0.05325
Bimaxillary subtense	−0.10719	−0.04811	−0.03264

When other mainland eastern and northern Asian samples are compared, all Japanese, including Ainu and Jomon, are members of a greater Asian grouping that includes cranial series from mainland China, Korea, Manchuria, Taiwan, and Hainan Island. These latter are eventually tied to Southeast Asia and ultimately Polynesia well separated from a second major constellation. The immediate origins of the Japanese, ancient and modern as well as the Ryukyu Islanders, is northeast Asia. Finally, there is no close connection between Jomon/Ainu and Pacific groups as advocated by Brace and colleagues (Brace and Tracer, 1992; Brace et al., 1990). Jomon and Ainu are members of a greater East/North Asian grouping, their presume ancestral homeland.

CONCLUSIONS

The tradition of applying analytical methods to metric data, which has characterized physical anthropology since its inception, continues to the present. While interest in this topic has diversified in recent years, determining

TABLE 14.11 Summary of Classification Results from Discriminant Function Analysis (Number of Cases Classified into Groups) 53 Groups, 29 Measurements

Group	Total Cases Orig. Assigned	No. Correct Assign.	% Correct Assign.	Jackknifed No. Correct Assign.	Jackknifed % Correct Assign.
Shanghai	50	15	30.0	5	10.0
Hong Kong	50	25	50.0	19	38.0
Chengdu	53	28	52.8	23	43.4
Hangzhou	50	10	20.0	6	12.0
Nanjing	49	16	32.7	8	16.3
Taiwan	47	20	42.6	13	27.7
Hainan Is.	47	15	31.9	13	27.7
Atayal	36	25	69.4	21	58.3
Manchuria	50	25	50.0	18	36.0
Anyang	56	28	50.0	22	39.3
Mongolia	50	41	82.0	40	80.0
Korea	32	10	31.3	4	12.5
Kanto	50	20	40.0	12	24.0
Edo	55	5	9.1	3	5.5
Kamakura	52	20	38.5	16	30.8
Kofun	62	26	41.9	18	29.0
Yayoi	62	22	35.5	15	24.2
Tohoku	53	18	34.0	13	24.5
Kyushu	51	18	35.3	11	21.6
Ainu	50	28	56.0	24	48.0
Ryukyu	62	17	27.4	14	22.6
Jomon	51	34	66.7	28	54.9
Cambodia-Laos	40	28	70.0	22	55.0
Thailand	50	23	46.0	18	36.0
Vietnam	49	19	38.8	13	26.5
Bachuc	51	30	58.8	23	45.1
Sulawesi	41	11	26.8	5	12.2
Sulu	38	18	47.4	11	28.9
Philippines	28	11	39.3	7	25.0
L. Sundas	45	10	22.2	4	8.9
Borneo	34	13	38.2	7	20.6
Java	50	17	34.0	11	22.0
Babuza-Pazeh	50	37	74.0	35	70.0
Bunun	26	20	76.9	16	61.5
Easter Is.	50	41	82.0	37	74.0
Hawaii	49	37	75.5	30	61.2
Marquesas	63	28	44.4	18	28.6
New Zealand	50	27	54.0	22	44.0
Tahiti	44	27	61.4	21	47.7
Guam	46	31	67.4	29	63.0
Caroline Is.	24	9	37.5	6	25.0
Admiralty	50	27	54.0	24	48.0
Vanuatu	47	24	51.1	14	29.8

(continued)

TABLE 14.11 *(Continued)*

Group	Total Cases Orig. Assigned	No. Correct Assign.	% Correct Assign.	Jackknifed No. Correct Assign.	Jackknifed % Correct Assign.
Fiji	32	15	46.9	9	28.1
New Britain	50	22	44.0	18	36.0
Sepik R.	50	30	60.0	23	46.0
Biak Islands	48	25	52.1	19	39.6
New Ireland	53	24	45.3	16	30.2
New South Wales	62	34	54.8	24	38.7
Queensland	54	22	40.7	17	31.5
Murray R.	50	30	60.0	24	48.0
Tasmania	26	19	73.1	17	65.4
N. Territory	50	27	54.0	23	46.0

past biological relatedness continues to attract considerable attention among skeletal biologists and physical anthropologists. Multivariate statistical procedures remain the most robust procedures available for analyzing metrical variables. Discriminant function analysis and Mahalanobis' generalized distance constitute two of the most popular multivariate procedures for determining biological relatedness and for the classification of unknown specimens. Various clustering procedures and other methods of ordination provide an important means of visualizing multivariate results.

A lingering reluctance among anthropologists and skeletal biologists to use multivariate statistical procedures stems, in part, from the complex, often daunting, mathematical theory that underlies these methods. Recent refinements of the methodological and theoretical concerns, many critical of the inappropriate application of these methods, have resulted in the recommendation of sometimes complex mathematical adjustments or "corrections" to the existing procedures. The latter have done little to advance the easy acceptance and use of these methods among the less mathematically inclined members of the discipline. As this chapter has endeavored to demonstrate, the use of these methods, many of which are now readily available in statistical packages designed for personal computers, although requiring a basic understanding of the general concepts that underlie these procedures, does not necessarily require that the potential user first be highly trained as a mathematician or statistician.

Some of the major concepts that underlie the use of these analytical procedures including the underlying assumptions of multivariate data, preparation of data, and other guidelines are further outlined in this chapter. Examples, which concentrate on the biohistorical relationships of Japan's early and more recent inhabitants, serve as an illustration of the application of multivariate procedures.

Coinciding with anthropologists' earliest applications of multivariate statistical procedures to metric data, the principal concern has been determining past relationships and classification or allocation of individual (usually fossil) specimens. This trend, which primarily addresses biohistorical issues, is likely to continue well into the twenty-first century. A great many of these earlier studies have encompassed vast geographical regions (big picture studies). Skeletal biologists, especially those who work closely with archaeologists and with archaeological human remains, will very likely focus more on regional analyses

TABLE 14.12 Mahalanobis' Generalized Distances and Level of Significance for 53 Male Groups Using 29 Cranial Measurements

Group	SHA	HK	CHE	HAN	NAN	TAI	HAI	ATY	BUN	BPZ
Shanghai	—									
Hong Kong	4.165	—								
Chengdu	4.122	7.930	—							
Hangzhou	0.734[b]	4.140	3.839	—						
Nanjing	2.425[b]	4.338	2.612[a]	1.667[b]	—					
Taiwan	10.603	8.641	8.941	9.635	7.772	—				
Hainan	8.154	6.902	9.658	8.238	7.280	3.371[a]	—			
Atayal	13.743	13.322	11.574	12.598	10.715	7.908	6.967	—		
Bunun	13.062	13.407	15.534	12.501	12.712	17.693	14.430	12.059	—	
Babuza-Pazch	13.945	18.407	17.113	13.771	13.445	15.855	13.257	18.241	13.107	—
Manchuria	6.590	6.556	6.268	6.008	3.740	6.666	6.188	9.779	13.127	17.866
Anyang	9.428	8.430	9.452	8.167	6.203	3.807	3.612	7.703	15.666	14.326
Mongolia	12.210	20.966	11.233	10.885	12.294	22.749	21.548	23.331	19.490	22.066
Korea	6.680	7.094	7.491	5.913	4.783	4.009[b]	2.563[b]	5.826[a]	11.458	11.793
Kanto	7.699	7.333	11.832	7.915	8.006	9.149	6.725	9.321	8.494	14.859
Edo	6.056	6.225	7.823	6.009	5.047	7.134	4.600	6.795	8.183	13.498
Kamakura	10.980	10.510	11.589	10.143	8.654	7.986	7.311	8.212	10.280	14.088
Kofun	7.892	9.389	8.153	7.035	6.956	7.987	7.102	9.967	11.662	15.473
Yayoi	6.695	9.143	7.164	5.807	5.379	9.124	8.055	9.480	9.689	12.578
Tohoku	9.337	10.082	10.232	8.935	7.054	8.167	6.969	6.933	8.117	14.724
Kyushu	9.071	7.655	12.025	9.074	8.362	7.843	5.488	6.998	10.035	15.551
Ainu	13.617	14.400	17.323	12.768	12.976	16.227	14.270	12.414	9.297	17.640
Ryukyu	8.877	7.926	9.904	7.832	6.523	6.588	5.015	7.537	10.921	13.729
Jomon	14.993	16.789	19.548	14.238	15.185	16.820	13.406	16.176	11.165	16.208
Camb/Laos	11.306	13.783	14.298	11.123	12.205	13.700	8.306	14.803	20.665	15.358
Thailand	6.124	5.623	11.798	6.594	9.025	8.720	5.066	12.503	16.092	16.602
Vietnam	6.409	5.141	7.232	5.668	6.063	6.352	4.756	9.046	11.784	13.025
Bachuc	9.836	8.220	13.842	9.625	11.812	9.278	4.810	14.404	20.786	16.966
Sulawesi	7.235	9.810	9.934	6.736	8.104	11.617	6.829	10.685	15.252	13.834
Sulu	11.269	14.589	13.833	11.083	13.194	15.310	10.659	16.115	17.393	13.383

TABLE 14.12 (*Continued*)

Group	SHA	HK	CHE	HAN	NAN	TAI	HAI	ATY	BUN	BPZ
Philippines	7.463	6.690	8.315	6.415	6.614	7.711	5.750[a]	8.269	14.613	15.358
L. Sundas	8.298	8.828	10.285	8.480	8.945	11.613	7.911	10.114	14.713	18.038
Borneo	8.499	9.754	11.156	8.011	8.932	12.369	8.493	10.165	11.488	13.705
Java	7.291	10.289	12.107	7.514	9.512	11.895	7.129	14.735	19.462	14.611
Easter Is.	27.067	25.236	26.928	25.260	21.689	23.008	24.753	25.142	21.505	27.754
Hawaii	15.067	17.092	17.516	14.926	15.467	18.702	16.588	25.244	20.717	19.131
Marquesas	17.930	20.331	15.723	17.178	16.169	18.368	18.528	21.471	17.572	22.035
New Zealand	16.603	18.302	15.983	15.932	14.376	17.401	16.042	15.755	12.866	18.708
Tahiti	21.219	22.710	21.376	21.424	19.810	19.707	20.244	26.099	27.104	27.357
Guam	14.082	18.060	13.745	14.535	12.039	18.141	16.632	19.841	23.739	17.905
Caroline	17.078	16.865	18.114	16.828	15.331	19.533	18.534	18.417	21.160	26.116
Admiralty	14.703	15.484	14.744	13.207	14.328	16.223	15.821	17.712	16.251	20.987
Vanuatu	24.578	25.609	25.210	25.674	26.200	30.959	27.138	24.251	24.817	36.515
Fiji	20.280	21.046	21.966	20.504	20.387	25.843	24.176	23.776	22.670	29.549
New Britain	23.084	23.002	24.404	23.307	23.356	27.657	25.342	21.658	26.830	35.890
Sepik R.	23.519	22.820	26.967	24.101	24.867	28.235	23.131	24.116	26.760	34.231
Biak Is.	18.098	17.740	18.579	18.065	18.823	22.171	20.475	18.116	20.070	28.686
New Ireland	20.490	20.413	21.688	20.548	19.948	24.726	21.560	20.617	22.864	30.341
New South Wales	27.701	31.028	30.847	29.011	31.468	37.560	32.294	26.992	31.806	42.587
Queensland	28.666	29.327	31.230	29.400	31.123	34.358	30.162	24.979	28.924	40.523
Murray R.	38.060	40.533	40.989	39.081	41.387	47.099	41.540	33.769	39.490	49.860
Tasmania	32.494	31.441	34.409	33.769	36.782	40.640	34.550	28.863	25.472	44.112
N. Territory	32.793	32.927	35.811	33.665	35.453	39.360	33.971	29.921	34.711	43.514

(*continued*)

TABLE 14.12 *(Continued)*

Group	MAN	ANY	MOG	KOR	KAN	EDO	KAM	KOF	YAY	TOH
Manchuria	—									
Anyang	6.859	—								
Mongolia	16.215	20.480	—							
Korea	4.245[a]	3.365[b]	16.295	—						
Kanto	6.743	8.395	21.705	4.416[a]	—					
Edo	3.546	6.039	18.281	2.777[b]	2.634[a]	—				
Kamakura	7.734	5.116	20.516	5.528	7.065	3.633	—			
Kofun	6.946	6.293	13.421	4.111	7.477	4.208	2.940	—		
Yayoi	6.235	6.975	10.318	4.758	6.725	4.030	3.230	1.635[b]	—	
Tohoku	5.097	6.868	20.859	3.586[b]	3.059[a]	1.762[b]	3.805	5.190	4.571	—
Kyushu	5.894	6.144	24.311	3.415[b]	2.752[a]	1.412[b]	3.081[a]	4.897	5.640	2.210[b]
Ainu	11.407	13.162	21.902	9.201	6.872	4.643	4.367	6.613	5.783	5.295
Ryukyu	6.412	4.429	17.711	3.816[a]	6.661	3.181	1.445[b]	2.444	2.296[a]	4.206
Jomon	15.040	13.163	22.047	9.907	8.498	7.631	5.301	5.196	5.347	7.053
Camb/Laos	14.023	12.459	20.242	9.919	14.202	11.533	15.547	14.831	13.591	16.472
Thailand	10.490	9.465	20.102	5.668	6.587	6.962	12.698	9.643	10.048	11.254
Vietnam	8.886	7.725	18.703	4.624[a]	7.331	4.951	7.802	6.890	6.762	7.919
Bachuc	12.402	10.284	25.776	7.162	10.390	9.002	14.728	12.605	13.154	13.351
Sulawesi	9.242	9.024	15.264	6.008	10.044	7.098	9.974	8.369	7.998	11.103
Sulu	14.800	14.162	20.917	10.668	13.458	10.491	13.697	13.468	12.394	14.726
Philippines	10.066	7.635	19.539	5.492[b]	10.489	7.202	10.685	10.121	9.718	10.904
L. Sundas	9.790	10.392	22.027	8.428	9.692	5.317	7.556	9.123	9.474	9.732
Borneo	11.426	9.911	20.324	7.654	9.869	6.916	7.343	8.462	8.052	9.346
Java	11.287	10.899	20.006	7.786	11.332	8.444	12.052	11.234	10.814	13.254
Easter Is.	20.317	19.455	35.542	20.485	21.083	15.946	14.330	20.621	21.220	18.523
Hawaii	15.588	16.821	21.790	13.591	15.397	12.015	14.516	14.395	15.042	18.335
Marquesas	13.236	16.394	25.251	15.480	16.863	11.554	13.478	14.668	15.091	15.590
New Zealand	13.743	14.016	28.958	14.256	13.061	9.254	10.977	14.801	14.828	12.036
Tahiti	13.807	20.143	34.546	18.297	19.025	13.992	16.153	18.723	19.484	18.483
Guam	16.914	15.221	21.696	13.955	18.133	12.992	14.191	15.703	14.985	18.063

TABLE 14.12 *(Continued)*

Group	MAN	ANY	MOG	KOR	KAN	EDO	KAM	KOF	YAY	TOH
Caroline	14.118	18.897	33.431	17.943	16.529	12.129	16.432	20.498	19.924	16.019
Admiralty	13.986	19.659	27.400	16.896	16.225	12.601	16.102	18.618	16.927	16.634
Vanuatu	24.225	29.358	39.865	28.948	25.201	20.405	21.515	25.294	26.480	25.322
Fiji	18.943	24.433	35.980	23.128	20.400	14.199	16.469	21.490	20.961	18.593
New Britain	22.910	26.780	39.588	26.013	23.101	18.702	19.240	23.566	24.731	23.296
Sepik R.	23.210	27.681	45.255	26.868	23.998	18.765	22.921	29.379	29.007	24.214
Biak Is.	17.966	21.423	35.735	21.000	20.122	13.854	15.547	20.095	20.514	18.025
New Ireland	18.028	24.619	37.243	21.776	19.930	14.340	17.785	21.360	22.100	18.798
New South Wales	31.094	34.847	43.856	32.946	28.265	23.703	27.025	31.674	32.472	29.939
Queensland	30.466	32.106	42.309	31.531	27.454	23.127	25.139	30.228	31.231	29.304
Murray R.	39.981	42.914	52.756	41.880	36.859	32.689	33.671	39.238	40.393	39.449
Tasmania	35.057	38.413	42.349	34.918	28.401	27.323	28.195	30.570	32.242	31.967
N. Territory	34.639	37.649	50.634	36.700	32.648	26.793	29.270	35.176	36.267	34.507

(continued)

TABLE 14.12 (Continued)

Group	KYU	AIN	RYU	JOM	CAM	THI	VIN	BAC	SLW	SUL
Kyushu	—									
Ainu	4.841	—								
Ryukyu	3.477	6.016	—							
Jomon	7.466	4.288	6.069	—						
Camb/Laos	14.374	20.837	12.142	20.706	—					
Thailand	8.344	15.033	8.982	15.600	5.999	—				
Vietnam	7.249	10.993	5.500	11.692	8.215	4.375	—			
Bachuc	10.316	19.896	10.749	19.081	6.747	3.269	5.167	—		
Sulawesi	9.284	13.286	7.112	14.905	2.636[b]	4.797	6.113	6.432	—	
Sulu	12.831	17.497	11.670	17.745	3.197[b]	7.526	7.998	6.998	3.648[b]	—
Philippines	9.849	14.612	7.158	15.941	6.838[a]	5.805	2.815[b]	6.241	4.767[b]	8.068
L. Sundas	7.255	10.681	6.547	15.053	6.573	7.226	5.227	8.777	3.583[a]	6.003
Borneo	7.828	11.697	6.845	13.161	5.922	7.310	4.948	8.374	3.846[b]	4.506[b]
Java	11.006	15.036	9.540	16.695	3.456[a]	4.549	6.176	5.952	2.463[b]	4.129
Easter Is.	17.373	16.160	16.741	22.851	23.791	26.405	20.894	29.700	20.549	20.750
Hawaii	14.590	15.016	14.466	18.482	11.516	12.977	13.096	16.436	10.029	8.568
Marquesas	14.527	16.429	15.017	21.297	17.044	19.151	16.238	20.757	13.734	11.707
New Zealand	11.471	14.159	12.544	18.045	14.452	17.669	14.561	20.140	12.071	10.380
Tahiti	15.907	19.368	17.334	25.060	20.166	21.272	19.688	22.291	16.966	15.036
Guam	15.488	19.214	14.473	22.483	11.814	16.700	12.243	19.335	12.062	10.596
Caroline	14.436	20.372	16.602	27.907	13.582	17.040	15.836	18.510	12.526	12.232
Admiralty	16.721	19.472	15.062	24.727	11.859	14.629	10.901	15.909	11.180	8.953
Vanuatu	22.590	25.267	23.661	32.337	22.109	25.886	23.377	30.842	18.463	19.411
Fiji	16.395	18.136	19.170	26.621	19.138	22.027	18.619	23.700	17.034	13.858
New Britain	20.369	22.376	20.550	30.646	20.063	23.351	21.088	28.238	15.873	19.198
Sepik R.	21.043	25.955	22.500	34.855	17.406	21.644	20.025	22.685	16.063	15.216
Biak Is.	15.736	19.796	16.777	27.315	17.820	19.827	15.399	20.257	14.057	12.656
New Ireland	17.101	19.586	18.340	26.770	15.132	19.682	17.115	22.809	13.004	13.742
New South Wales	25.996	25.847	30.434	36.992	25.587	28.532	26.858	32.958	21.675	23.192
Queensland	25.032	26.205	28.591	35.347	23.062	26.990	25.034	31.146	21.513	21.922
Murray R.	33.308	34.062	38.016	45.695	31.811	37.623	37.186	42.412	27.779	29.745
Tasmania	27.613	28.118	31.217	34.584	28.583	29.350	28.861	36.991	24.428	25.598
N. Territory	28.728	30.981	31.792	41.996	25.423	30.805	29.154	32.792	23.116	23.833

TABLE 14.12 (Continued)

Group	PHL	LSU	BOR	JAV	EAS	HAW	MAR	NZ	TAH	GUA
Philippines	—									
L. Sundas	5.542[a]	—								
Borneo	6.736[a]	3.245[b]	—							
Java	5.870	4.070	5.179	—						
Easter Is.	21.920	15.665	16.432	24.042	—					
Hawaii	14.512	10.558	11.465	9.823	10.918	—				
Marquesas	18.151	12.671	12.520	17.009	8.710	6.870	—			
New Zealand	14.532	9.047	9.644	15.280	7.644	10.173	3.892	—		
Tahiti	22.398	14.154	16.282	17.619	11.051	9.198	4.429	9.071	—	
Guam	13.946	10.302	10.534	12.101	13.944	7.516	13.096	11.742	15.371	—
Caroline	16.578	7.798	9.730	15.531	10.784	15.403	10.312	6.602	10.373	13.679
Admiralty	12.710	8.095	9.261	10.923	19.778	15.485	12.188	9.499	14.676	19.426
Vanuatu	25.504	10.123	15.061	20.850	24.344	24.891	19.576	13.378	20.846	24.418
Fiji	22.197	8.461	10.926	16.603	14.016	15.664	12.250	9.481	12.577	14.679
New Britain	21.468	7.608	13.744	17.677	21.900	23.965	22.514	14.712	22.008	21.802
Sepik R.	20.173	8.452	13.849	16.825	21.635	23.384	19.731	13.173	18.603	24.866
Biak Is.	16.234	6.275	9.570	15.797	18.093	20.122	13.701	9.343	15.189	19.003
New Ireland	18.302	6.707	11.282	15.104	16.661	18.468	15.385	9.624	15.194	18.992
New South Wales	28.075	11.660	18.364	21.296	29.240	27.371	27.386	20.780	28.190	25.255
Queensland	26.743	11.792	16.500	22.298	24.621	25.774	25.450	18.711	27.590	22.673
Murray R.	38.076	18.215	23.830	29.462	34.221	33.824	33.114	25.861	33.940	30.522
Tasmania	32.145	17.550	21.225	28.308	36.716	31.343	32.292	25.079	38.670	33.715
N. Territory	30.028	12.622	18.872	24.071	27.788	29.124	27.465	20.565	28.032	26.602

(continued)

TABLE 14.12 *(Continued)*

Group	CAR	ADR	VAN	FIJ	NBR	SEP	BIK	NIR	NSW	QLD	MRB	TAS	NT
Caroline Is.	—												
Admiralty	9.105	—											
Vanuatu	10.530	13.262	—										
Fiji	5.097[b]	10.891	7.904	—									
New Britain	9.219	12.810	2.775[b]	8.478	—								
Sepik R.	6.767	8.856	7.385	8.989	6.959	—							
Biak Is.	5.824[a]	8.052	5.125	4.225[a]	5.925	4.986	—						
New Ireland	4.409[b]	8.622	4.654	5.638	3.401	4.325	4.657	—					
New South Wales	15.689	20.406	6.340	9.778	5.950	11.369	9.945	10.026	—				
Queensland	13.221	19.709	6.101	8.420	6.531	12.423	9.303	9.743	2.259	—			
Murray R.	19.946	27.830	7.794	13.717	7.789	17.175	14.589	14.319	2.861	3.520	—		
Tasmania	24.611	24.632	8.178	18.546	11.250	20.184	15.793	15.464	10.760	8.982	10.713	—	
N. Territory	13.015	19.460	6.251	9.431	5.306	9.123	8.763	8.702	3.264	3.001[a]	3.263[a]	13.229	—

All distances are significant at 1% level when variance ratios are tested unless otherwise indicated: [a] = Significant at 5% level; [b] = Not significant involving skeletal series of more restricted temporal or geographical boundaries for examining the internal as well as external factors which have influenced their biological structure.

With the recognition by bioarchaeologists of the importance of determining biological relatedness to contextualize issues pertaining to health, disease, nutrition, demography, and epidemiology in past populations, studies that apply multivariate statistical procedures to metric and nonmetric data are expected to increase in number. The use of multivariate statistical procedures for classificatory purposes will undoubtedly continue to find applications in the

relatively new field of forensic anthropology as well as issues involving repatriation claims and NAGPRA (Native American Graves Protection and Repatriation Act) legislation (see Walker, Chapter 1).

Finally, given the statistical and mathematical underpinnings of the method and the problems associated with interpreting the results of multivariate statistical analyses, physical anthropologists and skeletal biologists, especially those highly tutored in quantitative methods, are expected to continue to refine the methodological and theoretical concerns associated with these methods. It is anticipated that these endeavors will make

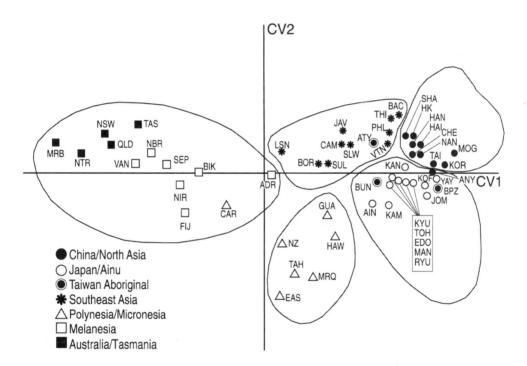

Figure 14.4 Plot of 53 male group means on the first two canonical variates using 29 cranial measurements. RYU = Ryukyu Islands, KAN = Kanto, TOH = Tohoku, KYU = Kyushu, EDO = Edo, KAM = Kamakura, KOF = Kofun, YAY = Yayoi, JOM = Jomon, AIN = Ainu, SHA = Shanghai, HAN = Hangzhou, NAN = Nanjing, CHE = Chengdu, HK = Hong Kong, ANY = Anyang, TAI = Taiwan Chinese, HAI = Hainan Island, MAN = Manchuria, KOR = Korea, MOG = Mongolia, ATY = Atayal, BUN = Bunun, BPZ = Babuza-Pazeh, VTN = Viet Nam, BAC = Bachuc, CAM = Cambodia & Laos, THI = Thailand, PHL = Philippines, LSN = Lesser Sundas, BOR = Borneo, SLW = Sulawesi, JAV = Java, SUL = Sulu, EAS = Easter Island, HAW = Hawaii, MRQ = Marquesas, NZ = New Zealand, TAH = Tahiti, GUA = Guam, CAR = Caroline Islands, ADR = Admiralty Islands, VAN = Vanuatu, FIJ = Fiji, NBR = New Britain, SEP = Sepik R., BIK = Biak Islands, NIR = New Ireland, MRB = Murray R., NSW = New South Wales, QLD = Queensland, NT = Northern Territory, TAS = Tasmania.

these methods more germane to analyzing and interpreting anthropological and skeletal biological data.

ACKNOWLEDGMENTS

Assistance with statistical analysis of the data presented in this chapter was provided by Ms. Rona Ikehara-Quebral. Ms. Billie Ikeda, of the Center for Instructional Support of the University of Hawai`i-Manoa, is responsible for the diagrams. Permission to examine the cranial series used in the present study has been previously acknowledged (Pietrusewsky, 1992, 1994, 1995; Pietrusewsky and Chang, 1996). Many thanks are also extended to Professor Keiichi Omoto and the International Research Center for Japanese Studies, Kyoto, where some of the results presented in this chapter were first presented in an international symposium organized by Omoto. Finally, my sincere thanks to Dr. Michele Toomay Douglas for reading and commenting on earlier versions of this chapter.

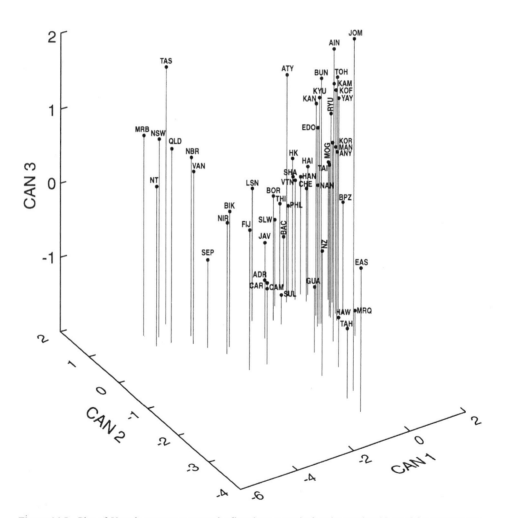

Figure 14.5 Plot of 53 male group means on the first three canonical variates using 29 cranial measurements (see Fig. 14.4 for explanation of abbreviations).

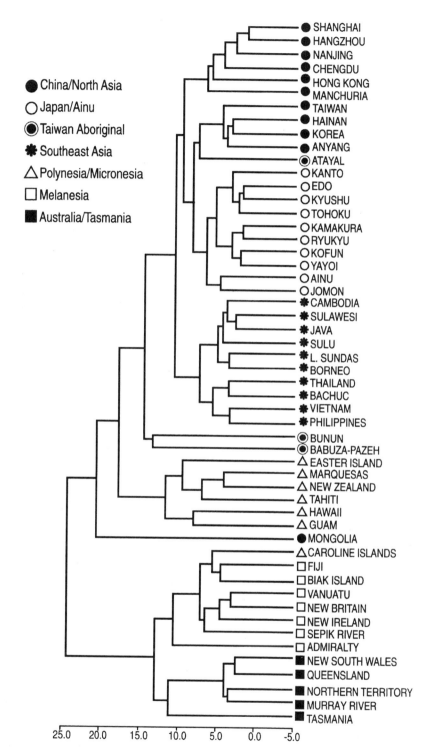

Figure 14.6 Diagram of relationship based on a cluster analysis (UPGMA) of Mahalanobis' generalized distances using 29 cranial measurements recorded in 53 male groups.

REFERENCES

Albrecht G. 1992. Assessing the affinities of fossils using canonical variates and generalized distances. Hum Evol 7:49–69.

Brace CL, Brace MC, Dodo Y, Leonard WR, Li Y-g, Shao X-q, Sangvichien S, Zhang Z-b. 1990. Micronesians, Asians, Thais and relations: a craniofacial and odontometric perspective. Micronesica Supplement 2:323–348.

Brace CL, Brace MC, Leonard WR. 1989. Reflections on the face of Japan: a multivariate craniofacial and odontometric perspective. Am J Phys Anthropol 78:93–113.

Brace CL, Hunt KD. 1990. A nonracial craniofacial perspective on human variation. (A)ustralia to (Z)uni. Am J Phys Anthropol 82:341–360.

Brace CL, Tracer DP. 1992. Craniofacial continuity and change. A comparison of late Pleistocene and recent Europe and Asia. In: Akazawa T, Aoki K, Kimura T, editors. The Evolution and Dispersal of Modern Humans in Asia. Tokyo: Hokusen-sha. pp. 439–471.

Bräuer G. 1988. Osteometrie. In: Knussmann R, editor. Anthropologie Handbuch der vergleichenden Biologie des Menschen Band 1. Stuttgart: Gustav Fischer Verlag. pp. 160–232.

Broca P. 1875. Instructions craniologiques et craniométriques. Mémoires de la Societé d'Anthropologie de Paris, Vol. 2, Ser. 2, pp. 1–204.

Brown P. 1996. The first modern East Asians?: Another look at Upper Cave 101. Liujiang and Minatogawa 1. In: Omoto K, editor. Interdisciplinary Perspectives on the Origins of the Japanese. International Symposium. Kyoto: International Research Center for Japanese Studies pp. 105–124 and 7 pages references.

Brown T. 1973. Morphology of the Australian Skull Studied by Multivariate Analysis. Australian Aboriginal Studies No. 49. Canberra: Australian Institute of Aboriginal Studies.

Buikstra JE, Frankenburg SR, Konigsberg LW. 1990. Skeletal biological distance studies in American physical anthropology: recent trends. Am J Phys Anthropol 82:1–7.

Buikstra JE, Ubelaker D, editors. 1994. Standards for Data Collection from Human Skeletal Remains. Arkansas Archaeological Survey Research Series 44. Fayetteville, Ark.: Arkansas Archaeological Survey.

Buranarugsa M, Leach F. 1993. Coordinate geometry of Moriori crania and comparisons with Maori. Man and Culture in Oceania 9:1–43.

Campbell NA. 1978. Multivariate analysis in biological anthropology: some further considerations. J Hum Evol 7:197–203.

Campbell NA. 1984. Some aspects of allocation and discrimination. In: Van Vark GN, Howells WW, editors. Multivariate Statistical Methods in Physical Anthropology. Dordrecht: D. Reidel Publishing Co. pp. 177–192.

Chernoff H. 1973. The use of faces to represent points in k-dimensional space graphically. J Am Stat Assoc 68:361–368.

Chernoff H. 1978. Graphical representation as a discipline. In: Wang PCC, editor. Graphical Representation of Multivariate Data. New York: Academic Press. pp. 1–11.

Corruccini RS. 1973. Size and shape in similarity coefficients based on metric characters. Am J Phys Anthropol 38:743–754.

Corruccini RS. 1975. Multivariate analysis in biological anthropology: some considerations. J Hum Evol 4:1–19.

Corruccini RS. 1987. Shape in morphometrics: comparative analyses. Am J Phys Anthropol 73:289–303.

Dean D. 1995. The analysis and collection of coordinate data in physical anthropology. In: Boaz NT, Wolfe LD, editors. Biological Anthropology. The State of the Art. Bend, Ore.: International Institute of Human Evolutionary Research. pp. 169–181.

Dixon WJ. 1990a. BMDP Statistical Software Manual. Vol. 1. Berkeley: University of California Press.

Dixon WJ. 1990b. BMDP Statistical Software Manual. Vol. 2. Berkeley: University of California Press.

Dixon WJ, Brown MB, editors. 1979. BMDP-79. Biomedical Computer Programs P-Series. Berkeley: University of California Press.

Dodo Y. 1986. Metrical and non-metrical analyses of Jomon crania from eastern Japan. In: Akazawa T, Aikens CM, editors. Prehistoric Hunter-Gatherers in Japan. University Museum Bulletin 27. Tokyo: University of Tokyo Press. pp. 137–161.

Dodo Y, Ishida H. 1990. Population history of Japan as viewed from cranial nonmetric variation. J Anthropol Soc Nippon 98:269–287.

Everitt BS, Dunn G. 1992. Applied Multivariate Data Analysis. New York: Oxford University Press.

Feldesman MR. 1997. Bridging the chasm: demystifying some statistical methods used in biological anthropology. In: Boas NT, Wolfe LD, editors. Biological Anthropology: The State of the Science. Bend, Ore.: International Institute for Evolutionary Research. pp. 73–99.

Fisher RA. 1936. The use of multiple measurements in taxonomic problems. Annals of Eugenics 7:179–188.

Giles E, Elliot O. 1962. Race identification from cranial measurements. J Forensic Sci 7:147–157.

Giles E, Elliot O. 1963. Sex determination by discriminant function. Am J Phys Anthropol 21:53–68.

Goldstein M, Dillion WR. 1978. Discrete Discriminant Analysis. New York: Oxford University Press.

Gower JC. 1966. Some distance properties of latent root and vector methods used in multivariate analysis. Biometrika 53:325–338.

Gower JC. 1967. A comparison of some methods of cluster analysis. Biometrics 23:623–637.

Gower JC. 1972. Measures of taxonomic distance and their analysis. In: Weiner JS, Huizinga J, editors. The Assessment of Population Affinities in Man. Oxford: Claredon Press. pp. 1–24.

Green MK. 1990. Prehistoric Cranial Variation in Papua New Guinea. Ph.D. Dissertation. The Australian National University, Canberra.

Hair JF, Anderson RE, Tatham RL, Black WC. 1998. Multivariate Data Analysis. 5th ed. Upper Saddle River, N.J.: Prentice Hall.

Hanihara K. 1985. Origins and affinities of Japanese as viewed from cranial measurements. In: Kirk R, Szathmary E, editors. Out of Asia. Peopling the Americas and the Pacific. Canberra: The Journal of Pacific History. pp. 105–112.

Hanihara K. 1991. Dual structure model for the population history of the Japanese. Japan Review. Bulletin of the International Center for Japanese Studies 2:1–33.

Hanihara K, Hanihara T, Koizumi K. 1993. The Jomon-Ainu and Pacific population groups. Japan Review. Bulletin of the International Center for Japanese Studies 4:7–25.

Hanihara T. 1993. Dental affinities among Polynesian and circum-Polynesian populations. Japan Review. Bulletin of the International Center for Japanese Studies 4:59–82.

Hanihara T. 1996. Comparison of cranialfacial features of major human groups. Am J Phys Anthropol 99:389–412.

Heathcote GM. 1986. Exploratory Human Craniometry of Recent Eskaleutian Regional Groups from the Western Arctic and Subartic of North America: A New Approach to Population Historical Reconstruction. British Archaeological Reports. International Series 301.

Heathcote GM. 1994. Population history reconstruction based on craniometry I. The backtracking approach and initial results. Hum Evol 9:97–119.

Hemphill BE. 1998. Biological affinities and adaptions of bronze age Bactrians III. An initial craniometric assessment. Am J Phys Anthropol 106:329–348.

Hotelling T. 1933. Analysis of a complex of statistical variables into principal components. J Ed Psych 24:417–441, 498–520.

Howells WW. 1957. The cranial vault: factors of size and shape. Am J Phys Anthropol 15:159–192.

Howells WW. 1966. The Jomon Population of Japan: A Study by Discriminant Analysis of Japanese and Ainu Crania. Cambridge: Papers of the Peabody Museum of Ethnology and Archaeology. Vol. 57:1–43.

Howells WW. 1969. The use of multivariate techniques in the study of skeletal populations. Am J Phys Anthropol 31:311–314.

Howells WW. 1972. Analysis of patterns of variation in crania of recent man. In: Tuttle R, editor. The Functional and Evolutionary Biology of Primates. Chicago: Aldine-Atherton Inc. pp. 123–151.

Howells WW. 1973. Cranial Variation in Man. Cambridge: Papers of the Peabody Museum of Archaeology and Ethnology. Vol. 67.

Howells WW. 1984. Introduction. In: Van Vark GN, Howells WW, editors. Multivariate Methods in Physical Anthropology. Dordrecht: D. Reidel Publishing Co. pp. 1–11.

Howells WW. 1986. Physical anthropology of the prehistoric Japanese. In: Pearson RJ, editor. Windows on the Japanese Past. Ann Arbor:

Michigan Center for Japanese Studies. pp. 85–99.

Howells WW. 1989. Skull Shapes and the Map. Craniometric Analyses in the Dispersion of Modern *Homo.* Cambridge: Papers of the Peabody Museum of Archaeology and Ethnology. Vol. 79.

Howells WW. 1995. Who's Who in Skulls. Ethnic Identification of Crania from Measurements. Cambridge: Papers of the Peabody Museum of Archaeology and Ethnology. Vol. 82.

Jantz RL. 1973. Microevolutionary change in Arikara crania: a multivariate analysis. Am J Phys Anthropol 38:15–26.

Konigsberg LW, Blangero J. 1993. Multivariate quantitative genetic simulations in anthropology with an example from the South Pacific. Hum Biol 65:897–915.

Konigsberg LW, Buikstra JE. 1995. Regional approaches to the investigation of past human biocultural structure. In: Beck LA, editor. Regional Approaches to Mortuary Analysis. New York: Plenum Press. pp. 191–219.

Konigsberg LW, Ousley SD. 1995. Multivariate quantitative genetics of anthropometric traits from the Boas data. Hum Biol. 67:481–498.

Kowalski CJ. 1972. A commentary on the use of multivariate statistical methods in anthropometric research. Am J Phys Anthropol 36:119–132.

Kozintsev AG. 1990. Ainu, Japanese, their ancestors and neighbours: cranioscopic data. J Anthropol Soc Nippon 97:493–512.

Lachenbruch PA, Goldstein M. 1979. Discriminant analysis. Biometrics 35:69–85.

Lahr MM. 1996. The Evolution of Modern Human Diversity: A Study of Cranial Variation. Cambridge: Cambridge University Press.

Larsen CS. 1997. Bioarchaeology: Interpreting Behavior for the Human Skeleton. Cambridge: Cambridge University Press.

Mahalanobis PC. 1930. On tests and measures of group divergence. Journal and Proceedings of the Asiatic Society of Bengal 26:541–588.

Mahalanobis PC. 1936. On the generalized distance in statistics. Proceedings of the National Institute of Sciences, Calcutta. 12:49–55.

Mahalanobis PC, Majumdar DN, Rao CR. 1949. Anthropometric survey of the United Provinces, 1941: a statistical study. Sankhya 9:89–324.

Marks GC, Habicht J-P, Mueller WH. 1989. Reliability, dependability, and precision of anthropometric measurements. Am J Epidemiol 130:578–587.

Martin R, Saller K. 1957. Lehrbuch der Anthropologie. Revised 3rd ed. Stuttgart: Gustav Fischer Verlag.

Matsumura H. 1989. Geographical variation of dental measurements in the Jomon population. J Anthropol Soc Nippon 97:493–512.

McHenry HM, Corruccini RS. 1975. Multivariate analysis of early hominid pelvic bones. Am J Phys Anthropol 43:263–270.

Mizoguchi Y. 1986. Contributions of prehistoric Far East populations to the population of modern Japan: a Q-mode path analysis based on cranial measurements. In: Akazawa T, Aikens CM, editors. Prehistoric Hunters-Gatherers in Japan. The University Museum Bulletin No. 27. Tokyo: University of Tokyo. pp. 107–136.

Moore-Jansen PM, Ousley DS, Jantz RL. 1994. Data Collection Procedures for Forensic Skeletal Material. 3rd ed. Report of Investigation No. 48. Knoxville: The Univeristy of Tennessee.

Omoto K, Hirai M, Harihara S, Misawa S, Washio K, Tokunaga K, Saitou N, Yamazaki K, Du R, Hao L, Yuan Y, Xu J, Jin F, Hu J, Wei X, Li S, Zhao H, Zhang Z, Niu K, Du C, Liu B. 1996. Population genetic studies on national minorities in China. In: Akazawa T, Szathmary EJE, editors. Prehistoric Mongoloid Dispersals. New York: Oxford University Press. pp. 137–145.

Omoto K, Saitou N. 1997. Genetic origins of the Japanese: a partial support of the dual structure hypothesis. Am J Phys Anthropol 102:437–446.

Ossenberg N. 1986. Isolate conservatism and hybridization in the population history of Japan. The evidence of nonmetric cranial traits. In: Akazawa T, Aikens CM, editors. Prehistoric Hunters-Gatherers in Japan. The University Museum Bulletin No. 27. Tokyo: University of Tokyo Press. pp. 199–215.

Ossenberg N. 1992. Microevolutionary parallels in the population history of Japan and aboriginal North America: the evidence of cranial nonmetric traits. In: Hanihara K, editor. International Symposium on Japanese as a Member of the Asian and Pacific Populations. Kyoto: International Research Center for Japanese Studies. International Symposium 4. pp. 64–77.

Ousley SD, Jantz RL. 1996. FORDISC 2.0: Personal Computer Forensic Discriminant Functions. Knoxville: The University of Tennessee.

Pearson K. 1926. On the coefficient of racial likeness. Biometrika 18:105–117.

Penrose LS. 1947. Some notes on discrimination. Annals of Eugenics 13:288–337.

Penrose LS. 1954. Distance, size, and shape. Annals of Eugenics 18:337–343.

Pietrusewsky M. 1990. Craniofacial variation in Australasian and Pacific populations. Am J Phys Anthropol 82:319–340.

Pietrusewsky M. 1992. Japan, Asia and the Pacific: a multivariate craniometric investigation. In: Hanihara K, editor. International Symposium on Japanese as a Member of the Asian and Pacific Populations. Kyoto: International Research Center for Japanese Studies. International Symposium 4. pp. 9–52.

Pietrusewsky M. 1994. Pacific-Asian relationships: a physical anthropological perspective. Oceanic Linguistics 332:407–429.

Pietrusewsky M. 1995. Taiwan Aboriginals, Asians, and Pacific Islanders: a multivariate investigation of skulls. In: P Li J-k, Tsang C-h, Huang Y-k, Ho D-a, Tseng C-y, editors. Austronesian Studies Relating to Taiwan. Taipei: Academia Sinica. Vol. 3. Taiwan, Republic of China: Symposium Series of the Institute of History and Philology. pp. 295–351.

Pietrusewsky M. 1997. The people of Ban Chiang: an early Bronze-Age site in northeast Thailand. Bulletin of the Indo-Pacific Prehistory Association. 16:119–148.

Pietrusewsky M. 1996. Multivariate craniometric investigations of Japanese, Asian, and Pacific Islanders. In: Omoto K, editor. Interdisciplinary Perspectives on the Origins of the Japanese. International Symposium. Kyoto: International Research Center for Japanese Studies, pp. 65–104.

Pietrusewsky M, Chang C-f. 1996. Craniometric comparisons of Taiwan aboriginals and peoples of the Pacific-Asia Region. Paper presented during the Symposium on Cultural as well as Biological Affinities among the Indigenous Peoples of Taiwan and Southeast Asia, Academia Sinica, Taipei, Taiwan, R.O.C., May 21–23, 1996.

Pietrusewsky M, Li Y, Shao X, Quyen NG. 1992. Modern and near modern populations of Asia and the Pacific: a multivariate craniometric interpretation. In: Akazawa T, Aoki K, Kimura T, editors. The Evolution and Dispersal of Modern Humans in Asia. Tokyo: Hokusen-sha. pp. 531–558.

Rao CR. 1948. The utilization of multiple measurements in problems of biological classification. Journal of the Royal Statistical Society B 10: 159–193.

Rao CR. 1952. Advanced Statistical Methods in Biomedical Research. New York: John Wiley.

Read DW. 1990. From multivariate to qualitative measurement: representation of shape. Hum Evol 5:417–429.

Relethford JH. 1994. Craniometric variation among modern human populations. Am J Phys Anthropol 95:53–62.

Relethford JH, Lees FC. 1982. The use of quantitative traits in the study of human population structure. Y Phys Anthropol 25:113–132.

Reyment DW. 1990. Reification of classical multivariate statistical analysis in morphometry. In: Rohlf FJ, Bookstein FL, editors. Proceedings of the Michigan Morphometrics Workshop. Special Publication No. 2. Ann Arbor: The University of Michigan Museum of Zoology. pp. 123–146.

Reyment RA, Blackith RE, Campbell NA. 1984. Multivariate Morphometrics, 2nd ed. New York: Academic Press.

Rhoads JG. 1984. Improving the sensibility, specificity, and appositeness of morphometric analyses. In: Van Vark GN, Howells WW, editors. Mulitvariate Methods in Physical Anthropology. Dordrecht: D. Reidel Publishing Co. pp. 247–259.

Richstmeier JT, Cheverud JM, Lele S. 1992. Advances in anthropological morphometrics. Ann Rev Anthropol 21:283–305.

Rightmire GP. 1970. Bushman, Hottentot and South African Negro crania studied by distance and discrimination. Am J Phys Anthropol 33:169–196.

Rightmire GP. 1972. Cranial measurements and discrete traits compared in distance studies of African Negro skulls. Hum Biol 44:263–276.

Rightmire GP. 1976. Multidimensional scaling and the analysis of human biological diversity in subSaharan Africa. Am J Phys Anthropol 44: 445–452.

Rightmire GP. 1979. Implications of Border Cave skeletal remains for Later Pleistocene human evolution. Current Anthropology 20:23–35.

Rohlf FJ. 1990. Morphometrics. Annual Review of Ecological Systematics 21:299–316.

Rohlf FJ. 1993. NTSYS-pc. Numerical Taxonomy and Multivariate Analysis System. Version 1.80. Setauket, N.Y.: Exeter Software.

Rohlf FJ, Bookstein, FL, editors. 1990. Proceedings of the Michigan Morphometrics Workshop. Special Publication No. 2. Ann Arbor: The University of Michigan Museum of Zoology.

Saitou N, Imanishi T. 1989. Relative efficiencies of the Fitch-Margoliash, maximum parsimony, maximum-likelihood, minimum-evolution, and neighboring-joining methods of phylogenetic tree construction in obtaining the correct tree. Mol Biol Evol 6:514–525.

Saitou N, Nei M. 1987. The neighbor-joining method: a new method for reconstructing phylogenetic trees. Mol Biol Evol 4:408–425.

Saitou N, Tokunaga K, Omoto K. 1991. Genetic affinities of human populations. In: Roberts DF, Fujiki N, Torizuka K, editors. Isolation, Migration and Health. Cambridge: Cambridge University Press. pp. 118–129.

SAS Institute, Inc. 1990a. User's Guide: Basics, Version 6. Cary, N.C.: SAS Institute, Inc.

SAS Institute, Inc. 1990b. User's Guide: Statistics, Version 6. Cary, N.C.: SAS Institute, Inc.

Sciulli PW. 1990. Cranial metric and discrete trait variation and biological differentiation in the terminal Late Archaic of Ohio: the Duff site cemetery. Am J Phys Anthropol 82:19–29.

Sjøvold T. 1984. A report on the heritability of some cranial measurements and non-metric traits. In: Van Vark GN, Howells WW, editors. Multivariate Statistics in Physical Anthropology. Dordrecht: D. Reidel Publishing Co. pp. 223–246.

Sneath PHA, Sokal RR. 1973. Numerical Taxonomy. San Francisco: Freeman.

Sokal RR, Uytterschaut H, Rösing FW, Schwidetzky I. 1987. A classification of European skulls from three time periods. Am J Phys Anthropol 74:1–20.

SPSS, Inc. 1990a. SPSS User's Guide, 4th ed. Chicago: SPSS, Inc.

SPSS, Inc. 1990b. SPSS Advanced Statistics Guide, 4th ed. Chicago: SPSS, Inc.

SPSS, Inc. 1992. SPSS/PC+ Version 6.0 Chicago: SPSS, Inc.

SPSS, Inc. 1993. SPSS for Windows, Version 6.0. Chicago: SPSS, Inc.

SYSTAT, Inc. 1992a. SYSTAT for DOS. Evanston, Ill.: SYSTAT, Inc.

SYSTAT, Inc. 1992b. SYSTAT for Windows, Version 5. Evanston, Ill.: SYSTAT, Inc.

Talbot PA, Mulhall H. 1962. The Physical Anthropology of Southern Nigeria. A Biometric Study in Statistical Method. Cambridge: Cambridge University Press.

Tatsuoka MM. 1970. Discriminant Analysis. Champaign: Illinois Institute of Personality and Ability Testing.

Tatsuoka MM. 1971. Multivariate Analysis: Techniques for Educational and Psychological Research. New York: John Wiley & Sons.

Torgerson WS. 1952. Multidimensional scaling I: Theory and method. Psychometrika 17:401–419.

Turner CG II. 1976. Dental evidence on the origin of the Ainu and Japanese. Science 193:911–913.

Turner CG II. 1987. Late Prehistoric and Holocene population history of East Asia based on dental variation. Am J Phys Anthropol 73:305–321.

Turner CG II. 1990. Major features of sundadonty and sinodonty including suggestions about East Asian microevolution, population history, and late Pleistocene relationships with Australian Aborigines. Am J Phys Anthropol 82:295–317.

Utermhole CJ, Zegura SL. 1982. Intra- and interobserver error in craniometry: a cautionary tale. Am J Phys Anthropol 57:303–310.

Utermhole CJ, Zegura SL, Heathcote GM. 1983. Multiple observers, humidity, and the choice of precision statistics: factors influencing craniometric data quality. Am J Phys Anthropol 61:85–95.

Vallois HV. 1965. Anthropometric techniques. Current Anthropology 6:127–143.

Van der Sluis DM, Schaafsma W, Ambergen AW. 1985. POSCON User Manual. Groningen, Netherlands: University of Groningen.

Van Vark GN. 1976. A critical evaluation of the application of multivariate statistical methods to the study of human populations from their skeletal remains. Homo 27:94–114.

Van Vark GN. 1985. Multivariate analysis in physical anthropology. In: Krishnaiah PR, editor. Multivariate Analysis VI. New York: Elsevier Science Publishing Co. pp. 599–611.

Van Vark GN. 1995. The study of hominid skeletal remains by means of statistical methods. In: Boaz NT, Wolfe LD, editors. Biological Anthropology: The State of the Science. Bend, Ore.: International Institute for Evolutionary Research. pp. 71–90.

Van Vark GN, Howells WW, editors. 1984. Multivariate Statistics in Physical Anthropology. Dordrecht: D. Reidel Publishing Co.

Van Vark GN, Pasveer JM. 1994. Mathematical multivariate analysis in physical anthropology, exemplified by the sex-diagnosis of archaeological skeletal series of *Homo sapiens sapiens*. In: Di Bacco M, Pacciani E, Borgognini Tarli S, editors. Statistical Tools in Human Biology. Singapore: World Scientific Publishing Co. pp. 231–254.

Van Vark GN, Schaafsma W. 1992. Advances in the quantitative analysis of skeletal morphology. In: Saunders SR, Katzenberg MA, editors. Skeletal Biology of Past Peoples: Research Methods. New York: Wiley-Liss. pp. 225–257.

Van Vark GN, van der Sman PGM. 1982. New discrimination and classification techniques in anthropological practice. Z Morphol Anthropol 73:21–36.

Williams-Blangero J, Blangero S, Towne B. 1990. Quantitative traits and populations structure: introduction. Hum Biol 62:1–4.

Willis CJ. 1999. 'The Dome of Thought, The Palace of the Soul' Interpreting the craniological morphology of ancient and near-contemporary Australian Aborigines. Ph.D. Dissertation. The Australian National University, Canberra.

Wilmink FW, Uytterschaut HT. 1984. Cluster analysis, history, theory and applications. In: Van Vark GN, Howells WW, editors. Multivariate Statistical Methods in Physical Anthropology. Dordrecht: D. Reidel Publishing Co. pp. 135–175.

Wilson SR. 1984. Towards an understanding of data in physical anthropology. In: Van Vark GN, Howells WW, editors. Multivariate Statistics in Physical Anthropology. Dordrecht: D. Reidel Co. pp. 261–282.

Wright RVS. 1992a. Identifying the origin of a human cranium: computerized assistance by CRANID. Sydney: University of Sydney.

Wright RVS. 1992b. Correlation between cranial form and geography in *Homo sapiens*: CRANID. A computer program for forensic and other applications. Archaeology in Oceania 273:128–134.

Yamaguchi B. 1982. A review of the osteological characteristics of the Jomon population in prehistoric Japan. J Anthropol Soc Nippon 90(suppl):77–90.

Yamaguchi B. 1985. The incidence of minor nonmetric cranial variants in the protohistoric human remains from eastern Japan. Bulletin of the National Science Museum, Tokyo, Series D 11:13–24.

Yamaguchi B. 1992. Skeletal morphology of the Jomon people. In: Hanihara K, editor. International Symposium on Japanese as a Member of the Asian and Pacific Populations. Kyoto: International Research Center for Japanese Studies. International Symposium 4. pp. 52–63.

CHAPTER 15

BUILDING THE BASES FOR PALEODEMOGRAPHIC ANALYSIS: ADULT AGE DETERMINATION

MARY JACKES

INTRODUCTION

In the 1970s, most North American osteologists accepted without question that methods of adult age assessment provided reasonably accurate estimates of the ages at death of human skeletons. We not only discussed rates of age-dependent pathology and trauma believing that our conclusions had some meaning, we undertook demographic analyses in the belief that we could make realistic statements about the structure of past societies. When Bocquet-Appel and Masset published their ideas in English in 1982, questioning methods of adult age assessment, they provided a lifeline to people who were struggling with data that did not make sense (Jackes, 1988). But there was a very strong reaction that received much attention (e.g., Van Gerven and Armelagos, 1983), so that Wood and colleagues could write in 1992 that the rebuttals had lain to rest the concerns raised by Bocquet-Appel and Masset.

Since 1982, there has been a shift in approach to adult assessment for the reconstruction of archaeological populations. Many ideas rejected in the early 1980s (Jackes, n.d.), are now widely accepted and can be restated word for word (Jackes, 1992). Where researchers

commonly dismissed adult age assessment as requiring little comment beyond the fact that "standard" methods were used, it is now standard to specify methods and acknowledge that there may be limitations to data (e.g., Storey, 1985; Storey and Hirth, 1997).

A general introduction to skeletal biology can now state: "At present, the lack of a wholly satisfactory technique for estimating age at death in adult skeletons from archaeological sites is one of the most thorny problems facing human osteoarchaeology" (Mays, 1998:50). Crubézy and Murail (1998:72) write: "The determination of the age at death of adults is at present the major problem within the whole field of anthropology" [*my translation*]. No longer do we hold to the simple acceptance that adult age assessment requires only an application of techniques summarized in standard laboratory books—Krogman (1962), Bass (1995), Brothwell (1981), Ubelaker (1989), Anderson (1969), the work of Acsádi and Nemeskéri (1970, and as summarized by members of the Workshop of European Anthropologists or WEA, 1980)—with choice of technique determined by mother tongue and geographical location rather than research considerations. The trend illustrated by, for example, Masset (1989) and Rose and Ungar (1998) of writing historical introductions to discussions on specific methods of age assessment, is a clear indication that adult age assessment is

Biological Anthropology of the Human Skeleton, Edited by M. Anne Katzenberg and Shelley R. Saunders.
ISBN 0-471-31616-4   Copyright © 2000 by Wiley-Liss, Inc.

an evolving and interesting field of study, not simply the routine application of standard methods.

Maples (1989) considered adult age assessment to be more an art than a science, and skeletal biologists may well practice that art with skill. But the description of an archaeological sample of skeletons is but one step in interpretation. The next step requires comparisons with other samples from other places and other time periods, analyzed by other researchers. We need to know how data are collected and what they are based on. It is clear that: (1) similar samples analyzed using different methods provide different results; and (2) different samples analyzed using the same methods provide similar results (e.g., Jackes, 1985, 1992).

We may assume that in the past skeletal biologists relied on their experience and their intuition: they applied their "art." But comparison requires systematization and standardization, and further effort at systematization has begun to lead to deeper questioning of the likelihood that we can achieve accurate adult age estimates for large samples of archaeological skeletons.

Meindl and Russell (1998:388) consider that "unknown age distributions could be approximated quite well by . . . multifactorial methods as long as actual adult life expectancy is low, that is, e_{15} is less than about 30 years," by which they mean that a 15 year old can expect to die at 45. Although many aspects of this approach have been criticized (as summarized in their review), the work of Meindl and colleagues has been a motivating force. Their insistence on examining indepth the age assessment methods accepted at the time of the analysis of the Libben site, their detailed publications, and their questioning of age estimation by "handbook-styled . . . comparison-matching a specimen to a series of discrete archetypes . . . (illustrating) mean age stages" (Meindl et al., 1990:356), have all contributed to the change in attitudes to adult age assessment.

The low adult life expectancy specified by Meindl and Russell (1998:388) seems to imply, as did Van Gerven and Armelagos (1983), that nearly everyone died by 50 and so it does not matter that we are unable to age older adults. But were there really no "old folks" (Weiss, 1973; Jackes and Lubell, 1985). Does it matter that we cannot age them? If we cannot rely on our ability to give accurate ages to all adults in a sample, then we must employ techniques that are not standard in demographic studies in order to examine basic demographic parameters such as fertility rates (Jackes, 1994). But, and this is more significant, we cannot get a clear idea of clear idea of incidences of caries and osteoarthritis, and cannot adequately study rates of cortical thinning.

There can be little doubt that people lived into old age—even in times of conflict, disease and famine—despite the fact that standard palaeodemographic methods would give no indication of this (Jackes, in press). Figure 15.1 (data from Russell, 1948) shows that, during the worst of the medieval period when the plague struck England again and again, the average age at death of males over 15 was around 47 years. In better times, males would live to an average age of 54. For married males of the aristocracy born before 1700 (and the seventeenth century condition of life was poor as a result of conflict and epidemics in England), the average age at death was 55 years (n = 1644): 60% of these men lived beyond age 50 (Westendorp and Kirkwood, 1998). Russell (1985:60–61) shows that, with variations with time and place over the first 1500 years A.D. across Europe and North Africa, quite a number of those who reached age 20 could expect to survive beyond 60. Ten percent survival beyond age 60 would be a conservative estimate, since reliable estimates of over a quarter, even a third, exist. As long ago as 1978, Sjøvold wrote of the "remarkable number of deaths between 70 and 80 years of age" that were recorded in an Austrian village in the 250 years prior to 1852. We have long known that it was possible for people to live to a great age prior to the twentieth century.

Mean age at death +/- 1sd
English males age 15 + (n = 2949)

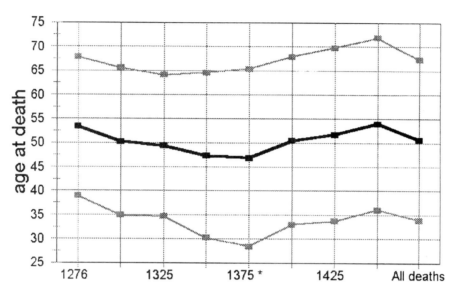

Figure 15.1 The mean age at death (±1 SD) for English medieval males who survived to age 15. The x axis records those born before 1276, 1276 to 1300, 1301 to 1325, 1323 to 1348, 1348 to 1375* (the period of the Black Death and its aftermath), 1376 to 1400, 1401 to 1425, and 1426 to 1450, and, finally, all deaths. (Data from Russell, 1948.)

Current research emphasizes both the genetic and nongenetic aspects of longevity (Vaupel et al., 1998). There must be a selection against frailty early in life, but not against "late-acting deleterious genes" (Promislow, 1998), so we cannot assume that those who survive early adverse circumstances must necessarily live into old age. On the other hand, there is no reason to maintain that archaeological mortality is by definition different from more recent mortality. In fact, Montagu (1994) maintains that those born before 100 B.C. had life spans equal to any but those recorded in the last 50 years.

The focus of our questions about adult age is slowly changing. We are beginning to accept that adults did live longer than osteologists have previously recognized and to accept that our methods of age assessment must be flawed. Many years after Howell (1982) first pointed out the inherent improbability of the Libben village composition, Harpending (1997:92)

wrote the following: "We must dismiss these [archaeological age distributions] as artifacts of the formation of the collection or of the aging procedures, else follow Lovejoy and colleagues and posit that human biology in the Precolumbian New World was different in kind from the biology of the rest of our species."

Skeletal biologists are now willing to question the accuracy of their age estimates for adult akeletons. It is not hard to understand why the trek to this point has been so drawn-out and hard-fought: questioning and drawing attention to the subjective, the intuitive basis of our age assessments seems to threaten the validity of much of our work in skeletal biology over many years.

Molleson (1995) has wondered whether those who die as young adults have "old bones," and those who die as old adults have "young bones," calling into question the uniformity of age changes even within one population. We can only hope that our skeletal samples are large enough, and the causes of mortality diverse enough, to provide us with a general picture that is acceptably close to reality in the study of paleodemography. The implications of this question for skeletal biology in general are beyond the scope of this chapter, but paleodemographers must be very wary of drawing generalizations from small, limited, possibly biased samples precisely because of possible variability

Variability within a population in the expression of age changes is a pressing concern if some methods of age assessment are more suitable for "older" individuals or for skeletal samples that are "older" (e.g. Molleson, 1995). Figure 15.2 (data from Galera et al., 1998) demonstrates that inaccuracy would be reduced if two methods of cranial suture assessment

could be used, one for younger, and another for older, adults. Meindl and Russell (1998:389) proposed that young and middle-aged adults be given ages "in a general way, such as the subjective estimation of clinical age," while different methods be applied to "those skeletons determined to be older than 40 years . . . [by] dental attrition and especially from the auricular surface." Aiello and Molleson (1993) suggest that the best compromise is to use the Todd/ Brooks or the McKern/Stewart/Gilbert pubic symphysis methods for those under 45 years of age, and the Acsádi/Nemeskéri technique for those over 45.

Meindl and Russell (1998) do not discuss the basic problem: while we may be able to identify someone in their early twenties, we do not know if a skeleton is from a fairly young, middle-aged or old adult. If we rely on

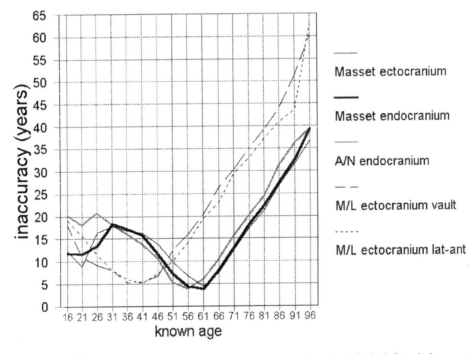

Figure 15.2 Differences among methods of analysis for cranial suture closure in individuals from the known age Terry Collection. Deviation of assessed age from real age is expressed as inaccuracy in years. The lines describe differences among the methods of three sets of researchers, based on internal or external suture closure: Masset, Acsádi and Nemeskéri (A/N), and Meindl and Lovejoy (M/L), who use both external vault closure with external closure in the lateral anterior portion of the cranium. The Masset and A/N methods give nearly identical results, the M/L results are different, but internally consistent. (Data from Galera et al., 1988.)

age-dependent skeletal changes to place people into age categories, and then analyse those skeletal changes to show the differences in the population as it aged, we are going in circles. Aiello and Molleson (1993) have suggested that initial sorting be done using bone histology, but there are acknowledged difficulties inherent in this method which will be discussed below.

Degenerative joint changes have been used as an adjunct to age assessment (e.g., by Kvaal et al., 1994), but this may well be invalid. Milner and Smith (1990) state that "The ages assigned to adult skeletons were generally consistent with subjective assessments based on the extent of dental attrition and arthritic lipping of the vertebrae, especially in the lumbar region, and of major joints." These authors are to be congratulated for stating openly that subjective assessments do enter into adult age estimation techniques. But we need to recognize that there are limitations: Molleson and Cox (1993:178) have shown that the correlation coefficient for real age and lumbar vertebral osteophytosis is .34 in females and .39 in males (see Jackes, 1977, for one explanation of this low correlation).

A skeptical attitude is now the norm, and the change in attitude has been quite revolutionary. In 1985, Buikstra and Konigsberg stated that adult age could be determined and proposed the value 30+/5+ years (used by Coale and Demeny, 1966) as a substitute for the paleodemographic estimator suggested by Bocquet-Appel and Masset (1977). Later amended by Konigsberg and colleagues (1989), the original statement of Buikstra and Konigsberg has remained in the literature as a frequently cited rebuttal of criticisms of paleodemography (e.g., Lanphear, 1989; Wood et al., 1992). It is clear that Konigsberg no longer supports his earlier ideas. Konigsberg and Frankenberg (1994:95), say that determining the sex of an adult "is not particularly problematic," but that "determination of age-at-death is an entirely different matter." In their wide-ranging summary of statistical approaches to paleodemography, these authors argue for the use of further statistical techniques to overcome the intransigent problems of paledemography

The question of adult age has relevance far beyond the problem of paleodemography. If age at death cannot be determined, then we can make no completely valid statements about any human characteristics that are subject to age-dependent changes (see, e.g., Caselitz, 1998, for a discussion of caries rates based on assumptions about archaeological life spans). That would certainly reduce the field of enquiry of skeletal biology to a very narrow focus. Nevertheless, it is legitimate to emphasize the importance of accurate adult age estimation to paleodemography. Paleodemography has three basic problems: (1) the accurate distribution of skeletons over the adult years, (2) the recognition of sample bias, and (3) the identification of population increase or decrease. Once these basics are dealt with, paleodemography can claim a place in skeletal biology. Therefore, we must enquire whether mathematical solutions will allow us to gain some reasonable approximation of the underlying adult age distribution of an archaeological sample, and to support Konigsberg and Frankenberg (1992) in saying that the time has come to stop fussing about the accuracy of age assessment techniques.

STATISTICAL APPROACHES

The idea that statistical techniques will solve a basic problem of paleodemography must be examined in some detail. Rather than discuss the techniques in a separate section, however, their value is tested here while examining methods of age assessment. Earlier concerns—mean age at death or life expectancy at birth, survivorship, prediction by linear regression analysis, probability distribution over 95% confidence limits (CL) of the mean age per age indicator stage—have been examined in Jackes (1992).

Konigsberg and co-authors (1997) discuss prediction of age by regression, but suggest that no method using regression is efficient.

Calibration of age by regression, with emphasis on multifactorial indicators, has been discussed by Lucy and colleagues (1995, 1996) and Aykroyd and colleagues (1999). These authors come to the conclusion that Bayesian approaches are worthy of more investigation. Here most emphasis will be given to Bayesian and iterative proportional fitting techniques for estimating age at death distributions (Bocquet-Appel and Masset, 1996; Konigsberg and Frankenberg, 1992), and to demonstrating how they function when applied to several methods of age assessment and known age samples.

The methods are illustrated for situations where reference population stage age data are available or can be reconstructed, so that the matrices can be used to calculate the prior probabilities. In other words, where the data used in the development of a method of age assessment have been published in detail, we can use those data to form a matrix. The matrix allows us to know how many individuals there are in each age category within the reference population who exhibit a particular stage of an age indicator. The basic idea is simple. For iterative proportional fitting, the cell frequency is divided by the total for that age category in order to give the probability that an individual with an indicator at a particular stage will fall into that age category (this probability is known as the "prior probability"). These probabilities are then used and multiplied by the stage distribution of the target sample in order to arrive at an estimate of the age distribution (the "target" always refers to the sample for which an age distribution is sought, while "reference" indicates the sample of known age individuals from which the prior probabilities are derived). Next, the operation is repeated (iterated). Experimentally, one example has been iterated 1165 times using femoral trabecular data from Bocquet-Appel and Bacro (1997) and stability is not reached. Thus, the program used here (written by N.G. Prasad), requires the setting of a tolerance level (e.g., 0.01 or 0.001) that limits the iterations at the point at which there is no change above the tolerance limit between one iteration and the next.

What is called Bayesian here could be iterated in the same way (but only the first iteration has been provided here). The prior probabilities are based on the cell frequency divided by the total for that stage (see the Appendix for an example). The probabilities provided by Masset (1989) for cranial sutures are no doubt of this type. The "proportional method" proposed by Boldsen (1988) should not be confused with the method referred to above as proportional fitting. Boldsen's method is a technique of smoothing adult age distributions: each individual is fractionally distributed across the entire assigned age range. It results in an age distribution similar to that given by the 95% confidence limits.

Another suggestion, hazard analysis (see for example Wood et al., 1992), is mentioned briefly. The hazard rate is, in fact, the m column (age-specific mortality) of a life table, and as such is highly correlated with the q column (probability of death within a certain age category). The m,q correlation coefficient rounds to .999 for the known age Christ Church, Spitalfields, London adults aged by three and four skeletal elements (Molleson and Cox, 1993), and for the assessed age distribution $r = .985$. Probability of death (q) has been used fairly consistently in paleodemography for the last decade and more (Jackes, 1992).

The hazard rate may be useful because it can be expressed plus and minus its standard error (SE, easily calculated using the Survival program in SPSS). As an example, we can use the people excavated from the church crypt in Spitalfields, London (Molleson and Cox, 1993) and reconstruct the real and assessed ages for 166 individuals who were aged by three or four skeletal elements. Figure 15.3 shows the Spitalfields known age adult distribution. The $\pm$SE hazard rate range for the real ages, calculated under the assumption that the population is stationary, is shown by the heavy lines. This range is so broad for the last 55 years of the distribution that it encompasses the m rates of up to $r = \pm.15$. The r here refers to the rate of natural increase, and the dashed lines show the range encompassed by the calculations based on the assumption of either population increase or decrease of 1.5%. What is clear is that the assessed age-at-death distribution, shown in solid thin lines, being inaccurate, cannot be adjusted by using hazard rates, or ranges derived from estimates of rates of natural increase. With the Spitalfields sample, the method of adult age assessment determines the distribution of assessed ages at death, and adjustments do not alter the basic form of the curve, which lies within the known age error range only at age 40 and between ages 55 and 60. Adjustments derived from estimates of rates of population increase or decrease do not overcome the basic inaccuracy of the estimated age distribution.

We can test the efficacy of age indicators only through analyses of known age samples.

Nevertheless, even if we were able to make a decision on the basis of work on known age samples, we still do not have an understanding of whether a method works better with one population rather than another. Bocquet-Appel (1986) and Masset (1976) have stated that a method will work best for a population with an age distribution similar to that of the original population, the "reference" sample around which the method was originally formulated. Thus, Molleson emphasizes (e.g., 1995) that the Spitalfields mean adult age at death is perhaps accurately estimated using the Acsádi and Nemeskéri complex method because the "reference" and "target" populations (the original sample used by Ascádi and Nemeskéri in developing their method and the Spitalfields sample to be given estimated ages) have the

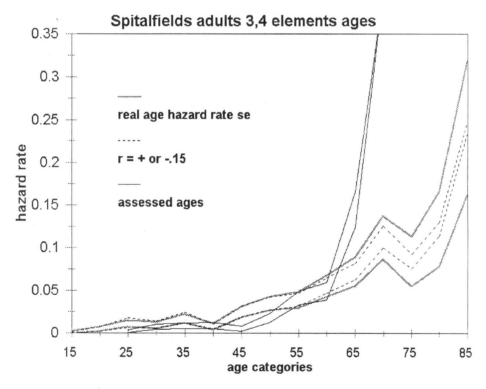

Figure 15.3   The hazard rate plus and minus its standard error for the best preserved Spitalfields known age adults. The stationary ±SE hazard rate range encompasses the hazard rates for natural increase of the population from +0.15 to –0.15. The assessed age distribution is also plotted here and is quite different from the true age distribution.

same general distribution of adult ages. The apparent accuracy of the method is not inherent in the method, but is predicated on the lucky chance of sample similarities in this case. Such a basic problem cannot be overcome by sophisticated statistical manipulation. It can only be dealt with by a better understanding of the course of human senescence over space and over time.

TAPHONOMY

Meindl and Russell (1998) argue that the taphonomic problems affecting age assessment of archaeological populations have been overstated. But it is, in fact, of paramount importance to be able to age samples for comparison in the same way, by the same methods. If preservation bias controls methods, the comparisons essential to an understanding of human population structure will not be valid.

Considerations of taphonomy and sample bias are fairly new in skeletal biology, as distinct from paleontology. Masset (1973) urged their importance many years ago; Toussaint (1991) and Tiley-Baxter (1997) have considered body part representation and Waldron (1987) and Walker and colleagues (1988) have discussed general implications of this. Detailed work on the taphonomy of Portuguese archaeological dentitions showed how age-dependent biasing of a sample gives rise to misleading information on age-dependent characteristics (Jackes and Lubell, 1996). In the past, paleodemographic comparison was based on life expectancy calculated from life tables, actually mean age at death. Mean age at death cannot be used as the basis for comparisons unless unbiased and comparable samples are analyzed by comparable techniques (Jackes, 1984, 1992). Hoppa and Saunders (1998) in testing these ideas, stress the importance of the representativeness of samples.

Taphonomy should be a major consideration for those researchers who maintain that the use of more than one age indicator leads to greater accuracy in age assessment. Meindl and Lovejoy's multifactorial method (1985; summary age computed by principal components analysis of the estimated ages), and Acsádi and Nemeskéri's complex method (1970) both require the conjoint use of several skeletal elements. Storey and Hirth (1997) use the multifactorial method for the site of El Cajón, but state that "relatively few individuals were aged by more than one indicator." Attrition and suture closure and alteration to the auricular surface of the hip bone were the osteological techniques employed, but 46% of the adults could not be assessed for age. The representativeness of this 46% is an important consideration.

Sciulli and colleagues (1996) provide details of their method of age assessment and the diversity of means they had to employ to assign an age to each of 209 individuals from the Pearson cemetery. This is an excellent example of how osteologists simply cannot provide standardized age estimates on more than a small percentage of adults. It is legitimate to enquire how the age estimates are affected by this problem that all osteologists have had to face.

There has been no exploration of how differential preservation of elements may alter age estimates. Bedford and colleagues (1993) tested the accuracy of the multifactorial method on a sample of 55 individuals from the Grant Collection. It appears that not all individuals had all four elements tested, and 13% lacked the auricular surface of the ilium. While these authors indicate that the summary age was more accurate than the individual indicators from ages 30 to 60, this cannot be fully evaluated without knowing the exact real age distribution of the indicators.

Two studies allow us to investigate the importance of evaluating the effect of taphonomy on age assessments. The data of Kemkes-Grottenthaler (1993) provide a very clear picture of the differences in representation of skeletal elements used for age assessment. Figure 15.4 demonstrates that there can be great differences even with two sites of the same general age, location, and type. Eltville, with a sample of 500 of which 317 are adult, is located in the ideal depositional environment for skeletal preservation (loess). Langenlonsheim contained 457 individuals, only 188 assessed as adult, and clearly offers a less satisfactory array of skeletal elements for adult age assessment. The information contained in Figure 15.4 would suggest that it is essential to consider cranial suture closure the major technique for adult age assessment, though it will not age more than about 70% of the sample. Such an approach would make comparison with some sites an impossibility, those with secondary or ossuary burial for example, which commonly retain no more than a small fraction of analyzable skulls.

At Christ Church, Spitalfields, only 76 of 219 (35%) individuals over age 17, of known age and sex, retained skull vaults, pubes, proximal femora, and proximal humeri (Molleson and Cox, 1993). The situation is actually worse since new analyses undertaken for this chapter have shown that very few individuals had cranial vaults sufficiently well preserved to allow a distribution among the Acsádi and Nemeskéri suture stages 1 to 5 (see Table 15.1).

There are no significant differences between the total sample known age and the age distribution for each individual skeletal element (all analyses done separately for males and females). There is, however a clear indication that the distribution by elements does not adequately represent the total known age sample.

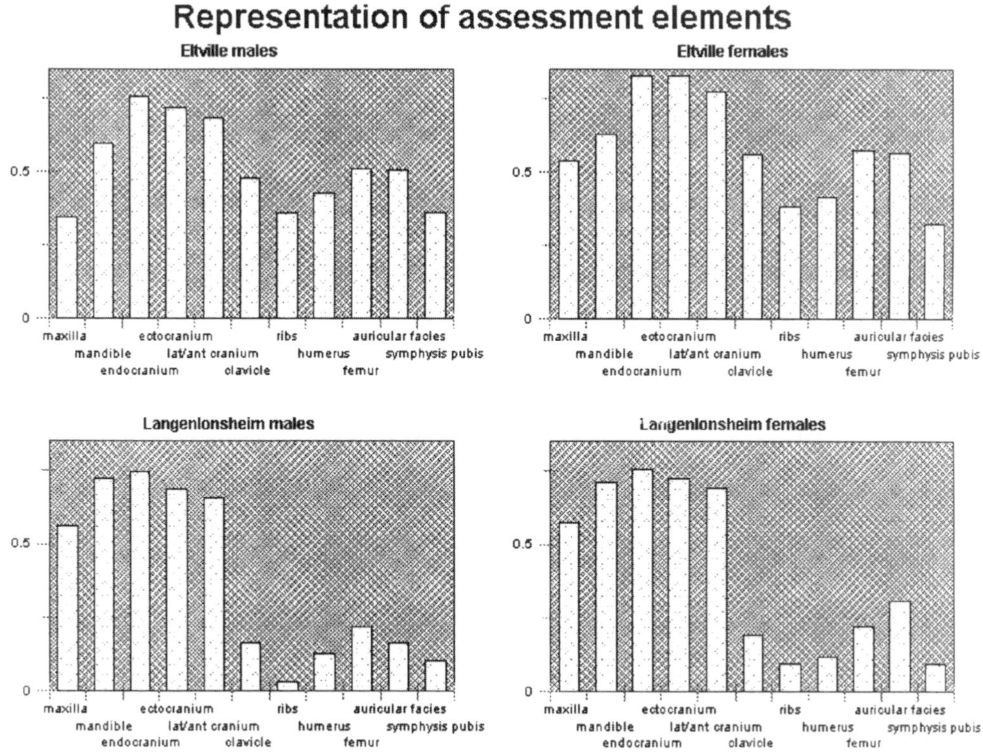

Representation of assessment elements

Figure 15.4 Differences in representation of skeletal elements used for age assessment between two German medieval sites. Y axes record ratio of numbers of elements present to total numbers of individuals. (Data from Kemkes-Grottenthaler, 1993.)

TABLE 15.1 Spitalfields Known Age Sample: Representation of Skeletal Elements for the Complex Method of Age Assessment

Known Age	Measurable Humeral Head %		Measurable Femur Head %		16 Endocranial Suture Points %		16 and Fewer than 16 Suture Points %		Pubic Symphyses %		Known Age n		Known Age n
	F	M	F	M	F	M	F	M	F	M	F	M	
20	0.0	66.7	100.0	66.7	0.0	0.0	0.0	0.0	100.0	33.3	1	3	
25	54.5	75.0	72.7	75.0	27.3	50.0	27.3	50.0	18.2	50.0	11	4	
30	50.0	18.2	100.0	54.5	50.0	0.0	50.0	0.0	100.0	36.4	2	11	
35	55.6	20.0	88.9	70.0	33.3	20.0	44.4	20.0	55.6	60.0	9	10	
40	16.7	75.0	50.0	75.0	16.7	0.0	16.7	0.0	33.3	75.0	6	4	
45	54.5	40.0	72.7	60.0	9.1	0.0	18.2	20.0	63.6	40.0	11	10	
50	78.6	73.3	71.4	80.0	21.4	20.0	28.6	33.3	42.9	46.7	14	15	
55	52.9	70.0	82.4	90.0	41.2	10.0	47.1	20.0	47.1	50.0	17	10	
60	63.6	57.1	81.8	76.2	45.5	19.0	45.5	23.8	63.6	66.7	11	21	
65	53.8	50.0	76.9	72.2	15.4	5.6	15.4	11.1	61.5	61.1	13	18	
70	43.8	50.0	56.3	61.1	12.5	11.1	12.5	16.7	50.0	50.0	16	18	
75	41.2	22.2	58.8	77.8	23.5	22.2	29.4	33.3	23.5	44.4	17	9	
80	75.0	25.0	62.5	75.0	25.0	0.0	25.0	0.0	50.0	50.0	8	4	
85	100.0	0.0	85.7	50.0	28.6	0.0	42.9	0.0	85.7	0.0	7	2	
Total	55.9	48.2	72.0	71.2	25.2	12.2	29.4	18.7	49.0	51.8	143	139	

The difference between the total male and female age distribution is significant.[1] But there is no difference between males and females on any specific skeletal element except, marginally, for the presence of a measurable humeral head (99% CI = 0.0455, 0.1065). In other words, there is a definite age at death difference between Spitalfields known age males and females, but this difference will not be evident from the surviving skeletal elements, perhaps caused by method of analysis, but more likely resulting from the very poor representation of crania and pubes. Of the total 836 adults excavated at Christ Church, Spitalfields, of both known and unknown age, only 70% retained at least one of the four elements used for age assessment, and only 425 (51%) could be given estimated ages based in whole or in part on pubes and/or skulls. In summary, taphonomical considerations are of great importance both in the calculation of the prevalence of any skeletal characteristic, and in paleodemography.

POPULATION DIFFERENCES

Fundamental to all comparative work in skeletal biology is the question of whether age changes are uniform across populations. Possible heterogeneity within samples has been mentioned, and there is an increasing recognition that aging differences between the sexes must be discussed. But our knowledge of population differences for skeletal age changes is still rudimentary.

While it is agreed that there are significant differences among population groups (Katz and Suchey, 1989), no analyses have been published that would allow confirmation of this. Such analyses have been urged (Jackes, 1992; Loth and İşcan, 1989), but existing reference samples are presently unavailable for this purpose. Katz and Suchey (1989) have stated that while they have been able to show aging differences among Americans of European, Mexican, and African origin, they believe that the "racial" ambiguity and mixture in their sample from southern California would frustrate efforts to reach a clear-cut result. Galera and colleagues (1998) argue for a population difference in rates of cranial suture closure, but this difference cannot be fully evaluated since they do not specify the difference between Black and White Americans. With the exception of the Black male/female age distributions, differences in age distributions among the samples are all highly significant. We would predict that Black males and White females are most different, based on the rounded value of 79, the highest in Table 15.2. This prediction is supported by the degree and direction of bias on all methods reported by Galera and co-workers.

Comparison of the work of Kemkes-Grottenthaler (1996b) and Galera and colleagues (1998) suggests that population differences in skeletal aging could be very important. The two known age samples examined by these researchers produce the same pattern of bias using the two Meindl/Lovejoy suture methods, but the deviation of assessed age from real age is greater for the Terry Collection sample than for the 109 skulls from Mainz. The specific details of the 236 crania from the Hamann-Todd Collection upon which the Meindl/Lovejoy method was originally based (Meindl and Lovejoy, 1985) have not been published, but the two American samples must be different in sex and age distribution, or in race, in order to generate differences in deviations of assessed age from real age in tests. The Hamann-Todd cranial sample probably consisted of about 54% individuals of European and about 45% individuals of African descent (see Lovejoy et al., 1985:table 1), while the Terry Collection sample used by Galera et al. (1998) comprises 42% individuals of European and 58% individuals of African descent. The two samples are thus different enough to suggest that population differences can lead to differing results in cranial suture closure.

---

[1] The 99% confidence interval (CI) of the Monte Carlo estimate of *P* is 0.0077, 0.0443. This analysis was done using StatXact-3, which provides an estimate of the probability by testing 500 tables, thus allowing a greater confidence that there is no error when describing a difference as significant.

A test of auricular surfaces (Murray and Murray, 1991) led to the conclusion that the method "is not equally valid for black and white individuals." This is not surprising since the age distribution for black males and white males is inverted. However, Murray and Murray re-tested using only those 69 individuals with a true age of 40 to 60, and found no difference in the performance of the auricular surface method by "race" in this age group. Thus, at present we simply do not know whether this method is equally valid across these two population groups. Loth and İşcan (1989) have noted very significant differences between Americans of European descent and Americans of African descent in age-dependent changes to the ends of ribs. More recently, Hoppa (2000) has discussed the possibility that inaccuracy in adult age assessment using pubic symphyses is related to population differences between the reference sample and the target sample.

If there is difficulty in fitting a sample to the type descriptions or illustrations of stages within a particular age indicator scheme, the difficulty will be reflected by assignment of one individual to multiple stages. Does the difficulty arise because the stages are not well defined and accurate, or are the age stages, as defined, inapplicable to the particular sample under study? Is this because of basic differences in the biology of the indicator and not just because of differences in age structure? This type of question must be answered before we can begin to have any confidence in "age" indicators as age indicators, rather than as relative stages in the senescence of the adult human skeleton, controlled by several factors. Genetics is certainly not the single controlling factor (Jackes, 1992), especially since secular change within a population is a possibility that has received a minimum of attention.

Masset (1989:98–99) discerned the possibility of diachronic changes in suture closure. Boldsen and Paine (1995) do no mention this when using ectocranial medial sagittal suture closure to hypothesize an increase in the length of life in Europeans over the last 9,000 years.

This allows room for temporal change, or for any factor other than a direct relationship between age and suture closure. A test on known age individuals from Spitalfields shows the relationship of midsagittal ectocranial suture closure with known age to be quite weak ($r = .44$). While the suture closure categories used (partial closure and complete closure) cover the whole spread of adult ages from the twenties to the eighties, the mean ages given the stages for a medieval Danish sample are very much younger than those for the later Londoners (many of Huguenot origin). Either diachronic change or inaccurate age estimation of the Danish sample used by Boldsen and Paine (1995) may be at work here. We cannot evaluate the factors until there is a different approach to skeletal changes; these changes have in the past been considered only in their capacity as "age indicators" but they merit study from other perspectives.

TABLE 15.2   Terry Collection Samples Used in Analysis of Cranial Methods of Age Estimation

Rounded χ^2 values for age distribution comparisons		Blacks		Whites	
		Males	Females	Males	Females
Blacks	Males	—	14	44	79
	Females		—	35	64
Whites	Males			—	34
	Females				—

Data from (Galera et al., 1998).

TESTS OF METHODS

Histology

Stout and co-workers (1996) have applied the method of predicting ages from the sum of intact and fragmentary osteons per unit area of the clavicular cortex to a sample of 83 nineteenth-century Swiss skeletons, apparently with cemetery records that report age at death. Estimated ages deviated from reported ages after age 40, so that the maximum estimated age was 54 years, while the maximum reported age was 75 years. The results indicate that the relationship of osteons per unit area with age is not linear. The authors note that there is "a loss of reliability in age prediction inherent in microscopic methods." At a certain point (which will differ for different bones and for the same bone from different individuals, depending on cross-sectional area, and factors affecting bone remodeling) the entire cortex will be remodeled, and the evidence of former remodeling will be removed by further remodeling. Thus, at some stage in the aging process, unknown for each population, indeed for each individual, histological age assessment cannot be applied (see also Robling and Stout, Chapter 7, for a discussion of these issues.

Although it was hoped that histological age assessment would provide accurate data for paleodemography (e.g. Buikstra and Konigsberg, 1985), histological aging has not lived up to its early promise. For example, Molleson and Cox (1993) report that a variety of histological techniques provided age estimates on the sample of known age individuals from eighteenth- and nineteenth-century coffin burials in the Spitalfields Christ Church crypt that were no better than macroscopic age estimates. Aiello and Molleson (1993) note that Kerley's histological techniques are no more accurate than the Acsádi/Nemeskéri pubic symphysis estimations, the latter also having the advantage of not requiring unaltered periosteal cortical bone.

Dudar and colleagues (1993) show that the regressions of morphological and histological age-at-death estimates derived from ribs of

known age at death do not differ significantly and suggest that a linked morphological and histological analysis will best estimate adult age at death. Pfeiffer (1998), in an important paper focusing on basic methodology in histomorphometry, has proposed that ribs should be used in histological examination because they may be less subject to interindividual and interpopulation variation in terms of osteon size.

The requirement of microscopically intact bone is a major problem for archaeological age assessment. Plate 1 illustrates examples of microbial decomposition, showing how the microstructure of cortical bone and tooth roots comes to be disrupted by the activities of bacteria that dissolve bone, extract collagen, and then redeposit the mineral fraction in a form that is denser and in which the crystals are altered. The bone cortex may appear to be very well preserved to the naked eye, but the bone in the outer portion of the cortex (specified in histological techniques) is very likely to be unusable (Aiello and Molleson, 1993; Jackes, 1992). Sampling location has a significant effect on cortical remodeling assessments (Pfeiffer et al., 1995).

Auricular Surface

Two tests allow us to examine this technique of age assessment first proposed by Lovejoy and colleagues (1985). Murray and Murray (1991) tested the auricular surface method of adult age estimation on a sample of 189 individuals aged over 20 from the Terry Collection (St. Louis, Missouri), a large cadaver collection of indigents from the first half of the twentieth century. Their subsample of the collection included both males and females, and Americans of both European and African descent. We do not know the actual age range of the sample, but those over 60 had average ages for males of 70 (Europeans) and 77 (Africans), and for females of 73 (Europeans) and 80 (Africans). Thus, the two identified population groups were also different in age. Sixty-seven percent of the sample was actually aged over 50 years, but the method placed only 21% over age 50. By contrast, although 28% of the sample actually fell between ages 30 and 50, the method gave 75% of the sample an age of 30 to 50. The difference between the real age distribution and the estimated age distribution (as derived from their figure 1) over the eight adult age categories is significant beyond expression.

Santos (1995, 1996, per. comm.) has tested the method on a known age population of indi- viduals born between 1824 and 1916, housed at the University of Coimbra, and has provided information that allows comparison of her re- sults with those of Murray and Murray (1991). The sample sizes are comparable (189 for Terry and 215 for Coimbra), as is the percent- age of females (52 and 51%). The major differ- ence is that 48% of the Terry sample is not of European extraction. The two samples tested are not different in terms of actual ages

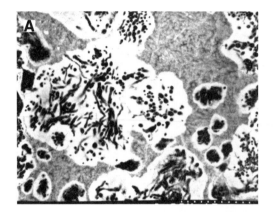

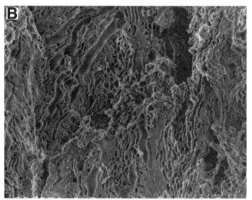

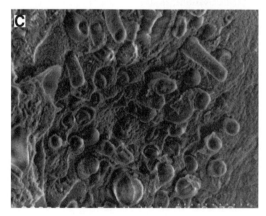

Plate 1   (A) Polished embedded thin section of left femoral mid shaft cortex (unnumbered sample given project designation 10DR). Normal bone matrix is compared with the redeposited and altered bone around the bacterial colonies from which the organic fraction has been removed. CM Barker SEM (Hitachi S-2700) 9/9/92 at 15kV, original magnification 2,000. (B) Broken surface of unpolished, unembedded section of Gruta da Caldeirão O14/34 right anterior femoral cortex, just below mid shaft. Bacterial tunnelling has been transected across and lengthways. R. Sherburne Field Emission SEM (Hitachi S-4100) 17/7/93:72 at 2.5 kV, original magnification 2,500. (C) Broken thin section of left anterior mid femoral cortex, just below the mid shaft, from Cabeço da Ar- ruda 35. Bacteria emerging from the break just at the margin of, not within, an Haversian canal. R. Sherburne Field Emission SEM (Hitachi S-4100) 17/7/93:81 at 2.5 kV, original magnification 11,000.

TABLE 15.3   Tests Showing that When Auricular Facies Estimates Are Tested They Demonstrate Method Control of Estimates, Not Sample Control of Estimates

χ^2 (7 df)	Collections	χ^2 Value	99% CI, 500 Tables, Monte Carlo Estimate of P
Real ages vs. stage "ages"	Terry	95.90	0.0000, 0.0092
Real ages vs. real ages	Terry vs. Coimbra	11.53	0.0948, 0.1732
Real ages vs. stage "ages"	Coimbra	80.53	0.0000, 0.0092
Stage "ages" vs. stage "ages"	Terry vs. Coimbra	0.02248	0.9908, 1.0000

(Table 15.3). When real ages of the collections are compared, the estimate of the probability (P) would be around 0.1 in 99% of 500 tests. Nor are the two samples different in terms of the distribution of auricular surface stages. In fact, since the estimate of the probability that there is any difference between the two would be 1.0 in 500 tests, we can say that the samples are identical with regard to stages.

On the other hand, the stage "age" distribution and the real age distribution in each case bear no relationship to each other. In the case of each of the two samples, the difference between the real age distribution and the estimated age distribution is so large that in over 500 tests the probability of the difference occurring by chance is more or less zero. For this reason, we can say that the method governs the "age" distribution, the estimated ages. The estimated ages are not characteristic of the target sample, they are in some way reflecting the built-in biases of the method, probably determined by the characteristics of the reference population. This is illustrated in Figure 15.5a. As shown in Figure 15.5b, it is likely that the method should be evaluated with the sexes separated.

Bradford and co-workers (1993) tested the method on a sample of 54 males and one female from the Grant Collection of unclaimed dead from the Toronto area dating to the middle of the twentieth century. The results were reported in terms of 10-year age intervals, so that it is not possible to show how each of the auricular age stages performs. Males from the

twenties to the fifties were over-aged by 5 to 10 years on average, while those over 60 were under-aged. An eight- to nine-year inaccuracy in age assessment of those from 30 to 60 years was demonstrated, similar to the results of Murray and Murray (1991), but the degree and direction of bias may have been different. Unfortunately, we do not know the age distribution of the sample tested. As such, this test of the method is not definitive as was found to be the case with a similar study by Saunders and colleagues (1992).

Ribs

Adult age assessment by means of the sternal ends of ribs has been proposed by İşcan (summarized in Loth and İşcan, 1989), based on the fourth rib. Molleson and Cox (1993) have noted that the second rib is the most robust and easily identified rib; even so, only 29% of the second ribs survived in the Spitalfields known age sample. The coding of the Spitalfields ribs was based on the work of İşcan and colleagues (1984), prior to the systematization proposed by Loth and İşcan in 1989, when it was recommended that males and females be scored separately. The work on the Spitalfields ribs is a clear demonstration of the value of this recommendation, since the correlation of total score with known age for males is .772, but for females is only .354. Dudar and co-workers (1993) also found a reasonably high correlation between rib end morphology and known age. Mann (1993) and Dudar et al. (1993) have

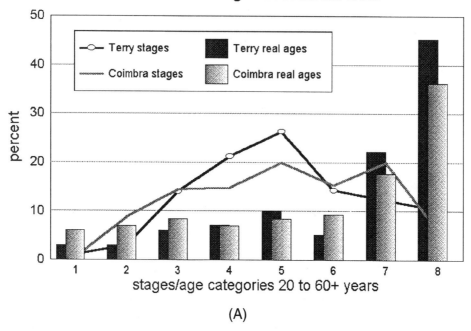

(A)

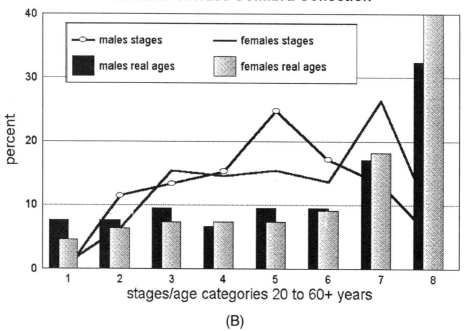

(B)

Figure 15.5 (A) Comparison of the Terry and Coimbra known age skeletal collections. (B) comparison of real age and facies auricularis stage "ages" for males and females in the Coimbra skeletal sample.

discussed the problems of identifying and using ribs in skeletal analyses.

Kemkes-Grottenthaler (1996a) has stated that ribs did not provide a good method of age assessment based on her two early medieval German samples. Analysis done for this chapter certainly showed "rib age" to be far removed from all other variables, when represented by midpoint of stage age range. A dissimilarity matrix (Euclidean distance proximity analysis) shows that rib changes, represented by the midpoint of the assessed age range, bear no relationship to other age markers and this is confirmed by hierarchical cluster analysis (average linkage between groups) of the matrix. Kemkes-Grottenthaler (1996a) suggests that preservation may be a factor here, causing difficulty in differentiating stages. Fully 43% of the 121 individuals she aged using ribs fell between two or more of the described stages, so that population differences should also be considered as one of the contributing factors.

Pubic Symphyses

The pubic symphysis, the most intensively studied of the age indicators and the one long believed to provide the most accurate age estimates, has actually received less than complete support in the literature. In 1955, Brooks noted: "regrettably [the results were] not very encouraging." Forty years later, Santos said: "the results of this study were not very encouraging" (1995).

The first systematization was that of Todd, who published his data on males (1920). Because the data were published, we are able to see that Todd's method was perhaps given too much clarity when it was published as a simple 10-point system in the first 1962 edition of Krogman's *The Human Skeleton in Forensic Medicine* (see Jackes, 1985, for a discussion). The method was re-evaluated by Brooks (1955), but it is not possible to reconstruct Brooks' data in its entirety. It would seem desirable to base tests on the Suchey/Brooks system, which has been well published (most

recently in Suchey and Katz, 1997) and can be reconstructed very easily from diagrams. The published diagrams differ slightly from the diagrams sent out with the casts and used for the construction of probabilities (Jackes, 1992). The new probabilities are therefore given in the Appendix.

The method of categorizing age changes in pubic symphyses developed by Meindl and Lovejoy derives from the Todd method, and the Acsádi/Nemeskéri method is also not completely independent in its origin (Acsádi and Nemeskéri, 1970). Because of this common origin, it is surprising that in Figure 15.6 the four methods of adult age assessment provide such different results (based on the work of Kemkes-Grottenthaler [1993], specifically the midpoints of the age ranges). Since the pubic symphysis has long been regarded as the standard skeletal element in adult age assessment (although pubes over age 35 have recently been characterized as "not particularly valuable for age estimation" by Meindl and Russell, 1998), it is important to emphasize that there is no certainty of adult age based on pubes.

While the Suchey/Brooks and Todd methods do provide some similarities in the ages individuals are given, skeletons that would be broadly distributed over a wide range of ages from 35–65 when the Suchey/Brooks method is used, would be grouped by the Todd method into the 40–50 age range. The Suchey/Brooks method is actually quite similar to the Acsádi/Nemeskéri method. Both would put Todd phase VI individuals into stage 3 and group males and females from Todd's phases VII and VIII into stage 4. Because Suchey/Brooks has six pubic symphyseal stages, the method would put individuals from Todd phase IX into stage 5 and the males would be distributed from stages 4 to 6, perhaps with most in stage 6. Todd's phase X individuals would go into stage 6. It seems to have been difficult to sort the younger adults in Kemkes-Grottenthaler's sample into Todd phases. Many individuals were put in I–II or I–III. Acsádi/Nemeskéri and Suchey/

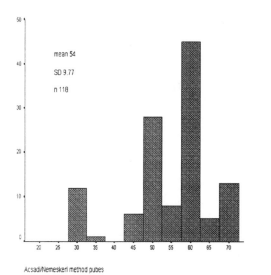

Brooks, however, are more or less equivalent at stages 1, 2, and 3.

Meindl/Lovejoy, on the other hand, have the following equivalencies with the Todd phases: 2 = VI; 3 = VII; 4 = VIII; 5 = IX, X. The Meindl/Lovejoy method groups all the Todd phase I–V pubes into stage 1. This leads to a high correlation between the results of the

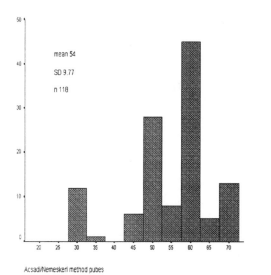

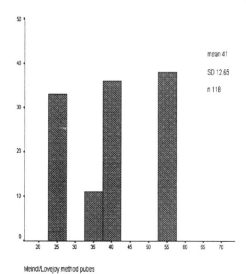

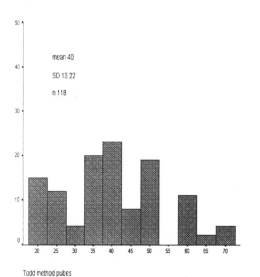

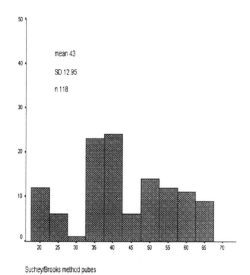

Figure 15.6 The distribution by midpoints of assessed age ranges illustrate, differences in four methods of adult age assessment based on the symphysis pubis. X axes represent assessed ages, y axes represent numbers of cases. (Data from Kemkes-Grottenthaler, 1993.)

TABLE 15.4   Distribution of Individuals over Pubic Symphysis Stages (Information Recalculated from Kemkes-Grottenthaler, 1993). The Double Ages Provided for the Suchey/Brooks Ranges Take Sex Differences into Account

Stage	Suchey/Brooks	Age	Acsádi/Nemeskéri	Age	Meindl/Lovejoy	Age
1	13	15–23/24	12.5	18–45	32.5	18–37
2	8	19–34/40	9	23–69	11	30–35
3	22	21–46/53	28.5	25–76	16.5	36–40
4	40	23/26–57/70	52.5	24–81	22	40–49
5	14	27/25–66/83	15.5	41–86	36	45–50
6	21	34/42–86/87	—	—	—	—

two methods. In Table 15.4, the frequency distributions have been simplified by assigning the individuals falling between two stages equally to the two stages, explaining why in the columns for the Acsádi/Nemeskéri and Meindl/Lovejoy methods fractional individuals are recorded. The Todd pubes frequencies were excluded since the number of individuals falling firmly within a stage was very limited (only 51/118 or 43.2% of pubes were classified as falling directly within a stage, all other pubes fell between two or more stages). Of the individuals in stage 1 in Table 15.4, 12 are placed there by both the Suchey/Brooks and Acsádi/Nemeskéri methods. These 12 individuals would be given an age of around 28 by the Acsádi/Nemeskéri method, but only about 20 by the Suchey Brooks method. Since it is generally possible to distinguish a 20 year old from a 28 year old, the problem is minor and could be resolved. However, the 14 individuals who fall into stage 4 by both methods, would certainly be given different ages based on the Suchey/Brooks (44 for males and 48 for females) and the Acsádi/ Nemeskéri (52.5 years) methods. The large number of individuals who fall into the Acsádi/Nemeskéri and Suchey/Brooks stage 4 are distributed over Meindl/Lovejoy stages 3 to 5, and would thus be given variously ages 38, 45, and 48. Since the data here are derived from Kemkes-Grottenthaler's research on early medieval populations, we have no way whatsoever of determining which age at death distribution is closest to reality. For that, we require tests on known age samples.

In Figures 15.7a and b the reconstructed Suchey/Brooks Los Angeles sample of individuals over 15 years of age (see Appendix) has been used to provide the prior probabilities. In other words, the Los Angeles sample provides the reference data from which we determine the probability that an individual with a pubic symphysis at a certain stage will be of a certain age. Figure 15.7a shows the results of different suggested methods of fitting symphysis stage to age for males, and Figure 15.7b illustrates the Suchey/Brooks method for female pubes. Distribution by iterative proportional fitting ("by iteration" in the legend), as suggested by Bocquet-Appel and Masset (1996) and Konigsberg and Frankenberg (1992), is shown to be completely ineffective in replicating the real age-at-death distribution. Proportional fitting is compared with two other methods that are also shown to be unsatisfactory as methods of deriving the real age distribution.

Figures 15.8a and b use data collected by Sheilagh Thompson Brooks on Spitalfields known age adults. Individuals with pathology or trauma and those whose pubic symphyses did not fall cleanly in a Suchey/Brooks stage have been excluded. Once again, as with the Coimbra sample pubes, we see that iterative proportional fitting does not provide reasonable age at death distributions. Comparison of Figures 15.7a and b and 15.8a and b demonstrates that programming for iteration of what are here called "Bayesian probabilities" would not provide accurate age distributions. The shapes of the curves are determined, not by the underlying real age distributions, but by the

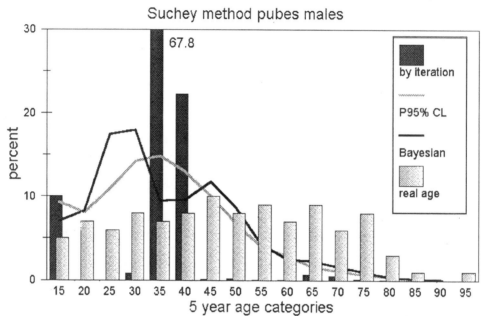

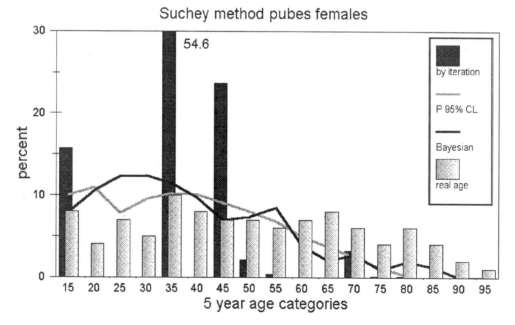

Figure 15.7   (A) Males and (B) females in Coimbra known age sample. Y axes represent numbers of cases. Real ages compared with assessed Suchey/Brooks ages distributed by probability over 95% CL of the stage mean, by Bayesian type calculation (given the reference indicator stage, this is the age class), and by proportional fitting (given the reference age class, this is the indicator stage distribution).

prior probabilities imposed by the method. Thus, while the Coimbra and Spitalfields real age distributions are quite different, the Bayesian curves are very similar, and this similarity would be intensified by iteration.

Reporting of Data

It is important that researchers publish their results in comparable forms, and in full, so that adequate evaluation by other researchers can be undertaken. In fact, there is no satisfactory method of economically summarizing a distribution. Reporting only the mean age of the distribution is inadequate. Molleson and Cox (1993) have suggested that the Spitalfields real and assessed ages are very similar because the target population (Spitalfields), and the reference population (the sample used by Acsádi and Nemeskéri as the basis for their method), are actually similar in age. Indeed, the 157 adults of known age in the Spitalfields sample who were assessed by Molleson using the symphysis pubis by the Acsádi and Nemeskéri method have a mean age of 59.12 years (15.75, standard deviation on five-year frequency data). The mean age by morphological phase for the symphysis pubis in the reference sample (Acsádi and Nemeskéri, 1970) is 57.60 years (SD = 8.88). From these figures, one would say that the pubic symphysis provides an accurate estimation of Spitalfields adult age. But Molleson's argument that this similarity is based on the similarity of the reference and target populations is justified when the Suchey/ Brooks symphysis pubis method is applied. (The Suchey/Brooks reference population has a younger mean age: males, n = 737, mean = 40.72 years, SD = 17.97; females, n = 273, mean = 37.61 years, SD = 17.25). Besides this problem, there is the added disadvantage that the mean age at death does not provide an adequate summary since mean age does not give a clear picture of differences in age distributions. It certainly gives no idea of the actual distribution of the real ages at death (compare Table 15.5 and Figures 15.7 and 15.8).

The normal type of scatter diagram does not allow a reconstruction of cell frequencies, and numerals or symbols to display cell frequencies are clumsy. Yet the next stage in our understanding of skeletal senescence involves finding ways of examining and testing the differences among matrices rather than trying to find ways of estimating distributions from prior probabilities. Thus, it is essential that we report results as fully as possible. The method established by Meindl and Lovejoy (e.g., 1989) of reporting results by inaccuracy and bias, as a replacement for a correlation coefficient expressing the relationship of real and estimated age, provides more information. But it limits methods of comparison, and renders the research data completely opaque to other methods of analysis and testing. The solution is to provide the data in matrix form.

Constandse-Westermann (1997) has provided real age (in years) by stage frequency data for her sample and it is obviously desirable to follow her example. It is then possible to use any age category necessary (5 or 10 years). Mean age by stage or mean stage by age can easily be calculated, and the information can be analyzed by parametric or nonparametric statistical tests. More, however, is needed. We need to have data by sex, and we must have data by population or subsample groupings so that the interaction of stage, age, sex, and ethnicity can be fully understood. For example, Hershkovitz and co-workers (1997a) provide interesting information on the closure of the jugular synchondrosis of the skull base, an element that has eluded the notice of osteologists in the past. But the 1869 skulls examined are not reported in such a way that we can judge the interplay of sex and ethnicity and possible biases in representation of subgroups in each age category. In fact, in view of the questions of asymmetry (Santos, 1996), laterality should also be checked by subgroup.

We also need to examine skeletal changes with regard to cause of death. Masset and de Castro e Almeida (1990) have demonstrated that, while tuberculosis does not seem to affect cranial synostosis, those who died of epidemic diseases are those whose external cranial sutures are likely to be in a more advanced state of closure. It is essential to our understanding of age changes that we know something of the life of the individuals within the reference population. Katz and Suchey (1989), for example, mentioned plans for a study relating to alcohol abuse, a very important consideration. There has been discussion that McKern and Stewart based their age estimates on a sample biased toward very young adults. But we should also recognize that in their sample 70% of the men 28 years and over had been prisoners of war before death. In fact, 60% of the men 28 to 50 years of age had been in captivity for anywhere from three months to over a year before they died (McKern and Stewart, 1957).

Cranial Sutures

Cranial suture observation for age assessment has a long history in anthropology, summarized by Masset (1989). Masset's work came at the end of a long period in which received wisdom stated that cranial sutures gave no clear idea of the ages of adults, whereas pubic symphyses gave the most reliable estimates (e.g., Brooks, 1955). Emphasis is again being placed on cranial sutures (Boldsen and Paine, 1995), but

there are clear signs of a healthy scepticism, leading to the provocative conclusion that "[sagittal] suture condition appears to be an age-independent, sexually biased phenomenon" (Hershkovitz et al., 1997b).

The detailed approach to cranial sutures, as laid out in Martin (1959), involves the observation of endocranial suture changes at 16 points on the vault. The results for these 16 points are expressed as a "mean closure stage" for each skull. Using a known age sample of 68 reasonably complete adult skulls from Spitalfields, the highest correlation between known age and mean closure stage ($r = .531$) is obtained from a quadratic regression model with age as the independent variable.

The Workshop of European Anthropologists (WEA, 1980) followed Acsádi and Nemeskéri (1970) in suggesting that the mean closure stage should be collapsed into five suture closure stages. For example, Spitalfields known age adults, males and females 20 years and over, in which all 16 points on the sutures were observable, can be redistributed into the five suture closure phases as shown in Table 15.6. We can add individuals for whom missing data could be estimated based on an assumption of symmetry in suture closure; however, care must be exercised since suture closure analysis

TABLE 15.5   Mean Age for Adults in Spitalfields (Brooks' data) and Coimbra (Santos, 1995, and in litt. 11/2/99) Known Age samples, and Mean of Ages Assessed for Symphysis Pubis by the Suchey/Brooks Method. Means Based on Frequency Data Within 5-Year Age Categories.

	Spitalfields				Coimbra			
	Males (n = 62)		Females (n = 56)		Males (n = 103)		Females (n = 100)	
	Mean	SD	Mean	SD	Mean	SD	Mean	SD
Real age	56.61	15.93	54.11	18.37	50.20	18.81	50.98	21.08
Using mean age for phase (Suchey & Katz, 1997:211)	42.04	12.72	41.02	11.65	38.12	10.72	40.24	12.51
Proportional fitting at .001	44.48	18.30	41.29	13.10	37.23	8.26	38.34	11.73
Number of iterations	548		144		470		822	
Bayesian fitting	42.54	16.13	41.62	16.22	38.62	14.24	40.87	16.84
Probability from reference stage mean age 95% CL	42.07	15.51	39.23	14.95	38.16	13.59	40.54	16.04

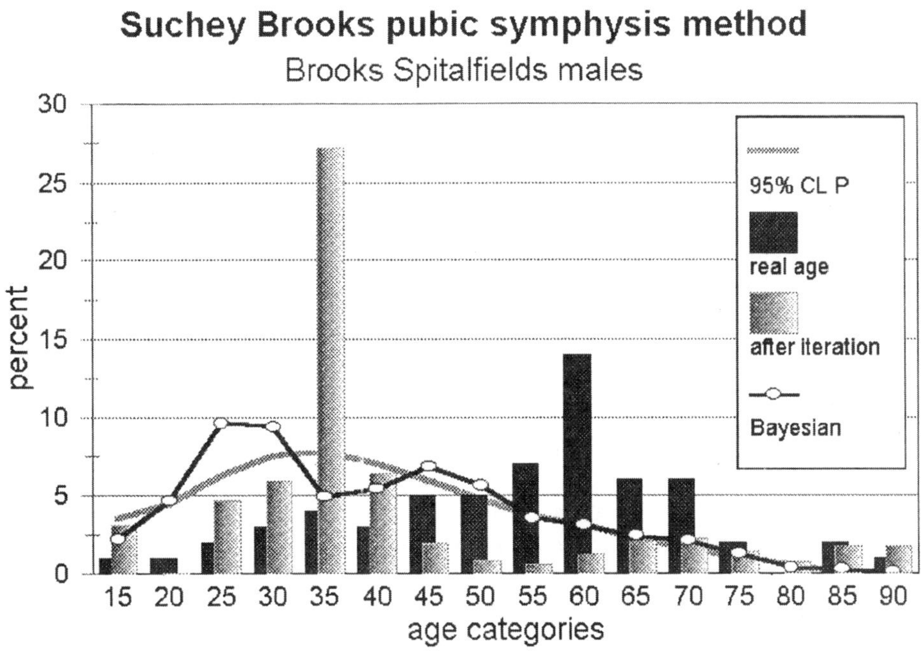

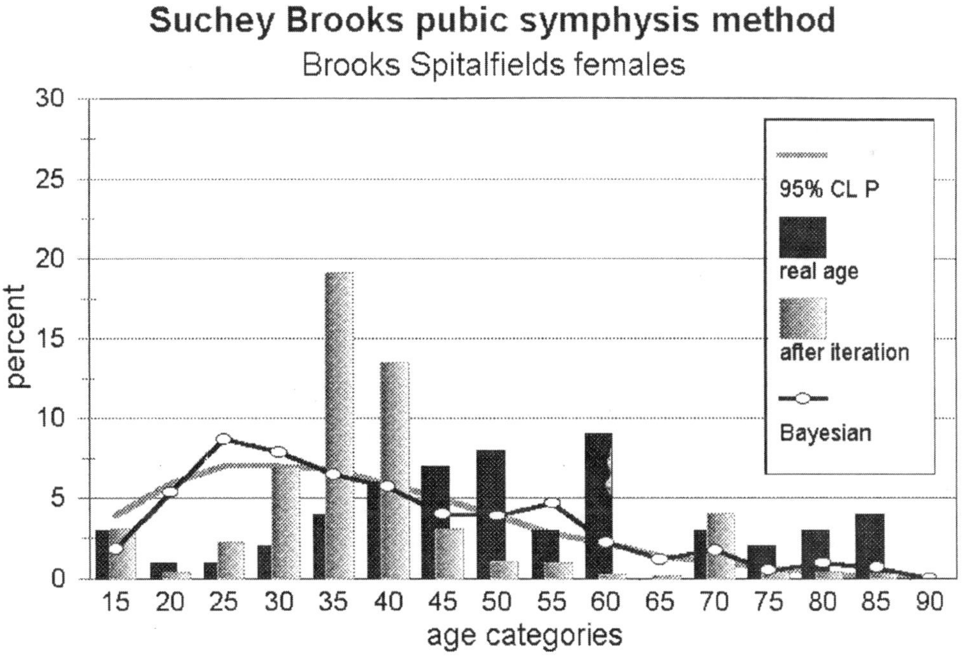

Suchey Brooks pubic symphysis method
Brooks Spitalfields males

Suchey Brooks pubic symphysis method
Brooks Spitalfields females

Figure 15.8   Pubic symphyses data on Spitalfields known age adults. Y axes represent numbers of individuals assessed for each five-year age category by Suchey/Brooks method redistributed by probability over 95% CL of the stage mean, by Bayesian type calculation (given the reference indicator stage, this is the age class), and by proportional fitting (given the reference age class, this is the indicator stage distribution), compared with real age distribution: (A) males, (B) females. (Data collected by Sheilagh Thompson Brooks.)

of this type "requires good preservation of the coronal, sagittal and lambdoidal sutures" (WEA, 1980). Overall, the left and right sides of the total Spitalfields adult sample seem equivalent, the mean suture closure and standard deviations being almost identical between sides, but symmetry is a concern. Acsádi and Nemeskéri (1970) actually seem to have chosen their reference sample on the basis of suture closure symmetry, 285 crania were used from a total of 402 available to them in Budapest.

Kemkes-Grottenthaler (1996b) has shown that the lateral anterior sutures (Meindl/Lovejoy system) are particularly vulnerable to asymmetry. Her sample of 109 known age skulls does not provide evidence of overall difference between left and right sides, but her data suggest that first one side of the skull and then the other passes through each of the Meindl/Lovejoy scores.

The Spitalfields known mean age is a little older for each stage (Table 15.7) than that found by Acsádi and Nemeskéri (1970), except in the case of stage 3. In stage 3 it is seven years older than the 49.1 years mean age for stage 3 in the Budapest medical school dissection specimens upon which the system was based, and the standard deviation is greater.

Acsádi and Nemeskéri (1970) gave 30-year ranges: stage 2, 30–60; stage 3, 35–65; stage 4, 45–75; stage 5, 50–80. With such broad ranges, it is hardly surprising that, in general terms, there is no contradiction between the two samples. While examination of the Spitalfields mean stage-for-age category

data (given in Table 15.8) show that suture closure is an age-dependent characteristic, the original Acsádi and Nemeskéri sample (1970) provided little assurance that age could be accurately estimated from cranial suture closure, as demonstrated by the last column in Table 15.8. Because the data for the original Acsádi and Nemeskéri reference sample are easily available, we can examine other methods proposed for generating adult age distributions. Our test target sample is the Spitalfield known age adults, and the reference sample (Acsádi and Nemeskéri, 1970) is 280 adults of age 20 and over with a mean age of 58.36 years (SD = 15.98). Iterative manipulation of the Spitalfields sample, deriving estimated age from suture closure stage, generates an age distribution that has no relationship to reality (Table 15.9). On the other hand, the estimated ages for the Spitalfields sample Bayesian type probability distribution is not significantly different from the actual known age distribution (the 99% CI of the P value = .63, .4).[2]

Bocquet-Appel (Bocquet, 1978) long ago proposed that assessed age distributions cannot be relied upon unless there is an almost perfect linear correlation between the indicator and age. However, Masset (1989) suggested that "an image of the unknown age sample" can be obtained by distribution over probable age classes. This is a much simpler process than that suggested by Jackes (1985, 1992). While Masset appears to have little confidence in the method of distributing based on prior probabilities when the indicator is not highly correlated with age, Table 15.9 belies that lack of confidence in this case with regard to the Bayesian type probabilities. In the Spitalfields adults aged 20 and over, the linear correlation coefficient between known age and mean points over all sutures is only $r = .486$.

TABLE 15.6 Frequency Counts for Acsádi and Nemeskéri Stages of Cranial Suture Closure for Complete Spitalfields Known Age Skulls

Stages	Males	Females	Total
1	0	0	0
2	2	9	11
3	3	4	7
4	6	10	16
5	3	6	9
Total	14	29	43

[2] The difference between the two methods of estimation is obvious: it is hardly necessary to point out that the χ^2 value for testing the difference from the real age distribution and the probability distribution is 3.74, while that for the estimation from iteration is 97.75.

TABLE 15.7   Acsádi and Nemeskéri Stages of Cranial Suture Closure by Known Age for Complete and Almost Complete Spitalfields Known Age Skulls

Known ages	WEA stages					Total n
	1	2	3	4	5	
20	0	3	2	0	0	5
30	0	4	2	1	0	7
40	0	3	1	1	0	5
50	0	5	1	9	4	19
60	0	2	1	7	4	14
70	0	1	2	4	6	13
80	0	0	2	2	1	5
Mean age	—	46.3	56.4	61.1	67.3	57.8
SD	—	14.1	22.4	11.5	9.1	15.8
Total	0	18	11	24	15	68

Masset (1989) considers that the use of 16 cranial suture points may not deal adequately with the correlation between sides of the coronal and occipital sutures. He thus proposes using the mean of each right/left pair of points, reducing the number of suture points to 10. While the difference appears to be minimal (tested using the 53 Spitalfields adults with all 16 points available, for ranges, means, and standard deviations), the Masset 10-point system is used to determine the age category/suture closure distribution of the Spitalfields adults with complete skulls by sex. Males and females are distributed among the seven age stages by Masset's distribution of mean suture closure points (Table 15.10), which allows for sex assignment. A test of age estimation by prior probabilities as suggested by Masset for endocranial sutures (Masset, 1989), with separate probabilities provided for males and females, provides a very fair approximation of the mean age of the samples. Although the estimated age distribution is not identical with the real one, there is no statistical significance to the differences (males, $P = .590$; females, $P = .868$).

The mean age of the Spitalfields known age adults can be estimated with almost perfect accuracy by the method of Masset (1989) based on cranial sutures, using the probabilities derived from his work on two Portuguese collections of known age adults. Galera and colleagues (1988), however, provide an interesting demonstration of the fact that the error in age assessment is not controlled solely by cranial sutures and their inherent variability, but by the methods utilized when examining cranial sutures (Figure 15.2). Since they point out that the Masset endocranial stage system is most accurate for those in their early sixties, we can only assume that Table 15.10 provides good support for the contention that age assessment will be accurate only when the target and reference samples are similar in age distribution. While it is impossible to test this conclusion on the basis of the Spitalfields sample, it appears possible that Masset's attempts (Masset and de Castro e Almeida, 1990) to circumvent the problem of the age structure of the reference population have not been successful.

Key and co-workers (1994) summarized discussions on whether or not there is sexual dimorphism in suture closure. They have devised a new method for dealing with suture closure by sex, based on the Spitalfields sample and taking into account the fact that the Spitalfields sample is biased towards individuals older than 50 years. Their test of this method, using a known age sample of South

Africans in the Dart Collection in Johannesburg, has produced "quite encouraging results." Key and co-workers (1994:205) state that, "further testing on populations with widely varying geographical, temporal and ethnic associations" is required and that "research should be directed towards understanding" suture closure. This is disconcerting given the long history of interest in cranial suture closure as a basic technique of age assessment.

Multifactorial Methods

This section examines the data of Kemkes-Grottenthaler, who has undertaken an interesting study of 505 adult skeletons from two medieval cemeteries in Germany (1993, 1996a). The skeletons were given ages, as ranges associated with stages, using 16 methods, with the idea of checking the complex method emanating from the work of Acsádi and Nemeskéri, and used as the basis for recommendations on age assessment (WEA, 1980). The 16 techniques employed are listed in Table 15.11. Since Kemkes-Grottenthaler (1993) provides data for each individual as age ranges, and sex assignments, it is possible to assess her results in detail.

The first multifactorial method is the summary age that Meindl and Lovejoy developed during the 1970s analysis of Libben, a large Ohio Woodland village cemetery (Lovejoy et al., 1985). The system was tested on the Hamann-Todd Collection at the Cleveland Museum of Natural History, skeletons collected from 1912 to 1938, of autopsied individuals born throughout the United States and in a number of other countries (Meindl and Lovejoy, 1989; Meindl et al., 1990). Tests of the method have been done on two known age samples, one of 130 skeletons and one of 131 each, as the authors say, "designed to match a known ethno-historical mortality profile" (Meindl et al., 1990). They chose a survivorship curve from a population in the literature and specimens from the known age samples were selected so that the age-at-death distribution would approximate the survivorship curve: (Meindl and Lovejoy, 1989:144; see Jackes 1992;196–197 for a discussion of this test methodology).

Principal components analysis using the results of several indicators provides the basis in the Meindl and Lovejoy method for the calculation of a summary age, the age estimates being derived by weighting based on the results

TABLE 15.8   Spitalfields Known Age Individuals with Almost Complete Skulls: Mean Suture Closure Stage for Real Age Compared with the Reference Population Data

Known Age	Mean	N	SD	Acsádi/Nemeskéri
25	2.4	5	.548	2.79
30	2	1	—	2.63
35	2.67	6	.816	3.23
40	4	1	—	3.36
45	2.25	4	.500	3.12
50	3.44	9	1.130	3.32
55	3.8	10	1.135	3.47
60	3.8	10	1.033	3.69
65	4.25	4	.957	3.57
70	4.25	5	.837	3.71
75	4.12	8	1.126	3.78
80	4.5	2	.707	3.52
85	3.33	3	.577	3.87
Total	3.53	68	1.113	—

TABLE 15.9   Comparison of Age Distributions for 68 Spitalfields Known Age Adults for Acsádi and Nemeskéri Suture Closure Stages Estimated by Proportional Fitting and Bayesian Probabilities

Age Categories	Spitalfields Adults Known Age	Estimation by Iteration	Estimation by Bayesian Probability
20–29	5	0.3	6.5
30–39	7	0.3	6.8
40–49	5	60.4	11.9
50–59	19	0.001	13.5
60–69	14	0	13
70–79	13	5.8	11.8
80–89	5	1.2	4.3
Mean	57.85	48.46	55.53
SD	16.52	9.94	17.15

of the analysis. Principal components analysis provides a way to examine relationships among variables when the data comprise a set of more than two variables. Principal components are a new set of variables computed from the original set, organizing the total variability so that it can be represented with fewer variables. This method is used at several points in this chapter. It allows the researcher to pinpoint ways in which the original variables are associated with each other. A further advantage of using a principal components analysis is that it allows graphing on two axes and the investigator can specify the cumulative percentage of variation accounted for by the two most important of the component variables. If more than two axes are taken into account, the data can be rotated so that the relationship among the data points can be understood in more detail.

Table 15.12 presents the results of a principal components analysis using the midpoint of the age range given by Kemkes-Grottenthaler (1993) for her sample of early medieval German skeletons. Here 58.44% of the variance is explained by the first principal component. In the Meindl/Lovejoy method, the correlation of each variable with the unrotated first principal component (in the first column of figures) "is then taken as its weight, and the final age of any individual is the weighted average of all

available age indicators for that specimen" (Lovejoy et al., 1985:4). Age assessment may be based on the assumption that there is a one-to-one relationship between an age indicator and a single age estimate, derived from the mean age per stage, but the Meindl/Lovejoy system assumes that the principal components analysis will show that some methods of assessment have a stronger relationship with real age than others. Table 15.12 shows that there are actually three sets among the age indicators used here. When the component matrix is rotated (third and fourth columns of figures), we can see more clearly that the three sets are based on (1) changes to os coxa surfaces, (2) dental attrition, and (3) cranial sutures. It appears here, especially from the rotated coefficients (in column 3, rotated first principal component), that mandibular attrition has the highest correlation with real age (0.896). It is not clear that introducing further variables such as cranial sutures actually increases the accuracy of the age assessment. However, we cannot test this because we cannot judge whether age-biased preservation differences are controlling the result of the principal components analysis.

Figure 15.4, based on the samples analyzed by Kemkes-Grottenthaler (1993), shows that no individual will be aged by all indicators, so that in using the Meindl/Lovejoy multifactorial method, we would have to weight final adult ages for these individuals when the majority could only be aged by suture closure. Age assessment would therefore be based on the indicator shown to have the weakest correlation with the first principal component (assumed to manifest age). Thus, in this example, age is controlled by taphonomic factors.

While it has long been considered that using more than one indicator in concert will give improved accuracy to age estimates (e.g., Brooks, 1955), it would seem desirable to have an improved understanding of the relationship among the indicators before multiple methods are used. This is because it is more difficult to assess the unique effects of each indicator and of taphonomic factors when elements are amalgamated. It would be cleaner in this case to use mandibular attrition as the age assessment method, and admit that a percentage of the adults must remain of indeterminate age at this stage of the analysis.

The "complex method" was first described in English by Acsádi and Nemeskéri in 1970 and then again by the Workshop of European Archeologists (WEA, 1980) with the tables for conjoint age assessment based on four or combinations of two or three age indicators calculated by Sjøvold. The basis for the method is a series of regression analyses (Acsádi and Nemeskéri, 1970) illustrating the relationship among the indicators. The complex method can be illustrated by again using the data provided by Kemkes-Grottenthaler (1993). Only 52 of 294 individuals from the medieval German cemetery at Eltville have all four age indicators, 24 males and 28 females. The situation for the Langenlonsheim site is even worse: two males and two females of a total of 181 individuals were the only individuals who retained all four indicators of the complex method.

The complex method scores derived from the Eltville sample were analyzed by principal components; only one component was extracted, explaining 54.6% of the variability. Assuming that the principal component extracted from these data actually expresses age, radiog-

TABLE 15.10   Distribution by Sex over the Masset Stages of Endocranial Suture Closure for Spitalfields Known Age Adults

Known Age Category	Masset Stage								Estimated from Prior Probabilities	
	4 Female	4 Male	5 Female	5 Male	6 Female	6 Male	7 Female	7 Male	Female	Male
20	2	—	1	1	—	1	—	—	2	1
30	1	—	3	—	—	2	—	—	4	2
40	1	—	—	—	1	—	—	—	5	3
50	2	—	1	1	4	—	3	3	6	3
60	—	—	1	—	4	—	2	5	7	3
70	1	—	—	—	1	2	4	2	7	3
80	—	—	1	—	2	—	1	—	4	1
	Females real age				Males real age					
Mean	57.83				56.26				57.65	55.83
SD	17.57				17.04				17.66	17.94

TABLE 15.11 Mean Ages Derived from Midpoints of Age Ranges for Age Indicators Applied to Two Medieval German Cemeteries. Group Statistics for Midpoint of Age Range

Indicator	Eltville Males (n = 145)			Langenlonsheim Males (n = 87)			Eltville Females (n = 149)			Langenlonsheim Females (n = 94)		
	N	Mean	SD	N	Mean	SD	N	Mean	SD	N	Mean	SD
Endocranial suture obliteration[a]	109	51.6	14.9	65	54.2	14.0	123	42.7	15.4	71	43.0	15.8
Femur[a]	74	50.7	5.6	19	50.1	4.2	85	48.4	6.6	22	47.3	5.0
Humerus[a]	62	55.3	4.9	11	54.8	5.6	62	56.5	4.5	11	54.3	5.3
Symphysis pubis[a]	52	54.7	8.9	9	58.3	6.0	48	53.1	10.6	9	51.8	12.6
Complex Method[a]	139	53.0	12.8	73	55.0	12.3	139	48.5	14.4	80	45.3	15.0
Maxillary attrition[b]	50	37.6	8.7	49	37.2	8.6	80	31.2	10.1	54	30.4	8.9
Mandibular attrition[b]	86	41.0	9.0	63	39.0	9.2	93	34.0	10.6	67	32.8	9.4
Ectocranial suture obliteration lateral-anterior[c]	99	38.0	5.4	57	38.4	5.6	115	35.4	5.4	65	35.3	5.4
Ectocranial suture obliteration vault[c]	104	38.3	7.0	60	38.6	7.1	123	34.9	7.2	68	33.2	6.5
Ribs[d]	52	31.3	9.5	3	36.3	2.0	57	24.4	11.7	9	20.0	4.1
Auricular surface[e]	73	40.7	10.2	14	37.9	7.8	84	37.9	11.4	29	40.0	11.5
Pubic symphysis[f]	52	40.9	12.4	9	44.4	12.6	48	40.0	13.2	9	38.3	12.5
Pubic symphysis[g]	52	40.2	11.4	9	45.9	11.8	48	44.7	14.1	9	41.7	15.1
Humerus spongiosa[h]	62	36.6	10.4	11	29.5	6.7	62	37.0	10.2	11	30.2	7.5
Femur spongiosa[h]	74	36.7	8.3	19	35.2	7.1	85	37.1	9.4	21	34.2	8.0
Pubic symphysis (Todd/Brooks)[i]	52	38.9	13.1	9	42.2	12.1	48	40.3	13.9	9	37.8	13.0

[a] WEA, 1980; [b] Lovejoy, 1985; [c] Meindl and Lovejoy, 1985; [d] Işcan and Loth, 1986a, 1986b; [e] Lovejoy et al., 1985; [f] Meindl et al., 1985; [g] Brooks and Suchey, 1990; [h] Szilvássy and Kritscher, 1990 (the overall difference between the sites is significant: $P = .000.$); [i] Krogman, 1962.

Data from Kemkes-Grottenthaler (1993).

raphy of the proximal humerus is least efficient in this sample as an age indicator. Proximal humeral trabecular stages are less correlated with this component than are the other three age indicators. Nevertheless, when all methods used by Kemkes-Grottenthaler (1993) are subject to Euclidean distance proximity analysis, a dissimilarity matrix is generated which shows that the femoral, humeral, and symphysis methods proposed by Acsádi and Nemeskéri for the complex method link closely, separated from all other techniques. This suggests that these three methods reinforce each other in giving older ages than those given by other age assessment methods. It is questionable then whether using four indicators of the complex method together will give a more accurate age; the central tendency of the indicators will simply be reinforced.

The matrix also reveals an interesting divergence between two methods of assessing radiographs of proximal femora. When examined in detail, it is clear that the Acsádi and Nemeskéri stages for femoral proximal trabecular alteration group individuals at around 35, 45, 55, and 65 years of age. On the other hand, the Szilvássy and Kritscher (1990) method, which provides a slightly different approach to femoral trabecular change produces a smoother distribution across all age groups from 20 to 70. This suggests that the reference population upon which the Acsádi and Nemeskéri complex method is based contributes to overaging in adults (as has been noted previously, e.g., Jackes, 1985).

Attrition and Other Dental Characteristics

Several age assessment methods are possible using the dentition. These are (1) for the occlusal and interproximal surfaces, observation of the removal of enamel and measurement of changes in crown dimensions; (2) radiographic examination of the height of the cemento-enamel junction above the inferior dental canal and radiographic or half tooth section examination of changes to the pulp chamber through the deposition of secondary dentin; and (3) histological studies of dentin and cementum. Rösing and Kvaal (1998) provide the most recent and comprehensive review of these methods.

Teeth are believed to be of particular value in age estimation (e.g. Hillson, 1998; Meindl and Russell, 1998). Attrition has even been used as the primary method of adult age estimation (Grauer, 1991). New methods of studying attrition using image analysis are proposed (Kambe et al., 1991; Mayhall and Kageyama, 1997) which require that dentitions be cast. Since casting before mandatory reburial is an obvious solution to the time-consuming nature of detailed dental analyses (Jackes, 1988), these suggestions are of great interest to researchers.

TABLE 15.12   Results of a Principal Components Analysis Using the Midpoint of Age Range Given by Meindl/Lovejoy Age Indicators

Component Matrix	Unrotated		Rotated (Varimax with Kaiser Normalization)	
Component	1	2	1	2
Auricular facies	0.653	−0.315	0.715	0.123
Pubic symphysis	0.731	−0.177	0.698	0.281
Maxillary attrition	0.845	−0.322	0.874	0.229
Mandibular attrition	0.875	−0.316	0.896	0.252
Lateral anterior sutures	0.733	0.609	0.242	0.922
Ectocranial vault sutures	0.726	0.602	0.241	0.912

Data from Kemkes-Grottenthaler (1993) for early medieval German skeletons.

The method proposed by Pot (Constandse-Westermann, 1997) appears to provide more detail than others similarly based only on removal of occlusal enamel. It has recently been tested by Constandse-Westermann on a known age and sex sample of middle-class Dutch from Zwolle who died between 1819 and 1828. Her study shows that, using attrition and alveolar resorption, it is possible to obtain a higher number of age estimates, and more accurate age estimates, than if the auricular surface, the pubic symphysis, or the Meindl/Lovejoy cranial suture methods are used. The average discrepancy from real age is 3.8 years for males, and 6.3 years for females. The difference between males and females in accuracy is not related to sex differences in attrition; it occurs because dental pathology is high in females in the sample.

The work on occlusal attrition in Portuguese teeth (e.g., Jackes, 1992; Lubell et al., 1994) has involved modifications of the Smith (1984) system. The modifications were introduced when the system was found to be unsatisfactory because teeth pass through wear levels at different rates, so that some wear levels must represent many years of adult life. The general applicability of the method has been tested on low attrition Chinese Neolithic teeth (Jackes and Gao, in press) and is being examined in high attrition Algerian Capsian teeth (sample discussed in Haverkort and Lubell, 1999). It would, even in its least detailed form, provide a much finer-grained picture of adult age than the Meindl/Lovejoy method. For example, in the Meindl/Lovejoy method of recording mandibular M1 attrition, their stages 2, 3, and 4 would be equivalent to the modified Smith stage 2; their 5 would be ca. 2.5; their 6 ca. 3 to 3.5; their 7 and 8 is equivalent to 4; 9 is 5; 10 is 6. There is no equivalent to the Smith stages 7 or 8. The Meindl/Lovejoy method examines cheek teeth as a unit, an approach that does not allow an understanding of differential wear between M1 and M2, and is therefore unable to compare rates of wear between samples based on coded differential wear among molars. Subtle changes in the rates of attrition occur even within samples that are separated by the minimum of dietary change (Jackes and Lubell, 1999; Lubell et al., 1994).

Jackes (1992) has proposed the use of dental changes beyond the simple removal of occlusal enamel. In fact, crown height by quadrant and details of enamel removal by quadrant are available for the Portuguese Neolithic, in association with changes in interproximal surfaces and wear plane angle. These data were gathered more than 10 years ago, but have not been analyzed in full. Others have used crown height as a variable in considering occlusion (Mayes et al., 1995; Walker et al., 1991; see Jackes, 1992, for discussion), and Molleson and Cohen (1990) experimentally studied the relationship of attrition stage to crown height reduction. Use of detailed type of information such as quadrant crown height is perhaps infrequent because of the enormous amount of time required for data collection and analysis.

Based on a very detailed method of scoring molar attrition, Dreier (1994) has shown a difference in attrition between males and females for a sample of Arikara of unknown age, with sex determined from crania and innominates. Other studies have shown a similar pattern (Larsen, 1997 provides a summary), but we cannot assume that the attrition in females was actually greater, unless the sample under study is of known age. Perhaps the females in the Arikara sample were actually older, on average, than the males (although the studies that have shown female dentitions to be more worn can generally associate female dental wear to the use of teeth as tools). In the unusual case of the Narrinyeri (84 male skulls and 72 female skulls from the nineteenth-century mass burials at the River Murray mouth in South Australia studied by Richards, 1984), some teeth do appear to wear relatively faster in females. In providing regression equations describing the relationship between tooth wear and age, based on known age individuals, Richards and Miller (1991) find no need to separate the sexes.

Bite force may be a factor in sex differences in tooth wear (Brothwell, 1989) although some evidence contradicts this idea (Hojo, 1954; Solheim, 1988). The need to consider sex in studies of the degree of cheek teeth attrition is not clearly determined, but not such study whether of occlusal or interproximal attrition, of secondary dentin deposition, or periodontal recession, should ignore the possibility of sex differences based on diet, activity, strength of jaw muscles, or jaw and tooth size.

Spitalfields individuals were coded for attrition using a simple grading system, derived from Brothwell (1981). Figure 15.9 shows the first right lower molars of males (n = 31) and females (n = 26) of known age and sex plotted against fit calculated by exact maximum likelihood. This is an estimation technique that finds those parameter estimates that are "most likely" to have produced the observed data (calculated for a sum of squares change of 0.001%, stability was reached at four iterations). Back plotting of the fit values against the actual wear codes shows clearly that predicted age from maximum likelihood would not be accurate. Categorical regression with optimal scaling of the five-year age categories and attrition scores as ordinal data provides a correlation coefficient of .578 and standard error of .11, but 66% of the sum of squares is unexplained.

It should be noted that the Lowess lines plotted on Figure 15.9 do not assume a linear or nonlinear relationship of the variables—either could be produced.[3] Figure 15.9 provides a clear indication that Spitalfields male attrition is greater than female attrition. Some of the analyses undertaken on the Spitalfields

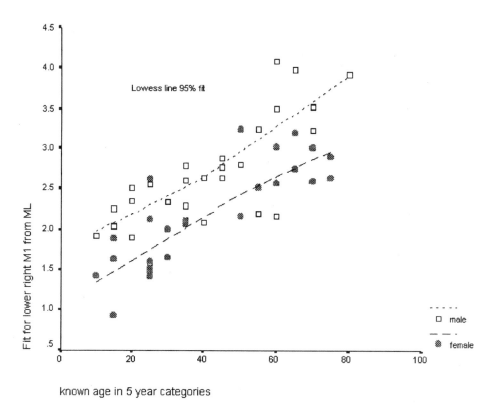

Figure 15.9 First right lower molars of males (n = 31) and females (n = 26) of known age and sex from Spitalfields plotted against fit calculated by exact maximum likelihood.

data suggest that female attrition levels off before male attrition. We can assume that the differential is not related to dietary or activity factors, but directly to the forces developed under male masticatory muscle strength. This would indicate that samples showing no sexual difference in attrition, or heavier female attrition, either have much reduced sexual dimorphism or strong differences in female diet and dental use. The standard error of the fit does not indicate that male attrition is more variable than female attrition. However, the information on the Spitalfields attrition is limited by the grading system used, which is not sensitive to subtle changes in crown wear, demonstrated by the fact that in most individuals the first molar was not recorded as more worn than second the molar. Santini and colleagues (1990) tested Brothwell's system on Chinese dentitions of known age at death and concluded that the inaccuracy of the method was too great for it to be useful. They did, however, note the differential rates of wear between first and second molars, asserting that the first molar actually wears faster than the second.

The use of maximum likelihood illustrates a growing concern that anthropologists have used regression analysis in an inappropriate way. It has been common to accept that, say, 11 attrition grades can be treated statistically as though they are continuous data. They could be more properly regarded as ordinal data. They can be used as frequency data for hazard analysis, or nonparametric analyses can be performed. In this latter case, performing a (nonlinear) regression analysis of stages used for the Spitalfields right lower first molars on five-year age categories yields an r of .468 (SE = 1.19).[4]

Future research on dental attrition rates should take into account that Richards and Miller (1991) have demonstrated the relationship between age and cheek tooth attrition to be nonlinear. They suggest the possibility that the first molars wear at a faster rate than the second molars. This idea deserves testing. The M1 comes into wear in association with the

dm2, which may provide less of a buffering effect than is provided by the M2 when it comes into wear. The difference in the force of the bite of a child, as against that of an adolescent, may, however, offset the difference between the dm2 and the M2 as the proximate tooth. Constandse-Westermann (1997) provides fascinating data from a series of Dutch cemeteries ranging over 1600 years suggesting that, not only the difference between M1 and M2 wear, but the trajectory of that difference (the comparison between the two teeth at different states of wear), has altered over time.

Along with attrition, radiographic examination of dentitions may provide important information on age-dependent changes, but radiographic techniques of age estimation have yet to be tested in full.

Kerr and Ringrose (1998) have summarized work on the compensatory eruption of teeth, a method that could be used to check age estimates in samples with severe attrition. The method is based on the proposal that as a tooth crown wears, bone is laid down at the root tip so that the occlusal level of the tooth is maintained. This compensatory bone can be observed on radiographs by measurements from the fixed point of the inferior dental canal. Data reconstructed from the diagrams provided by Kerr and Ringrose (1998) indicate that the inferior dental canal to tooth root tip measurement (AP) seen on mandibular radiographs does correlate with the inferior dental canal to occlusal surface (OS) measurement. But attrition does not bear a close relationship to these variables. Rather, we see a bimodal distribution of the AP measurement, requiring that sex be entered into the equation, and several outlying data points require explanation. At present, the hypothesis appears unproven.

---

[3]Lowess lines are locally weighted regression lines produced by smoothing collections of values along the X scale; the curve is produced by connecting successive smoothed values from left to right by line segments.
[4]Giles and Klepinger, 1988, and Rösing and Kvaal, 1998, urge that the SE of the regression estimate, also called m, be reported in age estimation by regression analysis.

Examination of dental radiographs for Portuguese Mesolithic and Neolithic material suggests that specialized radiography may be required, especially when root tip and the margin of the inferior dental canal must be identified with great precision. Perhaps because of heavy redeposition of minerals, or because of the radiographic techniques available under some study conditions, the Portuguese material is not easily amenable to this type of analysis.

Drusini and colleagues (1997) have proposed the use of panoramic radiography, and this was also used in my studies of Mesolithic Portuguese dentitions, with rather poor results. Enhanced radiographic techniques may have to be employed before accurate measurements can be made. Image enhancement techniques have not proved very useful thus far. It is probable that the measurements required by this method, which uses a ratio of crown height to the height of the coronal pulp cavity (Drusini et al., 1997) can be made with more accuracy using some form of image analyzer, than can the method of Kvaal and colleagues (1995), which requires that the root tip be clearly visualized. The tooth coronal index of Drusini appears to have a high correlation with real age, higher than the pulp height and width indices of Kvaal and co-workers.

There is a great deal more information on sectioned tooth root analysis than radiography. The examination of microscopic changes in conjunction with macroscopic features has a long history in forensic dentistry and anthropology since Gustafson (1950) first published his system based on six age-related characteristics. More recently, Solheim (1993) has proposed a new series of multiple regressions for dental age estimation. In each one, root translucency is an essential variable and color is a frequent variable. We need to enquire how important translucency is to age estimation. Lucy and colleagues (1995) have noted that it is impossible to use color and translucency when assessing archaeological teeth, and have suggested modifying dental estimation techniques to take this into account. Kvaal and co-workers (1994) suggest that the length of the apical translucent zone of the root be ignored in archaeological contexts.

It seems likely that cemental annulation will be of greatest value in the analysis of sectioned tooth roots from archaeological contexts (and Grosskopf, 1990, determined that this may even include cremations). Cipriano-Bechtle and colleagues (1996), using early medieval skeletons from a Bavarian cemetery, compared the results of age assessment derived from the complex method with those from microscopic examinations of the cementum of premolar tooth roots. Figure 15.10 demonstrates that the two distributions of adult ages, one derived from cemental annulations and the other from macroscopic methods of adult age estimation, are discrepant. The cemental annulation technique provides a distribution that has apparent biological validity, in contrast with standard macroscopic methods of adult age assessment, and gives a smoother distribution extending well beyond 60 years of age.

The counting of cemental annulations is not simple, however, and we cannot take it for granted (Jackes, 1992; Rösing and Kvaal, 1998). The most ambitious test of cemental annulation counting is that by Geusa and colleagues (1999). The roots of 150 canines and premolars (from 129 individuals) were sectioned and separately examined by phase contrast microscopy and digital enhancement of images of thin sections. Consequently, there are two separate cemental annulation age estimates to compare with age assessed by standard macroscopic methods. The degree of diagenesis is also recorded. Differences between teeth of the same individual, between estimates from the two separate laboratories (ranging from 0 to 29 years), and between estimates based on macroscopic age (which can be regarded as reasonably accurate up to age 25 or so) and those derived from cemental annulation, all raise questions as to the accuracy of cemental annulation age estimates. Testing indicates that there is no obvious effect of jaw, tooth, or sex on preservation, or interaction among these factors, nor indeed is there an in-

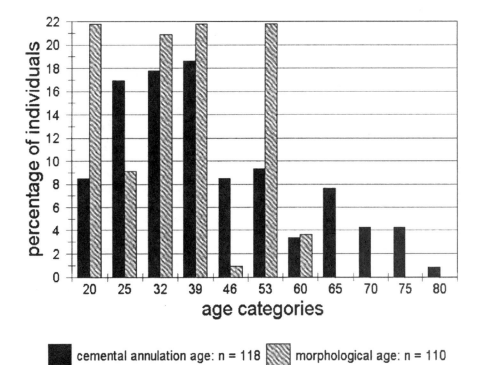

Figure 15.10   Comparison of distribution of adult ages derived from morphological indicators and from cemental annulation. (Data from Cipriano-Bechtle et al., 1996).

teraction between preservation differences and the discrepancy in the results from the two laboratories. Problems of preservation do not, therefore, explain the discrepancies.

DISCUSSION OF POSSIBLE SOLUTIONS

As yet we have no firm solutions to the problem of adult age assessment. We have seen that proposed statistical techniques do not provide the magic answer, and we could hardly expect that this would be so. If the "age indicators" do not directly manifest age, then redistributing frequencies of age indicators by a variety of statistical approaches will not lead to true ages. It would be beneficial to reexamine the reference data where possible, for example all the data of Acsádi and Nemeskéri, in such a way as

to confirm the relationships of indicators with age. The data on cranial suture closure given in Acsádi and Nemeskéri (1970) may well be best analyzed by categorical regression with optimal scaling. When the suture closure points are treated as ordinal data, age categories as numerical, the correlation coefficient is .571 with a standard error of .049. It should be noted that the residual sum of squares in this analysis, the unexplained error around the regression line, constitutes a full 67% of the total.

I believe that we must use indicator stages as they are—simply stages of skeletal change, which, like degrees of degenerative change in joints, have some relationship with age, but a relationship that is governed by many and complex factors. Age may contribute no more than 30% of the variability to these changes. I suggest that we observe and record age-dependent changes fully and in detail, seeking to compare them in systematic ways (as Kemkes-Grottenthaler, 1993, 1996a, has done). This will provide a foundation for analysis of these data across time and space. They will *not* be recorded and analyzed as age indicators, but rather as further data in our attempt to understand human populations in the past. In studying how the "erstwhile age-indicators"correlate with each other and with other skeletal characteristics, and gender, diet, activity, trauma, pathology, etc., we may begin to approach the "great unknown"(Jackes, 1992) of skeletal biology, the absolute age at death of adults in past populations.

What type of approach should be taken? As a first step and an example, Figure 15.11 shows the result of analyses of data from Kemkes-Grottenthaler (1993), but not in terms of age range or mean age or probability. These data were reworked into the original stage assignments. The Todd pubic age was excluded since the number of individuals falling firmly within a stage was very limited (only 51/118 or 43.2% of pubes were classified as falling directly within a stage, all other pubes fell between two or more stages). Acsádi/Nemeskéri complex age (which is derived from regression formulae) and clavicle age were also excluded. All other variables were analyzed as ordinal variables based on stage coding.

The data, as converted back into the defined stages, can be treated as multivariate ordinal data (in this analysis integer data only are used, so that all cases where the individual fell between predefined stages have been excluded). Optimal Scaling by Alternating Least Squares procedures using Nonlinear Principal Components Analysis (PRINCALS) in SPSS provides an easy method of analyzing such ordinal data.

It is obviously essential that such data be analyzed separately for males and females. Here I have simplified, not analyzing by site and choosing only one set of data for each indicator, attempting to use definitions provided and indicators proposed by a variety of researchers, in order to minimize the intercorrelations. The

following will be used: Suchey/Brooks pubic symphyses; Meindl/Lovejoy auricular facies and dental attrition; Acsádi/Nemeskéri suture obliteration; humeral and femoral spongiosa (Szilvássy and Kritscher, 1990); and rib stages (Loth and İşcan, 1989).

Figure 15.11a and b suggests that some "former age indicators" may function very differently from others. Several analyses have confirmed the grouping of suture, by whichever method, and dental stages. An obvious explanation for Figure 15.11 might be that individuals lacking skulls and teeth are different in "age" from those with skulls and teeth. This has been checked by comparing Suchey/Brooks pubes data for individuals with and without "dental age" (i.e., mandibular and maxillary ages combined): there is no significant difference (Monte Carlo estimate of $P = .42$).

The distribution of suture closure stages in skulls with and without "dental age" is significantly different ($P = .000$), however, but when the suture closure stage frequencies are translated into distributions over 10-year age categories by probability, there is no statistical significance to the difference: $P = .53$ (Monte Carlo estimate).

A more likely explanation for the grouping of attrition and suture closure is that both suture obliteration and the Meindl/Lovejoy attrition method have a very specific cutoff point. Once sutures are closed, no further changes can be recorded. Closure may well occur long before death. Thus, in the known age individuals at Spitalfields with complete suture closure, four died in their fifties, four in their sixties, six in their seventies, and one in the eighties. Similarly, the Meindl/Lovejoy attrition method has the characteristic of reaching its maximum level at a relatively early stage of dental wear, when the first molars still have some crown height and occlusal enamel remaining. The maximum stage would be reached well before death in most long-lived individuals.

Further analyses have indicated that the sternal ends of ribs, and humeral or femoral proximal spongiosa may provide results dif-

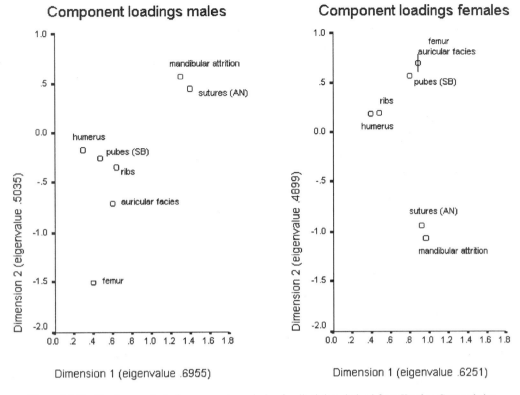

Figure 15.11   Nonlinear principal components analysis of ordinal data derived from Kemkes-Grottenthaler (1993): (A) males, (B) females. Component loadings show the relative contribution of the variables to the two dimensions.

ferent from those of other "age indicators." Pasquier and colleagues (1999) have proposed a new method of examining Suchey/Brooks male pubic symphysis stages, adding variables and recording both the right and left pubes, thereby increasing the linear correlation between pubic symphysis and true age to .86. While this computed tomography radiograph technique is hardly available to those working on archaeological samples, the idea that variables can be added to our present series will provide motivation for further research, perhaps using radiography.

Although not discussed in detail in this chapter, research into changes in spongiosa with age is of importance to the question of age-dependent changes in the human skeleton. Recent work is summarized by Brickley and

Howell (1999). But what methods can be used to get a true picture of age changes in cortical thickness and trabecular structure? Brickley and Howell (1999) show changes across their morphologically determined age categories, as is to be expected. But it is very unlikely that they have demonstrated the true pattern of change across older age categories, since females of age 36 and above show no significant differences across age categories.

Seriation of adults by many different "stage" methods, in a consistent manner and without preconceptions as to a necessary linkage of "stage" and "age," may free skeletal biology from something of a quagmire. The major focus will be to understand skeletal changes during the course of adult life, with emphasis on sex differences (evident from

Figure 15.11), on how to cope with sampling bias, and on sample differences. Thus we may begin to understand more clearly the impact of adult lives on skeletons. It would, of course, be desirable to have some age control for the particular sample being analyzed. In the recent past, it has been assumed that bone histomorphometry will supply all that is needed by way of age assessment, but this can no longer be accepted (e.g., Pfeiffer, 1998). There can be little doubt that, for the type of large archaeological samples under consideration, detailed analysis of dental attrition, including not simply loss of occlusal enamel but loss of crown height and other considerations (Jackes, 1992), will be a first step. Dental radiographs should be included in the analyses, especially if there is to be reburial.

While we cannot yet be certain that the methods used by Drusini and colleagues (1997), Kerr and Ringrose (1998), or Kvaal and colleagues (1995) will always provide useful information, such nondestructive methods must be explored for their potential. Selection of individual teeth, male and female, representative of stages of change identified by the seriation, can be made to allow the identification of the age of adults, and especially of those who appear oldest in a sample, as proposed by Jackes (1992) using cemental annulations. Rösing and Kvaal (1998) identify cemental annulations as the best choice for age estimation after amino acid racemization, which cannot be used on archaeological samples. Advances in the accuracy of cemental annulation counting (±2 years) are being reported (Wittwer-Bachofen, per. comm). Direct microscopy of various types, rather than image enhancement, contributes to the accuracy (also found to be true for our Portuguese thin section analysis). An important factor is likely to be the method of preparation of the unpolished thin sections.

We cannot doubt the necessity of using cemental annulations as a control when we read that "By the age of 40 years, occlusal wear (in almost all individuals prior to the seventeenth century [in a Scottish sample]) had reached the amelocemental junction with very few individuals retaining fully functional dentitions beyond the age of 40 years" (Kerr and Ringrose, 1998:245). These individuals had no evidence of hypercementosis, suggesting little heavy mastication. We can compare this with the situation reported by Richards and Miller (1991) of central Australian desert-living Aborigines who still, when studied in the 1950s and 1960s, maintained "food preparation, dietary preferences, and use of teeth for non-masticatory purposes" little removed from that of hunter-gatherers. The level of attrition reported for medieval Scots at age 40 (complete removal of occlusal enamel) would be highly unusual for desert Aborigines at age 70: most individuals from 60 to 80 years still maintained 20% of their occlusal enamel on the first molars. At age 40 in desert Aboriginal teeth, 60% of the occlusal enamel remained.

When tooth root microbial destruction is not too great, examination of tooth roots must be undertaken, and if facilities are not available, then it would seem essential that representative samples of roots be retained in event of reburial. Permission to take samples for cemental annulation counting should always be sought when arranging for samples for DNA amplification (whether for biological distance studies, or for confirming the sex of individuals for whom sex ascription is uncertain), for dating and for stable isotope analysis. Casts and radiographs of the dentition and the use of technology that will allow direct input of detailed dental measurements should be the very first steps in the recording of any skeletons that may be subject to reburial. A major consideration is the standization of radiographs when measurements are to be taken, unless all variables are expressed as ratios. The Portuguese femoral radiographs (Jackes, 1992) were taken in several facilities, but standardization is possible because all proximal femora were photographed in standardized ways that allow the checking of measurements made in the field with absolute accuracy using electronic scaling techniques. Radiographs can be laid over standardized photographic images and the scale adjusted electronically.

CONCLUSIONS

The effort here has been to try to establish viable methods for researchers working with samples large enough to allow reconstruction of population prevalences of age-dependent characters and of paleodemographic parameters. Our concern is to enquire into what is feasible under the conditions prevailing now, and considerations required by comparison of material being studied now with that studied in the past. Because large and representative samples are absolutely necessary in order to make valid statements about the adult age-at-death distribution of past populations, the question of feasibility is basic. One cannot, and should not, section all teeth within a large sample, saw through all long bone proximal ends (Molleson and Cox, 1993; WEA, 1980), or obtain readable thin sections from all femoral cortices, fourth ribs, or clavicles. A consideration here is what can most profitably be done to collect information quickly, accurately, and economically, especially when reburial is a possibility.

There must be detailed examination of dentitions, with careful consideration of which teeth might be sacrificed for root sectioning. Standardized photography and radiography of jaws and long bones must be undertaken, and casting of teeth should be undertaken where reburial is likely. No great advances have been published in recent years on the question of adult age assessment, and cemental annulation remains the method most likely to restore paleodemography to importance within skeletal biology. Work on known age samples has brought light to some dark corners, as has the vast amount of work undertaken by Kemkes-Grottenthaler. The increased interest of skeletal biologists in the use of categorical analyses will provide a new approach, freeing us from feeling coerced into estimating "ages" from stages. We will use indicator stages, not as age

estimators, but as categories of change during adult life, which will provide us with ways to understand how the human skeleton responds to the exigencies of adult life under many circumstances. The lack of age control will be an acknowledged limitation. Where possible, the limitation will be partially alleviated by the provision of a scale through cemental annulations. This scale will be a control for seriation based on detailed analyses of dentitions.

ACKNOWLEDGMENTS

I am particularly grateful to Theya Molleson for her generosity in making the Spitalfields data available to me, and her willingness to take the time and effort this required. I am asked by her to acknowledge the funders (the Greater London Council, the Nuffield Foundation, English Heritage (London Division), the Wellcome Trust, Mrs. Elizabeth Frayne), the British Museum (Natural History) and Dr. Suzanne Evans, Department of Statistics, Birkbeck College, University of London, whose MSc students entered the data. Thanks to Robert Hoppa and Sheilagh Thompson Brooks for help with access to additional Spitalfields data. Eugénia Cunha helped me obtain the thesis of Ana Luísa da Conceição dos Santos, who kindly performed some extra calculations on her data at my request. Ariane Kemkes-Grottenthaler is thanked for sending me her thesis. N.G. Prasad of the Department of Mathematical Sciences, University of Alberta, provided invaluable help, confirming my iterative program and independently producing a flexible approach that enabled me to test the method over a number of techniques and samples. Christina Barker and Michael Wayman of Chemical and Materials Engineering and Richard Sherburne of Medical Microbiology and Immunology at the University of Alberta are thanked for their help in obtaining the fine images in Plate 1. David Lubell, as always, has contributed to this chapter in many ways.

APPENDIX: SUCHEY BROOKS PUBIC SYMPHYSEAL DISTRIBUTION REFERENCE DATA

TABLE A1 Midpoint of Age Categories: Male Sample Distribution by Age and Stage

Stage	17.5	22.5	27.5	32.5	37.5	42.5	47.5	52.5	57.5	62.5	67.5	72.5	77.5	82.5	87.5	92.5	Total
1	73	30	0	0	0	0	0	0	0	0	0	0	0	0	0	0	103
2	6	52	12	4	1	0	0	0	0	0	0	0	0	0	0	0	75
3	0	11	24	7	4	2	3	0	0	0	0	0	0	0	0	0	51
4	0	12	41	47	23	18	14	11	2	0	2	1	0	0	0	0	171
5	0	1	9	15	11	19	35	23	13	4	2	0	1	1	0	0	134
6	0	0	0	6	2	11	15	25	27	37	27	27	16	4	4	2	203
Total	79	106	86	79	41	50	67	59	42	41	31	28	17	5	4	2	737

TABLE A2 Mid point of Age Categories: Female Sample Distribution by Age and Stage

Stage	17.5	22.5	27.5	32.5	37.5	42.5	47.5	52.5	57.5	62.5	67.5	72.5	77.5	82.5	87.5	92.5	Total
1	25	22	1	0	0	0	0	0	0	0	0	0	0	0	0	0	48
2	3	23	16	2	1	2	0	0	0	0	0	0	0	0	0	0	47
3	0	10	11	15	4	1	1	1	0	1	0	0	0	0	0	0	44
4	0	0	10	7	7	7	3	1	2	0	0	2	0	0	0	0	39
5	0	0	2	5	8	5	4	7	6	2	1	0	1	2	1	0	44
6	0	0	0	0	0	4	7	6	11	8	5	5	1	2	2	0	51
Total	28	55	40	29	20	19	15	15	19	11	6	7	2	4	3	0	273

TABLE A3   Males Bayesian Probabilities Cell/Stage Total

Midpoint of Age Category	Stage 1	Stage 2	Stage 3	Stage 4	Stage 5	Stage 6	Total
17.5	0.709	0.080	0.000	0.000	0.000	0.000	0.789
22.5	0.291	0.693	0.216	0.070	0.007	0.000	1.278
27.5	0.000	0.160	0.471	0.240	0.067	0.000	0.938
32.5	0.000	0.053	0.137	0.275	0.112	0.030	0.607
37.5	0.000	0.013	0.078	0.135	0.082	0.010	0.318
42.5	0.000	0.000	0.039	0.105	0.142	0.054	0.340
47.5	0.000	0.000	0.059	0.082	0.261	0.074	0.476
52.5	0.000	0.000	0.000	0.064	0.172	0.123	0.359
57.5	0.000	0.000	0.000	0.012	0.097	0.133	0.242
62.5	0.000	0.000	0.000	0.000	0.030	0.182	0.212
67.5	0.000	0.000	0.000	0.012	0.015	0.133	0.160
72.5	0.000	0.000	0.000	0.006	0.000	0.133	0.139
77.5	0.000	0.000	0.000	0.000	0.007	0.079	0.086
82.5	0.000	0.000	0.000	0.000	0.007	0.020	0.027
87.5	0.000	0.000	0.000	0.000	0.000	0.020	0.020
92.5	0.000	0.000	0.000	0.000	0.000	0.010	0.010
	1	1	1	1	1	1	6

TABLE A4   Females Bayesian Probabilities Cell/Stage Total

Midpoint of Age Category	Stage 1	Stage 2	Stage 3	Stage 4	Stage 5	Stage 6	Total
17.5	0.521	0.064	0.000	0.000	0.000	0.000	0.58
22.5	0.458	0.489	0.227	0.000	0.000	0.000	1.17
27.5	0.021	0.340	0.250	0.256	0.045	0.000	0.91
32.5	0.000	0.043	0.341	0.179	0.114	0.000	0.68
37.5	0.000	0.021	0.091	0.179	0.182	0.000	0.47
42.5	0.000	0.043	0.023	0.179	0.114	0.078	0.44
47.5	0.000	0.000	0.023	0.077	0.091	0.137	0.33
52.5	0.000	0.000	0.023	0.026	0.159	0.118	0.33
57.5	0.000	0.000	0.000	0.051	0.136	0.216	0.40
62.5	0.000	0.000	0.023	0.000	0.045	0.157	0.23
67.5	0.000	0.000	0.000	0.000	0.023	0.098	0.12
72.5	0.000	0.000	0.000	0.051	0.000	0.098	0.15
77.5	0.000	0.000	0.000	0.000	0.023	0.020	0.04
82.5	0.000	0.000	0.000	0.000	0.045	0.039	0.08
87.5	0.000	0.000	0.000	0.000	0.023	0.039	0.06
92.5	0.000	0.000	0.000	0.000	0.000	0.000	0.00
	1	1	1	1	1	1	6

TABLE A5 Revised Probabilities over 95% CL for Suchey/Brooks Pubic Symphysis Method, Males

5-Year Age Categories	Stage 1	Stage 2	Stage 3	Stage 4	Stage 5	Stage 6
15	0.7226	0.1490	0.0691	0.0311		
20	0.2172	0.4975	0.1923	0.0866	0.0011	
25		0.2966	0.2905	0.1513	0.0430	
30		0.0114	0.2535	0.2010	0.0872	
35			0.1278	0.2029	0.1411	0.0186
40			0.0213	0.1556	0.1819	0.0510
45				0.0907	0.1869	0.0871
50				0.0352	0.1531	0.1262
55					0.1000	0.1549
60					0.0520	0.1612
65					0.0083	0.1423
70						0.1064
75						0.0675
80						0.0363
85						0.0030

TABLE A6 Revised Probabilities over 95% CL for Suchey/Brooks Pubic Symphysis Method, Females

5-Year Age Categories	Stage 1	Stage 2	Stage 3	Stage 4	Stage 5	Stage 6
15	0.5521	0.1276	0.0670	0.0251	0.0007	
20	0.3947	0.3464	0.1476	0.0657	0.0265	
25		0.3491	0.2248	0.1132	0.0462	
30		0.1315	0.2367	0.1586	0.0719	
35			0.1723	0.1809	0.0995	0.0222
40			0.0867	0.1678	0.1228	0.0581
45			0.0160	0.1266	0.1349	0.0994
50				0.0777	0.1320	0.1416
55				0.0388	0.1151	0.1679
60					0.0894	0.1658
65					0.0618	0.1363
70					0.0381	0.0932
75					0.0154	0.0531
80						0.0168

REFERENCES

Acsádi G, Nemeskéri J. 1970. History of Human Life Span and Mortality. Budapest: Akadémiai Kiadó.

Aiello LC, Molleson T. 1993. Are microscope ageing techniques more accurate than macroscopic ageing techniques? J Archaeol Sci 20:689–704.

Anderson JE. 1969. The Human Skeleton: A Manual for Archaeologists: Rev ed. Ottawa: The Queen's Printer for The National Museums of Canada.

Aykroyd RG, Lucy D, Pollard AM, Roberts CA. 1999. Nasty, brutish, but not necessarily short: a reconsideration of the statistical methods used to calculate age at death from adult human skeletal and dental age indicators. Am Antiq 64:55–70.

Bass WM. 1995. Human Osteology: A Laboratory and Field Manual of the Human Skeleton, 4th edition. Columbia, Mo.: Missouri Archaeological Society.

Bedford ME, Russell KF, Lovejoy CO, Meindl RS, Simpson SW, Stuart-Macadam PL. 1993. A test of the multifactorial aging method using skeletons with known ages at death from the Grant Collection. Am J Phys Anthropol 91:287–297.

Bocquet J-P. 1978. Estimation methods of age at death in adult skeletons and demographic structure of the populations of the past. In: Garralda MD, Grande RM, editors. I Simposio De Antropologia Biologica De Espana. Madrid: Facultad de Biología Cuidad Universitar. pp. 37–47.

Bocquet-Appel J-P. 1986. Once upon a time: palaeodemography. In: Herrmann B, editor. Innovative Trends in der prähistorischen Anthropologie. Mitteilungen der Berliner Gesellschaft für Anthropologie, Ethnologie und Urgeschichte 7. Berlin: Free University.

Bocquet-Appel J-P, Bacro JN. 1997. Estimates of some demographic parameters in a neolithic rock-cut chamber (approximately 2000 BC) using iterative techniques for aging and demographic estimators. Am J Phys Anthropol 102:569–575.

Bocquet-Appel J-P, Masset C. 1977. Estimateurs en paléodémographie. L'Homme 17:65–70.

Bocquet-Appel J-P, Masset C. 1982. Farewell to paleodemography. J Hum Evol 11:321–333.

Bocquet-Appel J-P, Masset C. 1996. Paleodemography: expectancy and false hope. Am J Phys Anthropol 99:571–583.

Boldsen JL. 1988. Two methods for the reconstruction of the empirical mortality profile. Hum Evol 3:335–342.

Boldsen JL, Paine RP. 1995. The evolution of human longevity from the Mesolithic to the Middle Ages: an analysis based on skeletal data. In: Jeune B, Vaupel JW, editors. Exceptional Longevity: From Prehistory to the Present. Odense, Denmark: Odense University Press. pp. 25–36.

Brickley M, Howell PGT. 1999. Measurement of changes in trabecular bone structure with age in an archaeological population. J Archaeol Sci 26:151–157.

Brooks ST. 1955. Skeletal age at death: the reliability of cranial and pubic age indicators. Am J Phys Anthropol 13:567–589.

Brooks ST, Suchey JM, 1990. Skeletal age determination based on the os pubis: a comparison of the Acsádi-Nemeskéri and Suchey-Brooks methods. Hum Evol 5:227–238.

Brothwell DR. 1981. Digging Up Bones: The Excavation, Treatment and Study of Human Skeletal Remains third edition. London: British Museum (Natural History) and Cornell University Press, Ithaca, NY.

Brothwell D. 1989. The relationship of tooth wear to aging. In İşcan MY, editor. Age Markers in the Human Skeleton. Springfield, Ill: Charles C. Thomas. pp. 303–324.

Buikstra JE, Konigsberg LW. 1985. Paleodemography: critiques and controversies. Am Anthropol 87:316–333.

Bush H, Zvelebil M, editors. 1991. Health in Past Societies. BAR International Series 567. Oxford, England.

Caselitz P. 1998. Caries—ancient plague of humankind. In: Alt KW, Rösing FW, Teschler-Nicola M, editors. Dental Anthropology: Fundamentals, Limits and Prospects. New York: Springer-Verlag. pp. 203–226.

Cipriano-Bechtle A, Grupe G, Schröter P. 1996. Ageing and life expectancy in the early Middle Ages. Homo 46:267–279.

Coale AJ, Demeny P. 1966. Regional Model Life Tables and Stable Populations. Princeton, N.J.: Princeton University Press.

Constandse-Westerman TS. 1997. Age estimation by dental attrition in an independently controlled early 19th century sample from Zwolle, the Netherlands. Hum Evol 12:269–285.

Crubézy E, Murail P. 1998. Structure par âge et par sexe de la population inhumée. In: Crubézy E., Causse L, Delmas J, Ludes B, editors. 1998 Le Paysan Médiéval en Rouergue: cimetière et église de Canac (Campagnac, Aveyron). pp. 71–76.

Dreier FG. 1994. Age at death estimates for the protohistoric Arikara using molar attrition rates: a new quantification method. Int J Osteoarchaeol 4:137–147.

Drusini AG, Toso O, Ranzato C. 1997. The coronal pulp cavity index: a biomarker for age determination in human adults. Am J Phys Anthropol 103:353–363.

Dudar JC, Pfeiffer S, Saunders SR. 1993. Evaluation of morphological and histological adult skeletal age-at-death estimation techniques using ribs. J Forensic Sci 38:677–685.

Galera V, Ubelaker DH, Hayek L. 1998. Comparison of macroscopic cranial methods of age estimation applied to skeletons from the Terry Collection. J Forensic Sci 43:933–939.

Geusa G, Bondioli L, Capucci E, Cipriano A, Grupe G, Savorè C, Macchiarelli R. 1999. Dental cementum annulations and age at death estimates. Osteodental biology of people of Portus Romae (Necropolis of Isola Sacra, 2nd–3rd cent. AD). In: Bondioli L, Macchiarelli R, editors. Digital Archives of Human Paleobiology, Vol. 2. Rome: Museo Nazionale Preistorico Etnografico "L. Pigorini."

Giles E, Klepinger LL. 1988. Confidence intervals for estimates based on linear regression in forensic anthropology. J Forensic Sci 33:1218–1222.

Grauer AL. 1991. Patterns of life and death: the palaeodemography of medieval York. In: Bush H, Zvelebil M, editors. Health in Past Societies. BAR International Series 567.

Grosskopf B. 1990. Individualaltersbestimmung mit Hilfe von Zuwachsringen im Zement bodengelagerter meschlicher Zähne. Z Rechtsmed 103:351–359.

Gustafson G. 1950. Age determination on teeth. J Am Dent Assn 41:45–54.

Havercourt CM, Lubell D. 1999. Cutmarks on Capsian human remains: implications for Maghreb Holocene social organization and palaeoeconomy. Int J Osteoarchaeol. 9:147–169.

Harpending H. 1997. Living records of past population change. In: Paine RR, editor. Integrating Archaeological Demography: Multidisciplinary Approaches to Prehistoric Population. Carbondale: Southern Illinois University Press. pp. 89–100.

Hershkovitz I, Latimer B, Dutour O, Jellema LM, Wish-Baratz S, Rothschild C, Rothschild B. 1997a. The elusive petroexoccipital articulation. Am J Phys Anthropol 103:365–373.

Hershkovitz I, Latimer B, Dutour O, Jellema LM, Wish-Baratz S, Rothschild C, Rothschild B. 1997b. Why do we fail in aging the skull from the sagittal suture? Am J Phys Anthropol 103:393–399.

Hillson S. 1998. Knowing your roots. Nature 396:640–641.

Hojo M. 1954. On the pattern of dental abrasion. Okajimas Folia Anat Jpn 26:11–30.

Hoppa R. 2000. Population variation in osteological aging criteria: an example from the pubic symphysis. Am J Phys Anthropol 111:185–191.

Hoppa R, Saunders S. 1998. The MAD legacy: how meaningful is mean age-at-death in skeletal samples. Hum Evol 13:1–14.

Howell N. 1982. Village composition implied by a paleodemographic life table. Am J Phys Anthropol 59:263–269.

İşcan MY, Loth SR, Wright RK. 1984. Metamorphosis at the sternal rib: a new method to estimate age at death in males. Am J Phys Anthropol 65:147–156.

İşcan MY, Loth SR. 1986a. Determination of age from the sternal rib in white males: a test of the phase method. J Forensic Sci 31:122–132.

İşcan MY, Loth SR. 1986b. Determination of age from the sternal rib in white females: a test of the phase method. J Forensic Sci 31:990–999.

İşcan MY, editor. 1989. Age Markers in the Human Skeleton. Springfield, Ill.: Charles C. Thomas.

Jackes M. n.d. Palaeodemographic Mortality. Unpublished ms in possession of author.

Jackes, M. 1977. The Huron Spine: A Study Based on the Kleinburg Ossuary Vertebrae. Ph.D. Dissertation. Department of Anthropology, University of Toronto.

Jackes M. 1985. Pubic symphysis age distributions. Am J Phys Anthropol 68:281–299.

Jackes M. 1988. The Osteology of the Grimsby Site. Department of Anthropology, University of Alberta.

Jackes M. 1992. Paleodemography: problems and techniques. In: Saunders SR, Katzenberg MA, editors. Skeletal Biology of Past Peoples: Research Methods. New York: Wiley-Liss. pp. 189–224.

Jackes M. 1994. Birth rates and bones. In: Herring A, Chan L, editors. 1994. Strength in Diversity. Toronto: Canadian Scholars' Press Inc. pp. 155–185.

Jackes M. (in press). Ethnohistory and osteology in southern Ontario. In: The Entangled Past: Integrating History and Archaeology. Papers of the 27th Annual Chacmool Conference (November 1997). Calgary: University of Calgary, Department of Archaeology.

Jackes M, Lubell D. 1985. Where are the old folks? Unpublished manuscript submitted to Advances in Archaeological Method and Theory.

Jackes M, Lubell D. 1996. Dental pathology and diet: second thoughts. In: Otte M, editor. Nature et Culture: Actes du Colloque International de Liège, 13–17 décembre 1993. Etudes et Recherches Archéologiques de L'Université de Liège, no. 68. pp. 457–480.

Jackes M, Lubell D. 1999. Human skeletal biology and the Mesolithic-Neolithic transition in Portugal. In: Thévenin A, editor, with Bintz P, direction scientifique. Europe des derniers chasseurs Épipaléolithique et Mésolithique: actes du 5ᵉ colloque international UISPP, commission XII, Grenoble, 18–23 Septembre 1995. Paris: Éditions du CTHS. pp. 59–64.

Jackes M, Lubell D, Meiklejohn C. 1997. Healthy but moral: human biology and the first farmers of western Europe. Antiquity 71:639–658.

Jackes M, Gao Q. (in press). Jiangzhai and BanPo (Shaanxi, PRC): new ideas from old bones. In: Jank L, Kaner S, Matsui A, Rowley-Conwy P, editors. From the Jomon to Star Carr. Oxford: Oxbow Books.

Kambe T, Yonemitsu K, Kibayashi K, Tsunenari T. 1991. Application of computer assisted image analyzer to the assessment of area and number of sites of dental attrition and its use for age estimation. Forensic Sci Int 50:97–109.

Katz D, Suchey JM. 1989. Race differences in pubic symphyseal aging patterns in the male. Am J Phys Anthropol 80:167–172.

Kemkes-Grottenthaler A. 1993. Kritischer Vergleich osteomorphognostischer Verfahern zur Lebensalterbestimmung Erwachsener. D. Phil. Thesis. Johannes Gutenberg-Universität, Mainz, Germany.

Kemkes-Grottenthaler A. 1996a. Critical evaluation of osteomorphognostic methods to estimate adult age at death: a test of the "complex method." Homo 46:280–292.

Kemkes-Grottenthaler A. 1996b. Sterbealterbestimmung anhand des ektokranialen Nahtverschlusses: eine Avaluierung der Meindl-Lovejoy-Methode. Rechtsmedizim 6:177–184.

Kerr NW, Ringrose TJ. 1998. Factors affecting the lifespan of the human dentition in Britain prior to the seventeenth century. Br Dent J 184:242–246.

Key CA, Aiello LC, Molleson T. 1994. Cranial suture closure and its implications for age estimation. Int J Osteoarchaeol 4:193–207.

Konigsberg LW, Buikstra JE, Bullington J. 1989. Paleodemographic correlates of fertility. Am Antiq 54:626–636.

Konigsberg LW, Frankenberg SR. 1992. Estimation of age structure in anthropological demography. Am J Phys Anthropol 89:235–256.

Konigsberg LW, Frankenberg SR. 1994. Paleodemography: "Not quite dead." Evol Anthropol 3:92–105.

Konigsberg LW, Frankenberg SR, Walker RB. 1997. Regress what on what? Paleodemographic age estimation as a calibration problem. In: Paine RR, editor. Integrating Archaeological Demography: Multidisciplinary Approaches to Prehistoric Population. Carbondale: Southern Illinois University Press. pp. 64–88.

Krogman WM. 1962. The Human Skeleton in Forensic Medicine. Springfield, Ill.: Charles C. Thomas.

Kvaal SI, Kolltveit KM, Thomsen IO, Solheim T. 1995. Age estimation of adults from dental radiographs. Forensic Sci Int 74:175–185.

Kvaal SI, Sellevold BJ, Solheim T. 1994. A comparison of different non-destructive methods of age estimation in skeletal material. Int J Osteoarchaeol 4:363–370.

Lanphear KM. 1989. Testing the value of skeletal samples in demographic research: a comparison with vital registration samples. Int J Anthropol 4:185–193.

Larsen CS. 1997. Bioarchaeology: Interpreting Behavior from the Human Skeleton. Cambridge Studies in Biological Anthropology 21. Cambridge: Cambridge University Press.

Loth S, İşcan MY. 1989. Morphological assessment of age in the adult: the thoracic region. In: İşcan

MY, editor. 1989. Age Markers in the Human Skeleton. Springfield, Ill.: Charles C. Thomas. pp. 105–136.

Lovejoy CO. 1985. Dental wear in the Libben population: its functional pattern and role in the determination of adult skeletal age at death. Am J Phys Anthropol 68:47–56.

Lovejoy CO, Meindl RS, Mensforth RP, Barton TJ. 1985. Multifactorial determination of skeletal age at death: a method and blind tests of its accuracy. Am J Phys Anthropol 68:1–14.

Lubell D, Jackes M, Schwarcz H, Knyf M, Meiklejohn C. 1994. The Mesolithic-Neolithic transition in Portugal: isotopic and dental evidence of diet. J Archaeol Sci 21:201–216.

Lucy D, Aykroyd RG, Pollard AM, Solheim T. 1996. A Bayesian approach to adult human age estimation from dental observations by Johanson's age changes. J Forensic Sci 41:189–194.

Lucy D, Pollard AM, Roberts CA. 1995. A comparison of three dental techniques for estimating age at death in humans. J Archaeol Sci 22:417–428.

Mann RW. 1993. A method for siding and sequencing human ribs. J Forensic Sci 38:151–155.

Maples WR. 1989. The practical application of age estimation techniques. In: İşcan MY, editor. Age Markers in the Human Skeleton. Springfield, Ill.: Charles C. Thomas.

Martin R. 1959. Lehrbuch der Anthopologie in systematischer Darstellung, 1928. 3rd ed. revised by Saller K. volume 2. Stuttgart: Gustav Fischer Verlag. 1574 pp.

Masset C. 1973. Influence du sexe et de l'âge sur la conservation des os humains. In: Sauter M, editor. L'Homme, Hier et Aujourd'hui: Recueil d'Études en Hommage à André Leroi-Gourhan. Paris: Cujas. pp. 333–343.

Masset C. 1976. Sur quelques fâcheuses méthodes de détermination de l'âge des squelettes. Bull Mém Soc d'Anthro Paris. Sér 13, 3:329–336.

Masset C. 1989. Age estimation on the basis of cranial sutures. In: İşcan MY, editor. Age Markers in the Human Skeleton. Springfield, Ill.: Charles C. Thomas. pp. 71–103.

Masset C, de Castro e Almeida ME. 1990. Âge et sutures crâniennes. Catania, Italy: Proceedings of the Mediterranean Academy of Sciences. 277pp.

Mayhall JT, Kageyama I. 1997. A new, three-dimensional method for determining tooth wear. Am J Phys Anthropol 103:463–469.

Mays S. 1998. The Archaeology of Human Bones. London: Routledge.

Mays S, de la Rua C, Molleson T. 1995. Molar crown height as a means of evaluating existing dental wear scales for estimating age at death in human skeletal remains. J Archaeol Sci 22: 659–670.

McKern TW, Stewart TD. 1957. Skeletal age changes in young American males. Technical Report EP-45. Natick, Mass.: U.S. Army Quartermaster Research and Development Center.

Meindl RS, Lovejoy CO. 1985. Ectocranial suture closure: a revised method for the determination of skeletal age at death based on the lateral-anterior sutures. Am J Phys Anthropol 68:57–66.

Meindl RS, Lovejoy CO. 1989. Age changes in the pelvis: implications for paleodemography. In: İşcan MY, editor. Age Markers in the Human Skeleton. Springfield, Ill.: Charles C. Thomas. pp. 137–168.

Meindl RS, Lovejoy CO, Mensforth RP, Walker RA. 1985. A revised method for age determination using the os pubis, with a review and tests of accuracy of other current methods of pubic symphyseal aging. Am J Phys Anthropol 68:29–45.

Meindl RS, Russell KF. 1998. Recent advances in method and theory in paleodemography. Annu Rev Anthropol 27:375–399.

Meindl RS, Russell KF, Lovejoy CO. 1990. Reliability of age at death in the Hamann-Todd Collection: validity of subselection procedures used in blind tests of the summary age technique. Am J Phys Anthropol 83:349–357.

Milner GR, Smith VG. 1990. Oneota human skeletal remains. In: Archaeological investigations at the Morton Village and Norris Farms 36 cemetery. Illinois State Museum Reports of Investigations vol 45:111–148.

Molleson T, Cohen P. 1990. The progression of dental attrition stages used for age assessment. J Archaeol Sci 17:363–371.

Molleson T, Cox M. 1993. The Middling Sort. The Spitalfields Project. Vol. 2. The Anthropology. CBA Research Report 86. York Council for British Archaeology.

Molleson T. 1995. Rates of ageing in the eighteenth century. In: Saunders SR, Herring A, editors. 1995. Grave Reflections: Portraying the Past Through Cemetery Studies. Toronto: Canadian Scholars' Press Inc. pp. 199–222.

Montagu JD. 1994. Length of life in the ancient world: a controlled study. J R Soc Med 87: 25–26.

Murray KA, Murray TM. 1991. A test of the auricular surface aging technique. J Forensic Sci 36: 1162–1169.

Owings Webb PA, Suchey JM. 1985. Epiphyseal union of the anterior iliac crest and medial clavicle in a modern multiracial sample of American males and females. Am J Phys Anthropol 68: 457–466.

Pasquier E, de Saint Martin Pernot L, Burdin V, Mounayer C, Le Rest C, Colin C, Mottier D, Roux C, Baccino E. 1999. Determination of age at death: assessment of an algorithm of age prediction using numerical three dimensional CT data from pubic bones. Am J Phys Anthropol 108:261–268.

Pfeiffer S. 1998. Variability in osteon size in recent human populations. Am J Phys Anthropol 106:219–227.

Pfeiffer S, Lazenby R, Chiang J. 1995. Cortical remodeling data are affected by sampling location. Am J Phys Anthropol 96:89–92.

Promislow DE. 1998. Longevity and the barren aristocrat. Nature 396:719–720.

Richards LC. 1984. Principal axis analysis of dental attrition from two Australian Aboriginal populations. Am J Phys Anthropol 65:5–13.

Richards LC, Miller SLJ. 1991. Relationships between age and dental attrition in Australian Aboriginals. Am J Phys Anthropol 84:159–170.

Rose JC, Ungar PS. 1998. Gross dental wear and dental microwear in historical perspective. In: Alt KW, Rösing FW, Teschler-Nicola M, editors. Dental Anthropology: Fundamentals, Limits and Prospects. New York: Springer-Verlag. pp. 349–386.

Rösing FW, Kvaal SI. 1998. Dental age in adults—a review of estimation methods. In: Alt KW, Rösing FW, Teschler-Nicola M, editors. Dental Anthropology: Fundamentals, Limits and Prospects. New York: Springer-Verlag. pp. 443–468.

Russell JC. 1948. British Medieval Population. Albuquerque: University of New Mexico Press.

Russell JC. 1985. The Control of Late Ancient and Medieval Population. Philadelphia: The American Philosophical Society.

Santini A, Land M, Raab GM. 1990. The accuracy of simple ordinal scoring of tooth attrition in age assessment. Forensic Sci Int 48:175–184.

Santos AL. 1995. Certezas e incertezas sobre a idade à morte. Thesis. Departamento de Antropologia, Faculdade de Ciências e Tecnologia da Universidade de Coimbra.

Santos AL. 1996. How old is this pelvis? A comparison of age at death estimation using the auricular surface of the *ilium* and *os pubis*. In: Pwiti G, Soper R, editors. Aspects of African Archaeology. Papers from the 10th Congress of the PanAfrican Association for Prehistory and related Studies. Harare: University of Zimbabwe.

Saunders SR, Fitzgerald C, Rogers T, Dudar JC, McKillop H. 1992. A test of several methods of skeletal age estimation using a documented archaeological sample. Can Soc Forensic Sci 25:97–118.

Sciulli PW, Giesen MJ, Paine RR. 1996. Paleodemography of the Pearson Complex (22SA9) Eiden Phase cemetery. Archaeology of Eastern North America 24:81–94.

Sjøvold T. 1978. Inference concerning the age distribution of skeletal populations and some consequences for paleodemography. Anthrop Közl 22:99–114.

Smith BH. 1984. Patterns of molar wear in hunter-gatherers and agriculturalists. Am J Phys Anthropol 63:39–56.

Solheim T. 1988. Dental attrition as an indicator of age. Gerodontics 4:299–304.

Solheim T. 1993 A new method for dental age estimation in adults. Forensic Sci Int 59:137–147.

Storey R. 1985. An estimate of mortality in a pre-Columbian urban population. Am Anthropol 87:519–535.

Storey R, Hirth K. 1997. Archeological and paleodemographic analyses of the El Cajón skeletal population. In: Paine RR, editor. Integrating Archaeological Demography: Multidisciplinary Approaches to Prehistoric Population. Carbondale: Southern Illinois University Press. pp. 131–149.

Stout SD, Porro MA, Perotti B. 1996. A test and correction of the clavicle method of Stout and Paine for histological age estimation of skeletal remains. Am J Phys Anthropol 100:139–142.

Suchey JM, Katz D. 1997. Applications of pubic age determination in a forensic setting. In: Reichs KJ, editor. Forensic Osteology: Advances in the Identification of Human Remains. Springfield, Ill.: Charles C. Thomas. pp. 204–236.

Szilvássy J, Kritscher H. 1990. Estimation of chronological age in man based on the spongy structure of long bones. Anthropol Anz 48: 289–298.

Tiley-Baxter M. 1997. A taphonomic study of the human remains from Christchurch, Spitalfields. In: Sinclair A, Slater E, Gowlett J, editors. Archaeological Sciences 1995. Oxford: Oxbow Monograph 64. pp. 377–388.

Todd TW. 1920. Age changes in the pubic bone: I. The white male pubis. Am J Phys Anthropol 3:285–334.

Toussaint M. 1991. Étude spatiale et taphonomique de deux sépultures collectives du néolithique récent: l'Abri Masson et la Fissure Jacques à Sprimont, Province de Liège, Belgique. L'Anthropologie 95:257–278.

Ubelaker DH. 1989. Human Skeletal Remains: Excavation, Analysis, and Interpretation. 2nd ed. Washington: Taraxacum.

van Gerven DP, Armelagos GJ. 1983. Farewell to paleodemography? Rumors of its death have been greatly exaggerated. J Hum Evol 12:353–360.

Vaupel JW, Carey JR, Christensen K, Johnson TE, Yashin AI, Holm NV, Iachine IA, Kannisto V, Khazaeli AA, Liedo P, Longo VD, Zeng Y, Manton KG, Curtsinger JW. 1998. Biodemographic trajectories of longevity. Science 280:855–860.

[WEA] Workshop of European Anthropologists. 1980. Recommendations for age and sex diagnoses of skeletons. J Hum Evol 9:517–549.

Waldron T. 1987. The relative survival of the human skeleton: implications for paleopathology. In: Boddington A, Garland AN, Janeway RC, editors. Death, Decay, and Reconstruction: Approaches to Archaeology and Forensic Science. Manchester, UK: Manchester University Press. pp. 55–64.

Walker PL, Dean G, Shapiro P. 1991. Estimating age from tooth wear in archaeological populations. In: Kelley MA, Larsen CS, editors. Advances in Dental Anthropology. New York: Wiley-Liss. pp. 169–178.

Walker PL, Johnson JR, Lambert PM. 1988. Age and sex biases in the preservation of human skeletal remains. Am J Phys Anthropol 76: 183–188.

Weiss KM. 1973. Demographic Models for Anthropology. Memoirs of the Society for American Archaeology, Number 27. Am Antiq 38:1–186.

Westendorp RGJ, Kirkwood TBL. 1998. Human longevity at the cost of reproductive success. Nature 396:743–746.

Wood JW, Milner GR, Harpending HC, Weiss KM. 1992. The osteological paradox. Curr Anthropol 33:343–70.

CHAPTER 16

PALEODEMOGRAPHY

GEORGE R. MILNER, JAMES W. WOOD, AND JESPER L. BOLDSEN

INTRODUCTION

Paleodemography has developed into a lively, if contentious, field of study that promises to contribute much to our knowledge of past peoples. Estimates of age and sex from skeletal remains are critical to archaeological studies of mortuary practices, paleopathological analyses of skeletal and dental lesions, and research on the demographic characteristics of past populations. The potential significance of this work is undoubtedly why the paleodemographic literature has exploded since the first pioneering studies 30 years ago (Acsádi and Nemeskéri, 1970; Angel, 1969; Swedlund and Armelagos, 1969).

At first glance it would appear that skeletal age distributions should be readily interpretable, particularly in terms of mortality patterns. Yet it is precisely this issue that has prompted heavy attack both from within and outside the field (see Jackes, Chapter 15). These critiques, and the responses to them, have tended to focus on the means of deriving estimates of age from adult skeletons, the methods of extracting demographically useful and reliable information from age-at-death distributions, and the research questions that can be legitimately addressed with small samples of skeletons from archaeological sites. But rather than dismiss the field outright, as other

authors have done (Bocquet-Appel and Masset, 1982, 1985; Petersen, 1975), we would agree with Konigsberg and Frankenberg (1994) that each round of criticism has ultimately strengthened the field. The demographic aspects of paleopathological research have likewise been found wanting (Wood et al., 1992b), but here too there is room for optimism, although much work remains to be done by those who must rely on old bones.

Criticisms of paleodemography have focused mainly on methodological issues, leaving largely unaddressed the theoretical questions that inspire us to look at skeletons in the first place. The potential significance of paleodemographic results, regardless of how reliable they might be, is largely left as vague statements about the biological costs of changes in diet, population density, settlement size and duration, and the like. Certainly all would agree that knowing about the morbidity and mortality experience of ancient people is likely to tell us something about human existence in the past, reaching as far back as our hunter-gatherer forebears. Yet much more attention should be directed toward what we can learn from skeletons that cannot be learned from other sources, particularly archaeological remains and historical documents. Equally important is a realistic appraisal of what kinds of information we cannot get from bones. That is, what questions are unanswerable in principle, no matter how interesting they might be? Paleodemography is only worth pursuing if we can come up with a set of

Biological Anthropology of the Human Skeleton, Edited by M. Anne Katzenberg and Shelley R. Saunders.
ISBN 0-471-31616-4 Copyright © 2000 by Wiley-Liss, Inc.

important and coherent theoretical questions that can be addressed using osteological observations from mortality samples that number in the low hundreds, rarely more, and are subject to a variety of biases.

At the outset, we should emphasize the uniformitarian principle that underlies all of paleodemography. As Howell has put it,

> A uniformitarian position in paleodemography implies that the human animal has not basically changed in its direct biological response to the environment in processes of ovulation, spermatogenesis, length of pregnancy, degree of helplessness of the young and rates of maturation and senility over time. This does not imply that humans have not changed in the rates of *performance* of these processes, but only that the processes still respond in the same way to variations in environment, including the cultural and technological aspects of human society as part of the external environment. (Howell, 1976:26)

The essential point is not that demographic processes are invariant across human populations. If they were, there would be no need for paleodemographic reconstructions—or for that matter much of the demographic study of modern peoples. Variation is, however, constrained in predictable ways. We should not expect to see demographic patterns in prehistory that deviate wildly from what is known about modern human populations, for example, modal ages at death in the fourth or fifth decade of life as opposed to later ages (Howell, 1982). This fact places useful limits on the credibility of some of our demographic reconstructions. The uniformitarian principle is also a foundation for developing models of demographic processes for use in paleodemography. There are definite constraints on the range of variation that such models must be able to cover. Flexible models are needed, but not ones that achieve their flexibility by being too complicated to understand. This fundamental principle is implicit in every model reviewed in this chapter.

A BRIEF HISTORY

Anatomists and physical anthropologists have long been interested in using bones and teeth to estimate the age and sex of skeletons. But until the past few decades this work could not be considered paleodemography, except in the most general sense of the term. Mid-twentieth-century reports of cemetery excavations often included long lists of skeletons along with their age and sex, although these data were rarely used to address population-related issues. Osteologists were nonetheless concerned about the accuracy of their estimates, and some parts of the skeleton were found to be better for these purposes than others (Brooks, 1955; McKern and Stewart, 1957). The situation changed rapidly about thirty years ago when osteologists began to calculate life tables from cemetery samples and to compare these results with model life tables (Acsádi and Nemeskéri, 1970; Bennett, 1973; Buikstra, 1976; Lovejoy et al., 1977; Moore et al., 1975; Nemeskéri, 1971; Swedlund and Armelagos, 1969; Ubelaker, 1974). For the first time, data on archaeological skeletons were organized in such a way that demographic inferences could be drawn from them.

From the outset it was recognized that archaeological samples were typically biased, particularly in terms of infant underrepresentation, and the upper end of the age distribution was truncated because of an inability to estimate the age of skeletons beyond about 50 years. Some life-table figures were shown to be more heavily affected by infant underenumeration than others (Moore et al., 1975). In addition, cemetery samples were treated as if they were derived from stable populations. This assumption was consistent with the fact that populations usually reestablish the age structures determined by fixed fertility and mortality rates in no more than a few decades, depending on the severity and length of demographic disturbance (Weiss, 1975). In the absence of information about population growth, life tables were usually calculated as if the populations were stationary (a stationary population is a special case of a stable population whose growth rate equals zero). Nevertheless, the effects of population growth on life-table estimates were occasionally examined as well (Bennett, 1973; Buikstra, 1976; Moore et al., 1975). Finally, model life tables were generated specifically for use with the small populations typically studied by anthropologists, including those represented by skeletons (Weiss, 1973). Thus, in a matter of a few years during the 1970s, the study of ancient skeletons lurched forward from mere description to an attempt to use age-distribution data to reconstruct the demographic characteristics of past populations.

Despite these early advances, paleodemography was soon besieged by critics, many of whom intended their attacks to be fatal. The first self-avowedly devastating critique came from outside the field. In a wide-ranging article, the demographer Petersen (1975) argued that researchers dealing with ancient skeletons knew too little formal demography and had ludicrously small samples, which were likely to be unrepresentative of any real population. While it was true that some early paleodemographic analyses were rather naive, this hardly seems a necessary limitation of paleodemography, either then or now. The complaint that paleodemographic samples are typically small and produced by a complex and selective sampling process in comparison with mainstream demographic data sets was more justifiable. It was entirely accurate to say that skeletal ages at death are always estimated with error, more so in some parts of the life span than in others—though in fairness, much the same could be said about such widely accepted demographic data sets as the World Fertility Survey or the Demographic and Health Survey. The correct response to these problems, however, was not to give up on the field—it was less than a decade old at the time of Petersen's (1975) critique—but rather to invest the hard work needed to minimize errors and develop the means of dealing with the irreducible estimation error that is always present.

The second round of criticism was deemed so unanswerable by its authors that it was simply called a "farewell to paleodemography" (Bocquet-Appel and Masset, 1982). At the heart of this critique were two points: skeletal age distributions mimic those of the modern reference samples used to calculate them, and available methods for estimating ages are too imprecise to allow for a demographic signal to be detected amidst stochastic noise. On the basis of these criticisms, they concluded:

> Save unforeseen developments—unpredictable in the future at least—it would be futile to expect to have a working knowledge of the demography of ancient populations if we start only from the estimations of age at death. The scholars who persist in this course will only obtain artefacts; the information conveyed by the age indicators is so poor that the age distributions thus available can hardly reflect anything but random fluctuations and errors of method. (Bocquet-Appel and Masset, 1982:329)

This pessimistic appraisal provoked several responses (Buikstra and Konigsberg, 1985; Lanphear, 1989; Mensforth, 1990; Piontek and Weber, 1990; Van Gerven and Armelagos, 1983; cf. Bocquet-Appel and Masset, 1985). Although none of these replies was wholly successful, it quickly became apparent that Bocquet-Appel and Masset had overstated their case. While we agree with much of Bocquet-Appel and Masset's (1982) diagnosis, we reject their dismal prognosis. The confounding effect of the reference sample age distribution is indeed a serious problem with traditional methods of age estimation, but not a necessary one (Aykroyd et al., 1997; Koningsberg and Frankenberg, 1992, 1994; Konigsberg et al., 1997). It is also true that paleodemographic ages will always involve a considerable degree of error. Nonetheless, there are ways to minimize the error and, just as importantly, to deal with the remaining error. In fact, osteologists have increasingly become interested in the error structure of their age estimates (Jackes,

1985; Konigsberg and Frankenberg, 1992). As we discuss below, work by a number of paleodemographers over the past two decades provides just the sort of "unforeseen developments" that Bocquet-Appel and Masset thought were unlikely but necessary to rescue paleodemography from a well-deserved death.

A third round of criticism was set off by Sattenspiel and Harpending (1983) and Johansson and Horowitz (1986), who pointed out that nonzero population growth can distort age-at-death distributions so that they reflect fertility more than mortality. This phenomenon, long known in demography (Coale, 1957), has now become widely (but by no means universally) recognized in paleodemography (Buikstra et al., 1986; Koningsberg et al., 1989; Konigsberg and Frankenberg, 1994; Milner et al., 1989; Paine, 1989a, 1989b; Paine and Harpending, 1996, 1998). It has even given rise to a few attempts to estimate fertility from skeletal collections (Buikstra et al., 1986; Konigsberg et al., 1989; Paine, 1989a; for a cautionary note, see Horowitz et al., 1988). This issue can be called paleodemography's "non-stationarity problem." If all past populations were indeed stationary, we would still be wearing skins and living off the land, and certainly not writing this kind of essay. The non-stationarity problem has yet to be solved, although as detailed below it is now clear what must be done to solve it.

Finally, we come to the "osteological paradox" of Wood et al. (1992b)—namely, that heterogeneity in the risk of death and selective mortality can badly confound the interpretation of paleodemographic and paleopathological analyses, especially when the object is to compare skeletal lesion frequencies in cemetery samples.[1] From this perspective, we would argue that paleodemographic and paleopathological studies are—and ought to be—inextricably intertwined. The osteological paradox paper also prompted several responses (Byers, 1994; Cohen, 1994, 1997; Goodman, 1993; Jackes, 1993; Saunders and Hoppa, 1993; for a reply, see Wood and Milner, 1994). Incidentally, a separate interchange over the selectivity issue has broken out elsewhere (Bird 1996; Waldron, 1994, 1996).

All these critiques have posed important challenges for paleodemography, but they have scarcely succeeded in burying the field. In fact, they have strengthened it considerably by focusing attention on difficult methodological issues. Nonetheless, we believe that there remain several outstanding questions that must be addressed before paleodemography can take its rightful place as a legitimate branch of population science. Those problems, in the order they are discussed in the remainder of this chapter, are as follows:

- What theoretical questions should we be asking that can potentially be answered with skeletal samples?
- How can we best understand the complex sampling process that gives rise to an archaeological skeletal collection, and how can we correct for the selection biases that inevitably result from that process?
- How can we obtain unbiased sex and age estimates, in particular estimates that avoid the biases inherent in standard methods for estimating the age of adult skeletons?
- How can the error involved in age estimation be minimized while making full and

---

[1]A distinction should be drawn here between two distinct forms of paleopathology with fundamentally different research objectives. The first objective emphasizes the classification of skeletal lesions, the identification of disease processes that may have caused them, and the consequences of pathological conditions before the availability of effective medical treatment (e.g., Ortner and Putschar, 1985; Steinbock, 1976). This essential aspect of paleopathology can be practiced more or less in isolation from paleodemography (though the best studies of this sort do examine the age and sex of affected individuals when attempting to identify the diseases that may have produced particular kinds of bony lesions). In contrast, paleodemography is integral to the second research objective in paleopathology: the study of how healthy particular populations were in relation to other groups. This aspect of paleopathological research obviously encompasses all studies that address the biological effects of the transition to agriculture and the development of complex societies (e.g., Cohen and Armelagos, 1984a). Demographic issues, however, are typically given scant attention, except when the skeletal sample is subdivided into various groups defined by age and sex. In this chapter, we deal strictly with this second objective of paleopathology, sometimes dubbed *paleoepidemiology* (Boldsen, 1997a).

honest use of the error that necessarily remains?

- How can the non-stationarity problem be solved?
- How can we adjust for the interrelated problems of heterogeneous risk and selective mortality so that pathological lesions in individual skeletons can be linked to aggregate-level mortality patterns?

In an important sense, work on all of these problems must move forward simultaneously. What is needed is an analytical framework that allows this to happen. The work reviewed here represents an important step toward developing such a framework.

WHAT DO WE WANT TO LEARN FROM OLD BONES?

The issue that should be of foremost concern to paleodemographers is why this work is worth doing. What can skeletons from archaeological sites tell us about past peoples that cannot be better understood from other kinds of data? For convenience, we have divided the research questions into two categories, biological and cultural, although there is considerable overlap between them. This coverage of issues commonly found in the paleodemographic literature is not intended to be exhaustive, but is restricted to the topics we consider most important.

The central biological issue is how the distribution of individual health and well-being vary across time and space, and how this variation is related to population dynamics, environmental settings, and socioeconomic conditions. This issue is usually phrased along the lines of the demographic consequences of changes in the natural environment, subsistence strategies, and the organizational structure of preindustrial societies. Most of what can be subsumed under paleodemography, and much of paleopathology as well, has been oriented toward such topics for the past 30 years. Testable theoretical models are needed to answer these population-level questions. The empirical data in paleodemography are simply too spotty and hard to interpret to permit a purely empirical approach (a comment that could, of course, be directed at all areas of science).

To date, the only coherent school of thought on changes over great periods of time in health and demography crystallized about twenty years ago (Cassidy, 1980; Cohen and Armelagos, 1984b; Lallo et al., 1978; see also Cohen, 1989, 1994, 1997). It has gained wide currency because it accommodates a straightforward (but not necessarily correct) reading of much of the empirical evidence. Perhaps more importantly, no competing model linking health to socioeconomic change has been advanced until recently (Wood, 1998). The currently prevailing scenario can be summarized without too much violence to the argument as a two-step process resulting in increased morbidity and mortality. The first step occurred at the transition to agriculture, and the second with the origin of complex societies, particularly those labeled states or civilizations. This view of an unrelieved degradation of the human condition, at least as measured by disease and death, is the opposite of an earlier assumption of steady improvements in health accompanying technological progress.[2]

---

[2] Of course, much has been said over the past few centuries about the relationship between society, technology, and the human condition. Because of the nature of this review, we limit ourselves to the current view among anthropologists, and others, that health worsened from hunting-and-gathering days, not improved with the advent of agriculture and complex sociopolitical organizations, as was once commonly assumed. We cannot help notice, however, how similar certain elements of the currently popular two-step degradation scenario is to Rousseau's conjectures about the natural condition of humankind. The "good constitution of savages . . . reflect[s] that they are troubled with hardly any disorders, save wounds and old age"; further, "they lived free, healthy, honest, and happy lives." It was the ability to grow crops and to work metal, along with the development of inequities in property, that "first civilized men, and ruined humanity" (Rousseau, 1950:204, 243–244). In short, perspectives on the long sweep of human existence have varied from one extreme to another over the past few centuries, and until recently the means to evaluate them have been utterly lacking.

The two-step degradation scenario has several weaknesses. The typological thinking that underlies it misses numerous complications by forcing all populations into just a few pigeonholes. Many of the groups characterized as hunters-gatherers or agriculturalists were neither—they were somewhere in a "transition" from exclusive reliance on food collection to a firm commitment to agricultural production. In addition, this scenario limits attention to the major transitions, which, while lasting thousands of years, make up only a small part of human existence. It conflates changes in many different factors, including diet, sedentism, trade, and economic inequality, that should, at least initially, be analyzed separately since they did not occur in lockstep and may have had very different effects. Perhaps most fundamentally, as Pennington (1996) has noted, the two-step scenario fails to explain the growth in population that occurred over time—that is, the increase in human numbers that undeniably took place despite each purported round of degradation—and it provides no mechanism explaining why new subsistence practices were adopted when they had such adverse effects. Finally, the data themselves do not force this view on us (Jackes et al., 1997; Wood et al., 1992b).

This two-step model is virtually the only attempt that has been made to provide a coherent theoretical framework for paleodemography and paleopathology. Its proponents are to be congratulated for identifying a number of fundamentally important questions. Through long and arduous work, they have put the flesh of empirical data on the bones of centuries-old arguments about how the human condition might have changed over great spans of time. All this can be said even if we disagree with several of the inferences drawn from age-at-death distributions and skeletal lesion frequencies (Wood and Milner, 1994; Wood et al., 1992b).

Fundamental to this debate is the recent recognition of heterogeneous frailty and selective mortality as both theoretically and methodologically important, affecting both the demography and morbidity of modern and past populations. There are a number of important theoretical questions that must be tackled: where does the heterogeneity come from, how do its mean and variance change over time and differ among populations, and how do differing distributions of heterogeneity affect population dynamics? We suggest that a proper accounting for heterogeneity and selectivity might well alter our view of the linkages among changes in the natural environment, socioeconomic conditions, health, and population processes (Wood, 1998).

Paleodemography also has become harnessed to the archaeological study of past cultures. The composition of mortality samples in terms of age, sex, and social status is a critical source of information about the functioning of past societies. Furthermore, an understanding of the potential effects of social processes on cemetery composition is important in anticipating and countering selectivity bias, even when the questions being addressed are purely biological in nature.

Studies of past mortuary practices, important for their presumed relationships to social organization, would be severely crippled were it not possible to estimate age and sex from skeletons with some degree of reliability. These characteristics of the deceased are integral to investigations of what differences in body treatment, grave form, cemetery location, and artifact accompaniments might indicate about how past societies functioned. One of the first objectives of this work should be to see if the skeletal sample deviates markedly from the deaths expected in preindustrial societies, although all too often this step is omitted in archaeological mortuary analyses. In fact, this is one of the principal reasons why the simple pattern-matching of model and skeletal age-at-death distributions was advocated a decade ago (Milner et al., 1989; Paine, 1989a, 1989b). While such biased samples may be deeply flawed for biological studies, they may in fact be quite informative about what might have led to the formation of a particular cemetery. For example, a skeletal sample with an atypical age or sex distribution may have come from a burial ground for a special segment of society or people who were interred together because they died under unusual circumstances, such as the victims of a mass disaster.

SAMPLING ISSUES

Osteologists obviously base their inferences about past conditions on a tiny fraction of all people who were alive at a particular time and place. Samples usually number in the hundreds of skeletons, rarely more than that. Yet the absolute number of skeletons is not the most troublesome sampling issue that osteologists face. After all, sample size can always be increased through additional excavations, and extrapolating from small samples is commonplace in the sciences. The real problem is that osteologists can observe only those skeletons that have survived to modern times, were discovered by archaeologists, and were preserved in museums. It cannot be assumed that every skeleton has an equal chance of being studied. Furthermore, paleodemographers are interested in what happened in the distant past when these people were alive, but skeletal collections, being mortality samples, are highly selected samples of the people of a particular age who were once alive (Wood et al., 1992b).

The relationship between an ancient population and a museum's skeletal collection is far from straightforward. The skeletons available for study have been subjected to a highly selective sampling process that involves several stages: Living → Dead → Buried → Preserved → Found → Saved. There is nothing new about a concern over such issues. Over two centuries ago, Thomas Jefferson (1788:105) said of his excavation of an earthen mound in Virginia that "[t]he bones of infants being soft, they probably decay sooner, which might be the cause so few were found here." Jefferson did not elaborate on this point, but he clearly recognized that differential preservation could result in the preferential loss of part of the original sample of skeletons. Moreover, he must have had his own experience in mind—

high eighteenth-century infant mortality—when he noted there were fewer infants than expected in the mound. Thus he compared the skeletal sample to a model, albeit an implicit and primitive one. Despite this promising start, it has only been in the past few decades that osteologists have begun to address in systematic fashion the biases inherent in their skeletal collections.

A central issue is whether collections of skeletons can ever be considered representative of the communities from which they were derived, given that the Living → Dead transition is inherently selective (Saunders and Hoppa, 1993; Wood and Milner, 1994; Wood et al., 1992b). Skeletons from cemeteries are obviously mortality samples, and as such must be considered biased samples of the living. This bias stems from the fact that people are heterogeneous in their frailty or relative risk of death. Although Cohen (1994) has suggested that heterogeneous frailty was unlikely to be important in most preindustrial societies, especially small-scale, supposedly "egalitarian" ones, significant heterogeneity and selective mortality have been detected in many nonhuman animal species, ranging from nematodes to insects to birds (Carey, 1997; Carey and Liedo, 1995; Newton, 1998; Vaupel et al., 1994). It is difficult to believe that humans are less diverse. And, indeed, recent paleodemographic analyses have established that mortality risks were heterogeneous even in small-scale preindustrial societies (Boldsen, 1991, 1997a; Milner et al., 1991; Usher et al., 1997). Therefore, even if all members of a community were represented by skeletons—that is, everyone was buried in a completely excavated cemetery that yielded only well-preserved bones dug by skillful archaeologists—the individuals in each age interval would not represent a random sample of all individuals who were alive in that age interval. On the contrary, cemeteries are loaded with the sick, who are, on average, the most likely members of their cohort to die at a particular age.

The Dead → Buried transition has received more attention, especially from archaeologists.

Mortuary practices obviously affect the chances of a skeleton surviving to modern times. Yet even for societies that generally disposed of their dead in a way that favored preservation—such as simple and more-or-less immediate inhumation—all people were not always treated the same way. For example, historical and ethnographic accounts of many societies, including those roughly equivalent to the small-scale prehistoric societies that osteologists frequently study, indicate that newborns and older infants were often not buried in village cemeteries. It is not at all uncommon for skeletal samples to have too few infants, a problem in part related to mortuary customs. Unusual circumstances of death in these societies can also result in atypical ways of disposing of bodies or interment in places other than community cemeteries (e.g., Binford, 1971). To be sure, such practices normally result in the loss of relatively few skeletons from a cemetery sample, so few that they would be undetectable. More significant is the systematic handling of the dead from some fraction of the population in ways that were different from everyone else. Such practices were particularly likely to occur in hierarchically organized societies where high status people were buried in places other than the cemeteries used by the bulk of the population. There are, of course, many other situations where only a specially selected part of the entire population was buried in a particular place, such as medieval monasteries that served as hospitals for severely diseased or injured people (Møller-Christensen, 1982).

This sampling issue—what is represented by particular cemeteries—is especially important in societies consisting of socially and economically differentiated communities, such as the towns and rural villages of medieval Europe (Petersen, 1997). Here skeletons from single cemeteries cannot be considered representative of the full range of experience in both urban and rural settings. But even for smaller-scale societies it cannot be assumed that communities are essentially carbon copies of one another and, hence, that skeletons from any one

burial ground are necessarily representative of broader cultural, geographic, or temporal categories. One example is a group of late prehistoric tribal horticulturalists in the American Midwest who found themselves at the leading edge of a population expansion (Milner et al., 1991). Although intergroup conflicts were common at that time, an unusually large proportion of this village's inhabitants was attacked and killed, with at least one-third of all adults dying violently. To the extent that such conflict was socially and economically disruptive, it would be a mistake to assume that this particular skeletal sample was typical of culturally similar peoples at this time horizon.

The Buried → Preserved segment of the transition from living population to museum collection adds still more sampling bias. The characteristics of skeletal elements, especially the thickness of cortical bone, affect the chances of their surviving to modern times, as does their burial environment, particularly soil pH (Gordon and Buikstra, 1981; Mays, 1992; Waldron, 1987; Walker et al., 1988; Wiley et al., 1997). Slightly acidic soils that adversely affect bone preservation are quite common. As every excavator knows, small bones with thin cortices tend to disappear first, leaving behind the diaphyses of major limb bones, the cranial vault, and teeth. Sometimes all that is left of a burial are the enamel crowns of teeth, which are fragile and easily overlooked by inexperienced excavators. In general, the smallest skeletons, especially those of infants, are the ones most likely to be underrepresented whenever preservation is less than optimum.

Even if bones happen to make it to modern times, they do not necessarily survive the Preserved → Found → Saved part of the sequence that leads to study collections. Excavators differ in their experience and hence their ability to recognize poorly preserved bones or the skeletons of infants. Excavation strategies also introduce biases to skeletal samples. An emphasis on grave goods over skeletons has on many occasions led to uneven sampling of past populations because the places chosen for excavation are those with the greatest potential for yielding many artifacts. And even if bones are identified in the field, they do not necessarily become part of a museum collection. Particularly in the nineteenth and early twentieth centuries, obtaining skeletons was not an objective of excavations. If bones were taken from the field, often only pathological or intact specimens, and frequently just measurable skulls, were saved.

It is naive, then, to assume that skeletal samples are ever a simple and direct reflection of conditions in the living populations that generated them. On the contrary, selectivity is always operating and always needs attending to. Ironically, the main form of selectivity that we have emphasized in the past (Boldsen, 1991; Wood et al., 1992b) and that has met with most resistance (Goodman, 1993; Cohen, 1994, 1997)—namely, the selectivity involved in the Living → Dead transition—is probably the easiest to adjust for since it is based on predictable biological processes that can be modeled, a point to which we return later in this paper.

MEASUREMENT ISSUES

The classification of skeletons by age and sex is central to paleodemographic analysis. Accuracy, of course, is always a concern in such classifications, but we would also like to know how much confidence to place in our assessments of age and sex. The osteological methods used to produce estimates of age and sex are covered thoroughly elsewhere (Buikstra and Ubelaker, 1994; İşcan and Loth, 1989; Jackes, Chapter 15; St. Hoyme and İşcan, 1989). Here we focus on the logic of measurement and the errors involved in it.

Sex Estimation

Osteologists usually restrict their attention to adult skeletons when estimating sex from bone size and shape. The pelvis tends to be emphasized more for this purpose than the cranium, mandible, or the rest of the skeleton. The male and female distributions of skeletal features used to estimate sex overlap considerably. Some of these bony features are generally considered more reliable than others, and the degree of sexual dimorphism in skeletal characteristics varies among human populations. Thus, experience with handling bones—the more the better—is highly valued, as are multivariate statistical techniques used to characterize size and shape (St. Hoyme and İşcan, 1989).

It is now possible to extract and amplify ancient DNA from bones, which can in theory be used to determine the sex of all skeletons, regardless of age at death (Stone et al., 1996). Despite rapid advances in this field of research, there are practical limitations to the use of ancient DNA for estimating the sex of skeletons: not all skeletons yield DNA, contamination is a persistent problem, and the procedures are time consuming and expensive (Stone, Chapter 13). Because of labor costs, it is unlikely that ancient DNA will be used anytime soon for the routine determination of sex in studies of large skeletal collections from archaeological sites.

Traditional means of estimating sex, at least as employed before about 1970, tend to produce too many males, as noted by Weiss (1973). This problem stems at least in part from the great weight earlier osteologists placed on cranial morphology, sometimes to the near exclusion of pelvic characteristics. The principal cranial features used to estimate sex, including the supraorbital ridges, mastoid processes, and superior nuchal line, are generally considered indicative of males when one or more of them are robust. These features are less likely to be perceived as distinctively female, except in the case of very gracile individuals. The pelvis, in contrast, has several features that can be considered distinctly male or female characteristics. Furthermore, the cranial characteristics in older females can appear more like those of males; that is, they are more robust than those of young females (Meindl et al., 1985; Walker, 1995). This possibility should be examined more systematically, but it too would contribute to an overrepresentation of males whenever assessments of sex depend heavily on cranial features.

The reasonable inference that measurement error has resulted in an overrepresentation of males, particularly in older osteological studies, has been criticized (St. Hoyme and İşcan, 1989). But recent examinations of skeletal collections first studied several decades ago have found that errors in estimates of sex were more likely to be "females" misclassified as "males" than the reverse (Milner and Jefferies, 1987; Powell, 1988; Ruff, 1981). These results are consistent with both Weiss's (1973) finding and the shift over time in the relative weight osteologists place on crania and innominates when estimating sex.

Sex estimation is a statistical problem akin to other forms of estimation, and too little attention has been paid to it from this perspective (for some exceptions, see Giles and Elliot, 1963; Holman and Bennett, 1991; Konigsberg and Hens, 1998; Meindl et al., 1985). Thus far, two statistical approaches have predominated, discriminant function analysis (e.g., Giles, 1964; Robling and Ubelaker, 1997) and finite mixture analysis (e.g., Dong, 1997; Pearson et al., 1992). As Konigsberg and Hens (1998) have recently pointed out, sex estimation is a problem in Bayesian analysis, and thus involves inverse probability (see below).[3] If the proper inversion is not done, the sex composition of our sample will be biased toward that of the modern, known-sex reference sample that provides us with our osteological standards. Indeed, in formal analyses this problem could actually exacerbate the overrepresentation of males discussed by Weiss (1973), since most reference samples are dominated by male skeletons. Finally, no method will provide perfect, error-free classification by sex, not even the use of Y-linked DNA markers. Consequently, all paleodemographic analyses should ideally pool skeletons of both sexes and weight each one by its posterior probability of being one sex versus the other (see Konigsberg and Hens, 1998). As it happens, all these issues apply with even greater force to paleodemographic age estimation, where the problems are compounded by the fact that we need to locate individuals along an infinite array of continu-

ous age values rather than merely classify them into two discrete categories. In the next section these issues are examined in greater detail with reference to the problem of age estimation.

Age Estimation

The ages of juvenile skeletons can usually be estimated within an acceptable range of error, at least by the standards of paleodemography where all samples are small and suffer from a rich variety of biases. It is generally possible using dental development and epiphyseal closure to estimate the ages of juveniles to within several years or even, for the very young, within less than a single year (see Saunders, Chapter 5, FitzGerald and Rose, Chapter 6).

Estimating the ages of adults, however, has proved to be a persistent problem, and it becomes increasingly difficult with older skeletons. It is common, therefore, to lump all old people into an open-ended terminal interval such as 50+ years. This practice is an honest admission that it is nearly impossible to determine the age of the elderly with any precision. But it also makes it very difficult to say anything about senescent patterns of death, one of the dominant components of the human mortality curve.

Osteologists have traditionally been interested in obtaining either point estimates of age or relatively narrow interval estimates. In the latter case, the intervals used, often of constant width, are assumed to take into account much of the imprecision in estimating the age of adults. Thus, they are generally preferred over single-year estimates. However, while using point estimates on their own treats the esti-

---

[3] As explained in more detail below with respect to age estimation, Bayes's theorem provides a way to estimate the unknown probability that a skeleton has a trait that cannot be observed directly (e.g., a specific age or sex in an archaeological skeleton) given that it has a trait that can be observed (e.g., degree of cranial suture closure or sciatic notch angle). This method requires data on the joint distribution of both traits in a well-characterized modern reference sample. In Bayesian analysis, the conditional probability of having the unobservable trait given the presence of the observable trait is known as the *posterior probability*.

mates as known without error, using constant age intervals assumes that all individual ages have identical degrees of errors. All osteologists, of course, know that these assumptions are incorrect, but until recently only crude methods have been developed to deal with the problems posed by them.

When the age of a skeleton is estimated, it is never really believed that an exact age can be assigned to it, nor is it thought that all skeletons that look like they are in, say, their early twenties can be assigned with equal confidence into a single age interval such as 20 to 25 years. On the contrary, each skeleton has its own degree of error or precision depending upon the particular suite of traits available for age estimation. Consequently, what we really want to estimate is the probability density function $p(a|\theta_i)$ for each separate skeleton, where $p(a|\theta_i)$ is the probability that the skeleton died at age a given that it has characteristics θ_i, and θ_i is the set of skeletal traits observed in the i-th skeleton in our sample (Konigsberg and Frankenberg, 1992, 1994).

In order to estimate $p(a|\theta_i)$ we need access to an appropriate *reference sample*; that is, a collection of skeletons whose ages at death are known and in which the markers of aging we wish to use can be scored. Two such reference samples have been used widely by American paleodemographers: the Hamann-Todd and Terry collections (St. Hoyme and İşcan, 1989). However, these collections are highly selected samples in terms of the socioeconomic position and ages of the people included in them. The samples of early-twentieth-century deaths need to be treated with circumspection when used as standards of comparison for ancient bones. The age-at-death distributions of these two collections certainly cannot be regarded as representative of any real community. Another frequently used age estimation technique is based on the skeletal remains of Korean War dead (McKern and Stewart, 1957). For obvious reasons, this sample is composed entirely of males, most of them young adults. The heaping at comparatively early ages at death observed in this reference sample can result in massive

biases if not handled properly (Bocquet-Appel and Masset, 1982; Konigsberg and Frankenberg, 1992, 1994). This problem can create the illusion that adult mortality rates are extraordinarily high and accelerate much more rapidly than is the case in any historically well-documented human population. In earlier paleodemographic analyses, these biases were arguably the single most common source of error and misinterpretation, resulting in overall mortality curves that deviate substantially from those observed in living human populations (Lovejoy et al., 1977; cf. Howell, 1982; Milner et al., 1989; Paine, 1989a). If nothing else, this phenomenon, repeated in many studies, is a troubling violation of the uniformitarian principle (Howell, 1982).

Konigsberg and Frankenberg (1992, 1994; Konigsberg et al., 1997; also see Aykroyd et al., 1997, 1999) have provided good technical explanations of how these biases occur. Here we present a caricature of the faulty logic underlying the traditional analyses. In actual fact, no one (to our knowledge) has ever estimated ages in the naive way we describe—but the superficially more sophisticated regression methods that *have* been used are based on essentially the same reasoning. How, then, would an unimaginably naive paleodemographer estimate the value of $p(a|\theta_i)$? First, all individuals in the reference sample who display trait complex θ_i would be identified. Then, the fraction of those individuals who are, say ages $a = 30, 31, 32$, and so on would be computed and used—erroneously, as it happens—as estimates of $p(30|\theta_i), p(31|\theta_i), p(32|\theta_i), \ldots$. A moment's reflection will show that such estimates must be determined partly by the age composition of the reference sample. Suppose that the reference sample contains many 30-year olds but few 70-year olds. Then, even if trait complex θ_i is much more typical of *living* 70-year olds than of people in their thirties, $p(30|\theta_i)$ will be greater than $p(70|\theta_i)$ in the reference sample. In other words, our prehistoric skeleton will seem to be more like a 30-year old than a 70-year old, purely because of the biasing effect of the reference sample's age distribution.

This bias was pointed out almost twenty years ago by Bocquet-Appel and Masset (1982). In response, Van Gerven and Armelagos (1983) examined several paleodemographic data sets and showed that their estimated age distributions were not identical to those of the reference samples used. This response, unfortunately, missed the point. There is no reason to think that the traditional method will *duplicate* the reference sample, but only that it will produce estimates that are biased in the *direction* of the reference sample (Konigsberg and Frankenberg, 1992).

We hasten to add that this problem is no reason to abandon paleodemography, a point that even Bocquet-Appel and Masset (1996) now concede. The problem does, however, require a new approach to paleodemographic age estimation. More specifically, we need a method that will allow us to use a reference sample to obtain unbiased estimates of $p(a|\theta_i)$ for all a in a way that is not affected by the age distribution of the reference sample. As Konigsberg and Frankenberg (1992) have pointed out, this is another problem in inverse probability. The sorts of naive estimates described above are, quite simply, *not* estimates of $p(a|\theta_i)$ at all, but rather of its inverse $p(\theta_i|a)$. But we want $p(a|\theta_i)$, not $p(\theta_i|a)$. The relationship between these two probabilities is provided by an elementary formula from probability theory known as *Bayes's theorem*, which states that

$$p(a|\theta_i) = \frac{p(\theta_i|a)f(a)}{\int_0^\infty p(\theta_i|x)f(x)dx} \qquad (1)$$

The function $f(a)$ is the age-at-death distribution of the ancient population we are trying to analyze—that is, the probability that a randomly selected dead individual from that population is exact age a.

To apply equation (1), we must first have a set of unbiased estimates of $p(\theta_i|a)$ derived from an appropriate reference sample. There are two general approaches to this problem. The first is to use ordinary least-squares regression to relate some continuously distributed trait such as osteon count or degree of

epiphysial closure to age in the reference sample. If this approach is adopted, it is essential to use age as the independent variable ("classic" calibration) rather than regressing age on the skeletal trait ("inverse" calibration) if unbiased estimates of $p(\theta_i|a)$ are to be obtained (Aykroyd et al., 1997, 1999; Konigsberg et al., 1997). The second approach, which we call *transition analysis* (Boldsen, 1997b), is applicable to any skeletal trait that can be arranged into an invariant series of distinct developmental or senescent stages. The timing of transition from one stage to the next may vary widely, but the sequence itself can be assumed to be fixed so long as we are looking at biological structures that develop or degenerate in a regular manner. A standard transition function is derived by applying logit or probit regression to a known-age reference sample; the probability that an archaeological skeleton has attained or passed each morphological stage by age a is then estimated from the reverse logit or probit transform, providing just the sort of $p(\theta_i|a)$ estimates needed for equation (1). Examples of applications that would fall under the heading of transition analysis include Kolakowski and Bock (1981), Roche et al. (1988), Milner et al. (1997), and Herrmann (1998).

We also need an estimate of the function $f(a)$, the actual age-at-death distribution of the ancient population we are trying to reconstruct. But this places us in a quandary, for if we knew $f(a)$ there would be no need for all this effort. In Bayesian analysis, $f(a)$ would be called a *prior distribution,* and priors are often "noninformative" (i.e., partly or completely unknown). One tactic frequently adopted in such a case is to assume a uniform prior—in this case, a flat age-at-death distribution—and use it as a starting point for an iterative solution of the true distribution (Kimura and Chikuni, 1987; Konigsberg and Frankenberg, 1992). While this approach often works well, it is not guaranteed to converge on the proper age-at-death distribution. An alternative approach, more difficult to apply but perhaps less likely to go wrong, is to replace $f(a)$ in equation (1) with a mathematical formula for the age-at-death distribution derived from a parametric mortality model (for example, the Siler model discussed below) and then iteratively estimate the parameters of the model at the same time as the age-at-death distribution. Whichever approach is used, the Bayesian correction embodied in equation (1) is essential for any estimation of skeletal age at death, whether for paleodemographic or forensic purposes (for more technical detail, see Konigsberg and Frankenberg, 1992).

A final unresolved problem in paleodemographic age estimation is how best to combine information from different skeletal indicators of age. Certainly many different skeletal traits tell us something about age, for example, the pubic symphysis, the iliac auricular surface, the sternal ends of ribs, and even the much-maligned cranial sutures. It has long been recognized, especially by Lovejoy and colleagues (1985), that multiple age indicators need to be combined in a meaningful way.[4] The problem is that multiple age indicators can be correlated with each other, so the information they contain is not independent. In our work, we simplify things by assuming that the correlation among traits is purely attributable to age, so that the traits would be independent if they could be conditioned on age (Boldsen, 1997b; for similar assumptions, see Lucy and Pollard, 1995; Roche et al., 1988). The assumption of *conditional independence* may work well with certain traits, but we would never argue that it accurately reflects the biology of all traits. And when the assumption is incorrect—that is, when traits really are correlated at each age—the standard errors of our age estimates will be biased downward (Boldsen et al., 1998b). One promising approach to this problem is the recent suggestion that the correlation matrix among traits can be estimated by the EM algorithm and used to condition traits properly (Konigsberg and Frankenberg, 1992).[5] This approach is computer-intensive, and it is not yet clear that it produces markedly different age estimates from the assumption of conditional independence. But it unquestionably solves the problem, if by brute force. We suspect that

more elegant and less costly methods may be waiting around the corner.

ANALYTICAL ISSUES

Paleodemographic Mortality and the Non-Stationarity Problem

If we have attended successfully to the problems discussed in the previous section, we are now in possession of an age-at-death distribution broken down by sex. This distribution provides the basic data for the purely demographic part of paleodemographic analysis, the part intended to tell us something about the fundamental forces of population change. Before the 1980s it was usually assumed—quite reasonably, everyone thought—that ages at death are primarily a reflection of mortality, and that the obvious thing to use them for was estimating age-specific mortality rates. This was usually done by aggregating the observed ages at death into discrete intervals (usually 5 to 10 years wide) and treating the resulting distribution as if it were proportional to the $_nd_x$ column in a life table (i.e., the expected stationary age-at-death distribution). Age-specific mortality rates were then back-estimated using some simple modifications of standard life-table analysis (Acsádi and Nemeskéri, 1970).

---

[4]The use of multiple indicators by itself does not eliminate the influence of the reference sample age distribution on our estimates of age at death. The Bayesian correction is still necessary. Multiple indicators also create problems about how to combine information from different reference samples, since not all informative age indicators have been measured on any single reference sample.

[5]The EM algorithm is a computer-based numerical method for producing a series of parameter estimates that, under fairly general conditions, converge to proper maximum likelihood estimates (see below for maximum likelihood estimation). The algorithm proceeds in two stages: the expectation (E) step and the maximization (M) step. The E step computes the expected likelihood function conditional on the current parameter estimates, and the M step then maximizes that likelihood to provide updated parameter estimates. The two steps are alternated until the estimates converge.

This widely used method is based on the implicit assumption that exact ages at death are known, so that they can be assigned to discrete age intervals without any classification error. Obviously, that assumption is never correct in paleodemography. But there is another, more troubling assumption underlying this approach: that the living population giving rise to the skeletal sample was *stationary* in the technical demographic sense of the term. In other words, the population is assumed to have been closed to migration and to have had an intrinsic rate of increase equal to zero, age-specific schedules of fertility and mortality that were unchanging over time, and an equilibrium age distribution induced by those age-specific birth and death rates (Lotka, 1922). Otherwise, the effects of population growth on the living population's age distribution would confound the relationship between the age-at-death distribution and the $_nd_x$ function.[6]

These assumptions may sometimes hold true in an approximate way, but it seems rash to take them for granted as a matter of course. In particular, the growth rate of the population (whether positive, negative, or equal to zero) is one of its most important demographic characteristics. By assuming that the growth rate is always zero, we are taking for granted one of the most important things we could hope to learn.

While the assumption of stationarity was explicitly recognized in the earliest paleodemographic life-table analyses, the papers by Sattenspiel and Harpending (1983) and Johannson and Horowitz (1986) restated the problem in a forceful fashion. As those authors pointed out, two populations with *identical* age-specific mortality rates but *differing* levels of fertility (and hence differing growth rates) would produce different age-at-death distributions. If the assumption of stationarity were made, the two populations would produce different life-table estimates of mortality even though their actual mortality patterns were the same. In other words, classic life-table methods would mistake a difference in fertility and population growth for one in mortality, even when age-specific mortality rates were identical in the two samples.

To understand the origin of the non-stationarity problem—and to provide a basis for any attempt to solve it—we need to understand the basic determinants of the age-at-death distribution. To this end, it will be helpful to assume that the population of interest is *stable,* but not necessarily stationary; that is, we make all the assumptions listed above for the stationary population, except that we allow for the possibility of a non-zero growth rate. The assumption of stability is much less restrictive than the assumption of stationarity. Even when fertility and mortality rates are changing and substantial migration is taking place, most human populations still closely approximate a stable age distribution at any given time (Bourgeois-Pichat, 1971; Coale, 1972:117–61; Keyfitz, 1977: 89–92; Parlett, 1970). This property, known as *weak ergodicity* (Lopez, 1961: 66–68), ensures that stable models almost always fit reasonably well, unless the populations to which they are being fit have been subjected to unusually rapid, cataclysmic change.

The age-at-death distribution is only partly a function of age-specific mortality. It is also influenced by the number of living individuals at risk of death at each age, which can be influenced in turn by population growth. More precisely, the number of deaths at age a is proportional to the product of the age-specific hazard of death at a, $h(a)$, and the fraction of the total population that is age a, $c(a)$. In a stationary population, $c(a)$ is proportional to $S(a)$, the probability of surviving from birth to age a, which makes the age-at-death distribution a reflection of mortality alone. In a stable population with a nonzero growth rate equal to r, in contrast, the value of $c(a)$ is proportional to $S(a)e^{-ra}$. The quantity e^{-ra} corrects for the fact that the absolute number of newborns entering the population each year is changing as a result of population growth, thus distorting

---

[6]There are additional confounding effects of migration, which have received far less attention in paleodemography (Boldsen, 1984; Paine, 1997b).

the age distribution that would have been expected under conditions of stationarity. For a positive growth rate, for example, there are more individuals born this year than, say, 10 years ago: if B babies are born this year into a stable population, then $B \times e^{-10r}$ babies must have been born 10 years ago. This change in the number of individuals entering the population at birth means that the number of people dying at each subsequent age must be a function not only of the hazard of death, but of the growth rate as well.

These ideas can be made more precise by assuming that we have a mathematical function for $h(a)$ that adequately describes the risk of death at all ages across the life course. It is then possible to derive the associated survival function by solving $S(a) = e^{-\int_0^a h(x)dx}$ (Wood et al., 1992a). If the population were stationary, its age-at-death distribution—that is, the probability density function (PDF) of individual ages at death—would be

$$f_0(a) = \frac{h(a)S(a)}{\int_0^\infty h(x)S(x)dx} \qquad (2)$$

When the population is growing at some nonzero rate r, however, we must take into account the fact that the number of people born into it changes each year by a multiplicative factor equal to e^r. As a consequence, the number of people surviving to each age is proportional to $S(a)e^{-ra}$. Those survivors are then exposed to the age-specific mortality rate $h(a)$. Thus, the PDF for deaths in a population with growth rate r is

$$f_r(a) = \frac{h(a)S(a)e^{-ra}}{\int_0^\infty h(x)S(x)e^{-rx}dx} = \frac{f_0(a)e^{-ra}}{\int_0^\infty f_0(x)e^{-rx}dx} \qquad (3)$$

The effects of population growth on the age-at-death distribution are illustrated in Figure 16.1. In the top panel, the solid curve shows the age-at-death distribution expected in a stationary population ($r = 0$) under the mortality regime specified in the figure caption. The broken lines show the age-at-death distributions for four populations with exactly the

same age-specific mortality rates as the stationary case, but with different growth rates: two populations are declining in size ($r = -0.01$ or -0.02) while the other two are increasing ($r = 0.01$ or 0.02). The positive values of r increase the number of deaths at early ages relative to those at later ages; the resulting decline in the mean age at death is purely a reflection of the fact that successive birth cohorts are increasing in size because of population growth. Population decline has the opposite effect on the age-at-death distribution because the numbers entering the population are shrinking over time. If we were to assume that all five populations are stationary, we would estimate the age-specific survival curves shown in the bottom panel of Figure 16.1, curves that differ markedly from each other despite the fact that all five populations really have identical mortality rates.

If two stable populations have identical mortality rates but differing growth rates, there must be some difference in fertility between the two. Thus any difference between populations in age-at-death distributions may be attributable to a difference in mortality patterns, or it may reflect a difference in fertility. As Sattenspiel and Harpending (1983) emphasize, the age-at-death distribution is actually more sensitive to small changes in fertility than to similar changes in mortality, which has led to the use of age-at-death distributions to estimate fertility rates. However, the actual amount of *recoverable* information about fertility in such distributions is quite limited. The most we can ever hope to estimate about fertility from skeletal samples is the crude birth rate, b, which mainstream demographers consider to be uninformative about fertility processes.[7] Equation (3) contains a wealth of information about age-specific mortality in the form of the $h(a)$ and $S(a)$ functions, which have a unique, one-to-one relationship to each other. Unfortu-

---

[7] To quote one text (Newell, 1988:37), "The reason [b] is a 'crude' rate is that it includes all ages and both sexes in the denominator. No attempt is made to relate the births to the women at risk of having those births. Because of this it is strictly not a measure of fertility at all."

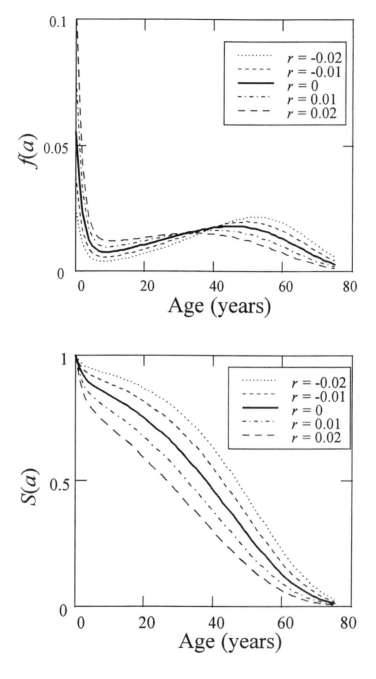

Figure 16.1   The effects of population growth or decline on the age-at-death distribution and associated estimates of age-specific survival (the probability of surviving from birth to each subsequent age). (A) The distribution of ages at death in five stable populations with identical age-specific mortality rates but different population growth rates (r). In all five cases, the age-specific mortality rates are generated by a mixed Makeham model (O'Connor et al., 1997) with parameter values $\alpha_1 = 0.05$, $\alpha_2 = 0.0005$, $\alpha_3 = 0.005$, $\beta_3 = 0.05$ and $\rho_0 = 0.1$. (B) The age-specific survival functions estimated from the age-at-death distributions in (A) under the erroneous assumption that *all five populations are stationary* ($r = 0$). Positive values of r make it appear as if survival is lower at each age, whereas negative values have the opposite effect.

nately, all the information about *fertility* is packed into the single parameter r. If we know the $h(a)$ schedule and the value of r, we can compute the crude death rate d of the population. The crude birth rate b is then $b = r + d$. But that, unfortunately, is as far as we can go in reconstructing fertility, because any given set of r and $h(a)$ values can be combined with an infinite number of different age-specific fertility schedules to produce a single value of b in a stable population (Keyfitz, 1977:174–175). In other words, age-specific fertility rates are nonidentifiable from data on skeletal samples. Fertility, alas, is one of those things that we will never be able to say much about, except in the most general sort of way, from paleodemographic data.[8] Yet we may be able to obtain unbiased estimates of the population growth rate, which would be a great boon to the study of ancient populations. The value of r is of profound demographic importance in its own right, and estimates of it from skeletal remains would be useful checks on independent estimates, such as those derived from archaeological settlement data.

Several attempts have been made to correct mortality estimates for population growth within the context of classic life-table analysis, none of them entirely successfully. Carrier (1958) developed an approach in which growth rates are mathematically incorporated into the life table; the effects of non-stationarity on the mortality distribution can then be examined by recalculating the life table under varying assumptions about population growth (Bennett, 1973; Jackes, 1986; Moore et al., 1975; O'Connor, 1995). By this method, a plausible range of mortality distributions can be computed from an equally plausible range of growth rates. Unfortunately, this approach is of little use unless we have strong prior notions about what the plausible range of growth rates is likely to be. Another idea, developed by Paine (1989a), is more or less the opposite of Carrier's. Paine begins by assuming a mortality regime in the form of a family of model life tables (those consistent with the regression coefficients used to generate the Coale-Demeny "West" Level 7 mortality

function; see Coale and Demeny, 1983). The level of mortality and the growth rate are then estimated from a skeletal sample by maximum likelihood methods. The advantage of this approach over Carrier's is that we end up with one set of mortality rates and the single best estimate of the growth rate conditional on those mortality rates. But Paine's method requires us to make some strong assumptions about the shape of the mortality function; it does not allow unrestricted estimation of both the age pattern of mortality and the population growth rate simultaneously. A further difficulty is that the likelihood surfaces produced by this method are relatively flat for paleodemographic samples, preventing precise estimation of any population characteristics.

All these methods involve either the direct estimation of life tables from skeletal data or the fitting of model life tables to age-at-death distributions. But it may be time to abandon life-table methods on the grounds that they are not well suited to paleodemographic data. The statistical properties of life-table estimates are well-characterized only when they are computed from the ratio of observed deaths at a given age during a precisely defined reference period to the number of person-years of exposure within the corresponding age × period interval (Smith, 1992:108–117). These are precisely the data that are unavailable to the paleodemographer. Model life tables do not help much: they are selected by ad hoc methods and do not allow for special statistical problems such as inexact age estimation. In addition, every available set of model life tables— whether those of Weiss (1973), Coale and Demeny (1983), or the United Nations (1983)—has important limits on the range of mortality patterns it can fit.

Parametric models of age-specific mortality, models that can be estimated (along with

[8]It was once thought that the number of births could be estimated from pitting that can occur on the dorsal surface of the pubic bone adjacent to the symphyseal margin, the so-called parturition scars (Angel, 1969). There is, however, no direct relationship between such scars and births (Kelley, 1979; Stewart, 1970; Suchey et al., 1979).

the population's growth rate) by maximum likelihood methods, are an attractive alternative to life-table analyses. By making fewer initial assumptions about the details of the mortality curve, this approach permits greater freedom to study the age pattern of mortality. This approach still requires the shape of whatever mortality distribution we are trying to reconstruct to fall within the range covered by the parametric model. Thus, it is important to choose a model of mortality that is flexible enough to approximate all human mortality experience.

One general model that has already found some application in paleodemography is the five-parameter competing hazards model developed by Siler (1979, 1983) and investigated by Gage (1988, 1989, 1990, 1991, 1994). The Siler model assumes that an individual's risk of death at each age is determined by a combination of three sets of competing causes: juvenile causes, senescent causes, and causes that are independent of age ("accidental" causes). The joint effect of these three groups of causes varies with age. The juvenile component is specified as a negative Gompertz function, and the age-independent and senescent components as a Gompertz-Makeham model (Siler, 1979). Assuming that the three components do not interact, the resulting age-specific hazard function is

$$h(a) = \alpha_1 e^{-\beta_1 a} + \alpha_2 + \alpha_3 e^{\beta_3 a} \qquad (4)$$

The parameters α_1 and β_1 describe the pattern of juvenile mortality, α_2 captures age-independent mortality, and α_3 and β_3 describe senescent mortality.

Although Gage (1989, 1991, 1994; also Gage and O'Connor, 1994) has shown that the Siler model can yield deep insights into the biology of death, at present we are interested in the model primarily for its ability to capture a wide range of human mortality experience. The applicability of the model to humans has been examined by Siler (1983), Gage (1990), and Gage and Dyke (1986). The Siler model is considerably more flexible than the four-parameter

Brass logit model frequently used by demographers (Gage and Dyke, 1986), and it covers an even wider range of mortality patterns than the Coale-Demeny model life tables (Gage, 1990). More recently, O'Connor (1995) has shown that the model is able to span the extraordinarily wide range of human mortality patterns that have been reported in the paleodemographic literature (some part of which is likely to represent biased age estimation rather than genuine variation in human mortality). Indeed, the model even works well when applied to data on nonhuman primates (Gage and Dyke, 1988) and other animals (Siler, 1979). The only features of human mortality that cannot routinely be captured by the Siler model are the so-called adolescent mortality hump (Mode and Bushy, 1982) and the apparent deceleration in mortality sometimes observed at very late ages (Manton et al., 1986). Although it is possible to develop more complicated versions of the Siler model to correct these deficiencies (Gage, 1989; Wood et al., 1992a), it is by no means clear that these two problems are serious enough to warrant a more complicated specification that would be difficult to apply to skeletal samples, especially since neither the adolescent mortality hump nor the senescent deceleration in mortality is a universal feature of human populations (Gage, 1989; Gage and Dyke, 1986). Besides, we doubt that such fine details of the mortality function can ever be reconstructed from skeletal samples, which even in the best of circumstances are small and biased. The Siler model hits just about the right level of detail for paleodemography: it shows us the overall pattern of mortality while preventing us from being distracted by all the squiggles in the age-specific curve.

We have, then, at least one simple but flexible model for age-specific mortality, a model that is able to cover a wide range of human mortality experience. Other useful model specifications are discussed by Holman et al. (1997) and O'Connor et al. (1997). As we show in the next section, a parametric model such as the Siler model provides the basis for solving such fundamental problems as non-stationarity and the error inherent in age estimation. An additional advantage of parametric models such as the Siler model for paleodemographic analysis is that, unlike standard life-table methods, they allow us to find reliable estimates for mortality at *all* ages, even those ages for which precise age estimates are impossible. For example, once we estimate the parameters of the Siler model, we can use equation (4) to generate the age-specific mortality rate for any age of interest, no matter how advanced. Thus, parametric mortality models allow us to examine patterns of mortality at later ages that are effectively inaccessible to standard life-table methods.

Maximum Likelihood Estimation for Paleodemography

How can parametric mortality models, such as the Siler model, be fit to age-at-death distributions while allowing for the full distribution of errors inherent in aging skeletons and correcting for the distorting effects of non-stationarity? As it happens, all these problems can be handled fairly easily in the context of *maximum likelihood estimation,* a standard body of statistical techniques that is starting to find widespread application in paleodemography (Boldsen, 1984, 1988; Buikstra, 1997; Holman et al., 1997; Konigsberg et al., 1997; O'Connor, 1995; Paine, 1989a, 1989b). As we have discussed in detail elsewhere (Wood et al., 1992a), maximum likelihood methods provide a natural and powerful way to fit parametric mortality models. In this section we show that the age-at-death distribution is, in principle, all that is needed to yield maximum likelihood estimates of the parameters of interest.

Maximum likelihood estimation requires us to specify the probability of obtaining each individual age observed in a skeletal sample. A general mathematical expression for the probability of observing a skeleton of a particular age can be derived from whatever parametric model is chosen for the analysis. The product of all the individual probabilities is known as the likelihood function, denoted L. Ultimately, we end up trying new parameter estimates, de-

riving probabilities for each observation, computing the overall likelihood, and then redoing the whole rigmarole until we find the parameter values that maximize L. Those parameter values are called maximum likelihood estimates (MLEs). MLEs have many desirable statistical properties, among the most important of which is efficiency (the lowest possible standard error for each parameter estimate), which makes them especially useful for small paleodemographic samples.

Holman et al. (1997) have developed a series of likelihood functions that can be maximized numerically to yield simultaneous estimates of the population growth rate and the age-specific mortality function from data on skeletal age at death. More recently, they have also done simulation studies to verify that they can recover the parameters of interest, including the growth rate, without bias (Holman et al., 1998). Holman and his colleagues consider several special cases depending on the kind of error affecting the age-at-death data, including when exact ages are known and when skeletal ages can be classified without error into discrete age intervals. As discussed above, however, we should be working strictly with estimates of the probability density function $p(a|\theta_i)$ for each skeleton. Under this kind of "distributed" aging, the likelihood for a sample of N skeletons is

$$L = \prod_{i=1}^{N} \int_0^\infty p(a|\theta_i) f_r(a)\, da =$$
$$\prod_{i=1}^{N} \frac{\int_0^\infty p(a|\theta_i) f_0(a) e^{-ra}\, da}{\int_0^\infty f_0(a) e^{-ra}\, da} \qquad (5)$$

In this expression, each skeleton contributes a likelihood, $f_r(a)$, of showing up in the mortality sample if it were age a, weighted by the probability that the skeleton actually is age a based on its observed traits, and integrated over all possible ages. This procedure, in effect, smears out the probabilistic age for each skeleton across the age-at-death distribution, thereby directly incorporating the full range of errors inherent in the age estimates into the likelihood function. In addition, each possible age that could be assigned to an individual skeleton is weighted by an exponential term containing r, which both adjusts for non-stationarity and allows r to be estimated from the likelihood function. To find $f_r(a)$, we take our parametric mortality model—equation (4) if we are using the Siler model—solve for the $S(a)$ function associated with it, and plug these expressions into equation (3). Equation (5) has never actually been used, for the simple reason that individual-level estimates of $p(\alpha|\theta_i)$ have not yet been published for any skeletal sample.[9] Nonetheless, this likelihood function should be the preferred way to fit mortality models to skeletal age-at-death distributions in future analyses.

Heterogenous Frailty and Selective Mortality

How can we extend this analytical framework to deal with the problem of individual-level heterogeneity? In paleodemography, the heterogeneity of most immediate concern is that affecting the risk of death, for it means that not all individuals enter the skeletal sample at the same rate. Such heterogeneity may stem from many sources. For example, social and economic differentials often translate into differences in mortality risks. These factors influence mortality via differences in nutrition, growth and development, exposure to infectious agents, and so forth. Individuals may also have "built-in" differences, such as a familial predisposition to certain cancers or cardiovascular disease.

Heterogeneity in the risk of death is both a nuisance and an opportunity to explore some interesting population biology. To date, most demographic, epidemiological, and statistical work on heterogeneity, including our paper on the "osteological paradox" (Wood et al., 1992b), has emphasized its nuisance value. Heterogeneity is a nuisance precisely because, if the heterogeneity is "hidden" (not captured by measured variables), it can confound and bias the results of aggregate-level analyses of

mortality (Manton et al., 1992; Vaupel and Yashin, 1985a, 1985b; Wood et al., 1992a).

This problem can be illustrated with a very simple model. Imagine a cohort of newborns, each of whom experiences an absolutely constant risk of death but who vary among each other in their risks. We might model the mortality rate experienced by the i-th child at age a as $h_i(a) = z_i \times h_c$, where h_c is the part of the rate shared by all members of the cohort, and z_i is the individual child's relative risk of death, the part specific to that child. To use terminology first proposed by Vaupel et al. (1979), z_i can be referred to as the i-th child's individual *frailty*. In this absurdly simple model, we assume that neither z_i nor h_c changes with an individual's age, so that each child's individual risk of death, $h_i(a)$, is itself constant for that particular child. But we also assume that z_i varies among newborns following the probability density function $g_0(z)$. In other words, frailty is heterogeneous in this cohort.

Generalizing a bit, we can write $g_a(z)$ for the distribution of z among children who have survived to age a. Even though z_i and h_c are constant for each child, the overall distribution $g_a(z)$ changes with age, for mortality progressively removes children of higher frailty from the cohort as time goes on. The *mean* risk of death for all children at age a is $\bar{h}(a) = \int_0^\infty g_a(z)zh_c dz = \bar{z}(a)h_c$, where the bars indicate means. In other words, the aggregate-level mortality rate at age a is just the product of the common hazard and the mean of the frailty distribution at that age.

The crucial point here is that $g_a(z)$ changes with age, because deaths of children at any given age are selective with respect to the frailty distribution: the greater a child's frailty, the more likely it is to die. Thus, the frailty distribution shifts with age as high-frailty individuals are eliminated by death (Fig. 16.2). As a result, the mean frailty of surviving children

[9]Just such data have been collected for the pubic symphysis, iliac auricular surface, and cranial sutures by Boldsen and Milner, and they are currently the subject of analysis (Boldsen, 1997b; Boldsen et al., 1998a, 1998b; Milner et al., 1997).

declines with age, causing the aggregate death rate to decline as well, even though the individual-level risks of death remain absolutely constant. Thus, where there is heterogeneity in frailty, changes in aggregate-level death rates (as might be estimated using conventional life-table methods) do not necessarily reflect the risks experienced by *any* of the individuals making up the aggregate.

As described to this point, the twinned problems of heterogenous frailty and selective mortality affect all areas of population biol-

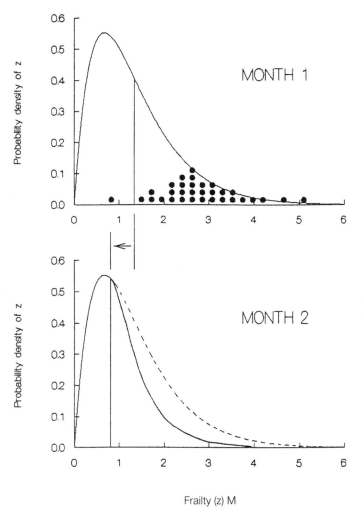

Figure 16.2   A simple model of heterogeneous frailty and selective mortality in a cohort of newborns. Each child's hazard of death is assumed to be constant and proportional to its individual-level frailty (*z*). Frailty is assumed to be distributed as a gamma random variable among newborns (A). Deaths during the first month of life (dots) are selective with respect to the frailty distribution; i.e., children of high frailty make up a disproportionately large fraction of all deaths. As a consequence, the frailty distribution shifts downward by the second month of life (B), and mean frailty decreases (arrow). Since the aggregate-level hazard of death at each age is proportional to the mean frailty of survivors at that age, the aggregate hazard declines even though the hazards of the individual children remain constant. (From Wood et al., 1992a. Hazards Models for Human Population Biology, Yearbook of Physical Anthropology, Copyright © 1992 Wiley-Liss, Inc. Reprinted by permission of John Wiley & Sons, Inc.)

ogy. But they are compounded for paleodemography and paleopathology because we observe only the black dots in Figure 16.2, never the smooth curve. It is the latter that tells us something about the health of the living population. In other words, any skeletal traits that may reveal something about an individual's health are observed only in the dead, not the living. And as the figure suggests, the dead are unrepresentative of the living, precisely because mortality is selective with respect to the frailty distribution.[10]

Solving this problem requires us to make proper use of paleopathological information on one or more kinds of skeletal or dental lesions and how those lesions are distributed by age. We emphasize the word "proper." In the past, it was not unusual for paleopathologists to assume that lesion frequencies in a mortality sample are a direct reflection of the prevalence of particular conditions in once-living populations (for some exceptions using skeletal and dental lesion and size data, see Cook, 1981; Cook and Buikstra, 1979; Guagliardo, 1982; Ortner, 1991; Palkovich, 1985; Saunders and Hoppa, 1993; Wood et al., 1992b). Cohen (1994) has argued that this assumption is appropriate because the conditions that caused the lesions commonly found on skeletons had little, if any, effect on the risk of dying. A similar position has been adopted by Waldron (1996) who, while acknowledging the effects of selective mortality for diseases that increase the risk of death, still maintains that for many diseases the frequency of skeletal lesions is equivalent to their prevalence in living populations. If it is true that certain illnesses have no influence, either direct or indirect, on the risk of death, the frequency of any associated skeletal lesions in the mortality sample should indeed be proportional to their prevalence in the living population.[11] But such illnesses strike us as supremely uninteresting. If we restrict our attention to illnesses that do not have any influence on the risk of dying—however weak or strong, direct or indirect—are we likely to learn anything meaningful about past health? If conditions are truly uninformative about un-

derlying frailty, they are of no use whatsoever in revealing the extent of heterogeneous frailty and selective mortality.

Paradoxically, then, we should actually seek out lesions that are likely to be subject to selective mortality, because these are the informative ones. It should be emphasized that we are referring not only to conditions that directly cause death, but also to those associated with an elevated risk of death. For example, many adults from a 700-year-old village cemetery in the American Midwest were killed by their enemies in ambushes (Milner et al., 1991). Their skeletons often showed signs of debilitating conditions, including active infections, partially healed bone fractures, and dislocated limb joints. While these people did not die from these illnesses and injuries, their ability to protect themselves or to flee danger was certainly impaired. Thus, even the skeletons of victims of violence cannot be assumed to be a representative sample of all people who were once alive in a particular community (Wood and Milner, 1994; for a contrary view, see Cohen, 1994).

The relationship between the presence of a pathological lesion and the individual's frailty is by no means straightforward. To take a simple example, osteologists quite often differentiate bony lesions that were obviously active at the time of death from those that appear to have healed. This commonly made distinction highlights a deeper question raised by Ortner (1991): is it good or bad to have a skeletal or dental lesion? The presence of a lesion indi-

---

[10]In their thoughtful review of the problem of selective mortality, Saunders and Hoppa (1993) conclude that other biases, such as differential preservation and biased age estimation, are likely to be much larger and more worrisome. We agree that this will often be the case, but that does not remove the additional effects of selective mortality. In addition, the phenomenon of selectivity (unlike those of poor preservation or erroneous ages) is of fundamental biological importance and, therefore, something we would like to be able to make inferences about.

[11]Here we are ignoring the low sensitivity and specificity of bony lesions used as indicators of particular diseases. These two additional issues have long been recognized as particular problems for paleopathologists interested in the disease experience of past populations.

cates that the individual survived some disease, nutritional deprivation, or trauma long enough to undergo a recognizable alteration of the normal structure of bones or teeth. The mere fact that they had the lesion may indicate that these people were healthier than other cohort members who succumbed to this particular condition before a distinctive hard-tissue lesion had time to form. But undoubtedly some community members shrugged off the infection long before it affected their skeletons. Others might never have been exposed to one or more of the pathogens that cause bone lesions, never experienced nutritional hardship, or rarely if ever engaged in activities that were likely to led to certain kinds of bone fractures. Sorting out what might be meant by the presence or absence of any skeletal or dental indicator, regardless of whether it is directly related to a particular disease or is nonspecific in the sense that it might have a number of causes (e.g., stunted growth), is by no means a simple task.

An important first step is to look at the age pattern of lesions, as advocated by many paleopathologists. Even when overall lesion frequencies are similar, the patterning across age groups may not be the same. For example, Boldsen (1997a) has shown that the risk of developing dental caries in the molars was markedly different for adult males and females in a medieval Danish village. When these people were treated simply as adults—that is, the age structure of the skeletal sample was ignored—the proportions of males and females with decayed teeth were similar. These conditions need not have been causes of death, only somehow associated with increased risks of dying. Thus, Boldsen (1991) has found that advanced dental attrition in a medieval Danish village was associated with an elevated risk of death. Here attrition served as a marker of whatever social or environmental conditions acted to shorten the life span. The people with greater occlusal wear were for some reason being winnowed out, and hence they were disproportionately represented in the younger age intervals of the adult mortality sample. In other words, it is the age distribution of lesions that

is providing information about heterogeneity and selectivity.

There are three things that need to be done to deal with heterogeneous frailty. First, some theory must be developed about the distribution of frailty and how it changes with environmental, economic, and social conditions. Second, a better understanding is needed of how frailty is related to an individual's risk of death. Third, measurable characteristics of skeletons must be identified that are informative about an individual's frailty.

Recently, some progress has been made on these separate goals. For example, Wood (1998) has started to develop some theory about how frailty distributions vary with economic and demographic change, while Weiss (1990) has drawn on theoretical models from population genetics to help explain variation in frailty. Saunders and Hoppa (1993) have done interesting simulation studies to address the question of whether stature is likely to be an informative indicator of frailty. We have also addressed the question of whether heterogeneity and selectivity can be identified using observable skeletal traits (Usher et al., 1997). In that work, the Cox proportional hazards model was generalized to allow for both a main effect of the presence of skeletal lesions or other indicators of health on the age at death and an interaction between the bony traits and age at death. Mathematically, it can be shown that the interaction term captures age-specific changes in the frailty distribution resulting from selective mortality. After validating the method against simulated data, we applied it to two skeletal samples: the medieval Danish peasant village of Tirup and the 700-year-old Norris Farm site in Illinois. Even with comparatively small samples similar to those from many archaeological sites, we found clear evidence of heterogeneity and selectivity in femur length, with somewhat more equivocal results using porotic hyperostosis and cribra orbitalia. These results convince us that heterogeneous frailty and selective mortality can be detected using skeletal traits, but not all traits are equally informative about individual frailty.

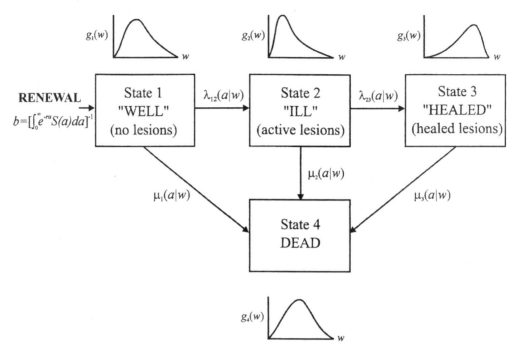

Figure 16.3   A multistate stationary renewal model for interpreting the frequency of skeletal or dental lesions in mortality samples. Each newborn enters the living population in the "well" state (i.e., without detectable lesions) and is assigned a value of frailty (z) drawn at random from the probability density function $g_1(z)$. Transitions to subsequent states among the living, including "ill" (with active skeletal or dental lesions) and "healed" (with healed lesions), occur at age-specific rates λ that are conditioned on the individual's frailty. Frailty also influences the age-specific rates μ at which people in various states die and enter the mortality sample. Because all the transitions in the model are selective with respect to frailty, the frailty distribution $g_i(z)$ shifts with age and state. The observed skeletons are a mixture of individuals from all three living states, as indicated by their age-specific lesion frequencies. The age-specific distribution of active and healed lesions, along with the associated ages at death, provide the data needed to fit such a model by the method of maximum likelihood. (From Usher et al., 1997).

As useful as all this work has been, it has still approached the problems of heterogeneity and selectivity in a rather piecemeal fashion. We still need a comprehensive analytical framework to handle all aspects of the problem simultaneously. Our colleague Bethany Usher is currently working toward that goal.[12] Her most important contribution to date has been to develop a modeling framework, based on stochastic renewal theory and multistate survival processes, within which to study all important aspects of heterogeneity and selectivity at the same time (Fig. 16.3). With respect to any particular skeletal lesion, she assumes that we can classify a skeleton as "well" at the time of

death (which in this context merely means that it did not have the lesion in question), "ill" (it had an active lesion at the time of death), or "healed" (it had a healed lesion). Living newborns enter the "well" state through a renewal process that adjusts for population growth. At birth, each cohort is assigned an initial frailty distribution, based on a functional form that makes theoretical sense. The hazard rate for each possible transition (e.g., "ill" to "healed"

[12] The model described here is part of Ms. Usher's doctoral dissertation work in the Department of Anthropology, Pennsylvania State University, and we are grateful to her for her willingness to let us discuss her work in print before she had has an opportunity to do so.

or "dead") is modeled as conditional on the individual's frailty, which allows the frailty distribution to change with age and state. As osteologists, we only observe individuals in the "dead" state, and this sample is a mixture of individuals drawn from the "well," "ill," and "healed" states. The information on the age-at-death distribution *and* the age-specific frequency of active and healed lesions among the skeletons provides the information from which the rest of the model can be estimated by maximum likelihood methods.[13] The parameter estimates so obtained will allow us to make inferences about the living population such as the actual prevalence of lesions, the influence of lesions (or rather their associated pathological conditions) on the risk of death, and the age-specific frailty distribution. Thus, we can draw unbiased conclusions about the health status of the actual population, as opposed to the skeletal sample, and test theoretical models about the ways in which frailty distributions change under different environmental and cultural conditions. This model, or something like it, should help us move from an exclusive concern about the possible confounding effects of heterogeneity (although these will remain important) to an attempt to understand its central role in population dynamics. It is important to emphasize that such models require us to use both paleodemographic data (ages at death) and paleopathological data (lesion frequencies) in the same analysis, which is precisely why we believe that paleopathology needs to be made an integral part of paleodemography.

CONCLUSION

In this selective review of paleodemography, several troubling issues and possible solutions to them have been identified. The most difficult issues include those related to age-at-death estimation, population non-stationarity, hetero-

geneous frailty, and selective mortality. In contrast to the outlook of a few decades ago—a time when it could be claimed that there was no future for paleodemography and, by extension, much of paleopathology (Bocquet-Appel and Masset, 1982; Peterson, 1975)—we see signs of progress in dealing with issues that have long plagued the field.

In this chapter, we have deliberately adopted a narrow definition of paleodemography as the study of the demographic characteristics of past populations using skeletal samples in isolation from other kinds of data. However, as a recent book by Paine (1997a) has shown, there is much more to paleodemography than the study of skeletons. It is essential to embed the results of osteological analysis in a broader theoretical and empirical discussion of population processes spanning the great periods of time known primarily through archaeological research. In addition, other kinds of data—settlement numbers and sizes, household distributions, environmental information—ought to be used to investigate demographic topics such as population growth or decline. The study of past populations should very definitely include analysis of skeletal samples, but much else besides.

ACKNOWLEDGMENTS

We thank Rebecca Ferrell, Darryl Holman, Lyle Konigsberg, Kathy O'Connor, and Bethany Usher for their helpful comments and suggestions. We also thank Darryl Holman and Bethany Usher for producing the figures.

REFERENCES

Acsádi G, Nemeskéri, J. 1970. History of Human Life Span and Mortality. Budapest: Akadémiai Kiadó.

Angel JL. 1969. The bases of paleodemography. Am J Phys Anthropol 30:427–437.

Aykroyd RG, Lucy D, Pollard AM, Roberts CA. 1999. Nasty, brutish, but not necessarily short: a

---

[13]For examples of how to estimate such complex multistate models, see Manton and Stallard (1988) and Wood et al. (1994).

reconsideration of the statistical methods used to calculate age at death from adult human skeletal and dental age indicators. Am Antiq 64:55–70.

Aykroyd RG, Lucy D, Pollard AM, Solheim T. 1997. Regression analysis in adult age estimation. Am J Phys Anthropol 104:259–265.

Bennett KA. 1973. On the estimation of some demographic characteristics of a prehistoric population from the American Southwest. Am J Phys Anthropol 39:223–232.

Binford LR. 1971. Mortuary practices: their study and their potential. Am Antiq Memoir 25:6–29.

Bird J. 1996. Prevalence studies in skeletal populations. Int J Osteoarchaeol 6:320.

Bocquet-Appel JP, Masset C. 1982. Farewell to paleodemography. J Hum Evol 12:353–360.

Bocquet-Appel JP, Masset C. 1985. Paleodemography: resurrection or ghost? J Hum Evol 14: 107–111.

Bocquet-Appel JP, Masset C. 1996. Paleodemography: expectancy and false hope. Am J Phys Anthropol 99:571–583.

Boldsen JL. 1984. Paleodemography of two southern Scandinavian medieval communities. Meddelanden Från Lunds Universitets Historiska Museum 5:107–115.

Boldsen JL. 1988. Two methods for reconstruction of the empirical mortality profile. Hum Evol 3:335–342.

Boldsen JL. 1991. Ageing and dental attrition in a medieval rural Danish Population. Int J Anthropol 6:217–224.

Boldsen JL. 1997a. Estimating patterns of disease and mortality in a medieval Danish village. In: Paine RR, Integrating Archaeological Demography: Multidisciplinary Approaches to Prehistoric Population. Occasional Paper No. 24. Carbondale: Center for Archaeological Investigations, Southern Illinois University. pp. 229–241.

Bolden JL. 1997b. Transition analysis: a method for unbiased age estimation from skeletal traits. Am J Phys Anthropol Supplement 24:76 (abstract).

Boldsen JL, Milner GR, Usher BM. 1998a. The quality of osteological age estimation based on transition analysis: the effect of lack of conditional independence. Presented at the annual meeting of the American Anthropological Association, Philadelphia, Pa.

Boldsen JL, Milner GR, Wood JW. 1998b. Transition analysis: a new method for obtaining unbiased age estimates from human skeletons. In preparation.

Bourgeois-Pichat J. 1971. Stable, semi-stable populations and growth potential. Popul Stud 25: 235–254.

Brooks ST. 1955. Skeletal age at death: The reliability of cranial and pubic age indicators. Am J Phys Anthropol 13:567–597.

Buikstra JE. 1976. Hopewell in the Lower Illinois Valley. Scientific Papers 2. Evanston, Ill.: Northwestern Archeological Program.

Buikstra JE. 1997. Paleodemography: context and promise. In: Paine RR, editor. Integrating Archaeological Demography: Multidisciplinary Approaches to Prehistoric Population. Occasional Paper No. 24. Carbondale: Center for Archaeological Investigations, Southern Illinois University. pp. 367–380.

Buikstra JE, Konigsberg LW. 1985. Paleodemography: critiques and controversies. Am Anthropol 87:316–333.

Buikstra JE, Konigsberg LW, Bullington J. 1986. Fertility and the development of agriculture in the prehistoric Midwest. Am Antiq 51:528–546.

Buikstra JE, Ubelaker DH. 1994. Standards for Data Collection from Human Skeletal Remains. Research Series 44. Fayetteville: Arkansas Archeological Survey.

Byers SN. 1994. On stress and stature in the "osteological paradox." Curr Anthropol 35:282–284.

Carey JR. 1997. What demographers can learn from fruit fly actuarial models and demography. Demography 34:17–30.

Carey JR, Liedo P. 1995. Sex mortality differentials and selective survival in large medfly cohorts. Exper Gerontol 30:315–325.

Carrier NH. 1958. A note on the estimation of mortality and other population characteristics given deaths by age. Popul Stud 12:149–163.

Cassidy CM. 1980. Nutrition and health in agriculturalists and hunter-gatherers: a case study of two prehistoric populations. In: Jerome NW, Kandel RF, Pelto GH, editors. Nutritional Anthropology: Contemporary Approaches to Diet and Culture. Pleasantville, N.Y.: Redgrave. pp. 117–145.

Coale AJ. 1957. How the age distribution of a human population is determined. Cold Spring Harbor Symp Quant Biol 22:83–88.

Coale AJ. 1972. The Growth and Structure of Human Populations: A Mathematical Investigation. Princeton: Princeton University Press.

Coale AJ, Demeny P. 1983. Regional Model Life Tables and Stable Populations, 2nd ed. New York: Academic Press.

Cohen MN. 1989. Health and the Rise of Civilization. New Haven: Yale University Press.

Cohen MN. 1994. The osteological paradox reconsidered. Curr Anthropol 35: 629–631.

Cohen MN. 1997. Does paleopathology measure community health? A rebuttal of "the osteological paradox" and its implication for world history. In: Paine RR, editor. Integrating Archaeological Demography: Multidisciplinary Approaches to Prehistoric Population. Occasional Paper 24. Carbondale: Center for Archaeological Investigations, Southern Illinois University. pp. 242–260.

Cohen MN, Armelagos GJ, editors. 1984a. Paleopathology at the Origins of Agriculture. Orlando, Fla.: Academic Press.

Cohen MN, Armelagos GJ. 1984b. Paleopathology at the origins of agriculture: editors' summation. In: Cohen MN, Armelagos GJ, editors. Paleopathology at the Origins of Agriculture. Orlando, Fla.: Academic Press. pp. 585–601.

Cook DC. 1981. Mortality, age-structure and status in the interpretation of stress indicators in prehistoric skeletons: a dental example from the lower Illinois valley. In: Chapman R, Kinnes I, Randsborg K, editors. The Archaeology of Death. Cambridge: Cambridge University Press. pp. 133–144.

Cook DC, Buikstra JE. 1979. Health and differential survival in prehistoric populations: prenatal dental defects. Am J Phys Anthropol 51:649–664.

Dong Z. 1997. Mixture analysis and its preliminary application in archaeology. J Archaeol Sci 24: 141–161.

Gage TB. 1988. Mathematical hazard models of mortality: an alternative to model life tables. Am J Phys Anthropol 76:429–441.

Gage TB. 1989: Bio-mathematical approaches to the study of human variation in mortality. Yrbk Phys Anthropol 32:185–214.

Gage TB. 1990. Variation and classification of human age patterns of mortality: analysis using competing hazards models. Hum Biol 62: 589–617.

Gage TB, 1991. Causes of death and the components of mortality: testing the biological interpretations of a competing hazards model. Am J Hum Biol 3:289–300.

Gage TB. 1994. Population variation in cause of death: level, gender, and period effects. Demography 31:271–296.

Gage TB, Dyke B. 1986. Parameterizing abridged mortality tables: the Siler three-component hazard model. Hum Biol 58:275–291.

Gage TB, Dyke B. 1988. Model life tables for the larger old world monkeys. Am J Primatol 16:305–320.

Gage TB, O'Connor KA. 1994. Nutrition and variation in levels and age patterns of mortality. Hum Biol 66:77–103.

Giles E. 1964. Sex determination by discriminant function analysis of the mandible. Am J Phys Anthropol 22:129–136.

Giles E, Elliot O. 1963. Sex determination by discriminant function analysis of crania. Am J Phys Anthropol 21:53–68.

Goodman AH. 1993. On the interpretation of health from skeletal remains. Curr Anthropol 34: 281–288.

Gordon CC, Buikstra JE. 1981. Soil pH, bone preservation, and sampling bias at mortuary sites. Am Antiq 46:566–571.

Guagliardo MF. 1982. Tooth crown size differences between age groups: a possible new indicator of stress in skeletal samples. Am J Phys Anthropol 58:383–389.

Herrmann NP. 1998. Age-at-death distribution estimation: an example at Indian Knoll. Presented at the annual meeting of the American Anthropological Association, Philadelphia, Pa.

Holman DJ, Bennett KA. 1991. Determination of sex from arm bone measurements. Am J Phys Anthropol 84:421–426.

Holman DJ, O'Connor KA, Wood JW. 1997. Correcting for nonstationarity in paleodemographic mortality models. Am J Phys Anthropol Supplement 24:132 (abstract).

Holman DJ, O'Connor KA, Wood JW. 1998. Estimating population growth rates from skeletal samples. Presented at the annual meeting of the American Anthropological Association, Philadelphia, Pa.

Horowitz S, Armelagos, GJ, Wachter K. 1988. On generating birth rates from skeletal populations. Am J Phys Anthropol 76:189–196.

Howell N. 1976. Toward a uniformitarian theory of human paleodemography. In: Ward RH, Weiss KM, editors. The Demographic Evolution of Human Populations. New York: Academic Press. pp. 25–40.

Howell N. 1982. Village composition implied by a paleodemographic life table: the Libben site. Am J Phys Anthropol 59:263–269.

İşcan MY, Loth SR. 1989. Osteological manifestations of age in the adult. In: İşcan MY, Kennedy KAR, editors. Reconstruction of Life from the Skeleton. New York: Alan R. Liss. pp. 23–40.

Jackes MK. 1985. Pubic symphysis age distribution. Am J Phys Anthropol 68:281–299.

Jackes MK. 1986. Mortality of Ontario archaeological populations. Can J Anthropol 5:33–48.

Jackes MK. 1993. On paradox and osteology. Curr Anthropol 34:434–439.

Jackes M, Lubell D, Meiklejohn C. 1997. Healthy but mortal: human biology and the first farmers of western Europe. Antiquity 71:639–658.

Jefferson T. 1788. Notes on the State of Virginia. Philadelphia, Pa: Prichard and Hall.

Johannson SR, Horowitz S. 1986. Estimating mortality in skeletal populations: influence of the growth rate on the interpretation of levels and trends during the transition to agriculture. Am J Phys Anthropol 71:223–250.

Kelley MA. 1979. Parturition and pelvic changes. Am J Phys Anthropol 51:541–546.

Keyfitz N. 1977. Introduction to the Mathematics of Population. rev. ed. Reading, Mass.: Addison-Wesley.

Kimura DK, Chikuni S. 1987. Mixtures of empirical distributions: an iterative application of the age-length key. Biometrics 43:23–35.

Kolakowski D, Bock RD. 1981. A multivariate generalization of probit analysis. Biometrics 37: 541–551.

Konigsberg LW, Buikstra JE, Bullington J. 1989. Paleodemographic correlates of fertility. Am Antiq 54:626–36.

Konigsberg LW, Frankenberg SR. 1992. Estimation of age structure in anthropological demography. Am J Phys Anthropol 89:235–256.

Konigsberg LW, Frankenberg, SR. 1994. Paleodemography: "Not quite dead." Evol Anthropol 3:92–105.

Konigsberg LW, Frankenberg SR, Walker RB. 1997. Regress what on what? Paleodemographic age

estimation as a calibration problem. In: Paine RR, editor. Integrating Archaeological Demography: Multidisciplinary Approaches to Prehistoric Population. Occasional Paper 24. Carbondale: Center for Archaeological Investigations, Southern Illinois University. pp. 64–88.

Konigsberg LW, Hens SM. 1998. Use of ordinal categorical variables in skeletal assessment of sex from the cranium. Am J Phys Anthropol 107: 97–112.

Lallo J, Armelagos GJ, Rose JC. 1978. Paleo-epidemiology of infectious disease in the Dickson Mounds population. Med Coll Virginia Quart 14:17–23.

Lanphear KM. 1989. Testing the value of skeletal samples in demographic research: a comparison with vital registration samples. Int J Anthropol 4:185–193.

Lopez A. 1961. Problems in Stable Population Theory. Princeton: Office of Population Research.

Lotka AJ. 1922. The stability of the normal age distribution. Proc Nat Acad Sci USA 8:339–345.

Lovejoy CO, Meindl RS, Mensforth RP, Barton TJ. 1985. Multifactorial determination of skeletal age at death: a method and blind tests of its accuracy. Am J Phys Anthropol 68:1–14.

Lovejoy CO, Meindl RS, Pryzbeck TR, Barton TS, Heiple KG, Kotting D. 1977. Paleodemography of the Libben site, Ottawa County, Ohio. Science 198:291–293.

Lucy D, Pollard AM 1995. Further comments on the estimation of error associated with the Gustafson dental age estimation method. J Forensic Sci 40:222–227.

Manton KG, Singer B, Woodbury MA. 1992. Some issues in the quantitative characterization of heterogeneous populations. In: Trussell J, Hankinson R, Tilton J, editors. Demographic Applications of Event History Analysis. Oxford: Oxford University Press. pp. 9–37.

Manton KG, Stallard E. 1988. Chronic Disease Modelling: Measurement and Evaluation of the Risks of Chronic Disease Processes. London: Charles Griffin.

Manton KG, Stallard E, Vaupel JW. 1986. Alternative models for the heterogeneity of mortality risks among the aged. J Am Stat Assoc 81:635–644.

Mays S. 1992. Taphonomic factors in a human skeletal assemblage. Circaea 9:54–58.

McKern TW, Stewart TD. 1957. Skeletal Age Changes in Young American Males. Technical Report EP-45. Natick, Mass.: Quartermaster Research and Development Command.

Meindl RS, Lovejoy CO, Mensforth RP, Don Carlos L. 1985. Accuracy and direction of error in sexing of the skeleton: implications for paleodemography. Am J Phys Anthropol 68:79–85.

Mensforth RP. 1990. Paleodemography of the Carlston Annis (Bt-5) Late Archaic skeletal population. Am J Phys Anthropol 82:81–99.

Milner GR, Anderson E, Smith VG. 1991. Warfare in late prehistoric west-central Illinois. Am Antiq 56:581–603.

Milner GR, Boldsen JL, Usher BM. 1997. Age-at-death determination using revised scoring procedures for age-progressive skeletal traits. Am J Phys Anthropol Supplement 24:170 (abstract).

Milner GR, Humpf DA, Harpending HC. 1989. Pattern matching of age-at-death distributions in paleodemographic analysis. Am J Phys Anthropol 80:49–58.

Milner GR, Jefferies RW. 1987. A reevaluation of the WPA excavation of the Robbins Mound. In: Pollack D, editor. Current Archaeological Research in Kentucky: Vol. 1. Frankfort: Kentucky Heritage Council. pp. 33–42.

Mode CJ, Busby RC. 1982. An eight-parameter model of human mortality: the single decrement case. Bull Math Biol 44: 647–659.

Møller-Christensen V. 1982. Æbelholt Kloster. Copenhagen: Nationalmuseet.

Moore JA, Swedlund AC, Armelagos GJ. 1975. The use of life tables in paleodemography. Am Antiq 40:57–70.

Nemeskéri J. 1971. Some comparisons of Egyptian and early Eurasian demographic data. J Hum Evol 1:171–186.

Newell C. 1988. Methods and Models in Demography. New York: The Guilford Press.

Newton I. 1998. Population Limitation in Birds. San Diego: Academic Press.

O'Connor KA. 1995. The Age Pattern of Mortality: A Micro-analysis of Tipu and a Meta-analysis of Twenty-nine Paleodemographic Samples. Ph.D. Dissertation. Albany: State University of New York.

O'Connor KA, Holman DJ, Boldsen JL, Wood JW, Gage TB. 1997. Competing and mixed hazards models of mortality: osteological applications. Am J Phys Anthropol Supplement 24:180 (abstract).

Ortner DJ. 1991. Theoretical and methodological issues in paleopathology. In: Ortner DJ, Aufderheide AC, editors. Human Paleopathology: Current Syntheses and Future Options. Washington: Smithsonian Institution Press. pp. 5–11.

Ortner DJ, Putschar WGJ. 1985. Identification of Pathological Conditions in Human Skeletal Remains. 2nd ed. Washington: Smithsonian Institution Press.

Paine RR. 1989a. Model life table fitting by maximum likelihood estimation: a procedure to reconstruct paleodemographic characteristics from skeletal age distributions. Am J Phys Anthropol 79:51–61.

Paine RR. 1989b. Model life tables as a measure of bias in the Grasshopper Pueblo skeletal series. Am Antiq 54:820–825.

Paine RR, editor. 1997a. Integrating Archaeological Demography: Multidisciplinary Approaches to Prehistoric Population. Occasional Paper No. 24. Carbondale: Center for Archaeological Investigations, Southern Illinois University.

Paine RR. 1997b. Uniformitarian models in osteological paleodemography. In: Paine RR, editor. Integrating Archaeological Demography: Multidisciplinary Approaches to Prehistoric Population. Occasional Paper 24. Carbondale: Center for Archaeological Investigations, Southern Illinois University. pp. 191–204.

Paine RR, Harpending HC. 1996. Assessing the reliability of paleodemographic fertility estimators using simulated skeletal distributions. Am J Phys Anthropol 101:151–159.

Paine RR, Harpending HC. 1998. Effect of sample bias on paleodemographic fertility estimates. Am J Phys Anthropol 105:51–61.

Palkovich AM. 1985. Interpreting prehistoric morbidity incidence and mortality risk: nutritional stress at Arroyo Hondo pueblo, New Mexico. In: Merbs CF, Miller RJ, editors. Health and Disease in the Prehistoric Southwest. Anthropological Research Papers 34. Tempe: Arizona State University. pp. 128–138.

Parlett B. 1970. Ergodic properties of populations, I: the one sex model. Theoret Popul Biol 1: 191–207.

Pearson JD, Morrell C, Brant LJ. 1992. Mixture models for investigating complex distributions. J Quant Anthropol 3:325–346.

Pennington RL. 1996. Causes of early human population growth. Am J Phys Anthropol 99:259–274.

Petersen HC. 1997. Population structure and patterns of variability within Danish medieval town and village cemeteries. Am J Phys Anthropol Supplement 24:185 (abstract).

Petersen W. 1975. A demographer's view of prehistoric demography. Curr Anthropol 16:227–245.

Piontek J, Weber A. 1990. Controversy on paleodemography. Int J Anthropol 5:71–83.

Powell ML. 1988. Status and Health in Prehistory: A Case Study of the Moundville Chiefdom. Washington: Smithsonian Institution Press.

Robling AG, Ubelaker DH. 1997. Sex estimation from metatarsals. J Forensic Sci 42:1062–1069.

Roche AF, Chumlea WC, Thissen D. 1988. Assessing the Skeletal Maturity of the Hand-Wrist: Fels Method. Springfield, Ill.: Charles C. Thomas.

Rousseau JJ. 1950. The Social Contract and Discourses. Cole GDH, translator. New York: E.P. Dutton.

Ruff CB. 1981. A reassessment of demographic estimates for Pecos Pueblo. Am J Phys Anthropol 54:147–151.

St. Hoyme LE, İşcan MY. 1989. Determination of sex and race: Accuracy and assumptions. In: İşcan MY, Kennedy KAR, editors. Reconstruction of Life from the Skeleton. New York: Alan R. Liss. pp. 53–93.

Sattenspiel L, Harpending HC. 1983. Stable populations and skeletal age. Am Antiq 48:489–498.

Saunders SR, Hoppa RD. 1993. Growth deficit in survivors and non-survivors: biological mortality bias in subadult skeletal samples. Yrbk Phys Anthropol 36:127–151.

Siler W. 1979. A competing-risk model for animal mortality. Ecology 60:750–757.

Siler W. 1983. Parameters of mortality in human populations with widely varying life spans. Stat Med 2:373–380.

Smith DP. 1992. Formal Demography. New York: Plenum Press.

Steinbock RT. 1976. Paleopathological Diagnosis and Interpretation: Bone Diseases in Ancient Human Populations. Springfield, Ill.: Charles C. Thomas.

Stewart TD. 1970. Identification of the scars of parturition in the skeletal remains of females. In: Stewart TD, editor. Personal Identification in Mass Disasters. Washington: Smithsonian Institution. pp. 127–135.

Stone AC, Milner GR, Paabo S, Stoneking M. 1996. Sex determination of ancient human skeletons using DNA. Am J Phys Anthropol 99:231–238.

Suchey JM, Wiseley DV, Green RF, Noguchi TT. 1979. Analysis of dorsal pitting in the *os pubis* in an extensive sample of modern American females. Am J Phys Anthropol 51:517–540.

Swedlund AC, Armelagos GJ. 1969. Une recherche en paléo-démographie: La Nubie soudanaise. Annales 24: 1287–1298.

Ubelaker DH. 1974. Reconstruction of Demographic Profiles from Ossuary Skeletal Samples: A Case Study from the Tidewater Potomac. Smithsonian Contributions to Anthropology 18. Washington: Smithsonian Institution Press.

United Nations. 1983. Model Life Tables for Developing Countries. New York: United Nations.

Usher BM, Boldsen JL, Wood JW, Milner GR. 1997. A general approach to the detection of heterogeneity and selective mortality from skeletal lesions. Am J Phys Anthropol Supplement 24:230 (abstract).

Van Gerven DP, Armelagos GJ. 1983. "Farewell to paleodemography?" Rumors of its death have been greatly exaggerated. J Hum Evol 12:353–360.

Vaupel JW, Johnson TE, Lithgow GJ. 1994. Rates of mortality in populations of *Caenorhabditis elegans*. Science 266:826.

Vaupel JW, Manton KG, Stallard E. 1979. The impact of heterogeneity in individual frailty on the dynamics of mortality. Demography 16:439–454.

Vaupel JW, Yashin AI. 1985a. Heterogeneity's ruses: some surprising effects of selection on population dynamics. Am Statis 39:176–185.

Vaupel JW, Yashin AI. 1985b. The deviant dynamics of death in heterogeneous populations. In: Tuma NB, editor. Sociological Methodology 1985. San Francisco: Jossey-Bass. pp. 179–211.

Waldron T. 1987. The relative survival of the human skeleton: implications for palaeopathology. In: Boddington A, Garland AN, Janaway RC, editors. Death, Decay and Reconstruction. Manchester: Manchester University Press. pp. 55–64.

Waldron T. 1994. Counting the Dead: The Epidemiology of Skeletal Populations. Chichester: Wiley.

Waldron T. 1996. Prevalence studies in skeletal populations: a reply. Int J Osteoarchaeol 6:320–322.

Walker PL. 1995. Problems of preservation and sexism in sexing: some lessons from historical collections for palaeodemographrs. In: Saunders, SR, Herring A, editors. Grave Reflections: Portraying the Past Through Cemetery Studies. Toronto: Canadian Scholars Press. pp. 31–47.

Walker PL, Johnson JR, Lambert PM. 1988. Age and sex biases in the preservation of human skeletal remains. Am J Phys Anthropol 76: 183–188.

Weiss KM. 1973. Demographic models for anthropology. Am Antiq Memoir 27.

Weiss KM. 1975. Demographic disturbance and the use of life tables in anthropology. Am Antiq 40:46–56.

Weiss KM. 1990. The biodemography of variation in human frailty. Demography 27:185–206.

Willey P, Galloway A, Snyder L. 1997. Bone mineral density and survival of elements and element portions in the bones of the Crow Creek massacre victims. Am J Phys Anthropol 104: 513–528.

Wood JW. 1998. A theory of preindustrial population dynamics: demography, economy, and well-being in Malthusian systems. Curr Anthropol 39:99–135.

Wood JW, Holman DJ, Weiss KM, Buchanan AV, LeFor B. 1992a. Hazards models for human population biology. Yrbk Phys Anthropol 35:43–87.

Wood JW, Holman DJ, Yashin AI, Peterson RJ, Weinstein M, Chang M-C. 1994. A multistate model of fecundability and sterility. Demography 31:403–426.

Wood JW, Milner GR. 1994. Reply. Curr Anthropol 35:631–637.

Wood JW, Milner GR, Harpending HC, Weiss KM. 1992b. The osteological paradox: problems of inferring prehistoric health from skeletal samples. Curr Anthropol 33:343–370.

INDEX